GOD'S EXEMPLARY GRADUATES

CHARACTER-ORIENTED GRADUATE ATTRIBUTES
IN THEOLOGICAL EDUCATION

Edited by
Peter G. Bolt and Peter Laughlin

God's Exemplary Graduates
Character-Oriented Graduate Attributes in Theological Education
Edited by Peter G. Bolt and Peter Laughlin

SCD Press
PO Box 1882
Macquarie Park NSW 2113
scdpress@scd.edu.au

© SCD Press and Contributors 2021

ISBN-13: 978-1-925730-21-0 (Paperback)
ISBN-13: 978-1-925730-22-7 (E-book)

Internal layout and design: Lankshear Design Pty Ltd.
Cover design based on design by: ben taylor creative enterprises, btce.com.au

GOD'S EXEMPLARY GRADUATES

CHARACTER-ORIENTED GRADUATE ATTRIBUTES
IN THEOLOGICAL EDUCATION

**Edited by
Peter G. Bolt and Peter Laughlin**

**SCD Press
2021**

Publications associated with SCD Learning & Teaching Theology Conferences

1. Les Ball, *Transforming Theology. Student Experience and Transformative Learning in Undergraduate Theological Education* (Preston, Vic.: Mosaic, 2012).
2. Les Ball & James R. Harrison (eds.), *Learning & Teaching Theology. Some Ways Ahead* (Northcote, Vic: Morning Start, 2014).
3. Yvette Debergue & James R. Harrison (eds.), *Teaching Theology in a Technological Age* (Cambridge: Cambridge Scholars Publishing, 2015).
4. Les Ball & Peter G. Bolt (eds.), *Wondering About God Together. Research-Led Learning & Teaching in Theological Education* (Macquarie Park, NSW: SCD Press, 2018).
5. Peter G. Bolt & Peter Laughlin (eds.), *God's Exemplary Graduates: Character-Oriented Graduate Attributes in Theological Education* (Macquarie Park, NSW: SCD Press, 2021).

CONTENTS

Introduction
    1 *God's Exemplary Graduates.* Peter Laughlin   vii

Part 1: **TOWARDS GOD'S EXEMPLARY GRADUATES**   1
    2 *Student Formation in Tertiary Education.* Bill Salier   3
    3 *'Integration' in The Ancient World.* David Wright   22
    4 *Educating for Eternity.* Peter G. Bolt   32
    5 *Fit for Purpose.* Neil Holm   58
    6 *Graduate Attributes in the Australian College of Theology.* Geoffrey R. Treloar   72
    7 *Graduate Attributes and Theological Education.* James Dalziel   90
    8 *Graduate Attributes for Roman Catholic Seminaries.* Debra Snoddy   105

Part 2: **SCRIPTURE AND GRADUATE CHARACTER**   129
    9 *Appreciating the Creative Artistry of the Hebrew Text.* Laurence Woods   131
    10 *Psalms and Popular Songs.* Sarah L Hart   145
    11 *Character and Pedagogy in the Book of Proverbs.* Andrew Errington   156
    12 *The Power of Persuasion.* Claire Smith   165
    13 *Graduate Attributes and the New Covenant.* Peter Carblis   181

Part 3: **TEACHING FOR GRADUATE DEVELOPMENT: PEDAGOGICAL PRINCIPLES** — 211

    14 *Religious Higher Education at the Crossroads.* Trevor Cairney — 213

    15 *Religious Freedom and the Theological Academy.* Neil Foster — 226

    16 *The Role of Curriculum in Developing Character-Oriented Graduate Attributes with an Illustration from Church History.* Les Ball — 251

    17 *The Virtues of Religious History.* Michael Gladwin — 265

    18 *'But Only One Thing is Necessary'.* Peter Mudge — 294

Part 4: **TEACHING FOR GRADUATE DEVELOPMENT: PRACTICAL CONSIDERATIONS** — 313

    19 *Facilitating Student Formation in Tertiary Education.* Bill Salier — 315

    20 *Educating for the Kingdom.* James Pietsch — 333

    21 *God's Exemplary Graduates in Times of Ecological Crisis.* Sebastian Salaske-Lentern — 346

    22 *Language Learning in Theological Education.* Constantine R. Campbell — 365

    23 *Designing Effective Fieldwork Experiences.* Peter Laughlin — 373

    24 *Cults in the Classroom.* Bernard Doherty — 385

Part 5: **IMPLICATIONS FOR THE PASTORAL GRADUATE** — 403

    25 *Private Study, Social Learning, and Embodied Practice.* David B. McEwan — 405

    26 *Unbounding Learning Communities.* Steve Taylor, Rosemary Dewerse — 420

    27 *Curiosity-Based Learning.* Stephen Smith, Murray Bingham, Catherine Kleemann — 435

    28 *Should Ministers be Graduates Anyway?* Dennis Nutt — 450

Epilogue *Theologically-Shaped Character in an Increasingly Polarized Environment.* Peter G. Bolt — 463

INTRODUCTION
1 | GOD'S EXEMPLARY GRADUATES

Theological institutions and their faculty work hard to produce curriculum, programs and immersive experiences that develop, shape and form students along a defined set of graduate attributes. Indeed, producing quality graduates of character, expertise and a commitment to life-long learning is a corporate endeavour for the sake of the whole Church. But what is an 'exemplary graduate'? A different question yet again, is what are 'God's Exemplary Graduates'? To answer this question the Sydney College of Divinity invited scholars to contribute to a conference discussion at SCD in 2019. The results of that conference are now here offered as the fourth volume in SCD's ongoing series of Learning and Teaching publications.

This volume of essays continues the discussion that began in the preceding volume, *Wondering About God Together* (SCD Press, 2018). There the practice of research-led learning and teaching was recognised to influence graduate outcomes and prompted the present discussion as to what kind of graduates were being produced. The areas addressed in this volume provide a set of lenses through which an answer to this question might begin to emerge. They include a discussion on what it might mean to move *towards the forming of God's exemplary graduates*; reflections upon the *biblical foundation of graduate character*; *pedagogical principles for graduate development* and a robust discussion on practical ways that teachers can *engage in the classroom with graduate outcomes in mind*. The final section which brings the discussion to a fitting conclusion reflects on *relevant implications for the successful pastoral graduate*. It was initially hoped that this volume would appear much earlier but due to the COVID-19 pandemic, contributors requested and were granted more time to complete their submissions. We believe the extra time has been worth the wait and this volume is now the stronger for it. The editors would like to thank the contributors for fulfilling their commitments during this difficult, and in many ways unprecedented, time.

Part 1 of this volume explores how desired graduate attributes inform the educational task. In the lead essay, 'Student Formation in Tertiary Education', Bill Salier notes how character formation has always been a key concern of a holistic approach to tertiary education. This is all the more relevant in theological education which endeavours to produce graduates who not only work in ministry contexts effectively but display a life of character and virtue commensurate with such a vocation. Salier therefore suggests that the goal and theory of formation must be established before a consideration of practice and evaluation can take place. As in Christian formation in general, the goal of graduate character formation, says Salier, is conformity to the image of Christ. This essay explores this theme and in so doing lays the groundwork for the latter discussion on practice and evaluation which appears in Chapter 19 of this volume.

The following two essays consider the historical background to desired graduate outcomes. In '"Integration" in the Ancient World—An Anachronistic Concept?', David Wright notes that the integration of theological knowledge, ministry skills and godly character is a consistent theme across the Classical, Hellenistic, and New Testament eras. Arguing that this integration was consistently a desired outcome, he highlights some of the ways that the ancient world sought to achieve it. He then draws out two implications for us today. The first is that it is plausible to ground this integration in the pages of the New Testament thus giving biblical support to its implementation. If this is granted, then the second is to ensure that in our teaching today the development of godly character should not be treated in isolation from growth in theological understanding and practical skills. Thus, God's exemplary graduates will be 'integrated' graduates. In the second of these two essays, 'Educating for Eternity: Ultimate Learning Outcomes in Colonial NSW', Peter Bolt takes a look back to the early Australian context and asks what it was that the developing colony education system hoped to achieve. Tracing the educational practices as the young region transitioned from a penal colony to a free society, Bolt adeptly demonstrates that the prevailing view of the times was that the rising generations had to be educated, not just for profit in this world but for their salvation in the next. Not only does this intriguing exploration of recent history remind Australians of their Christian roots, it points to the interplay and interconnections between graduates of ministry and graduates of life. In a similar vein, theological educators are not merely training graduates for ministry today, they are in a very real way, educating them for eternity.

The next four chapters move away from the historical perspective to address graduate attributes today. Commencing with Neil Holm's 'Fit for Purpose: Graduate Attributes Grounded in Ecclesiology', the question is asked as to whether the many graduate attributes proposed by theological higher education institutions today are really 'fit for purpose'. Of particular concern is the tendency for theological institutions to be overly influenced by secular understandings of graduate outcomes, outcomes which are designed for different professions and industries. In contrast, Holm suggests that theological institutions need to focus their graduate attributes on the formation and ministry skills of the graduate. Drawing upon a number of metaphors (*landscape*, *letter*, and *mirror*) he explores the nature of godly attributes and how graduates—whatever their context—will be called to lead alongside rather than from above. Particular attributes are then given by way of example for a specific ecclesiological context. Following on is the chapter by Geoff Treloar, 'Graduate Attributes in the Australian College of Theology—Rhetoric or Reality?' The chapter is presented in two parts. The first is an analysis of a recent audit undertaken by the Australian College of Theology which exposed the 'wide gap between the rhetoric and the reality' in the implementation of graduate attributes within the College. The second part is an explanation on how the College responded to the challenge of closing the gap. Two important elements arise from the discussion. The first is that the institution must have clearly identified what graduate attributes they are seeking to develop. Without clear, measurable attributes the institution will not be able to assess their performance. The second element is just how to assess that performance and here Treloar identifies four characteristics of graduate attributes that enable that analysis to be done: They are *owned*; they are *promoted*; they are *integrated into the curriculum framework*; and they are *monitored and measured*. With these characteristics it is possible for all institutions to track their own engagement with graduate attributes against their stated outcomes.

The third of the four chapters addressing graduate attributes today is from James Dalziel in his essay, 'Graduate Attributes and Theological Education: Interactions between Organisational Change, Spiritual Formation, Online Learning and Business Models'. While an imposing title, Dalziel deftly navigates the various topics in an integrated fashion drawing the reader's attention to a number of salient points. Key among them is the important need for graduate attributes to incorporate spiritual formation elements. Dalziel notes that it is possible to create graduate attributes that align with regulatory requirements whilst still incorporating the graduate formational needs of future employers whether they be ecclesiastical or para-church organisations. What is required is creativity and focus on the part of the institution. The subsequent question that must then be addressed is how such formation is to be achieved. Traditional classroom-based institutions have chapel services, prayer groups, community service etc. to help form students, whereas online theological educators must find alternative avenues. However, in either case, intentional spiritual formation must be implemented through activities, assessments and graduate outcomes or students will not be fully formed as the industry requires.

The final essay in this first part is from Debra Snoddy, 'Graduate Attributes for Roman Catholic Seminaries'. Here graduate attributes from various Roman Catholic universities are compared to determine points of congruence and incongruence. This data is then evaluated against relevant documents from the Magisterium to consider how well they align with what is considered to constitute appropriate training for the priesthood. Noting four dimensions in particular–the human, the spiritual, the intellectual and the pastoral, Snoddy goes on to suggest eight specific graduate outcomes that could be considered to achieve these dimensions: authenticity, creativity, humility, discernment, critical thinking, the capacity to work both autonomously and collaboratively, ethical praxis and finally, communication. It is argued that graduates who possess these attributes will begin pastoral life on a sure and steady footing.

Part 2 comprises five essays offering an exploration of graduate character formation through the lens of Scripture. Leading the way is Laurie Woods, 'Appreciating the Creative Artistry of the Hebrew Text and the Difficulties Faced by Modern Translators'. What Woods offers up is an analysis of two specific Old Testament texts–Genesis 2 and Isaiah 57:15, in which the artistry of the Hebrew text is revealed over against the prose of most English translations. Unfortunately, the difficult decisions that translators make to render the Hebrew in ways that make sense in English also tend to obscure and deflect the reader away from the rhetorical character of the Hebrew. Woods therefore argues that graduates need to be aware of the importance of Hebrew literary style if they are to correctly interpret and apply the biblical text.

The next contribution from Sarah Hart, 'Popular Songs and Psalms' is an interesting discussion on how the development and use of popular songs can help the biblical interpreter explore the Psalms. Her contention is that the writing and subsequent use of popular songs provides an appropriate parallel by which to approach the background to these biblical songs. Drawing from her class work in which students analysed a number of popular songs, Hart highlights five in particular to explore. Her conclusion is that each song has a different context, background and purpose even though they share classification as a popular song. This analysis helps the student to assess the Psalms as individual expressions of worship rather than a single whole to be approached with a collective hermeneutic.

Following on is Andrew Errington's 'Character and Pedagogy in the Book of Proverbs'. Beginning with a reflection on the present state of virtue ethics drawn from Alasdair MacIntyre, Errington argues that the book of Proverbs provides an important lens to view character-oriented development. Not that Proverbs provides a simple solution, says Errington, for in many ways it leaves us with ongoing questions. But what it does do is provide a correlation between acts and character that underpins a very distinctive way of understanding wisdom. He notes, 'wisdom is about creation's hospitality to forms of action; and so "being wise" or "getting wisdom" is not merely about the development of certain subjective attributes, but about a relation to the reality and moral structure of the world'. This relation has to do with action and thus the expression or enacting of virtuous action. Errington then shifts gear a little to include a reflection on Thomas Aquinas' contribution to prudence and virtue, noting that for Aquinas virtues supply the 'principles of action' needed in any given situation. Notwithstanding that Proverbs draws a connection between actions and virtue, what is more important, he argues, are the words of instruction that guide us even when 'what is within us' fails. That is, for Proverbs, what guarantees right action or virtue is not the human ability to do so but the faithful adherence to trustworthy instruction.

Claire Smith shifts us into the New Testament with an evaluation of the 'Power of Persuasion' in Paul's letters. Paul often uses the verb *parakaleō* to exhort his communities to particular action or thought. This instructional technique, Smith argues, demonstrates Paul's commitment to the well-being of the recipients and his concern for their holistic development. Basing his appeals in his own personal relationships with the community, Paul as teacher, invests himself into the instructional relationship with the desired purpose of motivating them to learn and thus to change. What we see in Paul's *parakaleō* appeals is therefore an awareness of the transformative power of the gospel and the way in which education and instruction can lead to newness and wholeness of life.

The final essay of this section is from Peter Carblis entitled, 'Graduate Attributes and the New Covenant'. In continuity with Geoff Treloar's early study, Carblis argues that effective theological education produces graduates that are able to serve as co-labourers with God. That is, graduate attributes are not cognitive alone but must be based in the outworking of the *missio Dei*. Drawing on illustrations in both vocational and higher education, Carblis explores what competencies and skills would be considered appropriate in dialogue with significant New Testament texts. He concludes with two categories of attributes that theological institutions can utilise to shape their focus on graduate development.

Part 3 'Teaching for Graduate Development: Pedagogical Principles' consists of five essays which focus on the underling pedagogy behind the effective producing of graduates attributes. Trevor Cairney leads us off with 'Religious Higher Education at the Crossroads: The Need to Reconsider Epistemology, Pedagogy and Formation'. Noting that in recent years there has been a tendency for religious higher education providers to idealise their secular university counterparts, Cairney highlights the uniqueness of theological institutions and their ongoing need to focus on the holistic formation of graduates. Three dangers are singled out as being of particular concern of secular universities: the loss of community and collegiality, a corresponding rise in individualism and an increasing failure to study in depth. But these dangers can be avoided, says Cairney, if priorities are established that reflect our faith basis. Fundamental to these priorities are a faith-based epistemology, a pedagogy that reflects our collective mission, and formation that builds character for that mission. If such can be maintained, then theological institutions will not just produce graduates that a technically capable but ones that are more aptly fit for Christian life itself.

The next essay from Neil Foster is an important analysis on 'Religious Freedom and the Academy'. Highlighting recent cases in both Australia and international contexts, Foster demonstrates the eroding freedom that religious academics have in university contexts around the Western world. This fact necessitates that theological educators, even those in privately funded institutions, have a working knowledge of the principles of religious freedom and their corresponding rights and duties under those provisions. This is also a pedagogical matter as it goes to the heart of forming graduates along confessional lines. Having provided examples of current challenges to religious freedom in the university sector, Foster then turns to analyse religious freedom as a fundamental human right before turning to evaluate current university policies relevant to the issue. Whilst he concludes that some protections are in place, there are 'several areas where there are uncertainties and gaps'. Foster has provided us with a timely reminder for the present context.

The next two essays form an integrated pair inasmuch as they are both from the perspective of teaching church history. Les Ball discusses the 'Role of Curriculum in Developing Character Oriented Graduates' with specific illustrations from church history and Michael Gladwin reminds us of the significant 'Virtues of Religious History'. Ball begins his discussion with a foundational analysis of curriculum as the central plank in student formation. There is a clear link, he argues, between 'curriculum design and delivery' and 'desired graduate outcomes'. This link can be leveraged towards student formation by ensuring that curriculum design yields a threefold perception that any given unit is important, doable and enjoyable. In such a context, an intrinsic motivation is unlocked that opens the student to a willingness to be formed by the learning experience. Ball then illustrates how this can work with two specific examples from the discipline of church history.

Gladwin continues the theme by describing how the discipline of religious history can help to shape the character attributes and dispositions of students towards desired virtues. In particular three sets of virtues can be developed each with their own subsets. The first, which Gladwin terms 'historical' virtues include a commitment to 'truth-telling, honesty, and balance, humility, empathy, charity, and justice'. The second termed 'epistemic' virtues include 'carefulness, patience, perseverance, diligence, and attentiveness'. The third is labelled, appropriately enough for Christian higher education, 'theological' virtues which includes, 'faith and hope' but also aesthetic virtues of beauty and indeed, one may add, love. What Gladwin succeeds in doing is demonstrating how it is possible, through a study of Christian history, to shape the common life of the present in positive ways.

The final paper in Part 3 is from Peter Mudge entitled, 'But Only One Thing is Necessary'. Deliberately evoking Jesus' comment to Martha in Luke 10:42, Mudge opens his essay with a reflection on what that 'one thing' is that is necessary in fostering exemplary graduates. Like a number of other contributors, the answer says Mudge, lies along the lines of suitable virtues. But what are the essential virtues of an exemplary graduate? Drawing upon the notion of *epektasis*–the 'stretching towards one's full potential of Christ in God', Mudge explores a four-fold movement towards essential virtue creation. But at its heart is the challenge to always go beyond the 'customary threshold of virtue' to cultivate compassion that translates into self-giving.

Part 4 turns from reflection to praxis and includes six essays that deal with practical considerations around the theme of graduate development. In the first essay, Bill Salier completes the reflections begun in Chapter 2 of this volume by focussing on how to 'Facilitate Student Formation in Tertiary Education'. The key to praxis is knowing where you are going and, in that sense, one must begin with the end in mind. This is particularly true in character formation where the journey one takes is crucial to where one ends up. Thus, Salier argues, 'clearly articulated goals at an institutional level help set direction and establish priorities, which enable a consistent approach and commitment to student learning …and…formation across all levels of the college's life and teaching'. This includes both formal (curriculum) and informal (chapel; retreats etc.) elements of the student experience. The challenge, as always, lies in effective assessment of the formation program. When assessing character virtues of graduating students, one cannot look for a numerical grade. Instead, Salier suggests that we can find a level of quantification through the student's capacity, sophistication and maturity of personal reflection. This can be done through both formal and informal means, but it must become an intentional practice if meaningful assessment is to be achieved.

The next four essays form a group around learning practice. James Pietsch in 'Educating for the Kingdom' notes how the New Testament describes character formation that begins in this age in preparation for the age to come. In a similar way, educational learning activities, whilst grounded in the student's present understanding and knowledge, help prepare the student with the capability to tackle more advanced tasks in the future. To educate for the kingdom is therefore to focus on the creation of suitable learning activities in the present, which will work together to foster the development of graduate virtues that will ultimately evidence the new creation. Continuing the creation theme, Sebastian Salaske-Lentern then invites us to explore the practical possibilities of educating students towards an ecological understanding of virtue. That is, God's Exemplary Graduates, will be individuals who care not just for ethical, moral and religious conversion but a 'spiritual ecological conversion' as well. As stewards of God's creation, theological graduates are well-placed to take the lead in advocating for suitable action to protect and nurture the world in which we live.

Constantine Campbell then turns our attention to 'Language Learning in Theological Education'. He asks the question as to what extent language learning (particularly Greek, Hebrew and Aramaic) can shape Christian character? Deliberately, and with tongue firmly planted in cheek, he misquotes the Apostle Paul, noting that perhaps students should 'rejoice in [their] language studies, because [they] know that language study produces endurance, endurance produces proven character, and proven character produces hope' that does not disappoint! What is intriguing about Campbell's study is he adroitly argues for why language learning should be understood to include character and virtue development and its value not be limited to the academic and theological outcomes. In a similar way, though within a completely different context, Peter Laughlin explores how 'Designing Effective Fieldwork Experiences' can lead to character formation which in many ways surpasses the ministry outcomes the experience is designed to achieve. Laughlin articulates how the unit design phase is crucial in ensuring that any given experience will enable the student to meet the necessary learning outcomes. But what results from the experience is not just the desired academic learning but overt formational outcomes involving character, self-awareness and a willingness to explore growth areas. Two case studies are given by way of example to demonstrate the formational power of these types of fieldwork experiences.

The final essay in this section is from Bernard Doherty entitled, '"Cults" in the Classroom: Some Neglected Challenges of Religious Pluralism and Multiculturalism to Pedagogy and Curriculum in Theological Education'. Here Doherty notes that with the growth of religious pluralism and multiculturalism across the Australian landscape, it has correctly been perceived that there is a need to equip graduates with the skills to engage with those of other faiths and cultures. But what has been neglected in this shift to examine the major world religions, has been adequate education around various cults, such as the Hare Krishnas, the Moonies, the Children of God and other lesser known groups on the fringes of mainstream religions. But, Doherty argues, simply adding in an apologetic against the views of specific cult groups fails to adequately prepare the student for engaging with their adherents. Rather, an integrated theological approach that borrows from the work done in the sociology of religions and religious studies will better enable graduates to engage in the task of witnessing to these groups.

Part 5 is the final section of this volume and contains four essays collected around the theme of 'Implications for the Pastoral Graduate'. Recognising that graduates of theological institutions will most often be engaged in some form of pastoral or Christian ministry, these essays attempt to chart out a path for graduate effectiveness. The first essay by David McEwan is entitled 'Private Study, Social Learning and Embodied Practice: Insights from John Wesley's Framework for Preparing Effective Ministers in Early Methodism'. Framing his discussion through the lenses of neuroscience, social psychology and higher education, McEwan analyses John Wesley's model for ministry training. For Wesley, education was an instrument of personal–and hence–social reform, which meant that training was designed to equip the student to develop their character through personal transformative practices and should not only be limited to intellectual outcomes. Highlighting, 'private reading, community conference, and personal involvement', as three specific examples, McEwan explores how investment in such practices helps to shape graduates long after they leave the formal academy.

Taylor and Dewerse then turn our attention to the theme of lifelong learning in 'Unbounding Learning Communities'. Drawing from Richard Osmer's four-core tasks for developing an educational strategy, the authors examine the spiral of action-reflection as it relates to fifty-five ordained ministers of the Presbyterian Church in New Zealand. What they discovered was that the 'bounded communities' of traditional theological education (that is, 'groups that form within a structured teaching or training setting'), cause difficulties for ministers attempting to integrate into the 'real-world' communities upon graduation. What was suggested was that instead of seeing the institution as the place of learning, such communities should become 'unbounded', deliberately connecting and integrating with local contexts and in so doing, create an atmosphere of 'lifelong learning' for the students as well as to those to whom they minister.

Smith, Bingham and Kleemann continue this lifelong learning theme by examining the role that curiosity plays in educational development. 'Curiosity-Based Learning: Stretching Fearlessly into the Unknown' explores how curiosity not only motivates learning but encourages students to continue to learn, to press into what it is that they do not yet know or understand. However, as people habitually believe they understand more than they actually do, it is crucial to coach students to be aware of their own 'information gaps'. This means not providing excessive direct instruction to which the student may incorrectly perceive as not being relevant to them, and instead getting them to 'have a go' and discover for themselves where their limitations lie. Such a process requires adequate coaching and here the authors provide us with an 'Action Coaching Approach' that demonstrates one model for effectively helping people to engage in curious learning.

The final essay of this volume is a reflective piece by Dennis Nutt entitled, 'Should Ministers be Graduates Anyway?' Grounded in a historical reflection on the educational practices of the Churches of Christ in Australia, Nutt describes the initial impetus to graduate ministry in the early years of the Church. Not everyone believed, however, that institutional graduates were a 'good thing', preferring on-the-job experience, character and proficiency over qualifications. But gradually the importance of having educated ministers became apparent as the educational level of congregations also began to rise. Soon, it was considered essential 'that the minister needed to be as well-educated as the society at large'. Nutt concludes that theological institutions are necessary, we do need 'graduates' because 'we need ministers of the soul… ministers, who in an age of doubt…command the respect and confidence of their people because of their zeal, loyalty, faith, and piety'. The College is the ideal place to birth such attributes.

As the fruit of the Learning and Teaching Conference of 2019, the essays within this volume ably demonstrate the heart, soul and passion that theological educators have for forming students within their care to be God's Exemplary Graduates. The many suggestions and reflections within will no doubt prove helpful to current faculty and teaching practitioners but, it is hoped, they will also prepare the way for further discussion and experimentation around the formation of graduates into the future. Ultimately, however, it should be remembered that such formation is not a work of institutions, teachers or even of the student themselves but remains a work of the Spirit of God. God's Exemplary Graduates, can be taught, coached and encouraged but we must never forget that it is the Spirit that brings transformative life, character and power for ministry. With that in mind we commend the present volume to you.

Peter Laughlin

PART 1
TOWARDS GOD'S EXEMPLARY GRADUATES

2 | STUDENT FORMATION IN TERTIARY EDUCATION

Abstract

Student formation, especially in terms of character, has always been a key concern when taking a holistic approach to tertiary education. The issues are arguably even more acute in light of the widespread dismay over the apparent lack of character revealed by corrupt and immoral practices in a series of professions. This paper surveys aspects of current practice and thinking with respect to student formation and suggests some theological resources to inform the practice of student formation. This will establish a base from which to consider practices to facilitate student formation (Chapter 19).

1. What Are We Talking About?

When we think about 'God's exemplary graduates', we are generally talking about the formation and shape of graduates of the theological colleges with whom they are engaged. This may or not be expressed in a list of graduate attributes, but somewhere in the minds of theological educators, there will be a picture of what they want to see in their graduates when they leave their programme of study. While this will be largely framed in terms of the growth and development of knowledge and skills relating to the overall discipline, there will also be the expectation of growth and change in a personal sense. This is usually understood as personal formation.

The language of formation can be vague, with terms like character formation, human formation, spiritual formation, and personal formation jostling for attention. The common denominator is formation, or even transformation, understood as a contribution to what a student is becoming in the holistic sense of their personhood. Vocational formation is another significant term but not so relevant to this particular discussion, which will be broader. Much instruction in theological colleges is conducted in the context of formation for various types of paid church ministry, but the reality is that the majority of students enrolled in Australian theological institutions are not necessarily vocationally oriented in this sense.[1] That said, many are studying with a view to general service or ministry in a Christian context. Regardless of vocational intentions or outcomes, a college's formational goals pertain in a general sense to spiritual, personal, or character formation.

The focus here will be on formation or transformation in a general sense. This is not to discount skills or intellectual development, and, in a holistic sense, these other areas are clearly inter-related, but the focus of this series of essays and the conference from which they sprang is the development of personal qualities and convictions expressed in practices that are best thought of within the character realm. I will use the term formation in a general sense and try to avoid lapsing into discussions on specific vocational formation.

2. Why Are We Talking About This?

It might seem a silly question to ask, with a blindingly obvious answer, but it is worth pausing for a moment to consider why we would be discussing the issue of formation. There are at least four reasons.

2.1. It Is What Educators Talk About

First, it is what educators talk about, or perhaps should talk about. At whatever stage education takes place, primary, secondary, or tertiary, there is an awareness that what is happening is more than informing students. Student formation has always been central to a holistic approach to education. Whether it is talk about head, hand, and heart, or competencies, convictions, and character, or another trio of terms, the point is clear: Educators are not just interested in knowledge but are vitally concerned with what kinds of persons are produced by our efforts

---

1   Sherlock, *Uncovering*, 32.

at whatever level of education they participate. To this end, education courses at every level have always paid attention to matters of character and formation.

In the tertiary sector, this has usually been expressed in terms of graduate attributes. These statements attempt to encapsulate and communicate an institution's aspirations for their graduates and provide a guide for the curriculum and its teaching. My own early experience with graduate attributes came via engagement with the Teaching and Learning Centre at the University of Sydney in 2004-6.[2] The list of graduate attributes usually begins with 'hard' attributes; knowledge to be mastered related to a particular discipline and skills essential to its practice. Then, finally comes attitudes that are the expression of desired character traits. In my experience, this final area was the most contested, with a whole host of questions raised about their framing and implementation: What were they to be; how could they be expressed in the curriculum, how could we know if it was working; were they realistic or simply aspirational, and what difference did they really make in the curriculum? Often, it seemed that a beautiful list of attributes could be drawn up and promptly shelved and brought out only occasionally, almost as a curiosity piece.[3]

Institutions in the tertiary sector regularly revise their lists of attributes. When revisiting the graduate attributes of a number of universities for this essay, it was interesting to note what I felt was a more modest attempt at framing attributes, especially in the area of formation and character, where the emphasis seems to fall on professional identity and practice. This is certainly ambitious and needed in its own way, but the tenor of these attributes is general. It encompasses things like building integrity, confidence, and personal resilience and the capacity to manage challenges and uncertainty. At a more micro level, attributes expressed an ambition for ethical responsibilities pertaining to the particular discipline, knowledge of professional standards, and working professionally with others.[4] I read this as an acknowledgement of the difficulty

---

2   The key texts were Ramsden, *Learning to Teach*, Biggs and Tang, *Teaching for Quality*, and a key figure was Simon Barrie, 'A Research-Based Approach'.
3   Treloar, *Graduate Attributes*, 7 notes that 'GAs are not well promoted in Non-University Higher Education Providers, See also Oliver and De St Jorre, *Graduate Attributes*.
4   See the following examples from New South Wales universities https://teaching.unsw.edu.au/sites/default/files/upload-files/unsw-graduate-attributes_0.pdf
    https://webcentral.mq.edu.au/teaching/curriculum_assessment/curriculum_design/graduate_capabilities/
    https://www.sydney.edu.au/students/graduate-qualities.html
    https://www.uts.edu.au/research-and-teaching/learning-and-teaching/uts-model-learning/graduates-attributes

of framing formational goals that are too personal and so the tendency to focus on professional practice.

2.2 Our Culture Looks to Its Institutions for Student Formation

Educators have always instinctively looked to this kind of holistic formation, but they also realise that formation is what the surrounding culture looks to its educational institutions to do.

At the time of presentation, in the Australian context, there is a general interest in formation and ethical practice amongst the graduates of tertiary institutions. This is partly because these are perennials, but also in the immediate context because of some spectacular failures. We only need to refer to the series of Royal Commissions in Australia and the #metoo movement and its exposure to unhealthy attitudes and workplace practices. Cray laments the corrosion of character in contemporary culture, precipitating what he terms a civic crisis or a crisis of citizenship.[5]

Cray's interests are social fabric and citizenship, and he suggests that the corrosion of character is an important factor in this civic or citizenship crisis. He observes a slow fracturing and failure of community in which character is forged and increased fragmentation into special interest groups with specific identities. This is accompanied by an overall lack of respect and concern for institutions that used to act as a stable bedrock in our society.

Cray sees this as expressed particularly in individualisation, consumerism, and constructivism, noting that the modern turn to the self for meaning and purpose precipitates the erosion of social capital. The soft hedonism at the heart of consumerism and the triumph of subjectivism in the self-made person reigns supreme, and ever-changing personal identities result in a problematic discourse about character in general as there is little room for the concept of a stable self that grounds talk of character. Regardless of whether there is agreement with his actual diagnosis, many would recognise at least the symptoms.[6]

Questions are rightly asked regarding not only the skill levels of graduates from our various tertiary institutions but also their character as professionals.

---

5   Cray, *Disciples*. Although the book is relatively old, and the diagnosis may be disputed, the concerns raised are contemporary.
6   Similar concerns were expressed by both Catherine McGregor and John Carroll as they reflect upon some of the less than helpful behaviours expressed during the response to the COVID-19 pandemic in NSW at the time of writing. See *The Australian*, Saturday, 14 March 2020.

How has the institution helped to shape this individual so that the greater good is being served?

This is true in the tertiary theological sector as well. The reputation of churches generally has suffered greatly due to the catastrophic moral failures recorded at the Royal Commission into Institutional Responses to Child Sexual Abuse.

The stakeholders of theological institutions expect this as well. There is abundant anecdotal evidence of complaints about the quality of graduates and their lack of preparedness for ministry. There are discussions about unhealthy, even toxic, work environments within denominations, along with instances of moral failure. Much of this prompts theological institutions to look again at their effectiveness or otherwise in forming students.

2.3 We Claim to Be Doing This Already

From the perspective of the tertiary theological sector, the third reason we are interested in this topic is because we already claim to be doing this, and I assume we want to do it better.

In his excellent study of transformative learning in the tertiary theological sector, Les Ball notes 'a high level of consensus that theological education needs to incorporate the whole life of the student, while anchoring theology in the faith tradition which has given rise to it, that is to make theological education transformative rather than merely cognitive'.[7]

In his scoping study, surveying the field of Australian theological education, Charles Sherlock noted the 'sector-wide swing (that) has taken place towards "integrated", "holistic" or "transformative" learning–words appearing time and again in college websites, promotional materials, and handbooks'.[8] We will return to see how this claim has been assessed shortly.

2.4. A Contribution to Make?

The final basis for our reflection is the possibility that the tertiary theological sector can make a significant contribution to the broader discussion about student formation. Theological colleges already contribute to their culture through their 'exemplary graduates'. The bolder claim is that the theological colleges of Australia have great advantages when it comes to student formation.

---

7 Ball, *Transforming*, 5.
8 Sherlock, *Uncovering*, 58.

These advantages are a function of the theological resources they have on hand. These resources include the legacy of a long and rich concern for the importance of personal formation as well as a history of experimentation and innovation in attempting to facilitate it. They also include relative clarity concerning the goal of personal formation and a vigorous discussion amongst various traditions as to the how of formation is facilitated with respect to both theory and attendant practices. More controversially, from a secular perspective, they also have an understanding that encompasses assistance beyond their own resources in the form of the person and work of the Holy Spirit.

This is a pertinent discussion for the following reasons: It is a natural discussion for educators at any level. Our culture has expectations of formation from our institutions, theological colleges claim to be doing this, and there is a significant contribution to be made in the general area of formation. Before turning to examine three Scriptural perspectives on formation, we will briefly explore some of the context in which this discussion takes place in our colleges.

Now, these simple and somewhat bold statements hide a depth of confusion and discussion amongst various Christian traditions as to the precise answers to these questions, as well as the precise contributions we can make. We will now consider a brief historical perspective and detail some commentary on contemporary claims by theological colleges concerning their commitment to formation. Theological colleges may have a significant contribution to make, but they need to keep their own house in order.

3. In What Context Are We Talking About It?
3.1. Changing Ways of Operating

One of the cornerstones of theological education in general and personal formation, in particular, has been personal interaction with a teacher or rabbi. This has often meant a group of individuals, living with or near a teacher or rabbi, and receiving face-face instruction and exhortation and interaction. We find this model in Jesus' relationship with his disciples, as he taught, trained, and reflected with his disciples concerning their ministry in his name.[9]

---

[9] The outline that follows is indebted to discussions in Liefield & Cannell, 'Spiritual Formation'; Banks, *Reenvisioning*; , Steubing, 'Spiritual Formation'; Cheesman, 'Spiritual Formation'; Sherlock, *Uncovering*; Cheesman, 'History'; Ball, *Transforming*; Tang, 'Elements'; Tang, 'Process'; Gonzalez, *History*, and discussions at the SCD 'God's Exemplary Graduates' Conference, 2019.

This same model of close connection between teacher and student continues in the early desert fathers, monasteries, and some university colleges. Both students and teachers were members of a residential community. There are domestic variants as well, with puritan nurseries for young preachers involving students residing in the home of a respected minister as apprentices.

This model was inherited by theological colleges and Bible colleges in the 19th and 20th centuries. They focused on vocational training in residential communities. In the case of theological colleges, young men (usually) would leave home, live in close, intense residential communities, and remain single for their training.

This ideal has been modified in more recent years, often under external pressure. This has seen a reduction in focus on intentional close communal formation, especially in a residential context. The external pressures impinging upon theological colleges include the increasing age of those going to colleges and the admission of married students and their families, non-residential students, part-time students, and non-vocational students (due in part to a rise in government funding). A (welcome) rise in academic standards has sometimes distracted teachers and students from their commitment to student formation in the broader sense, and the demands of formal accreditation has increased this pressure. In the Australian context, the advent of the government loan scheme for private education (Feehelp) saw many colleges increase in size, reducing the level of interaction between teacher and student. The rise of distance education and the sheer cost of providing residential education are other significant contextual factors. Colleges are being forced to consider how they can do the same formational job in ever-changing contexts.

3.2. Claims About Student Formation Questioned

Locally and internationally, theological colleges affirm the importance of formation and claim to be doing it.[10] However, this aspiration is often noted and then followed by questions concerning its implementation.

In the Australian context, the two most comprehensive treatments are to be found in the studies conducted by Charles Sherlock and Les Ball. Despite most colleges' claims to be engaged in transformative education, Sherlock could find no evidence of any clear definition of a transformative experience, nor of any indication that it was, in fact, intentionally or strategically incorporated into

---

10   See Ball, *Transforming*, cf. Naidoo, 'Call'.

any set curriculum. Finally, he could find no evidence of any formal means of demonstrating or recognising such experience.[11]

For his part, Ball builds on Sherlock's observations and observes that while what he calls transformative learning is an aspiration and affirmed, he suggests that, perhaps, not much is happening. He notes that while most parties strongly desire it as an aspirational outcome, great variability exists in its implementation. There are few deliberately structured transformative elements within the formal degree programme, with most relying on the relatively unstructured extra-curricular life of campuses to provide this dimension.[12]

When he presents the findings of his investigation, Ball finds little evidence that theological colleges actually produce transformation, suggesting the sector assumes that the study of theology involves a significant personal transformation but with little evidence produced to support such an assertion.[13] Students reported little transformation, and what they did report was mainly intellectual: they reported that their studies were overly intellectual and unconnected to real life.[14] Ball also questioned how formative the college community is in students' lives. He observed that faculty tended to deem it a major factor, but graduates did not.[15]

Ball's study is a stimulating and important piece of work for the Australian context, and it stands as one of the few detailed investigations into the area of formation. It raises so many important questions, such as the place of student formation in the college context: What are the elements that make for effective formation? Can and should formation be done within the curriculum, or should it be left to extra-curricular pursuits? How important is the community context? Are there modes of pedagogy and curriculum design that are best suited to facilitating these goals? How can we know that what we are doing is actually working? What can reasonably be expected from a college in this area given the time and resources available?

While being critical and posing difficult questions, Ball is also able to make suggestions and point to helpful examples of good practice.[16] His work, overall,

---

11 Sherlock, *Uncovering*, 105–8.
12 Ball, *Transforming*, 2.
13 Ball, *Transforming*, 5, 109.
14 Ball, *Transforming*, 66-69.
15 Ball, *Transforming*, 74.
16 Ball, *Learning and Teaching*. See, for example, the models noted by the Hibberts as well as their own suggestion, Hibbert & Hibbert, 'Addressing the Need'.

testifies to the presence of a vigorous conversation and general concern over the issues he lists and makes an important contribution.[17]

3.3 A Contrary View

Against this discussion, there is a school of thought represented by the writer Carl Trueman that questions the extent and responsibility of the theological college's involvement in the process of formation. In a typically robust fashion, he suggests:

> This is a real challenge for theological educators as it is one area where seminaries cannot go very far in meeting the need. Indeed, I find the whole notion of 'spiritual formation' within seminaries to be somewhat problematic: seminaries impart knowledge and skills which are essential for ministry and which cannot be acquired with like ease in a practical mentoring situation; they also provide a context for developing important and useful friendships which will last a lifetime; but they cannot really engage in spiritual formation in any deep way. Certainly, the professor can and should strive to model Christian behaviour; but the real, deep, lasting spiritual formation for ministerial candidates takes place in a church context just as it does for every other Christian. The church is where the word is preached, the sacraments administered and discipling takes place.[18]

He goes on to suggest that seminaries need to work with local churches and understand their limits with respect to formation. While there is an element of truth here, Trueman overstates the case, and his work begs numerous questions.[19] The college is a legitimate place for student formation to take place, and to not attend to the possibilities afforded by the experience would be neglectful. That said, Trueman's statements alert us to the limits of what can be reasonably achieved. The college experience is a moment in time; significant but a moment nonetheless. It is an experience that occurs in the extended

---

17 Hibbert & Hibbert, 'Addressing the Need', and Frame, 'Proposals', 379–80.
18 Truman, 'On Witsius'.
19 As these observations are made, it is important to note that this is an online opinion piece and not a fully articulated essay.

context of the work of God in the believer's life and their participation in a variety of other formational communities, not least the local congregation.[20]

4. What Can We Say?

The New Testament theologian N.T. Wright suggests any theory of character education needs three elements: the right goal, steps to take to get there (a theory), and the practices necessary to make those steps habitual.[21] I would add a fourth from an educational perspective: a sense of how to evaluate.

Using Wright's schema, I want to explore the goal and theory of formation in the section that follows. This will lay the ground for a consideration of practices and an evaluation to come in Chapter 19 of this volume. Throughout this discussion, I want to think about what we might be able to say from three New Testament writers about personal formation. I am not claiming this investigation has any unique status and will be drawing on the work of New Testament (NT) scholars, but I am hoping that there might be some material of interest to further stimulate thinking about our practices and also for us to see what we might be able to offer the broader conversation.

There is, of course, a vast amount of material in the Scriptures to inform thinking about the shape and development of character, and the discussion below contains only part of that. It is suggested, though, that this is a significant sampling that highlights the shape of the goal and some fundamental pointers as to the theology of personal formation and the practices that facilitate it. It does so from a New Testament perspective—the perspective of fulfilment and clarity in light of the revelation of Jesus Chris—so, arguably, it reflects a drawing together of many strands of thinking that find their culmination in this revelation.

4.1 The Goal of Spiritual Formation

What is the goal of formation? A brief survey of three of the major writers in the NT, Peter, Paul, and John, reveals a general unanimity that the goal or endpoint of spiritual formation is conformity to the image of Christ. Paul expresses his concern for the believers in Galatians 4:19, describing himself by way of the pains of childbirth until Christ is formed in them. Earlier in the letter,

---

20 This discussion will be picked up in the accompanying essay.
21 Wright, *Virtue*, 27.

he can speak of his own identity as having been reshaped, supplanted even, when he suggests that it is 'no longer I who live, it is Christ who lives in me'. He goes on to state that the life he now lives in the flesh is being done so in faith in the Son of God who 'loved me and gave himself for me' (Gal. 2:20). In Colossians 1:28, he speaks of his labours to present every believer mature in Christ (cf. Eph. 4:11-16, which expresses a similar concern oscillating between individual and corporate horizons). Peter speaks of the goal of sharing in the divine nature (2 Pet. 1:4), while John states that the eschatological goal for believers is that 'we will be like Him because we will see him as he is' (1 John 3:2).

So, too, does the articulated goal of character formation in the Christian college or institution often reflect some form of this urge to find Christ likeness or Christ being formed in the graduate. This may be a list of virtues, but a Christ-like character expressed in love in all its fullness is most likely a prominent feature of such formulations.

I am not suggesting this simple formulation ensures consistent agreement as to the precise shape of this goal. We only need to look at the history of Jesus research to realise that there are many ways to answer the question 'who is Jesus Christ?' What does it mean to be formed in the image of Christ? The contribution from the Apostle Peter will provide stimulus to consider this further.

a. Some Thoughts from Peter: 'Christ driven identity formation'

In his recent study, Bayer explores a biblical perspective of character formation through the lens of the Apostle Peter as he appears in the New Testament.[22] In a semi-narrative approach, Bayer first traces the story of Peter through Mark's Gospel, then through Luke's narrative account Acts, and then finally through the Petrine correspondence.

The foundational insight Bayer articulates is that of Christ-driven identity. By this, Bayer means that Christ shapes the character of his followers in their increasing dependency upon him. Bayer suggests that the person of Christ and the disciples' developing identity are inseparable and interrelated entities. He sees a consistent testimony in Peter's story with the dynamic between Christology and the identity formation of the Christian believer, and this is crucial to Christian formation.[23]

---

22 Bayer, *Apostolic Bedrock*.
23 Bayer *Apostolic Bedrock*, 4.

Bayer is insistent that we see Christian maturity (character formation) as a function of the work and ongoing presence of the triune God, by the Holy Spirit, predicated on the atoning work of Christ. This process takes place within the individual and occurs in the midst of the Christian community. This does not take place for its own sake but as part of the calling of God's people to be the new temple of God. This identity as the new temple of God is expressed publicly. Christian character formation is, therefore, embedded in a missional context whereby the purified people of God worship and glorify Him, reflecting Christ, individually and corporately, amidst a watching and often hostile world.

Bayer identifies six character traits that are the focus of this concentration on Peter's story.[24] These traits are:

> 1. Growth in faith and trust towards God. This calls for personal involvement on a practical basis (1 Pet. 2:23; 4:19; 5:6). It is personal and childlike (Mark 9:42; 10:52); expressed in prayer (Mark 11:24) and worship (1 Pet. 3:15). It is not immune to unbelief or doubt (Mark 9:24) but does not give way to fear.
>
> 2. Becoming a courageous witness (Mark 8:36) who naturally speaks about Christ and who is (Mark 5:20). The book of Acts generally traces Peter's development here as well as recording the courageous witness of the people of God, usually in the context of adversity and persecution.
>
> 3. Pursuing purity of heart. The holistic sense of the heart suggests that this attribute is focused on both will and direction (Mark 6:52; 8:17-21) as well as a moral dimension (Mark 7:21-23; Acts 5:3-4; 1 Pet. 1:22).
>
> 4. Growth in humility and service. Humility is not seen as weakness, indecision, or lack of will.[25] Rather humility lets go of a self-serving agenda because of a greater trust in the supreme purpose, power, and wisdom of God; and uses strength for the service of others (Mk. 10:45). It is not a self-generated virtue but comes about as a result

---

24 Bayer *Apostolic Bedrock*, 230–267.
25 Bayer *Apostolic Bedrock*, 244 compares this conception with the understanding prevalent in the first-century Roman context.

of the encounter with God and others (cf. Acts 10; Gal. 2; 1 Pet. 5:5-7).[26]

5. Overcoming purifying trials and persecutions. External pressure is placed on the disciple through temptation and persecution (1 Pet. 3:16; 4:12-14) and prayer and watchfulness are required (Mark 14:34,37-38), so the temptation to deny undivided dependence upon Christ is not succumbed to.[27] Peter also points to the purifying and maturing function of suffering (1 Pet. 1:6-7).

6. Progressing in surrender and obedience. Bayer summarises this as the transfer of 'the primary allegiance from the self to Christ... surrendering control of self-determination'.[28] As with all the other characteristics, this is both exemplified by Christ and taught to his disciples (Mark 8:34-37).

Bayer demonstrates how 'Christ driven identity formation spawns a rich array of character traits, which lie at the centre of sustained transformation'.[29] There is much to ponder on here for colleges who seek to facilitate growth in their students as these traits give more structure to the notion of what it means to be formed by the image of Christ. Further, these traits are generative in that lines can readily be drawn from them to political, social, and ethical engagement.[30]

4.2 The Pathway to Formation

a. What is the Pathway to Character?

We have looked at some perspectives offered by the Apostle Peter to see what Christian formation might look like. In order to gain some biblical perspectives on how that formation might be facilitated, we turn to Paul and John.

b. Perspectives from Paul

Paul will provide three contributions to our thinking in this area. Colossians 3 provides an overall perspective concerning God's action in this area, while two

---

26 Bayer *Apostolic Bedrock*, 252 identifies a series of encounters Peter has on his 'downward mobility' into true and healthy humility.
27 Bayer *Apostolic Bedrock*, 253.
28 Bayer *Apostolic Bedrock*, 266.
29 Bayer *Apostolic Bedrock*, 267.
30 Bayer *Apostolic Bedrock*, 272–3.

other perspectives from Romans point to some important dynamics.

Colossians 3 is a classic exposition of a key dynamic that lies at the heart of Paul's contribution to our thinking about personal formation. Paul's perspective is profoundly eschatological. It reflects his understanding that in the death and resurrection of Jesus, there is a real sense in which the future event to which the whole creation is heading and the revealing of Christ and his people with him in glory has already begun. Colossians 3:1 states that the believers have been raised with Christ, and their life is hidden with Christ in God (Col. 3:3). In these phrases, there is a real sense in which 'in Christ' the process of transformation is complete, achieved for the believer through the cross of Christ. This understanding has profound implications for the individual. After Paul has declared the reality of what has happened for the believer and its coming revelation at the return of Christ (Col. 3:1-4), he goes on to outline the believer's response. They are to live to become the people they are destined to be.[31] This is then played out in parallel sequences of putting to death certain things (Col. 3:5-11) and putting on others like a new set of clothes (Col. 3:6-17). At the centre of this sequence is the promise that the new self of the believer is being renewed in the image of God, implying that this is the work of God for the believer by the Spirit (Col. 3:10).

This is a description of the formation, in the present time, of a character that properly anticipates the guaranteed future state. Paul's teaching charts a careful course between establishing a set of rules or practices that simply need to be followed to bring about formational success and the idea that formation can simply come naturally, as if no further reflection or effort is required.[32] It is a communal vision as much as an individual one, as the qualities to adopt are expressed relationally, and Colossians 3:16 implies a communal context.

Paul's eschatologically driven ethic provides a clear vision of participation in the new creation in the full human maturity and dignity that comes from having Christ formed in the individual and a consequent call to action that follows from the apprehension of this vision.

In Romans 12, Paul outlines one key element of the whole dynamic of formation. In Romans 12:2, he exhorts his readers to be transformed by the renewing of their minds. This is in the context of an appreciation of God's

---

31 While Paul may state this most clearly and fully it is not a perspective alien to other New Testament writers: see 1 John. 2:28-3.2 and 2 Pet. 1:4ff.
32 Wright, *Virtue*, 39–51 helpfully contrasts Paul's approach with these two other broad approaches.

mercies and with a view to proper worship (Rom. 12:1). This renewal of the mind answers to the debasing of the mind that has taken place due to rebellion (Rom. 1:21). The mind is central to Christian formation, and character development is the result of thought and choices based on a growing knowledge of the work of God and its implications. So, in Romans 6:11, Paul exhorts his readers to reckon themselves dead to sin on the basis of the understanding that, because of the work of God, they died and have been raised 'in Christ' (Rom. 6:3-11). The believer will, therefore, not let sin reign in their bodies and will pursue righteousness rather than wickedness (Rom. 6:12-14). A similar dynamic is outlined in Ephesians 4:17-24. Thinking clearly in the light of gospel realities is an essential part of personal formation in Paul's framework.

In Romans 5:3, Paul points to the role of suffering in the development of character when he describes the process of suffering as producing endurance, endurance character, and character hope. Other passages in Paul hint at the same insight in Romans 5 (cf. Rom. 8:18; 2 Cor. 4:10; Phil. 3:10-11). Paul makes explicit here a more general understanding in the New Testament concerning the place of suffering in personal formation (cf. 1 Pet. 1:5-8; Jas. 1:2-4; cf. Heb. 2:10). Two impulses would appear to support the process: the first is the suffering of Jesus, and the second is Paul's own suffering and its part in his call and mission. Paul made Jesus' crucifixion thematic for his own life, and we see a link to Peter's perspective described above by Bayer as 'Christ-driven identity formation'.

4.3 A Perspective from John

In a recent study, Cornelis Bennema highlighted the significance of mimesis, or imitation, for Johannine ethics as the newly (re?)discovered field of Johannine ethics slowly gains momentum.[33]

Drawing on the occurrences of conjunctions and constructions such as 'just as', 'even as....so also', 'thus' Bennema points to the theme of imitation or mimesis that is present in the Gospel. This begins with the imitation of the son by the Father. The key verse is John 5:19 where Jesus states that he 'can do nothing on his own, but only what he sees his Father doing; for whatever the Father does, the Son does likewise'. This is at once a statement of complete dependence and complete identity and ability. John's focus is primarily on the

---

33 Bennema, *Mimesis*.

Son-Father mimesis, though Bennema also detects a latent Spirit-Son mimesis in the description of the Spirit as another Paraclete (John 14:15) and the statements that the Spirit only speaks what he hears and sees from Jesus (John 16:13-15).

There is also a mimesis appropriate to the believer. Bennema describes this in two dimensions. In John 13 and 15, there is a performative mimesis where the disciple is urged to go and do likewise (John 13:14 and John 15:12 [the love command as it appears through the Gospel]). Here, the disciples are urged to understand Jesus' original actions and creatively deploy the original sense in their own context.[34] Bennema notes that the 'Jesus' method of using personal example to move his followers towards the kind of behaviour He expects from them by way of mimesis did not arise in a vacuum but was learned from his Father. So, the believer-Jesus mimesis imitates the Son-Father mimesis.[35]

Bennema describes a second kind of believer-Jesus mimesis as 'existential'. Here, he reflects on passages such as John 17:16,18,21,23,24, where believers are to imitate certain qualities of the Godhead, such as unity, otherworldliness, sent-ness (*sic*); communion, and ultimate location being where Jesus is. There is clearly a performative element to this level of mimesis, but the association is even more direct.[36]

The idea of imitation is extended in 1 John 3:11 to the models (good and bad) John is outlining in his letter. The idea of imitation is not unique to the Johannine corpus. Paul exhorts his readers at Philippi to imitate himself and other godly models (Phil. 3:17; cf. 1 Cor. 11:1), and Peter will also speak of the example of Christ (1 Pet. 2:21). Paul's quotation of Menander's epigram in 1 Corinthians 15:33 sums up the theme of imitation with its warning about the corrosive effects of 'bad company' and its implied exhortation to keep good company.

4.4 Summary

From this brief survey, biblical perspectives on personal formation can be gleaned. The overall goal or shape of Christian character is closely identified with the formation of a character that is modelled on the character displayed by Jesus Christ. This process is closer than modelling as the NT writers have a notion of Christ being formed in the believer, and the believer conforms to the image of Christ.

There is the understanding that this occurs within an eschatological frame-

---

34 Bennema, *Mimesis*, 104–5, 124–5.
35 Bennema, *Mimesis*, 142.
36 Bennema, *Mimesis*, 125–135.

work where the believer is working out or growing into that which has already been achieved for them. In this sense, character is a gift received. This points in turn to the work of God taking place, in the power of his Spirit in and for the believer. The development of character is a task within this gift framework as the believer strives (empowered by the Spirit) to become what they already are by grace and faith.

The pursuit of character as a task involves some structures and tasks, including the renewing of the mind, putting off old practices and putting on new practices, and attending to the model of Jesus Christ and other models of Christian character. We have also seen the important role that suffering has in this economy in the formation of the believer.

This summary is not exhaustive, and there are doubtless other perspectives and aspects to be observed. However, this will suffice for the moment as a solid foundation upon which to consider some more concrete strategies to facilitate student formation in the next essay/chapter.

5. Coda: The Politics of Christian Character Formation in the Public Square

Having presented some of the fruitful avenues for reflection in the area of formation in the theological college, I want to briefly return to an earlier question posed: Does the theological education sector have anything to offer to the wider sector with respect to thinking about student formation? I want to say, 'yes…but'.

On the one hand, there are two considerable barriers to a positive contribution. The first is the public failure of Christian character as evidenced by many of the findings unearthed by the Royal Commission into Institutional Responses to Child Sexual Abuse. This has not been a good look, to put it mildly, and the reputation of the 'church', broadly conceived, has suffered as a result.

Second, the eschatological and spiritual understanding expressed above makes the translation to a secular context difficult. The New Testament writers confidently point to the work of God, by his Spirit in working in the believer to grow and transform them to an end that has already been gifted. This is received and understood within the faith. This will be both incomprehensible and a source of despair for the secular institution. It points to the impossible possibility of student formation.

That said, there may be two contributions possible as well. There are hints, clues, and models that can be picked up and applied as is the case with many Christian teachings and practices. These may be pale imitations and lacking the power that comes through being embedded within the Christian story, but they may be good and a blessing nonetheless. Such contributions will include the importance of the renewal of the mind and the attention that is given to the deliberate formation of character, the importance of modelling, and perhaps even the place of suffering.

The second contribution is a potentially prophetic one whereby God's exemplary graduates from theological colleges can point to a more excellent way—a good goal and a different process—inviting further investigation that may lead the Lord knows where. Of course, the prophetic task is not easy, and more often than not, it is the path of suffering. But this suffering may be part of the testing and proving of our own institutions.

There is a contribution to be made, but we need to continue to get our own house in order. Fortunately, there are ample materials to work with.

Bibliography

Banks, R. *Reenvisioning Theological Education. Exploring a Missional Alternative to Current Models* (Grand Rapids, Michigan: Eerdmans, 1992).

Ball. L. *Transforming Theology. Student Experience and Transformative Learning in Undergraduate Theological Education* (Preston, Victoria: Mosaic Press, 2012).

Ball. L. *Learning and Teaching Theology. Some Ways Ahead* (Eugene, Oregon: Wipf & Stock, 2015)

Barrie, S. 'A Research-Based Approach to Generic Attributes Policy', *Higher Education Research and Development* 23 (2004), 26-76.

Barrie, S. 'Understanding What We Mean by the Generic Attributes', *Higher Education* 51.2 (2006), 215-41.

Biggs, J & C. Tang. *Teaching for Quality Learning at University* (4th edn; Maidenhead: McGraw Hill, 2011).

Bayer, H.F. *Apostolic Bedrock. Christology, Identity, and Character Formation According to Peter's Canonical Testimony* (Milton Keynes: Paternoster, 2016).

Bennema, C. *Mimesis in the Johannine Literature. A Study in Johannine Ethics* (New York: T&T Clark 2017).

Cheesman, G. 'The Spiritual Formation of Students–A Personal Selection from the Literature', *The Theological Educator* 2.1 (2007), 4-7.

Cheesman, G. A. History of Spiritual Formation in Theological Education. Theological Education. net (2012) <http://theologicaleducation.net/articles/view.htm?id=198>.

Cray, G. *Disciples and Citizens: A Vision for Distinctive Living* (Nottingham: IVP, 2007)

Liefield, W.L. & L.M. Cannell. Spiritual Formation and Theological Education. 238-252, in J.I. Packer (ed.) *Alive to God: Studies in Spirituality* (Downers Grove, Illinois: IVP, 1992)

Naidoo, M. 'The Call for Spiritual Formation in Protestant Theological Institutions in South Africa'. *Acta Theological Supplementum* 11, (2008).

Ramsden. P. *Learning to Teach in Higher Education*. (2nd edn; London: Routledge, 2003).

Sherlock, C. *Uncovering Theology. The Depth, Reach and Utility of Australian Theological Education* (Adelaide: ATF Press, 2009).

Stuebing, R. 'Spiritual Formation in Theological Education: A Survey of the Literature', *Africa Journal of Theology* 18.1 (1999), 47-70.

Tang, A. The Process of Spiritual Formation (2014) <https://www.academia.edu/10783130/The_Process_of_Spiritual_Formation>

Tang, A. The Elements of Spiritual Formation (2014) <https://www.academia.edu/18311996/The_Elements_of_Spiritual_Formation>

Trueman, C. On Witsius, Character and Cleaning Rosters. Postcards from Palookaville (2012). <https://www.reformation21.org/on_witsius_character_and_clean>.

Wright, N.T. *Virtue Reborn* (London: SPCK, 2010).

Bill Salier
Youthworks College, Sydney
bill.salier@youthworks.net

3 | 'INTEGRATION' IN THE ANCIENT WORLD

AN ANACHRONISTIC CONCEPT?

Abstract

There is widespread agreement that theology, skills, and godly character should be integrated as part of a student's experience of theological education. This paper will argue that it was a common societal practice in the ancient world to educate people through the integration of theology, skills, and character.

The paper concludes by drawing out two implications. First, given that integration was part of the ancient world, it is plausible that the practice of integration may be found in the New Testament. If this is the case, the second implication is that the development of godly character should not be treated in isolation from the growth in theological understanding and practical skills if we are to produce 'God's exemplary graduates'.

1. Introduction

Richard and Evelyn Hibbert argue for the importance of integration, saying 'theological education cannot focus only on understanding God and his ways, but must help people grow in Christlikeness and develop skills for ministry'.[1]

---

[1] Hibbert and Hibbert, 'Better Integration', 107.

Even more boldly, they claim 'the key to enhancing theological education is the intentional integration of knowing, being and doing, of theory and practice, and of theology with life and ministry'.[2] Given this bold claim, integration is a concept worth exploring.

What is integration? The working definition this chapter will use is: 'the process by which Christian theology, practical ministry skills, and godly character, are combined and developed in a person for the goal of exercising ministry'. This leaves open the question of what is the nature of the ministry to be exercised; it could be lay or ordained, paid or unpaid, full-time or part-time.

The question I want to ask is, as we look to the world of the NT, is integration an anachronistic concept? In other words, was integration part of the fabric of the ancient world, whether or not the term was used, or is it only a contemporary concept? To answer that, this chapter will briefly survey Greek, Jewish, and Roman literature before making some conclusions.

2. Greek Literature

Paideia (παιδεία) was a dominant feature of classical Greek culture. It was a combination of civilisation, culture, tradition, education, and literature and can be summarised as enculturation through education.[3] At the heart of the content of paideia was arete (ἀρετή). The term was broadly applied and meant 'excellence', but in Greek philosophy, it came to refer to a person's character, meaning 'virtue'.[4] The aim of education was to produce virtue in people.[5] Aristotle said that 'the good of man is the active exercise of his soul's faculties in conformity with excellence or virtue, or if there be several human excellences or virtues, in conformity with the best and most perfect among them'.[6] Exercising virtue was the greatest act of devotion to the gods.[7] A person's character was, therefore, the most important aspect of paideia.

Plato and Aristotle agreed that a person's virtuous conduct flowed from the right knowledge.[8] Knowledge of the truth was required to produce virtue

---

2 Hibbert and Hibbert, 'Better Integration', 107.
3 Jaegar, *Paideia*, vi.; White, *Where is the Wise Man*, 29-30.
4 *TDNT*, 1:458.
5 Isocrates, *Panath.* 12.30-33.
6 Aristotle, *Eth. nic.* 1.7.15.
7 Isocrates, *Nic.* 20.
8 Plato, *Resp.* 2.377c.; Aristotle, *Eth. nic.* 2.2.2.

because knowledge nourishes the soul.[9] The highest knowledge a person could have is knowledge of the divine (although Plato and Aristotle differ on the content of divine knowledge).[10] For Plato, it was, therefore, of critical importance that the material used to teach children and young people presents the right 'pattern of theology'.[11]

Skill (techne - τέχνη) and virtue appeared to mutually influence each other as part of paideia. Plato recognised rhetoric as a skill. While identifying that it was a skill open to abuse, he argued that this should not preclude it being taught. Rather, the character of the person using the skill is the key issue.[12] Conversely, Aristotle argued that young people should only be taught skills that helped them grow in virtue.[13] Thus, character was to shape the use of skills, and skills were to be used to grow character.

The content of Greek paideia displays interconnections between virtue, right knowledge of the divine, and skills. Virtue was shaped by right knowledge and was displayed in the exercising of skills. Skills, in turn, could be combined with right knowledge to produce virtue. Xenophon believed this was embodied in the Persian leader Cyrus the younger, who was of outstanding character, skilful with horses, and intellectually sharp.

> Here, then, Cyrus was reputed to be, in the first place, the most modest of his fellows and even more obedient to his elders than were his inferiors in rank; secondly, the most devoted to horses and the most skilful in managing horses; he was also adjudged the most eager to learn and the most diligent in practising military accomplishments, such as the use of the bow and the javelin.[14]

Although Plato disagreed with Xenophon's assessment of Persian education, he too believed leaders needed to know the truth, conform their character to the truth, and be skilful in expressing the truth.[15]

---

9   Plato, *Prot.* 2.313c.
10 Plato, *Leg.* 12.966c.; Aristotle, *Metaph.* 12.1072b-c.
11 Plato, *Resp.* 2.379a.; Nightingale, 'Liberal Education', 138.
12 Plato, *Gorg.* 456d-457c.
13 Aristotle, *Pol.* 8.1337b.
14 Xenophon, *Anab.* 1.9.5-6.
15 Plato, *Leg.* 12.966b.

3. Jewish Literature

Running across Jewish literature is the ideal of the wise person. The paideia of Sirach begins with the Lord who alone is wise and from whom all wisdom comes.[16] As such, 'to fear the Lord is the beginning of wisdom'.[17] Sirach 1:11–20 says the fear of the Lord brings joy, happiness, flourishing, and long life because wisdom from the Lord is full and complete. Living wisely begins with fearing the Lord; God is the source of wisdom, and only those who approach him with humility and reverence will access his wisdom. Fearing the Lord leads a person to keep his law, and so obtain wisdom, thus making the law a chief expression of his wisdom. The wise person fulfils the law by carrying it out.

Virtue is a dominant feature of Philo's understanding of paideia. Philo cites prudence, courage, temperance, and justice as the overarching virtues from which others flow.[18] Virtue is the fruit of paideia for as it grows the virtues, it purifies the soul, thus allowing a person to control the passions that undermine good character. Even though Philo strongly emphasises the importance of philosophy and reason, he also argues that the commands of God found in the Hebrew Scriptures are central.[19] Wisdom comes from the word of God working with divine reason.[20] The Mosaic law exemplifies virtues because the law is the closest representation of the universal law that pervades the cosmos.[21]

For Josephus, all things in the conduct of life are to have piety as their goal because virtue is the greatest reward for a person and a blessing for themselves and others.[22] Conducting a life characterised by godly and virtuous behaviour was of vital importance.[23] According to Josephus, piety is grounded in God who is the source of everything good and possesses perfect virtue.[24] The appropriate response for all people is, therefore, to worship him.[25] God makes himself known through divine revelation contained in his laws, the law of Moses.[26] The law contains God's wisdom and is the best education for people because it

---

16 *Sir* 1:1, 8. The NRSV translation of Sirach is used throughout.
17 *Sir* 1:14.
18 Philo, *Post.* 128.
19 Attempting to acquire virtue without the law is to be reduced to a sophist. Philo, *Post.* 130.; *Sobr.* 9.
20 Philo, *Fug.* 137.
21 Philo, *Mos.* 2. 10.; Borgen, 'Philo – An Interpreter', 77-78.; Zurawski, 'Mosaic *Paideia*', 493.
22 Josephus, *C. Ap.* 2.175.; *A.J.* 4.182-183.
23 For the apologetic impact of Jewish piety according to Josephus see, Feldman, *Jew and Gentile*, 230-232.
24 Josephus, *A.J.* 4.180; 1.23.
25 Josephus, *C. Ap.* 2.192.
26 Josephus, *A.J.* 4.183.

teaches true piety.[27] Therefore, it is the knowledge of God that drives true piety.[28]

In addition, for Sirach, Josephus, and Philo, to be wise also involves being skilful. All skill comes from the Lord, and people rely on these skills as they go about their work.[29]

The Jewish literature points to the integration of the knowledge of God expressed through the law of Moses, virtuous and godly character, and skills. Moses is the great hero throughout the Jewish literature, and the following example from Philo captures what integration looks like:

> He exhibited the doctrines of philosophy in all his daily actions, saying precisely what he thought, and performing such actions only as were consistent with his words, so as to exhibit a perfect harmony between his language and his life, so that as his words were such also was his life, and as his life was such likewise was his language, like people who are playing together in tune on a musical instrument.[30]

In addition, Philo lauds Moses for being the most skilful shepherd of his generation and argues that shepherding is the ideal training for the skills needed in leading God's people.[31]

4. Roman Literature

In the Roman world, virtue was defined in terms of loyalty and duty, first to the gods and then in relation to family and the state, and is summed up in the word pietas.[32] For Seneca, a person of virtuous piety is one who loyally fulfils their duty to the gods, empire, and household. Plutarch describes virtue as more important than gold because it is a quality of God. Therefore, a leader reflects the likeness of God by his virtuous life.[33]

Cicero calls oratory the greatest skill.[34] Therefore, a skilled orator who is virtuous is both rare and embodies all that is honourable. Cicero says it glorifies

---

27 Josephus, *A.J.* 12:37; *C. Ap.* 2.175; 291-294.
28 Josephus, *A.J.* 1.21.; Spilsbury, 'Josephus and the Bible', 130-131.
29 *Sir* 38:3-6, 31.
30 Philo, *Mos.* 1. 29. See also 1. 48.
31 Philo, *Mos.* 1. 60-64.
32 Seneca, *Ep.* 76.23; 66.37; 49:12; 74:12.
33 Seneca, *Adv. Col.* 30; *Sera* 5; *Princ. iner.* 3.
34 Cicero, *De or.* 1.129.

the community to see "an outstanding orator who is also a man of worth".[35] An example of the ideal of integration comes from Quintilian. He says,

> It is no hack-advocate, no hireling pleader, nor yet, to use no harser term, a serviceable attorney of the class generally known as causidici, that I am seeking to form, but rather a man who to extraordinary natural gifts has added a thorough mastery of all the fairest branches of knowledge, a man sent by heaven to be the blessing of mankind, one to whom all history can find no parallel, uniquely perfect in every detail and utterly noble alike in thought and speech.[36]

5. Findings

Our very brief survey of Greek, Jewish, and Roman literature reveals a great diversity of approaches to education in the ancient world, both between these groupings and within the groupings themselves.[37] Blanket statements cannot be made about a single approach to education across the Mediterranean; nor can it be said there was a purely uniform Graeco-Roman or Jewish approach to education. This variety is seen in the content and goals of education.

Even though the most common feature mentioned by the writers is the importance of virtuous character, the content of what this involves varied widely. For example, Josephus emphasised piety and virtue, as did Plutarch, even though Plutarch endorsed sexual relations between men and boys —an anathema to the Jews known for their distinctive morality.[38] Both championed virtuous character, but the content was vastly different. Another example is the use of virtuous character. Quintilian said there needed to be consistency between an orator's character and their speaking. Cicero and Tacitus took a much more utilitarian approach in which the orator's character is one rhetorical tool, and, therefore, truth and character are subservient to winning over an audience.

There are also large differences in what was regarded as theology or knowledge of the truth. At a foundational level, the question of whether it is

---

35 Cicero, *De or.* 2.85.
36 Quintilian, *Institutes* 12.1.25
37 E.g. Barton and Boyarin, *Imagine No Religion*, 170-171 argue that Philo and Josephus approach godliness very differently.
38 Meeks, *Moral World*, 94-96.

even possible to know the gods produced a variety of answers.[39] Plato and Aristotle differed on the content of divine knowledge; Seneca's view of God was vastly different from Sirach's portrayal. Coupled with differences in the content of theology are epistemological differences. Philo maintained an important role for reason, philosophy, and the law of Moses, and Sirach incorporates non-biblical wisdom with the law, but this was different to Cicero, saying that truth is known through reason. How each writer regarded revelation and reason varied markedly. This translated into differences in the selection of texts to be studied (e.g. Homer or the law of Moses).

There were also important variations in the aims of education. Broadly speaking, Graeco-Roman education sought to produce good citizens who would serve the interests of the state. On the other hand, Jewish education wanted to grow people who would live wisely in accordance with the law of Moses. The goals of these approaches to education were fundamentally different.

Recognising the variegated nature of the content and aims of education in the ancient world, nonetheless, it is still possible to identify some common features. Our survey reveals that virtuous character held an important place in education, regardless of the theological or cultural background of the writer. The virtuous person who lived a pious life was an ideal to be aspired to and one that writers on education promoted. Related to this was the importance of theological knowledge because it was knowledge that produced virtuous character. Whether it was Plato calling for the selection of poetry chosen for children to contain sound theology, or the Jewish emphasis on the law of Moses, or the place of reason in Cicero and Seneca, all strands of education believed that understanding theological truth resulted in more virtuous people. And because the goal of Graeco-Roman education was to produce virtuous citizens to serve the interests of the state, the skill of rhetoric was indispensable. The ideal orator would be ineffective without rhetorical skills. The Jewish literature also identifies the importance of skills but does not focus as narrowly on rhetoric. It instead includes skills such as leadership, management, music, and writing, as well as life skills. The importance of virtuous character influencing the use of skills in an appropriate and helpful manner is also a consistent theme across most of the texts.

Although education in the ancient world was very diverse. Nonetheless, our survey reveals that it sought to produce citizens (and especially leaders) in whom

---

39 Schnabel, 'Knowing the Divine and Divine Knowledge', 287-312.

theology, skills, and character were woven together. It is reasonable to conclude that integration was a part of the ancient world.

6. Implications

There are two implications I would like to highlight that flow from what we have examined. First, given that the integration of theology, skills, and character was part of the ancient world, it should alert us to the possibility of finding the concept of integration in the pages of the New Testament. As you read the following examples, consider whether they display the concept of integration:

> Are all apostles? Are all prophets? Are all teachers? Do all work miracles? Do all have gifts of healing? Do all speak in tongues? Do all interpret? Now eagerly desire the greater gifts. If I speak in the tongues of men or of angels, but do not have love, I am only a resounding gong or a clanging cymbal.
>
> 1 Cor. 12:30–13:1

> Command and teach these things. Don't let anyone look down on you because you are young, but set an example for the believers in speech, in conduct, in love, in faith and in purity. Until I come, devote yourself to the public reading of Scripture, to preaching and to teaching. Do not neglect your gift, which was given you through prophecy when the body of elders laid their hands on you. Be diligent in these matters; give yourself wholly to them, so that everyone may see your progress. Watch your life and doctrine closely. Persevere in them, because if you do, you will save both yourself and your hearers.
>
> 1 Tim. 4:11-16

> Remember your leaders, who spoke the word of God to you. Consider the outcome of their way of life and imitate their faith.
>
> Heb. 13:7

> The end of all things is near. Therefore be alert and of sober mind so that you may pray. Above all, love each other deeply, because love covers over a multitude of sins. Offer hospitality to one another

without grumbling. Each of you should use whatever gift you have received to serve others, as faithful stewards of God's grace in its various forms. If anyone speaks, they should do so as one who speaks the very words of God. If anyone serves, they should do so with the strength God provides, so that in all things God may be praised through Jesus Christ. To him be the glory and the power for ever and ever. Amen.

1 Pet. 4:7-11

If these passages point to the concept of integration, it is also worth noting that they come from different authors, suggesting it was reasonably widespread rather than being identified as a feature of one particular writer.

A second implication is that we should not treat character in isolation from theology and skills. This is particularly important in a volume dedicated to thinking about the formation of character in the graduates of theological education. The ancient world deemed character formation as very important, and, although it has been beyond the scope of this chapter, the passages cited above are indicative of the high value the New Testament places on godly character. Our survey should at least encourage us to pause and think before we focus on character formation in isolation. The ancient world linked character formation to knowledge (of the gods/of God) and the use of skills. I would argue that to produce God's exemplary graduates, we need to do the same.

Bibliography

Aristotle. Translated by Rackham. H and H. Tredennick. 23 vols. LCL (Cambridge: Harvard University Press, 1926-1991).

Barton, C. A. & D. Boyarin. *Imagine No Religion: How Modern Abstractions Hide Ancient Realities* (New York: Fordham University, 2016).

Borgen, P. 'Philo - An Interpreter of the Laws of Moses', in Seland T. (eds.), *Reading Philo: A Handbook to Philo of Alexandria*. (Grand Rapids, Michigan: Eerdmans, 2014): 75-101.

Cicero. *On the Orator*. Translated by E. W. Sutton and H. Rackham. 2 vols., LCL (Cambridge: HUP, 1948).

Feldman, L. H. *Jew and Gentile in the Ancient World: Attitudes and Interactions from Alexander to Justinian* (Princeton: Princeton University Press, 1993).

Hibbert, R. & E. Hibbert. 'Addressing the Need for Better Integration in Theological Education', in Ball, L. & J. L. Harrison (eds.), *Learning and Teaching Theology: Some Ways Ahead* (Northcote: Morning Star, 2014): 107-17.

Isocrates. Translated by G. Norlin. 3 vols. LCL (Cambridge: Harvard University Press, 1928-1945).

Jaeger, W. *Paideia: The Ideals of Greek Culture*. Translated by G. Highet. 3 vols. (Vol. 3. Oxford: Blackwell, 1947).

Josephus. *The Works of Josephus: Complete and Unabridged*. Translated by W. Whiston (Peabody: Hendrickson, 1987).

Meeks, W. A. *The Moral World of the First Christians* (Philadelphia: Westminster Press, 1986).

Nightingale, A. W. 'Liberal Education in Plato's Republic and Aristotle's Politics', in Too, Y. L. *Education in Greek and Roman Antiquity* (Leiden: Brill, 2001): 133-73.

Philo. Translated by F. H. Colson and G. H. Whitaker. 10 vols. (LCL. London: Heinemann, 1924-1962).

Plato. Translated by R. G. Bury. 12 vols. (LCL. Cambridge: Harvard University Press, 1967-1968).

Quintilian. *Institutio Oratoria*. Translated by H. E. Butler. 4 vols. (LCL. Cambridge: HUP, 1920-1922).

Seneca. *Moral Essays*. Translated by J. W. Basore. 3 vols. (LCL. Cambridge: HUP, 1928-1935).

Schnabel, E. J. 'Knowing the Divine and Divine Knowledge in Greco-Roman Religion', *TynBul* 68, 2 (2017), 287-312.

Spilsbury, P. 'Josephus and the Bible', in Chapman H. H. & Z. Rogers (eds.), *A Companion to Josephus* (Oxford: John Wiley & Sons, 2016): 123-34.

White, A. G. Where is the Wise Man? Graeco-Roman Education as a Background to the Divisions in 1 Corinthians 1-4. Vol. 536, *LNTS*. (London: Bloomsbury T & T Clark, 2015).

Xenophon. Translated by C. L. Brownson and J. Dillery. (LCL. Cambridge: Harvard University Press, 1998).

Zurawski, J. M. 'Mosaic Paideia: The Law of Moses within Philo of Alexandria's Model of Jewish Education', *JSOJ* 48 (2017), 480-505.

David Wright
Bible College of South Australia
david.wright@biblecollege.sa.edu.au

4 | EDUCATING FOR ETERNITY

ULTIMATE LEARNING OUTCOMES IN COLONIAL NSW

Abstract

Education in NSW was instituted and overseen by the first Chaplains. Given the peculiar and experimental circumstances of a penal colony gradually moving towards a free society, the educational institutions strained to keep pace with the needs presented by colonial children growing in both age and number. After parochial schools had provided 'primary' education for decades, and 'secondary' had been dealt with in piecemeal fashion, the 1830s saw the opening of a public discussion about a National Education system. The discussions gave rise to the publication of three separate plans to institute grammar schools to feed into a (tertiary) college. Variations between the plans stemmed from the best way to include religious education.

After forty years of existence, NSW had a population very different in makeup than in 1788. Just after these plans were formulated, Governor Bourke attempted to institute a General System of Education to meet the needs of the day. The System sparked heated controversy during the 30s before failing in favour of a 'Denominational system'. Further bitter debates followed in the 40s, when Governor Gipps moved against the 'Denominational System' with more success than his predecessor. These two decades of controversy surrounding the role of religion in education inevitably influenced the shape of higher education when it was introduced, first in the late 40s with St James College and then

St Mary's College, both of which soon failed. Finally, in the 50s, the University of Sydney and Moore College were established, which both survive to this day.

Although obscured in the earliest period by the pressing concerns of a chaotic colony and in the later debates by the sectarian language of 'denominational distinctives', a strongly held view, nevertheless, emerges that 'the rising generations' had to be educated, not merely for profit in this world but chiefly for their salvation in the next. This view is expressed most clearly in discussions about the earlier levels of education, but this was also the perspective some applied to higher education as it emerged. Because 'Revealed Religion' allowed humanity to know God, Australia's early Christian educators believed that they were educating for eternity.

1. Introduction

The first chaplains of NSW were clergymen of the Church of England, and they were all known to themselves as the evangelical party and to their detractors as 'Methodists'— used as a derogatory term. The chaplains opened and supervised primary schools from the early days of the colony. Although they saw the need to educate all, they were only ever able to educate some. For the chaplains, education was part of the overall goal of individual moral improvement with a view to the betterment of society. But they believed that this goal would be achieved by children learning to read so that they could read the Bible and learn about the work of Jesus Christ for their salvation, and, therefore, find assurance of their secure place in the kingdom of God in the world to come. Yes, education aimed at the transformation of life through the transformation of moral character, but that transformation of moral character only came about through a Christ-based assurance about eternity. Thus, when the chaplains instituted schools, they were educating for eternity. This perspective, however, was not unique to the Anglican chaplains and was shared not only by their co-religionists but even by those proposing a 'secular' education. When Australia's first tertiary institutions began to come into existence, they were also envisaged against this perspective of eternity—even, in its own way, the most 'secular' proposal, that of the University of Sydney.

2. Australian Tertiary Education in Prospect
2.1 The Vision of Thomas Hobbes Scott

The prospect of an Australian university first surfaced in the English Government's communications with the Colony of NSW in 1823, when Earl Bathurst 'instructed Governor Brisbane to remember that the School Reserves should be of such an extent as to suffice for schools of a higher order and ultimately for a university'.[1]

Although he might be the first official mouthpiece for the idea of a tertiary college, Bathurst was not its originator. From September 1819 to 1821,[2] Thomas Hobbes Scott was in NSW as the Secretary to Commissioner Bigge. As part of his inquiry into the administration of the Colony, Commissioner Bigge had been asked to report on the state of education, and Scott took a particular interest in this aspect of their responsibilities. When he returned home, he wrote a report for the Home Government recommending an educational system for NSW, which envisioned the establishment of a university. When Bathurst recommended the reservation of land for this proposed institution, he would have been already implementing Scott's recommendations,[3] even though Scott's official report was not dated until March the following year.[4] By that date, Scott had already been ordained[5] and appointed as the first Archdeacon of NSW and commissioned to proceed to NSW to implement his educational proposals.[6] When the papers announced his appointment, they did so with a touch of convict humour: 'The Rev. Hobbs Scott will speedily be *transported* to New South Wales, where he is to officiate as Archdeacon, with a salary of £2000 per year'.[7]

His enormous salary, second only to that of the Governor, provoked constant

---

1   Ward, 'Foundation of the University of Sydney', 295-296; followed by Campbell, 'John Dunmore Lang', 48.
2   Macquarie's journal, [1819] Sunday 26. Sept.
3   Border, 'Scott, Thomas Hobbes (1783–1860)', is aware that a report was made earlier: 'He returned to England with Bigge, was consulted at the Colonial Office and submitted plans for chaplains and schools in the colony'.
4   T.H. Scott, Plan for a permanent provision for the Church establishment.
5   He was made deacon and ordained priest in 1821, and in 1822 was appointed rector of Whitfield, in the diocese of Durham; Border, 'Scott, Thomas Hobbes'.
6   On 14 Feb 1824, the papers announced that 'The Rev Hobbs Scott is appointed Archdeacon of Australasia, in New South Wales, with a salary of 2000l per annum. This is the highest Ecclesiastical Authority in that colony'; *Jackson's Oxford Journal* (Oxford, England), Saturday, 14 February 1824; repeated in *The Aberdeen Journal* (Aberdeen, Scotland), Wednesday, 10 March 1824. These newspaper reports show that the later date often given for his appointment, 2/10/1824, as given, for example, by Border, 'Scott, Thomas Hobbes', is mistaken. Burton, *State of Religion*, 9–10, gives the date 24 October 1824.
7   *Trewman's Exeter Flying Post or Plymouth and Cornish Advertiser* (Exeter, England), Thursday, 18 March 1824.

criticism in the colony, almost from the moment Scott arrived in NSW on 7 May 1825.[8] But that was not his only problem, and on 26 October 1829, after four and a half tumultuous years in the colony, he departed.[9] Although Scott was roundly criticised by the press on a number of fronts, in one way or another, his presence advanced education. In 1826, Governor Darling, who 'was inspired by a belief in the value of religion',[10] commenced a school for convict boys under Master John Kingsmill, which was run on Dr Bell's system, and his wife, Eliza, helped to create the Female School of Industry.[11] Darling urged Scott to pursue a more active policy, hoping that the clergy could help in the 'moral and religious improvement' of the young people.[12] Ironically, as Scott departed NSW, the *Sydney Gazette* began a series of articles attempting to stir public interest in education.[13] By January of the next year, the paper boasted of its success, since two plans had emerged for two separate tertiary colleges growing out of their own grammar schools. By the end of 1831, there would be three.

2.2 Plans for Three Universities

a. Sydney College

After commencing an earlier secondary school in 1820,[14] in September 1825,[15] Dr Laurence Hynes Halloran, a gifted teacher of dubious character, gave notice of the formation of the Sydney Public Free Grammar School and issued a plan.[16] Although opening in November, a series of misbehaviours from Halloran and

---

8   SG 12 May 1825: 'On Saturday arrived from England, with 133 male prisoners, all in good health, the ship *Hercules*, Captain Vaughan. The Guard consists of a detachment of the 41st and 48th Regiments, under orders of Lieutenant Stewart. Passengers, the Rev. Archdeacon Scott, Captain Rossi (Superintendent of Police), Mrs Rossi, and two children; Mr Surveyor Ralph; Mr Stewart, and four servants. The Surgeon Superintendent is Dr Goodsir, R.N'. Having arrived on the Saturday, Scott remained on board until Sunday, so that he could preach to the prisoners.
9   SG 27/10/1827.
10 Fletcher, *Ralph Darling*, 205.
11 Fletcher, *Ralph Darling*, 113–114, 202–204.
12 Fletcher, *Ralph Darling*, 202.
13 SG 28 January 1830: 'Not much more than two months have elapsed since we endeavoured, by means of the example of Cape Town, to arouse our countrymen to a sense of the great duty of providing for the intellectual improvement of their offspring. Happily, the appeal was not in vain'.
14 Austin, 'Halloran, Laurence Hynes (1765–1831)'. See also Grose, 'Dr. Halloran'.
15 SG 22 September 1825.
16 Halloran, *Proposals for the Foundation*. The initiative was initially well-received by the *Gazette*; SG 3/11/1825, but soon Halloran's infamous ability to get into trouble with his words cooled attitudes towards his institution.

his son led to suspension of operations in October 1826.[17] Because of drought and economic downturn in the late twenties, it struggled to re-open, but in January 1830, a revised plan was published and, on Australia Day, a foundation stone was laid. The plan made it clear that the grammar school would not be oriented towards any particular religious denomination and that it was the first step towards a tertiary college. After a subsequent change of name, the 'Sydney College' was the kernel from which the University of Sydney eventually grew.

b. The King's Schools and Moore College

January 1830 also saw the publication of a plan from the Church and Schools Corporation.[18] This Corporation was a direct product of Archdeacon Scott's educational initiatives for NSW and one of the major triggers of the reactions against him. Now, led by Scott's recently arrived successor, Archdeacon (and later Bishop) William Grant Broughton, and including the colony's most ancient educators, the Revs. Samuel Marsden and William Cowper, the Committee of the Church and Schools Corporation outlined their plans for two grammar schools to be known as the King's Schools—one in Sydney and one in Parramatta—that would feed into a tertiary college. Both grammar schools were subsequently opened, but only the one at Parramatta has survived. The tertiary college that grew out of this plan was Moore College, which opened at Liverpool in 1856 purely as a theological college, before moving to Newtown in 1891, where it still continues to operate conveniently situated alongside the University of Sydney.

c. The Australian College

The third proposed college was the brainchild of Australia's first Presbyterian minister, the Rev. John Dunmore Lang. After arriving in 1823, the energetic and abrasive Scotsman began to institute his own grand vision for Presbyterianism in NSW, in which education played a key role. Starting with primary education, in June 1826, he announced the opening of the Caledonian School[19] to be modelled on the Scottish parish school system, but it failed to get off the ground. In the late 20s, Lang was associated successively with the plans for Halloran's

---

17   Austin, 'Halloran, Laurence Hynes (1765–1831)'.
18   Corporation of Church & School Lands, *Plan for the Formulation and Regulation of the King's Schools*.
19   In the *Australian* 21 June 1826, Lang announced it would open on 3 July 1826. The plan was published in May, stating that the school was 'to be conducted on principles similar to High Schools in Scotland', *SG* 6 May 1826.

Sydney Public Free Grammar School, then the King's Schools, then the Sydney Grammar School again, before finally deciding to open his own school. Seeking a competitive edge by opening before the King's Schools, his Australian College commenced classes on 15 November 1831, even before completing its buildings.[20] Claiming that the 'Australian College promises at no distant period to be the first and the most influential institution for the education of youth in the Southern Hemisphere', Lang always planned that it would eventually become a tertiary college. Although the Australian College had a brief period of success, it mostly struggled to survive before effectively collapsing by 1845.[21] It nevertheless continued to exist notionally in J.D. Lang's vision for tertiary education, which eventually resulted in St Andrew's College taking its place as an affiliated college within the grounds of the University of Sydney.

Thus, by the end of 1831, three plans had been issued, each recognised as heading towards higher education:

> EDUCATION being the ground-work of all moral and social good, the enlightened Colonists of every class and 'grade' in this community are consequently interested in promoting either by their good wishes or their purses or both, where they can, all institutions which have for their end the dissemination and diffusion of useful knowledge. Accordingly, the various ACADEMIES already established throughout the Colony, and such as may be, together with the several UNIVERSITIES yet in embryo, of which latter there are now projected no fewer than THREE.[22]

As Australian tertiary education began to emerge in the early 1830s, it did so within the generally held belief that education was for the betterment of society through the moral improvement of the individual. The three proposed colleges would also, each in their own way, express the larger vision behind that belief. They would educate the rising generation with an eye on eternity.

---

20 Rosenhain, 'John Dunmore Lang', 64.
21 For the story of the collapse, see Rosenhain, 'John Dunmore Lang', 81–87, who notes that from 1845–1850, 'the College did not exist as an educational institution'.
22 *Australian* 16 December 1831.

3. Educating for Eternity

3.1 Australia's Earliest Educators & the King's School

The King's Schools arose in direct continuity with the education provided by the Anglican Chaplains, who were Australia's first educators. Products of the eighteenth-century Evangelical Revival, these men lived their lives and conducted their ministries with their eyes fixed on the blessed hope made certain by the death and resurrection of Jesus Christ. Whether dealing with adults or children, they wanted them to learn to read so that they could read the Scriptures to discover the work of Christ for themselves. This would certainly renovate their life in this present evil age, but it would do so by firstly making them ready to meet their maker in the age to come.

Although this eternal perspective was shared by the second and third of the Chaplains with oversight of education in NSW, Samuel Marsden and William Cowper, their predecessor, Australia's first Chaplain and educator, Rev. Richard Johnson, can be taken to exemplify them all.

Along with being the first Chaplain to NSW, Rev. Richard Johnson is recognised as 'the pioneer of education in the Colony'.[23] As for his own teacher training, if Johnson's early preparation followed that of the Elland scholars, like Samuel Marsden, he may have acted as an assistant teacher to Joseph Milner when he was at Hull Grammar School.[24] Despite not having a dedicated facility in about 1790, Johnson opened a small school conducted by convict William Richardson and his wife and wrote to the Society for the Propagation of the Gospel (SPG) in an attempt to fund some schoolmasters.[25] Although Governor Phillip was instructed on 20 August 1789 to have a spot set apart for a minister and schoolmaster, the first church only opened on 3 September 1793 after Johnson built it himself.[26] By the time Johnson's church was burned down on 1 October 1798, 150 to 200 children had been in attendance at the school he ran in the building.[27]

Johnson complained that he could do little for education in the first couple of years after the First Fleet arrived in January 1788 because of the 'unsettled confused state' of the colony.[28] But an additional factor in these early days

---

23   Rainey, *The Real Richard Johnson*, 20 and 30.
24   As suggested by Macintosh, *Richard Johnson*, 32.
25   R. Johnson to Secretary for SPG, 6 December 1794; Mackaness, *Some Letters*, part 2, No. 22.
26   Mackaness, *Some Letters*, part 1, n.5.
27   Mackaness, *Some Letters*, Part 1, Letter 16, n.2.
28   Johnson to Morice, 21 March 1792 (SPG Archive), as quoted in Macintosh, *Richard Johnson*, 88.

would have been that the children of the colony had not yet reached the age at which their education could begin, which, according to Johnson's own rules drafted in 1798, was the age of three.[29] In the unusual and experimental situation of the transplantation of an entire population into a new colony, any educational strategies had to keep pace with the growing age of the first cohort of potential pupils. Despite the earlier start under the Richardsons, probably by the first part of 1792, their numbers had grown sufficiently for Johnson to take concerted action:[30]

> there being several children of age to be instructed, I proposed to [Governor Phillip] to have a person appointed at different places to instruct them to read; to this he readily consented, and myself was appointed to superintend them; we have now one school established at *Sydney* and another at *Parramatta*; a schoolmistress appointed for each. These teach the children belonging to the *Convicts* gratis; the Military officers etc. making them some little acknowledgement for their trouble.[31]

At the same time as he began organising an education system for the whole colony, towards the end of 1792 and now almost five years in NSW,[32] Johnson delivered An *Address to the Inhabitants of the Colonies, Established in New South Wales and Norfolk Island*, which he subsequently published in 1794 so that many more inhabitants might read it—the first piece of Australian literature published. The two-part *Address* firstly outlines Johnson's understanding of the gospel of Christ and then provides some practical advice for putting that gospel into practice in everyday life. At every point, the *Address* drips with Johnson's perspective shaped by eternity.

It is there at the beginning as he entreats his hearers to consider the gospel message well:

> Oh, I intreat you, brethren, to consider what is contained in these two words, *salvation* and *damnation*! The one implies every thing

---

29 'Rules or Articles to be Observed Respecting the School at Sydney, New South Wales, 1798', Mackaness, *Some Letters*, part 2, No 31; Macintosh, *Richard Johnson*, 108. Rule #3: 'no child is to be admitted till he or she shall arrive at the age of three years'.
30 Macintosh, *Richard Johnson*, 88.
31 Johnson to Morice, 21 March 1792 (SPG Archive), as quoted in Macintosh, *Richard Johnson*, 88.
32 Since the First Fleet arrived in New South Wales in January 1788, the year of delivery can be calculated from his comment 'we have now been here almost five years', Johnson, *Address*, 1.

that an immortal soul can want or desire to make it happy. The other includes an idea, the most gloomy and dreadful that can be conceived. The former will be the admiration of angels, and the song and joy of the redeemed; the latter will be the torment of devils, and of all impenitent sinners, for ever and ever.

Remember likewise, that ere long, either this endless inconceivable happiness, or unutterable misery will be your portion, or your doom, and mine. Our glass of life is running away apace. Our time is fast hastening to a period. Death is making sure and speedy strides towards us daily, judgment is at hand, and the judge himself is at the door. And oh! consider, when the breath we now draw shall depart, the tender thread of life be cut, our state will be unalterably and for ever fixed; either to live with God, with angels, and glorified saints, in heaven; or to dwell with devils, in the darkness and torments of hell.

On these accounts your souls are, as I have already observed, very precious, not only in the sight of God, but also to me. My brethren, God is my record, how greatly I long after you all, in the bowels of Jesus Christ. Next to the salvation of my own soul, nothing in this world lies so near my heart, as the conversion and salvation of my fellow creatures; and especially of you, over whom I am appointed more immediately to watch, as one who must give an account.[33]

Although he was an ordained Church of England minister, he assured his hearers that the good news of Jesus Christ was not a sectarian concern, and it was eternity that was the great leveller:

Brethren, I do not ask you, what religious persuasion or denomination you have espoused. I fear, that, if I may judge of your hearts by your actions, too many are destitute of any sense of religion at all. But I do not address you as Churchmen or Dissenters, Roman Catholics or Protestants, as Jews or Gentiles; I suppose, yea, I know, that there are persons of every denomination amongst you. But I speak to you as men and women, as intelligent creatures, possessed of understanding and reason. I speak to you as mortals, and yet immortals [...]

---

33 Johnson, *Address*, 3–5.

> The great point is, how we shall die? whether as believers or unbelievers, as saints or sinners. One soul, according to our Lord's declaration, is of more value than the whole world. If you lose your soul, you lose all at once. You lose heaven and happiness for ever. Whatever, therefore, you do, or leave undone, for God's sake, and for your own sakes, neglect not for one day or hour longer, the vast concerns of another life.[34]

When Johnson embarked on the First Fleet, he had taken with him a collection of Bibles and other reading material for distribution. Amongst the Evangelicals, reading in itself was regarded as 'hygenic', for 'useful knowledge' was a health-bringing activity, assisting the individual to be morally transformed into a better human being for the greater good of society.[35] This was possible even for the convicts and soldiers of NSW. But even more importantly, if a person could read, they could then read the Bible for themselves, and in so doing, they could discover the great things achieved by Christ all for their benefit.

This first piece of Australian literature, therefore, urges the first Australians to learn to read for the sake of their eternal souls:

> I intreat you, therefore, to read the word of God carefully. Many of you have had Bibles or New Testaments given to you, and others might have them, if they had but an inclination to read.
>
> Some of you will perhaps object, and say, as you have already said to me, We cannot read. Others, We have no time given us. If you cannot read yourselves, you might prevail on some of your comrades to read to you.* As to your having no time, I much question it. Rather you have no inclination. Too many of you can find time to jest, to talk obscenely or profanely, to read and sing idle songs; why might not some, or rather the whole of this time be employed in reading, or hearing the Bible? You might find time, if you could find a will. But remember, that such excuses as you now make, will stand you in no stead when you appear before God in judgment.[36]

---

34 Johnson, *Address*, 24–26.
35 Gribben, 'Introduction'; Horde, 'The Library'; and for one Australian case-study, see Bolt, 'Thomas Moore's Bookshelf', 191, 195, and Bolt, 'Moore, Thomas (1762–1840)', 516–517, 521.
36 Johnson, *Address*, 38–39.

At this point in the published *Address*, and perhaps even in the original spoken version, Johnson as an educator adds a footnote (*) offering his every assistance in learning to read.[37] And even though he is addressing adults presumably at this stage of the colony's life, the address was delivered in exactly the same year that he was first gathering the children of the colony into classrooms.[38] We can, therefore, see in the *Address* the framework within which Johnson set the need to read, whether for adults or children. In his view, he was educating for eternity.

Certainly, the next world was demonstrably on Johnson's radar in all his pastoral ministrations. The year before he delivered *An Address*, he wrote to his 'old hostess' at Boldrewood of the next world, and with some excitement:

> In the first place then, permit me to condole with you respecting the death of your husband, & I pray God that he may be your husband & friend for you & yours all things needful & good for you both for this world, & for that which is to come.
>
> I hope that my worthy & kind friend is still above all things, seeking after the one thing needful. Ah, what are all the riches or honours of this world, when compared to the unsearchable Riches of Jesus, & those honours which God has laid up for the righteous in his heavenly & everlasting kingdom. I trust & hope by this time you have been led to see, to feel, & to experience the thrill [?] of those things of which you have been instructed.[39]

In his opinion, his views in Australia have not changed from what he preached in England:

> I do & ever shall rejoice with you though now several years have elapsed since I saw you, I have not even any cause why I'd alter or change my religious sentiments; nay, the more I study the word of God, & the more I become acquainted with men & things, the more am I established in the truth & importance of the doctrines which I have espoused, & which to the best of my judgment, & to the utmost of my poor abilities, I did whilst with you, inculcate & inforce upon the friends of the people, & that not only publicly but

---

37 Footnote * p.39: 'if there could be a convenient building created for this purpose, I should think myself happy, not only to furnish you with books, as far as I am able, but also personally to attend and assist you, as much as my immediate calls of duty would permit'.
38 Probably in the first part of 1792, cf. Macintosh, *Richard Johnson*, 88.
39 R. Johnson to Mary King, 17 September 1791 (Hampshire RO: 90M90/1).

also, (after the example of the great apostle) privately & from house to house testifying, Repentance towards God, & faith toward our Lord Jesus Christ. In that way I hope & trust I have hitherto studied to keep a conscience void of offence towards all; & by the Grace of God, I have long since come to this resolution & conclusion, that I will make Jesus Christ, & him crucified, the sum & substance of my preaching, well aware that whatever does not tend or aim to exalt the Saviour & to debase & humble the sinner, is antichrist & will never be accompanied or followed with any good success either in the conversion of sinners here or the eternal salvation hereafter.

[…] I once more exhort my f^d to be looking [firm]ly to this Jesus by an eye of faith. Be ass[ured] that he alone can do you good. I am go[in]g to preach to morrow from these two texts Luke 24:47 & Heb 7:25. I trust I find great pleasure at times in exalting this Jesus & preaching a free & full salvation through what he has done & suffered. Look to him, believe in him, live upon him. He can & will make afflictions & death itself easy & desirable. We are not to live here for ever & by & by, if we are the Lord's servants, he will call us to himself, & reward us with a 'well done good & faithful servant enter then into the joy of thy Lord.

His audience, however, has certainly changed, but despite the various blocks to their hearing, he is hopeful that the message of eternity will nevertheless penetrate:

I need not tell you that I am here situated amongst a set of people the most ignorant & abandoned that can be well conceived; & truly many of them too justly answer their description. Uncleanness, theft & other notoriously wicked practices are practiced too openly, too generally amongst them and after all the admonitions, warnings, threatenings promises &c given them, they seem to remain as insensible & stupid as ever—yet I'd hope that some are wrought upon; are convinced of their past folly, madness & the danger they have been in & are now seeking & enquiring the way to Zion. Oh that more & more may be so influenced, as to be wise to think of & purpose for their latter end.[40]

---

40 R. Johnson to Mary King, 17 Sept 1791 (Hampshire RO: 90M90/1).

Even his sign-off is touched by the eternal future:

> Through mercy we are all well. Have an increase of one daughter as sweet a babe as was ever born. Mrs J. unites in love to you & all f^ds. Remember me to Mrs Millys, & hope she is still pressing forward towards the prize.—'tis those that endure to the end that shall be saved'.

When Johnson died, long after he left NSW, H.G. Watkins preached a funeral sermon that mentioned that Johnson's final sermon (on Phil. 1:23) looked forward to his own departure to be with Christ. Noting that their pastor had often pressed these things upon them, Watkins cited more biblical texts that looked to the kingdom of God and heavenly rest and echoed one of the themes of Johnson's life by stating that parents:

> should bring up their children in the nurture and admonition of the Lord; i.e. that they should train them up in the way they should go, so that they may be useful in the world, and attain to heaven at the last.[41]

Johnson lived, served, and educated with a view to eternity.

A few examples from Johnson's two successors will suffice to show that they shared his eternal perspective. In a sermon on parents raising their children, Samuel Marsden exhorted his hearers:

> Endeavour to get a clear and strong persuasion of the reality of the Christian religion, the necessity of becoming acquainted with God here, before you can be entitled to the enjoyment of him in the eternal world.[42]

Or, on another occasion, both adults and children had to reckon with the same future:

> God has blessed you with his gospel. To you and your children is the word of this salvation sent. Repent therefore and turn unto the Lord and receive the benefits of his death and intercession. One would think the joys of heaven, the glories of the upper world, the favour and love of God, and the eternal happiness which he promises

---

41 Watkins, *A Sermon*, 12, 9–10, 6.
42 Marsden, Sermon 81 (Hebrews 11:19).

to all them who obey him, would be sufficient to draw all men to Jesus, that all would run to obtain this blessed prize of eternal life as soon as they were told that they might enjoy it. But alas, few believe the report. Few think it worthwhile to pay any attention to the concerns of their souls.[43]

Likewise, after a lengthy period of illness, William Cowper spoke of human beings facing 'daily mortality' and, therefore, having a 'duty of preparing for another world'.[44]

Following in Johnson's footsteps, Marsden and Cowper were instrumental in setting up the first primary-level education in NSW.[45] After Archdeacon Scott formed the Church and Schools Corporation, they both sat on its committee. This was, therefore, the perspective from which the King's Schools were formed and the perspective that looked towards their subsequent tertiary college. They were educating for eternity.

To return to the institutions as they were emerging, and taking them slightly out of order, this was also the perspective of The Australian College.

3.2 The Australian College

John Dunmore Lang never lost what had been impressed upon him by his own teachers, 'a lively impression of the joys of the elect and the eternal torments of the damned'.[46] His 1826 Caledonian School Prospectus demonstrated his outlook on education:

> The ultimate and legitimate end of all education is the formation of a moral and religious character and not merely the advancement of the human intellect in literature, philosophy and science.[47]

When Lang launched the newspaper *The Colonist* in January 1835, the first issue entered the debate, already gathering steam in the colony, over the proposal to introduce a General System of Education, such as that introduced by Lord Stanley into Ireland in 1831. One of the major concerns about what became

---

43 Marsden, Sermon 95 (Ephesians 2:18).
44 W. Cowper, [Sermon on Ps. 141:7], 14 October 1849.
45 Lieut. Gov. Sorrell also asked Cowper for advice in regard to setting up the system of education in Tasmania; see Bolt, *William Cowper*, 155.
46 Campbell, 'John Dunmore Lang', 9, citing Clark, *A Short History*, 70.
47 'Prospectus of an Institution proposed to be formed in Sydney under the designation of The Caledonian Academy', in Lang Papers, Vol.16, pp.1–3, cited from Campbell, 'John Dunmore Lang', 21.

known as 'the Irish System'—and a somewhat unjust concern due to a prevailing ignorance of the scheme—was that it removed religious instruction from schools. On this question, Lang was immediately forthright:

> Whether religious instruction of any kind should be imparted to the youth attending a public school [...] On this most momentous question we maintain the affirmative.[48]

This then led to several issues expounding his views on education, and he continued to raise the issue of education across the short life of the newspaper. These editorials, therefore, provide a window into his view of the aims of the Australian College. Certainly, education must prepare the student to take their place in society in the future, for 'the design of education [is] to fit men for filling their places and discharging their respective duties in society'. More importantly, however, it must have a role in moral transformation, for:[49]

> knowledge unaccompanied with virtuous principle, is like a sword in the hand of a madman. It may be used for the benefit, but the chances are ten to one that it will be used to the serious injury, not only of him who wields it, but of society at large.

But even this moral improvement is set within a larger goal:

> But if, as professed Christians, we believe that the existence of man shall not be terminated with this transitory state of being, and if we believe that his condition in a future life will depend on his discharge or neglect of his individual duties in the present, education will assume an importance infinitely greater than we should otherwise feel disposed to assign to it—it will appear to be nothing less than the training up of an intelligent being for immortality, and, its objects will appear commensurate with the duration of eternity. [...]
>
> In accordance with this view of the nature and design of education, we hold it of prime—of indispensible necessity —that along with the effort to impart mere knowledge to a child or pupil, there should be conjoined a systematic endeavour to imbue his mind with those principles of morality and religion that will fit him for the proper discharge of his relative duties in this world and prepare him for the next.

---

48 *Colonist* 29 January 1835.
49 *Colonist* 29 January 1835.

In other words, the Australian College was also educating for eternity.

But if the first two institutions discussed sought to be closely aligned with particular denominations, what of the Sydney College, which aimed to be open to all persuasions?

3.3 The Sydney College

After failing to get started in 1825, the idea of the Sydney Public Free Grammar School was revived in 1828, and a prospectus was written. In January 1830, its name was simplified to 'The Sydney College', and on Australia Day, a foundation stone was laid.[50] The revised prospectus published in February declared that: 'That the institution be available to all parties, of whatever religious persuasion', and in order to ensure this in the classroom, 'that no religious book be used, by authority'.[51] The one concession to that ban was 'the Old and New Testament'. However, signalling that the school had adopted what was known as 'the Lancaster system' of education propagated by the British and Foreign Schools Society, the Bible was to be read in the classroom 'without note or comment'.

Thus, despite attracting criticism in some circles for being 'non-religious', this was not strictly true. Rather, in the interests of extending education to all, the catechisms and secondary writings of the various Christian denominations were laid aside in favour of Christianity's primary text, regarded as being powerful enough to speak for itself.

The *Prospectus* concluded with the Committee 'expressing their sincere desire' for the future success of their institution:

> that as the Sydney College has been established under still more favourable auspices than many other academic institutions which have afterwards risen to eminence both in Europe and in America, its future advancement may keep pace with the best wishes of its founders.

Alongside this wish for temporal success, they also prayed for more ultimate outcomes for their graduates, desiring

> that, under the blessing of Almighty God, it may be extensively and increasingly efficient in diffusing useful knowledge, and promoting

---

50 *Prospectus of the Sydney College*, 7–8.
51 Resolution 11, *Prospectus of the Sydney College*, 6.

> the temporal *and eternal* welfare of many, throughout this most interesting part of the habitable globe.[52]

In what may sound a strange paradox to later generations who do not take the time to understand the nuances of the nineteenth-century debates, just as much as those of the Church of England King's School and the Presbyterian Australian College, the founders of the 'non-religious' Sydney College prayed to God that their students would be educated for eternity.

Despite the heated calumnies at the time, the issue was not about religion set against no religion, or even eternity set against a purely temporal horizon. Even at the time, the *Gazette* noted the real difficulty that was being negotiated:

> We are far, very far, from wishing to discourage any efforts for the mental improvement of the Colony, and we will only repeat our hope that the Sydney College, in endeavouring to steer clear of the Scylla of party in religion, will be equally cautions to avoid the Charybdis of Latitudinarianism and infidelity.[53]

Nobody wanted 'infidelity', that is, the lack of Christian faith, and nobody wanted 'party in religion', that is, the presence of sectarian division.

3.4 The Bitter Sectarian Battles

In December 1831, as these three educational plans were beginning to come into effect, each looking towards the establishment of a tertiary college, and each in their own way educating for eternity, Richard Bourke arrived as the next Governor of NSW. His attempt to bring in the 'Irish System' of general education inflamed the already simmering sectarian differences over education.[54] Although he failed in this aim, his Church Act of 1836 set all denominations on a firmer footing by providing subsidies for clerical salaries and for new church construction, ultimately available to all denominations. But it quickly became apparent that this 'Denominational System' was very expensive for the government. When Governor Gipps arrived on 24 February 1838, he soon returned to the question of a National System of Education, even though he favoured the Lancaster system being promoted by the British and Foreign

---

52 *Prospectus of the Sydney College*, 14. [my emphasis]
53 *SG* 28 January 1830.
54 See King, *Richard Bourke*, 226–232.

Schools Society and, in terms of our three emergent NSW institutions, having similarity to the Sydney College and the Australian College. Under Bourke and Gipps, the public debates over education grew heated, and, looking back, it is evident that sectarian concerns had polarised the discussion, and both sides were missing the point with the other.

But even in the midst of the heated discussions about which educational plan was best amongst the church groups, it is possible to find some voices amongst the clamour that still spoke about education in the light of the world to come. And, perhaps to the surprise of the hardened sectarian, they appear to have come from people on all sides of the various divides.

Amongst the speeches as the St Philip's Parochial Association met on 12 October 1841 for its first anniversary, Colonel Wodehouse spoke against

> the fallacy of that pernicious system which would confine the training of youth to the mere acquirement of those accomplishments which fit him for providing for the necessities, or ministering to the gratification of the perishing body, while it makes no provision for the more important concerns of the *immortal soul*; and while it professes to fit them for the various situations in which they may be placed in *this* world, totally neglects instructing them to make any preparation for the *next*.[55]

When the same group met in 1844 to organise a petition against the general education system about to be proposed by the Legislative Council, Rev. Robert Allwood declared that:

> mere secular instruction has no right to be called education; it is part of education, but not education itself. We find man endowed with the highest moral and intellectual powers, which are incapable of being satisfied in this world, and we consider that only as education which is addressed to the full development of these powers, which trains them to their proper end, their holy exercise in a future world.
>
> We consider any system of instruction which would fasten his mind down upon the concerns of this life unworthy of a being that is to live for ever; and that too a system which will not admit of his

---

55 *SG* 16 October 1841 (my emphasis).

> continuing long in this world without discovering that a void has been left in his heart which religious principles should have filled, and for which there is no substitute. For the day must come when another life will obtrude itself upon the thoughts, however we may now endeavour to evade it. In sickness and in sorrow, events which will sooner or later come upon every one, that education surely is faulty that does not provide against them—and I need scarcely say that it is not mental endowments nor intellectual acquirements which will then profit. The broken heart is not to be bound up by the smattering of a science, nor the bed of death smoothed by being able to range over the secrets of nature; but by that knowledge, which is able to make wise unto salvation.[56]

At the same time, but across town, about 500 Roman Catholics heard Rev. Dr Murphy express similar sentiments:

> Excellent as secular education was, without spiritual education it was nothing, and it was better that they should be wholly without the former, than that they should be deprived of the latter.[57]

Later in the century, when the Public Education Act 1880 withdrew all state support from denominational schools, Dean Cowper (the first William Cowper's son) remarked on 'the peculiar signification which was given to the word "secular" by this legal enactment'.[58] In comparison to the 'aggressively secular' 1872 Act in Victoria, that in NSW was 'religion-friendly',[59] permitting clergy to visit state schools for the purposes of giving denominational instruction.[60] Henry Parkes, the promoter of the Bill in NSW, insisted:

> It was never the intention of the framers of this Bill to exclude such a knowledge of the Bible as all divisions of the Christian church must possess, or a knowledge of the great truths of Revelation.[61]

---

56 *SG* 4 September 1844.
57 *SMH* 10 September 1844.
58 W.M. Cowper, *Autobiography and Reminiscences*, 184.
59 Piggin & Linder, *The Fountain*, 391.
60 Piggin & Linder, *The Fountain*, 390, citing the Act.
61 Piggin & Linder, *The Fountain*, 390.

Far from meaning 'the complete exclusion of the teaching of religion from state schools',[62] 'secular' was understood to mean 'anti-sectarian, not anti-Christian', for 'under this Act the teaching shall be strictly non-sectarian, but the words "secular instruction" shall be held to include general religious teaching as distinguished from dogmatical or polemical theology"'.[63] The roots of education in NSW had not been forgotten. As Bishop Barker affirmed to the Sydney Diocesan Synod in June 1879, public discussion continued:

> there are many persons in this community who owe all their hopes of heaven as well as their well-being in this life to the principles inculcated by the clergy in Church of England schools. [...] Education, to deserve the name, should be of the whole man—body, soul, and spirit.[64]

Thirty years earlier, at the end of almost two decades of bitter sectarian discussion about education, William Charles Wentworth rose in the Legislative Council to propose the University Bill that resulted in the foundation of the University of Sydney. When the Act received Royal Assent on 1 October 1850, it allowed for degrees in Arts, Law and Medicine and 'expressly stated that [the University] must belong to no religious denomination and require no religious test'.[65] This, too, was a stand against sectarianism. Even the founders of the University of Sydney did not want to stand in the way of a moral vision of education, with eternity in view.

4. The University of Sydney and Eternity

Although it might be true to say that the University of Sydney is Australia's oldest surviving tertiary institution, it was not Australia's first. Despite disputing with each other over the merits or otherwise of a national education system, the various denominations were still getting on with the educational job. While the Sydney College and the Australian College were dreaming of a future tertiary college rising from their ashes, the pressing needs for clergy in the colony moved both the Anglicans and the Catholics to actually start one—even if neither

---

62 Piggin & Linder, *The Fountain*, 391.
63 Piggin & Linder, *The Fountain*, 390, citing the Act.
64 Cowper, *Episcopate*, 367.
65 Dallen, *University of Sydney*, 9.

survived for very long. For the Anglicans, St James Grammar school was exalted to St James College at Lyndhurst in Glebe,[66] and the Catholics commenced training Benedictines at St Mary's College.[67]

In September 1849, when William Charles Wentworth promoted the University Bill in the Legislative Council, he dealt with several objections that had been raised against his proposed plan for that institution. As summarised by the *Gazette*, Wentworth declared its fundamental principle.

> It was to be an Institution merely for secular education. This principle was absolutely indispensable; if they once introduced the principle of sectarian interference, all government of such an institution was at an end, because if any one sect asserted its supremacy, all other sects would retire from it, and thus be virtually excluded from a participation in the benefits.[68]

Wentworth's proposal sought to manage the introduction of a university in such a way as to head the sectarian battle off before it even began and to remove the possibility of sectarian battles from Australia's future tertiary sector.[69] But the principle of secular education and the consequent prohibition of clergy on the Senate, or even from the lecture hall, should in no way be construed to mean that the proposed university was an 'infidel institution'. On the contrary, Wentworth shared the prevailing view that education was necessary to bring about moral transformation. He pushed this view even further, claiming that higher education was necessary for the greater prosperity, not just of the cause of morality but also of Christianity in particular.[70]

Against the charge that the exclusion of clergy was an 'irreligious measure', he hoped that

> however confined its provisions might be to the mere object of secular instruction, this Bill was not without provision to satisfy those who might have higher notions. The 21st clause provided

---

66 St James was the first to explicitly make the transition from Grammar School to Tertiary College, as noted by Campbell, 'John Dunmore Lang', 49. See further, Bolt, "Training Colonial Clergy'.
67 St Mary's Seminary was opened on 26 January 1838, *Monitor* 22 January 1838.
68 *SG* 5 October 1849.
69 After the collapse of the Church & School Corporation, at the departure of T.H. Scott, Wentworth had crowed over 'this triumph of justice over corruption and imbecility', as a rejection of an Established Church in the Colony, rejecting this feature of old England and looking instead to the US 'where all religions are tolerated and supported by their several disciples'; *Australian* 9 May 1829.
70 *SG* 5 October 1849.

> that, though religion might not be taught at the University, it might be instilled. Still would be left to pastors the task of impressing on the minds of students the tenets to which their parents clung.

This clause alone, he said, refutes the charge that it was an 'infidel institution'. Wentworth believed that

> to the higher extent education was carried, the more elevated the state of morality of the colony would become. He believed that the best mode of proving the divinity of the great Christian code, was to advance the intellect of those who trusted and relied upon it. He did not believe that the great truths of Christianity were safely entrusted to the uneducated man. [...] the cause of religion would rest more securely on the educated mind.

He ended his speech with accelerating rhetoric and with a vision of eternity:

> this measure was to enlighten the mind—to refine the understanding and to elevate the soul of their fellow-man— this, of all their acts, alone contained the germ of immortality. This, he trusted would live—would live to commemorate the Council who passed it [and give] a long line of heroes who would shed a deathless halo, not only on their country, but upon that University which called them into being.[71]

Wentworth's 'educational experiment' was modelled on the University of London,[72] which was a non-teaching body that provided examinations for multiple colleges around the country. One of those colleges (University College, London) was specifically non-religious to allow for people of non-Christian religions who might come from far-flung corners of the British Empire. But other colleges included denominational colleges and even colleges that taught theology, so in its wider constitution, the University of London was far from anti-religious or even non-religious and could hardly be described as 'an infidel

---

71 *SG* 5 October 1849.
72 See his speech to the Legislative Council, as reported in *SG* 5 October 1849.

institution'.⁷³ The one difference Wentworth's proposed university had from London was that it would be a teaching university, not just an examining body. But the plan clearly allowed for other affiliated colleges, who could teach their own courses and gain degrees, while at the same time taking advantage of the 'secular' education provided by the university professors. In fact, Wentworth's model specifically envisaged the incorporation of the Anglican theological college, St James, Lyndhurst (Glebe), and the Roman Catholic theological college, St Mary's, into the university system for he explicitly mentioned them in his speech to the Legislative Council.⁷⁴ Wentworth declared that, as with the University of London, the provision for affiliated colleges would mean in the near future 'the erection of such establishments in every part of the colony'.⁷⁵ By 1854, this model had become enshrined in the Affiliated Colleges Act.

It is also worth noting that, although it may have taken some members of the Legislative Council by surprise, when Wentworth introduced the University Bill in 1849, clause 20 specifically noted that the students would be required to have a religious attainment certificate signed by their churches before they were able to graduate with a degree from the university:⁷⁶ 'no religious tests to be administered, but regulations may be made for recording the due attendance of students at their respective churches'.⁷⁷

In other words, even if the university itself did not engage in it directly, its provision for affiliated colleges assumed that others would continue to operate within the tertiary environment, educating for eternity.

---

73 Objecting to the proposed ban on clergymen in the University, the *Sydney Morning Herald* (3 October 1849) noted that it was only the University College that had a principle of no religious tests, allowing people from all over the globe to attend. Listing a further 26 of the university's colleges, it noted that some were 'strictly theological seminaries', whether Church of England, Roman Catholic, Independent, or Wesleyan, and that 'all of them avail themselves of the University degrees, of course all teaching in their own halls their own peculiar tenets'.
74 This was to allow 'every sect' to compete for the University's degrees and honours, 'whether it was a candidate from St Mary's, or from Lyndhurst, the broad principle on which the University was founded, would admit all'; *SG* 5 October 1849.
75 *SG* 5 October 1849.
76 This was later removed by the University's first principal, John Woolley, an import from England and a Unitarian unsympathetic with the history or desires of Sydney's Christian denominations; Cable, 'Woolley, John (1816–1866)'.
77 *SG* 5 October 1849.

Conclusions

Wentworth was Australian-born. Although there were established churches in Ireland, England, and Scotland, there had never been and nor would there be an established church in Australia. The educational context in Australia was, therefore, different too, and although Christianity has a significant role to play, the sectarian squabbles of the home countries must not be allowed to be repeated to the detriment of higher education in Australia.

In many ways, the contemporary theological sector may find itself sitting somewhat uncomfortably within the contemporary Australian higher education environment. But it needs to be remembered that, from its beginning, Australian education operated with the goal of the betterment of society through the moral improvement of the individual, deeply motivated by the prospect of eternity. As tertiary education emerged, it had to allow for the sectarian differences within the peculiar context of a land without an established church. The unique and experimental model that emerged, and which became the model for all Australian universities,[78] was one in which secular education and Christianity could co-exist and mutually benefit one another.

Alongside the university, Christianity ought to grow in strength, depth, and persuasiveness as it is subjected to the rigour of critical inquiry. But alongside tertiary institutions thoroughly committed to Christianity, the university ought to be constantly reminded not only that we share a common goal in the betterment of society through the moral improvement of the individual but, like it or lump it, we are all educating for eternity.

Bibliography

1. Primary Sources

Corporation of Church & School Lands *Plan for the Formation and Regulation of the King's Schools, Preparatory to the Institution of a College* (Sydney: R. Mansfield, 1830; 21832).

Cowper, W. *A Sermon [on Ps. 141:7] Preached in St. Philip's Church, Sydney on Sunday, October 14, 1849* (Sydney: W.R. Piddington, [1849]).

Halloran, L.H. *Proposals for the foundation and support of a public free grammar school, in ... Sydney ... : respectfully submitted to the consideration of the Governor & Council, and of the inhabitants* (Sydney: Government Printer, 1825). http://nla.gov.au/nla.obj-52756556.

Johnson, R. *An Address to the Inhabitants of the Colonies, Established in New South Wales and Norfolk Island* (London: Goff & Amey, 1794). http://setis.library.usyd.edu.au/ozlit.

---

78 Cable, 'Woolley, John (1816–1866)'.

Johnson, R. Letter to Mary King, 17 Sept 1791 (Hampshire RO: 90M90/1).

Lang, J.D. 'Prospectus of an Institution proposed to be formed in Sydney under the designation of The Caledonian Academy', in *Lang Papers*, Vol.16. Education 1826–1871 (Mitchell: A 2236).

Mackaness, G. *Some Letters of Rev. Richard Johnson, B.A. First Chaplain of New South Wales* (2 parts; Sydney: D.S. Ford, 1954).

Macquarie, L. Journal. *Lachlan and Elizabeth Macquarie Archive.* https://www.mq.edu.au/macquarie-archive/lema/.

Marsden, S. Sermons 81 & 95; see D.B. Pettett, *Transcription of Samuel Marsden's Sermons.* https://myrrh.library.moore.edu.au:443/handle/10248/5508.

Scott, T.H. *Plan for a permanent provision for the Church establishment, submitted to the Secretary of State for the Colonies, 30 March 1824.* NSW Governor's Despatches, vol. 5, 1823–24, pp. 709–760 (Mitchell: A1194).

Sydney College *Prospectus of the Sydney College, New South Wales, with a Short Statement of the Proceedings of the Committee of Management* (Sydney: R. Mansfield, 1830). digital.slv.vic.gov.au/dtl_publish/pdf/marc/1/1324563.html

Watkins, H.G. *A Sermon on the Occasion of the Decease of the Rev. Richard Johnson B.A., Rector of St Antholin's and St John Baptist, preached on Sunday, March 25th, 1827* (London: W. Gilbert, 1827).

2. Secondary Sources

Austin, A.G. 'Halloran, Laurence Hynes (1765–1831)', *Australian Dictionary of Biography*, vol. 1 (Melbourne: Melbourne University Press, 1966). http://adb.anu.edu.au/biography/halloran-laurence-hynes-2149/text2741.

Bolt, P.G. 'Moore, Thomas (1762–1840)', in C. Stitz (eds.), *Australian Book Collectors. Some Noted Australian Book Collectors & Collections of the Nineteenth and Twentieth Centuries.* Second Series Part II: I–Z (Brighton, Vic.: Green Olive Press, 2013): 509–529.

Bolt, P.G. *William Cowper (1778–1858): The Indispensable Parson. The Life & Influence of Australia's First Parish Clergyman* (Camperdown, NSW: Bolt Publishing Services, 2009).

Bolt, P.G. 'Training Colonial Clergy after Moore's Will and Before Moore's College', in *Thomas Moore of Liverpool: One of our Oldest Colonists. Essays and Addresses to Celebrate 150 Years of Moore College* (Camperdown, NSW: Bolt Publishing Services, 2007): 249–293.

Bolt, P.G. 'Thomas Moore's Bookshelf', *Thomas Moore of Liverpool. One of our Oldest Colonists. Essays & Addresses to Celebrate 150 Years of Moore College* (Camperdown, NSW: Bolt Publishing Services, 2007): 115–210.

Border, R. 'Scott, Thomas Hobbes (1783–1860)', *Australian Dictionary of Biography*, vol. 2 (Melbourne: Melbourne University Press, 1967) http://adb.anu.edu.au/biography/scott-thomas-hobbes-2645/text3685.

Burton, W.W. *The State of Religion and Education in New South Wales* (London: J. Cross & Simpkin & Marshall, 1840).

Cable, K.J. 'Woolley, John (1816–1866)', *Australian Dictionary of Biography*, vol. 6 (Melbourne: Melbourne University Press, 1976). http://adb.anu.edu.au/biography/woolley-john-4885/text8173.

Campbell, K.R. 'John Dunmore Lang, Presbyterianism and Tertiary Education in New South Wales, 1831–1875' (Unpublished MA thesis, University of NSW, 1967). http://unsworks.unsw.edu.au/fapi/datastream/unsworks:48462.

Clark, C.M.H. *A Short History of Australia* (London: Penguin, 2006 [1963]).

Cowper, W.M. *The Autobiography and Reminiscences of William Macquarie Cowper, Dean of Sydney* (Sydney: Angus & Robertson, 1902).

Cowper, W.M. *Episcopate of the Right Reverend Frederic Barker, D.D. Bishop of Sydney and Metropolitan of Australia. A Memoir* (London: Hatchards, 1888).

Dallen, R.A. *The University of Sydney. Its History and Progress* (Sydney: Sydney University Union, 21925 [1914]).

Fletcher, B.H. *Ralph Darling. A Governor Maligned* (Melbourne: Oxford University Press, 1984).

Gribben, A. 'Introduction', in *Reading for Moral Progress: Nineteenth Century Institutions Promoting Social Change*. Papers from the Conference on Faith and History, Messiah College, Grantham, Pennsylvania, 7–8 October 1994 (Occasional Papers, Graduate School of Library and Information Services, University of Illinois at Urbana-Champaign; 1997): 1–4.

Grose, K. 'Dr. Halloran: Pioneer Convict Schoolmaster in New South Wales: A Study of His Background', *Australian Journal of Education* 14.3 (1970), 303–324.

Horde, D.M. 'The Library is a Valuable Hygenic Appliance', in *Reading for Moral Progress: Nineteenth Century Institutions Promoting Social Change*. Papers from the Conference on Faith and History, Messiah College, Grantham, Pennsylvania, 7–8 October 1994 (Occasional Papers, Graduate School of Library and Information Services, University of Illinois at Urbana-Champaign; 1997): 19–42.

King, H. *Richard Bourke* (Melbourne: Oxford University Press, 1971).

Macintosh, N.K. *Richard Johnson. Chaplain to the Colony of New South Wales. His Life and Times 1755–1827* (North Sydney: Library of Australian History, 1978).

Piggin, S., & R.D. Linder, *The Fountain of Public Prosperity. Evangelical Christians in Australian History 1740–1914* (Melbourne: Monash University Publishing, 2018).

Rainey, W.H. *The Real Richard Johnson* (Melbourne: Marshall, Morgan, & Scott, 1947).

Rosenhain, G. 'John Dunmore Lang. His Work and Influence in Australian Education' (Unpublished MA Thesis, University of Adelaide, 1949). https://digital.library.adelaide.edu.au/dspace/handle/2440/109997.

Ward, J.M 'Foundation of the University of Sydney', *JRAHS* 37.5 (1952).

Peter G. Bolt
Sydney College of Divinity, Sydney
peterb@scd.edu.au

5 | FIT FOR PURPOSE

GRADUATE ATTRIBUTES GROUNDED IN ECCLESIOLOGY

Abstract

This genesis of this paper lies in a concern that the graduate attributes proposed by theological higher education institutions in Australia are not always fit for purpose. Given the state of regulation in Australian higher education today, there is a danger that theological institutions will be overly influenced by secular understandings of the nature of appropriate graduate attributes. Graduate attributes are grounded, consciously or unconsciously, on assumptions about the purpose of higher education or the nature of the profession that graduates will enter. This paper grounds the graduate attributes for a theological higher education institution in a descriptive and imaginative account of the local congregation as a learning community.

1. Introduction

This paper begins with a review of developments in the scope of graduate attributes in higher education in Australia and considers their implications for theological education. All graduate attributes have a back story. Their development draws on some form of narrative that provides a history or background context. The theological graduate attributes that I propose in

Section 3 of this paper stem from a particular, perhaps idiosyncratic, narrative.

Section 2 describes this narrative in terms of a certain ecclesiology. This ecclesiology views the local church as a learning community within which graduates will participate as the 'first among equals'. I argue for a clear focus on refreshed forms of Christian relationship within the local church that lead to transformation that enables a different way of living. In order to equip graduates to serve in such a context, Section 3 proposes and describes six graduate attributes: teamwork and leadership skills; interpersonal relationship skills; skills in problem-solving and generating solutions; global citizenship and cultural competence; competence in reflective practice; and knowledge of the ecclesiology upon which these graduate attributes are built.

2. Graduate Attributes

The focus of graduate attributes in higher education has changed recently. In 2000, a commonly quoted definition of graduate attributes was:

> Graduate attributes are the qualities, skills and understandings a university community agrees its students should develop during their time with the institution. These attributes include but go beyond the disciplinary expertise or technical knowledge that has traditionally formed the core of most university courses. They are qualities that also prepare graduates as agents of social good in an unknown future.[1]

By 2015, the definition had changed to emphasise employability and further study:

> on completion of a course of study, students [must] have demonstrated the learning outcomes specified for the course of study, whether assessed at unit level, course level, or in combination... [and] the learning outcomes for a course (degree) must include generic skills important to employment and further study, and independent and critical thinking skills suitable for life-long learning.[2]

---

1   Oliver & Jorre de St Jorre, *Graduate Attributes*, 822.
2   Oliver & Jorre de St Jorre, *Graduate Attributes*, 822.

Some commentators see a conflict between preparing students for employment and preparing students as agents of social good. They argue that preparing students for citizenship erodes the true function of higher education. However, this is a false distinction. Employees must be good citizens in the workplace. They must contribute to the good of the firm and, thus, to the good of the nation.[3]

According to Oliver and Jorre de St Jorre, the most common graduate attributes in Australian higher education in 2011 and 2015 were (1) written and oral communication; (2) critical and analytical (and sometimes creative and reflective) thinking; (3) problem-solving (including generating ideas and innovative solutions); (4) information literacy, often associated with technology; (5) learning and working independently; (6) learning and working collaboratively; (7) ethical and inclusive engagement with communities, cultures, and nations. However, by 2015, there was increased emphasis on information literacy, global citizenship, and problem-solving.

In addition to the broad categories of graduate attributes above, Oliver and Jorre de St Jorre noted some 'Other Attributes' that included (1) self-reliance and confidence; (2) leadership; (3) scholarly integrity; (4) numeracy; and (5) interdisciplinarity. Of these 'Other Attributes', emphasis on leadership changed little between 2011 and 2015. Self-reliance and confidence, scholarly integrity, and numeracy, although not highly rated overall, received much less emphasis in 2015. Interdisciplinarity did not feature in 2011 but by 2015 was receiving equal emphasis with leadership. Interdisciplinarity refers to 'to the capacity to acquire knowledge and understanding of fields of study beyond a single discipline or to understand one's discipline across interdisciplinary contexts'.[4]

For theological education, the decreasing support for scholarly integrity may be a warning. On the other hand, the emergence of interdisciplinarity may be a pointer to the future. In the context of theological education, interdisciplinarity suggests attention might be well paid to close integration of the traditional theological disciplines. Many theological universities organise the curriculum around Old Testament studies; New Testament studies; church history; systematic theology and ethics; and practical theology, missiology, and pedagogy of religion. Each discipline is separated from the other, and there is an emphasis on specialisation. Interdisciplinarity requires a reduction in separation and specialisation.

---

3   Oliver & Jorre de St Jorre, *Graduate Attributes*, 822.
4   Oliver & Jorre de St Jorre, *Graduate Attributes*, 825.

Most theological universities will have no difficulty recognising the common graduate attributes identified by Oliver and Jorre de St Jorre: communication; critical, analytical, creative and reflective thinking; problem-solving; information literacy; learning and working independently and collaboratively; and ethical and inclusive engagement with communities, cultures, and nations. Indeed, most of them are central to the formation of theological graduates. However, in this paper, I will focus on attributes related to ethical and inclusive engagement of several kinds, reflective thinking, working collaboratively, and interdisciplinarity. This emphasis relates strongly to the fourth of Oliver and Jorre de St Jorre's seven key actions. The fourth key action is that higher education institutions should continue to emphasise attributes associated with global citizenship, teamwork and communication; give more emphasis to independence, critical thinking and problem-solving, and the fundamental foundational skills of written and spoken communication.[5]

Before proceeding to consider graduate attributes more deeply, let us take Oliver and Jorre de Jorre's first three key actions: higher education institutions should:

- Publish the attributes they focus on, aligning the emphasis with the needs of their students and the aims of their institutions
- Ensure that attributes are contextualised and communicated at a course level, including in the curriculum, course handbooks, and marketing materials
- Be more explicit with students: Those who teach students and support their learning should communicate intended outcomes and explain their importance repeatedly throughout the course.[6]

3. A Back Story for the Development of Graduate Attributes that Equip Graduates to Fulfil the Calling— Do Justice, Love Kindness, Walk Humbly

Although it might seem a little sententious or platitudinous, perhaps we should begin by asking, 'What does God require of the graduates of theological institutions?' What does God have in mind for graduates? What does God have

---

5   Oliver & Jorre de St Jorre, *Graduate Attributes*, 833.
6   Oliver & Jorre de St Jorre, *Graduate Attributes*, 833.

in mind for those church members the graduates will work with and for? First, God's requirements for graduates of theological institutions are no different to God's requirements of any person: 'He has told you, O mortal, what is good; and what does the Lord require of you but to do justice, and to love kindness, and to walk humbly with your God?' (Mic. 6:8 NRSVA). Second, speaking to God's people in Ephesus, Paul indicated that God has given his people grace. This grace came from Christ, whose purpose in ascending into heaven was to 'fill all things'. Paul emphasises that God's people, be they apostles, prophets, evangelists, pastors, teachers, or others, have a calling, a vocation, a purpose. They are called to use their giftedness to 'equip the saints for the work of ministry, for building up the body of Christ, until all of us come to the unity of the faith and of the knowledge of the Son of God, to maturity, to the measure of the full stature of Christ. . . . [S]peaking the truth in love, we must grow up in every way into him who is the head, into Christ' (Eph. 4:11-16 NRSVA).

The church is the body of Christ (Col. 1:24). Rowan Williams translates this vision for the graduates of theological institutions using contemporary language. The church is 'first of all a kind of space cleared by God through Jesus in which people may become what God made them to be (God's sons and daughters)'. These children of God are to inhabit the body of Christ, the church, 'as a climate or a landscape'. Williams does not elaborate on these terms, but it is worth looking more closely at what he might mean by inhabiting the body of Christ, the church, as a landscape.[7]

3.1 Church as a Landscape

When we think of landscape, we may imagine ourselves in the bush, in nature, where we become aware of some trees, creeks, waterfalls, open plains, clouds, hills, houses, roads, and so on. In the main, we see individual objects or groups of objects, or some objects in relation to others. Rarely do we perceive 'landscape'. Rarely does our consciousness become aware of 'a wholeness, a unity, over and above its component elements, without being tied to their specificity or mechanistically composed of them'.[8]

Tony Campolo told a story of a 'landscape experience' when he visited the Empire State Building in Grade 9.

---

7   Williams, *The Christian Priest Today*.
8   Simmel, *The Philosophy of Landscape*, 20.

> Like most boys my age, I was chasing girls and crawling around the observation area. Then suddenly, I caught myself! I walked to the railing and peered over the edge of the building. The magnificence of the skyscrapers of New York lay before me and I stood there, stunned into reverence. In one mystical moment, I absorbed the city. I gazed at it with such intensity that if I were to live a million years that moment would still be part of my consciousness. I was so fully alive at that moment, that I sensed it had become part of my eternal now.[9]

If we are fortunate enough to become aware of this wholeness, when we become aware of 'nature,' we sense an 'infinite interconnectedness' between all that lies around us. We become aware of 'the uninterrupted creation and destruction of forms'. When something happens before us, we sense its 'flowing unity' as it expresses itself over time or in the space that lies before us. Nature is the 'unity of a whole'. It is unbounded. It is real. It exists. It has no connection with 'art and artifice' or 'something intellectual or historical'.[10]

The scene in John 12:1-8 expresses something of the landscape quality. According to the disciple John, the scene follows soon after Jesus raised Lazarus from the dead. The family of Lazarus and his sisters, Martha and Mary, host Jesus for a meal, perhaps an overnight stay. This is an intimate family scene. Jesus loved Lazarus (John 11:3). He loved this family, and they loved him. Mary suddenly took it all in. Jesus was part of the family. There was no shame here. A woman could let down her hair at home with her family. Mary loves Jesus for the brotherly-sisterly relationship they have and for the way he treats Martha and her as equals. She loves him because he brought Lazarus back to life. Martha had already recognised Jesus as 'the Messiah, the Son of God, the one coming into the world' (11:27). As Jesus approached the home before raising Lazarus, Mary had knelt at his feet saying that Lazarus would have died had Jesus not been there. It seems as though during the meal, Mary suddenly sees the landscape before her. She is aware of its 'flowing unity'. She intuits who Jesus is. She senses Jesus' impending death. Then, she is shattered by the significance of the chief priests' and Pharisees' order that 'anyone who knew where Jesus was should let them know' (3:57). Overcome with emotion, she anoints him in preparation for his death as any sister anoints her dead brother in preparation for his burial. Jesus understands what she has done with his

---

9   Campolo, *Let Me Tell You a Story*, 73.
10 Simmel, *The Philosophy of Landscape*, 21.

comment in 12:7: 'she bought it [the nard] so that she may keep it for the day of my burial'. She uses her hair because, in this way, Jesus is also anointing her. This was Mary's mystical moment.

Viewed in these ways, when followers of Jesus inhabit the body of Christ, the church, as a landscape, they become aware of the unity, the wholeness. Without losing sight of the individual elements, they become aware of the flow that exists between these brothers and sisters in the body; they become aware of the flow of Christ's presence in the body. They sense the reality of the body. They, too, have mystical moments, perhaps not as momentous as Campolo or Mary, but mystical nevertheless. This reality is not the church as an institution because the institution is an artifice.

Williams says that God's people, ordained or otherwise, must be what Habakkuk and Ezekiel called watchmen. The church, the body of Christ, is a place where people dwell and where they can see the wholeness, the unity. They can see God, God's creation, and themselves properly. In order to fulfil their role, God's people, ordained or otherwise, must be free to see. They must occupy a position where they can see what is going on, where the danger lies, what the patterns are, what is the best way forward. They must be able to read the world around them, to read the surrounding cultures, to read the various expressions of emotion, to read the myths of the contemporary world, and to read human hearts. They must be able to watch out that they do not fall (1 Cor. 10:12). In this context, God's people must build the Christian community. They must build up the body of Christ, until all God's people come to the unity of the faith and of the knowledge of the Son of God, to maturity, to the measure of the full stature of Christ. They must help each other 'to make sense to each other and of each other'.[11] They are to see each other as new creations, see Christ in each other, and to assist each other in the process of becoming the righteousness of God (2 Cor. 5:21). The righteousness of God, the character of God, the justice of God will be revealed for all to see in the right relationships with God, with each other, and with the world. Within the church community, God's people must help each other to work together, to cooperate, to collaborate, to recognise and release each other's gifts. For all these various functions to be released, there must be a degree of overall coordination—a person or people who

---

11   See also Romans 15 where Paul refers to the strong putting up with the failings of the weak; building up the neighbour; living in harmony so that together they may with one voice glorify God; welcoming one another; instructing one another.

orchestrates the various activities, who bring a degree of coordination to the enterprise, and who are committed to building a 'differentiated unity'.[12]

3.2 Letter from Christ

There is another way we can understand this principle of 'seeing' one another. In 2 Corinthians 3, members of the church in Corinth show that collectively they are a letter from Christ. The message that the church in Corinth revealed to the world was written by the Spirit of the living God and delivered by Paul. This message was written directly on human hearts. It was not written in ink or on tablets of stone. These Christians showed Christ's message. They showed the good news. They showed the world, and they showed each other. They looked at each other, and they saw the good news of Christ at work. Verse 12 points to a collective transformation. Paul then used the image of a mirror rather than a letter. In this image, the glory of the Lord fell on them and in them. Like a mirror, they reflected this glory to each other. The presence of the Holy Spirit in their lives allowed them to see through unveiled eyes. Then, they truly saw each other and saw the glory of God within each other. As they contemplated the Lord's glory, they were being 'transformed into his image with ever-increasing glory, which comes from the Lord, who is the Spirit'. (v. 18 NIVUK). This transformation was a multi-sensory experience. God put each Christian on display in Christ. Through each Christian, God

> spreads the aroma of the knowledge of Him in every place. For to God we are the fragrance of Christ among those who are being saved and among those who are perishing. To some we are an aroma of death leading to death, but to others, an aroma of life leading to life. (2 Cor. 3:14-16 (Holman))

3.3 Reflections from the Mirror

Gregory of Nyssa also picked up on the mirror image. Gregory was interested in Christian formation. Christian formation takes place when God's people are actively engaged in receiving the very life of God. It also occurs as they grow in their understanding of themselves as living by participation in God. This last statement recalls Williams' comment on deeply seeing ourselves. For Gregory,

---

12 Williams, *The Christian Priest Today*.

the quality of activity that enables proper reception is the key to receiving the life of God. Gregory used the mirror image in the following way. The sun shines a beam of light on the mirror. The mirror receives the beam and then emanates a beam or ray into the surrounding environment. The soul is like the mirror. The soul receives the light of God and reflects it. The soul reflects the activity of God. The quality of the reflection depends on the receptivity of the mirror. The reception is limited if the mirror is dirty or clouded over. This then affects the quality of the reflection. In this way, each person, created in the image of God, exhibits a likeness to God. However, while all are created in the likeness of God, not all partake in the likeness to the same degree. Gregory uses a musical instrument to illustrate. The instrument can sit idle, or it can be played or activated. In the same way, the image of God must be activated within each person. The ultimate goal of each human being is to participate in God's complex plan of loving the whole world. In order to grow into greater likeness to God and more fully participate in God's plan, human beings, in the grace of God, must engage in consistent personal and spiritual discipline. This discipline or ascetic practice clears away the grime on the mirror. According to Gregory, Christians must examine constantly their own thoughts, their own words, and their own actions in their innermost depths to see whether they are oriented to Christ or are drifting away from him.[13] Gregory's emphasis on actively growing into God echoes various New Testament emphases on growing in righteousness: 'In him we might become the righteousness of God' (2 Cor. 5:21); 'strive for the kingdom of God and his righteousness' (Matt. 6:33). This cleaning the mirror provides the opportunity to move towards a life of what Gregory calls 'virginity'. This life is one of divine beauty and of purity. The soul is engaged with God. It is disengaged from the distractions of the world but continues to be engaged in loving the world. The soul is free from corruption.[14]

If I understand Gregory correctly, each follower of Jesus within the body of Christ, within the church, continually reflects the image of God to others. As they engage in cleaning the mirror, that image is more clearly and brightly reflected on others. 'Now we see in a mirror, dimly, but then we will see face to face' (1 Cor. 13:12). However, in this life, that mirror may always be somewhat dim, but under God's grace and with ascetic practice, that mirror may become less dim. As it does, so the clearer image of God is reflected on each other in the

---

13   Benedict XVI, Saint Gregory of Nyssa (2).
14   Volpe, *Rethinking Christian Identity*, 154–163.

church. However, in most churches, Christians sit in rows looking forward to the minister or song leader. They are not particularly conscious of each other except, perhaps when the Gospel is read from the centre of the church with everyone looking to the reader but conscious of fellow Christians standing all around. Christians may also be conscious of each other if the church practises 'passing the peace' when people move around the church greeting each other with 'The peace of the Lord be with you'. Even when a church follows these rituals, most Christians do not perceive these moments as a conscious movement toward being 'transformed into his image with ever-increasing glory, which comes from the Lord, who is the Spirit'. When Christians participate in small study groups or other interactive and communicative settings, they stand a greater chance of truly being aware of each other, of actually seeing each other. In the main, however, followers of Jesus are not conscious that God's image within each one is shaping and forming them through each other. Church members are more prone to seeing faults or limitations in each other, yet teaching on the body of Christ urges them to look at each other. Rather than seeing others as less honourable, they should extend greater honour to them. God has put the body together and has given greater honour to the less honourable. Gregory encouraged his readers to see Christ in those around them. Christ is present in the poor. Christians should not despise the poor. The poor have worth and dignity in God's eyes:

> They represent the Person of the Saviour. And this is how it is: 'For in his goodness, the Lord gives them his own Person so that through it, those who are hard of heart and enemies of the poor may be moved to compassion [...] Gregory speaks of rising to God in prayer through purity of heart, but also rising to God through love of neighbour. Love is the ladder that leads to God'.[15]

Love is the power to 'act-each-other-into-well-being'.[16] Love is the power to act-each-other-into-righteousness.

When Christians fail to look at each other, they are like the Israelites in the wilderness when Moses came down from the mountain with the tablets. Moses had been face to face with God. His 'mirror' shone brilliantly. The image of God was revealed in a remarkable way, but the people refused to allow that

---

15 Benedict XVI, Saint Gregory of Nyssa (2).
16 Beverley Harrison cited in Chopp, *Saving Work*, 41.

image to be reflected onto them. They demanded that Moses cover the image with a cloth. When Christians refuse to look at God's glory reflected to them through their brothers and sisters, they refuse to allow that image of God to penetrate them and to shape their very being. They turn away from 'acting-each-other-into-wellbeing'.

3.4 Proposed Graduate Attributes

The graduates of theological institutions may be those entering the priesthood or some other form of ordained ministry. They may work in missionary service or in parachurch settings. They may be laity who simply want to be better equipped Christians capable of expressing their faith appropriately in everyday life. In whatever sphere they serve, the model of the church outlined above will require them to work alongside others either in congregational or other contexts. These graduates will practise a form of servant leadership where they lead from alongside rather than above. They might be the 'first among equals', but essentially they will share parity with other members of the body of Christ.[17]

The ecclesiology outlined above presents the ideal church as a community of learning. In this context, a learning community is a community in which members assist each other in achieving their spiritual development needs. This community focuses on social interaction and identity rather than individual action. Members collaborate in the learning process. They are actively engaged in problem-solving and in generating solutions to the problems that arise in their joint enterprise. In the main, status and rank are set aside. All members of the community interact with each other in ways that demonstrate mutual appreciation that is expressed in the richness of their discourse. There is a strong and growing sense of interdependence and active engagement in the construction of knowledge as the community continues as a learning cohort over time.[18]

The graduate attributes proposed below are by no means comprehensive. They focus on attributes that are easily overlooked but which are essential for the preparation of graduates to contribute to the kinds of ministry described above. Clearly, graduates will also need knowledge of certain academic disciplines. However, in a learning community, the same degree of competence in the disciplines may be less significant. The skills in problem-solving referred

---

17 Greenleaf, *Servant Leadership*, 66.
18 This description of the church as a learning community is adapted from the literature review of learning communities in Smith and Bath, *The Role of the Learning Community*.

to below may, to some degree, offset the need for highly developed discipline knowledge. Taking the foregoing into account, graduates will have the following attributes:

GRADUATE ATTRIBUTES	DESCRIPTORS[19]
Teamwork and leadership skills	Seeks and considers feedback from others. Exhibits sensitivity and understanding of others' perspectives in a respectful manner. Maintains healthy, mutually beneficial relationships with others. Effectively weaves and analyses information from multiple sources and perspectives into a cohesive narrative. Employs narrative to engage people and call them to action. Acts in congruence with personal, organisational, and community values and beliefs. Demonstrates leadership through role modelling, influence, and service.
Interpersonal relationship skills	Accepts responsibility for actions. Works collaboratively with others. Recognises how one's personal actions affect other people and communities. Constructively resolves interpersonal conflicts.
Skills in problem solving and generating solutions	Creatively elicits ideas and proposals from others in a way that builds on their knowledge and leads to active engagement in the construction of knowledge. Develops creative and effective responses to communal, personal, intellectual, professional, and social challenges.
Global citizenship and cultural competence	Demonstrates the ability to work with people of different genders, sexual orientations, races/ethnicities, nations, religions, socioeconomic statuses. Exhibits the ability to connect with others across communities. Adapts behaviours appropriately to live and work in an evolving, diverse world. Demonstrates care and concern for the welfare of others. Engages in community involvement and/or affiliation with suitable organisations.

---

19   The ideas in the table were guided by Fitzell, Reflective Practice and Northwestern University, Learning Domain - Interpersonal Competence.

Competence in reflective practice	Understands and employs the reflective practice cycle that includes experiencing certain events or situations, reflecting on them and subjecting them to critical analysis, interpreting the reflection with a view to informed action taking in future situations. Employs the reflective practice cycle in interpersonal relationships, in pastoral settings, and in reflecting on broader societal and cultural trends. Employs the reflective practice cycle as a personal, a communal, and a spiritual discipline.
Knowledge of the ecclesiology upon which these graduate attributes are built	Understands that the body of Christ, the local congregation, is actually an interconnected whole, in which each part is equally valuable and visible and where each part seeks to form relationships with other parts in order to build each other and build the church and wider community.

Conclusion

The graduate attributes proposed above prepare graduates to participate in local congregations that are learning communities. The choice of congregations as learning communities is not driven by educational theory, personal preference, or institutional demands. It is driven by a particular vision of what it means to be 'the body of Christ'. This vision tries to imagine what the body of Christ might look like in 2020. It is a vision that rejects my current experience of what the church is today in 2019.

This paper has attempted to start with a view of what the church might be and then let that view drive the development of graduate attributes. Given the state of regulation in Australian higher education today, there is a danger that theological institutions will be overly influenced by secular understandings of the nature of appropriate graduate attributes. There is a risk that theological graduate attributes will echo the graduate attributes of universities. Graduate attributes must be fit for purpose, and what is fitting for theological institutions may be quite different from other higher education institutions. The attributes proposed here focus more on reflective thinking than critical thinking, on interdependence rather than independence, on mutuality rather than autonomy, self-reliance, and confidence, and on caring for and service to others rather than personal success and achievement.

Bibliography

Benedict XVI, *Saint Gregory of Nyssa (2)*, General Audience, Saint Peter's Square, Wednesday, 5 September 2007 <https://w2.vatican.va/content/benedict-xvi/en/audiences/2007/documents/hf_ben-xvi_aud_20070905.html> [accessed 4 March 2019]

Campolo, T. *Let Me Tell You a Story: Life Lessons from Unexpected Places and Unlikely People* (Nashville, Tennessee: Thomas Nelson, 2000) https://books.google.com.au/books?id=gRyXIbfNXEgC&printsec=frontcover&dq=Let+Me+Tell+You+a+Story:+Life+Lessons+from+Unexpected+Places+and+Unlikely+People&hl=en&sa=X&ved=0ahUKEwiUt52Xla_lAhXNbSsKHRXUD_kQ6AEIKTAA#v=onepage&q=Let%20Me%20Tell%20You%20a%20Story%3A%20Life%20Lessons%20from%20Unexpected%20Places%20and%20Unlikely%20People&f=false [accessed on 8 April 2019]

Chopp, R.S. *Saving Work* (Louisville, Kentucky: Westminster John Knox Press, 1995)

Fitzell, J. *Reflective Practice: A Personal Productivity Tool for Managers* (2013) <http://www.professionalsaustralia.org.au/blog/reflective-practice-a-personal-productivity-tool-for-managers/> [accessed 22 October 2019].

Greenleaf, R.K. *Servant Leadership* (Mahwah, NJ: Paulist Press, 1977)

Northwestern University, Division of Student Affairs. Learning Domain - Interpersonal Competence (n.d.) <https://www.northwestern.edu/studentaffairs/assessment/learning-outcomes/student-learning-outcomes/interpersonal-competence/index.html> [accessed 22 October 2019]

Oliver, B. & Jorre de St Jorre, T. 'Graduate Attributes for 2020 and Beyond: Recommendations for Australian Higher Education Providers', *Higher Education Research & Development* 37 (2018), 821-836.

Simmel, G. 'The Philosophy of Landscape', *Theory, Culture & Society* 24 (2007), 20-29.

Smith, C.D. & Bath, D.M. 'The Role of the Learning Community in the Development of Discipline Knowledge and Generic Graduate Outcomes', *Higher Education* 51 (2006), 259-286.

Volpe, M.A. *Rethinking Christian Identity* (Chichester, West Sussex: Wiley-Blackwell, 2013).

Williams, R. *The Christian Priest Today: Lecture on the Occasion of the 150th Anniversary of Ripon College, Cuddesdon, Friday, 28 May 2004.* <http://aoc2013.brix.fatbeehive.com/articles.php/2097/the-christian-priest-today-lecture-on-the-occasion-of-the-150th-anniversary-of-ripon-college-cuddesd> [accessed 18 December 2018]

Neil Holm
Sydney College of Divinity
neilh@scd.edu.au

6 | GRADUATE ATTRIBUTES IN THE AUSTRALIAN COLLEGE OF THEOLOGY

RHETORIC OR REALITY?

Abstract

The Australian College of Theology (ACT) is a self-accrediting Higher Education Private Provider (HEPP) in the Australian higher education system. Established by the Church of England in Australia and Tasmania in 1891, it has evolved into an ecumenical consortium that enables eighteen affiliated theological colleges to deliver courses from diplomas (AQF level 5) through to doctorates (AQF level 10).[1] A perennial driver of its operations is the need to reconcile the aspirations of the affiliated colleges, each of which has its own history and identity, with the centralising requirements of the legally recognised 'provider'. The implementation of graduate attributes (GAs) is one area in which the effects of this dualism have been recently encountered. This paper chronicles how the issue arose and how the ACT has responded to date.

The paper is divided into two parts. Part I is a revised version of the paper that arose from the invitation of the Sydney College of Divinity (SCD) to reflect upon graduate attributes at its 2019 Learning and Teaching Conference. It is worth preserving because it reports the results of the audit prompted by the SCD invitation, namely, the exposure of a wide gap between the rhetoric and the reality in the implementation of GAs in the ACT. Part II provides an account of

---

1   Treloar, *Theological Education*, 101–18.

how the ACT responded to the challenge arising from the results of the initial diagnostic phase. It may be regarded as an outline of a work in progress, driven by the need to close the gap between what is said and what is actually being done in relation to Gas. It thus seeks to ensure institution-wide clarity of purpose and teaching and learning coherence in a federal model that is unusual in the Australian higher education sector. In its account of how a pedagogical problem has been identified and addressed, the paper provides new knowledge and understanding of how such problems are managed in a theological consortium in Australia.

1. Introduction and Context

The FOCUS statement for the conference noted the function of graduate attributes as a statement of the aspirations of an institution of learning 'which can guide and shape the learning experiences of the students on their journey towards those goals'.[2] It posed the question: 'how can the student learning experience be guided by such Graduate Attributes in order to bring the aspirations into reality?'

The FOCUS statement also recognised that the consequences extend well beyond the institution and those who come under its influence: 'Higher educational Institutions produce graduates who then take their place as leaders in society for years to come'. Again, an important question arose: 'Can an institution of Higher Education hope to graduate better human beings prepared to build a better society?'

Prioritising character formation over intellectual formation, the FOCUS statement asked, thirdly: 'Given the increasingly obvious need for societal leaders being decent human beings who act ethically and with integrity, how can institutional Graduate Attributes aspire to shape these kinds of human beings?'

Given the interest of Christian people and the churches in personal and social transformation, and given the awful discrediting of the churches and theological colleges by the Royal Commission Into Institutional Responses to Child Sexual Abuse, and given the underlying and accelerating decline of Christian adherence (and even belief in God) in contemporary Australian society,[3] this is an agenda that cannot fail to attract the ongoing attention of theological educators.

2   https://scd.edu.au/2019-learning-teaching-theology-conference/.
3   Sheridan, *God Is Good For You.*

The presumption of the conference was that GAs are well-established among the theological providers in the Australian higher education sector. This presumption prompted the question: Is this really the case in my own institution and, indeed, the other institutions operating in this space? Does the reality match the rhetoric? The investigation coincides with a similar concern in the higher education sector at large.[4] Diagnoses of practice in the universities provide lines of investigation also appropriate to theological providers; the prescriptions are also more or less transferrable to theological education.

2. Graduate Attributes in the ACT

GAs were adopted by the ACT in 2014-15.[5] So far as I am aware, no attempt has been made to monitor their impact or measure their effect.

In 2015, their existence was commended by the external review panel that assessed ACT courses with a view to their reaccreditation.[6] However, the absence of an affective dimension was identified as a shortcoming. Under the direction of the Academic Board, the GAs were modified to include affective qualities. At the time of writing, there has been no further discussion of GAs in the Academic Board. Currently, the ACT has four Graduate Attributes: ACT graduates will be: 1) Christian people; 2) Christian scholars; 3) Christian professionals; and 4) Christian leaders.[7]

The qualifier 'Christian' makes clear that the ACT is concerned with Christianity in the Religious Studies strand in the Australian Standard Classification of Education (ASCED). This means that it provides learning and teaching from within the Christian tradition for its reproduction and development. The ACT recognises that this tradition is itself diverse and contested, but, while it is evangelical in flavour, it remains open in principle to all the varieties in which Christianity is manifested in the world.

---

4   Hammer, 'Graduate attributes as components of curriculum quality assurance? Critically examining examples of sector practice as part of institutional policy renewal,' unpublished presentation at the 2018 HERDSA conference. Four other papers at this conference were devoted to this matter.
5   Minutes of the Academic Board, AB1411-09.1 and AB1503-09.1. All of the ACT documents cited in this paper are held in the ACT database.
6   Minutes of the Academic Board, AB1509-09.1.
7   They are set out and their place in the Teaching and Learning Framework explained in 'Learning Outcomes – Principles and Rules (2019)', a document not yet publicly accessible but available on request. This document is a substantial revision of 'Learning Outcomes Principles (2015)'.

Each of the substantives is non-technical and inclusive. 'People' refers to men and women of conviction and character. 'Scholars' means students (they will be learners). 'Professionals' means work-ready and capable. 'Leaders' signifies the ability to influence the thinking and conduct of others—individuals, groups, communities, societies. Each of the attributes is qualified by a set of sub-attributes. ACT graduates will be:

1. Christian people, who:

    1.1 Are committed representatives of the Christian faith
    1.2 Value the life of faith and the service of others
    1.3 Engage with human experience intellectually and emotionally
    1.4 Act on the basis of an informed Christian world view
    1.5 Contribute to society as members of the church and local, national, and global communities

2. Christian scholars, who:

    1.1 Study and think to the glory of God
    1.2 Understand the discipline of theology in its various aspects
    1.3 Appreciate the main Christian traditions and how they have developed
    1.4 Faithfully present the Christian tradition of belief and practice to the contemporary world
    1.5 Are capable of independent and collaborative inquiry
    1.6 Contribute theological perspectives to the questions of human understanding

3. Christian professionals, who:

    3.1 Are capable of both self-directed practice and also working with others and in teams
    3.2 Apply the disciplines of theology to Christian ministry and service and other professional practice
    3.3 Bring a Christian perspective to bear on social and cultural engagement
    3.4 Communicate effectively in a range of contexts
    3.5 Reflect critically on Christian knowledge and experience as the basis for lifelong learning and practice; and

4. Christian leaders, who:

    4.1   Provide purpose, direction, influence, and enablement to others as individuals and in communities

    4.2   Minister to others

    4.3   Manage churches and other Christian communities

    4.4   Apply their outlook and skills to local, national, and international settings

Evaluation of the ACT GAs suggests, initially, that they are neither glamorous nor trendy. Yet their ordinariness may be their strength. They are intelligible, realistic, achievable, and defensible as fit for purpose. They combine the personal and cognitive skills and social dimensions of higher education and training. They also look beyond the classroom to work and life settings. At the same time, they do not reflect cultural captivity to the *Zeitgeist*, so that they are not merely fashionable and do envisage the capacity to be independent of social influence ('in the world but not of the world'). *Prima facie* at least, the GAs of the ACT follow the agenda of the conference FOCUS statement.

3. Evaluating the Implementation of Graduate Attributes

What part, then, have the GAs actually played in the life of the ACT? Have they made any difference? Have they been a genuine influence on ACT graduates? Closely related questions are: How would we know? By what methods can we discover answers? What are the conditions of GA effectiveness?

Here, I am indebted to research carried out by Dr Sarah Hammer from the University of Southern Queensland.[8] On the basis of her investigation of the 41 Australian universities, she identified four characteristics of successful implementation of GAs.

    i.   They are owned. That is, somebody within the organisation (normally a Deputy VC or, usually, the academic developers) takes responsibility for them, a sign that the organisation actually cares.

    ii.   They are promoted; that is, they are published and proclaimed.

---

8   See note 4 above.

iii. They are integrated into the curriculum framework; that is, in learning and teaching policy and procedure and in course and unit learning outcomes.
iv. They are monitored and measured.

Another presenter at the HERDSA 2018 Conference reported on what has been done by Griffith University to promote the development of graduate attributes.[9] Attention was directed to 'The Griffith Graduate', a website that sets out the rationale for each GA, displays student videos that illustrate the benefits of cultivating each GA and assist developing a portfolio to evidence GA attainment, and shares faculty suggestions and resources (including teaching tips, learning activities, and assessment instruments) to embed the GAs into their curriculum.[10] The means of operationalising the University's Graduate Attributes Policy[11] and, distinguished by this dual engagement of students and faculty, this website has a fair claim to being industry best practice, at least in Australia. It suggests three further tests by which to evaluate effectiveness in implementing GAs: adoption of a policy; engagement and support of students;[12] and engagement and support of faculty.

4. Graduate Attributes in the ACT

How does the ACT fare when operations are assessed by these criteria?[13] Are they owned? The ACT structures that might take responsibility are the bodies within the organisation that administer the curriculum, the Academic Board, the Coursework Committee, and the Academic Quality Committee. None of these bodies appears to have taken much interest in the GAs. Then, there are the functionaries with responsibility for the character and quality of learning and teaching, the Dean, the Director of Teaching and Learning, and the Director of

---

9   Williams, 'Academic Futures'.
10 See https://www.griffith.edu.au/the-griffith-graduate. Consulted most recently on 9 October 2019.
11 Available at https://policies.griffith.edu.au/pdf/the Griffith Graduate.pdf.
12 The importance of engaging students was emphasised at this conference by Les Ball, 'The Role of Curriculum in Developing Character-oriented Graduate Attributes With an Illustration From Church History,' (Chaptger 16 of this volume); and illustrated operationally by Stuart Schonnell, 'Students As Partners in Learning in Individual Units For Authentic Student Engagement and as a Lead Indicator of Teaching Effectiveness,' unpublished presentation, 2018 HERDSA Conference.
13 This question was posed in the period from September 2018 to early March 2019. Since then, the position has changed, as section II below, 'A work in progress', indicates.

Risk and Compliance. None has been charged specifically with responsibility for the GAs. Are they promoted, publicised? At the very least, can they be found on the ACT website? The clear and telling answer is that they are not. It is reasonable to assert that the GAs are not part of the public face of the ACT.

The ACT is not alone in this. Apparently, GAs are not well-promoted by Non-University Higher Education Providers.[14] Similarly, of the three comparable organisations (ACT, Sydney College of Divinity, and the University of Divinity), only the UD (significantly, a university) publishes its GAs on the website. Of the other theological providers, Alphacrucis College, Avondale College, Excelsior College and Christian Heritage College do publish their GAs. The Australian College of Christian Studies, Moore College, Perth Bible College, and Tabor College do not. Alphacrucis also has a publicly available GA Policy.

Are the GAs integrated into the curriculum framework? The current answer is 'to some extent'. The best indicator of the place of GAs in the teaching and learning framework is the document titled 'Learning Outcomes - Principles and Rules' (2019), in which the GAs are identified and mapped to the Course Learning Outcomes.[15] The unit learning outcomes (which govern teaching and learning activities and assessment schemes) are, in turn, mapped to the course learning outcomes. By means of this alignment, the GAs are part of the teaching and learning framework and bear indirectly on teaching and learning.

Are they monitored and measured? Here, the answer is 'not overtly'. It can be maintained reasonably that they are involved in the monitoring of Higher Education Standards 1.4.1-4, which, in terms of compliance, attracts a 'confident' rating. The 'Graduate Outcomes Survey 2017' extracted from the SES data also provides some evidence of performance in this respect. This shows high levels of satisfaction (75% +—except in numeracy). However, it should be noted that the graduate attributes of the GOS do not (yet) align with the ACT GAs.

---

14 Oliver & De St Jorre (2018), 'Graduate attributes for 2020 and beyond', 826.
15 Note 7 above.

5. The ACT Graduate Attributes in the Affiliated Colleges

A similar picture emerges from a survey of the web sites of the ACT affiliated colleges.[16] None of the affiliated colleges displays (or mentions) the ACT GAs on their websites. Only four mention GAs (their own) at all. The identity of the colleges are signalled in other ways—statements of mission, vision and values, of beliefs, lists of faculty, answers to 'why this college?', and graduate profiles. Where colleges publish the approved course learning outcomes, they reflect the ACT GAs to which the CLOs are mapped.

In the discussions leading to the adoption of GAs, the Academic Board noted that several affiliated colleges had their own GAs. It was not anticipated that this would be problematic provided that the GAs of a college are consistent with those of the ACT. So far as I am aware, this relationship has never been scrutinised.

Whatever can be said of qualification, it appears that: 1) GAs are not a significant component of the self-presentation of the affiliated colleges; and 2) outwardly the ACT GAs do not have a significant influence on the teaching and learning culture of the ACT colleges. This indicates that promoting the GAs generally and those of the ACT is not seen as an important function of the affiliated colleges. This is hardly surprising. Again, as far as I am aware, there has been no conversation between the ACT and the colleges on this subject.

To some extent, this picture is complicated by a (rudimentary) survey of the academic deans' attitudes towards GAs.[17] Responses ranged from warm support to scepticism about their value. In relation to teaching and learning activities, responses again ranged from giving the GAs no thought at all to actively working to integrate them. It would be good to carry out a similar survey of a selection of the faculty. Yet, while there is clearly counter-evidence, it does

---

16 That this method may be simplistic is suggested by Ian Hussey (2015) 'Spiritual formation in an Australian Baptist theological college: a survey-based case study,' *Journal of Adult Theological Education* 12.2: 137-52, who refers to the graduate attributes of Malyon College as a driver of the development of spiritual formation of students. These graduate attributes are not referred to on the Malyon College website.

17 The survey was conducted in September 2018. The questions were: 1) Could you explain your understanding of the GAs; 2) Who would you describe your attitude towards the GAs?; 3) To what extent, and how, do you connect your own teaching with ACT GAs and course learning outcomes?; 4) Does your college have its own GAs? If so, where are they published or otherwise made visible?; 5) Does your college acknowledge and promote the ACT GAs? If so, where are they published or otherwise made visible? 6) Who in your college has responsibility for the GAs? 7) To what extent to ACT GAs influence curriculum delivery in your college? 8) What part do you think GAs (might) play in theological education?

generally appear to be the case that faculty in the affiliated colleges do not engage with the GAs. The ineffectiveness of the implementation of GAs in the ACT is evident in Table 1.

Table 1: Implementation of Graduate Attributes in the ACT in early 2019

Aspects of effective implementation of GAs	Are these aspects of effective GA implementation a feature of ACT operations?
Ownership	No
Promotion	No
Integration into the curriculum framework	Partial
Measured and monitored	No
Faculty engagement and support	Limited
Student engagement and support	Unknown

5. What Does This Mean? Does This Matter?

If these observations are sound, it follows that the ACT itself and the affiliated colleges are not garnering the benefits of having a set of clearly stated and realistic GAs. This, in turn, gives rise to several effects.

One is the perpetuation of a historical lack of clarity about the purpose of ACT courses. Prior to the adoption of GAs, the purpose of theological education in the affiliated colleges was widely claimed to be 'formation'. A consultation on formation in 2014 revealed that: 1) there was no shared view of what this term means; and 2) it referred very often to extra-curricular activities, such as chapel attendance, prayer and pastoral groups, and informal interactions during breaks in teaching. This suggested that the contribution of the curriculum was either not well understood or simply taken for granted. The commitment to 'formation' also assumed that most students would be on-campus. Against this background, GAs provide content for the ideal of formation. They also provide focus for the challenge of forming students studying online.

Another effect is that the teaching and learning framework is not well understood so that its influence on the academic culture of the ACT is attenuated. Understandably, the attention of faculty tends to be on the unit(s) they have to teach. To the extent that teaching, learning, and assessment activities are constructively aligned with the unit learning outcomes, and to the extent that unit learning outcomes are aligned with the course learning outcomes, the GAs have an unrecognised influence on the teaching and learning culture of the ACT. However, until they become more visible at the over-arching level of the teaching and learning framework and are promoted more intentionally, their impact will be limited.

A third effect is that the emphasis in the self-representation of colleges is on the college, not the student —on the producer, not the product. This is partly the result of traditional higher education practice and partly the result of the religious culture in which the colleges were founded and developed. In that context, denominational identity and theological purity are highly prized commodities. However, in light of the decline of denominationalism and the progress of ecumenical engagement, and given the shift in higher education generally to student success and well-being, these aspects of college identities may have lost their market salience. Greater emphasis on student formation through the lens of GAs may be worth considering.

6. Recommendations

Of the seven actions proposed on the basis of a recent survey of GAs in Australian higher education,[18] it appeared that the ACT would do well to consider four:

1. 'Publish the attributes [...] aligning the emphasis with the needs of their students, and the aims of their institutions';
2. 'Ensure that attributes are contextualised and communicated at a course level, including in the curriculum, course handbooks and marketing materials';
3. 'Be more explicit with students: those who teach students and support their learning should communicate intended outcomes and explain their importance repeatedly throughout the course';
4. 'Draw on more objective measures to test achievement of the attributes by students, inculcating them more directly into assessments in the curriculum'.

---

18   Oliver and De St Jorre, 'Graduate attributes for 2020 and beyond,' 833.

7. A Work in Progress

7.1 Role of the Academic Board

On the eve of the SCD GAs conference, this analysis was presented to the Academic Board at its meeting in March 2019 with the recommendations that the ACT:

1. Determine who (if anybody) should take ownership for GAs in the ACT and the affiliated colleges.
2. Co-ordinate the presentation of GAs by the ACT and the affiliated colleges.
3. Publish the GAs on the ACT website and the websites of the affiliated colleges.
4. Incorporate GAs into the policies and curriculum documents that govern teaching and learning in the ACT.
5. Engage students with the GAs.
6. Monitor and assess the attainment of the GAs more closely.

The AB responded positively, affirming the importance of the GAs on the grounds that they are an indication of what the ACT is actually doing (or seeking to do) in its programs, provide a trajectory for the future, and position the ACT to defend its operation in the higher education sector.[19] The AB also endorsed the propositions that: 1) the GAs help to elaborate what is meant by 'formation'; and 2) provide a means for evaluating online delivery of courses (by providing criteria by which to judge what is gained and what is lost in different modes of delivery).

The AB accepted the claim that the ACT does not derive the full benefit of the GAs. While not in a position to accept the six recommendations, it made arrangements to continue the discussion at subsequent meetings. It also made 'in-principle' commitments to:

1. Secure and strengthen the place of the GAs;
2. Revise and publicise the GAs on the ACT website;
3. Devise methods for assessing and measuring attainment of the GAs; and
4. Improve integration of the GAs into the teaching and learning framework through the relevant policies and procedures and by strengthening the alignment with the course and unit learning outcomes.

---

19 Minutes of the Academic Board, AB1903-09.1.

The AB further requested that the GAs be made a subject for consideration at the annual professional development conference. The AB noted as an additional benefit that the review and mapping process across all levels of curriculum and strategy within a consortium would be a first in the theological sector in Australia and, when properly reported, provide a new body of knowledge and pedagogy for the benefit of all participants.

At its second meeting for the year in May, the AB considered a paper titled 'A New Theological Degree Proposed by the Bible College of South Australia, April 2019'.[20] The effect of the paper was to challenge the adequacy of the approved GAs by providing an alternative vision of formation and how it might be achieved. Its particular concern was to incorporate into the formal curriculum extra-curricular activities such as chapel attendance and small groups that are vital to personal and ministry formation. The discussion supported genuine incorporation of formational aspects of college life into the curriculum but noted that the new course proposal fitted well in the established GA framework. This framework is evidently capable of accommodating curriculum innovation.

The discussion was further extended at the third meeting in August.[21] It was prompted by a position paper titled 'How Do We Know What We Are Doing is Working?'. The paper and subsequent discussion took up the all-important question of measurement and monitoring. It was noted that there is no readily available data on what ACT graduates are doing five years after their graduation, so that impacts of courses are difficult to gauge with any precision. Both the difficulty and importance of this kind of research was emphasised. The possibility of financing the necessary investigation through the DMin program was brought forward, and a working party appointed to devise a pathway for the consideration of the Board.

8. Other Developments

Running parallel and sometimes intersecting with the AB discussions were other developments with a bearing on the implementation of GAs in the ACT.

The place of the GAs in the curriculum framework was strengthened by the development by the Coursework Committee of Courses, Units and Assessment

---

20 Minutes of the Academic Board, AB1905-06.
21 Minutes of the Academic Board, AB1908-06.

Policies. These Policies assign a specific place to the GAs in each of these areas and, thereby, clarify their function in the Teaching and Learning Framework.

Developments in the affiliated colleges also improved the implementation of the GAs. In a step unrelated to the initiatives of the AB, one college developed a video titled 'Graduate Attribute Led Theological Education' that carefully identified and justified the role of GAs in the delivery of its courses. This video extended the established practice in this college of explicitly relating each unit in a course to the GAs. However, these sound practices appear still to be rare in the ACT and forge a pathway other colleges might consider following.[22]

Christ College is one of the few affiliated colleges that publicises GAs on its website.[23] Table 2 shows how these GAs can be co-ordinated with those of the ACT. Co-ordination along these lines appears to offer one method for promoting GAs in a structure that sustains a dualism between the legally recognised 'provider' and the affiliated colleges that deliver its programs.[24]

Table 2: Graduate Attributes of the ACT and of Christ College

ACT Graduate Attributes	Christ College Graduate Attributes
1. Christian people	Knows God in Christ Loves God in Christ Knows self in Christ Loves people like Christ
2. Christian scholars	
3. Christian Professionals	Preaches and teaches Christ from the Scriptures
4. Christian leaders	Leads God's church under Christ

This juxtaposition shows both how the GAs of the ACT are reflected in the GAs of Christ College and how Christ College is distinctive in the ACT collective. The substantial correlation in the area of 'Christian People' indicates that Christian character formation is paramount in the approach of this college. Preparation for professional ministry also emerges as the primary purpose of

---

22　A small-scale study of 17 unit outlines from eight other colleges found explicit reference to GAs in only one outline.

23　https://christcollege.edu.au/study/graduate-attributes/.

24　Laidlaw College has a highly developed Graduate Profile (https://www.laidlaw.ac.nz/about-us/graduate-profile/) that correlates very strongly with the GAs of the ACT. However, this profile was developed about a decade ago in response to the requirements of the New Zealand higher education system. Because of its different provenance, this Graduate Profile is not included in the current analysis.

the education and training provided. The one domain in which there is no clear correlation appears to marginalise the function of the curriculum, no doubt an unintended consequence. This suggests as a benefit of the comparison to the college a way in which the local GAs might be developed to identify how the teaching of courses can be expected to impact the students and also enhance the mission of Christ College.

Another affiliated college which publishes its GAs is the Sydney Missionary and Bible College (SMBC).[25]

Table 3: Graduate Attributes of the ACT and of SMBC

ACT Graduate Attributes	Sydney Missionary and Bible College Graduate Attributes
1. Christian people	People of bold conviction, perseverance, obedience, and prayer People of warmth and love Fired by a zeal for God's honour
2. Christian scholars	Gospel-focused
3. Christian professionals	People who have a heart for mission Godly communicators
4. Christian leaders	Responsible and resourceful people

The juxtaposition of these GAs with those of the ACT again discloses an emphasis on character formation. Although real enough, the correspondence with the other three ACT GAs is not substantial and may afford scope for some reconsideration. A missionary focus also emerges very clearly as the distinguishing mark of the College.

These comparisons point to the possibilities for branding and market differentiation for affiliated colleges by developing their own GAs as an interpretation of the ACT GA framework. Yet, they also indicate that presently, while there is consistency between the GAs of 'the provider' and the college, the co-ordination is loose and uneven. Given that neither set of college GAs was formulated with reference to those of the ACT, this was to be expected. Yet, the diagnostic and possible remedial benefits are such that the value of co-ordinating GAs at both nodes of the ACT operation may be regarded as demonstrated.

---

25 https://www.smbc.edu.au/study/graduate-attributes. The gloss on each attribute assists the correlation with the GAs of the ACT.

This suggests in turn that, given the benefits of GAs that have yet to be garnered by the majority of colleges, comprehensive and systematic coordination of the ACT GAs with those of the affiliated colleges offers a further means of effective implementation at the same time as enhancing the coherence of the ACT teaching and learning culture without jeopardising the cherished diversity of the affiliated colleges.

9. A Way Forward

The Academic Board returned to the GAs at its final meeting in 2019 with a view to drawing together the results of a long-running discussion and devising a strategy with which to move forward.[26] It received a report that described the progress that had been achieved since the issue was first raised, noting in particular that two of the recommendations tabled in March have been addressed. The remaining four were retained in a revised set of recommendations brought forward as a possible agenda for continued work on closing the gap between the rhetoric and the reality in the implementation of GAs in the ACT:

1. Develop a Graduate Attributes Policy
2. Create a Graduate Attributes page on the ACT website
3. Co-ordinate the presentation of GAs by the ACT and the affiliated colleges and oversee the publication of the co-ordinated GAs on the websites of the affiliated colleges
4. Engage students with the GAs.
5. Engage faculty with the GAs
6. Monitor and assess the attainment of the GAs more intentionally
7. Commission a longitudinal study of ACT graduates with a view to ascertaining the attainment of Graduate Attributes as one means of measuring the effectiveness of ACT courses.

In the discussion, the Board reaffirmed its commitment to the GAs as a means of clarifying institutional identity and purpose. The importance of improving the visibility of the GAs was emphasised as the basis of developing the all-important engagement of the faculty and students. The need to collect relevant data as the means of determining whether the GAs are having an appreciable

---

26 Minutes of the Academic Board, AB1910-06.

effect and, indeed, determining whether they are fit for purpose was also reiterated. How best to co-ordinate the GAs of the ACT with those of the affiliated colleges was identified as a task of the sub-committee appointed in August to lead the implementation of the GAs.

In order to enact its determination to make the GAs of the ACT effective, the Board adopted the first recommendation and tasked the Dean with developing a Graduate Attributes Policy in the expectation that this Policy would be the means of responding to the other six recommendations.

10. Conclusion

This review of engagement with GAs in 2019 indicates that, in a manner reflecting the situation in the higher education sector at large, the ACT is wrestling with the challenge of strategising for the development of GAs in students and demonstrating how this is being achieved. Table 4 indicates the progress that has been made.

Table 4: Implementation of Graduate Attributes in the ACT by Late 2019

Aspects of effective implementation of GAs	Are these aspects of effective GA implementation (now) a feature of ACT operations?
Ownership	Yes
Promotion	Developing
Integration into the curriculum framework	Improved
Measured and monitored	Under consideration
Faculty engagement and support	Still limited
Student engagement and support	Partial

A comparison of Tables 1 and 4 points to a clear improvement in the ACT's implementation of its GAs. After engaging with the issue for almost a year, significant progress has been achieved in two areas. The AB has taken ownership of the GAs and incorporated their effective implementation into its operations. While there remains scope for further development, the place of the GAs in the Teaching and Learning Framework has been established by their incorporation into the Courses, Units, and Assessment Policies. The next steps in the strategy have been identified, and arrangements have been made for the development of a policy to direct the process.

When GAs were first adopted in 2014, it was observed that this marked the beginning of a change in the teaching and learning culture of the ACT that would take ten years to be realised fully. By identifying shortcomings in the implementation and the requirements for effectiveness, this assessment at the half-way point seems to have provided much needed impetus to ensuring that the rhetoric in the ACT in relation to the GAs matches the operational reality.

Bibliography

Australian College of Theology, Minutes of the Academic Board 2018-19.

Ball, L., 'The Role of Curriculum in Developing Character-oriented Graduate Attributes with an Illustration from Church History,' (Chapter 16 of this volume).

Barrie, S. C. 'Understanding What We Mean by the Generic Attributes of Graduates. *Higher Education* 51.2 (2016), 215-41.

Green, W., Hammer, S. & Starr, C. 'Facing up to the Challenge: Why Is it so Hard to Develop Graduate Attributes?' *Higher Education Research and Development* 28.1 (2009), 17-29.

Hammer, S. 'Graduate attributes as components of curriculum quality assurance? Critically examining examples of sector practice as part of institutional policy renewal' (Unpublished presentation at the 2018 HERDSA Conference).

Hussey, I. Spiritual Formation in an Australian Baptist Theological College: A Survey-Based Case Study', *Journal of Adult Theological Education* 12.2 (2015), 137-52.

Kensington-Miller, B. et al. 'From Invisible to SEEN: A Conceptual Framework for Identifying, Developing and Evidencing Unassessed Graduate Attributes', *Higher Education Research and Development* 37.7 (2018), 1439-53.

Oliver, B. 'Graduate Attributes as A Focus For Institution-Wide Curriculum Renewal: Innovations And Challenges', *Higher Education Research and Development* 32.3 (2013), 450-63.

Oliver, B. & De St Jorre, J. 'Graduate Attributes For 2020 and Beyond: Recommendations For Australian Higher Education Providers', *Higher Education Research and Development* 37.4 (2018), 821-36.

Ruge, G. & McCormack, C. 'Building and Construction Students' Skills Development for Employability – Reframing Assessment for Learning in Discipline-Specific Contexts', *Higher Education Research and Development* (2017) DOI: 10.1080/17452007.138351.

Schonnell, S. 'Students as Partners in Learning in Individual Units for Authentic Student Engagement and as a Lead Indicator of Teaching Effectiveness', (unpublished presentation, 2018 HERDSA Conference).

Sheridan, G. *God Is Good For You: A Defence of Christianity in Troubled Times* (Crows Nest: Allan & Unwin, 2018).

Treloar, G. R. 'The Three (or Four) Identities of the Australian College of Theology', in Andrew Bain and Ian Hussey (eds.), *Theological Education: Foundations, Practices, and Future Directions* (Eugene, Oregon: Wipf & Stock, 2018): 101-18.

Williams, J. 'Academic Futures: Personalised, Role-based Professional Learning to Develop and Enhance Learning and Teaching Capabilities,' and 'The Evolution of the Griffith Learning and Teaching Capabilities Framework', (unpublished presentations, 2018 HERDSA Conference).

Geoffrey R. Treloar[27]
Australian College of Theology
gtreloar@actheology.edu.au

---

[27] Best thanks are due to my Higher Education Research and Development Society of Australasia (HERDSA) reference group – Dr John Gilchrist, Dr Gesa Ruga, and Mr Stuart Schonnell – for fruitful interaction during the development of this paper. I also acknowledge the willingness of colleagues in the Australian College of Theology to support my investigation by participating in surveys and supplying various documents.

7 | GRADUATE ATTRIBUTES AND THEOLOGICAL EDUCATION

INTERACTIONS BETWEEN SPIRITUAL FORMATION, ONLINE LEARNING, AND BUSINESS MODELS

Abstract

Developments over the past decade have sparked concerns that online theological education may not provide an equivalent spiritual formation experience compared to traditional on-campus modes of education. There is also rising concern that the provision of online theological education with limited spiritual formation may result in a mode of teaching that is less expensive to conduct, and hence this could undermine the business models of on-campus colleges while at the same time producing graduates who are less developed in personal character and spiritual maturity. But on-campus education may also struggle with effective spiritual formation if it is haphazard and poorly monitored. In both cases, the need is to ensure that graduate attributes for spiritual formation are clearly articulated and then implemented in activities, assessments, and graduate outcomes and that weaknesses in outcomes are identified and improved. Comprehensive, effective online spiritual formation may prove just as costly (or more so) than effective on-campus spiritual formation.

1. Background

In recent years, a number of seemingly disparate concerns have arisen in theological education—issues about how to conduct fully online courses, about e-learning technology, about spiritual formation in both face-to-face and online contexts, and about the appropriate fees to charge for theological education. This paper is a personal reflection on these issues from a sympathetic observer (but not a 'product') of (broadly-based) evangelical theological education based on my experiences in education, psychology, technology, and higher education regulation.

These recent concerns touch on a deeper issue that could be phrased as 'how does theological education in a digital age remain true to its traditions of best preparing graduates for serving the Body of Christ?' (This service may take many forms—as clergy, as workers in church-related and other organisations, and in informal roles within church and society.) Another way the issue is expressed is 'can spiritual formation be done online?' It can also be articulated in terms of graduate attributes: 'Are we preparing and forming our students to become the kind of graduates that are expected of us?'

There is sometimes a concern that a move towards digital education, especially fully online courses, will lead to poorer theological education overall, particularly in relation to the challenging goal of spiritual formation. If technology leads to poorer education, all other things being equal, should it not rightly be resisted?

My own sense is that the issues are more complex. There are certainly risks to adopting technology in theological education, and in the case of fully online theological education, I would hazard that the risks are sufficiently large that without quite deliberate steps to mitigate them, spiritual formation outcomes can indeed be poorer in some situations. But I believe there are several different problems conflated here, so this paper offers an attempt to explicate and disentangle these issues, together with some suggested future steps.

'Spiritual formation' is defined in different ways—Foster et al.'s study of US clergy preparation identifies three 'apprenticeships': cognitive, practical, and normative—with normative referring to the development of professional identity.[1] In Diane Hockeridge's recent research on this topic, she combines Foster et al.'s approach with a framework from Mayer and de Freitas to describe

---

1   Foster et al., *Educating Clergy*.

the first element as cognitive/constructivist—'building a framework for understanding'; the second as associationist/practical—'learning as behaviour'; and the third as situative/normative—'learning as social practice'.[2]

My sense is that many evangelical theological colleges are relatively strong on the cognitive side, moderate on social learning, and weak on practical experience. But more importantly, the challenge is integrating these three dimensions to foster the development of the whole person—that is, graduate attributes need to be holistic, not simply cognitive. In particular, a key graduate attribute should be the development of a Godly character that shows visible signs of faith, hope, and love, as well as the Fruits of the Spirit in the way that students apply their theological understanding to their work in the Body of Christ. As Ball suggested, this often requires transformative learning in the life of the student.[3] In this paper, 'spiritual formation' will refer to the broad development of Godly character that can be applied effectively in daily life with others, particularly in Christian leadership roles.

2. Is Modern Theological Education Biblical?

Before considering online theological education and spiritual formation, it is worth stepping back for a moment to reflect on the structures of modern theological education and their relationship to the modes of learning exhibited in the Bible, particularly in the ministry of Jesus and the subsequent actions of the apostles.

The degree of similarity among today's theological colleges in their practices is quite striking. The typical structure of weekly lectures/seminars over a semester of around four months, together with essays and exams for assessment, has become very common; and most innovations concern relatively modest adjustments around the edges of this pattern. However, if we conduct a thought experiment to imagine transporting the typical church leaders from the period of Paul's letters to see how God's leaders are trained in the Twenty-First Century, I think they would find our modern approaches surprising. Yes, we have the Bible in a form that they did not; but my concern is more the mode of learning—the way that these leaders learned to be effective church leaders. I suspect our

---

2   Hockridge, 'Challenges for Educators'. See also Mayes & de Freitas, 'Technology-Enhanced Learning'.
3   Ball, *Transforming Theology*.

time travellers would find our ways of educating strangely regimented and relatively weak in 'on the job' learning and in experiences that foster personal transformation leading to the Fruits of the Spirit. That is, our modern holistic graduate attributes are weak in practice, despite the rhetoric.

This thought experiment is all the more intriguing given how much importance many Christians place on returning to the essence of Jesus' life and the life of the early church. Why is there not a similar interest in getting back to similar modes of learning to those experienced with Jesus and in the early church? For example, these modes of learning seem to be based more on interactions with everyday 'working' life; are more opportunistic in their teaching based on immediate events; are assessed by doing hands-on tasks such as preaching and caring (sometimes with 'pass/fail' assessments; never with scores); and involve searching judgements of the heart (not writing essays). Put another way, Paul did not train and guide church leaders using weekly lectures and written exams.

I am not suggesting that the structures we use today are entirely inappropriate—there are many good, practical reasons for these structures. My point is simply that where these structures limit some of the kinds of learning that would seem central to the development of church leaders in the first-century church—notably spiritual formation—then it would be worth considering how our current structures might be astray rather than assuming these structures are a 'given'.

3. Regulatory Environment

Christians are called to be in the world, but not of it, and this challenge is relevant to the regulatory regime that applies to theological education. There is much that is beneficial in the modern quality assurance approach to higher education of agencies, such as Australia's Tertiary Education Quality and Standards Agency (TEQSA) and similar bodies overseas. Frameworks for explicit statements about course structures and requirements, progression rules, and other similar information can be of considerable benefit to students, educators, and external agencies.

However, one of the downsides to the modern quality assurance approach is its struggle to deal with educational issues that are not easily 'pinned down' within formal quality structures. This is particularly notable for issues such as character development in a range of helping professions—doctors, nurses, social workers, psychologists, teachers, and others. In many modern universities, there is limited willingness to make character judgements about students and their suitability for a profession. While some professions have developed 'personal and professional development' activities (or similar), they are often limited in scope and narrow in their chosen moral values (typically tolerance is the primary moral value taught). In truth, it is incredibly rare for students to be blocked from completing a degree for reasons of personal character (except in cases of criminal behaviour).

In theological education, this issue is even more acute—because 'character development', as an alternative phrasing for spiritual formation, is so central to the wider goals of theological education. Indeed for some, it would be described as the most important goal. The difficulty is that this educational goal does not easily fit within the regulatory structures and educational practices of modern higher education. While this is not a problem for theological education alone (as the professions noted above suggest), the difficulties are great and pressing for theological education.

In practice, many theological colleges find ways around this problem by instituting processes and activities that will (hopefully) contribute to spiritual formation, and yet these are often outside the formal structures recognised by regulatory bodies (such as TEQSA in Australia). While some limited success has been achieved in creating small 'official' units such as 'Guided Spiritual Formation' (and these are well used by some colleges), the truth is that even these official units are usually on the margins of the overall theological degree structure. Many other key spiritual formation activities (such as chapel, shared meals and living arrangements, prayer partners, mentors, etc.) are entirely absent from TEQSA-based structures, despite their crucial importance to the goals of theological education.[4]

To what extent are theological colleges called to work within the regulatory structures arising from society even when they are a poor fit for the spiritual goals of colleges? To what extent should theological colleges push back against unhelpful constraints on spiritual formation arising from regulatory structures? It is not my intention to suggest full answers here, but I do think that a clear-eyed appreciation of this problem is needed in order to reflect on the question of spiritual formation and technology. Technology itself is of little direct

---

4   But see Shaw, *Transforming Theological Education* for an interesting example of including these activities within degree structures, based on the European Bologna process.

relevance to this regulatory blindness, but it has the potential to exacerbate an existing weakness in the way the wider regulatory context applies to theological education, as will be discussed in the sections below.

One promising way to address these challenges is through carefully crafted 'Graduate Attributes' that articulate the spiritual formation goals of theological education and then ensures that these are part of the educational process, including appropriate use of assessment. While more work is needed in this area, it provides a promising way of working within current regulatory structures while still giving significant emphasis to this central aspect of theological education.

4. E-Learning Technology and Fully Online Courses

When educators think of learning technology, or 'e-learning', they often think specifically of fully online courses. While this is an important subset of technology in education that raises specific issues for the current discussion, it is worth first acknowledging that the impact of technology on tertiary education has been much broader.

Many on-campus courses today use technology as a helpful adjunct to face to face teaching, such as the use of Learning Management Systems for providing course information, lecture slides (and sometimes lecture recordings), links to library readings, and potentially other features such as practice test questions and course discussion forums. These technologies can have beneficial impacts on student learning (such as a lecture recording, which allows students to stop and replay a section they have found difficult to understand, especially for those whose native language is different to that of the lecture). Technology can also have deleterious impacts on learning (such as students who do not attend lectures because they can listen to a lecture recording later and then try to cram many hours of recorded lectures into a short space of time before an exam). While there is no guarantee that technology will always be used well (or will always be used badly), it has the potential to be a helpful adjunct to face-to-face teaching.

When it comes to fully online courses, it is common for those who have not taught these courses to assume that the educational experience must be less than face-to-face, especially for activities such as discussion. In some ways, this is quite true—current video conferencing is not the same as being together physically, and the loss of non-verbal cues can significantly diminish the educational experience for both student and educator in discussions.

But one of the surprises of successful fully online courses is that the depth of discussion can sometimes be greater than that of a face-to-face classroom. Asynchronous discussion forums, where students can post messages to each other in a 'threaded' format, can allow for rich conversations and deep personal reflections. The asynchronous aspect of this technology allows students to reflect on their responses at length and to rewrite and edit a response before posting it. This can create a deeper and broader discussion among students than the classroom (which tends to favour outspoken and quick-responding students over others).

I have taught units in a Master of Education where the online discussion was of a deeper quality than I would anticipate for face-to-face. More students participated in this deeper discussion because there is 'time' to hear every voice in an online discussion forum, unlike a classroom of limited duration. Online discussion is not always deep, and students can be quiet and shallow just as much online as in a classroom. But I would take issue with those who suggest that online is always worse and face-to-face is always better.

So, where does spiritual formation fit within e-learning? For topics that benefit from ongoing deep reflection, shared with a community of like-minded students, then an online discussion forum can be very useful. Also, an online diary (or its equivalent) of personal reflections over the course of study can have benefits for later reflection (or for potentially sharing with a mentor). For the brave, a blog can act as a public reflective diary.

For 'real-time mentoring' interactions, such as discussion or prayer between a student and a mentor about deep personal issues, the role of technology can be more mixed. These discussions can be held over synchronous technology such as audio or video conferencing tools, and they can be effective if the limitations of these technologies are kept in mind and addressed (e.g. fewer non-verbal cues may require more active listening on the part of a mentor to check that any cues they perceive are indeed accurate). Asynchronous technologies as simple as email can be quite beneficial in student-mentor relationships, especially where the history of email discussions over time provides a foundation for later reflection, and where occasional personal contact complements the contact via email.

Technology is not neutral in spiritual formation interactions because every technology can have hidden dimensions that may benefit and/or degrade some aspect of communication. But there are some technologies that do have beneficial aspects that are potentially superior to the classroom (e.g. a well-used asynchronous forum), and others that may be used in place of face-to-face contact (such as audio/video conferencing). Even where the fidelity of the online interaction is less than face-to-face contact, there are ways of acknowledging this problem and adjusting to it as best as possible given the circumstances (such as more active listening). All this does not necessarily mean that fully online spiritual formation is the ideal option—but it is to counteract the assumption that it is impossible.

5. Haphazard Spiritual Formation in Face to Face Contexts

When I have pressed colleagues on how they know that spiritual formation is taking place for their on-campus students (and how the students themselves would know what it would look like), the response is often along the lines of 'well, you just know'. While there is something to be said for this kind of 'tacit knowledge' in such a complex area, my sense is that more could be done to be explicit about spiritual formation processes and expectations without removing the need for complex, hard-to-describe mentoring judgements.

For example, many students in theological education also work part-time in a church or Christian organisation (hereafter 'church' for simplicity), and I have often heard it said that this allows them to work out their theological knowledge in practice. While I agree strongly with this idea, when I have pressed colleagues on the details, the connection between theological college and church is often quite limited; for example, there is little alignment between pastoral challenges in church with the subjects being studied at college in a given semester.

If the student has a mentor in the church, there is often little contact between this mentor and the theological college. When pressed on this issue, I often hear about the difficulties of busy people and the difficulties of finding time to make contact between a church mentor and a theological college mentor and sometimes a kind of 'sink or swim' assumption that a bit of tough love would be good for the student (i.e. 'tough love' here means a lack of guidance on how to relate college and church life and that students need to work this out for themselves).

If spiritual formation really matters as a graduate attribute, and if one of the key ways of encouraging this formation is through the intersection of knowledge and practice, then shouldn't support and guidance for students in their experiences in local churches or Christian organisations rank very high on the list of priorities of theological education? I have sometimes heard this explained as a job for churches: Churches should form clergy, not theological colleges. But surely both should do all they can to ensure head knowledge is translated into heart and action?

This problem is not unique to theological education—trainee teachers have some similar challenges in integrating their education theory lectures with their 'prac teaching' experiences in schools. Similar challenges can exist for doctors and nurses in linking lectures on the scientific basis of medicine to clinical practice in hospitals.

Indeed, it sometimes seems to me that the whole educational enterprise has been built backwards. I believe that for many kinds of learning for 'helping professions', it is important to be 'doing' as part of the learning process because the 'doing' helps you to reflect more deeply on the 'thinking'. We need many tight cycles of 'theory-practice-reflection' and 'practice-theory-reflection'. In teacher training, this often falls down because students get several years of theory, and only towards the end of their degree do they get much 'practice', when ideally they would have had rich experiences of both practice and theory from their first year of study. For doctors and nurses, the problem is often that their areas of clinical rotation in hospitals do not match the topics in their concurrent on-campus lectures.

In theological education, the combination of church experience and theological learning often occurs at the same time, but there is little deep connection where each enriches the other explicitly. That is, I think many theological educators hope that this enriching interplay occurs, but in reality, there is little that is explicit or documented to ensure it occurs. I would hope for a great deal more scaffolding for students about how to connect theory and practice and regular opportunities for discussion and reflection on the interplay between them. And this should count significantly towards their theological degree. In terms of graduate attributes, this means ensuring regular effective assessment of spiritual formation outcomes in order to evaluate whether a student's graduate outcomes are as expected.

For those who doubt my general concerns, I would suggest taking an honest look at assessment. Students respond strongly to assessment as a marker of what is important. So, if spiritual formation and practical church experiences are absent from assessment, then this sends a powerful message to students that they are not as important as, say, theology essays and Greek exams.

While there is much that could be done to improve spiritual formation within current degree structures, more radical possibilities deserve consideration. I find fascinating the story of Bonhoeffer and his 'illegal' theological seminary under Hitler[5], and his book 'Life Together'[6] describes a kind of theological education quite different to current structures. I am also fascinated by the description of the Servant Leadership School at the start of Henri Nouwen's 'In the Name of Jesus': a theological education that starts from a basis of shared community, prayer, and service of inner-city poor, where theological training evolves out of these experiences.[7]

An example of how existing theological degree structures can be adapted to new teaching approaches without breaching typical regulatory requirements is described in 'Transforming Theological Education' by Perry Shaw.[8] He gives an example of a theological college where instead of weekly lectures on different topics, the approach is based around single integrated units over shorter periods (e.g. five weeks)—where one topic is considered at a time. Each integrated unit is viewed through four lenses (Biblical-Theological; Historical-Theological; Sociological-Cultural, and Personal-Ministerial). The three-year degree structure outlined in the book has a range of integrated units to cover the core curriculum, taught in a problem-based learning style; together with a range of spiritual formation activities such as chapel, mentoring, small groups, and individual learning plans, which have been created in a way that earns credit points towards the overall degree. This example illustrates how theological education could be done differently, with a particular focus on explicit spiritual formation within the degree as an articulated graduate attribute yet aligned to a regulatory framework (in this case, the European Bologna process).

In summary, much could be done to improve spiritual formation in face-to-face theological education, and while online spiritual formation brings its own challenges, they are not insurmountable; nor is face-to-face education any guarantee of good spiritual formation outcomes. I have often asked colleagues, 'how would you know if a student has 'failed' spiritual formation? How would the student know, in order to seek to improve?' I believe there is much that could be done to make spiritual formation more explicit and improve integration between college and practical experiences.

---

5   Metaxas, *Bonhoeffer*.
6   Bonhoeffer, *Life Together*.
7   Nouwen, *In the Name of Jesus*.
8   Shaw, *Transforming Theological Education*.

6. Online Spiritual Formation

I know many theological educators who are quite worried about online spiritual formation—they can't see how it can be done effectively. I understand their concerns, but they often arise from a lack of personal experience with sustained, intense interaction via online technology. For those who have successful taught fully online courses that involve rich student discussion, the idea of online spiritual formation may sound challenging, but not insurmountable.

Some of the tools that would assist face-to-face formation, such as diaries/journals and discussion among students, can be replicated effectively online, so long as students are familiar with the strengths and weaknesses of these online tools (such as online forums). Real-time mentoring can be achieved through audio or video conferencing; and as noted already, non-verbal cues are weaker with current technology, but it is possible to adapt to these limitations if student and mentor are keen to openly explore how they could make the experience work as best as possible. Praying over audio/video conferencing may sound strange to those who haven't tried it before; but with some experience, it becomes unremarkable. There are times when physical contact, such as a hand on the shoulder, can be a great encouragement during the struggles of life. So, the (potential) benefits of face-to-face contact should not be forgotten, but much can still be done without physical co-location.

The challenge for online spiritual formation is to work out how it can best be achieved within the constraints of technology and degree structures. I think an open discussion of the potential difficulties of relating 'virtually' should be part of this process; and greater effort (and skill) in 'active listening' can be required to overcome some limits of the technology.

Ironically, online spiritual formation has the potential to be better than some face-to-face experiences, because people who are relating online are more aware of the challenges of doing so, and hence are more deliberate, explicit, and active in their attempts to achieve appropriate spiritual formation outcomes. By comparison, some face-to-face contexts are assumed to lead to effective spiritual formation, and yet there is little in place to explicitly foster it, and so in reality, the outcomes may be quite uneven.

One final point is that hybrids of technology and face-to-face contact can provide additional benefits to either alone. For example, imagine a mobile phone 'app' that reminds students each week at a particular time (e.g. an hour after finishing their church tasks) to reflect on their experiences and how they relate to their learning at college. These accumulated reflections over a semester could then be used for a reflective essay and/or be discussed with college and church mentors.

For fully online courses, it can be beneficial if students have a chance to meet face to face at some point, ideally early in their studies. While this may be impractical in some cases where students are spread around the world, my own experience in teaching online Master of Education units is that students often like to come together if at all possible. One of the benefits of doing this is that online discussion is often richer (or becomes richer faster) when students have met each other face-to-face previously. So, I think that where circumstances permit it, an opportunity for face-to-face contact early in an otherwise fully online degree can be of great benefit; for example, an initial one- or two-week intensive on campus at the commencement of studies.

7. Online Education, Spiritual Formation, and Business Models in Theological Education

With the rise of online education, some theological colleges may worry that other (online) colleges may lower their fees and hence 'undercut' other colleges in an attempt to gain market share. I believe that concern over fee discounting has an important connection to the various issues of spiritual formation and technology outlined above. So, I will summarise my earlier concerns as applied to this issue as a structured argument:

If

- spiritual formation is poorly recognised within existing regulatory structures, and
- spiritual formation is sometimes haphazard, or rarely made explicit and scaffolded in college practices and assessment

and

- fully online courses can meet existing regulatory requirements, but
- due to the lack of explicit detail on spiritual formation in regulations and college practices, online spiritual formation may be weak or absent in some online degrees

and assuming that

- there are many hidden costs to on-campus theological education that arise from the aspiration of spiritual formation (shared living, chapel, mentoring, etc.), so that even when these practices may not be as explicit or effective as they could be, they nonetheless represent a significant component of the overall cost of on-campus theological education,

then
- online courses have the potential to undercut face-to-face courses on price due to 'hidden' cost savings arising from reduced spending on spiritual formation activities, but
- with a final outcome of poorer spiritual formation outcomes for online graduates if online spiritual formation is not addressed in very active and deliberate ways.

My point is not that online theological education should be avoided but rather that spiritual formation is challenging to get right in all of theological education, but even more so online. My suspicion that if a college sets out to address the challenges of online spiritual formation comprehensively, the results could be quite effective. But this dedicated effort would be unlikely to lead to cost savings. This would echo a more general experience in higher education that online courses, done well, rarely lead to cost savings, and are sometimes more expensive to run than face-to-face courses.

However, given a regulatory environment where spiritual formation graduate attributes are rarely a focus of government oversight, and uneven college practices in relation to spiritual formation, I think it is quite possible that a college could create an online theological degree that meets all the necessary regulatory requirements, and may even appear to address online spiritual formation, but in practice does not expend much effort on online spiritual formation. This, in turn, leads to potential cost savings, and hence the possibility of lower prices and undercutting of other colleges.

Conclusion

This paper attempts to bring together a number of distinct but connected issues in order to foster more discussion within theological education of the implications of the digital age, and particularly the move to fully online courses and the impact of this move on spiritual formation.

As happens so often with new educational technology, the technology uncovers wider educational issues that deserve consideration, and so the uneven state of spiritual formation in face-to-face contexts seems to me to be just as relevant as concerns about online spiritual formation. For those who are willing to consider it, I think the whole structure of modern theological education deserves a fresh look in light of the practices of the early church—and this has direct implications for spiritual formation and graduate attributes.

I have given some examples in this paper of how online technology can lead to effective education experiences (online discussion forums) and also of how some weaknesses of technology can be mitigated (active listening to deal with the degradation of non-verbal cues). I would recommend more work on these issues, leading to general guidelines for students and lecturers in theological colleges.

In regards to online spiritual formation, I believe that theological colleges should investigate this issue in some detail to develop policies and processes that ensure that their work in spiritual formation is explicit, comprehensive, and effective. For example, Diane Hockridge and colleagues at Ridley College in Australia have been actively addressing spiritual formation in an online context, and others no doubt are as well, so an appropriate next step could be to see what general structures can be gleaned from the effective practices of colleges engaging in this issue while recognising that the particular details of how a college does this would remain unique to that college.

It is my suspicion that once online spiritual formation is addressed comprehensively and effectively, it is unlikely to lead to cost savings that would encourage pricing competition. Indeed, it may prove quite expensive to implement very effective online spiritual formation experiences. But given the gaps in regulatory frameworks, I believe that more work on graduate attributes for spiritual formation is needed in order to avoid the possibility of online education leading to 'undercutting' within the marketplace for theological education.

Bibliography

Ball, L. *Transforming Theology: Student Experience and Transformative Learning in Undergraduate Theological Education* (Preston, Victoria: Mosaic Press, 2012).

Bonhoeffer, D. *Life Together* (Vol. 27, SCM Press, 1954).

Foster, C. R., Dahill, L. E., Golemon, L. A., & Tolentino, B. W. *Educating Clergy: Teaching Practices and the Pastoral Imagination* (San Francisco: Jossey-Bass, 2006).

Hockridge, D. 'Challenges for Educators Using Distance and Online Education to Prepare Students for Relational Professions', *Distance Education* 34 (2013), 142-160.

Mayes, T., & de Freitas, S. 'Technology-Enhanced Learning: The Role of Theory', in H. Beetham & R. Sharpe (eds.), *Rethinking Pedagogy for a Digital Age* (Oxford: Routledge, 2013).

Metaxas, E. *Bonhoeffer: Pastor, Martyr, Prophet, Spy* (Nashville, Tennessee: Thomas Nelson, 2010).

Nouwen, H. J. *In the Name of Jesus: Reflections on Christian leadership* (St Pauls BYB, 1999).

Shaw, P. *Transforming Theological Education: A Practical Handbook for Integrative Learning* (Cumbria, UK: Langham Global Library, 2014).

James Dalziel
Morling College, Australian College of Theology & University of Divinity
jamesd@morling.edu.au

8 | GRADUATE ATTRIBUTES FOR ROMAN CATHOLIC SEMINARIES

A PROPOSAL

Abstract

This paper will begin by examining what is meant by the phrase graduate attributes. From there it moves to critically evaluate the stated graduate attributes from other Roman Catholic Australian universities and determine points of congruence and incongruence. After completing research from the universities, an analysis of the pertinent Roman Catholic documents will be undertaken to establish the Magisterium's view as to what constitutes a solid education for men training for the priesthood. This research has been undertaken with a view to establishing what is current best practice regarding the development of graduates in Australian universities and proposing a range of graduate attributes for the consideration of the Australian Roman Catholic Church as it moves to align itself with best practice in Australia and the relevant documents for priestly training from Rome.

1. Introduction

In the wake of the Royal Commission into Institutional Responses to Child Sexual Abuse[1] and its damning indictment of the Roman Catholic (RC) Church in particular, we feel that the time is ripe for looking at what kind of graduates RC seminarians ought to aspire to be upon completion of their studies in tertiary education. We are undertaking this study to specifically address the Commission's Recommendation 16.20, which reads as follows:

> In order to promote healthy lives for those who choose to be celibate, the Australian Catholic Bishops Conference and all Catholic religious institutes in Australia should further develop, regularly evaluate and continually improve, their processes for selecting, screening and training of candidates for the clergy and religious life, and their processes of ongoing formation, support and supervision of clergy and religious.[2]

What Recommendation 16.20 seems to be saying is that current processes for the selection, screening, and training of such candidates have been inadequate up until this point. One can hardly argue with this given the findings of the Royal Commission. That said, it is equally relevant to point out that the RC community of faith is currently enduring collective trauma as a result of the failings of these processes in the past, to adequately identify deviant sexual pathologies in adolescents and young men coming forward for holy orders. It is also true to say that, currently, there are few programmes for ongoing formation and support, and those that exist are dependent on voluntary take up among clergy. Further, it is only in the wake of the Royal Commission that professional supervision has been mandatory in some dioceses, and participation by clergy is patchy at best. Therefore, there is a felt need by the RC laity to see that the Royal Commission is taken seriously by the RC hierarchy and that change happens in a manner that is conducive to more openness, transparency, and accountability.

For my part, we shall confine ourselves to the training of seminarians into

---

[1] The Royal Commission was established in 2013 by the Australian Government pursuant to the Royal Commissions Act 1902 to inquire into, and report upon, responses by institutions to instances and allegations of child sexual abuse in Australia.

[2] Royal Commission into Institutional Responses to Child Sexual Abuse, Final Report Recommendations, 53, see https://www.childabuseroyalcommission.gov.au/sites/default/files/final_report_-_recommendations.pdf

graduates worthy of holy orders. What then can a biblical scholar contribute to the conversation around the formation of candidates for the priesthood in particular? What kind of graduate ought to be considered for ordination? In order to answer these questions, we will begin by examining what is meant by the phrase graduate attributes, a term that may not be familiar to those in authority in the RC Church. From there, we will critically evaluate the stated graduate attributes from three Australian universities with RC connections and determine points of congruence and incongruence. The universities are:

- Australian Catholic University
- The University of Divinity
- The University of Notre Dame in Australia

Once the critique of graduate attributes from the universities is complete, an analysis of the pertinent Roman Catholic documents will be undertaken. Particular attention will be given to:

- The Apostolic Constitution, *Veritatis Gaudium*[3] (The Joy of Truth), which establishes the norms that govern ecclesiastical faculties.
- *Ratio Fundamentalis Institutionis Sacerdotalis*[4] (The fundamentals of priestly education), which governs who may be considered for holy orders in the universal Roman Catholic Church, and how suitable candidates are to be educated for mission.
- *The Ratio Nationalis Institutionis Sacerdotalis*[5] (The national system for priestly education), which governs who may be considered for holy orders in the Australian Roman Catholic Church is undergoing revision to conform with the norms ascribed by the Apostolic Constitution from Rome. As such, and until the updated national Ratio is available, we will only refer to this document as may be essential for clarification of my approach. Other relevant documents will not be excluded but will be used only as they contribute to the conversation on what is current best practice in the tertiary education sector. In doing so, we hope to be better positioned to propose a range of credible graduate attributes for the consideration of all interested stakeholders as we move beyond the Royal Commission and

---

3   Pope Francis, *'Veritatis Gaudium'*.
4   Congregation for the Clergy, *'Ratio Fundamentalis Institutionis Sacerdotalis'*. Hereafter, simply referred to as the *Ratio*.
5   Australian Catholic Bishops Conference, *'Ratio Nationalis Institutionis Sacerdotalis'*.

into the reordering of established practises for the good of the RC Church, local and universal.

2. What Are Graduate Attributes?

There was very little consensus as to what constitutes graduate attributes (GAs) when they were first muted as a possibility in the late Twentieth Century. However, by the turn of the millennium, some convergence had taken place. Indeed, J Bowden's definition, which is commonly cited in the literature dealing with GAs, states that graduate attributes are 'the qualities, skills and understandings a university community agrees its students would desirably develop during their time at the institution and, consequently, shape the contribution they are able to make to their profession and as a citizen'.[6] They are, in essence, generic skills that are defined as 'those transferable skills which are essential for employability at some level for most'.[7] They have also been called 'core skills', 'key competencies', 'transferable skills', or 'underpinning skills'.[8] As Ruth Bridgstock notes,

> Bowden et al.'s (2000) definition encompasses two main types of attributes: (1) those which pertain to an individual's capacity for citizenship (including involvement in democratic processes, social cohesion, equity and human rights, and ecological sustainability) and thus [the] ability to contribute towards a well-functioning society (Rychen & Salganik, 2005); and (2) those which pertain to an individual's capacity to obtain and maintain work (Harvey, 2001; McQuaid & Lindsay, 2005) and thus contribute to economic productivity.[9]

The research done by these scholars aligns very well with TEQSA's own definition of what constitutes graduates attributes, '[g]eneric learning outcomes that refer to transferable, non-discipline specific skills that a graduate may achieve through learning that have application in study, work, and life contexts'.[10]

---

6   Bowden, Generic Capabilities of ATN University Graduates, Para 1.
7   Kearns, Generic Skills for the New Economy, 2.
8   Mayer, Putting General Education to Work.
9   Bridgstock, 'The graduate attributes we've overlooked', 32.
10 See https://www.teqsa.gov.au/glossary-terms under G for graduate attributes.

3. What Is Their Purpose?

Using the definitions and clarifications from the authors above, it becomes clear that the purpose of GAs is really related to the employability of graduates after they finish tertiary training. Employability may be seen as the possession by an individual of the qualities and competencies required to meet the changing needs of employers, clients, and/or customers.[11] So, how then are they relevant to colleges committed to the mission of the Christian traditions, which is about service to the community of faith and the wider society and not about finding a job *per se*? We are unsure that we can furnish an answer to that question. What we can say is that other colleges and universities with similar commitments to the Christian traditions have endeavoured to articulate what they see as desirable qualities in their graduates. Their efforts are presented below.

The obvious result of successfully finishing academic studies is the awarding of a diploma/ degree, and much of the priestly candidates' days are spent in class. However, as one scholar writes, '[w]ithout committing to integrate human maturation, spiritual development, intellectual acuity, and pastoral charity within the man himself, a seminary risks simply being at school'.[12] The new *Ratio* asserts that the mission of integration is to be at the forefront of a seminary's work such that the 'successful completion of the requirements of study cannot be the only criterion for determining the length of the formative *iter* [sic, Latin for 'path'] of the candidate [...] because study [...] is but one aspect of integral formation'.[13] In order to further the holistic development of the candidates, the *Ratio* recommends that '[f]ormators shall ensure the cooperation of the professors [...] and shall meet regularly with them, in order to address teaching-related matters, so as to promote more effectively the integral formation of the seminarians'.[14] The purpose of this is clear—there is much more to seminary formation than academics, and for true integration to happen, no single aspect of formation ought to be allowed to dominate. Indeed, Jorge Carlos Patrón Wong has identified some of the dangers that may ensue when one method of formation dominates over another. He argues that a monastic formation may lead to Spiritualism, and in a similar way then, forming good organisers may lead to Pastoralism, while forming ministers of the cult

---

11   See Confederation of British Industry, *Making Employability Work*, 1.
12   Keating, 'Beyond Schooling', 37. See further Keating. 'The Seminary and Western Culture', 1099-1111.
13   Congregation for the Clergy, *Ratio Fundamentalis Institutionis Sacerdotalis*, §118.
14   Congregation for the Clergy, *Ratio Fundamentalis Institutionis Sacerdotalis*, §141.

can lead to Liturgism. He goes on to say that '[t]hese types of imbalances, often part of the tradition of our seminaries, tend to deform priestly identity'.[15]

As such, care is needed to maintain a balance in the elements of formation to enable the maturation of the seminarian to proceed over time, thereby enabling the full flourishing of the candidate as both person and priest. In this, we follow Alasdair MacIntyre in understanding flourishing as independent practical reasoning, which also needs self-knowledge.[16] However, as MacIntyre states, there is no self-knowledge without input from others who act as a touchstone to test one's beliefs about oneself. Self-knowledge implies, then, the virtues that facilitate one's agency to form and sustain relationships and so accept criticism from trusted friends.[17] One's ability to form and sustain relationships implies both the ability to care for others and pursue common goods with.[18] Indeed, this is exactly what candidates for the priesthood are called to be.

4. Existing Graduate Attributes in the Australian University Sector

Below are the stated GA's from Australian Catholic University (ACU), University of Divinity (UD), and the University of Notre Dame in Australia (UNDA).

ACU[19] courses enable graduates to be:

[e]thically informed and able to

1. demonstrate respect for the dignity of each individual and for human diversity
2. recognise their responsibility to the common good, the environment and society
3. apply ethical perspectives in informed decision making

Knowledgeable and able to

4. think critically and reflectively
5. demonstrate values, knowledge, skills and attitudes appropriate to the discipline and/or profession

---

15 Wong, 'Foundations of Priestly Formation', *Congregation for the Clergy*, 43.
16 MacIntyre, *Dependent Rational Animals*, 97.
17 MacIntyre, *Dependent Rational Animals*, 97.
18 MacIntyre, *Dependent Rational Animals*, 98.
19 https://www.acu.edu.au/about-acu/employers-and-industry/why-hire-acu-graduates

6. solve problems in a variety of settings taking local and international perspectives into account

Skilful and able to

7. work both autonomously and collaboratively
8. locate, organise, analyse, synthesise and evaluate information
9. demonstrate effective communication in oral and written English language and visual media
10. utilise information and communication and other relevant technologies effectively.

In addition, graduates of research degrees should demonstrate the ability to construct knowledge through research.

Highlighting the values of their GAs, ACU says that it 'summons the University to attend to all that is of concern to human beings. ACU brings a distinctive spiritual perspective to the common tasks of higher education, while being an open and inclusive community'. To that end then, 'ACU explicitly engages the social, ethical and religious dimensions of the questions it faces in teaching and research and service. In its endeavours, it is guided by a fundamental concern for justice and equity, and the dignity of all human beings'. As such,

> ACU is committed to the pursuit of truth and academic freedom. The University seeks to develop its students as educated, skilled and ethical graduates, who are sensitive to injustice and work for the common good. In line with this commitment and drawing on the Identity and Mission of the University, the ACU graduate attributes are unique in the sector in highlighting the values that inform all aspects of the University.

It clear that ACU's graduate attributes are aspirational and centred on three pillars, ethics, knowledge, and skills development. While it is possible to measure both knowledge and skills development, it is difficult, if not impossible, to quantify their success in regard to any ethical development in their graduates. Therefore, it is with some doubt we read further that, 'ACU undertakes to ensure that all graduates develop the University's graduate attributes. This development is achieved through explicitly teaching and assessing the University's graduate attributes within each course'.

The University of Divinity (UD)[20] approved five graduate attributes in 2012. These attributes are said to shape all their courses of study, as well as establishing UD's aspirations for all of its graduands. They are 1) **Learn** understood as, '[g]raduates [who] are equipped for critical study, especially of Christian texts and traditions'. 2) **Articulate meaning** that, '[g]raduates [are able to] articulate theological insight and reflection' 3) **Communicate**, which indicates that '[g]raduates communicate informed views through structured argument'. 4) **Engage** such that, '[g]raduates engage with diverse views, contexts and traditions'. 5) **Serve**, so that [g]raduates are prepared for the service of others'.

UNDA is the only university to begin their GA statement by offering a definition of what they mean by graduate attributes and then present their generic GAs with what they term as 'graduate abilities'. Closer examination shows that the graduate abilities spell out in concrete terms what the aspirational generic attributes are.

> ... For Notre Dame,[21] graduate attributes are the qualities, skills and understandings which the University aspires to enable in its students. These attributes include, but go beyond, the disciplinary expertise or technical knowledge that has traditionally formed the core of most university courses. They are qualities that also prepare its graduates as agents for social action and global citizenship.

---

20 https://divinity.edu.au/study/graduate-attributes/
21 https://www.notredame.edu.au/about/learning-and-teaching-at-notre-dame/graduate-attributes

The University of Notre Dame Australia Graduate Attributes Statement

Generic Graduate Attributes	Graduate Abilities
Communication	The ability to communicate effectively in all domains within a range of contexts, using oracy, literacy, numeracy and information skills.
Critical and Reflective Thinking	The ability to be a reflective practitioner with sound decision making abilities, through the use of clear, critical and creative thinking and effective problem solving skills.
Technical competence and Interdisciplinarity	A comprehensive technical knowledge of a field of study, in addition to inter-professional knowledge extending beyond a single discipline.
Life-long Learning	Acceptance of personal responsibility for ongoing life-long learning and professional development, with a capacity to be self-directed and utilise effective time-management skills.
Ethical Responsibility	A capacity for high ethical standards both personally and professionally, underpinned by the ability to apply ethical thinking skills to social/societal problems and challenges.
Philosophical and Religious Approaches to Life	The ability to be an open and reflective individual, sensitive to and accepting of others' values and beliefs, whilst recognising and challenging prejudice and bias from a sound intellectual base.
Team work	A capacity to contribute in a positive and collaborative manner in order to achieve common goals.
Research and Information Retrieval Skills	The ability to construct new concepts or create new understanding through the process of research and inquiry.
Internationalisation	A capacity for international and global perspectives based on an understanding and appreciation of social and cultural diversity and individual human rights.
Commitment to Active Citizenship	A commitment to connect with and serve the community through active participation, engagement and reflection.

Having seen how briefly and succinctly the universities qualify their graduate attributes, it seems to be *apropos* to see what the RC bishops would desire in their candidates. However, such information is not readily available in Australia. In the United States, however, the Bishop Conference is clear in what they desire in candidates for preparing for the priesthood:[22]

- A personal relationship with God integrated through prayer and seen as an important and vital part of his life
- Has the ability and willingness to talk about his faith
- Has some involvement in his local parish
- Has a desire to serve others and make a difference in people's lives
- Motivated by the mission of Jesus and ability to articulate it
- Willing to sacrifice personally for the service of the Gospel and the church
- One who is approachable
- Possesses a psycho-sexual-socio maturity
- Has the ability to collaborate with others
- Takes initiative and assumes responsibility for his actions
- Recognizes the importance of the church and the role of the church as teacher.
- Possesses the skills of self-mastery and discipline
- Has shown the capacity and evidence of living a chaste celibate life
- Has healthy relationships with men, women and children
- Has average intelligence, common sense, good physical & emotional health
- Recognizes the need to both give and accept support from others
- Possesses a keen sense of empathy
- Has leadership skills
- The celebration of the Sacraments are important to him
- Has the ability to nurture another person's growth
- He is open and respectful of all people
- A person of integrity
- An awareness of God's omnipotent presence
- Others have mentioned that he would make a good priest

---

22 http://usccb.org/beliefs-and-teachings/vocations/upload/vocations-fishers-men-2005-appendixk.pdf

The US bishops finish the list by saying, 'this list does not exhaust all of the qualities needed to be an effective & (*sic*) holy priest'. Given the extensiveness of this list, one cannot help but wonder if any human person can meet these criteria. It is worthy of note that these are the criteria to *begin* training, not the qualities and attributes one might expect a graduate candidate for priesthood to attain over the course of his studies and formation at seminary. Therefore, we are cognizant of the need to make sure that any attributes we suggest are real and not ideal, are practical for mission, and are achievable by human persons.

5. Points of Congruence and Incongruence

To that end then, we note that one of the points of congruence among the universities we have surveyed is the emphasis on the need for critical thinking. UD in Melbourne adds a special emphasis on the ability to engage critically with Christian texts and traditions. Communication skills, including IT skills and competencies, were also seen as positive attributes to develop in graduands. Added to this, the universities aspire to have graduands that focus on serving the common good and so live from an informed ethical perspective. Further, UNDA and UD encourage their graduands to engage with diverse views, contexts, and traditions, and UNDA and ACU favour and value the ability to work as part of a team.

As regards the points of incongruence, we note that ACU values the ability to work autonomously and the capacity to solve problems. UNDA aspires to interdisciplinarity and graduands' commitment to life-long learning and what they call 'internationalisation'. By this term, they mean '[a] capacity for international and global perspectives based on an understanding and appreciation of social and cultural diversity and individual human rights'.[23] UD seeks to enable its graduands to articulate theological insight and reflection, though exactly what this means in concrete terms is not stated.

---

23   *Vid. supra.*

6. What can the Roman Catholic Church Contribute to the Development of Graduate Attributes?

Veritatis Gaudium (The Joy of Truth) 2016 favours that pastoral concern given to the entire training of the students, such as to overcome the divorce between theology and pastoral care, between faith and life (§2). Indeed, this is of paramount concern for the training of men for the priesthood. It continues by saying that there is a need for the integration of the different levels of human knowledge—theological and philosophical, social and scientific—and it recognises that this is already happening with the People of God and that it ought to become part of ecclesiastical studies (§2 and §3). 'We lack leadership capable of striking out on new paths' in an age of continuous change. What is needed is a radical paradigm shift that is open to new situations and ideas (§3). Essentially, this is re-calling the maxim from Cardinal Newman, for a clergy with clear heads and holy hearts.[24] By this, he means that there is a need for a union of devotional and ethical praxis, on the one hand, and for critical self-reflection, on the other. This author would add that this critical self-reflection needs to the done in conversation with others in order to promote the fullness of human flourishing *à la* MacIntyre.[25]

Philosophy and theology, therefore, need to be undertaken 'with an open mind and on one's knees. The theologian who is satisfied with his complete and conclusive thought is mediocre' (§3). The document goes on the reiterate the four criteria first articulated by Vatican II for the renewal and revival of ecclesiastical studies for the missionary outreach of the church. These are 1) the Gospel of Jesus Christ as the 'joyful and life-giving contemplation of the face of God… [that allows] our hearts and minds to heed the cry of the poor and to give concrete expression to the social dimension of evangelisation' (§4); 2) Dialogue that promotes a culture of encounter between authentic and vital culture wherein a reciprocal exchange of gifts may take place. In *Caritas in Veritate*, Benedict XVI asserts, 'truth … is *logos* which creates *dia-logos* and hence communication and communion'.[26] To that end, *Veritatis Gaudium* states that the academic curriculum needs to rethink and update the integration of the different disciplines so as to 'reach the places where new narratives and paradigms are being formed' (§4). From this second criterion, a third naturally follows; 3) That an inter- and

---

24 Newman, *The Via Media of the Anglican Church*, lxxv.
25 MacIntyre, *Dependent Rational Animals*, 97.
26 Benedict XVI, Encyclical, 'Caritas in Veritate' (Charity in Truth), see especially § 4.

cross- disciplinary approach to studies at the level of both content and method be undertaken that ultimately leads to the integration of science into faith (§4); And finally, 4) networking between institutions to set up suitable channels of cooperation while maintaining specialised centres of research.

It is in such an environment that the church seeks to foster the development of candidates that must be well-rounded (§2) through the integration of all levels of knowledge (§4, c1). Therefore, candidates must be able to engage in critical thinking (§5) to follow the interdisciplinary and cross-cultural approach that the ecclesial institute is to pursue (§5).

Section IV of *Veritatis Gaudium* contains a brief sketch of the requirements that are to be fulfilled for the studies of a student to be considered valid. There are no personal criteria given for anything that might be considered a graduate attribute, save mention of 'legitimate documentation ... about the student's moral life' (Art. 26:1,1). However, Section V of the General norms of the new *Ratio* from Rome is more explicit in naming the elements, stating that there is a need for integrated formation (§10) that can foster the development of candidates in the human (§94), spiritual (§101), intellectual (§116), and pastoral (§119) dimensions of their personhood.[27] It further encourages the concept of on-going formation (§152) once the candidate becomes an ordained minister. These dimensions must interact concurrently in the path of formation and the life of the priest with the aim of transforming and assimilating the heart 'in the image of the heart of Christ' (§89). Seminarians are to 'enter into communion with the charity of Christ the Good Shepherd'.[28] As a shepherd after the model of Christ, the ordained minister is to be a leader supporting and promoting community among the People of God (§90) since the mission of the church is the goal and horizon of all formation (§91). For this to happen, there needs to be an integral formation of the whole person who is to serve the Christian community. This requires a sound interior life, co-operation with the Holy Spirit, and for formators to be vigilant for merely formal and external respect being paid to the demands of formation that may lead to, consciously or unconsciously 'a purely 'servile and self-serving' obedience' (§92). With all this in mind then, what does the Roman Church see as the necessary requirements for priestly formation?

---

27   The four dimensions are dealt with at length in the Apostolic Exhortation *Pastores Dabo Vobis* (I will give you shepherds [after my own heart: Jer. 3:15]).
28   *Pastores Dabo Vobis*, n. 57.

6.1 The Human Dimension

In his *Summa Theologiae*, Aquinas favours the view that 'grace builds upon nature'.[29] By this, he means that a correct and harmonious spirituality perfects what nature has already given.[30] As such, human formation is the 'foundation of all priestly formation' (§94), and the candidate for priesthood is called to develop his personality to promote integral growth in all its dimensions, physically, psychologically, and morally. This is such that he may develop an objective perceptive of persons, men and women of all ages and social backgrounds (including himself, one supposes), to improve his capacity for social interaction (§94). Further, he is called to develop his awareness of the social environment (§94).

This begins with cognisance of his own life history and his own weaknesses so that he may become capable of self-determination even in moments of crisis which, if 'adequately understood', can become occasions of renewal and conversion (§96). Human formation is necessary for evangelisation as the gospel is mediated by his humanity (Acts 1:8). These days, evangelisation includes the use of the media and ease with the digital world that offer possibilities for evangelisation (§97 and 98), all the while being attentive to the risks, including forms of addiction, that are part and parcel of these platforms (§99).

6.2 The Spiritual Dimension

The dictum the *Ratio* uses to introduce the formation of the spiritual dimension of the candidate is taken from Jerome: Ignorance of the Scriptures is ignorance of Christ.[31] The Word of God 'holds a preeminent place in the process of spiritual growth' by 'being welcomed in the depth of the heart' (§103). Spiritual formation seeks intimate personal union with Christ through prayer (especially *lectio divina*), liturgy (especially the Eucharist), and the sacraments (especially reconciliation), marking the seminarian with that sacrificial love that is the beginning of pastoral charity. The liturgy of the hours and the divine office must not be lacking in the life of the priest (§104 and 105). Regular spiritual direction, an annual retreat, and true and mature obedience are essential characteristics of the well-formed minister of the church (§106-109). A significant part of spiritual formation is 'perfect continence in celibacy' (§110), and an equally significant

---

29 Aquinas, *Summa Theologiae*, I, q. 2, a. 2 ad 1.
30 Aquinas, *Summa Theologiae*, I, q. 1, a. 8 ad 2.
31 Jerome, *Commentarii in Isaiam*, Prologus: CCL 73, 1.

part of the *Ratio* is given over to repeating the Latin Church's teaching on this.[32] Seminarians should cultivate:

- the spirit of poverty to develop a proper relationship with the world and worldly goods (§111)
- authentic and filial devotion to Mary and the saints (§112)
- knowledge of, and mediation on, the Fathers of the church (§113)
- certain expressions of popular piety and religion, especially those approved by the Magisterium (§114)
- the specific virtues of those called to priesthood (§115)

6.3 The Intellectual Dimension

Gaudium et Spes (Joy and Hope)[33] determined that the knowledge of philosophy and theology helps one to 'hear, distinguish and interpret the many voices of our age, and to judge them in the light of the divine word, so that revealed truth can always be more deeply penetrated, better understood and set forth to greater advantage'.[34] Therefore, candidates for Holy Orders need a solid competence in the philosophical and theological sciences as well as more general educational preparation to enable them to enter into fruitful dialogue with the contemporary world (§116). Intellectual formation enriches human and spiritual formation, helping the person to listen profoundly to the Word of God and the ecclesial community and so learn to read the signs of the times (§117). In this way, the *forma mentis* (mentality) interprets the questions and challenges encountered in ordained ministry in the light of faith. However, the successful completion of study requirements cannot be the only criterion used to determine the 'length of the formative *iter* [path] of the candidate' (§117).

6.4 The Pastoral Dimension

The Ratio asserts that 'priestly formation must be permeated by a pastoral spirit... summed up as pastoral charity [so that the seminarian] acquire[s] the inner freedom to live the apostolate as service... and to be present as a man of communion' (§119). In order to facilitate this, future priests need to become

---

32 We do not enter into dialogue with the many documents referred to in the *Ratio*. Instead, we direct the reader to look at §110 and the copious footnotes there.
33 Vatican Council. *Pastoral Constitution on the Church in the Modern World*.
34 *Gaudium et Spes*, n. 44.

expert in the art of pastoral discernment, which necessitates leaving behind preconceived certainties to listen deeply and openly to God and the community of faith that he will serve. This will enable him to interpret wisely and with understanding all kinds of things and so be capable of good judgment when making decisions, as well as offer spiritual and pastoral possibilities that are attainable in the socio-cultural context in which they are found (§120). By taking the stance of the Good Shepherd (Jn. 10), he will be serene in disposition and an attentive companion 'without falling into legalistic or rigorist obsessions' (§120). The candidate for ordination needs to be able to proclaim Christ to all, including those searching for 'an authentic response to their deepest questions', those who profess another religion, the non-practising and non-believers. As such, he will need to create new spaces and new pastoral opportunities and go out and meet those who do not share his faith tradition (§121).

The formation of the seminarian's pastoral dimension necessitates his study of pastoral theology and the useful contributions made by the human sciences—psychology, sociology, and pedagogy (§122). But the study of these sciences alone is insufficient. He ought to have exposure through pastoral placement to the myriad experiences of human life, especially to people who, for a variety of reasons, are living life on the margins. In this respect then, pastoral placement in a parish should be given particular importance where the future priest is guided by those already in Holy Orders, consecrated persons and laypeople who are 'truly expert and prudent' advising and supporting him appropriately and reflecting with him on his service (§124).

These are the requirements as set out by the Roman *Ratio* of 2016. But how is one to discern what might be construed as GAs from the requirements for formation? What kind of person ought the candidate for Holy Orders be after finishing such an intensive *iter* of formation? The final section of this paper offers eight GAs for the consideration of interested stakeholders.

7. A Preliminary Proposal of Graduate Attributes for Consideration of Interested Stakeholders

Academics have long understood education to have three essential elements, the acquisition of knowledge, the development of skills, and the successful application of both knowledge and skills. But for the man preparing to be a shepherd of the church, something more is required than knowledge, skills, and application. So, using the categories provided by the *Ratio*, of human, spiritual, intellectual, and pastoral formation, we propose the following.

As to the human dimension of the human person, we suggest that a graduate of seminary training ought to manifest both authenticity and creativity. By authenticity, we follow Aoife McGrath's understanding 'that no matter the share in Christ's mission, discipleship or ministry, it is the whole person (and integral subject) who is called and who serves. Thus, in theological education generally, and no less in ministry formation, a student's character or personality should not remain unmoved or unchanged by the theological endeavour, [but] should become integrated into who the person is'.[35] Achieving authenticity is a very ambitious goal, but given the nature of the ministry the graduate will undertake, it is of paramount importance. Following Charles Taylor, we see authenticity as marked by both a self-determining freedom when a person is free to decide for him/herself alone[36] and a person having an original way of being human, being their true selves and not merely imitating others.[37] However, this is not a form of egoism, but more an ethic of authenticity, the proper way to be, how one ought to live and discover their true identity in relationship with God and not merely conforming to external demands.

By creativity, we mean the 'entry of God's Spirit into the human spirit [which] actuates the gifts of human creativity in the highest degree. Grace calls forth the latent powers of the human person; the initiative of God blesses the talents of believers'.[38] These talents are then put to the service of the community of faith, which can often mean doing something challenging and out of one's comfort zone. Being creative in ministry is following the pattern of Christ himself. Jesus' ability to be creative within the strictures of first-century Palestine is one of the reasons he was so attractive to individuals despite his radical message. 'To be able to think of something new and greater and to achieve it is creativity. An ordinary person wants to do what everyone else is doing. A leader is someone who is prepared to be creative and to chart new territories'.[39] Of course, this creativity must be channelled into positive and healthy outcomes for the benefit of the People of God and the church universal.

---

35   McGrath, 'Striving for authenticity in ministry formation and practice', pre-print copy, 3.
36   Here, Taylor acknowledges his debt to Jean Jacques Rousseau.
37   Here, he acknowledges his debt to Johann Gottfried von Herder. See Taylor, *The Ethics of Authenticity*, 27-29.
38   Wiest & Smith, *Ethics in Ministry*, 182.
39   Heward-Mills, *Church Administration and Management*, 327.

In reference to the human person's spiritual dimension, we consider that humility and discernment are critical attributes for the future priest.[40] Humility is best understood as under the authority of the Good Shepherd *par excellence*, as any authority in ministry is given by God alone and grounded in the being of Godself. 'A humble understanding of ourselves will prevent us from performing for the crowd and instead encourage us to play to the audience of One… Instead of playing God, we do well to remember one of the most beloved titles we hold: *under-shepherd*'.[41] A fundamental text for the mediation on what humility in action looks like are the Beatitudes from the Gospel of Matthew (Mat. 5). This text is by no means an exhaustive treatment of humility, but it is a very good place to start! Also, we know that '[a]lthough Paul's ministry was characterized by humility, it was not a "poor me, woe is me" kind of humility'.[42] Neither was it insipid and weak or mealy-mouthed. His attitude was very much like Jesus'— he never forced his message on people who 'did not come to be served, but the serve, and give his life as a ransom for many' (Mat. 20:28). That said, Paul never hesitated to preach anything that would be helpful to conversion, teaching openly and publicly in a straightforward and clear manner and with great, sometimes even fierce, passion. Humility then is not to be confused with docility, but the preacher preaching the gospel in the manner of Paul. In this way, then the natural pair for humility is discernment.

Discernment is an art, skill, and gift. It requires humility so that we can be free to respond to God, being mindful of Jesus, in relation with the Scripture and watching how one's sense of God's calling resonates with the life of Jesus.[43] 'Discernment is not a one-time event, but an ongoing practice. We return again and again, constantly seeking to deepen our awareness of God's presence and calling. The hope of discernment is that over time our lives and ministries will become more transparent to God's life and more faith to Jesus' way of love'.[44] Discernment also involves the participation of others, and discernment for ecclesial ministry requires the participation of the ecclesial community since it is in their name that ministry is given. The community tests the personal discernment of the individual to ascertain that the personal desire for ministry is accompanied by the appropriate human and spiritual characteristics, which

---

40   Here, I acknowledge my debt to my colleague Dr Peter McGregor at the Catholic Institute of Sydney.
41   Wilson & Hoffmann, *Preventing Ministry Failure*, 20. Emphasis is original.
42   Salter, *What Really Matters in Ministry*, 172.
43   Yaconelli, *Contemplative Youth Ministry*, 162.
44   Yaconelli, *Contemplative Youth Ministry*, 162

are essential to this public service, and that the individual has acquired the necessary formation and education to be effective.[45]

The intellectual dimension of the graduate candidate for priesthood is possibly the easiest way to identify suitable GAs for the seminarian finishing formation. Again, we see two important attributes that are necessary for efficacy in ministry. These are critical thinking and the capacity to work both autonomously and collaboratively. From our own experience of teaching seminarians from different cultures in a tertiary education environment, there are many challenges to overcome. There are constant issues around language, comprehension, and writing skills in English for students from Asia and Africa, for whom English is sometimes a third or even fourth language. Added to this mix is that critical thinking—following the Western Enlightenment model—is something alien, particularly for students from parts of Asia.[46] However, without education on forms of critical thinking,[47] it will be difficult for the future priest to form his own authentic judgments. Ministry carries an important burden, which can make of the pastor a self-important ass of little, if any, use to the People of God and the church universal. In order to embody Christ to the world truthfully, the future priest must have critical cognitive skills, such that embodiment will not be built on the expression of personal and subjective convictions. Education is rational, and logical analysis can lead to a spiritual awakening that will direct the candidate in achieving Christlikeness. By internalising and personifying what he learns, the dichotomy between the subject studying and the object of his study is overcome. The objective of his critical study is to achieve non-dualistic unity with the object of that study—Christ.

The capacity to work both autonomously and collaboratively may seem to be self-explanatory. However, to illustrate our point briefly, we will reflect on what this might look like in one key area of ministry: problem-solving. Ongoing ministry effectiveness is dependent on how the future priest goes about solving the inevitable problems that will surface in pastoral ministry. There is a fundamental danger here that must be considered. Few candidates have difficulty

---

45 Here, I would like to acknowledge my debt to Cahoy, *In the Name of the Church*, 100. Though he is talking about lay ministry, the same is true for ordained ministry.
46 Davies & Barnett, *The Palgrave Handbook of Critical Thinking in Higher Education*, 299-316.
47 We leave moot the form of critical thinking that ought to form the basis of seminarian training. It is our view that each of the disciplines of philosophy, theology, and the human sciences do critical thinking following different models. Instead, we refer the reader to the pertinent chapters in *The Palgrave Handbook of Critical thinking in Higher Education*, particularly chapter 19.

in taking the Lone Ranger[48] method to problem-solving. However, we must add that even the Lone Ranger had Tonto. It is working collaboratively in this area where many experience difficulties and frustrations. While the Lone Ranger method is undoubtedly quicker, the one using this approach may, in fact, miss a moment for evangelisation. By including others with suitable gifts in making decisions, where authentic participation is fostered and promoted, the graduate seminarian can add a tremendous spark and impetus that encourages people to participate in the messiness of pastoral life. Collaboration itself is often messy and, sometimes, even painful, but these reasons alone are not sufficient to discount its use. The benefits outweigh the disadvantages, not least of which is the building up of the faith community and the individual members therein.

When it comes to the pastoral dimension of the graduate candidate, two attributes are of principal importance, ethical praxis and communication. Ethical praxis means that the future priest thinks and behaves with moral uprightness leaving him beyond reproach because the slightest excess or omission will be well and truly capitalised upon. Christian existence *is* faith in practice. Of course, there will be lapses; he is a human with all the ordinary human frailties. These lapses may even prove to be points of renewal and reconversion to the mission of the church, thus enriching his life and ministry as a priest and pastor to other equally frail human beings. In this regard, the Word of God is of particular import, especially the prophets of the Hebrew Scriptures.[49]

The final attribute we proffer for consideration is communication. Again, one example must suffice for this paper. So, we shall examine briefly what communication as an interpersonal skill might look like for the seminary graduate. The purpose of interpersonal communication is to advance one's relationships with the people of the church, in one-to-one ministry and group activities. Indeed, much of his future mission in the church is person-to-person ministry of some sort. Many seminarians contend that with God's call comes God's grace to help them meet the demands of ministry. We do not dispute this. However, it may be that it is only when he finds himself in ministry that he learns that '[e]ffective communication is not instantaneous, and relational skills to not appear as if by magic when they are needed […] interpersonal skills must

---

48 For more on the Lone Ranger mentality, see Osborne, *Surviving Ministry: How to Weather the Storms of Church Leadership*, 57ff. Indeed, Osbourne asserts that resisting the Lone Ranger mentality is key to effective pastoral ministry (p. 59).
49 Jensen, Ethical Dimensions of the Prophets, 172ff for the relevance of the prophets to our contemporary world.

be learned and developed through careful study and precise training'.[50] Skills in communicating ideas, concepts and information to the People of God are vital to his mission in the church. If one cannot communicate, one cannot lead, and the priest is more than a theologian. He is first and foremost, in our opinion, a preacher, an effective communicator of God's own Word. While the message of the Scriptures does not change, the audience hearing it does, and so must God's messenger. Therefore, he must continue to hone his skills to continue reaching those sitting in the pews.

We are aware that the attributes identified above are selective and may be limited. However, we are of the opinion that were graduates preparing for ordination to be in possession of these attributes, they will begin pastoral life with a sure and steady footing. Clearly, these attributes interact and interrelate across the multiple aspects of the human person, each building, enabling, and perfecting the others. We favour the view that seminarians will need to continue to refine and develop these attributes over the course of their life as ministers in the church. Doing so will show those who they are ordained to serve that they are truly God's Exemplary Graduates.

Selected Bibliography

Apostolic Exhortation *Pastores Dabo Vobis* (I will give you shepherds [after my own heart: Jer. 3:15]) <http://www.vatican.va/content/john-paul-ii/en/apost_exhortations/documents/hf_jp-ii_exh_25031992_pastores-dabo-vobis.html>.

Aquinas, T. *Summa Theologiae*, Latin Text and English Translation, Introductions, Notes, Appendices, and Glossaries (Cambridge: Blackfriars; New York: McGraw-Hill, 1964-1967).

Australian Catholic Bishops Conference. 'Ratio Nationalis Institutionis Sacerdotalis' (Programme for Priestly Formation Australia, 2007, with revisions in 2014 and 2015). <https://www.catholic.org.au/acbc-media/downloads/bishops-commissions/bishops-commission-for-church-ministry-1/1863-program-for-priestly-formation/file>.

Bowden, J. with G. Hart, B. King, K. Trigwell, and O. Watts. *Generic Capabilities of ATN University Graduates* (2000) <http://www.clt.uts.edu.au/ATN.grad.cap.project.index.html>.

Bridgstock, R. 'The Graduate Attributes We've Overlooked: Enhancing Graduate Employability through Career Management Skills', *Higher Education Research & Development* 28.1 (March 2009), 31–44.

Cahoy, William J. et al. (eds.). *In the Name of the Church: Vocation and Authorization of Lay Ecclesial Ministry* (Collegeville, Minnesota: Liturgical Press, c2012).

---

50 Neff, *A Pastor's Guide to Interpersonal Communication*, 5. Future priests could learn much from this very practical guide.

Confederation of British Industry. *Making Employability Work: An Agenda for Action* (London: Confederation of British Industry, 1999): 1.

Congregation for the Clergy. *Ratio Fundamentalis Institutionis Sacerdotalis* (The Gift of the Priestly Vocation) (2016) <http://www.clerus.va/content/dam/clerus/Ratio%20Fundamentalis/The%20Gift%20of%20the%20Priestly%20Vocation.pdf>.

Davies, M. & R. Barnett. *The Palgrave Handbook of Critical Thinking in Higher Education* (New York: Palgrave Macmillan, 2015).

Heward-Mills, D. *Church Administration and Management* (Bloomington, Ind.: WestBow Press, 2011).

Jensen, J. *Ethical Dimensions of the Prophets* (Collegeville, Minn.: Liturgical Press, 2006).

Jerome. *Commentarii in Isaiam*, Prologus: Corpus Christianorum Latina. 73. Turnhout: Brepols, 1953-.

Kearns, P. *Generic Skills for the New Economy – Review Of Research*. (Adelaide: National Centre for Vocational Education Research, 2001).

Keating, J. 'Beyond Schooling: Seminaries, Integral Formation, and the Role of Academics' *Seminary Journal* (Theme: Priestly Formation Today, 2017), 37-43 <http://www.clerus.va/content/clerus/en/biblioteca.html>.

Keating, J. 'The Seminary and Western Culture', *Nova et Vetera*, English Edition 14.4 (2016), 1099-1111.

MacIntyre, A. *Dependent Rational Animals: Why Human Beings Need the Virtues* (Chicago, Ill.: Open Court, c1999).

Mayer, E. *Putting General Education to Work: The Key Competencies Report* (Canberra: Australian Education Council and Ministers for Vocational Education, Employment and Training, 1992).

McGrath, A. 'Striving for authenticity in ministry formation and practice', in *Weaving Theology in Oceania: Culture, Context and Practice* (Newcastle-upon-Tyne: Cambridge Scholars, forthcoming 2020, pre-print copy).

Neff, B. J. *A Pastor's Guide to Interpersonal Communication: The Other Six Days* (New York: Routledge, 2006).

Newman, J. H. *The Via Media of the Anglican Church: Illustrated in Lectures, Letters, and Tracts written between 1830 and 1841* (Vol. I, Preface 3) (London: Basil Montagu Pickering, 1877): lxxv.

Osborne, M. E. *A Pastor's Guide to Interpersonal Communication: The Other Six Days* (New York: Routledge, 2006).

Pope Benedict XVI. Encyclical, 'Caritas in Veritate' (Charity in Truth)... *On Integral Human Development in Charity and Truth*, 7 July 2009, see especially § 4 <http://www.vatican.va/content/benedict-xvi/en/encyclicals/documents/hf_ben-xvi_enc_20090629_caritas-in-veritate.html>.

Pope Francis. *Apostolic Constitution*, 'Veritatis Gaudium' (The Joy of Truth) on Ecclesiastical Universities and Faculties, 29 January 2018 <https://press.vatican.va/content/salastampa/en/bollettino/pubblico/2018/01/29/180129c.html>.

Royal Commission into Institutional Responses to Child Sexual Abuse Final Report Recommendations <https://www.childabuseroyalcommission.gov.au/sites/default/files/final_report_-_recommendations.pdf>.

Salter, D. *What Really Matters in Ministry: Profiling Pastoral Success in Flourishing Churches* (Ada, Miss.: Baker, 1990).

Taylor, C. The Ethics of Authenticity (London: Harvard, 1991).

Vatican Council. *Pastoral Constitution on the Church in the Modern World*: Gaudium et Spes; Promulgated by His Holiness Pope Paul VI on December 7, 1965 (Boston: Pauline Books and Media, 1998).

Wiest, W. E. & E. A. Smith. *Ethics in Ministry: A Guide for the Professional* (Minneapolis, Minn.: Fortress, 1990).

Wilson, M. T. & B. Hoffmann. *Preventing Ministry Failure: A ShepherdCare Guide for Pastors, Ministers and Other Caregivers* (Downers grove, Ill.: IVP, 2007).

Wong, J. C. P. 'Foundations of Priestly Formation', *Congregation for the Clergy*. <http://www.clerus.va/content/clerus/en/notizie/new4.html>.

Yaconelli, M. *Contemplative Youth Ministry: Practicing the Presence of Jesus* (London: SPCK, 2006).

Additional Websites

http://usccb.org/beliefs-and-teachings/vocations/upload/vocations-fishers-men-2005-appendixk.pdf.

http://www.newmanreader.org/works/viamedia/volume1/preface3.html

https://divinity.edu.au/study/graduate-attributes/.

https://www.acu.edu.au/about-acu/employers-and-industry/why-hire-acu-graduates.

https://www.notredame.edu.au/about/learning-and-teaching-at-notre-dame/graduate-attributes.

https://www.teqsa.gov.au/glossary-terms under G for graduate attributes.

Debra Snoddy[51]
Catholic Institute of Sydney
dsnoddy@cis.catholic.edu.au

51 ORCID Number https://orcid.org/0000-0001-6778-8515.

PART 2
SCRIPTURE AND GRADUATE CHARACTER

9 | APPRECIATING THE CREATIVE ARTISTRY OF THE HEBREW TEXT

AND THE DIFFICULTIES FACED BY MODERN TRANSLATORS

Abstract

This paper offers a survey of two samples of biblical writing in order to highlight the literary craft that makes up the world of these texts. An understanding of the language and culture of an author enables the interpreter to gain some awareness of the intention of the writer. The paper offers an approach to familiar passages that could be part of an education program that seeks to expose students to the value of a literary appreciation of Hebrew texts. In the process of literary appreciation, it becomes clear how some modern English translations struggle to accurately reflect the tone, rhythm, and rhetorical nuances of the original Hebrew.

It is impossible to gain a full appreciation of biblical writing without hearing the text spoken or read aloud in its original language. With this in view, the texts under consideration in this paper were read in Hebrew to allow participants to gain some grasp of how the storytellers of the past might have brought out the rhythm, cultural nuances, repetitions, and the various literary and rhetorical devices that characterise these extracts. Hebrew citations are taken from *Biblia Hebraica Stuttgartensia*. English translations are the author's except where specified.

1. Genesis 2

Any study of Genesis 2 needs to begin with the readers imagining that they are hearing the text read or narrated by a storyteller. More authentically, the Hebrew storyteller (*ha-mesaper sipurim*) would be relating the chapter in Hebrew and thus showcasing the effect of literary devices such as wordplay, assonance, repetitions, cultural allusions, word choice, along with instances of particular emphasis that are explicit or implied in the written text. In this dynamic setting, the narrative or poetry would gain texture, energy, and colour designed to grip the listener's imagination and convey a message.

That Genesis 2 and 3 form a literary unit is indicated by the parallel motifs of a) paradise gained and human innocence, and paradise lost with the accompanying loss of innocence, b) the contrast between the human tilling the garden in a state of blessedness (2:15) and then tilling the ground with hard work after expulsion from the garden (3:23), and c) the recurring reference to the tree of life and the tree of the knowledge of good and evil. Generally recognised as written by the Yahwist, Genesis 2 deals with human beginnings in a vivid corporeal way. God does not create from a distance by word alone, as in the Priestly account of Genesis 1, but is personally involved in fashioning human and animal life with hands-on activity. The contrast in this divine activity is conveyed by the Hebrew verbs *bara* (create) and *yatsar* (fashion).

The chapter opens with a string of subordinate clauses that only come to a climax with the main clause at v.7 where God forms the *'adam* from the dust of the *'adamah*. Most English and Western European translations do not even attempt to reflect this particular wordplay that so clearly points to humanity's connection with the earth.[1] But hearing this narrated or read aloud, the Hebrew listener would immediately perceive the relationship between the earth creature (*'adam*) and the earth (*'adamah*) from which it is formed and would understand the implication, particularly when it is reinforced later on in 3:19 when the *'adam* is reminded that it came from the dust and will return to the dust of the earth. The writer is obviously making a statement from human experience and points out that in view of human origins, there is no room for hubris:

wayitser yhwh elohim	And the Lord God fashioned the earth
et-ha'adam	creature
'afar min ha-'adamah	[from] dust from the earth. (Gen. 2:7a)

---

1 One notable exception is the *Inclusive Bible*, which translates 2:7 as: 'So YHWH fashioned an earth creature out of the clay of the earth,' thereby affirming the connection so explicit in the Hebrew.

From this point to the end of chapter 2, the listener will become used to the action of God expressed regularly with the construction: verb + YHWH-elohim + object. This is a formula that trumpets the divine action and points to the original oral delivery of the narrative with the kind of repetition that serves as an aide-mémoire to both storyteller and listener.

The formation of *ha-'adam* begins with the action of God, who is depicted as a kind of potter or sculptor shaping the *'adam* personally by hand. This divine metaphorical involvement generates connection and initiates a relationship, which is further emphasised when the absolute breath or spirit of life is given to the mortal, thereby creating a living person:

vayipakh beapav nishmat khayim	And he blew into his nostrils the breath of life,
vayehi ha'adam lenefesh khayah	and the earth creature became a living person.
	(Gen. 2:7b)

The alliteration here has the effect of onomatopoeia with the strong and obvious bilabial plosives in *vayipakh beapav* imitating the blowing of the breath of life into the creature. The balance of the phrases, the breath of life (*nishmat khayim*) and the creature becoming a living being (*nefesh khayah*) is plain enough for the storyteller to highlight. Humanity has life because of the spirit of God, and sharing in the life of God now brings the gift of self-consciousness by which the human can willingly and wholeheartedly respond to the divine. A two-way connection is established. The reader can now see how this account is not shaping up to be solely a creation story but is rather beginning to emphasise relationship and connection between the human and the divine.

Next, God provides a physical environment for the earth creature. The planting of the garden assumes the creation of the world, reinforcing the point that this is not exclusively a creation account. Eden is introduced as a place of luxurious fertility, in effect, a mythical paradise from a Middle-Eastern point of view. The placing of the *'adam* in this paradise is expressed in v.8 with measured rhythm, assonance, and alliteration:

vayita' yhwh elohim gan be'eden miqedem	And the Lord God planted a garden in Eden in the east
vayasem sham ha-'adam 'asher yatsar	and he placed there the human which he had fashioned.
	(Gen. 2:8)

The introduction of the two featured trees is also done with balanced phrases that highlight the idyllic nature of the garden: trees pleasant to look at and trees good for food:

vayatsmakh yhwh elohim	And the Lord God made to grow out
min ha-'adamah kal 'ets	of the ground every tree,
nekhmad lemar'e vetov	pleasant to look at and good for food;
lema'akhal	and the tree of life in the midst of the garden
ve'ets hakhayim betokh hagan	and the tree of the knowledge of good and evil.
ve'ets hada't tov vara'	(Gen. 2:9)

The specific focus on the beauty and function of the trees indicates that the human is to be well provided for in a beautiful setting. God is putting at the human's disposal everything necessary for sustaining life. But into the mix are added two trees of entirely different genre. Both the tree of life and the tree of the knowledge of good and evil are by their very titles allegorical and function on a different plane. While the tree of life may well be an allusion to the search for immortality and squandered opportunities that form a major motif in the Mesopotamian Epic of Gilgamesh and the story of Adapa, the Yahwist has no intention of featuring this common non-Jewish motif in his account. The tree of life slips into the background only to reappear near the end of the story at Genesis 3:22,24. It is the tree of the knowledge of good and evil that becomes a pivotal item as the metaphorical eating of its fruit should impart the knowledge it has to offer.

The flow of the narrative is interrupted by the description of the four rivers. This creates some tension that needs resolution. When the narrative resumes, the writer repeats the statement of the human being placed or set down (נוּחַ) in the garden but this time with the added responsibility of working it (עָבַד) and watching over it (שָׁמַר). In spite of the vast geographical landscape implied in the introduction of the four rivers, the setting of the account is restricted to the immediate surroundings of the *'adam*. For the sole purpose of the narrative, the focus is on one human being in a garden that he can work and take care of and the two specified trees that are within his reach. Here is another example of the function of myth; namely, to present the general by concentrating on details of the particular.

The human is now given a test that will assess his mettle. Herein lies another ancient mythic motif whereby a character's virtue is only confirmed when he or she has passed whatever ordeal or test has been set. In this case, the tree of life is sidelined, and the prohibition is against eating the fruit of the tree of the knowledge of good and evil. The discerning reader could well stop and wonder what this tree looks like and might even come to appreciate how Christian artists, particularly those of the Renaissance, have shaped our thinking. Conventionally, artists have depicted this tree as a fruit tree with real physical fruit, when, in reality, it is a figurative symbol featured in a metaphorical tale. The essence of the Hebrew metaphor lies in the way eating or tasting connotes experience through personal contact. Some examples of how this works will illustrate the point.

Job is comparing the deaths of two men, one who dies after a full and prosperous life while another dies in bitterness:

> And another dies with a bitter soul,
> And has not tasted of the good. (Literally, eaten אָכַל of good).
> (Job 21:25)

Psalm 34:8 has 'Taste and see (טַעֲמוּ וּרְאוּ) that the Lord is good'. Nobody would miss the force of the image where the verb טעם (taste) is a metaphor for experience. Experience of the Lord gives understanding that the Lord is good. The NRSV translation of Psalm 119:103 reads:

> How sweet are your words to my taste,
> sweeter than honey to my mouth.

A more literal rendering would be:

> How pleasant to my palate are your words
> more than honey to my mouth.

But again, the metaphor of eating or tasting conveys the notion of experiencing something, in this case, the wisdom and support of the Torah, and the psalmist glories in the Torah are an ideal guide for living.

> The woman in the Song of Solomon delights to sit in the shadow of
> her lover as she acclaims,
> and his fruit was sweet to my taste (or literally, to my palate).
> (Song 2:3 NRSV)

The main point here is that eating or tasting is a metaphor for experience. In essence, then, this is a narrative about human behaviour, not about forbidden fruit. Theological education programs would do well to dispense with misleading terms like 'our first parents' and 'eating forbidden fruit' so that graduates might not be guilty of perpetuating the fiction of 'Adam and Eve eating the apple'.

The next step in the story follows on from a realisation that the *'adam* on his own is incomplete and, as such, can never achieve fulfilment or grow to wholeness and thereby become what he can be. He needs a partner who will be *negdo* (נגדו); that is, standing beside him to be a fitting and complementary life companion who will complete his humanity.

The narrator then takes the reader/listener on a false path by showing God creating the animals out of the *'adamah* in an effort to arrive at a partner who can be a sustaining helper and companion to the *'adam*. It is worth noting that the noun עז meaning both help and helper more frequently refers to God as sustaining help or succour and certainly does not have an automatic connotation of assistant, servant, or subordinate. The implication here is that the companion to the *'adam* will be his equal and, therefore, a fit and capable support and sustainer. The narrator and the reader/listener know full well the creation of animals is no solution; it is not going to provide a suitable partner for the man, and this creates suspense in the story.[2]

True, there is a connection between the animals and the human. They are both fashioned from the *'adamah,* and the relationship between them is established by the naming of the animals. This connection is particularly underpinned when God is depicted as bringing the animals and flying creatures (*kal 'of ha shamay'im*) to the *'adam* so that he might give them names. Moreover, the allocated names will be abiding identity markers for these creatures.

vekol 'asher yiqra 'lo ha 'adam nefesh khaya hu shemo	And whatever the human called a living creature, that was its name (Gen. 2:19)

The Hebrew text pointedly uses the qal perfect to say that God was the one who did not find a suitable partner for the man. God's search was clearly unproductive and, at this stage, does not fulfil the divine intention uttered in 2:18.

---

2   Westermann, *Genesis 1-11*, 226. Westermann discusses the theories that point to the mythical background of God making a futile attempt to create a partner for the *'adam*. He notes the particular similarities and differences between Enkidu's situation in the Gilgamesh Epic and Genesis 2:19-20.

> וּלְאָדָם לֹא־מָצָא עֵזֶר כְּנֶגְדּוֹ ule'adam lo' matsa 'ezer kenegdo And for the man he did not find a suitable helper (Gen. 2:20)

Rabbinic reflection on this text highlights the contrast between the animals and the human. The human's lament in the Midrash underlines the unsatisfactory outcome of God's creation of the wild and domestic creatures of the animal kingdom. We read in *Bereshit Rabbah* 17:4:

He made them pass by in pairs. He said, 'Everything has its partner, but I have no partner'.

The Aramaic of the direct speech reads:

> לכל יש בן זוג ולי אין בן זוג   lakol yesh ben zug uli 'eyn ben zug.

The tension is unresolved; the human is still incomplete. A truly suitable matching partner who can relate to the earth creature on every level—physical, mental and spiritual—must be someone of the same species, and the only way to achieve this is to take some part of the original human and fashion a partner. To accomplish this, God has to render the *'adam* unconscious, and the narrator describes God taking a rib from the human and building it into a woman.

The use of three different verbs in three different stages of the divine creative process is intentional and significant:

bara' – create by mere word (Gen. 1:1),
yatsar – fashion out of earth (Gen. 2:7),
banah – build from raw material (Gen. 2:22).

God then brings the woman to the original earth creature. In light of the marriage context specified in Genesis 2:24, it is quite conceivable that this is a reference to the Jewish wedding ceremony where the attendant brings the bride to the groom. The tension is now resolved, and woman arrives as the climax of the whole scenario. This highpoint is reinforced, with literary overkill, in fact, when the *'adam* utters his enthusiastic response to God, saying, 'This time (*ha-pa'am*) this woman is bone of my bones and flesh of my flesh'. No English translation of this response adequately reflects the rising force contained in the Hebrew text, where the woman is intentionally emphasised with three occurrences in the one outburst of the feminine demonstrative *zo't*. Likewise, no English translation is able to imitate the obvious poetic form of this spontaneous exclamation. Noteworthy are a) the parallelism of bone and flesh in lines 2 and 3, and of *zo't/ishah* and *meish/zo't* in lines 4 and 5, b) the assonance and wordplay of *'ish* and *'ishah,* and c) the chiastic structure of lines 4 and 5 (ABC/C¹B¹A¹), 'this…called woman // man…taken this'.³

The literal English rendered below highlights the difficulty of arriving at a fluent translation and, at the same time, accurately replicating the rhythm and structure of the original Hebrew:

zo't hapa'm 2 beats	This one, this time,
'etsem mea'tsamaiy 2 beats	is bone of my bones
uvasar mibsariy 2 beats	and flesh of my flesh;
zo't yiqare' 'ishah 3 beats	this one shall be called woman
ki me'ish luqakhah zo't 3 beats	for from man was she taken, this one. (Gen. 2:23)

It is worth noting here that *La Bible de Jérusalem* makes a commendable attempt to imitate the Hebrew but can only bring this about in 2:23b:

Pour le coup, c'est l'os de mes os
et la chair de ma chair!
Celle-ci sera appelée "femme",
car elle fut tirée de l'homme, celle-ci!

The climactic tone of this statement is reinforced with the term *hapa'm*, meaning now finally, this time, now at last,⁴ and the repeated feminine *zo't,* one at the beginning of each of the two halves of the *'adam*'s enthusiastic cry, and a third at the end of the verse. This newly arrived feminine person is greeted with animated recognition that she is of the same species as the *'adam* and clearly the high point of the chapter.

Contained in the verse is the Hebrew idea of the closest kind of relationship where two people are of the same kind. Now, the woman is with the man as a sustaining companion. Now, at last, all is good because he is no longer alone but has a partner to complement him and make him complete.

To highlight the gender difference, the man establishes a relationship with the woman and gives her the generic name that corresponds to his own. He declares, 'She shall be called *'ishah* because she was taken from *'ish'*. In this breath, the man names both his woman and himself. Here, the narrator's

---

3   Wenham, *Genesis 1-15*, 70.
4   Clines, *Dictionary*, s.v. הַפַּעַם.

deliberate wordplay is designed to underscore the unique closeness of their relationship inasmuch as their names sound almost identical. This would be immediately evident coming from the speech of the storyteller who would stress the effect of the unmistakable assonance, as it creates the impression of connection and likeness between man and woman.[5] Many interpreters over the centuries, apparently unfamiliar with Hebrew, have missed the pun and, blind to the rising climax of the narrative, have not taken full account of its resolution with the arrival of the woman. Far from being a secondary or subordinate character, the woman is the culmination of the creative process in this chapter of Genesis.

Failure to appreciate this literary conclusion has led some commentators to regard woman as subordinate because she comes last in the creation agenda.[6] This, then, has given rise to all kinds of anthropological and theological interpretations that do not do justice to the escalating structure of the narrative and the literary impact of the emphatic *zo't* in Genesis 2:23.

Following the man's ecstatic cry, the narrator inserts an etiological observation of his own, which serves as a commentary on the ideal relationship of a man and a woman who cling to each other and become one in a marriage of commitment. It acts as a kind of *inclusio*, which bookends with Genesis 2:18. Its function as a conclusion or deduction is indicated by עַל־כֵּן (so, therefore, thus, in this way),[7] an adverbial expression of manner that, coming from the mouth of the storyteller, points the listener to the purpose or at least a traditional outcome of the preceding narrative. This addition by the narrator adds an extra dimension to this whole account:

'al-ken y'azav 'ish 'et 'aviv	Consequently, a man leaves his
ve 'et 'imo	father and his mother
vedavaq be'ishto	and clings to his wife
'vehayu levaser 'ekhad	and they become one flesh.

(Gen. 2:24)

Even in early Israelite society where arranged marriages were the norm, the narrator draws a picture of the loyalty and commitment that should sustain the perfect bond between husband and wife. It is this, after all, that forms the solid

---

5   It is the assonance that produces the effect as *'ish* and *'ishah* have different origins and do not share the same etymology. See Speiser, *Genesis*, 18; Cotter, *Genesis*, 32, n.15.
6   Augustine, *On Genesis*, 114; John Chrysostom, *Homilies*, 111; Hooke, 'Genesis', 179; Maly, 'Genesis', 12.
7   Clines, *Dictionary*, s.v. עַל־כֵּן.

foundation of a healthy and productive society.

Yet again, the Hebrew of this verse has a rhythm and progression that traces a man's movement from his original family—from which he derives his identity—to his wife with whom he becomes one and with whom he will cooperate in the formation of a new identity as someone's husband and someone's father. The literary implication is that the marital bond overtakes filial ties. Here is a fitting conclusion to the matrix of relationships that is presented in this second chapter of Genesis. Calling this a second creation story places the focus on creation and risks overlooking the literary design in the structure of the narrative and the building of tension with its climactic resolution. Furthermore, the narrator's inserted statement regarding the relationship of man and woman in marriage lifts Genesis 2 beyond a mere creation story to a commentary on the marital commitment that forms the foundation of human society. What may well have been a stand-alone creation account has become something more through the addition of verse 24.

Most English Bibles set out the text of Genesis 2 as prose, thereby deflecting attention from the rhetorical character of the vocabulary, style, and arrangement of the Hebrew. Even some versions that have explanatory footnotes do not highlight the rising tension in this chapter and the climactic resolution with the arrival of the woman.

2. Isaiah 57:15

Another passage that has a vibrant poetic character and yet suffers from translations that do not do justice to the semantics, structure, and rhythmic flow of the language is Isaiah 57:15. This verse is preceded by the prophet's condemnation of misplaced priorities and warped values that gave rise to blatant hypocrisy as people of wealth and power took part in acts of ritual and piety when their lives were characterised by oppression and wickedness. Speaking for God, the prophet sets up a pointed contrast between the high and holy dwelling place of the Shekhinah and the lowly wretchedness of the oppressed.

ki ko 'amar ram venissa'	For so says the high and lofty one
shokhen 'ad veqadosh shemo	who dwells forever and holy is his name:
marom veqadosh 'eshkon	In the high and holy place I dwell
veetdakka' oushefal ruakh	and with the crushed and humiliated in spirit;
lehakhayot ruakh shefalim	to give life to the spirit of the humiliated
lehakhayot lev nidkka'im	to give life to the heart of the crushed.

The difficulty with many English translations of this verse is that the impact of the contrast is diminished by the inadequacy of terms like contrite and humble. The few examples below demonstrate this failure to give full force to the Hebrew *dakka* (crushed) and *shefal* (brought low). The primary connotation of the root *dakha* (דכא) is to crush, reduce to dust, and oppress, and the root *shefal* (שפל) bears the connotations of low, be brought low, abased, and humiliated.[8] In the context of ancient Israelite society, this would be tantamount to dishonour. The literary contrast intended here is between the stark opposites of the lofty and holy dwelling place of the Holy One and those who have been crushed and brought low. These latter have been passed through the hardship of divine punishment and have been brought low to the point of seeing the light and being prepared to open themselves to *teshuvah*; that is, the way back to God.

While this return implies a movement through remorse and contrition, it does not suggest that the redeemed are primarily triggered by virtue of humility. If it were, we might expect to see verbs such as ענה, כנע or the adjective עָנָו, which have a more direct application to a deliberate humbling of self or being humble in the sight of God. Rather than voluntary humility, it is imposed punishment that has brought them down, rendering them depressed and rudderless. Realisation now brings them to their most profitable option, which is to abandon the way of error and return to God.

Below are some sample English translations that, like most English versions, have a shared concentration on humility and contrition over the primary Hebrew focus on being crushed and brought down:

---

8   Clines, *Dictionary*, s.v. שפל.

also with those who are contrite
and humble in spirit,
to revive the spirit of the humble,
and to revive the heart of the
contrite.
NRSV

and also with him who is of a
contrite and lowly spirit,
to revive the spirit of the lowly,
 and to revive the heart of the
contrite.
ESV

Yet with the contrite and the lowly
in spirit—
Reviving the spirits of the lowly,
Reviving the hearts of
the contrite.
Tanakh

With him who has a contrite and
humble spirit,
To revive the spirit of the humble,
And to revive the heart of the
contrite ones.
NKJV

but also with the broken and humble,
in order to revive the spirit of the
humble
and revive the hearts of the
broken ones.
CJB

I dwell in a high and holy place,
but also with the contrite and lowly
of spirit,
To revive the spirit of the lowly,
to revive the heart of the crushed.
NABRE

Of this selection, the revised version of the *New American Bible* comes closest to the semantics and poetic intent of the original Hebrew, but even this does not give full account of the two verbs that describe those who have been crushed (דכא) and brought low (שפל). Neither does it give a voice to the parallelism and repetition of those two verbs in the last two lines, which state the purpose of the Holy One's focus on the crushed and humiliated of Israel. The majority of translations miss the full causative force of the hiphil in the infinitive construct *lehakhayot* (לְהַחֲיוֹת), which occurs in the last bicola. While 'revive' is an adequate translation, it does not have the same weight as 'give new life' or 'bring to life' the heart and spirit of the chastened. Causing new life to re-animate the crushed and devastated is the essential idea in this expression. And, of course, no translation can achieve the brilliant economy of the Hebrew poetry in these bicola. Notice the addition of the *vav* before the second *lehakhayot* to maintain the balance of rhythmic syllables:

lehakhayot ruakh shefalim	לְהַחֲיוֹת רוּחַ שְׁפָלִים
lehakhayot lev nidkka'im	וּלְהַחֲיוֹת לֵב נִדְכָּאִים:

The majority of English translations of Isaiah 57:15 do not point up the force of the contrast between the loftiness of the One who is set apart, the *qadosh*, and the depressed state of the *nidkka'im* and the *shefalim*. The synonymous parallelism, repetition, and rhythm in the Hebrew text are not generally given full rhetorical value. That said, there is no denying the enduring difficulty, and in many cases, the impossibility, of satisfactorily rendering the poetry of one language into an equivalent translated form in another language. The above examples highlight this difficulty by demonstrating the marked difference in the stylistics of classical Hebrew and modern English.

Conclusion

This all too brief focus on the poetics of two Hebrew passages highlights some of the many literary and stylistic devices employed by writers of biblical Hebrew narrative and poetry. Appreciation of these techniques allows the modern reader to gain a complete understanding of the meaning and intention of a given text. The process of conducting an informed literary analysis will also alert the modern reader to the difficulties faced by translators as they struggle to render biblical writing in a way that does some justice to the rhythm, flow, and stylistics of the original language. As a corollary, it is incumbent upon designers of programs of pastoral and theological education to see that students have some exposure to the literary style of biblical Hebrew. This will enable them to appreciate the artistry in a given text and become aware of the obstacles faced by translators. Students need to hear Hebrew text read fluently and with expression so that they can develop some sense of its literary character. It is easy to overlook the fact that the rhetorical characteristics of a biblical text function as an essential vehicle of its spiritual and inspiring message.

Bibliography

Biblia Hebraica Stuttgartensia: With Westminster Hebrew Morphology.(electronic ed; Stuttgart; Glenside PA: German Bible Society; Westminster Seminary, 1996).

Clines, D. J. A. (ed.) *The Dictionary of Classical Hebrew* (Sheffield: Sheffield Phoenix Press, 2011).

Cotter, D. W. *Genesis* (Berit Olam, Studies in Hebrew Narrative and Poetry; Collegeville: The Liturgical Press, 2003).

Hooke, S.H. 'Genesis', *Peake's Commentary on the Bible* (London: Thomas Nelson, 1962).

Maly, E. 'Genesis', in Raymond E. Brown et al. (eds.), *The Jerome Biblical Commentary* (Englewood Cliffs N.J.: Prentice-Hall, 1968): 7-46.

Saint Augustine. *On Genesis: Two Books on Genesis Against the Manichees; And, On the Literal Interpretation of Genesis, an Unfinished Book* (Fathers of the Church, 84; Washington, D.C.: Catholic University of America, 1990).

Speiser, E.A. *Genesis* (The Anchor Bible; Garden City: Doubleday, 1962).

St John Chrysostom. *Homilies on Genesis, 1-17* (Fathers of the Church, 74; Washington, D.C.: Catholic University of America, 2010).

Wenham, G. *Genesis 1-15*, (Word Biblical Commentary; Nashville: Thomas Nelson, 1987).

Westermann, C. *Genesis 1-11. A Commentary* (London: SPCK, 1984).

Laurence Woods
Independent researcher
lmwoods74@bigpond.com

10 | PSALMS AND POPULAR SONGS

NEW INFORMING OLD

Abstract

Exemplary theology graduates are those able to apply their studies in daily life. Students in a 2018 course on the Psalms were required to present a modern popular (pop) song, five of which are discussed in this essay. Analysing pop songs using Ricoeur's idea of the world behind the text, the world of the text, and the world in front of the text is one way to understand the complexity of the study of Psalms. Psalms and pop songs are art forms that communicate through poetic language. Both genres express feelings we have as human beings, address social issues, and offer values that may motivate. Pop songs can facilitate an understanding of psalms, and vice versa.

1. Introduction

The title for one of the Sydney College of Divinity (SCD) conferences in 2019 was God's Exemplary Graduates. I understand exemplary graduates to be those who complete courses within one of the nine theological institutions accredited by SCD. Thereafter, they are able to apply their studies not only within church contexts but also within the various contexts in which they live. I lecture in Biblical Studies at Good Shepherd College (GSC), Auckland, New Zealand, which is affiliated with the Catholic Institute of Sydney. GSC is the sole tertiary theological provider in the Roman Catholic tradition in New Zealand—focused on offering a theological education to men preparing for ordination (seminarians) and to laypeople desiring such studies. Lay people study theology for varied reasons, such as a prerequisite for teaching religion in Catholic schools, for chaplaincy work, or for personal development.

On average, GSC has thirty effective full-time students (EFTS) per semester. The percentage of seminarians to lay students fluctuates, though, on average, the percentage can be considered as thirty per cent seminarians to seventy per cent laity.

The training for seminarians consists of theological, spiritual, and pastoral elements. The spiritual development of seminarians belongs within the realms of the seminary community. Mentors in the seminary choose appropriate pastoral projects for seminarians. Lay people may have a spiritual director or mentor. They generally live within a communal unit, such as a family or religious congregation. Their pastoral field is broad—from their family to the workplace or a specified ministry, such as Catholic schools, hospital, or prison chaplaincy.

In the first instance, my role is to teach biblical studies, one discipline within the broader field of theology, not spiritual or pastoral training. It is too simple to say that theology is the education of the head in contrast to spirituality feeding the soul, and pastoral work is the field of action, as the head, soul, and body in action function together as a unity. However, I do see my obligation as offering solid training in biblical studies—providing input to the head and teaching the skills required for biblical interpretation. My teaching role in biblical studies makes up only one part of the much larger whole of theology studies.

Basic interpretative skills have to be taught in biblical studies, but to become an exemplary graduate, the skill in biblical studies must be useable; that is, able to be applied in the contemporary world. The sub-title for the 2019 SCD Learning Conference is 'Character-Orientated Graduate Attributes in Theological Education'. I understand character-orientated attributes as related to applicable skills. The Bible has the power to inspire and transform—to nourish life-giving values and positive action. It can move its readers to change themselves and the world for the better.

One link between the Bible and today's world is popular (pop) songs. Psalms and pop songs are forms of art communicated through the spoken or sung word and taken in through the ears. Their message often addresses important human values and social justice issues. In semester two, 2018, I taught a course on Psalms and experimented with popular songs as a way to integrate old psalms with the modern world. For the Psalms course, besides an obligatory exegesis of a psalm and compulsory reading of a stipulated article every week, each student had 15 minutes to present one popular song of their choice. The idea was that exploration of a modern song facilitates the study of an old psalm. If students have a song that they like, then their analysis of the pop song may help them to see how the words of the song reflect the joys and pains of the period in which we live with an immediacy or validity, as did the psalms for Jewish communities in the biblical period (fourth to first-century BCE). Analysis of new (Western) lyrics put to music can facilitate analysis of old (ancient Near Eastern) poetry. The analysis involves applying Paul Ricoeur's concepts of the world behind the text, the world of the text, and the world in front of the text.

Songs chosen by the students listed alphabetically are:

- *Ah, Non Giunge*, aria from Bellini's opera La Somnabula
- *Kyrie*, sung by the band Mr Mister
- *Livin' on a Prayer*, sung by Jon Bon Jovi
- *Malhari*, from the Hindi film Bajirao Mastani
- *Never Enough*, a song from the film The World's Greatest Showman
- *Sons of Gallipoli*, lyrics and music composed by Chris Skinner
- *Te Waka Huia*, a Maori protest haka (dance) with narrative
- *The Rose*, sung by Westlife
- *Where is the Love?* sung by the band Black Eyed Peas
- *You Raise me Up*, sung by Josh Groban.

Not all the songs chosen are songs or, for that matter, pop songs or music of the West. The aria *Ah, Non Giunge* is from an opera by the nineteenth-century Italian composer Vincenzo Bellini. *Malhari* is a victory dance set within a Hindi film—the choreographed physical movement has visual rather than aural impact, as a sense of rhythm is more intensive than the words or any musical harmony. *Te Waka Huia* is a Maori protest song with action. Similar to *Malhari*, the energy and visuals of the dance, though reinforcing the words, came across stronger than the aural dimension. Nearly all the songs were played in class on YouTube; that is, sound with visuals, not as a sound bite alone. The visuals were sometimes the group performing their own song; for example, *Kyrie* performed by the band Mr Mister, or in the case of *The Rose*, Westlife, an Irish boyband, sang and enacted a prenuptial scene as a narrative to the song.

Thanks are due to the ten students who all completed the 2018 course on Psalms at GSC. I had their presence before me as I explored their chosen songs for this essay. Regrettably, the scope of the essay does not permit addressing every song. An analysis of five of the compositions follows—*Kyrie, Never Enough, Where is the Love? Livin' on a Prayer,* and *The Rose*. They are then commented on with reference to Ricoeur's methodology.

2. Analysis

Kyrie is sung by the pop/rock group Mr Mister. Richard Page, a member of the band, wrote the music and a relative, John Lang, composed the words. The first line of the chorus, 'Kyrie eleison, down the road that I must travel', is the most-repeated phrase in the song. Many who listen to the song do not know that the background to the phrase 'Kyrie eleison' is traditional Christian liturgy or that the words are Greek and mean 'Lord have mercy' when translated. A search on what the phrase means for various listeners brings up interesting results. When words are not heard or not understood, readers seek to fill the gap. The human tendency is to create meaning or produce coherence. 'Kyrie eleison' is then rendered as 'Carrying a laser down the road', or as 'Kireyae lays upon the road that I must travel' or yet again as 'Carry me I'm lazy down the road that I must travel'.[1]

John Lang says he went to an Episcopal Church as a child; hence, his knowledge of the phrase 'Kyrie eleison' and its meaning. The band Mr Mister is not a Christian band. However, the lead singer, Richard Page, considers this song a prayer, as in an interview, he says, 'I got a lot of power from meditation, from being still and realizing that what I am doing is insignificant compared to the universe. That is what this song is all about'.[2] How Lang and Page, composers of the song, understand and feel about the song is not necessarily how listeners understand and feel about the song.

Never Enough is a song from the film The Greatest Showman (2017), based on the life of P. T. Barnum and his involvement with the entertainment industry.[3] Barnum organised a US tour for the famous Swedish singer Jenny Lind. During the course of the tour, Lind fell in love with Barnum, which is the background

---

1 https://www.songfacts.com/facts/mr-mister/kyrie
2 https://www.songfacts.com/facts/mr-mister/kyrie
3 https://www.classicfm.com/discover-music/never-enough-the-greatest-showman/

for the first singing of *Never Enough*. The word love is not used in the song, though a relationship is suggested by the term of endearment 'darling' and by the words 'these hands could hold the world'. Stars and the night sky are mentioned in two of the short verses, which can be understood as metaphors for spotlights that light up an otherwise dark stage. The song is repeated later in the film, but in the second setting, the context is Barnum's rejection of Lind's advances. In the initial context, the song is about the love of one person for another, but in the second context, unrequited love morphs into universal love and hope. Nearly all the phrases within the song are ambiguous, open to different interpretations, and hence, the meaning is variable.

Justin Paul, one of the two writers of the lyrics, describes the song as a pop ballad. Use of the word ballad by Paul is surprising, as a narrative or storyline is almost non-existent in the song. Paul comments that repetition, a technique to attract people to a song, is deliberately used.[4] The catch-phrase of the song, 'For me, never enough …', with its constant repetition is also the song's title. Some of Paul's skill with the few phrases that make up the song is the metaphorical nature of the phrases—multiple meanings and understandings are possible. The meaning of the phrases is not confined to the narrative of the film.

Where is the Love?, sung by Black Eyed Peas, was presented in class as a YouTube clip.[5] My lasting memory of the clip is of a person running through streets plastering a poster with a big red question mark painted on a black background on any surface possible. The red question mark urgently carried becomes iconic and recurs throughout disparate scenes. The big red question mark shrieks communal protest at me.

In the world of the text, some of the words of the song are 'people killin'', 'people dyin'', 'people gets colder', 'something's wrong with it'. The sense of inhumanity and a lack of social care conjured up by these words is strengthened by further phrases such as 'nations droppin' bombs', 'chemical gasses fillin' lungs', or 'to discriminate only generates hate'. The phrases solicit different interpretations and refer to varied contexts, from terrorism to racism and ageism to materialism, or from war to drug addiction. Contrasting words used in the song, such as peace and love and fairness and equality, appeal to positive human attributes.

The verses are sung in rap style with an accusatory chant tone. The essential

---

4   https://www.songfacts.com/facts/loren-allred/never-enough
5   https://www.youtube.com/watch?v=WpYeekQkAdc

phrase of the refrain is the question, 'Where is the love?' Or, is the refrain a rhetorical cry meaning love has disappeared—love is no more? The refrain is sung by several voices and echoed by a choir of further voices.

The world behind the text is multi-faceted. The song is attributed to several members of the group Black Eyed Peas, with a first version appearing in 2001.[6] The song was released again in 2003 as a single sung by Black Eyed Peas but did not gain the popularity of a more recent version. When Black Eyed Peas changed the style of their music to a more mainstream pop sound, as heard in the video clip, the song became a hit. The song has taken on a life of its own as other artists appropriate the words and tune to make their own versions; for example, Inbal Bibi in Israel, or Sho Sakurai singing a Japanese version for a Japanese audience.

Livin' on a Prayer and *Where is the Love?* are examples of songs written by friends from similar backgrounds.[7] The lyrics for *Livin' on a Prayer* date to the Reagan era (1981-89), also known as a time of trickle-down or neo-liberal economics. In New Jersey, in the basement of one of their parents' houses, Bon Jovi and Richie Sambora created the characters of Gina and Tommy for their song.

Livin' on a Prayer is the lament of a couple and tells of their woes. The song opens with the phrase 'once upon a time', which evokes the idea of a story from a long time ago, but then almost immediately an unusual twist is added as the words 'not so long ago' follow. We are now on the alert. Tommy and Gina are on the verge of financial ruin, then in a state of ruin. Tommy has lost his job as a dock worker and pawned his guitar. Gina works long hours at a diner, US English for a small cheap eatery. They attempt to live from her meagre income. What they have is love for one another and faith in God, expressed with the often-repeated phrase 'livin' on a prayer'. As the song progresses, there is less and less story to tell. More and more, their plight is apparent as the words of the refrain 'woah, livin' on a prayer' recur more frequently. It seems too simple to say, but the words referring to prayer suggest hope. Prayer somehow keeps Gina and Tommy going.

---

6   Early members of the band were Will.i.am, Apl.de.ap, Taboo, Justin Timberlake, Printz Board, Michael Fratantuno, and George Pajon.

7   *Where is the Love?* is the collaboration of several members from the band Black Eyed Peas. The change in their style of music is significant. See https://www.bbc.com/news/blogs-magazine-monitor-25120899 or https://www.lyricsondemand.com/b/bonjovilyrics/livinonaprayerlyrics.html. Desmond Child later joined as a co-writer of the song. See https://www.tennessean.com/story/entertainment/music/2014/06/20/story-behind-song-livin-prayer/11103409/

Amanda McBroom wrote the words for *The Rose* and sang the song in clubs (1977-78). It was then chosen for Bette Midler to sing in a film with the same title (1979).[8] In class, the song was shown as on YouTube sung by Westlife (2006).[9] The performance background of *The Rose* moves through several contexts—from a song composed in the late seventies, used a couple of years later for a film with the same title, then sung by an Irish boy band called Westlife, with nuptial visuals added in the early Twenty-First Century. In the course of forty years, the setting for the song has moved from live music in a club, to a song sung in a film viewed at a cinema, to a YouTube video accessible on a home computer.

The song is a short ballad without a refrain. The story progresses as three verses, each verse made up of eight lines, are sung. Alternate lines rhyme. For example, in verse one, the final word of line one 'river' loosely rhymes with 'razor' at the end of line three, then 'hunger' rhymes with 'flower' in lines five and seven. The final words of the even lines more obviously rhyme; 'reed' with 'bleed' and 'need' with 'seed'. The first verse is dense with images—love is compared to a river, to a razor, and to hunger and likened to a flower.

The second verse is about breaking through thresholds that hinder one from moving forward in life. Hindrances are portrayed in four different ways. The first sentence refers to holding back as something negative with the words—'It's the heart afraid of breaking that never learns to dance'. For me, this means trust is necessary in relationships. You have to follow the gut. Life is a risk. The fear of pain or hurt cannot be managed in advance—at some point, you just have to trust. This is expressed better than my words by Amanda Broom with her final sentence in verse two, 'And the soul afraid of dyin' that never learns to live'.

The final verse offers the promise of joy that love can bring—'Just remember in the winter far beneath the bitter snows lies the seed that with the sun's love in the spring becomes the rose'.

The song offers a non-typical take on love. It is not about love as a romantic relationship or as a fun state of being in togetherness. The title of the song, The Rose, alludes to love and pain, as the rose is a classic metaphor for love. Beauty and attraction can come with thorns and pain.

In class, the song was presented as a black and white video in a YouTube version. The clip begins with shots of an anxious groom and an anxious bride

---

8 The story of the film is loosely based on the life of singer Janis Joplin. https://en.wikipedia.org/wiki/The_Rose_(song)
9 https://www.youtube.com/watch?v=VTCQBuYhq_s

shortly before the marriage ceremony. Then, the best men, band members clad in suits, are seen in a room with a chequered floor (resembling a chessboard), while the bridesmaids are in another room helping the bride prepare. At the beginning of the clip, a sense of human separation is apparent, despite all preparing for the same event. Connectedness is absent as there is no touching. The first human touch is when the bride walks down the aisle with her hand on her father's arm. From this point on, the separate groups of people start to come together to become a larger single group. As the ceremony progresses, the bride comes in contact with the groom, and then, finally, the entire wedding party is seen dancing at the post-ceremony function. For me, the nuptial narrative of the YouTube clip detracts from the strength of the poetry—visual effects override the sung words. It was on studying the words of the song that I came to discover how amazing Broom's poetry is—strong yet supple, severe but gentle.

3. Implications

One of the goals of the presentation of pop songs as part of a course on Psalms was to show issues that scholars have to deal with in the interpretation of biblical texts. Researching the development of pop songs sheds light on the complexity of the world behind the text. Two of the pop songs were written by two people—*Kyrie* and *Livin' on a Prayer*. *Where is the Love?* was written by a team of composer artists. If pop songs are often written by a team, then it is not so difficult to conceive of psalms being written by a team, or in biblical speak, by scribes from a scribal school. As a biblical text may evolve over generations, so some pop songs develop over decades. A second point needs to be made regarding authorship. Some students referred to *The Rose* as *Bette Midler's The Rose*. This nomenclature attributes the song to Bette Midler, the singer through whom the song first really became known, but, in fact, Amanda Broom was the author of the words. The person through whom a song becomes popular can become the person to whom a song is attributed—thereby, the performer seems to take precedence over the composer/originator. Attribution of *The Rose* to Bette Midler facilitates an understanding of the attribution of some psalms to David, with words such as 'a Psalm of David', as found in the superscription of several psalms.

The words of the song *The Rose* have remained the same for over forty years, but the medium and context have changed—from night club to film to

YouTube clip played, for example, on a mobile phone. When the group Black Eyed Peas changed the music style for *Where is the Love?*, the song became much more popular. Similarly, the setting for performances of psalms changed—for example, from a Levitical choir singing at the Temple in the late monarchic period to a community of exiled Jews praying together in Babylonia. In the world behind the text, settings for performance can change. Furthermore, the appropriateness of a text may wax or wane according to the social interests of the time.

Genres, vocabulary, and literary techniques are features of the world of the text. *Where is the Love?* can be understood as a contemporary protest song related to the psalm genre 'communal lament' as categorised by Herman Gunkel in Form Criticism. In the song, references to killin' and dyin' contrast with references to peace, love, and truth. The content appeals to universal humanity, as all have to continue to live together on this single planet. Similarly, in the psalms, the tone can alternate between sentences. In one sentence, the psalmist feels mocked and belittled by an enemy, then in the next sentence, turns to speak of God as the One who gives hope and confidence. The rapid and frequent change of voice between sentences is typical of pop songs and psalms.

Livin' on a Prayer is an example of a song of petition. Gina and Tommy more and more frequently call out 'Woah, we're half way there. Woah, livin' on a prayer'. The song is in the style of Gunkel's psalm genre 'individual lament'. The narrative ceases to move forward, as the increasingly repeated refrain suggests a static state and reinforces a sense of the young couple's impoverishment. The use of words such as 'diner' for a cheap eatery or 'six string' for a guitar suggests North American authorship. Similarly, sometimes vocabulary in the psalms suggests different sources or origins. Use of the word Horeb instead of Sinai may suggest deuteronomistic influence (Ps 106:19) in biblical writing, or Ephraim can be a synonym for the Northern Israelite kingdom of Israel (Ps 78:67).

A psalm such as Psalm 22 can be interpreted very differently depending on the tradition within which it is read. In the Jewish tradition, the lions and encircling bulls with wide-open mouths can be read as metaphors for the Babylonian oppressors and Nebuchadnezzar when recited by Judean communities in the Babylonian exile. In the Christian context, the Matthean Passion narrative in chapter 27 draws on Psalm 22 in its interpretation of Christ. The opening words of Psalm 22, 'My God, My God, why have you forsaken me', are assigned to Jesus on the cross. Further phrases from the psalm, such as 'words of my groaning' or 'all my bones are out of joint', give insight into how Jesus may have felt in his suffering. The soldiers mock Jesus and cast lots for his clothing—actions mentioned in Psalm 22. Over time, Jewish and Christian traditions have produced different interpretations of Psalm 22. Similarly, interpretative variations are apparent with pop songs. Lang. as the author/composer (the world behind the text) of *Kyrie*, and audiences today (the world in front of the text) have different understandings of the words of the same song.

One sees how both old and new texts take on a life of their own—apart from the authors/composers. The meaning of a text is influenced by the medium through which it is transmitted (sound and/or visual) and the contexts (temple or assembly, bar or headphones of a mobile phone) in which it is performed. The world of the composer/s or author/s is different from that of the current listener/s or audience. In the case of the song *Kyrie*, some listeners created their own sense out of the words 'kyrie eleison', which were incomprehensible to them. Or, *The Rose* began as a song sung by the author in night clubs, but now it is most often heard and seen in the medium of YouTube. One current format of the song sung by Westlife keeps the original words, but the medium has greatly changed. The original words continue, but the newer medium is multilayered with sound, visuals, and a nuptial narrative. The wedding scene visuals interpret the song in the context of a marriage—love becomes confined to that setting rather than the broader meaning of love as suggested by the words of the lyric.

An analysis of pop songs can facilitate the study of biblical psalms. The authors behind some pop songs such as *Livin' on a Prayer* and *Where is the Love?* cry out, like the Hebrew prophets, on social justice issues. Some songs offer values to strive or hope for, speaking of love and peace and equality. Hebrew values often mentioned in the psalms are justice (mishpat), righteousness (tsedekah), and steadfast love (chesed). Exemplary students are those able to integrate the Bible into their lives such that it inspires positive action in the circles in which they move. The composers of pop songs can be understood as today's poets and prophets. They find images and metaphors and ways to describe the joys and pains of living in this contemporary world.

The writings of the Bible offer a norm or standard by which to view the texts of pop songs today. The biblical writings are regarded as inspired, but some contemporary pop songs are also inspired. Truths are disclosed in the Bible, but some pop songs reveal truths about life in today's world, too. The two different textual worlds can mutually inform and offer ideas on how to live more dynamically today.

Websites

Kyrie by Mr Mister, www.songfacts.com/facts/mr-mister/kyrie

Livin' On A Prayer Lyrics, Lyrics On Demand, https://www.lyricsondemand.com/b/bonjovilyrics/livinonaprayerlyrics.html

Never Enough by Loren Allred, www.songfacts.com/facts/loren-allred/never-enough

"Never Enough" from the Greatest Showman, www.classicfm.com/discover-music/never-enough-the-greatest-showman

Smashed Hits: Livin' On a Prayer, www.bbc.com/news/blogs-magazine-monitor-25120899

Story Behind the Song: 'Livin on a Prayer', The Tennessean, https://www.tennessean.com/story/entertainment/music/2014/06/20/story-behind-song-livin-prayer/11103409/

The Black Eyed Peas – Where is the Love? (Official Music Video), www.youtube.com/watch?v-WpYeekQkAdc

The Rose (song), https://en.wikipedia.org/wiki/The_Rose_(song)

Westlife – The Rose (Official Video), https://www.youtube.com/watch?v=VTCQBuYhq_s

Sarah L Hart
Good Shepherd College, Te Hepara Pai
Sarahhart324@gmail.com

11 | CHARACTER AND PEDAGOGY IN THE BOOK OF PROVERBS

Abstract

On first impression, the book of Proverbs appears to provide significant support to a character-focused approach to education. It abounds with character terms, names for virtues and vices, and is centrally concerned with the qualities and prospects of certain kinds of persons: the wise, fools, the righteous. For this reason, it has been drawn on by advocates of virtue ethics. However, the book of Proverbs also presents problems for such views. As Anne Stewart has highlighted, it lacks any clear narrative structure or clear implications about character development. Furthermore, in certain respects, its approach to pedagogy and moral reasoning pays scant attention to virtues. This paper will outline these issues and then illustrate their significance by reference to Thomas Aquinas's understanding of prudence. It will conclude with some suggestions as to how this should moderate emphasis on character-oriented attributes in theological education.

1. Education After Virtue

The widespread appeal of the virtues in modern moral philosophy and Christian ethics has something to do with the moral malaise and interminable ethical conflicts of the public culture of contemporary Western societies. Perhaps the virtues, we think, will allow people—perhaps, especially Christian people—to carve a path through the chaos and confusion of modern moral life, where principle-based or other theoretical approaches to ethics are failing. Enthusiasm for character-oriented graduate attributes is in certain respects cut from the same cloth.

At the beginning of the book that in some ways ignited this contemporary interest in virtue, *After Virtue*, Alasdair MacIntyre described our situation by analogy with the following scenario:

> Imagine that the natural sciences were to suffer the effects of a catastrophe. A series of environmental disasters are blamed by the general public on the scientists. Widespread riots occur, laboratories are burnt down, physicists are lynched, books and instruments are destroyed. Finally a Know-Nothing political movement takes power and successfully abolishes science-teaching in schools and universities, imprisoning and executing the remaining scientists. Later still there is a reaction against this destructive movement and enlightened people seek to revive science, although they have largely forgotten what it was. But all they possess are fragments.[1]

MacIntyre suggests that something analogous to this is our actual situation in relation to 'the language of morality'.[2] Though far less obvious and dramatic, the modern history of the West has produced such a catastrophe in moral language, so that today, although we know the names of many moral concepts, we do not really know how they work. 'What we possess' MacIntyre writes, 'are the fragments of a conceptual scheme, parts which now lack those contexts from which their significance derived'.[3]

The irony of this is that if MacIntyre's account of things is right, then the solution cannot be merely to attempt to retrieve something called 'virtue ethics' and plug it into the contemporary world and its institutions of learning. On MacIntyre's account, such a move can only involve the recovery of another fragment, like the children in his imaginary scenario who are taught to 'learn by heart the surviving portions of the periodic table and recite as incantations some of the theorems of Euclid'.[4] It is not hard to imagine how an embrace of 'character-oriented graduate attributes', especially in the context of a tertiary education system driven by the logic of neo-liberalism, could be just such a forlorn attempt to recall a dislocated piece of earlier wisdom. And while theological education, insofar as it maintains deep contact with the Christian tradition, may have resources to avoid such a disconnection from its earlier

---

1 Alasdair MacIntyre, *After Virtue*, 1.
2 *After Virtue*, 2.
3 *After Virtue*, 2.
4 *After Virtue*, 1.

moral visions, it would surely be foolish to overestimate its capacities.

Is such a pessimistic conclusion warranted? In this chapter, I want to agree that the enthusiasm for the virtues within contemporary education contexts is overheated; but I want to disagree with the reasons MacIntyre gives, in a way that I think leaves us in a slightly less dire situation. I want to do so through a consideration of the book of Proverbs and the assumptions about moral reasoning that are implicit within it.

2. Character and Action in the Book of Proverbs

The book of Proverbs can be seen as a text that gives fulsome support to a character-oriented way of thinking. After all, it appears to abound with virtue terms: wisdom, folly, the sluggard, coolness of spirit, the wicked, the righteous. So, at least, argues William P. Brown, 'the idea of character constitutes the unifying theme or centre of the wisdom literature, whose raison d'être is to profile ethical character'.[5] 'Education in ancient Israel', he maintains, 'was devoted primarily to the task of "moral formation", or "the building of character"'.[6] Brown argues that, in the book of Proverbs, there is an implied narrative arc, in which the son of the household (in view in chapters 1–9) enters into the social world (chapters 10–29) before finally returning home again (chapters 30–31).[7] The book begins with a wayward son (1:8-19) and ends with the mature, successful husband in the background of the final poem (31:10-31). The various proverbial sayings contribute to a whole in which there is a progression from basic 'to more advanced, variegated fare' and increased 'reliance upon the reader's discriminating powers of discernment'.[8]

Yet things are not so simple. To take the most obvious point, the book of Proverbs contains no straightforward portrait of the wise man. The capable wife of the final poem is beautifully pictured, and she is the counterpart to personified wisdom in chapters 1–9. But her husband, who sings her praise (31:28), is not depicted—in a sense, the only wise thing he has done is apparently to have married her. Moreover, the passage that introduces the poem allows no room for the satisfaction of having arrived: 'No, my son! No, son of my womb!

---

5 Brown, quoted in Anne W. Stewart, *Poetic Ethics*, 11.
6 Brown, 'The Pedagogy of Proverbs 10:1–31:9', 150.
7 See Stewart, *Poetic Ethics*, 27–28.
8 Brown, 'The Pedagogy of Proverbs 10:1-31:9', 181.

[...] Do not give your strength to women!' (31:2-3).⁹ We are still not, it seems, very far from the son of chapter 1. Brown's claim that Proverbs is dedicated to moral formation and building character, therefore, needs questioning, for it is not at all clear that much formation or progress ever takes place.

This is one of the reasons that Anne W. Stewart, in her recent book *Poetic Ethics in Proverbs* (Cambridge, 2016), argues that in Proverbs, 'character is not linked to a larger narrative arc', and that Proverbs does not operate with a 'narrative model of selfhood'.¹⁰ The poetic form of Proverbs, she suggests, drives a focus not on the development of character over time but on moments, the particular courses of action that make up one's character. Proverbs, Stewart writes, 'privileges discrete episodes, conjures up the emotions evoked by particular moments and features a string of isolated situations that are not of necessity connected into a coherent whole'.¹¹ Stewart notes that this means Proverbs 'bears some resemblance to a rule-based ethic that privileges acts, not character'. However, she maintains that Proverbs is still primarily focused on character. 'The emphasis remains on the quality of the agent rather than the act itself'.¹²

I think, though, that Proverbs does privilege acts over character, though not in quite the 'rule-based' sense Stewart has in mind. It is true that, as Stewart notes, the emphasis in Proverbs is not simply on individual actions. Nor is it simply on qualities of the agent. In fact, virtue terms are not quite as abundant in Proverbs as we might expect. To take one striking example, the description of the *ēšet-ḥayîl* in chapter 31 makes no reference to virtues.¹³ In my view, it is more accurate to say that what Proverbs is most interested in is kinds of action—determinate, identifiable forms of human acting, which can be identified both in individual instances and when extended over a life-course. In relation to speech and anger, for example, Proverbs can give particular advice —'put your hand over your mouth!' (30:32)—but it can also name more settled policies of action—'one who spares words is knowledgeable' (17:27). Note that this is not

---

9 Unless otherwise stated, Scripture quotations are from the *New Revised Standard Version Bible: Anglicized Edition*, copyright © 1989, 1995 National Council of the Churches of Christ in the United States of America. Used by permission. All rights reserved worldwide.
10 Stewart, *Poetic Ethics*, 207, 209.
11 Stewart, *Poetic Ethics*, 209.
12 Stewart, *Poetic Ethics*, 213.
13 With the possible exceptions of the terms ḥayîl (v. 10), and 'ōz-wᵉhāḏār (v. 25). The first is intended as an encompassing description, and the second double term is not really a virtue but rather a description of her standing and impressiveness.

a description of a character trait, a quality of an agent, but of a way of acting: restraining your words. Such policies of action do lead naturally to virtue language: 'those who are slow to anger calm contention' (15:18); 'one who is cool spirit has understanding' (17:27). The virtues certainly have a place in Proverbs; but they are not primary in a straightforward sense; they depend upon the coherence of kinds of action. The virtues in Proverbs are correlated with kinds of action, and it is these that in are in a sense the primary focus.[14]

Behind this interest in kinds of action stands a distinctive way of understanding wisdom. Wisdom, in the book of Proverbs, is not simply something human individuals have, neither just a quality nor attribute. Wisdom is also, and perhaps more fundamentally, an aspect of the world that God has made 'by wisdom'. 'The LORD by wisdom founded the earth; by understanding he established the heavens' (Prov. 3:19). And this wisdom, this skill[15] by which God made the world, comes to have a kind of distinct presence within the created world. As Gerhard von Rad put it, wisdom is the 'primeval order' or 'world reason', 'the mystery behind the creation of the world', 'not an attribute of God but an attribute of the world, namely that mysterious attribute, by virtue of which she turns towards men to give order to their lives'.[16] Wisdom is something determinate, and in some real sense, external to the human subject. That is also why Proverbs abounds with images of paths and ways: Wisdom is something to be taken hold of (Prov. 3:18), walked in, not merely developed. It is also why wisdom, in one of the most distinctive literary features of Proverbs, calls (Prov. 1:20; 8:1; 9:3) and why wisdom is personified as another standing over against the subject (Prov. 1:20-33; 8:1-36; 9:1-6).

Proverbs foregrounds kinds of action because it understands wisdom in this way: Wisdom is about creation's hospitality to forms of action; and so 'being wise' or 'getting wisdom' is not merely about the development of certain subjective attributes but about a relation to the reality and moral structure of the world. This relation has fundamentally to do with action: Wisdom's paths are the kinds of action that, by virtue of God's creative work, lead to life. This

---

14 This reading of Proverbs, and the discussion that follows, is developed in detail in Andrew Errington, *Every Good Path*.
15 As Raymond Van Leeuwen has highlighted, the other key terms with which wisdom (ḥokmâ) is constantly linked in Proverbs, especially tĕbûnâ and daʿat, are terms frequently associated with practical skill. See Raymond Van Leeuwen, 'Cosmos, Temple, House: Building and Wisdom in Mesopotamia and Israel', 83. Note the parallels in 1 Kings 7:13-14; 10:4-8,23-24 and Exodus 31:3; 35:31; 36:1; 35:35.
16 Gerhard von Rad, *Wisdom in Israel*, 155-157, 161.

is why the *Ðēšet-ḥayîl* in chapter 31 is not described by listing her virtues but by listing the kinds of things she does.

For this reason, also, Proverbs places a heavy emphasis on the importance of listening and paying attention to particular words, teaching, and instruction. 'Hear, my child, your father's instruction, and do not reject your mother's teaching' (1:8). 'Let your heart keep my commandments' (3:1). 'Keep hold of instruction; do not let go' (4:13). This emphasis is one of the central features of the book's pedagogy, though it is quite alien to most traditions of virtue ethics. Virtue ethics tends to see the cultivation of internal habits as the key to making the right choices in moments of difficulty. For Proverbs, though, the key to good choices is not just good habits, but good words closely remembered.

3. Thomas Aquinas on Prudence

The significance of this difference can be seen if we observe an interesting point of contact between Proverbs and the moral thought of Thomas Aquinas. Aquinas begins his treatise on prudence with the question, 'Whether prudence is in the cognitive or in the appetitive faculty'.[17] He holds that it is the former because prudence is about knowledge of the future, of what is 'far off'[18]; and through the sensitive faculty, we know only 'what is within reach and offers itself to the senses'. Yet, Aquinas also insists that prudence depends upon moral virtues. His thinking is shaped by Aristotle's statement that in practical matters, 'virtue makes the aim right, and practical wisdom the things towards it'.[19]

For Aquinas, prudence depends on the moral virtues because our thinking can be thrown off course by our passions. 'It happens sometimes', he says, 'that general principles known by understanding or science are swept away in the particular case by a passion'. Hence, in order to be able to see, in a particular instance, what is the right kind of thing to aim at, a person 'needs to be perfected by certain habits, whereby it becomes, as it were, connatural to him to judge rightly about an end. This is done by moral virtue'. The virtues supply the 'principles of action' needed in the particular moment.[20]

---

17   Thomas Aquinas, *Summa Theologiae* ii-II.47.1.
18   'The prudent man thinks about matters far ahead'. *Summa Theologiae* ii-II.47.1.
19   Aristotle, *Nicomachean Ethics*, 6.12, 1144a9. On Aquinas's interpretation of Aristotle here see Tobias Hoffmann, 'Prudence and Practical Principles', 165-183.
20   *Summa Theologiae* i-II.58.5. On this passage, see Errington, *Every Good Path*, ch. 2.

Aquinas gives an example of such a moment in which reason may be swept away by passion: 'to one who is overcome by lust, the object of his desire seems good, although it is opposed to the universal judgment of reason'.[21] In broad terms, this is a situation familiar to the reader of the book of Proverbs, with its repeated warnings about the peril of the 'strange woman'.[22] In Proverbs 7:6-23, for example, the father paints a picture of a young man 'steered' (*hiṭṭattû*) by her speech, 'overwhelmed' (*taddîḥennû*) by her 'smooth talk', so that 'all of a sudden' (*piṯ'ōm*) he goes with her (vv. 21–22). The verbs used suggest a powerful moving force that resonates with Aquinas's language of being 'swept away' and 'overcome'. Yet, this similarity highlights an accompanying dissimilarity between the two perspectives. For Aquinas, this possibility is an argument for the necessity of moral virtues. For Proverbs, however, it is an argument for the critical importance of words of instruction. What the son needs, above all, is to keep the father's words, to hide them close, to 'not depart from the words of my mouth' (5:7; cf. 7:1–3,24). What will save the son when his thinking is scrambled in the face of temptation is not so much his virtues within, but the recollection of words of guidance that have come from without and that put him in contact with wisdom, with the reality of the world's hospitality to action. The virtues might remind us of the path of wisdom, but will they do so with enough force and clarity to enable right action? For Proverbs, it is words that enable us to discern the right path.

Conclusion

To what conclusions might these observations lead us? I began by noting MacIntyre's 'disquieting suggestion' that our situation today is one in which our knowledge of moral concepts is at best fragmented and partial, a result of a massive cultural disconnection from the traditions in which they arose, and that gave them coherence so that the attempt to do something like introduce or enhance the importance of character-oriented attributes in theological education is doomed to failure because of its inevitably partial and fragmented character. This argument depends upon a way of thinking in which a particular socio-

---

21 *Summa Theologiae* i-II.58.5.
22 See Prov. 2:16-19; 5:1-23; 6:20-35; 7:1-27; 23:26-28. In this figure, see especially Stuart Weeks, *Instruction and Imagery in Proverbs 1–9*, 128–141.

cultural context, a tradition and narrative rich with shared practices, is the necessary context for the exercise of practical wisdom. MacIntyre takes this to be Aristotle's view of things, in which, in MacIntyre's phrase, there is 'no practical rationality outside the polis'.[23] In this, he has been followed by a number of figures in Christian ethics, including Stanley Hauerwas and Charles Pinches.[24] In my view, the book of Proverbs does not quite support this way of thinking. For the context that secures the possibility of practical rationality is creation. Behind the narratives, histories, and traditions that shape our actions stands, closer than we tend to imagine, the world God has made by wisdom, calling to us, extending hospitality to human action.

This leaves us in a slightly less hopeless position than MacIntyre's argument suggests. For the world God has made is a world in which the meaningfulness of descriptions of virtues is stabilised by their connection to real structures of the world. At least, this is true of much of the terminology that is used to describe virtues. Slowness of anger, coolness of spirit, perceptiveness, discernment, truthfulness, cautiousness—these are meaningful names that serve as signposts to Wisdom's pleasant ways, all her paths that are peace (Prov. 3:17). We are not wrong to hope that graduates will exhibit such virtues, nor perhaps to try to name them in lists of outcomes. We should, however, be wary of virtues without pedigree in the tradition, or apparent connection to demonstrably good forms of action—like, perhaps, 'agility'.

However, our enthusiasm for such an orientation needs to be tempered because on my reading, Proverbs also implies that virtues are only ever of limited use when it comes to the actual task of living well, the business of acting well in the particular, complex moments we will face in life and in the work of Christian service. Aristotle thought that it was the virtues that make the aims of our action right; and Aquinas understood this in connection with practical reasoning in difficult situations. But Proverbs does not appear to think this way. What people need to meet the challenges of complexity and temptation thrown up by ministry and, indeed, just by life is not so much virtue, but trustworthy words of instruction, words that come from without and that, when what is within fails us, can still guide us. This may be an argument not so much for character-oriented graduate attributes as for an emphasis on knowledge of 'the

---

23 MacIntyre, *Whose Justice? Which Rationality?*, 141. See also MacIntyre, *Three Rival Versions of Moral Enquiry*, 58-68.
24 See Charles R. Pinches, *Theology and Action: After Theory in Christian Ethics* (Grand Rapids: Eerdmans, 2002), 15-18, 50-58, 199-232.

sacred writings that are able to instruct you for salvation through faith in Christ Jesus' (2 Tim. 3:15). 'Trust in the Lord with all your heart, and do not rely on your own insight. In all your ways acknowledge him, and he will make straight your paths' (Prov. 3:5-6).

Bibliography

Aristotle. *Nicomachean Ethics*. Edited and translated by Roger Crisp (Cambridge: Cambridge University Press, 2000).

Brown, W. P (ed.) 'The Pedagogy of Proverbs 10:1–31:9', in *Character and Scripture: Moral Formation, Community, and Biblical Interpretation* (Grand Rapids: Eerdmans, 2002): 150-182.

Errington, A. *Every Good Path: Wisdom and Practical Reason in Christian Ethics and the Book of Proverbs* (Edinburgh: T&T Clark, 2019).

MacIntyre, A. *After Virtue: A Study in Moral Theory* (3rd edn; London: Duckworth, 2007).

———. *Whose Justice? Which Rationality?* (London: Duckworth, 1988).

———. *Three Rival Versions of Moral Enquiry* (London: Duckworth, 1990).

Pinches, C. R. *Theology and Action: After Theory in Christian Ethics* (Grand Rapids: Eerdmans, 2002).

Rad, G. V. *Wisdom in Israel*. Translated by James D. Martin (London: SCM, 1972).

Stewart, A. W. *Poetic Ethics in Proverbs: Wisdom Literature and the Shaping of the Moral Self* (New York: Cambridge University Press, 2016).

Thomas A. *Summa Theologiae* (61 Vols; Cambridge: Blackfriars, 1964–1981).

Van Leeuwen, Raymond. 'Cosmos, Temple, House: Building and Wisdom in Mesopotamia and Israel', in Clifford R.J. (ed.), *Wisdom Literature in Mesopotamia and Israel* (SBL Symposium Series 36. Atlanta: Society of Biblical Literature, 2007): 67-90

Weeks, S. *Instruction and Imagery in Proverbs 1–9* (Oxford: Oxford University Press, 2007).

Andrew Errington
Lecturer, St Mark's National Theological Centre, and Research Fellow, Public and Contextual Theology Research Centre, Charles Sturt University School of Theology.
aerrington@csu.edu.au

12 | THE POWER OF PERSUASION

PAUL'S ΠΑΡΑΚΑΛΕΩ APPEALS

Abstract

The paper explores Paul's use of *parakaleō* vocabulary as a means of persuasion and dissuasion in the educational environment of the early Pauline communities. English Bible versions translate the verb with a variety of terms with a range of meanings including 'to exhort', 'to urge', 'to comfort', 'to beseech', and 'to encourage'.

Parakaleō vocabulary appears in all the Pauline epistles except Galatians. Paul often uses the vocabulary to make epistolary appeals or refer to his own activity in other contexts. It is also used for the activity of those in ministry and for mutual activity within the Christian community.

Some commentators argue that Paul's *parakaleō* appeals are coercive commands for obedience, in which he imposed his will against the will of the recipients. However, the paper will show that while Paul was utilising his apostolic authority in issuing the appeals, he did so as one committed to the welfare of the recipients, and within relationships established and shaped by the gospel. His own will was part of the persuasive force of the instruction. He cared if the recipients learned, and so he appealed to them within the context of existing benevolent relationships established in the gospel to persuade them to learn and so be shaped and transformed.

Paul's use of *parakaleō* vocabulary for his own activity provides educators with a model of the relational nature of teaching and learning in early Christian communities, and the way in which personal familiarity and benevolent relationships, and the personal investment and commitment of the 'teacher', may be used to facilitate transformation and development of Christian character, beliefs and conduct.

1. Introduction

It is the nature of 'graduate attributes' lists that they focus on the desired outcome in the graduate, and not on the attributes of the teacher or contribution of the relationship and interaction between teacher and learner needed to produce those outcomes.

One of the purposes of the New Testament (NT) epistles was to develop what might be called 'graduate attributes'. The letters were educational enterprises intended to produce transformed live, and so sought to teach recipients about the right belief, right conduct, and right character to produce those mature in Christ.

Paul's παρακαλέω epistolary appeals—where Paul uses the verb to call for a response from his readers—provide an opportunity to examine the educational enterprise in both directions. We can see the desired outcomes in the learners, but also certain attributes of Paul as a teacher, and the way in which the relationship between Paul and his addressees is integral to both the educational process and outcome.

2. Παρακαλέω-Appeals and Graduate Attributes

Παρακαλέω occurs 109 times in the NT, sixty-two times in the epistles, of which, fifty-four occur in fifty verses in the thirteen-letter Pauline corpus. Paul uses the word group to make epistolary appeals and refer to his own activity outside the letters. It is also used for divine activity, as well as the activities of those in ministry and regular church members. Neither the verb nor cognate noun (παράκλησις) appears in Galatian; otherwise, παρακαλέω-appeals occur in all letters, except Colossians, 2 Timothy, and Titus. Παρακαλέω-appeals are also found outside the Pauline corpus (Heb. 13:19,22; 1 Peter 2:11; 5:1; cf. Jude 3).

Paul uses παρακάλεω fourteen times in first-person singular present indicative appeals (Rom. 12:1; 15:30; 16:17; 1 Cor. 1:10; 4:16; 16:15; 2 Cor. 2:8; 10:1;

Eph. 4:1; Phil. 4:2[x2]; 1 Tim. 2:1; Phlm 9–10); and five times in first-person plural present indicative appeals (2 Cor. 6:1; 1 Thess. 4:1,10; 5:14; 2 Thess. 3:12). A further first-person singular use refers to and effectively repeats a historical appeal (1 Tim. 1:3 aorist indicative).

If Paul's παρακαλέω-appeals can serve as a window to examining the desired attributes of the teacher and the relationship between teacher and student, we must first establish that these appeals were concerned with the production of what might be called 'graduate attributes'.

The appeals in Romans 12, Ephesians 4, and 1 Thessalonians 4 most succinctly indicate this was the case. All three function as introductions for extended paraenetic material and as summary statements that embrace the whole of life in its individual and corporate dimensions.[1]

a) In Romans 12:1, Paul urges readers to present their whole selves (σῶμα)[2] to God, as living sacrifices in true spiritual worship. They were not to conform to the ways of this world but be transformed by the renewing of their minds so they might know and do the will of God.

b) In Ephesians 4:1, Paul enjoins readers to live their whole lives (περιπατῆσαι) in a manner worthy of the calling they have received in the gospel.

c) In 1 Thessalonians 4:1, Paul and his co-senders urge readers to live out in increasing measure what they had received from them, as instructions telling them how they ought (δεῖ) to walk (περιπατεῖν) and please God (4:2).

All other appeals show similar interest in the beliefs, character, and lives of the recipients. They were to imitate Paul and his ways in Christ Jesus (1 Cor. 4:14); not receive the grace of God in vain (2 Cor. 6:1); avoid and resist those who caused divisions and opposed genuine faith (Rom. 16:17; 1 Tim. 1:3); be united and love one another (1 Cor. 1:10; 2 Cor. 2:8; Phil. 4:2; 1 Thess. 4:10; Phlm. 10); ensure everyone works and provides for the needy (1 Thess. 5:14; 2 Thess. 3:12); respects those in ministry, and prays for the welfare of all people, especially with respect to the progress of the gospel (Rom. 15:30; 1 Cor. 16:15–16; 1 Tim. 2:1).

In summary, then, Paul's παρακαλέω-appeals addressed the whole of life—belief, prayer, character, relationships, love, unity, financial and occupational matters, practical care of the needy, and protection from false teaching, as well as conformity with the broader Christian community and with the will of God. These were personal and communal 'attributes' recipients were to display in

---

1   Moo, *Romans*, 748. Baugh, *Ephesians*, 287. Bruce, *Thessalonians*, 77.
2   So, Moo, *Romans*, 751, taking σῶμα theologically to refer to the whole person.

increasing measure until Christ was formed in them—a goal that would be only realised when he returns (cf. 1 Thess. 3:13).[3]

Moreover, as 'graduate attributes' today reflect the values and ethos of an institution and the hope that graduates will display the distinctives of the institution,[4] so too were Paul's appeals concerned with the ethos of believing communities—with creating, delineating, and maintaining their Christian identity—and with the personal distinctives of those within them.

Stylistically, Paul's παρακαλέω-appeals display common elements,[5] including 1) first-person present-indicative παρακαλέω; 2) conjunction (δέ or οὖν); 3) recipients addressed in accusative (ὑμᾶς); 4) vocative address (ἀδελφοί); 5) prepositional clause with theological rationale for request (usually διά); 6) content of request using infinitive, imperative, or ἵνα clauses.

Four appeals have all six elements.[6] The appeal in Philemon is unusual as it lacks most elements, including a clear statement in the immediate context of the content, except that it is for (περί) Onesimus (Phlm. 9-10).

Previous studies have explored the literary 'form' and antecedents of Paul's παρακαλέω-appeals,[7] which are not our interest here, except to note that the different elements map loosely onto the following lines of enquiry: the lexical value of παρακαλέω; the epistolary context of the appeals; Paul's relationship to and depiction of the recipients; Paul's self-depiction; and qualifying statements about the nature of the appeal.

3. Lexical Considerations

Παρακαλέω is a strengthened and compounded form of καλέω, which has the sense 'to call to oneself' rather than 'to call to (someone)'.[8] It is regarded as one of the most important verbs for speaking and influencing in the NT, yet displays a wide semantic range, and it can be difficult to know which meaning was

---

3 Cf. Thomas, 'παρακαλέω', 26.
4 E.g., Sydney University: https://sydney.edu.au/education-portfolio/ei/teaching@sydney/graduate-qualities-important/ [accessed 22 March 2019].
5 Noted by Aasgaard, '"Brotherly Advice"', 247.
6 Rom. 12:1; 15:30; 16:17; 1 Cor. 1:10 display all six features. The remaining appeals omit elements, e.g., conjunction (Phil. 4:2); ἀδελφοί (1 Cor. 4:16; 2 Cor. 2:8; 6:1; 10:1; Eph. 4:1); prepositional clause (1 Cor. 4:16; 16:15; 2 Cor. 2:8; 6:1; Eph. 4:1; Phil. 4:2; 1 Thess. 4:10; 5:14; 1 Tim. 1:3; 2:1).
7 E.g., Sanders, 'Transition'; Bjerkelund, *Parakalô*. Mullins, 'Petition'.
8 Schmitz, 'παρακαλέω', 774.

intended.[9] For example, in 2 Corinthians, the verb appears eighteen times and is translated as 'comfort' in nine (ESV: 1:4[x3], 6; 2:7; 7:6,7,13; 13:11),[10] but in 1 Thessalonians, where it appears eight times, it is translated as 'comfort' only once (ESV 3:7), and otherwise, 'exhort' (ESV 2:12; 3:2), 'urge' (ESV 4:1, 10; 5:14), and 'encourage' (ESV 4:18; 5:11).[11] The context should control the translation, but differences between Bible versions illustrate the difficulties translators face.[12]

One of the issues in translation is the type of 'power' or influence Paul was utilising in these appeals. It is widely recognised he was seeking to exert influence and do so on the basis of his divinely-appointed apostleship. However, some post-modern and feminist interpreters see in Paul's use of this vocabulary a *misuse* of power for his own purposes, rather than an exercise in persuasion for the benefit of his audience.[13]

This raises the broader question of the paradigmatic relations of παρακαλέω with other verbs of appeal and command. Where does παρακαλέω fit in the range of words Paul uses where the will of the subject—in this case, Paul—is brought to bear upon others?

At one end of the spectrum are verbs expressing command where the expected response is obedience.[14] Παρακαλέω can be distinguished from these—for instance, the contrast in Philemon where Paul claims to forego the right to 'command' (ἐπιτάσσω) and instead 'appeals' (μᾶλλον παρακαλῶ) rests on the different semantic values of the verbs in terms of authority or coercion.[15] Elsewhere, Paul uses other verbs of command.[16]

At the other (softer) end of the spectrum are words expressing 'desire' or 'wish', which Paul uses to express his hopes for those to whom he writes, in the expectation they would learn from the disclosure and respond accordingly, but without asking for the response.[17]

---

9 Smith, *Pauline Communities*, 275-6.
10 NIV is similar, although uses 'encourage' at 2 Cor. 7:13 and 13:11.
11 NIV is similar, although replaces 'comfort' with 'encourage' at 1 Thess. 3.7, and replaces 'exhort' with 'encourage' (2:12; 3:2). NIV does not translate παρακαλέω as 'comfort' outside of 2 Corinthians.
12 See, Grayston, 'Problem of Translation', 27-31.
13 Smith, *Pauline Communities*, 275. E.g., Schütz, *Paul*, 221–24. Polasky, *Paul*, 56–72. Elliot, '"Thanks"', 51-64.
14 Paul's apostolic command was also expressed grammatically, for example, through the imperative mood.
15 This is the case irrespective of any *literary or rhetorical* force Paul may be utilizing.
16 E.g., παραγγέλλω: 1 Cor. 11:17; 1 Thess. 4:11; 2 Thess. 3:4, 6,10,12; 1 Tim. 6:13. Διατάσσω: 1 Cor. 11:16,34; 16:1; Tit. 1:5. Cf. Makujina, 'Verbs', 365–66.
17 E.g., βούλομαι: 1 Tim. 2:8; 5:14; Tit. 3:8; θέλω: Rom. 16:19; 1 Cor. 7:32; 10:20; 14:5; cf. 11:3; οὐ θέλω: Rom. 1:13; 11:25; 1 Cor. 10:1; 12:1; 2 Cor. 1:8; 1 Thess. 4:13.

The force of παρακαλέω for Paul's epistolary activity is between these two ends. It is the language of personal appeal, petition, and persuasion rather than command—even *benevolent* command[18]—and yet it explicitly attempts to bring about change.[19] Paul's use is similar to that in first-century letters between family and friends and diplomatic letters,[20] which did not use a command-obedience dynamic, but sought co-operation, participation, and acceptance within relationships of trust.[21] Παρακαλέω-appeals, then, functioned as personal appeals where the subject sought to align the will of another to their own will through persuasion or dissuasion within relationships of trust and goodwill.

Linda Belleville distinguishes between παρακαλέω and ἐρωτάω, a word of similar force and meaning, by saying παρακαλέω was used for 'an appeal by one who has the authority to command but the tact not to', whereas ἐρωτάω was used more for requests made between equals (e.g. Phil. 4:3).[22] However, Paul is able to use both verbs with the same audience in the same sentence (1 Thess. 4:1), so this distinction should not be overpressed (cf. ἐρωτάω: 1 Thess. 5:12; 2 Thess. 2:1). Similarly, δέομαι, which appears in requests with a stronger sense of urgency (cf. 2 Cor. 5:20; 10:2; Gal. 4:12)[23], is used with the same audience in the same sentence, so again a sharp distinction is unlikely (2 Cor. 10:1-2).

Paul could, and frequently did, issue instructions using the imperative mood.[24] His will, in those instances, was expressed grammatically. However, with verbs of request and command, the will of the subject is explicit and integral to the act itself, and so enabled Paul to signal his desire for and investment in the requested outcome, with the lexical value of the verbs indicating the nature and force of that request.

Paul's use of παρακαλέω for these requests reflects his intention to draw forth a *voluntary* response from his addressees using his will to persuade them to bring their wills, beliefs, and conduct into alignment with his own. He is saying that it matters *to him* if his audience accepts his appeal—he is *willing* them to learn.

---

18 Grayston, 'Problem', 28.
19 Mullins, 'Petition', 48, claims it is the 'most personal and intense of the verbs of petition'. Louw and Nida, §33.168, semantic domain 'ask for, request'.
20 Bjerkelund, *Parakalô*, 188. Mullins, 'Petition', *passim*.
21 Smith, *Pauline Communities*, 278, Ehrensperger, *Paul*, 175.
22 Belleville, 'Authority', 56.
23 E.g., 'implore', 'beg', 'plead'.
24 *Accordance* (12.3.4) identifies 323 occurrences, in 251 verses, of 166 lexemes.

4. Epistolary Context of the Appeal

The literary context also provides insights into the nature of an appeal and is evident in the conjunctions used, and more broadly throughout the letter. Conjunctions appear in fifteen appeals.[25] Some function as simple transitional articles,[26] however, others are used to link the content of the appeal with what has preceded as its natural outworking.

a) In Romans, Paul appeals to his readers to present their whole selves as living sacrifices to God, which is their appropriate response to God's saving actions set out in the previous chapters (12:1, cf. οὖν ['therefore']).[27]

b) In 1 Corinthians, Paul's appeal to become imitators of him arises from his example in the previous chapters, and his relationship to them as their father in Christ Jesus, which is on view in the immediate context (1 Cor. 4:14–16, οὖν).[28]

c) In 2 Corinthians, Paul's appeal (2 Cor. 2:8) that they reaffirm their love for the repentant offender is based (διό ['therefore']) on the preceding request that they forgive and comfort him.[29]

d) His appeal to the Ephesians to live in a manner worthy of the calling they have received rests on the nature of that calling, which Paul has been expounding in the letter (Eph. 4:1, οὖν; cf. 1:3–3:21).[30]

e) Paul's appeal to the Thessalonians 'more and more' to live as they ought and to please God corresponds with his immediately prior prayer that the Lord would increase their love for each other and that they will have hearts that are holy and blameless before God when the Lord Jesus comes (1 Thess. 4:1, οὖν; cf. 3:11-13).[31]

f) In 1 Timothy, Paul's appeal for prayer seeking the salvation of all people is a corollary of Timothy's task to remain in Ephesus to rebuke false teachers and advance the gospel for all people—even the worst of sinners (1 Tim. 2:1, οὖν; 1:3-20; 2:1-6).[32]

That is, the *content* of the παρακαλέω-appeals has strong theological connections with what has gone before, which is made explicit with the use of

---

25 Οὖν: Rom. 12:1; 1 Cor. 4:16; Eph. 4:1; 1 Thess. 4:1 (+ λοιπόν); 1 Tim. 2:1. Δε: Rom. 15:30; 16:17; 1 Cor. 1:10; 16:15; 2 Cor. 6:1 (+ και); 10:1; 1 Thess. 4:10; 5:14; 2 Thess. 3:12. Διό: 2 Cor. 2:8.
26 E.g., δέ Rom. 15:30; 16:17; 1 Cor. 1:10; 1 Thess. 5:14.
27 Moo, *Romans*, 748.
28 Smith, *Pauline Communities*, 364-66.
29 Barnett, *Second Epistle*, 127.
30 Baugh, *Ephesians*, 291-92.
31 Hiebert, *Thessalonians*, 173.
32 Mounce, *Pastoral Epistles*, 76.

inferential conjunctions. Even when the conjunction is more transitional, the appeal is not an isolated request but reflects the broader concerns of the letter.[33]

This thematic connection with the broader literary context is evident even in Philippians 4:2, where Paul's twin παρακαλέω-appeals to Euodia and Syntyche are asyndetic, but where the content of the appeals repeats key themes and vocabulary in the letter (e.g. Phil. 1:15; 2:2-7).[34] Even the repetition of the appeal formula to each woman may have been intended to avoid taking sides and minimise the risk of envy, rivalry, and division that have been themes throughout (cf. 1:15; 2:3).

The appeals, then, are not isolated requests that can be understood or interpreted on their own. Nor are they arbitrary requests calling for arbitrary responses. Rather, their *content* flows naturally from the content of the letters. Paul's appeals and the 'attributes' they sought to produce are embedded in and rest upon the themes and concerns of the letters. Thus, readers were shown the 'logic' of the appeals and that they sought to align readers with God's will and God's work on their behalf.

5. Paul's Relationship to and Depiction of the Recipients

The relationship of Paul and the wider Christian community with the recipients of his παρακαλέω-appeals provide further insight into the development of 'graduate attributes'. These come into view both in the terms of address he uses for them and the depictions he gives them.

The vocative plural address ἀδελφοί occurs in eight appeals.[35] By this, Paul signals that his appeal is made within the context of their existing sibling relationship, where together they belong to the one family of God, as brothers and sisters, with a common experience of God's grace and love. The term communicates love, warmth, and affection and connotes relationships of trust, harmony, and symmetry,[36] and culturally-shared and accepted notions of mutual obligation and commitment.[37]

---

33 Cf. Rom. 15:30 with Rom. 1:9-15; 1 Cor. 1:10 with 1 Cor. 1:4-9. Smith, *Pauline Communities*, 96, 102.
34 Particularly, the semantic links with τὸ αὐτὸ φρονεῖν (Phil. 4:2). Cf. Fee, *Philippians*, 185, 200, 389-92.
35 Rom. 12:1; 15:30*; 16:17; 1 Cor. 1:10; 16:15; 1 Thess. 4:1; 4:10; 5:14. *Cf. Moo, *Romans*, 907, on textual variant.
36 This symmetry does not exclude the possibility of hierarchy in human relationships—rather the point is that all believers enjoy the same relationship to God as Father. Cf. Clarke, 'Equality or Mutuality'.
37 Cf. Aasgaard, "Role Ethics", 513–30; "'Brotherly Advice'", 243–44.

In addition, most appeals make some reference to the recipients' relationship with Paul and/or their association with the wider Christian community, where a positive response to the appeal will increase their identification with and belonging to that community.

a) His appeal in Romans 15 connects Paul and his readers to the welfare of the saints in Jerusalem and looks forward to the refreshment he hopes to receive from them in person in answer to their prayers (15:31-32). His appeal in Romans 16 goes on to mention that the recipients' obedience is 'known to all' and that Paul rejoices over them (16:17-19).

b) In 1 Corinthians, the first appeal is a response to what Paul has heard from Chloe's people and goes on to rehearse his previous contact with the Corinthian believers (1 Cor. 1:4,11,14-16). His second appeal arises directly out of his relationship with them, as well as his intention to send his 'son' Timothy so they can imitate Paul as their father in Christ Jesus—according to Paul's 'ways' that he teaches everywhere in every church (1 Cor. 4:14-17). And his third appeal is set in the context of the exemplary devotion and service of the household of Stephanas and Paul's joy that some of that household is currently with him (1 Cor. 16:15-18).

c) In 2 Corinthians, Paul's appeal for them to reaffirm their love for the repentant brother is set in the context of his previous letter, as well as his desire for restored unity and harmony with them and within the church (2 Cor. 2:5-11). His later appeal that he will not have to be bold when he visits Corinth also clearly references his previous time among them (2 Cor. 10:1-2).

d) In Philippians, the appeal to Euodia and Syntyche is sandwiched between a reference to the whole Philippian Christian community as Paul's 'joy and crown', whom he loves, and his description of the women to his 'true companion', as those who worked alongside him (συνήθλησάν) in the gospel with Clement and others (Phil. 4:1-3).

e) In 1 Thessalonians, the first appeal refers to Paul's previous visit to them (1 Thess. 4:1-2), and the second acknowledges that Thessalonians' love had already extended to other Christian communities in Macedonia (4:10, cf. 1:7-8).

f) The appeal against idleness in 2 Thessalonians responds to reports Paul has received, and points to Paul's and his co-workers' lived example among them (2 Thess. 3:7-1).

g) Paul's personal appeals to Timothy (1 Tim. 1:3) and Philemon (Phlm 9–10) explicitly mention their existing relationships.

In short, the relational dynamic is not limited to the lexical value of παρακαλέω. Many appeals use the strong and evocative ἀδελφοί-address to signal the divinely established sibling bonds between Paul and his addressees, and most reference his relational history with recipients and/or their connection to the broader Christian community. Only three appeals lack this relational context.[38] More broadly, the appeals reflect the ethos of the wider believing community (in purpose and content) and would increase identification and conformity with and belonging in that community.

Interestingly, this relational dynamic sought to operate through a written medium, in the physical absence of Paul, and even where there had been no prior face-to-face contact (cf. Romans). Nevertheless, Paul appeals to recipients, in the context of these personal connections and shared history, as someone who knows them and is known by them and is a representative of the wider Christian community—and who, like them, is a member of God's family.

6. Paul's Self-Depiction

As noted above, the qualitative nature of the power or influence Paul sought to use in his παρακαλέω-appeals has been a focus of recent research. Paul's self-conception and self-depiction have rightly been recognised as a key consideration in this regard.

The previous discussion about ἀδελφοί and the relational matrix of the wider Christian community drew attention to Paul's awareness of the mutual and symmetrical familial bonds of affection between the recipients of the appeals and himself, as well as their shared role in the wider Christian movement.

Yet, there is also asymmetry in these relationships. Paul begins many of his letters noting his appointment as an apostle, appointed by Christ Jesus, with God-given responsibility and authority.[39] This is an important consideration in identifying the force and function of his παρακαλέω-appeals.[40]

Yet, several factors indicate his authority more generally, and its role in the appeals, was moderated. His apostleship was valid only as long as he adhered

---

38 Appeals lacking ἀδελφοί or reference to personal history with Paul or other believers: 2 Cor. 6:1 (although Paul is a fellow-worker with God); Eph. 4:1; 1 Tim. 2:1.
39 Rom. 1:1; cf. 1:5; 11:13; 16:7; 1 Cor. 1:1; cf. 4:9; 9:1–5; 15:9 'least of all'; 2 Cor. 1:1; cf. 12:12; Eph. 1:1; 1 Tim. 1:1; cf. 2:7. Body of letter: 1 Thess. 2:6; δοῦλος: Phil. 1:1 (with Timothy).
40 Dunn, *Theology*, 571-580. Holmberg, *Paul*, 80-89. Ehrensperger, *Paul*, 81-97. Polaski, *Paul*, 11,24-28.

to the true gospel (Gal. 1:6-9),[41] and the nature of his apostleship being 'through Jesus Christ' cut both ways: It was a source of authority, but it also placed him under Christ's authority.[42] Significantly, too, his apostleship is not mentioned in *any* παρακαλέω-appeal, nor do all letters with appeals mention his apostleship (Philippians, 2 Thessalonians, Philemon), and four appeals are issued by Paul *and* his co-senders (παρακαλοῦμεν; 1 Thess. 4:1,10; 5:14; 2 Thess. 3:12).

Additionally, Paul's self-presentation in the appeals does not use a command-obedience paradigm. Rather, he uses images of 'soft power' based on respect, which are further modified by the phrase 'in the Lord/Christ Jesus'.[43] This 'soft' kind of power was:

> passive rather than active, ascribed rather than exerted. While "rank" remains, it is never "pulled," but rather "pulls," like gravity. Any existing power differential is used not to enforce control but rather to elicit participation.[44]

At first glance, the appeal in 2 Corinthians 6 might be an exception—where Paul writes he works together with God (6:1 συνεργοῦντες),[45] when he has also just written that God makes his appeal through him (5:20), effectively making Paul's appeal 'God's appeal'.[46] However, Paul's polemic against the super-apostles depends on his weakness and him *not* using and seeking personal power as they do, so it would be counterproductive for him to utilise *personal* authority and power in his appeal.

Finally, Paul's use of the παρακαλέω-word group for activities by regular Christians, and for acts of comfort and entreaty, also weighs against an authoritarian force of the lexeme in his appeals in the absence of other indicators.[47]

Paul's self-depiction in his παρακαλέω-appeals then shows that he was not seeking to utilise his 'rights' as an apostle by demanding obedience. He 'claims the position of the "subject-who-knows" who is able and willing to give

---

41 Smith, *Pauline Communities*, 136-137,161.
42 Barnett, 'Apostle', 48–50. Belleville, 'Authority', 55-57.
43 I.e., *prisoner*: δέσμιος: Eph. 4:1; Phlm 9; *old man*: πρεσβύτης: Phlm 9; *father*: ἐγέννησα: 1 Cor. 4:16; Phlm 10 cf. 19c. Brookins, '"Auctoritas"', 309, 315–16. Cf. Ehrensperger, *Paul*, 126–136, 145–46.
44 Brookins, '"Auctoritas"', 321. This comment relates to the operation of *auctoritas* in Paul's appeal in Philemon, however, seems apt for other παρακαλέω-appeals.
45 Martin, *2 Corinthians*, 165.
46 Barnett, *Second Epistle*, 311.
47 Ehrensperger, *Paul*, 176.

guidance' to his fellow siblings in Christ[48]—but as brothers and sisters with independent wills and mutual responsibilities.

Moreover, the relational dynamic of παρακαλέω-activities, which sought to align the will of the object with that of the subject, requires that Paul himself display the attributes, character, belief, and conduct he sought in recipients—and have a reputation for doing so. That is, the persuasive power of his appeals depended on the integrity and consistency of his own life with the appeals' content and manner. This is most obvious where imitation of him is on view (1 Cor. 4:16; cf. Phil. 3:17–4:2,9; 2 Thess. 3:7-9) but is a necessary condition for the persuasive nature of all his appeals.

Even when his appeal came with some urgency or strong concern, its persuasive potency lay in relationships of trust, where recipients could be sure that his appeal for change was in their best interests. He did not speak to them as an unknown or outsider, but as a fellow child of God, whose own life displayed the 'attributes' he sought, and who was an appointed and trustworthy servant of the gospel.

7. Qualifying Statements about the Nature of the Appeal

Paul's παρακαλέω-appeals sought transformation, and he expected them to be accepted. However, the ultimate motivating power for change did not come from him, and neither was allegiance to him *personally* the goal. The motivation and source of the appeals was God—Paul was an agent or mediator of God's love and power. In six appeals, this is made explicit when Paul includes a statement about the nature of his activity in a prepositional clause (usually διά)[49]—the inclusion of which marks a deviation from the standard form of appeal in Hellenistic letters of the time.[50]

a) In Romans, Paul's first appeal (12:1) is 'by (διά) the mercies of God'; that is, the basis or source of Paul's activity is the saving mercies of God—'Paul is simply the instrument through whom "the mercy of God" is itself exhorting'.[51] His second appeal asking for prayer has two prepositional clauses: 'by our Lord Jesus Christ and by the love of the Spirit' (15:30, διά [x2]) and indicates the

---

48 Ehrensperger, *Paul*, 177.
49 Διά: Rom. 12:1; 15:30 (x2); 1 Cor. 1:10; 2 Cor. 10:1; ἐν: 1 Thess. 4:1; 2 Thess. 3:12.
50 Aasgaard, '"Brotherly Advice"', 247. Mullins, 'Petition', 53, 'divine authority phrase'.
51 Moo, *Romans*, 749.

manner of his appeal; namely, it comes with the authority of Christ and is an expression of love that comes from the Spirit.[52]

b) In 1 Corinthians, Paul's appeal for the Corinthians to all agree is consonant with and invokes the character, authority, and reputation of Christ[53] (1:10, διά 'by the name of our Lord Jesus Christ', ESV), who had been named nine times already in the letter.[54]

c) In 2 Corinthians, his appeal is made in the manner of Christ—in all meekness and gentleness (10:1, διά).[55]

d) In the Thessalonian correspondence, the two appeals with prepositional clauses both add a second verb for speaking (1 Thess. 4:1; 2 Thess. 3:12),[56] and both verbs are modified by the phrase 'in (ἐν) the Lord Jesus (Christ)'. This identifies the manner of the appeal—reflecting the love, character, and authority of Jesus (cf. 1 Thess. 3:11-13; 2 Thess. 3:6).[57]

These prepositional phrases then identify the grounds or manner of Paul's appeals. They are theological in nature—relating to God's acts in salvation, the person and work of Christ, and the love of the Spirit. Hence, it is not surprising that these clauses are a Pauline addition to the usual Hellenistic form of epistolary appeals.[58] Whereas the conjunctions in appeals draw attention to the reasons or grounds of the *content*, the prepositional clauses identify the specific grounds or manner of *Paul's* activity itself.

Why Paul states the theological rationale for his activity explicitly in some appeals and not in others is unclear. However, the distinctively Christian nature of even those appeals without a prepositional clause can be seen from the broader discourse context.[59] Either way, Paul gives his readers information so they would know how to interpret and understand the benevolence of his appeals and their dependence on the will and character of God.

---

52 Moo, *Romans*, 909. Campbell, *Paul*, 250-251.
53 Thiselton, *Corinthians*, 115.
54 I.e., 1 Cor. 1:1, 2 (x2), 3, 4, 6, 7, 8, 9.
55 Campbell, *Paul*, 252. Moo, *Romans*, 749 fn.21, observes that in all these occurrences just reviewed 'the object of διά is that which is ultimately making the appeal that is expressed'.
56 Ἐρωτῶμεν and παραγγέλλομεν respectively. Cf. 1 Thess. 5:12, 14 ἐρωτῶμεν + παρακαλοῦμεν.
57 Campbell, *Paul*, 165-67.
58 They do not appear in non-Pauline epistolary appeals, i.e., Heb. 13:19; 22; 1 Pet. 2:11; 5:1; Jude 3.
59 E.g., Rom. 16:18; 1 Cor. 4:14-15; 16:13-14; 2 Cor. 2:5-11; 5:20-21; Eph. 4:2-3; 4:1, 3; 1 Thess. 5:12-13; 1 Tim. 1:5,18-20; Phlm. 8.

Conclusion

Paul's παρακαλέω-appeals illustrate the contribution of the teacher and the relationship of teacher and student to the development of 'graduate attributes' in the faith, character, life, and conduct of individual Christians and believing communities. Paul's contribution was not neutral, disengaged, or disinterested. Rather, his personal role in the appeals was integral to their pedagogical force, despite his physical separation from his audience and the written medium of the letters.

Put simply, Paul's appeals sought to *persuade* his 'students' to learn (in response). His will was brought to bear upon them in order to bring about voluntary transformation so that they would display the 'graduate attributes' desired by God.

We have seen that there were several aspects to that persuasive force. These include the *relational context* of divinely established relationships of familiarity, goodwill, and trust; the *contents* of the appeals being consonant with the broader theological message of each letter; the *grounds and manner* of the appeals arising from the activity and character of God and Paul's desire to see change in the recipients; and, finally, in the *alignment of Paul personally* with the responses sought in the appeals as an authentic lived-expression of those 'graduate attributes', all to the glory of God.

Bibliography

Aasgaard, R. '"Brotherly Advice": Christian Siblingship and New Testament Paraenesis', in Staff, J. & Engberg-Pedersen, T. (eds.), *Early Christian Paraenesis in Context*. 237-266 (Berlin: de Gruyter, 2004).

Aasgaard, R. '"Role Ethics" in Paul: The Significance of the Sibling Role for Paul's Ethical Thinking', NTS 48 (2002), 513-30.

Barnett, P. W. 'Apostle', in Hawthorne, G. F, Martin, R. P. & Reid, D.G. (eds.), *Dictionary of Paul and his Letters*. 45-51 (Downers Grove: IVP, 1993).

Barnett, P. W. *The Second Epistle to the Corinthians*. New International Commentary on the New Testament (Grand Rapids, MI: Eerdmands, 1997).

Baugh, S. M. *Ephesians*. Evangelical Exegetical Commentary (Bellingham, WA: Lexham, 2016).

Belleville, L. L. 'Authority', in Hawthorne, G, Martin, R.P., & Reid, D. G. (eds.), *Dictionary of Paul and his Letters*. 54-59 (Downers Grove: IVP, 1993).

Bjerkelund, C. J. Parakalô: Form, Funktion und Sinn der parakalô-Sätze in den paulinischen Briefen. Bibliotheca Theologica Norvegica 1, Oslo: Universitetsforlaget, 1967.

Brookins, T. A. '"I Rather Appeal to Auctoritas": Roman Conceptualizations of Power and Paul's Appeal to Philemon', *CBQ* 77 (2015), 302-321.

Bruce, F. F. *1 & 2 Thessalonians*, WBC (Waco, TX: Word, 1986).

Campbell, C. R. *Paul and Union with Christ: An Exegetical and Theological Study* (Grand Rapids, MI: Zondervan, 2012).

Clarke, A. D. 'Equality or Mutuality?: Paul's Use of "Brother" Language', in Williams, P. J. et al. (eds.), *The New Testament in Its First Century Setting: Essays on Context and Background in Honour of B. W. Winter on His 65th Birthday.* 151-64 (Grand Rapids, MI: Eerdmans, 2004).

Dunn, J. D. G. *The Theology of Paul the Apostle* (Grand Rapids, MI: Eerdmans, 1998).

Ehrensperger, K. *Paul and the Dynamics of Power: Communication and Interaction in the Early Christian Movement.* Library of New Testament Studies 325 (London: T&T Clark, 2007).

Elliot, S. S. '"Thanks, but no Thanks": Tact, Persuasion, and the Negotiation of Power in Paul's Letter to Philemon', *NTS* 57 (2010), 51-64.

Fee, G. D. *Paul's Letter to the Philippians*, New International Commentary on the New Testament (Grand Rapids, MI: Eerdmans, 1995).

Grayston, K. 'A Problem of Translation: The meaning of Parakaleo, paraklesis in the New Testament', *Scripture Bulletin* 11/2 (1980), 27-31.

Hiebert, D. E. *1 & 2 Thessalonians* (Chicago: Moody, 1992).

Holmberg, B. *Paul and Power: The Structure of Authority in the Primitive Church as Reflected in the Pauline Epistles* (Philadelphia: Fortress, 1978).

Louw, J. P. & E. A. Nida, *Greek-English Lexicon of the New Testament based on Semantic Domains* (New York: United Bible Societies, 1988).

Makujina, J. 'Verbs Meaning "Command" in the New Testament: Determining the Factors Involved in the Choice of Command-Verbs', *Estudios Bíblicos* 56 (1998), 357-369.

Martin, R. P. *2 Corinthians.* Word Biblical Commentary 40 (Waco, TX: Word, 1986).

Moo, D. J. *The Epistle to the Romans* (Grand Rapids, MI: Eerdmans, 1996).

Mounce, W. D. *Pastoral Epistles.* Word Biblical Commentary 46 (Nashville, TN: Thomas Nelson, 2000).

Mullins, T. 'Petition as a Literary Form', *Novum Testamentum* 5 (1962), 45-54.

Polaski, S. H. *Paul and the Discourse of Power.* Gender, Culture, Theory 8; The Biblical Seminar 62 (Sheffield: Sheffield Academic Press, 1999).

Sanders, J. T. 'The Transition from Opening Epistolary Thanksgiving to Body in the Letters of the Pauline Corpus', *JBL* 81 (1962), 348-62.

Schmitz, O. 'παρακαλέω, κτλ', in Kittel, G. et al. (eds.) *Theological Dictionary of the New Testament.* trans. Geoffrey W. Bromily. 773-799 (Grand Rapids: Eerdmans, 1964–1976), translation of Theologisches Wörterbuch zum Neuen Testament, vol. 5, Zehnter Band. Stuttgart: W. Kohlhammer Verlag, 1933.

Schütz, J. H. *Paul and the Anatomy of Apostolic Authority* (Louisville, KY: Westminster John Knox Press, 2007, republished from 1975).

Smith, C. S. *Pauline Communities as 'Scholastic Communities': A Study of the Vocabulary of 'Teaching' in 1 Corinthians, 1 and 2 Timothy and Titus.* Wissenschaftliche Untersuchungen zum Neuen Testament 2:335 (Tübingen: Mohr Siebeck, 2012).

Sydney University. Graduate Qualities <https://sydney.edu.au/education-portfolio/ei/teaching@sydney/graduate-qualities-important/> [accessed 22 March 2019].

Thiselton, A. C. *The First Epistle to the Corinthians: A Commentary on the Greek Text (New International Greek Testament Commentary* (Grand Rapids, MI: Eerdmans, 2000).

Thomas, J. 'παρακαλέω', in Balz, H. & Schneider, G. (eds.), *Exegetical Dictionary of the New Testament.* 23-27 (Grand Rapids, MI: Eerdmans, 1990–93).

Claire Smith
Independent Researcher

13 | GRADUATE ATTRIBUTES AND THE NEW COVENANT

Abstract

The paper will provide a New Covenant based appraisal of the development of Key Competencies in the Australian context. It will overview the development of these concepts through the Finn Review, the Mayer Report, the emergence of Employability Skills, Core Skills, the AQF related concept of Generic Skills and the discussion surrounding Graduate Attributes. It will also draw on the key competencies research of the OECD's DeSeCo project. The content and trajectory to the discourse surrounding the Key Competencies will be compared with qualities of character implied in the promise of the New Covenant.

1. Introduction

I remember being in a lively discussion about means, methods, outcomes, objectives and ends in an industrial education and training seminar. As we were about to slide into a hair-splitting, definition-demanding discussion about competencies, capabilities, and contexts, Rod, a ruddied workplace trainer, cut us short and said, 'Before you get into all of that stuff ... the way I think about it is that nobody ever needs a quarter-inch drill. What they need is a quarter-inch hole'. He was saying, in as simple a way as possible, that the most important thing is to know what you are trying to achieve before considering how you are going to achieve it. His homespun wisdom was a curt reminder of Stephen

Covey's apt insistence that in for success in any pursuit, you must begin with the end in mind.[1]

What, then, is the 'quarter-inch hole' of Christian theological education? What is the end we should have in mind before we start planning? Accepting that all theological education ultimately prepares its students for some sort of service or ministry, whether it is theoretical or practical, or in the academy or the field. The answer is simple. Christian theological education must help its students become practitioners in ministries that are validly in accord with New Testament distinctives and follow the *Missio Dei*. In Biblical terms, graduates must be competent as ministers of the New Covenant.[2] They must be competent in whatever context they serve, to serve as co-labourers with God as He writes His law on the minds and hearts of those they serve and forms them into His people.[3]

The question then becomes, what are the attributes of a competent minister of the New Covenant? Whatever these may be, they must be central to the purpose of all Christian theological education, and graduates must exhibit them. However, these attributes are specified; they must incorporate validly criteria defined by and derived from the New Covenant and engage effectively with the social contexts of their situation.

Formal considerations of graduate attributes in education for policy development emerged in the 1990s and has continued apace ever since.[4] The terminology has varied. Terms used to describe sets of attributes include key-competencies, employability skills, foundation skills, transversal skills, and graduate attributes.

The underlying purposes that have guided the definition and selection of such attribute sets have varied. In many schemes, the dominant driver is

---

1   Covey, *The 7 Habits of Highly Effective People*.and it continues to be a business bestseller with more than 10 million copies sold. Stephen Covey, an internationally respected leadership authority, realizes that true success encompasses a balance of personal and professional effectiveness, so this book is a manual for performing better in both arenas. His anecdotes are as frequently from family situations as from business challenges. Before you can adopt the seven habits, you'll need to accomplish what Covey calls a \"paradigm shift\"--a change in perception and interpretation of how the world works. Covey takes you through this change, which affects how you perceive and act regarding productivity, time management, positive thinking, developing your \"proactive muscles\" (acting with initiative rather than reacting.
2   Covenant and testament are essentially synonymous. They are both translations of *diatheke*. The difference between these terms lies in the idea that a testament requires the death of the testator to come into effect. Reference to the New Covenant as the New Testament draws attention to the centrality of the cross in the establishment of the New Covenant and greatly amplifies it force and priority.
3   CF. 2 Cor. 3:6; Heb. 8:10-11.
4   Holdsworth, *Producing Sustainability Professionals*.

employment-related economics.[5] Others are social or humanistic in focus and emphasise community improvement and 'the Good Life'.[6] Others again focus on social and environmental sustainability.[7] Many overlap. While none of these approaches has foregrounded moral or spiritual considerations, it would be wrong to say that such concerns have been entirely absent. Most, if not all, are expressions of a desire for some form of social equity or environmental responsibility. New Covenant-based attributes rarely compete with or contradict such desires. In many cases, New Covenant-based attributes reinforce or supplement them.

What follows explores the development of the idea of graduate attributes as educational objectives over the past few decades. It includes consideration of

- developments in vocational education,[8]
- developments in higher education,[9] and
- the Organisation for Economic Cooperation and Development's (OECD's) Definition and Selection of Competencies (DeSeCo) project.[10]

It then discusses the incorporation of New Covenant-based attributes.

2. Developments in Vocational Education

This section considers the developments in the identification and selection of graduate attributes in the Australian vocational education sector. These developments were driven primarily by utilitarian employment-related economic considerations. They began with the 1991 Finn Review. In the decades that followed, it progressed through the use of the terms *Key Competencies*, *Employability Skills*, and *Foundational Skills*.

The Finn Review focused on the convergence of general and vocational education. It argued for the continual trans-disciplinary development of societal

---

5 E.g. Finn, 'Young People's Participation in Post-Compulsory Education and Training';Mayer, 'Key Competencies';ASQA, 'VAC 7.4'.; Fontelles & Enestam, 'Recommendation of the European Parliament', 10–18.
6 E.g. Rychen, 'Key Competencies', 63-108.
7 E.g. Holdsworth, *Producing Sustainability Professionals*.
8 Finn, 'Finn Review'.; Mayer, 'Key Competencies'.; BCA & ACCI, *Employability Skills for the Future*.;ASQA, 'VAC 7.4: User's Guide About the Standards'.
9 Monash University, 'Monash Graduate Attributes'.; University of Adelaide, 'Graduate Attributes'.; University of Melbourne, 'The Melbourne Graduate'.; University of New South Wales, 'UNSW Graduate Attributes'.; University of Queensland, 'Graduate Attributes'.; University of Sydney, 'Graduate Qualities'.
10 Rychen, 'Key Competencies: Meeting Important Challenges in Life'.

and workforce skills and knowledge[11]. It listed six 'essential things which young people need to learn in their preparation for employment' and which should be developed 'regardless of the education or training pathway that they follow'[12]. These were styled *Key Competencies* and were as follows:

- language and communication;
- mathematics;
- scientific and technological understanding;
- cultural understanding;
- problem-solving; and
- personal and interpersonal characteristics.

The Finn Review also recommended the establishment of a standards framework for these competencies.[13]

The Mayer Report followed the Finn Review and set out to further identify the Key Competencies and develop a means of describing them. It intended to provide a common reference point for curriculum and teaching in both the school and training sectors.[14] Building on the work of the Finn Review and developments in the UK, US, and New Zealand,[15] the Mayer report identified and described seven Key Competencies.[16] It precluded values and attitudes. In response to those that argued for the inclusion of values and attitudes, the Mayer Committee writes,

> The Committee acknowledges and shares this commitment to the importance of values and attitudes. In doing so, however, it maintains the view that a set of Key Competencies can only contain those things which can be developed by education and training, which do not require some innate predisposition or adherence to a particular set of values and which are amenable to credible assessment.[17]

---

11 Finn, 'Finn Review', ix.
12 Finn, x.
13 Finn, xi.
14 Mayer, 'Key Competencies'.
15 Mayer, 15.
16 Mayer, viii.
17 Mayer, 15.

The Mayer Key Competencies became an integral part of the unit of competency as it was mandated for vocational education by the then Australian National Training Authority (ANTA).[18] See Table 1.

Table 1 Mayer Key Competencies and Descriptions

Key Competence	Description
Collecting, Analysing, and Organising Information	The capacity to locate, sift, and sort information in order to select what is required and present it in a useful way, and evaluate the information itself and the sources and methods used to obtain it.
Communicating Ideas and Information	The capacity to communicate effectively with others using the range of spoken, written, graphic, and other non-verbal means of expression.
Planning and Organising Activities	The capacity to plan and organise one's own work activities, including making good use of time and resources, sorting out priorities, and monitoring one's own performance.
Working with Others and in Teams	The capacity to interact effectively with other people both on a one-to-one basis and in groups, including understanding and responding to a client and working effectively as a team to achieve a shared goal.
Using Mathematical Ideas and Techniques	The capacity to use mathematical ideas, such as numbers and space, and techniques, such as estimation and approximation, for practical purposes.
Solving Problems	The capacity to apply problem-solving strategies in situations where the problem and the desired solution are clearly evident and in situations requiring critical thinking and a creative approach to achieve an outcome.
Using Technology	The capacity to apply technology, combining the physical and sensory skills needed to operate with the understanding of scientific and technological principles needed to explore and adapt systems.

---

18   ANTA, *Competency Standards from the Training Package Development Handbook*.

The turn of the millennium saw further review.[19] Despite the consensus that Key Competencies were necessary, dissatisfaction existed about their clarity and relevance to employment and further learning. This review included consideration of developments in the US, UK, Canada, Europe, and the OECD.[20] It led to a change in terminology. 'Generic Employability Skills' replaced 'Key Competencies'. Incorporating international developments, it expanded upon the Mayer Key Competencies to include:

- a capacity to learn, adaptability, and a willingness to embrace change,
- a business orientation, and
- an achievement orientation.[21]

The skills identified were grouped into three sets: basic skills, intellectual abilities, and personal attributes.[22] See Table 2 for a brief outline.

Table 2 Generic Employability Skills

Generic Skill	Description
Basic	Foundation skills in literacy and numeracy, and in using information and communication technology
Intellectual abilities	Critical and creative thinking, and planning and organisation
Personal Attributes	Attitudes and abilities of self-management, on-going learning, and collaboration

The most significant departures from the Mayer Key Competencies were in the category of Personal Attributes, which included a limited approach to values and attitudes.

The outcome of this review integrated the personal attributes in the descriptions of the final list of eight skills and de-emphasised foundation skills in literacy and numeracy.[23] See Table 3.

---

19   Curtis & McKenzie, 'Employability Skills for Australian Industry'. See also: Curtin, 'Employability Skills for the Future', 38-52. For criticisms, see: Williams, 'The Discursive Construction of the "competent" Learner-Worker', 33–49.; Sheldon & Thornthwaite, 'Employability Skills and Vocational Education and Training Policy in Australia', 404-425.
20   Curtis and McKenzie, 'Employability Skills Report', 27–36, Appendix 2.
21   Curtis and McKenzie, x.
22   Curtis and McKenzie, ix, 51-53.
23   Allen Consulting Group, *Employability Skills: Final Report*, 2.Science and Training, 2004; BCA & ACCI, *Employability Skills for the Future*, 7.

Table 3 Mandated Employability Skills

Employability Skill	Description
Communication	Communication skills that contribute to productive and harmonious relations between employees and customers;
Teamwork	Teamwork skills that contribute to productive working relationships and outcomes
Problem-solving	Problem-solving skills that contribute to productive outcomes;
Initiative and Enterprise	Initiative and enterprise skills that contribute to innovative outcomes
Planning and Organising	Planning and organising skills that contribute to long-term and short-term strategic planning
Self-management	Self-management skills that contribute to employee satisfaction and growth
Learning	Learning skills that contribute to ongoing improvement and expansion in employee and company operations and outcomes
Technology	Technology skills that contribute to the effective execution of tasks

This list subsumed the Mayer Key competencies. It added initiative and enterprise and learning.[24]

The next phase of development re-emphasised the foundational skills in literacy and numeracy omitted from the list of Employability Skills. This iteration has seen the term *Foundation Skills* replace *Employability Skills*. Foundation Skills are now a combination of Language Literacy and Numeracy (LLN) and Employability Skills.[25]

3. Developments in Higher Education

Since at least the 1980s, economic imperatives have become the predominant drivers of the higher education sector. In this, it is not unlike the vocational

---

24 Cleary, Flynn, & Thomasson, *Employability Skills,* 10.
25 SCOTESE, *National Foundation Skills Strategy for Adults,* 2.For the purpose of this Strategy, foundation skills are defined as the combination of : English language, literacy and numeracy (LLN ASQA. (2018). VAC 7.4 VET Accredited Source Standard 7.1 [Text].

education sector. These imperatives have arisen from the linking of education to national prosperity in the knowledge economy and have given rise to constant calls for universities to produce employable graduates.[26]

A clear example of this link may be found in the *Council Recommendation on Key Competencies for Lifelong Learning* presented to the European Commission in 2018. This document focuses strongly on a set of eight key competencies that are expected to guide education and training in all sectors, including early childhood, vocational education and training, adult education, non-formal learning, and higher education.[27] These competencies are as listed below. They are fully defined in *Key Competencies for Lifelong Learning: European Reference Framework*.[28]

- Communication in the mother tongue,
- Communication in foreign languages,
- Mathematical competence and basic competences in science and technology,
- Digital competence,
- Learning to learn,
- Social and civic competences,
- Sense of initiative and entrepreneurship,
- Cultural awareness and expression.

This linking of education to the economy gave rise to the massive global expansion of the higher education sector in the late Twentieth Century. The public investment that enabled and accompanied this expansion has led to the demand that all such institutions justify the public funds they receive by demonstrating that they are achieving relevant and worthwhile outcomes. This demand typically requires a statement of the generic outcomes of the education provided by an institution as a condition of funding. Education authorities typically now use quality assurance methodologies to provide evidence that the institutions are achieving the outcomes thus claimed.[29]

Not surprisingly, these developments are often contested and have revived

---

26 Barrie, 'Understanding What We Mean by Generic Attributes of Graduates', 217.
27 European Commission, 'Proposal for a Council Recommendation on Key Competences for Lifelong Learning'.
28 Figel, *Key Competencies for Lifelong Learning*.
29 Barrie, 'Understanding What We Mean by Generic Attributes of Graduates', 217.; Nightingale & O'Neil, *Achieving Quality Learning in Higher Education*.

debate about the purpose and nature of higher education. While resistance to the reduction of higher learning due to the constraints of the employability skills agendas has not always been successful, the social changes arising from the information explosion and the impact of post-modernism have been recognised.[30] *Generic graduate attributes* generally include, therefore, qualities that contribute to graduates being 'agents of social good in an unknown future', in addition to disciplinary expertise.[31]

Progress toward the definition and selection of such attributes differs from institution to institution and has been slow and fragmented. See Appendix 1 for a selection of graduate attribute statements from a selection of major Australian universities. Institutions have generally been unable to make the systemic changes needed to foster the development of the attributes they have so far declared as their aims.[32]

4. DeSeCo

The DeSeCo project was an OECD initiative aimed at developing a coherent strategy for defining, selecting, and measuring competencies and skills. It asked 'What competencies are needed for the individual to lead an overall successful and responsible life and for contemporary society to face present and future challenges?' and 'What are the normative, theoretical, and conceptual foundations for defining and selecting a limited set of the most relevant competencies?'[33]

---

30 Barrie, 'Understanding What We Mean by Generic Attributes of Graduates', 217.
31 Barrie, 217.; Bowden et al., 'Generic Capabilities of ATN University Graduates', para 2.; University of Bologna, 'Transversal Competencies -'."plainCitation":"University of Bologna, 'Transversal Competencies -', Alma Mater Studiorum Universitá di Bologna, 2019, https://www.unibo.it/en/teaching/Transversal-competencies-and-other-learning-opportunities/transversal-competencies.","noteIndex":31},"citationItems":[{"id":34972,"uris":["http://zotero.org/users/4735130/items/89XMRSHL"],"uri":["http://zotero.org/users/4735130/items/89XMRSHL"],"itemData":{"id":34972,"type":"webpage","abstract":"Acquiring transversal competencies provides students with the basic knowledge, abilities and qualities required to translate competences into suitable behaviour for organizational purposes.","genre":"Alma Mater Studiorum Universitá di Bologna","language":"en","title":"Transversal competencies -","URL":"https://www.unibo.it/en/teaching/Transversal-competencies-and-other-learning-opportunities/transversal-competencies","author":[{"family":"University of Bologna","given":""}],"accessed":{"date-parts":[["2019",4,6]]},"issued":{"date-parts":[["2019"]]}}}],"schema":"https://github.com/citation-style-language/schema/raw/master/csl-citation.json"} ; McIlvenny, 'Are Transversal Competencies the "New Black"?' 42.
32 Barrie, Hughes, & Smith, 'The National Graduate Attributes Project'.
33 OECD, *Definition and Selection of Competencies*, 2.

It set out to develop a globally valid theoretical framework for the identification of the competencies needed for a successful and responsible life.[34] Noting the multiplicity of concepts of both competence and key competence that existed in the literature, the DeSeCo authors developed an overarching frame of reference that included:

- a definition of key competencies,
- the level of competence required to meet the complex demands and challenges faced by individuals and societies, and
- a three-fold categorisation of key competencies.[35]

The authors set three criteria to define key competencies; these are that key competencies must[36]

- contribute to highly valued outcomes at the individual and societal levels in terms of an overall successful life and well-functioning society,
- are instrumental for meeting important complex demands and challenges in a wide spectrum of contexts, and
- are important for all individuals.

Concerning the complex demands faced by individuals and society, they argued for a normative starting point grounded in the values shared in international conventions related to human rights and sustainable development.[37] They also centred on the idea of 'the good life' accompanied by a level of reflective practice that enables individuals to navigate their social space, deal with differences and contradictions, and take personal responsibility.[38] Following Canto-Sperber and Dupuy, they defined the good life terms of key values 'that are consistent with any major moral theory' and are 'compatible with individual and social diversity'.[39] These include

- accomplishment,
- the elements of human existence ('choosing one course through life and having a life which is properly human')
- an understanding of one's self and one's world,

---

34 OECD, 3.
35 Rychen, 'Key Competencies: Meeting Important Challenges in Life', 66.
36 Rychen, 66–67.
37 Rychen, 71.
38 Rychen, 68–82.
39 Rychen, 70. Canto-Sperber & Dupuy, 'Competencies for the Good Life and the Good Society', 73-75.

- enjoyment, and
- deep personal relations.[40]

Following these considerations, they laid out a threefold categorisation of nine interrelated but conceptually distinct action-oriented key competencies understood as necessary to address globally common demands of life and society. These were as follows:[41]

- interacting in socially heterogeneous groups. This includes
    - relating well to others,
    - cooperating, and
    - managing and resolving conflict;
- acting autonomously. This includes
    - acting within the big picture or larger context,
    - forming and conducting life plans and personal projects, and
    - defending and asserting one's rights, interests, limits, and needs; and
- using tools interactively. This includes
    - using languages, symbols, and text interactively,
    - using knowledge and information interactively, and
    - using technology interactively.

5. New Covenant-based Attributes

Much, perhaps most, of the quest to define and select key competencies is of value to theological education. It is of particular value in the specification of practical and relational capabilities of graduates, theological or otherwise. None of it, however, explicitly addresses the moral or spiritual capabilities that might be expected of theology graduates. All theology graduates must be able, to some degree, to serve as *Ministers of the New Covenant,* whether they are in formal or informal settings in the academy or the field.

What follows examines two key New Covenant passages of Scripture and derives graduate attributes from them. These are 1 Corinthians 3:5-6 and Hebrew 8:10.

---

40 Rychen, 'Key Competencies: Meeting Important Challenges in Life', 70.
41 Rychen, 85-104.

5.1 2 Corinthians 3:5-6

2 Corinthians 3:5-6 connects ministry to the New Covenant.[42]

> Not that we are sufficient (competent) in ourselves to claim anything as coming from us, but our sufficiency (competency) is from God, who has made us sufficient (competent) to be ministers of a new covenant, not of the letter but of the Spirit. For the letter kills, but the Spirit gives life.

This declaration describes ministry as an authoritative God-enabled and Spirit-centred service involved in the causing of its recipients to become[43]

> A letter from Christ delivered by us, written not with ink but with the Spirit of the living God, not on tablets of stone but on tablets of human hearts.

2 Corinthians 3:5-6 is embedded in a lengthy defence of the validity and effectiveness of the ministries of Paul and his companions. This defence draws heavily on the gruesome metaphor of Roman triumphal processions in which Paul describes his companions and himself as both captives and incense bearers for Christ victorious.[44] It also draws heavily on the imagery of Moses at Sinai, Jeremiah's prophecy of the New Covenant, and Ezekiel's Spirit-centred prophecies.[45]

The concept of sufficiency or competency employed in this passage is multifaceted, pointed, and used in a polemic that confidently contrasts Paul's God-centred confidence with the self-sufficiency of his opponents.[46] The Greek word translated sufficiency or competence here is *hikanos* (ἱκανός). *Hikanos* is drawn from a root meaning to reach with the hand and was used to refer to the concept of competency currently employed in the vocational training.[47] *Hikanos* was also used extensively within the 'divine man' tradition contemporaneous

---

42 The claims that Paul is making about himself and/or those with him are readily seen to be applicable to ministry in general.Carblis, 'Educating for Virtue', 47.
43 2 Cor. 3:3.
44 2 Cor. 2:14; Carblis, 'Educating for Virtue', 40.
45 Carblis, 42–43.
46 Carblis, 44.
47 *Hikanos* and its cognates have a persistent double meaning in history and other languages. It refers to both the ability and skill to achieve something and the authority to do so. The European Union translation service provides examples of equivalents that include accreditation, appropriateness, approval, authorisation, certification, entitlement, jurisdiction, licence, responsibility, qualification, and right. Mulder, 'Competence: The Essence and Use of the Concept in ICVT', 6-7.

with Paul. It was also used in the Septuagint as an attribute of God.[48] Its use in this passage may, therefore, refer to both practical and spiritual capabilities.

The following table suggests ministerial dispositions or capabilities derived from this argument.[49] These might be incorporated into the graduate attributes of theological students.

Table 4 Dispositions or Capabilities of Ministers of the New Covenant

Verse	Image from 2 Corinthians	Ministerial Disposition or Capability
2:14	Captive	Surrender and obedience – A surrendered obedient follower, a captive of Christ victorious
2:14-16	Aroma of Christ	Worshipful follower – An incense bearer in the procession of Christ victorious, offers a public confession that is attractive to those who accept Christ but may be repulsive to those who reject or oppose Him.
3:3, 7-18	Ministers of the Spirit as distinct from the letter.	Rejects the juridicism, the approach of the letter, in favour of the internal liberating life-transforming work of the Spirit.
3:4-6	Sufficiency or competence	Draws capability from relationship with God. Rejects self-sufficiency.
3:5	Minister of the New Covenant	Works as a co-labourer with God as He executes the terms of the New Covenant in the lives of believers. The New Covenant is understood as a promise by God that He will transform the inner life of His people into conformity with the underlying precepts of His law.

---

48 Carblis, 'Educating for Virtue', 43.; Fallon, 'Self's Sufficiency or God's Sufficiency: 2 Corinthians 2:16', 372.; Harris, *The Second Epistle to the Corinthians*, 269.; Martin, *2 Corinthians*, 270.
49 See Carblis, 'Educating for Virtue', 49–54, for a discussion on the place of human agency in the outworking of the New Covenant and the ministry of the Spirit and distinct from the letter.

5.2 Hebrew 8:10

There is little doubt that Paul and the Corinthians understood themselves as being in the community of the New Covenant as prophesied by Jeremiah.[50] The terms of this covenant promise the renovation of mind and heart by the direct action of God.[51] The opening statement of this covenant is:

> I will put my laws into their minds,
>   and write them on their hearts.[52]

This statement promises the internalisation of the laws of God in the minds and hearts of believers. It declares a process of spiritual and moral formation performed by God within those subject to the New Covenant. It promises an ensuing transformation of character into conformity with the precepts of that law. The reference to the law is understood to be the Decalogue.[53]

This statement thus grounds New Covenant ministry in the formation of New Covenant-based spirituality, character, and virtue.[54] It also implies an outcomes-based and recipient-centred approach to ministry. Any approach to ministry grounded in these terms must, therefore, be centred on Decalogue-based outcomes as declared by this covenant.[55]

New Covenant ministers should, therefore, demonstrate an accurately informed Spirit-led understanding of and commitment to the formation of Decalogue-based virtues in their lives. They must also be competent to encourage and assist the recipients of their ministries to develop similarly accurately informed and Spirit-led understandings and commitments. See Table 5 for a list of Decalogue-based character attributes or virtues.[56]

---

50 Jer. 33:31-34.
51 Carblis, 'Educating for Virtue', 4.
52 Jer. 31:33b; Heb. 8:10a, 10:16b.
53 Carblis, 'Educating for Virtue', 186-98.
54 Cf. Stanley Hauerwas, *A Community of Character'.*; MacIntyre, *A Short History of Ethics.*; Wright, *Virtue Reborn*.
55 Carblis, 'Educating for Virtue', 64.
56 For a fuller discussion on Decalogue-based virtues and their structure, see Carblis, chap. 7.

Table 5 New Covenant Decalogue-based Virtues

Precept		Character Attribute or Virtue
Preface	I am the Lord your God who brought you out of Egypt	Covenant faithfulness
First	No other Gods	Single-minded faithful devotion to God revealed in Christ
Second	No graven images	Exclusive commitment revealed in Christ
Third	Not take the name of the Lord your God in vain	Respect for the holiness of God's name
Fourth	Remember the Sabbath day	Mindful commitment to sacred time
Fifth	Honour your father and your mother	Respect and care for father and mother
Sixth	You shall not kill/murder	Respect for life
Seventh	You shall not commit adultery	Chastity-faithfulness and integrity in family life and relationships
Eighth	You shall not steal	Material justice - productivity and generosity
Ninth	You shall not bear false witness	Truthfulness and integrity
Tenth	You shall not covet	Appreciativeness (*Eucharistia*)

6. New Covenant Attributes — Summary

Consideration of the attributes that might be derived from 2 Corinthians 2–3 and Hebrew 8:10 yields a two-dimensional approach to define attributes of New Covenant ministers and, hence, of theological graduates.

The first dimension is derived from 2 Corinthians 2–3 and identifies a Spirit-embracing, surrendered, obedient, and worshipful follower of Christ, who:

- rejects juridicism,
- embraces the liberating life-transforming work of the Spirit,
- rejects self-sufficiency, and

- understands ministry as co-labouring with God in the inner transformation of lives into conformity with the underlying precepts of God's Law.

The second dimension is derived from Hebrew 8:10 and identifies a person who has an accurately informed Spirit-led understanding of the formation of Decalogue-based virtues. This person exhibits a competent commitment to growing in:

- covenant faithfulness,
- single-minded and faithful devotion to God revealed in Christ,
- exclusive commitment to God revealed in Christ,
- respect for the holiness of God's name,
- mindful commitment to sacred time,
- respect and care for father and mother,
- respect for life,
- chastity-faithfulness and integrity in family life and relationships,
- material justice—productivity and generosity,
- truthfulness and integrity, and
- appreciativeness (*eucharistia*)

7. Summary and Conclusion

Formal considerations of graduate attributes began in the Australian vocational education sector. Utilitarian in nature and driven by employment-related concerns, graduate attributes were examined in the 1991 Finn Review, followed by the 1992 Mayer Report. This stage of development focused exclusively on trainable vocational skills called *Key Competencies* and declined to incorporate values and attitudes. Dissatisfaction with this approach led to the adoption of *Employability Skills,* which extended the *key Competencies* to incorporate attitudes relating to the capacity to learn, adaptability, the willingness to embrace change, and an orientation to business and achievement. A further review adopted the terminology of *Foundational Skills* and incorporated language, literacy, and numeracy skills. Values remained unaddressed.

The latter half of the Twentieth Century saw the linking of the economy to education, which gave rise to the dramatic global investment in and expansion of the higher education sector. The economic imperatives of this investment and expansion led inexorably to demands that higher education providers demonstrate they are achieving worthwhile outcomes. The methodologies adopted typically require the use of quality assurance methodologies to provide evidence that they are achieving economically relevant generic outcomes in the attributes of their graduates. Progress toward the definition and selection of these attributes has been fragmented and slow. The reduction of educational goals to economic imperatives has been contested. Recognition of social changes arising from the information explosion and the impact of post-modernism has, however, resulted in the incorporation of values relating to social responsibility.

The DeSeCo project (1998-2003) ran parallel to many of these developments. This project was an initiative of the OECD. Unlike the development reviewed in the vocational and higher education sectors, this project set out to consider the issues involved on a more global, societal, and philosophical level. It was to avoid fragmentation and incoherence. While economic considerations remained important in this project, it set out to develop a globally valid framework for the identification of competencies needed for a successful and responsible life. Its final report proposed three categories of competencies. Those are that successful and responsible actors in the modern world must be able to productively

- interact in socially heterogeneous groups,
- act autonomously, and
- use tools interactively

Most of what the vocational and higher education sectors have arrived at fits comfortably into and may be refined by these categories.

While the DeSeCo categories also apply in theological education, they are entirely silent about the formational, spiritual, and moral dimensions essential to theological education. This silence becomes most apparent when considering the imperatives for Christian ministry as implied by its essential link to the New Covenant. An examination of 2 Corinthians 3:5-6 and Hebrew 8:10 arrives at two categories of attributes. These are that theological graduates must

- be a Spirit-embracing, surrendered, obedient, and worshipful follower of Christ, and
- exhibit a competent commitment to growth in the moral and spiritual virtues that underlie the Decalogue.

I, therefore, propose a combination of the DeSeCo categories and those derived above relating to New Covenant ministry as the attributes of theological graduates. This results in a five-part statement of overlapping and mutually conditioning generic graduate attributes. Mission- and ministry-related attributes may then be added. Together, these are the 'quarter-inch hole' toward which all curriculum and pedagogies should strain.

Table 6 Sample College Statement of Graduate Attributes

As a result of the training and education offered by ****** College, our Theological graduates will
1) be Spirit-embracing, surrendered, obedient and worshipful follower of Christ,   2) exhibit a competent commitment to growth in the moral and spiritual virtues that underlie the Decalogue.   3) interact effectively in socially heterogeneous groups,   4) act autonomously, and   5) use tools interactively

Bibliography

Allen Consulting Group. 'Employability Skills: Final Report: Development of a Strategy to Support the Universal Recognition and Recording of Employability Skills; A Skills Portfolio Approach' (Canberra: Department of Education, Science and Training, 2004).

ANTA. *Competency Standards from the Training Package Development Handbook* (Brisbane: Australian National Training Authority, 2001).

ASQA. 'VAC 7.4: VET Accredited Courses Identify Employability Skills Relevant to the Course Outcomes'. Australian Skills Quality Authority (ASQA): Users' guide to the Standards for VET Accredited Courses: About the Standards for VET Accredited Courses' <https://www.asqa.gov.au/standards-vac/7.4> [accesssed 6 July 2020].

Barrie, Simon. 'Understanding What We Mean by Generic Attributes of Graduates'. *Higher Education* 51 (3 January 2006): 215-41 <https://doi.org/10.1007/s10734-004-6384-7>.

Barrie, S., Hughes, C. & Smith, C. 'The National Graduate Attributes Project: Integration and Assessment of Graduate Attributes in Curriculum'. *Final Report - The National GAP* (Strawberry Hills, NSW: Australian Learning and Teaching Council, 2009) <http://citeseerx.ist.psu.edu/viewdoc/download?doi=10.1.1.178.9102&rep=rep1&type=pdf>.

BCA & ACCI. 'Employability Skills for the Future' (DEST, Australian Government Publishing Service, 2002).

Borrell F., J., & Enestam J. E. 'Recommendation of the European Parliament and of the Council of 18 December 2006 on Key Competences for Lifelong Learning', *Official Journal of the European Union* 394 (30 December 2006): 10-18.

Bowden, J., Hart G., King, B., Trigwell, K., & Watts O. 'Generic Capabilities of ATN University Graduates' (Teaching and Learning Committee, Australian Technology Network, Higher Education Division, 2001).

Canto-Sperber, M., & Dupuy, J.P. 'Competencies for the Good Life and the Good Society', in Rychen, D. S. & Hersh, L. (eds.), *Defining and Selecting Key Competencies* (Kirkland, WA, US: Hogrefe and Huber Publishers, 2001): 67-92.

Carblis, P. 'Educating for Virtue: The New Covenant as a Framework for the Development of Character' (Sydney College of Divinity, 2020).

Cleary, M., Flynn R., & Thomasson, S. *Employability Skills: From Framework to Practice: An Introductory Guide for Trainers and Assessors* (Melbourne: Precision Consultancy, 2006).

Covey, S. R. *The 7 Habits of Highly Effective People: Powerful Lessons in Personal Change* (New York and London: Simon and Schuster, 2004).

Curtin, P. 'Employability Skills for the Future', in Gibb, J (ed.), *Generic Skills in Vocational Education and Training* (Adelaide: National Centre for Vocational Education Research Ltd, 2004): 38-52.

Curtis, D. & McKenzie, P. 'Employability Skills for Australian Industry: Literature Review and Framework Development Report to: Business Council of Australia Australian Chamber of Commerce and Industry' (Australian Council for Educational Research, 2001).

European Commission. 'Proposal for a Council Recommendation on Key Competences for Lifelong Learning' (Brussels: European Commission, 2018) <https://eur-lex.europa.eu/legal-content/IT/TXT/?uri=CELEX:52018DC0024>.

Fallon, F. T. 'Self's Sufficiency or God's Sufficiency: 2 Corinthians 2:16', *Harvard Theological Review* 76.3 (July 1983), 369-70.

Figel, J. *Key Competencies for Lifelong Learning: European Reference Framework* (Luxembourg: Office for Official Publications of the European Communities, 2007) <http://hdl.voced.edu.au/10707/285153>.

Finn, B. 'Young People's Participation in Post-Compulsory Education and Training: Report of the Australian Education Council Review Committee' (Canberra: Australian Government Publishing Service, July 1991) <https://www.voced.edu.au/content/ngv%3A42925>.

Harris, M. J. *The Second Epistle to the Corinthians: A Commentary on the Greek Text. The New International Greek Testament Commentary* (Grand Rapids, Michigan: Eerdmans Publishing Company, 2005).

Hauerwas, S. *A Community of Character: Toward a Constructive Christian Social Ethic* (Kindle edition. Notre Dame, Indiana: University of Notre Dame Press, 1991).

———. *After Christendom: How the Church Is to Behave If Freedom, Justice and a Christian Nation Are Bad Ideas* (Kindle edition. Nashville: Abingdon Press, 1991).

———. *Character and the Christian Life: A Study in Theological Ethics* (Notre Dame, Indiana: University of Notre Dame Press, 1994).

———. 'Character, Narrative and Growth in the Christian Life (1980)', in *The Hauerwas Reader* (Duke University Press Books, 2001): 221-54.

Holdsworth, S. 'Producing Sustainability Professionals: Assessing Graduate Attributes in Sustainability' (Canberra: Australian Government Department of Education and Training, 2019) <https://nla.gov.au/nla.obj-1261486762>.

MacIntyre, A. *A Short History of Ethics: A History of Moral Philosophy from the Homeric Age to the Twentieth Century* (Second edition, Kindle edition. London: Routledge, 1998).

———. *After Virtue: A Study in Moral Theory* (Third edition. Notre Dame, Indiana: University of Notre Dame Press, 2007).

———. *Dependent Rational Animals: Why Human Beings Need the Virtues* (Chicago, Ill.: Open Court, 2001).

Martin, R. P. '2 Corinthians', in *World Biblical Commentary* (Second edition. Vol. 40. Grand Rapids, Michigan: Zondervan, 2017).

Mayer, E. 'Key Competencies: Report of the Committee to Advise the Australian Education Coulcil and Ministers for Education, Employment and Training on Employment-Related Key-Competencies for Post Compulsory Education and Training' (Australian Education Council and Ministers of Vocational Education, Employment and Training, 1992).

McIlvenny, L. 'Are Transversal Competencies the "New Black"?', *Professional Educator* 20.1 (2019), 42.

Monash University. 'Monash Graduate Attributes', 27 February 2017. <https://www.monash.edu/__data/assets/pdf_file/0009/786969/Course-Design-Policy.pdf>.

Mulder, M. 'Competence: The Essence and Use of the Concept in ICVT', *European Journal of Vocational Training* 40 (2007), 5-21.

Nightingale, P., & O'Neil, M. (eds.). *Achieving Quality Learning in Higher Education* (London: Routledge, 2012).

OECD. *Definition and Selection of Competencies: Theoretical and Conceptual Foundations* (DeSeCo). (Paris: OECD, 2000).

Rychen, D. S. 'Key Competencies: Meeting Important Challenges in Life', in Rychen, D. S. & Salganik, L. H (eds.), *Key Competencies for a Successful Life and a Well-Functioning Society* (Cambridge, MA, US: Hogrefe and Huber publishers, 2003): 63-108

SCOTESE. *National Foundation Skills Strategy for Adults* (Canberra: Standing Council on Tertiary Education Skills and Employment, 2012).

Sheldon, P. & Thornthwaite, L. 'Employability Skills and Vocational Education and Training Policy in Australia: An Analysis of Employer Association Agendas', *Asia Pacific Journal of Human Resources* 43.3 (2005), 404-425.

University of Adelaide. 'Graduate Attributes'. *Learning and Teaching: University of Adelaide.* <http://www.adelaide.edu.au/learning/resources-for-educators/graduate-attributes> [accessed 6 July 2020].

University of Bologna. 'Transversal Competencies -'. *Alma Mater Studiorum Universitá di Bologna*, 2019. <https://www.unibo.it/en/teaching/Transversal-competencies-and-other-learning-opportunities/transversal-competencies>.

University of Melbourne. 'The Melbourne Graduate'. *University of Melbourne Chancellery (Academic)*. The University of Melbourne, 20 June 2016 <https://provost.unimelb.edu.au/student-life/the-melbourne-graduate>.

University of New South Wales. 'UNSW Graduate Attributes'. *University of New South Wales*, 3 August 2020 <https://teaching.unsw.edu.au/sites/default/files/upload-files/unsw-graduate-attributes_0.pdf>.

University of Queensland. 'Graduate Attributes'. *Policies and Procedures Library. The University of Queensland, Australia*, 7 December 2017 <https://ppl.app.uq.edu.au/content/3.10.05-graduate-attributes#Procedures>.

University of Sydney. 'Graduate Qualities'. *The University of Sydney*, 24 June 2020 <https://www.sydney.edu.au/students/graduate-qualities.html>.

Williams, C. 'The Discursive Construction of the "competent" Learner-Worker: From Key Competencies to "Employability Skills"', *Studies in Continuing Education* 27. 1 (2005), 33-49.

Wright, N. T. *Virtue Reborn* (London: SPCK Publishing, 2010).

Peter Carblis
University of Newcastle/Sydney College of Divinity
petercarblis@gmail.com

Appendix 1
Graduate Attribute of Select Australian Universities

Graduate attributes from five Australian universities.
- Monash University
- University of Adelaide
- University of Melbourne
- University of New South Wales
- University of Queensland
- University of Sydney

Monash University

Graduate Attributes as at 6 July 2020.[57]
All Monash courses are designed to prepare Monash graduates to be:

1. responsible and effective global citizens who:
    a. engage in an internationalised world
    b. exhibit cross-cultural competence
    c. demonstrate ethical values

2. critical and creative scholars who:
    a. produce innovative solutions to problems
    b. apply research skills to a range of challenges
    c. communicate perceptively and effectively

University of Adelaide

Graduate attributes as at 6 July 2020.[58]
Attribute 1: Deep discipline knowledge and intellectual breadth
Graduates have comprehensive knowledge and understanding of their subject area, the ability to engage with different traditions of thought, and the ability to apply their knowledge in practice including in multi-disciplinary or multi-professional contexts.

---

[57] Monash University, 'Monash Graduate Attributes', 1.
[58] University of Adelaide, 'Graduate Attributes'.

Attribute 2: Creative and critical thinking, and problem solving
> Graduates are effective problems-solvers, able to apply critical, creative, and evidence-based thinking to conceive innovative responses to future challenges.

Attribute 3: Teamwork and communication skills
> Graduates convey ideas and information effectively to a range of audiences for a variety of purposes and contribute in a positive and collaborative manner to achieving common goals.

Attribute 4: Professionalism and leadership readiness
> Graduates engage in professional behaviour and have the potential to be entrepreneurial and take leadership roles in their chosen occupations or careers and communities.

Attribute 5: Intercultural and ethical competency
> Graduates are responsible and effective global citizens whose personal values and practices are consistent with their roles as responsible members of society.

Attribute 6: Australian Aboriginal cultural competency
> Graduates have an understanding of, and respect for, Australian Aboriginal values, culture, and knowledge.

Attribute 7: Digital capabilities
> Graduates are well-prepared for living, learning, and working in a digital society.

Attribute 8: Self-awareness and emotional intelligence
> Graduates are self-aware and reflective; they are flexible and resilient and have the capacity to accept and give constructive feedback; they act with integrity and take responsibility for their actions.

University of Melbourne

Graduate Attributes as at 6 July 2020.[59]

The University of Melbourne educational experience prepares well-rounded graduates who are academically outstanding, practically grounded, and socially responsible. Melbourne's graduates are distinguished by their broad outlook and openness to different perspectives.

Melbourne's degrees develop research and reasoning skills that equip graduates to be influential citizens with high leadership potential. The University's graduates engage with national and global issues and are attuned to social and cultural diversity. They have high levels of self-awareness and value their personal integrity and well-being.

Academic distinction

A Melbourne degree provides graduates with in-depth knowledge of their specialist disciplines and skills in examining issues with multiple disciplinary perspectives. Melbourne graduates are critical, creative thinkers with strong reasoning skills. They can apply knowledge, information, and research skills to complex problems in a range of contexts and are effective oral and written communicators.

The Melbourne educational experience prepares graduates to be entrepreneurial and innovative thought-leaders. Melbourne graduates bring research and inquiry skills to challenges in their workplaces and communities. They are adept lifelong learners who generate bold and novel ideas by critically evaluating alternative possibilities and viewpoints.

Active citizenship

Melbourne graduates have engaged with contemporary local, national, and global issues and developed an appreciation of the Asian region. They have a high regard for human rights, social inclusion, ethics, and the environment. Melbourne graduates are aware of the social and cultural diversity in communities and can work collaboratively with people from diverse linguistic and cultural backgrounds. In particular, they have an understanding of and deep respect for Indigenous knowledge, culture, and values.

The Melbourne experience supports a commitment to civic service in

---

59   University of Melbourne, 'The Melbourne Graduate'.

graduates' lives and careers, equipping them to be active, well-informed citizens who make substantial contributions to society. Graduates have the potential to be leaders in their professions and communities, with the capacity to work effectively across disciplines and cultures. Through advocacy and innovation, they are able to lead change for a sustainable future.

Integrity and self-awareness

Melbourne graduates are motivated, self-directed, and well-organised, with the ability to set goals and manage time and priorities. They are able to work effectively both independently and in groups. They are also highly self-aware and reflective, with skills in self-assessment, and place great importance on their personal and professional integrity.

The opportunities offered by the Melbourne experience help prepare graduates who are enthusiastic, self-assured, and confident of their knowledge, yet flexible, adaptable, and aware of their limitations. Melbourne's graduates are willing to explore, experiment, and learn from mistakes. They have empathy and concern for the welfare of others and can manage their own well-being.

University of New South Wales

Graduate Attributes as at 3 August 2020.[60]

UNSW graduates will be:
Scholars who are:
- understanding of their discipline in its interdisciplinary context
- capable of independent and collaborative enquiry
- rigorous in their analysis, critique, and reflection
- able to apply their knowledge and skills to solving problems
- ethical practitioners
- capable of effective communication
- information literate
- digitally literate

---

60   University of New South Wales, 'UNSW Graduate Attributes'.

Leaders who are:
- enterprising, innovative and creative
- capable of initiating as well as embracing change
- collaborative team workers

Professionals who are:
- capable of independent, self-directed practice
- capable of lifelong learning
- capable of operating within an agreed Code of Practice

Global citizens who are:
- capable of applying their discipline in local, national and international contexts
- culturally aware and capable of respecting diversity and acting in socially just/responsible ways
- capable of environmental responsibility

University of Queensland

Graduate Attributes as at 6 July 2020.[61]

In-depth knowledge & skills in the field of study
- A comprehensive and well-founded knowledge in the field of study.
- An understanding of how other disciplines relate to the field of study.
- An international perspective on the field of study.

In addition, bachelor with honours graduates will display
- where relevant, the ability to apply enhanced knowledge and core skills appropriate to the workplace.

Effective Communication
- The ability to collect, analyse, and organise information and ideas and to convey those ideas clearly and fluently, in both written and spoken forms.
- The ability to interact effectively with others in order to work towards a common outcome.

---

61 University of Queensland, 'Graduate Attributes'.

- The ability to select and use the appropriate level, style, and means of communication.
- The ability to engage effectively and appropriately with information and communication technologies.

In addition, bachelor with honours graduates will display
- The ability to clearly communicate the results of research in a format suitable for publication in the field of study; and
- The ability to explain clearly and defend research findings through oral presentations, including at conference standard.

Independence and Creativity
- The ability to work and learn independently.
- The ability to generate ideas and adapt innovatively to changing environments.
- The ability to identify problems, create solutions, innovate and improve current practices.

In addition, bachelor with honours graduates will display
- The ability to undertake supervised research, including the design and conduct of investigations, in a systematic, critical, and evidence-based manner, as an individual or as a member of a team; and
- The ability to apply and contribute skills and knowledge creatively and innovatively in a research environment.

Critical Judgement
- The ability to define and analyse problems.
- The ability to apply critical reasoning to issues through independent thought and informed judgement.
- The ability to evaluate opinions, make decisions and to reflect critically on the justifications for decisions.

In addition, bachelor with honours graduates will display
- The ability to identify problems appropriate for research and to pose research questions.
- The ability to make a critical analysis of the literature.
- The ability to analyse research data and to draw logical conclusions.

Ethical and Social Understanding
- An understanding of social and civic responsibility.
- An appreciation of the philosophical and social contexts of a discipline.
- A knowledge and respect of ethics and ethical standards in relation to a major area of study.
- A knowledge of other cultures and times and an appreciation of cultural diversity.

In addition, bachelor with honours graduates will display
- An appreciation of social and ethical responsibilities and the ability to apply ethical standards in research in the field of study.

University of Sydney

Graduate Attributes as at 6 July 2020.[62]

Graduate quality	Definition
Depth of disciplinary expertise	Deep disciplinary expertise is the ability to integrate and rigorously apply knowledge, understanding and skills of a recognised discipline defined by scholarly activity, as well as familiarity with evolving practice of the discipline.
Critical thinking and problem solving	Critical thinking and problem solving are the questioning of ideas, evidence, and assumptions in order to propose and evaluate hypotheses or alternative arguments before formulating a conclusion or a solution to an identified problem.
Oral and written communication	Effective communication, in both oral and written form, is the clear exchange of meaning in a manner that is appropriate to audience and context.
Information and digital literacy	Information and digital literacy is the ability to locate, interpret, evaluate, manage, adapt, integrate, create, and convey information using appropriate resources, tools, and strategies.
Inventiveness	Generating novel ideas and solutions.
Cultural competence	Cultural competence is the ability to actively, ethically, respectfully, and successfully engage across and between cultures. In the Australian context, this includes and celebrates Aboriginal and Torres Strait Islander cultures, knowledge systems, and a mature understanding of contemporary issues.
Interdisciplinary effectiveness	Interdisciplinary effectiveness is the integration and synthesis of multiple viewpoints and practices, working effectively across disciplinary boundaries.
Integrated professional, ethical, and personal identity	An integrated professional, ethical, and personal identity is understanding the interaction between one's personal and professional selves in an ethical context.
Influence	Engaging others in a process, idea, or vision.

---

62 University of Sydney, 'Graduate Qualities'.

PART 3
TEACHING FOR GRADUATE DEVELOPMENT: PEDAGOGICAL PRINCIPLES

14 | RELIGIOUS HIGHER EDUCATION AT THE CROSSROADS

THE NEED TO RECONSIDER EPISTEMOLOGY, PEDAGOGY, AND FORMATION.

Abstract

Religious Higher Education is at a significant crossroads in development, facing many strategic choices and challenges. Our institutions differ in discipline offerings, modes of delivery, theological focus, and pedagogy. As a result Religious Higher Education institutions can no longer be defined narrowly, and as such all face at times unique, although related challenges. However, could it be that in the midst of all this diversity today's universities have become disconnected from the key historical goals of scholarship–the search for wisdom, enlightenment, transformed lives, growth in intellectual, social and moral character, the virtue of 'charity', and of course 'quaint' ideas like devotion, fellowship and collegiality? In parallel, and in the face of criticism from within and without, universities now speak about desirable graduate attributes. Sadly, those described often have little relationship to human character, and even less to what universities actually do to and with students each day. In this paper, I will discuss what I see as three key dangers for Christian Higher Education, as well as three key priorities if we are to ensure that we don't follow the pathway towards mediocrity of many secular universities. The dangers are the loss of community and collegiality, a rise in individualism, and a failure to study in depth. The three priorities are the need to adopt an enhanced commitment to epistemology, pedagogy and formation as key components in reshaping and sustaining Christian higher education.

1. Conflicts of Culture, Pedagogy, and Purpose in Higher Education

After almost four decades of teaching, undertaking research, and filling varied leadership roles in universities, I want to step back to consider what I have learned about the state of higher education today. The sum total of my experiences within higher education has led me over time to reflect on what the modern university has become. As well, in the last twenty years in particular, I have considered faith-based institutions as a sub-category. And my broad conclusion? I see a very confused picture, characterised by conflicting messages about purpose, formation, and pedagogy. Forgive me for this somewhat cynical and frustrated reflection on how things are today.

Universities are very unhappy places; well, that's what every academic I know tells me. Academics are despondent about the way universities are run, they groan about the weight of their teaching and administration, they feel that there isn't enough funding, and they have difficulty forming relationships with colleagues. Students also have complaints. It's too expensive, workloads are too high, they have trouble balancing study, part-time work and life, and they decry the unavailability of academic staff. Almost no one attends lectures these days, and some don't even turn up for tutorials. The average full-time student can manage to spend no more than two to three days on campus each week. Administrative staff complain about both the academics and students, as well as how over-worked and underpaid they are.

Faculty in our universities seem to want less teaching and more research and scholarship. As well, they seek less time on campus and more time, well, off-campus, preferably overseas, doing research. I hope that our Christian academics never end up like this.

Administrative staff at universities would seem to dream of a place where they can administer higher education, while the students and faculty are off-campus causing them less disruption. As well, universities have become administrative fortresses, with office hours limited and minimal contact possible, except by email and occasionally phone. Impregnable websites are the repositories of the information students, and course applicants need to find answers to varied questions, largely unaided. In short, at most universities, it is almost impossible to find a lecturer or administrator by phone, and office doors are almost always shut.

Students also appear to have much simpler needs today; they want their degrees with minimal effort. And they want them in the shortest time possible, so they can get high-paying jobs, which allows lots of time to do things unrelated to their education.

Why is everyone so unhappy? What is at the base of such despondency on campuses? Surely not just being over-worked. Some academics in older universities point to a golden age in the 1950s and 1960s when teaching loads were lower, administration was minimal, professors had more time to 'profess', and scholarly interests were driven by one's interests. But if there was such a 'golden age', it has disappeared.

At one level, we could simply claim that the unhappiness is because the typical university lecturer is driven by personal ambition, the desire to achieve worldly acclaim, security of employment, and generous academic conditions. However, this seems at odds with previous generations where there was a desire to work, and in some cases, live on campus as Christians with different goals, ambitions, and priorities. Sadly, it also seems that Christian faculty in higher education is not immune to the behaviour of other faculty because they, at times, can be driven by the same goals. While, we would hope that Christian staff at Christian institutions might just be different, this doesn't always seem to be the case.

Today's secular universities have become disconnected from some of the key goals of scholarship—the search for knowledge, wisdom, enlightenment, transformed lives, growth in intellectual, social and moral character, an interest in the well-being of others, not to mention devotion, fellowship, and collegiality. I'm not suggesting these things are completely absent from the modern university, but when they are present, they stand out as a beacon, rather than being the norm.

I suspect that even some of our Christian institutions are losing sight of our ultimate purpose. I reviewed a major secular university recently over a period of six months. I concluded that the core motivation 'institutionally' seemed to be dominated by a desire to make money, and the overall intent being to get bigger and bigger. It seemed as I reviewed the university that it was beginning to look more like an ambitious business; a factory for graduates who deliver research headlines. In the process, the student body was changing. Students were wealthier and more ambitious than ever before and less interested in the life of the university except for what they were getting out of it. And all the while, I saw evidence that it was becoming increasingly disconnected from the things that once made it a great institution.

What DO universities aspire to in 2019? A perusal of some of their mission statements at the time of the conference was enlightening.[1]

The University of Sydney indicated that its mission/strategy was:

> To create a place where the best researchers and most promising students can achieve their full potential.

Western Sydney University saw its mission as:

> To be a university of international standing and outlook, achieving excellence through scholarship, teaching, learning, research and service to local and international communities, beginning with the people of Greater Western Sydney.

Cambridge University stated that:

> The mission of the University of Cambridge is to contribute to society through the pursuit of education, learning and research at the highest international levels of excellence.

Oxford University was suggesting their goal was:

> The advancement of learning by teaching and research and its dissemination by every means.

University mission statements are almost universally utilitarian in content and purpose. The best thing I could say is that, perhaps, they are undergirded by ethical and philosophical theory that is utilitarian in nature. That is, suggesting that the best action is the one that maximises utility, usually defined as that which produces the greatest well-being for the greatest number of people. Of course, we might well ask, just what do we mean by 'well-being' in the modern university?

Having critiqued some secular universities, we must ask, are the mission statements of our faith-based institutions better? You would hope so, but once again, they are quite mixed.

The Sydney College of Divinity at the time of the conference stated that its mission was to:

---

1 I should note that some of these may have changed since I presented my paper in April 2019.

> Provide high-quality, accredited courses in theology and related disciplines from undergraduate to postgraduate levels, including research degrees
>
> Encourage theological scholarship and train future theological scholars
>
> Prepare leaders who are well qualified to build up the Church
>
> Promote a theologically literate membership of the Church

Alphacrusis College simply stated that it exists for the purpose of:

> Equipping Christian leaders to change the world.

Avondale College suggested that it sought to:

> Foster a Christian higher education learning community that is dedicated to serving world needs.

Moore College, on the other hand, was seeking to:

> Enable men and women to deepen their knowledge of God, through higher education in the field of theology. This is so that they might faithfully and effectively live exemplary Christian lives, proclaim and teach the Word of God, and care for others in the name of Jesus Christ in all the world, to the glory of God.

There is considerable diversity in all of these statements.

Some quick observations.

Those I've picked from our faith-based institutions (randomly) are better than most of the universities but perhaps are still a little unfocussed. Dare I say it, I think some of our Christian institutions are becoming increasingly distracted as we grapple with survival in a sector that has ring-fenced us into a category that is penalised with reduced FeeHelp and a unique 25% additional penalty charge. How do we ensure our futures? Many of us are grappling with this question. And we do so as small institutions with varying levels of capital behind us. As well, we do this in a market that is limited by the size of the population who attend churches associated with us, as well as some that we manage to steal from other denominations. There is a small pool of students and some very doubtful funding.

This brings me to the second half of my paper, calling for our Christian institutions to ensure that they are not transformed increasingly into small-scale versions of secular universities. If we are to avoid this trap, there needs to be something distinctive about our epistemology, pedagogy, and formation that is reflective of our faith basis.

Some institutions have shown a desire to upscale operations, add diversity to the curriculum, and in some cases, new disciplines or fields of study that seem motivated by a desire to look more like universities. These are actions that I suspect are reflective of the need for survival rather than a vision that aligns with what we believe about our faith basis and our desire for student formation.

For over twenty years, I've been thinking much about how we might sustain institutions where we train our students to think theologically, by applying biblical truth to every current and future situation in life. One fundament that I feel strongly about is that everything we do in our colleges should be characterised by, or at least reflect, the Bible's teaching centred on the gospel of Christ and the human need for reconciliation with God. Even if an institution decides to have an MBA program, I'd hope that it would still be as committed to education and character formation based on learning in a Christ-centred community. Our Christian institutions need to be places where formal learning is just the beginning, as we shape people to become more effective Christian disciples, and as we experience learning and Christian growth together within a community. All that I've said so far leads me to ask everyone here to consider what pedagogy, community, and formation look like in your colleges.

2. What Does Pedagogy Look Like in my College, Subject, Class?

I believe that Christian pedagogy must be rooted in a clear understanding of God's purposes for his people 'in-between' this life and the next. The Bible suggests that our lives are to be centred on knowing and honouring God in the here and now, with an eye on the future as we await Christ's return and the coming of the kingdom of God. As we read in 1 Peter 1;2, our true and ultimate home is not on earth, for we are to live out our lives as 'aliens and strangers' (1 Pet. 1:17b; 2:9-12). We live between two worlds, and our pedagogy should reflect this 'in-between' existence.

In my book 'Pedagogy and Education for Life: A Christian Reframing of

Teaching, Learning, and Formation',[2] I argue that 'Education is the whole of life of a community, and the experience of its members learning to live this life, from the standpoint of a specific end goal'.[3] I want to suggest that it is the 'whole of life' that must continue to be our highest priority, for to do otherwise will lead us to become just like the universities many of us have fled.

My definition of education has two major propositions that gave shape to my book. First, education is indeed about the 'whole of life' of a community, not simply curriculum or method. Second, participants 'learn to live this life' together from a particular standpoint, goal, or purpose (telos). This is an education focused much more on the ends rather than simply the means; the 'why' rather than the 'what' and 'how'. Having said this, I must stress that any good degree in theology (like any discipline or field of study) must also give time to 'what' we teach and 'how' we do it. My use of the term pedagogy encapsulates (or attempts to make sense of) the orchestrated concern for the 'why', 'what', and 'how' of teaching.

As we train for ministry and life, the ends and means must always be seen in relation to the ultimate problems of life; problems that concern the nature and destiny of humankind. This should lead to a pedagogy that reflects an understanding that God made us in his image as creative, problem-solving beings, to seek him and live in relationship with Him and one another. While doing this, God also calls us to love, serve, and work with a knowledge of his risen Son in order to bring God the glory.

Education is a process of cultivation and formation. Put another way, the task of the teacher is the nurturing and transformation of habits of body and mind that enable our students to fulfil God's purposes for a life centred on Christ. This is a tough call given how little access we have to our students if you work in a university. And I probably should say, that even as tertiary educators—who might well be teaching a business course, teaching degree, or creative arts program—we must not lose sight of this imperative. Let me structure the rest of my paper around three questions that reflect my thesis within this conference paper. In doing so, I effectively offer a warning about the slippery slope we end may up on if we lose sight of the original purposes of our institutions.

---

2   Cairney, *Pedagogy and Education for Life*.
3   This definition was based on and inspired by a definition used by Montagu Vaughan Castelman Jeffreys in his book *Glaucon: An Inquiry Into the Aims of Education*. Although, I should add that the assumptions underpinning the words were not identical.

3. Understanding What We Mean by 'Pedagogy'

Any discussion of pedagogy is complicated today because the term has been used and abused in many ways. It has been captured by numerous interest groups.[4] However, if we look carefully at its etymology, we will find that the word is as old as formal education itself. For the ancient Greeks, its purpose was to lead the child as they grew in body, mind, and spirit. It involved 'an interaction between one who acts and one who is acted upon'.[5] Children were not assumed to find their own way into the community through a process of osmosis or discovery. They were led into it. It was also much more than teaching content, specific subjects, and skills.[6]

The emphasis on formation is critical to pedagogy. My view of pedagogy (and I'm pretty sure that of the early Greeks) is that learning and teaching is interwoven into the daily life of any community. I think similarly that such a process of formation, or even transformation, is what the Christian school or college desires to see. For the Bible's central message is about our transformation in and through Christ. We are what we live, not just what content is learned, the worldview the teacher holds, the exams we sit and pass, assignments completed, and so on. It is within the life of the community that lives and character are shaped, as we live, learn, and engage with others.

This is the view of pedagogy that I present in my book. When translated to our contemporary context, it leads me to suggest that pedagogy also encompasses '…how teachers orchestrate and sustain classroom learning and life, driven by an intent and telos'.[7]

This 'orchestration' of life in the Christian College (or school) should always be approached with the formation of the student for the glory of God as the priority. To consider a teacher's pedagogy, we also need to consider the teacher's knowledge, beliefs, and goals that shape their actions.[8]

In a sense, pedagogy is the embodiment (or enactment) of what good research, sound biblical understanding of personhood, and God's ultimate purposes for us in Christ would suggest we should do.

---

4   Cairney, *Pedagogy and Education for Life*, 32.
5   Gurley, 'Platonic Paideia', 351-377.
6   One of the best introductions to Paideia can be found in Peter C. Hodgson, *God's Wisdom: Toward a Theology of Education*.
7   Cairney, 33.
8   Beech, *Christians as Teachers*, 115-146. Beech's book includes an interesting discussion on the way that teacher beliefs impact even the most mundane of tasks in the classroom. He suggests that teaching Christianly means all activities can have pedagogical significance.

4. What Does Community Look Like in Our Colleges?

Closely related to pedagogy is the need for community. Community is at the heart of our Christian institutions. And nurturing effective Christian college communities requires an understanding that all educational institutions are complex places, made up of equally complex social groupings and relationships with reflected and embedded practices. They are not just physical places; they are relational places or spaces.

In effect, they are a patchwork of related and overlapping 'communities'. They are essentially communities of belief and practice.[9] I believe that understanding this is foundational to the creation of authentic Christian education and pedagogy. Lecturers and principals seek to create and shape metacommunities like colleges every day. It requires effort to influence culture and provide direction, and it is a very difficult and complex task.

One of the key tasks of the Christian educational institution is to reflect much on how we shape our classroom and institutional communities. These communities are shaped in part by the social groupings that are formed to help our students learn as they engage in different practices within the college community and beyond. Our aim should be to help them to see how they can live their lives across the numerous communities of practice that constitute their world and yet, all the while, be growing in Christ. And of course, we all live within many diverse communities. Some of these are 'controlled' by the educational institution, but many are not.

When students turn up at the institution's gate, ' … they come together to deal in their own fashion with the agenda of the imposing institution …'[10] They come as inhabitants of multiple communities of practice in which life is shared in meaningful ways. They participate as people who are existing members of varied groups, friendship cliques, churches, families, clubs, online communities, teams, and so on, often simultaneously. They participate socially just as much as they do intellectually, and as they do they exchange knowledge, beliefs, and practices, all of which has an impact on formation (more on this in a minute).[11]

How the institution manages or accommodates the interaction with, and relationship to such diverse intersecting and overlapping communities and their culture and practices, is critical. Our students are often members of families,

---

9   Cairney, 25.
10 Wenger, *Communities of Practice*, 78.
11 There was insufficient time to explore this point, but it is covered in depth in my book.

churches, friendship groups in and outside school, virtual communities via social media, sporting teams, clubs and so on. Can we help our students to negotiate and learn, in and from these communities, while also growing in faith and understanding of God within our institutions?

Having said this, I'm left with an uncomfortable question that I will leave with you to ponder. It might be all well and good to do what I'm suggesting for theology students, but what about Christian educators teaching education, business, media, accounting, and so on? How realistic is it to ensure that our faith remains at the very core of what we do in non-theological courses? I'm not sure. But if you are seeking to be a more comprehensive institution, then you, we, need to work it out because it is hard to point to many Christian universities around the world that moved from being theological colleges towards becoming comprehensive universities without the faith basis of these institutions becoming sidelined, ghettoised, or in some cases, lost completely.

5. How Concerned Am I with the Formation of My Students?

In 'Pedagogy and Education for Life', I argue that our pedagogy determines our focus and should be concerned very much with the formation of our students. We seek to place our mark on students in ways that should truly differentiate our colleges from secular universities. Our colleges, of course, are not meant to be completely separate or isolated from the world. After all, our graduates will often work in varied contexts around the world. If our colleges end up totally separate from the world, how will our students make their way in the world?

Pedagogy isn't the tool or strategy of the teacher as guard or overseer. It is more than curriculum, monitoring student behaviour, vetoing good and bad practices, or simply looking to squash ideas that don't fit within the teacher's worldview or beliefs. As well, as we seek to form our students, we must not confuse imparting knowledge with formation. Formation reflects and encapsulates all that we do in the classroom to create and sustain a community; a community focused on a coming 'Kingdom'. For you see, if it is an authentic 'Christian Education'—in all that we do, say, sanction, and plan—it should be centred on the end goal of seeing our students growing as people who understand, know, and seek the 'Kingdom of God'.[12]

---

12 Cairney, 34.

The ancient teacher, from whom many of our ideas on pedagogy have their foundation, had in focus a moral end, not a technocratic one. Hence, we need to ask ourselves, is my institution driven by the core propositions of our faith and a mission that centres on transformative pedagogy?

The model of pedagogy that I advocate in *Pedagogy & Education for Life* reflects a belief that pedagogy is not simply method, teaching strategies, or curriculum. Rather, it is our very practices, interwoven into the daily life of any community; such a pedagogy seeks to see classes, schools, and students transformed.

'Pedagogy' involves the formation of students, as well as the shaping of classroom and school cultural practices by teachers with the participation of many others.

Any discussion of pedagogy is complicated today because the term has been used and abused in many ways. The word is as old as formal education itself. It was derived from the Greek paidagogeo, a compound of paidos (child) and agogos (one who leads or guides).

For the ancient Greeks, its purpose was to lead the child as they grew in body, mind, and spirit. It involved 'an interaction between one who acts and one who is acted upon'.[13] Children were not assumed to find their own way into the community through a process of osmosis or discovery but were lead into it.

Pedagogy always was, and still is, much more than teaching content, specific subjects, and skills. The term as the ancient Greeks understood it gave rise to the word paideia, which for first-century Greeks meant the passage from boyhood to manhood, a process of becoming fully human or of turning young men into citizens.

The intent of paideia was to create a specific kind of Greek citizen who could take their place in Greek society as a leader. The ancient teacher had in focus a moral end, not a technocratic one. The word paideia is what Paul uses in Ephesians 6:4. It is often translated as 'discipline', which for the Greeks and Paul meant 'bring[ing] them up in the discipline and instruction of the Lord'.[14]

Pedagogy reflects and at the same time is interwoven into the daily life of the classroom. And the intent of Christian pedagogy must always have as its central goal the transformation of our students in and through Christ. Pedagogy encompasses the essence of how teachers orchestrate and sustain classroom learning and life. And this is always driven by intent and telos. This orchestration

---

13 Gurley, 'Platonic *Paideia*', 351-77.
14 Cairney, 33.

of the life of the classroom or school will always reflect the teacher's knowledge, beliefs, and goals that shape their actions.

Educational pedagogy is the collective shaping of the habits, beliefs, knowledge, dispositions, actions, and words of classroom or school members that will incline individuals and the institution toward the telos, end purpose, or goal of education. It incorporates how we teach (including method) and what we teach (curriculum), as well as why we teach.

In conclusion, an authentic Christian pedagogy will always reflect an understanding that Christian education is much more than the careful selection of method, content, strategy, and curriculum. Rather, as I have argued above, Christian education, like any education, should reflect the understanding that:

> Education is the whole of life of a community and the experience of its members learning to live this life from the standpoint of a specific end goal.

For those of us who teach theology embedded within courses that have vocational outcomes other than full-time Christian ministry, they still need to be situated within a broader understanding of God's purposes for our lives beyond vocational education. We could spend hours talking about Christian practices in our institutions. Craig and Dorothy Dykstra address such 'Christian Practices' and define them as:

> … the things Christian people do together over time to address fundamental human needs in response to and in light of God's active presence for the life of the world.[15]

While I like their definition, the central approach I explore in *Pedagogy and Education for Life* is not simply identifying and replicating Christian practices, or even 'secular liturgies' within life. Instead, my focus is on how Christian teachers and institutions can help their students to see, respond to, and navigate all of the practices of life (Christian and non-Christian) with a telos that is shaped by and directed toward the kingdom of God.

Alasdair Macintyre in his book 'After Virtue' reminds us that:

> Every activity, every inquiry, every practice aims at some good; for by "the good" or "a good" we mean that at which human beings aim.[16]

---

15 Dykstra, *Growing in the Life of Faith*, xii.
16 Macintyre, *After Virtue*, 173.

The question I leave you with is what do the practices of each of our institutions aim at?

Bibliography

Beech, G. *Christians as Teachers: What Might it Look Like?* (Eugene, Oregon: Wipf & Stock, 2015).

Cairney, T. H. *Pedagogy and Education for Life: A Christian Reframing of Teaching, Learning, and Formation.* (Eugene, Oregon: Wipf & Stock, 2018).

Dykstra, C. *Growing in the Life of Faith: Education and Christian Practices* (Louisville, Kentucky: Geneva, 1999).

Gurley, J. 'Platonic Paideia', *Philosophy and Literature* 23 (1999).

Hodgson, P. C. *God's Wisdom: Toward a Theology of Education* (Louisville, Kentucky: Westminster John Knox Press, 1999).

Jeffreys, M. V. C. *Glaucon: An Inquiry Into the Aims of Education* (London, UK: Pitman, 1950).

MacIntyre, A. *After Virtue: A Study in Moral Theory* (3rd ed. London: Bloomsbury, 2013).

Wenger, E. *Communities of Practice: Learning, Meaning, and Identity* (Cambridge, UK: Cambridge University Press, 1998).

Trevor Cairney
The University of Sydney
info@trevorcairney.com

15 | RELIGIOUS FREEDOM AND THE THEOLOGICAL ACADEMY

Abstract

Decent human beings who act ethically and with integrity, as one would hope graduates of theological study would be, should have a working knowledge of the principles of religious freedom for a number of reasons. First, extending liberty to other members of the community to make decisions about religious matters, and so far as possible, live out those commitments, is just the right thing to do. Humans created in the image of God should be given that respect. Second, such an attitude should be modelled on others in the religious communities they may be leading or guiding. Thirdly, the principles of religious freedom are vital for the ongoing mission of religious groups in Australia. Where such freedom is challenged, leaders may need to know enough about those principles to act to defend the mission of their community in the face of challenges from other groups or, in some cases, the government. Those who teach in the theological academy also need a working knowledge of these principles, as the legitimacy of the enterprise of theological education is increasingly challenged in the higher education sector, especially when conducted in accordance with the tenets of traditional faith communities. Indeed, theological education may increasingly need to equip students and staff for a godly response when opposition becomes persecution. The paper aims to provide a framework for these issues and identify areas where further work may be needed.

1. Introduction

The topic of 'religious freedom' has assumed more importance in Australia in the last few years. There are a number of reasons for this, including the increasingly ethnically and culturally diverse nature of Australian society, the shrinking number of persons who express commitment to what was previously the mainstream Christian consensus in society,[1] and a general move in the wider community away from a previously shared set of moral values about issues to do with sexuality and 'birth and death' issues.

For all these reasons, and perhaps others, there has been a heightened debate over the extent to which Australian society should support decisions of religious believers to live and act in ways that are mandated by their religion but which are not usually supported for the community at large or are unpopular. Given the role of universities as a key source of general education and research into important social issues, it is not surprising that some of these matters have started to affect the life of the university. While one might think at first that 'religious freedom' challenges are not applicable to those engaged in theological education, I would maintain that they will be relevant to theological teachers as they are relevant to all who are engaged in tertiary education.

Decent human beings who act ethically and with integrity, as one would hope graduates of theological study would be, should have a working knowledge of the principles of religious freedom for a number of reasons. First, extending liberty to other members of the community to make decisions about religious matters, and so far as possible to live out those commitments, is just the right thing to do. Humans created in the image of God should be given that respect. Second, such an attitude should be modelled to others in the religious communities they may be leading or guiding. Thirdly, the principles of religious freedom are vital for the ongoing mission of religious groups in Australia, and where such freedom is challenged leaders may need to know enough about those principles to act to defend the mission of their community in the face of challenges from other groups or, in some cases, the government. Those who teach in the theological academy also need a working knowledge of these principles, as there are more and more challenges in the higher education sector to the legitimacy of the enterprise of theological education, especially when conducted in accordance with the tenets of traditional faith communities. Indeed, theological education

---

1 See the most recent census data indicating only about 52% of Australians regard themselves as 'Christian'.

may increasingly need to equip students and staff for godly response when opposition becomes persecution. The paper aims to provide a framework for these issues and to identify areas where further work may be needed.

Here, I want to begin this discussion by outlining some of the challenges faced by believers who are part of university communities and to note how the law and other policies currently deal with these challenges. These lessons are applicable across a range of disciplines. They are particularly germane to theological educators working in 'secular' institutions, but many of these concerns may well arise even in confessional educations institutions.

The paper is not uniformly pessimistic about religious freedom on campuses in Australia but notes that there are areas where, arguably, change needs to take place to protect this important human right.

I work at the University of Newcastle, and most of my examples of law and policy relate to that context. I should say at the outset, however, that in my experience, our university has generally supported appropriate academic and religious freedom, and many of the most concerning developments that can be seen overseas are not present here. But 'the price of freedom is eternal vigilance',[2] and so it is worth being aware of possible future challenges.

2. Examples of Challenges to Religious Freedom at Universities

As mainstream Christian views have become more unpopular, there have been various challenges to those views being lived out, or spoken about, at universities, which are often, of course, made up of people from a more 'progressive' end of the political spectrum. Here are some brief examples. Some relate to students (and staff will, of course, be interested in what their religiously motivated students may experience), some to staff.

2.1 Challenges due to General Religious Activities

Student challenges Christian student groups have operated on university campuses for many years, in many cases being the largest active student groups.

---

2 As with many striking quotes, the source of this useful phrase is greatly disputed. It certainly was used in 1852 by Wendell Phillips in speaking about the abolition of slavery. This piece indicates it was around in other sources in the earlier part of the Nineteenth Century: http://www.thisdayinquotes.com/2011/01/eternalvigilance-is-price-of-liberty.html.

Those groups, since they exist for the purpose of sharing the Christian gospel with non-believers, and helping Christian students live out their faith, will usually want to ensure that their office-holders at least share the ethos of the group. But this may be challenged by a 'secular' student organisation that thinks that membership and offices in all student groups should be open to all.

This issue came up a few years at the University of Sydney, where the student newspaper (Honi Soit, 13 March 2016) reported that:

> The University of Sydney Union (USU) has threatened to deregister the Sydney University Evangelical Union (EU) from the Clubs & Societies program over the latter's requirement that all members must make a declaration of faith in Jesus Christ.[3]

In the end, this proposal was dropped after public concerns were expressed about the foolishness of an approach that singled out religious groups, as opposed to other 'viewpoint-based' groups, such as student political clubs, from being able to restrict leadership and membership to those who shared the ethos of the group. Sydney University Union withdrew its threat to de-register the Sydney University Evangelical Union for its policy requiring members to be Christians.

Nevertheless, this sort of pressure from universities, as well as from student unions, may be expected to continue. To take one more recent example, from the United States, at the University of Iowa, a Christian student group, Business Leaders in Christ ('BLinC'), had been penalised because it would not agree to appoint to its leadership a same-sex attracted student, who said that they would not undertake to comply with the group's commitment to biblical sexual values. The University claimed that this was a breach of its Policy on Human Rights, forbidding discrimination on the basis of, among other things, sexual orientation. BLinC claimed, however, that the issue was not the student's orientation but their express refusal to modify their behaviour to accord with biblical norms.

The student group succeeded in obtaining a preliminary order from a federal court staying the proposal to deregister it.[4] They have since been successful in

---

3   See my blog post 'Religious Ethos and Open Membership at Sydney University' (17 March 2016) at https://lawandreligionaustralia.blog/2016/03/17/religious-ethos-and-open-membership-at-sydney-university/ commenting on the episode.

4   See my comment on the case in 'Iowa University Christian student group reinstated by Federal judge' (26 Janurary 2018) at https://lawandreligionaustralia.blog/2018/01/26/iowa-university-christian-student-group-reinstated-byfederal-judge/ .

getting the judge to extend the order allowing them to operate on campus, pending a final hearing.[5] One of the reasons that the judge ruled in their favour was that many other 'viewpoint-based' clubs had also not included a formal commitment to 'nondiscrimination' in appointing leaders, but none of those other clubs had been penalised. This suggested to the judge that the real reason for the action was a disapproval of the specific doctrines favoured by the Christian club, which the judge said would be a breach of the 'free speech' First Amendment rights of the club.

Are there other challenges faced by students? We will comment on some 'hate speech' issues below. But another common challenge faced by student groups comes where a university suggests that they should not be involved in sharing the gospel with other students. Sometimes, this comes as a refusal to allow groups to hand out advertising materials. So far, as far as I am aware, no university has tried to completely ban students from talking to other students about religion, but as bizarre as this sounds, it may be worth noting that some such attempts seem to have been made in Queensland primary schools over the last few years.[6] So, it may not be impossible that a rule of this sort might be proposed at universities. (I should stress that such a proposal would probably be unlawful for reasons I will note later. But, at the moment, I am simply providing examples of possible issues.)

2.2 Staff Challenges

What Sort of Religious Freedom Challenges Do University Staff Face? It has to be said that, at least for academics, Australian universities still generally retain support for the idea of 'academic freedom'—that members of academic staff should be allowed liberty to pursue research as their academic judgment sees fit and to report their views honestly without fear of penalty. It is a little disturbing that it seems to be downplayed somewhat, but at our university, we do have a reference in the 'Code of Conduct' to this idea:

> (30) We promote collegiality by behaving inclusively and openly and fostering academic freedom.[7]

---

5   See https://www.insidehighered.com/news/2018/08/03/christian-student-group-sues-u-iowa-incites-debatereligious-freedom-and-lgbtq (3 August 2018).

6   See my comment in 'Can kids tell other kids about Jesus at school?' (15 April 2017) at https://lawandreligionaustralia.blog/2017/04/15/can-kids-tell-other-kids-about-jesus-at-school/ .

7   See https://policies.newcastle.edu.au/document/view-current.php?id=204&version=1.

Still, there can be challenges with a staff member expressing their views on a controversial topic in appropriate ways. Of course, Christian staff at secular universities are committed to serving the educational purposes of the university, and we ought in no way to misuse our position to turn lectures or seminars into evangelistic opportunities. (And even at confessional institutions, there will be appropriate times for such things and other times that are not appropriate.) But, in my view, it should be clearly acceptable when teaching areas that involve matters on which there are differing views in society for the Christian perspective to be presented as one of those views. And a staff member should feel no compunction to hide their private views when questioned. (There have certainly been many staff members from the 'progressive' end of the spectrum who have been very open about their Marxist or other critiques of orthodox opinions.)

There was one episode recently in Australia where a university academic faced calls to be dismissed because of their religious views. One blog reported it this way:

> Dr Steve Chavura, a Senior Research Associate at Macquarie University, has been the subject of calls for his dismissal from the university. What is Dr Chavura's sin? Dr Chavura is on the board of the Lachlan Macquarie Institute, a Christian organisation that serves to foster critical thinking and robust Christian contributions to public policy.[8]

In the end, Macquarie University, to its credit, paid no heed to the calls for Dr Chavura's dismissal or discipline for his religious views. But it was telling that someone thought that his mere association with a conservative Christian group could somehow justify this.

2.3 Challenges Faced due to 'Hate Speech' Prohibitions

While the area of so-called 'hate speech' is broadly a part of the general issue of challenges to religious freedom, there are enough specific cases on this sort of area that it is worth highlighting as a separate point.

Here, one of the problems we face is this contested phrase. If 'hate speech' meant 'calling for violence against someone on the basis of their identity', then no Christian would support a right to speak in this way. But sadly, in an example of

---

8   Murray Campbell, *Calls for Macquarie University to Distance Themselves from Christian Academic* (29 March 2017) <https://murraycampbell.net/2017/03/29/calls-for-macquarie-university-to-distance-themselves-fromchristian-academic/>.

the common phenomenon of 'verbal inflation', a phrase that all would agree is wrong in its most extreme example can come to be applied to much more innocent behaviour. For some people, 'hate speech' has come to mean 'speech implying hatred on the part of the speaker'. In particular, it is commonly used to refer to 'speech which somehow disagrees with a fundamental identity issue of someone'. The most obvious example is the Bible's teaching that homosexual activity is wrong. To relay that teaching is now sometimes seen as inciting 'hatred' for homosexual persons. In this way, what seems like a reasonable restriction of speech to avoid physical harm can become a means of censoring Biblical moral views.

2.3.1 Students

A student, then, who expresses the Bible's view may be accused of 'hate speech'. Two prominent examples will suffice. One comes from the UK, the case of Felix Ngole. To quote from an earlier online comment on the case:

> The decision, Ngole, R (On the Application Of) v University of Sheffield [2017] EWHC 2669 (Admin) (27 October 2017), was an application for judicial review of an administrative decision made by the Appeals Committee of the University of Sheffield Senate, on appeal from a disciplinary decision (made by a "Fitness to Practice" committee in the Department of Sociological Studies) to in effect expel Mr Ngole from his course of study. In making its decision the FTP committee and the Appeals Committee claimed that they were applying "professional practice" standards laid down by the relevant body which accredited social workers in the UK, the Health and Care Professions Council (HCPC).[9]

The heinous action for which Mr Nglole was dismissed from his post-graduate social work course was that, in a series of comments on the website of a US TV channel, he had explained (after being asked) what the Bible said on homosexuality. The university disciplined him for this.

---

9   See my post 'University student dismissed for expressing Biblical view on homosexuality' (3 November 2017).<https://lawandreligionaustralia.blog/2017/11/05/university-student-dismissed-for-expressing-biblical-view-onhomosexuality/ >.

When these online remarks were brought to the attention of the university authorities, they investigated and concluded that he was not fit to be a social worker. The initial departmental investigation 'had concerns about the condemnation of same-sex sexual relations, or "homosexuality", in the terms used, on a public forum to which people including social work service users could link him by name'.

Mr Ngole's dismissal is still being appealed through the courts. He recently had a hearing before the English Court of Appeal.[10]

The second example is closer to home. The Australian Christian Lobby reports on the case of 'Joshua', a university student who had simply offered to pray for a friend who was struggling who was then reported to campus authorities and was unbelievably suspended from his course until completing 'counselling' and told not to come onto campus until this was done.[11]

Thankfully, the involvement of lawyers organised by ACL meant that the university concerned subsequently completely reversed its disciplinary processes and cleared Joshua's record.

2.3.2 Staff

So far as I am aware, no staff member at an Australian university has been removed or disciplined for their speech. However, there have been a number of incidents in the US. Let me cite one. In the middle of the fevered recent debate about the nomination of Judge Brett Kavanaugh to the US Supreme Court, a US professor tweeted to a large number of students that due process required that people not be assumed guilty.

> Nearly 100 students at the University of Southern California attended a rally at noon on Monday demanding a tenured professor be fired after he sent a reply-all email last Thursday to the student body noting that 'accusers sometimes lie'.

Professor James Moore emailed:

> If the day comes you are accused of some crime or tort of which you are not guilty, and you find your peers automatically believing your

---

10 See https://www.premier.org.uk/News/UK/Christian-thrown-off-social-work-course-slams-judge-s-orwellian-ruling (Tues 12 March 2019).
11 There is a video report of the case here: https://youtu.be/rZbq7kc2rrY .

accuser, I expect you find yourself a stronger proponent of due process than you are now.[12]

The university so far has not met those demands, but reports indicate that the Dean of the Faculty met with protestors. Dean Knott said to the crowd:

> What [Professor Moore] sent was extremely inappropriate, hurtful, insensitive. We are going to try to do everything we can to try to create a better school, to educate the faculty.

In terms of free speech on our (Newcastle) campus, there are some helpful guidelines in the University's Media Policy.

> (8) In engaging with the media, expert commentators can expect the support of the University. This does not imply endorsement of a particular view put forward, but means that their right to speak as a University staff member in their area of expertise will be upheld.

> (9) The University recognises and respects the concept of academic freedom. It expects that staff and students will accept the responsibility that academic freedom imposes: to ensure that information provided to the media and public is supported by peer-reviewed evidence.[13]

But it would be useful to see a commitment to free speech which also covered a situation where a university staff member commented in private on something which they felt strongly about, even if it was not within their area of expertise, so long as it did not breach the law.

A number of concerns have been raised in recent years about a tendency for US universities to cave in to radical student demands that universities be made 'safe spaces', by which seems to be meant places where no student will ever have to be aware that others oppose their lifestyle decisions. Calls for controversial speakers not to even be heard (so-called 'no platforming' demands) have also become more common.[14]

---

12 See 'Students Demand Professor Be Fired After He Champions Due Process, Says 'Accusers Sometimes Lie', *PJMedia* (1 Oct 2018). <https://pjmedia.com/trending/students-demand-professor-fired-after-he-championsdue-process-says-accusers-sometimes-lie/>.
13 See https://policies.newcastle.edu.au/document/view-current.php?id=107&version=1 .
14 For a helpful review and critique of these movements, see the recent book by Lukianoff and Haidt, *The Coddling of the American Mind*.

But it is very encouraging to see that, recently, a number of Australian university chancellors have recently spoken out in favour of strong protection of 'free speech' on campuses and against the idea of so-called 'safe spaces'.[15] UWS Chancellor Dr Peter Shergold is quoted as saying:

> Universities need safe spaces for students, be they LGBTI or Muslim ... where they can go and talk to each other. But university campuses cannot be safe spaces in terms of ideas. People should be challenged by ideas, see a diversity of ideas. That's the heart of the institutional ethos of a university.

And ANU Chancellor Gareth Evans is also quoted:

> Lines have to be drawn, and administrators' spines stiffened, against manifestly unconscionable demands for protection against ideas and arguments claimed to be offensive. Keeping alive the great tradition of our universities—untrammelled autonomy and untrammelled freedom of speech—is a cause to which university chancellors [...] should be prepared to go to the barricades.

3. The Biblical Basis for Religious Freedom

So far, I have noted a number of issues that impact the freedom of Christian students and staff to live out their religious commitments. Let me more briefly spell out some of the reasons why religious freedom is an important value.

One is that the Bible, especially the New Testament, assumes that all people in society should be free to make their own choice about what religion to follow. Now, of course, the Bible is in no doubt as to who the true God is, that Jesus Christ is his Son, and that salvation is only found through him. But the assumption of the Bible is that God does not coerce people into faith but encourages them to freely choose.

While the position of the nation of Israel in the Old Testament was somewhat unique, being a political nation, which was meant to be made up of God's people, when we come to the New Testament the status of being one of God's

---

15   See 'University chiefs unite to defend free speech', *The Australian* (5 October 2018). https://www.theaustralian.com.au/higher-education/university-chiefs-unite-to-defend-free-speech/newsstory/96e87108a7a1559e3104997a93322000

people comes solely from putting faith in Jesus Christ. Christians are to take the message of Jesus into the world. This is not to be done with weapons or force but with the aim of persuading people to see the truth (see, for example, the reference to Paul's methods of evangelism in the book of Acts, where he sought to 'persuade' – Acts 18:4, 'Every Sabbath he reasoned in the synagogue, trying to persuade Jews and Greeks'.)

Historically, the commitment of Christians to putting the facts before others, so they could make their own choice, led over a period of time to a strong belief that all people should be free to make up their own minds.[16]

4. Religious Freedom as a Fundamental Human Right

In more recent years, especially following the terrible religiously based persecutions carried out by the Nazis in World War II, the international community has adopted a number of statements of fundamental human rights, and one of those rights has been said to be religious freedom.[17] One of these is the Universal Declaration of Human Rights, and another is the International Covenant on Civil and Political Rights which, in Art 18, provides:

> 1. Everyone shall have the right to freedom of thought, conscience and religion. This right shall include freedom to have or to adopt a religion or belief of his choice, and freedom, either individually or in community with others and in public or private, to manifest his religion or belief in worship, observance, practice and teaching.
>
> 2. No one shall be subject to coercion which would impair his freedom to have or to adopt a religion or belief of his choice.
>
> 3. Freedom to manifest one's religion or belief may be subject only to such limitations as are prescribed by law and are necessary to protect public safety, order, health or morals or the fundamental rights and freedoms of others.

---

16 For a recently published monograph on the origins of 'religious freedom' in the Christian world-view, see Wilken, *Liberty in the Things of God*.

17 For my most recent survey of laws in Australia protecting religious freedom, see Foster, N. J. 'Religious Freedom in Australia Overview 2017 Update', *Human Rights Law Alliance* (2017). <http://works.bepress.com/neil_foster/112/> .

Note here that religious freedom does not simply extend to 'the right to go to church' (though, that is important and challenged in some countries around the world) but also covers the right to 'manifest' religion in 'observance, practice and teaching'. Appropriate limits can be put on that right to manifest, under art 18(3), but only subject to certain strict requirements spelled out in that sub-article.

It is important to note that international treaty obligations (even treaties to which Australia has formally committed itself, like the ICCPR) are not binding under Australian domestic law until further implemented in Australian law in some way. So, it is not possible to rely directly on ICCPR art 18 as a remedy. But the courts have often said that a treaty like the ICCPR can at least be 'taken into account' in interpreting legislation that contains some ambiguities. And the fact that Australia has acceded to a treaty may give constitutional power to the Commonwealth Parliament to enact a law that implements the treaty.

Following the same-sex marriage 'postal survey' and enactment of amendments to the Marriage Act 1961 allowing such marriages, the then-Prime Minister commissioned an 'expert panel' chaired by the Hon Phillip Ruddock to enquire into the need to provide stronger protections for religious freedom.[18] The Ruddock Report was finally made public late last year, in the middle of an unhelpful controversy about the right of religious schools to take their religiously-based moral framework into account in dealing with students and staff.[19]

It may be as well to summarise this debate and current responses, as these matters may continue to be raised in the forthcoming election debates. The laws in question relate to 'educational institutions' generally, which, in some cases, will include confessional bible and theological colleges at the tertiary level, not just primary and secondary schools.

One of the ways that religious freedom is protected in Australia is that various laws prohibiting discrimination contain internal clauses that 'balance' religious freedom rights with rights not to be unjustly treated on irrelevant grounds.[20] One obvious example is that a theological college set up to teach in accordance with a specific theological tradition should be allowed to say that its academic staff must be adherents to that tradition. In NSW, at the moment, this

---

18 See https://www.pmc.gov.au/domestic-policy/religious-freedom-review for the review.
19 I have provided a summary and initial response to the Ruddock Report on my blog, starting with this one on Dec 13 (https://lawandreligionaustralia.blog/2018/12/13/the-ruddock-report-has-landed-part-1/) and extending into two later parts.
20 For a general analysis of such clauses, see N. Foster, 'Freedom of Religion and Balancing Clauses in Discrimination Legislation'.

is not a problem because there is no law in this state forbidding discrimination based on religious belief. But in other jurisdictions where this is a ground for unlawful discrimination, relevant clauses will allow selection of staff who are believers to teach.[21]

However, other problems may be presented where the law forbids discrimination on the grounds of 'sexual orientation'. For example, a theological college that wishes to operate in accordance with the long-standing biblical view that homosexual activity is contrary to God's purposes for humanity may be met with a claim that refusing to employ someone who wants to agitate against that view (because they are gay) is unlawfully discriminating. Or they may wish to ask students who are attending the college to commit to behaving in accordance with biblical sexual standards.

In NSW, there is a prima facie prohibition on discrimination against someone because of their sexual orientation under the Anti-Discrimination Act 1977. But s 56 of that Act contains a 'balancing clause' as follows:

> **56 RELIGIOUS BODIES**
>
> Nothing in this Act affects:
> (a) the ordination or appointment of priests, ministers of religion or members of any religious order,
> (b) the training or education of persons seeking ordination or appointment as priests, ministers of religion or members of a religious order,
> (c) the appointment of any other person in any capacity by a body established to propagate religion, or
> (d) any other act or practice of a body established to propagate religion that conforms to the doctrines of that religion or is necessary to avoid injury to the religious susceptibilities of the adherents of that religion.

Somewhat oddly, the NSW Act also contains a series of general exclusions, so that the Act does not apply to a 'private educational authority'. The definition of this term would seem to mean that the Act, in general, does not apply to

---

21 See this paper for some of the details of such clauses across Australia: 'Protecting Religious Freedom in Australia Through Legislative Balancing Clauses', paper presented at Freedom 17: Religious Freedom in a Secular Age? (Freedom for Faith, 14 June 2017, Canberra, ACT) <http://works.bepress.com/neil_foster/111/>.

confessional Bible or theological colleges or universities:

> '**Private educational authority**' means a person or body administering a school, college, university or other institution at which education or training is provided, not being:
>
> (a) a school, college, university or other institution established under the Education Act 1990 (by the Minister administering that Act), the Technical and Further Education Commission Act 1990 or an Act of incorporation of a university, or
>
> (b) an agricultural college administered by the Minister for Agriculture.

However, the Commonwealth has also enacted a prohibition on sexual orientation discrimination under the Sex Discrimination Act 1984 (Cth). Section 37 of that Act replicates the provisions in s 56 of the NSW law for 'religious bodies' generally, and there is a specific further clause in s 38 dealing with 'educational institutions':

> **Educational institutions established for religious purposes**
>
> 38 (1). Nothing in paragraph 14(1)(a) or (b) or 14(2)(c) renders it unlawful for a person to discriminate against another person on the ground of the other person's sex, sexual orientation, gender identity, marital or relationship status or pregnancy in connection with employment **as a member of the staff** of an educational institution that is conducted in accordance with the doctrines, tenets, beliefs or teachings of a particular religion or creed, if the first-mentioned person so discriminates in good faith in order to avoid injury to the religious susceptibilities of adherents of that religion or creed…
>
> 38 (3) Nothing in section 21 renders it unlawful for a person to discriminate against another person on the ground of the other person's sexual orientation, gender identity, marital or relationship status or pregnancy in connection **with the provision of education or training** by an educational institution that is conducted in accordance with the doctrines, tenets, beliefs or teachings of a particular religion or creed, if the first-mentioned person so discriminates in good faith in order to avoid injury to the religious susceptibilities of adherents of that religion or creed. (emphasis added)

An 'educational institution' is defined simply as 'a school, college, university or other institution at which education or training is provide'" (s 4(1)). Section 38(1) deals with the employment of staff, and s 38(3) relates to dealings with students.

This paper is not the place to rehearse the lengthy debate about the impact of these provisions and whether or not they should be amended, or how. In short, the Ruddock Report recommended preserving these provisions but making them more transparent by requiring students and staff be notified. There was then a press beat-up alleging that Christian schools, in particular, were expelling gay students. That this was not happening did not prevent politicians promising to see that it never happened. But the Coalition, the ALP, and the Greens all had different proposals as to how any change should take place. One particularly dangerous religious freedom, reflected in a bill supported by the ALP, would have taken away rights in relation to 'education' generally from all religious bodies, not just schools and colleges.[22]

The upshot of these arguments is that the Morrison government said they would refer these issues to the ALRC, but the Opposition seems to have indicated they would enact sweeping changes if elected. It is to be hoped that if elected, they will not simply press ahead with the previous bill, which was far too widely drawn.[23]

5. The Governance of Universities: A Mix of Law and Policy

So how is religious freedom legally protected at universities at the moment? The governance of Australian universities is a complex mix of federal and state legislation, as well as internal policies of different sorts. In brief, taking my university as an example, some are established formally under an Act of the NSW Parliament—see, for example, the University of Newcastle Act 1989 (NSW) ('UoNA'). Hence, our institution is governed by the laws of NSW. We are also, of course, subject to any valid Commonwealth legislation enacted under the powers given to the Commonwealth Parliament in s 51 of the Constitution.

Other private institutions may be set up simply as a company or an

---

22 See my comments at https://lawandreligionaustralia.blog/2018/11/29/alp-bill-on-religious-schools-andstudents/ .
23 See here for my latest update: https://lawandreligionaustralia.blog/2019/02/25/post-ruddock-report-developments/.

incorporated association or as part of a larger group.

Education as such is not a 'head of power' under the Constitution, but the way that taxation and funding operates in Australian means that the state of NSW receives money for the running of a public university by way of a grant from the Commonwealth. The Commonwealth then exercises a high degree of input into educational standards, degreeconferring rules, etc. So far as I am aware, the Commonwealth has not so far attempted to attach conditions relating to academic or religious freedom to the grants it makes for the operation of universities, but in theory, this would be possible. It is interesting to note that last year, the federal education minister urged universities to have in place policies supporting free speech, especially dealing with the question of who should pay for increased security when topics being discussed at university venues draw a hostile crowd.[24] Presumably, it would be possible to include requirements of this sort as a condition of a recurrent Commonwealth grant.

In addition to the above, universities are empowered to make subordinate legislation' of different types: 'by-laws' approved by the NSW Governor (see, e.g. UoNA s 28), 'rules' made by the University Council (UoNA s 29; see the University of Newcastle By-Law 2017, cl 20), and various other 'policies' and 'procedures' made by different internal bodies.

6. Legal Protection of Religious Freedom in NSW

So how is religious freedom protected legally in NSW at the moment? The previously linked lengthy paper gives a broad overview,[25] but I will aim to summarise it briefly.

Section 116 of the **Commonwealth Constitution** provides that the Commonwealth Parliament shall not make any law 'for prohibiting the free exercise of any religion', but as a general protection of religious freedom it has a number of weaknesses:

- It does not apply to state parliaments.
- It has so far been interpreted fairly narrowly by the High Court, but I

---

24 See 'You protest, you pay: Education Minister's bid to bolster free speech at universities', *Sydney Morning Herald* (22 September 2018) <https://www.smh.com.au/politics/federal/you-protest-you-pay-education-minister-s-bidto-bolster-free-speech-at-universities-20180921-p5057h.html>.
25 See Foster (2017), above n 17.

think there is scope for a more sensible interpretation in the future to provide some better protection.

There is some broad protection for 'free speech' on controversial issues through **an implied right of 'freedom of political communication'** recognised in a number of recent decisions by the High Court of Australia as a right attaching to all Australian citizens. This right cannot be breached by either the Commonwealth or the States, as it is a right that applies to both those levels of government.

In Attorney-General (SA) v Corporation of the City of Adelaide [2013] HCA 3, for example, the High Court held that a ban on 'street preaching' could be justified on 'traffic management' grounds, but not if the reason for the ban was related to the content of the message being conveyed. French CJ commented at para [43]:

> Freedom of speech is a long-established common law freedom. It has been linked to the proper functioning of representative democracies and on that basis has informed the application of public interest considerations to claimed restraints upon publication of information. (footnotes omitted)

Later in that case, at para [67], his Honour commented that even 'religious' matters fell within the protection of the implied freedom:

> Plainly enough, preaching, canvassing, haranguing and the distribution of literature are all activities which may be undertaken in order to communicate to members of the public matters which may be directly or indirectly relevant to politics or government at the Commonwealth level. The class of communication protected by the implied freedom in practical terms is wide.

All the members of the Court, in that case, made it clear that a law forbidding communication could be justified for traffic reasons, but not on the basis of some objection to the content of the communication:

> [T]he only purpose of the impugned provisions is to prevent obstruction of roads. It follows that the power to grant or withhold consent to engage in the prohibited activities must be administered by reference to that consideration and none other.[26]

---

26 See Attorney-General (SA) v Corporation of the City of Adelaide [2013] HCA 3. Hayne J at 140. http://proctors.com.au/

So, this freedom may in some cases provide protection for religiously-motivated free speech.[27]

There is, however, as mentioned previously, **no general prohibition against discrimination on the grounds of religion** in NSW (unlike most other states and territories).

There is limited protection against religious discrimination in employment under the Fair Work Act 2009 (Cth). While s 351 of that Act seems to provide general protection against 'adverse action' based on religion, s 351(2) means that it is not operative in NSW since our local law does not prohibit religious discrimination.

The only other FWA provision providing protection for an action based on religion is a little-used provision of the FWA that was enacted based on Australia's international law obligations, s 772. In Part 6-4, it 'contains provisions to give effect, or further effect, to certain international agreements relating to discrimination and termination of employment' (s 769). Under s 772, it is unlawful for an employer to terminate an employee's job for a range of reasons, including under s 772(1)(f) 'religion'. But note that this only applies to termination, and there are strict limitation requirements, including the need to file a claim within 21 days of the dismissal (s 774).

While, as noted above, international treaties are not directly enforceable, in at least one decision the Full Court of the Federal Court was prepared to strike down a state regulation impairing religious freedom (and free speech) on the basis that the courts will **read** general 'regulation-making' powers as not intended to unduly interfere with these internationally recognised human rights.[28]

Laws against discrimination on certain grounds do contain what I have elsewhere called '**balancing clauses**' designed to protect religious freedom, although mainly that of religious groups as opposed to that of an individual. Still, these may be useful should some student Christian group policies be challenged. For example, if a Christian student group declines to appoint a

---

27 The limits of this protection are presently being considered by the High Court of Australia in proceedings challenging state laws forbidding any communication about abortions being made within 150 m of abortion clinics. See Clubb v Edwards, the documents for the appeal being at http://www.hcourt.gov.au/cases/case_m462018 ; the case was heard from 9-11 October 2018, but we don't know when it will be handed down.

28 See Evans v NSW [2008] FCAFC 130, where the regulation prohibited protestors from 'annoying' participants in the Catholic World Youth Day celebrations. See also Aboriginal Legal Rights Movement Inc v South Australia and Stevens (1995) 64 SASR 551, [1995] SASC 5532, where a similar principle of 'legality' protecting religious freedom was said to be operational.

person advocating homosexual activity to an executive position, and is alleged to be guilty of discrimination on the basis of sexual orientation, it can probably rely on specific 'balancing clauses' in that legislation allowing them to operate in accordance with their beliefs.[29]

An important provision, however, relates specifically to universities, which seems to have been included in most state legislation establishing these. The UoNA, for example, provides as follows in s 24:

> 24 No Religious Test or Political Discrimination
> A person shall not, because of his or her religious or political affiliations, views or beliefs, be denied admission as a student of the University or be ineligible to hold office in, to graduate from or to enjoy any benefit, advantage or privilege of the University.

While so far as I am aware, this provision (and others like it) have never been referred to in court, it may be a very useful additional religious freedom protection for those in 'secular' universities.

7. Protection of Religious Freedom under Policy Guidelines

What about protections under university policies? I list the ones that I have found at my university. These examples may assist in finding similar policies in place at other institutions.

One slightly odd thing is that our university used to have a 'procedure' that referred to the display of banners and posters, which for some reason was repealed and not replaced during 2017.

However, there is still a reference to this 'Banner and Poster' procedure which includes the following:

> The policy aims to allow **freedom of expression and the free flow of information**, whilst ensuring that information posted on the campuses is respectful of all individuals, is not defamatory or derogatory, and is consistent with the University's Code of Conduct.[30]

---

29 For the Commonwealth sphere, see Sex Discrimination Act 1984, s 37; in the state area, see Anti-Discrimination Act 1977 s 56. Arguably, if the law of the land would allow a Christian group the privilege to run their group in accordance with their religious beliefs, then any attempt by a university to impose a stricter standard might be attacked as beyond the power of the university to make such rules.

30 https://uonmarketing.zendesk.com/hc/en-us/articles/201209874-Banner-and-PosterProcedure.

This is good as an affirmation of the need to support free speech. The University general Code of Conduct includes the following:

> (30) We promote collegiality by behaving inclusively and openly, and fostering **academic freedom**.

I noted previously the Media Policy, which says that:

> The University recognises and respects the concept of **academic freedom**.

And cl 3(b) in the Code of Ethical Academic Conduct, under Student Responsibilities, says that one such responsibility is:

> To act at all times in a way that respects the rights and privileges of others and shows commitment to **freedom of expression**.[31]

The University, for its part, undertakes in cl 2(a) of that Policy:

> To provide a work and study environment free from discrimination or harassment on the basis of race, nationality, sex, age, political conviction, sexual preference, marital status, **religious belief**, disability, family responsibilities or carers' responsibilities.

It is also good to see that the University Academic Promotion Policy contains the following:

> (9) The promotion process will have regard for the principles of equal opportunity, fairness and social justice. These principles require that there be **no discrimination** against any individual on the basis of personal characteristics such as sex, sexuality, ethnicity, age, disability, cultural background and **religion**.[32]

The University has a general policy designed to forbid discrimination or harassment: *Promoting A Respectful And Collaborative University: Diversity And Inclusiveness Policy*.[33] One important feature is the definition of 'harassment' in cl (33):

---

[31] https://policies.newcastle.edu.au/document/view-current.php?id=203&version=1.
[32] https://policies.newcastle.edu.au/document/view-current.php?id=238&version=1.
[33] https://policies.newcastle.edu.au/document/view-current.php?id=88&version=1.

> Harassment means any unwelcome behaviour that intimidates, offends, or humiliates, an individual, or group of people, and occurs because of race, colour, nationality or ethnic origin, **religion**, sex, pregnancy (actual, presumed and/or breastfeeding) marital status, age, disability, transgender status, homosexuality, sexual preference, carer's responsibilities, trade union activity or association, political opinion or irrelevant criminal record or some other characteristic specified under anti-discrimination or human rights legislation.

There are some dangers to free speech in this wide-ranging definition, which sets the bar very low, that behaviour simply has to 'offend' and be 'unwelcome' to someone. (Comments about a Biblical view of sexuality, for example, were alleged to be "offensive" in an action against the Roman Catholic Archbishop of Hobart a few years ago, although the action never proceeded to a final trial.)[34] However, there is a useful linked document that gives examples of the sort of thing that is intended to be caught, and in general terms that document refers to behaviour at the more serious end of the scale.[35] In fact, it is useful to note that item (xii) on the list illustrating 'harassment' is:

> (xii) making derogatory remarks about someone's race, **religion** and customs.

8. Applying these Protections to the Challenges

Finally, then, how do these protections currently apply to the challenges identified above? The following is just a general summary of the ways that some of these challenges might be addressed. In each case, one possible challenge has been chosen; others could be added.

8.1 General religious activities

(i) Students and student groups

Suppose a student Christian group told that it could not limit its membership, or its leadership, to those who adhered to a Christian ethos. One option would

---

34 See my blog post on the episode, "First they came for the Catholics..." (13 November 2015) https://lawandreligionaustralia.blog/2015/11/13/first-they-came-for-the-catholics/.

35 See https://policies.newcastle.edu.au/download.php?id=199&version=2&associated.

be to ascertain whether a prohibition on 'viewpoint-based' membership was being enforced against other religious groups and other 'viewpoint-based' clubs such as a political club or a feminist action group. If not, if the Christian group had been singled out, then this could be said (at my University) to be in breach of the University's general "Promoting" policy noted above, which includes the following statement:

> (13) The University does not tolerate any unwelcome or unfair treatment by any person or group of people whilst engaged in activity or business on behalf of or in association with the University, regardless of the day, time or place. Unwelcome or unfair treatment may be expressed through bullying, discrimination, **unlawful discrimination**.

And the following definition of 'unlawful discrimination':

> (37) Unlawful Discrimination is when an individual or a group of people, are treated unfairly or less favorably than another person or group on the basis of [...] **religion**...

So, to penalise a Christian group for doing something, but not to complain when that thing is done by non-Christian groups, seems to amount to unlawful discrimination. Without going into the details, there are various administrative law remedies that may be invoked if the University fails to act in accordance with its own published policies.

It may also be argued that in such a case, the University would have breached the law, by reference to s 24 of the UoNA, noted above, which forbids the University from making someone ineligible to 'enjoy any benefit, advantage or privilege of the University' on the basis of their 'religious... affiliations, views or beliefs'. Clearly, it is an advantage for a student club to be recognised by the University and to be able to book rooms and operate on campus. To deny a group such an advantage on the basis of their Christian beliefs would be to breach s 24, and again there would be a range of litigation options, especially in relation to breach of an act of parliament.

Of course, it may be that a rule of this sort was rolled out for all 'viewpoint' clubs. This would be unlikely (would the feminist club really want someone who was a Donald Trump supporter on their executive?). But if it happened, then perhaps a challenge may be possible under the 'free speech' remedies noted below.

(ii) Staff

Suppose a staff member was threatened with discipline or termination due to their membership of an unpopular religious group. As above, to do this would arguably breach the University's self-imposed 'Promoting' policy, but would also pretty clearly breach s 24 of the UoNA. It would also arguably be actionable in the Federal Court as a breach of s 772 of the Fair Work Act 2009.

If there was a threat that a person would not be promoted due to their openly but politely expressed religious views, then this would seem to be a breach of the Academic Promotion Policy cl (9) noted above.

8.2 Free speech issues

(i) Students and student groups

Suppose a Christian student group was told that it could not encourage its members to share the gospel of Jesus with other students. If this prohibition were simply imposed on the Christian group and not others, the above arguments about religious discrimination would apply.

In addition, however, there would be 'free speech' arguments that could be made. The University would arguably be in breach of its own policies in favour of 'freedom of expression' (see for Newcastle, e.g., the Banner and Poster policy still cited above.)

In particular, it could be argued that the principle of support for free speech is such an important legal value that parliament could not have intended to allow the University to restrict free speech in such a way without explicit authority (see the Evans case noted above.) Or one could argue that the 'implied freedom of political communication' would restrict the limits of any law made under authority of an enactment of the NSW parliament that would purport to restrict free speech in this way.

(ii) Staff

Suppose a staff member were told that because of their comments on an internet forum, they would be disciplined or terminated. Discrimination arguments would be possible here, especially under s 24 UoNA. It would also be possible to argue the 'free speech' points noted above. In particular, as it related to a member of academic staff, the University has expressed support for 'academic freedom' under its *Code of Conduct* cl (30), and this is likely to be a key point in arguing for academic free speech.

Conclusion

The above has been a quick survey of some areas that require more unpacking. But one thing that is fairly clear is that, while there is some support for religious freedom at Australian universities at the moment, there are several areas where there are uncertainties and gaps. It is to be hoped that future changes may prove useful in plugging those gaps and providing a framework where a healthy debate on religious issues can take place at Australian tertiary campuses.

Bibliography

Foster, Neil J. "Religious Freedom in Australia overvidew 2017 Update" *Human Rights Law Alliance* (2017).

Foster, Neil J. "Freedom of Religion and Balancing Clauses in Discrimination Legislation" *Oxford Journal of Law and Religion 5*, (2016), 385-430.

Foster, Neil J. "Protecting Religious Freedom in Australia Through Legislative Balancing Clauses", *Freedom 17: Religious Freedom in a Secular Age?* (2017).

Likianoff, Greg and Johnathan Haidt. *The Coddling of the American Mind* (Penguin, 2018).

Wilken, R. L. *Liberty in the Things of God: The Christian Origins of Religious Freedom* (Yale: Yale UP, 2019).

Websites

ALP Bill on Religious Schools and Students, lawandreligionaustralia.blog

Calls for Macquarie University to distance themselves from Christian Academics, murraycampbell.net

Can kids tell other kids about Jesus at school? lawandreligionaustralia.blog

Christian student group sues u iowa – www.insidehighered.com

Christian thrown off social work course, www.premier.org.uk

Eternal Vigilance is the price of liberty, www.thidayinquotes.com

First they came for the Catholics, lawandreligionaustralia.blog

Iowa University Christian student group reinstated by Federal Judge, lawandreligionaustralia.blog

Religious Ethos and Open Membership at Sydney University, lawandreligionaustralia.blog

Policies, policies.newcastle.edu.au

Post Ruddock Report Developments, lawandreligionaustralia.blog

Religious Freedom Review, www.pmc.gov.au

Students demand Professor be Fired, pjmedia.com

The Ruddick Report has Landed, lawandreligionaustralia.blog

University chiefs unite to defend free speech, www.theaustralian.com.au

University student dismissed for expressing Biblical view on homosexuality, lawandreligionaustralia.blog

You Protest, you pay, www.smh.com.au

Neil Foster
Newcastle Law School
neil.foster@newcastle.edu.au

16 | THE ROLE OF CURRICULUM IN DEVELOPING CHARACTER-ORIENTED GRADUATE ATTRIBUTES WITH AN ILLUSTRATION FROM CHURCH HISTORY

Abstract

The paper presents a philosophical and strategic platform for designing and implementing curriculum with the aim of producing decent human beings who act ethically and with integrity. It focuses on graduate attributes drawn from the Australian Qualifications Framework, specifically the capacity for critical analysis of complex knowledge and professional practice, the exercise of informed and balanced critical judgement in problem identification and solving, and the personal responsibility for one's own learning and autonomy in decision-making. The paper adopts the position that curriculum considerations have a key role in the development of such desirable character attributes. With an illustration from church history, it suggests an approach to curriculum design that is intentional and strategic in the progressive development of character, with the aim of producing graduates capable of taking critically informed, just, and autonomous stances in society.

1. Identifying Desirable Graduate Attributes

Graduate attributes are those aspirational qualities espoused by all higher education institutions as they seek to produce successful graduates of high calibre in a range of personal and professional life settings. Typically, these have been expressed in terms of proficient acquisition of specialist knowledge, adroitness of performance of professional skills, and expertise in the application of such knowledge and skills to their life settings. Such categories of attributes have been seen traditionally as demonstrable and measurable, thus by implication reliable, and so they have proved to be attractive to auditing bodies who rely on tangible outcomes in bench-marking institutional performance. In recent times, there has been a growing expression of dissatisfaction with such a limited perspective, as employers and community have called for a greater emphasis on integrated character formation and good citizenship as requisites of a good education.[1] This requires a re-orientation of aspiration, which leads us into the less comfortable zone of the intangibility of humanness, itself difficult to define, hard to identify, and evasive in evaluation. Such a re-orientation understandably sits awkwardly with the traditions of content mastery and performative skills, given its alarming association with a slide into emotive subjectivity at the cost of authentic academic rigour. The position of this paper is that such a re-focusing on character-forming attributes is not revolutionary, but rather already sits potentially within the currently accredited curriculum frameworks and may well be developed by a more strategic approach to structuring such attributes intentionally into the curriculum we deliver.

To contain this discussion within a short exercise, we will take three current statements of graduate attributes from the Australian Qualifications Framework,[2] which lend themselves directly to the kind of character formation that we seek to achieve in producing decent human beings who act ethically and with integrity. With varying nuances at undergraduate and graduate course levels, the following attributes feature prominently in higher education statements. Both bachelor and master courses seek to produce, inter alia, graduates who:

- critically review and analyse complex knowledge and professional practice (GA 1);
- exercise critical thinking and judgement in problem identification and solving (GA 2); and
- take responsibility for their own learning and autonomy in decision-making (GA 3).

---

1 For example: Ball, *Transforming Theology*, 81–85; Smith & O'Flynn, 'Responding to Complexity', 119–128; Hockridge, 'Rethinking our Approach to Student Formation', 200–214; Mudge & Fleming, '"To Take You Where You Do Not Wish To Go"', 123–139.
2 AQFC, *Australian Qualifications Framework*. This Framework is currently under review, but the examples used in this discussion are illustrative of current thinking about graduate attributes.

Such graduate attributes are more than academic skills; if developed intentionally and strategically, they can become a part of who the graduate is.

2. Curriculum Is Central to All Academic Programs

Higher education is, of course, a multi-faceted undertaking. It includes many tensions among factors such as recruitment and clientele, human and physical resources, learning environments and management systems, student welfare and support, vocational outcomes, community demand and engagement, as well as the formal and informal curriculum. Recently, in Australia, there has emerged a growing concern for the quality of the overall student experience. This has been voiced in a number of significant reports emanating from overarching bodies, such as the Council of Private Higher Education (COPHE) and the Tertiary Education Quality and Standards Agency (TEQSA).[3] The COPHE report was a benchmarking exercise that analysed the experience of first-year students, with a focus on the transitioning experience of commencing students. While it was not comprehensive, it provided a window into practices. The TEQSA report was more comprehensive and focused on first-year attrition rates in various higher education institutions. In both reports, the main focus was on what is being done or needs to be done in areas of contextual support, such as generic study skills, pastoral care, and student welfare. Observably high student attrition rates (most noticeably in theological education) are seen as a marker of inefficient systems of student support. Yet, neither report focused on courses. There were occasional references to learning management systems and teaching methods but virtually nothing significant on curriculum. With reference to theological education, in particular, traditional classical curriculum still dominates, with some tinkering only in matters of subject combinations and majors, and little attention given to the core elements of curriculum. Curriculum is the sacred cow of theological education, despite common criticism of the shortcomings of graduate outcomes. Yet, surely the link between curriculum design and delivery and desired graduate outcomes is clear. Ten years ago, Sherlock made the penetrating observation that statements of graduate attributes 'are of little use if they are not fed back into the design of learning outcomes for

---

3   COPHE, *Benchmarking First Year Institutional Student Engagement.* Australian Government, TEQSA, *Characteristics of Australian Higher Education Providers.*

disciplines and units'.[4] Today, as evidenced in these major reports, we are still focusing on contextual support systems without commensurate action on curriculum. The elements of student welfare and attrition are unquestionably important. However, the complexity of such contextual factors notwithstanding, the formal curriculum lies at the heart of every educational enterprise as the fundamental rationale for the institution's existence. This paper is an attempt to throw some specific light on the role of the formal curriculum in developing character, not as an adjunct to academic purpose, but as a central plank in the academic program.

A fundamental factor in improving student retention and enhancing graduate attributes is a curriculum designed to motivate and to facilitate successful progression through and completion of a course. Several generic issues arising from recent Australian research point to common features that de-motivate students and thus militate against the development of desirable graduate attributes, including:

- a lack of adequate preparatory skills development for successful study in theological fields
- a heavy overload in introductory units of academically and personally challenging content
- a lack of perceived connection to the contemporary student's prospective world in terms of applied content and learning processes
- a pervasive fragmentation of course units with a subsequent lack of integration of content knowledge, practical skills, and personal values.

Several further specific points emerge, including:

- the concern with the fragmented nature and the lack of effective integration within traditional theological curricula[5]
- the ideal of a staged developmental structure rather than, or in conjunction with, the traditional segmented content approach to fields and majors[6]
- the aspiration to move from competence to capability[7]
- the recognition of the learning characteristics of the iGeneration[8]

---

4   Sherlock, *Uncovering Theology*, 85-86.
5   Ball, *Transforming Theology*, passim.
6   Ball, *Transforming Theology*, 141-144.
7   Smith & O'Flynn, 'Responding to Complexity', 119-128.
8   Martin, 'Theology for the iGeneration', 147-157.

- the need for a strategic approach to transitioning first-year students into theological study.[9]

By taking such concerns into consideration, we may develop curriculum principles that facilitate character-oriented graduate attributes. A distillation of all associated factors leads to one overarching principle of curriculum design and delivery, namely, the primacy of hermeneutics over content and performative skills for character formation. This is not hermeneutics limited to biblical studies, but the hermeneutics of all content areas, where critical analysis, independent judgement, and autonomous learning are woven into the fibre of all study programs: biblical, theological, historical, and pastoral.

3. Curriculum Design

To develop a strategic proposal for constructing a curriculum that intentionally addresses student character formation, an appropriate starting point is a recognition of student perceptions and needs.

A student's perseverance and personal development are intrinsically motivated by students' perceptions of units and courses. Typically, there are three salient areas of perception, with success typically requiring a positive perception in at least two of these areas:

- The unit is important: to personal development; to ministry enhancement; to vocational pathways;
- The unit is doable: within learning capacity; with adequate resources and skills tuition to ensure success;
- The unit is enjoyable: engaging the learner actively; engaging with the learner's lifestyle and personal attributes.

Within a usual range of adult intellectual capacity, a positive perception of any two of these three characteristics will typically lead to perseverance; the absence of any two of them will typically lead to dissatisfaction, often contributing to attrition.

To facilitate successful and motivated progression through a course, a course needs to be seen to have the following three attributes:

---

9   COPHE, *Benchmarking First Year Institutional Student Engagement*.

- Order: especially with first things first; introductory units establish skills and transitional frameworks for ongoing success;
- Progression: with discernible links from introductory skills through to advanced skills and cognitive engagement;
- Coherence: with integration of disciplines; connected knowledge, skills, values; holistic and explicit connection with graduate attributes.

Within a usual range of individual tastes and interests, a positive perception of any two of these three characteristics will typically lead to course satisfaction, with the overall course seen as 'making sense'; the absence of any two of them will typically lead to dissatisfaction, with limited attainment of desired graduate attributes.

Flowing from such awareness, we can establish a strategic framework to lead to the ultimate goal of personal character formation. The first stage is designed to transition into theological thinking and study processes before encountering mass content:

- Set up a framework for exploration and integration to be revisited throughout the course
    - Locate the learner in relation to the program ahead
    - Establish realistic individual starting points
- How to study theology deeply, skilfully, and safely; establish that critical development is not anti-spiritual; initiate scholarship with a safety net
    - Rather than a heavy initial diet of Old Testament Survey, New Testament Survey, Greek I, Church History Survey, and Theology 1, which creates content overload and presents numerous internal conflicts.

The second stage is designed to explore rather than to impose a theological corpus:

- Provide the opportunity for personal selection, engagement, and application
    - With the goal to develop the person, not just knowledge
- Explore for discovery and discernment, not imposition and absorption.

The third stage is designed to integrate theological understandings and personal values:

- Incorporate identity formation alongside theological growth at all stages of the course

- Progressively focus on conceptual appropriation and living (lived) application
- Develop an integrative 'capstone' ethos by the end of the course.

A recommended curriculum structure that incorporates such stages will employ a three-level scaffold, which can readily apply to all content areas, no matter how courses are structured in terms of majors or specialisations:

- Level 1: position for the transition to theological education
  - establish personal and common goals; effective approaches to learning.

At this level, the focus is on GA 1: critically review and analyse complex knowledge and professional practice. The emphasis is on establishing a reliable framework for the critical analysis of content in the field of study. It takes cognisance of the learner's personal history and aspirations and provides the tools that will enable the learner to process content in ways that fit those aspects. This stage is not about masses of new information, but it is mainly concerned with setting the learner up for success and meaning in learning.

- Level 2: explore to discover theological and personal meaning
  - generate comprehensive ethos rather than comprehensive content.

At this level, the focus is on GA 2: exercise critical thinking and judgement in problem identification and solving. It builds on the platform of Stage 1 by using those tools to explore issues from various angles, to deal with differing perspectives and understand conflicts and resolutions, be they conceptual, pragmatic, or technical. Learners will be confronted by challenges and scenarios in research and dialogue, and they will need to have the liberty of exploring with an intellectual and spiritual safety net, as they learn to consolidate their spiritual awareness conjointly with their intellectual expansion. The development of informed and balanced problem-based judgement is a key element in character formation, which can be learnt in, but need not be limited to, any subject.

- Level 3: integrate to complete a phase of learning
  - not to 'complete' learning
  - promote spirit and structures of life-long autonomous learning.

At this level, the focus is on GA 3: take responsibility for their own learning and autonomy in decision-making. Building on the previous stages, this level focuses on the learner's integration and personal appropriation of principles and knowledge learnt, now applied to specific areas of personal relevance. It provides progressively for the learner's initiative in shaping and conducting the study. It does not aim to 'finish off' the learning, but it aims strategically to allow the learner to devise and take responsibility for personal actions and outcomes. In short, this is where the learner 'makes sense' of it all, as far as this phase of learning is concerned.

There are inevitable pedagogical considerations in all of this. While pedagogy is not strictly a part of curriculum, there needs to be an alignment of curriculum principles and pedagogical methods: We cannot expect the development of independent critical judgement if methods focus on content absorption and toeing an establishment line. Therefore, appropriate pedagogical philosophy and principles need to be employed in conjunction with curriculum design. A character-forming pedagogical ethos will focus more on developing flexible capability—the capacity to adapt to change and generate new, useful knowledge for improved practice—rather than mere content competence—what individuals know or do in terms of skills and knowledge. Learning approaches should utilise the contemporary reality of the iGeneration, in terms of learners sourcing their own information, learners controlling their learning, and learners engaging with technology. Recent research has aired numerous approaches to such formative methods. Some prime local examples have been detailed by Tim Cooper in his work on developing history activities,[10] by James Dalziel in his work on Developing Scenario Learning,[11] by Karina Kreminski and Michael Frost in their work on missional leadership,[12] by Steve Taylor and Rosemary Dewerse in their work on flipped learning,[13] and by Ben Chenoweth in his work on biblical fiction.[14] Excellent coverage of creative teaching methods is provided by Stephen Brookfield in his Skillful Teacher publication.[15] There are many more, and such creative methods are certainly within easy reach of most of our theological educators.

---

10 Cooper, 'Transformative Learning in Church History', 201-210.
11 Dalziel, 'Developing Scenario Learning', 17-25.
12 Kreminski and Frost, 'Theological Education for Missional Leadership', 175-186.
13 Taylor and Dewerse, 'Curiosity and Doubt in Researching the Future', 426-452.
14 Chenoweth, 'The Pedagogy of Biblical Fiction', 284-302.
15 Brookfield, *The Skillful Teacher*, especially ch. 6 'Lecturing Creatively', 69-82, and ch. 12 'Teaching Students to Think Critically', 155-167.

4. An Illustration from Church History

Let me now give a practical illustration of these ideas drawn from my own teaching of church history.

As a first step, I seek to establish a guiding rationale for studying history, of any kind, with specific application to the church. There are many approaches to such a rationale, all of which have merit, but we need to clarify where we stand at the outset, as this will shape our learning and teaching processes. Some of the main approaches often expressed, explicitly or implicitly, go along the following lines.

We study history in order:

- to study the past as 'pure' academics.

    This sees history as a chronicle of antiquities, studied for its intrinsic interest, with a focus on the narrative and characters of the evolving story. It keeps the subject of history at a remote, and therefore, safe distance from our contemporary situation.

- to learn about the past to understand the present.

    This approach brings the past into contact with the present, as a genuine quest to understand how we arrived at where we are today, and so has value in providing an informed base for discussion of our present condition.

- to learn about the past to justify our present.

    This is a (not always) subtle variation on the previous rationale, as it looks to the narratives of the past to validate rather than to evaluate our current position. We see regular references to our (American) constitution, our (Westminster) heritage, our (democratic) tradition, and the (Anglican, Baptist, Catholic) way of doing things. The appeal to tradition for vindication is seen as a strong safeguard against heresy and error, but it is not always used for the healthiest of developments.

- to learn from the past to avoid repeating its mistakes.

    This approach ushers in a note of critical engagement. Honest analysis and appraisal of our historical narrative can provide insights into principles and shaping factors at play in all eras, which can serve to guard against perpetuating the acknowledged sins of the past. 'If we don't learn from the mistakes of the past, we are doomed to repeat them' is a popular observation. This is a healthy approach, but it is typically self-critical and largely defensive in its focus on avoiding wrong rather than developmental in generating progress.

- to learn from the past to evaluate our present.

    This approach is more dynamic, as it takes the previous approach into a balance of positive and negative appraisal, wherein we learn to value our good history and acknowledge our bad history. It is far more generative of desirable and balanced character formation than the previous approaches.

- to learn from the past to appreciate our present and to steer our future with integrity.

    Naturally, being the last in my list, this approach is the one I espouse as a philosophy of history. To me, this sits at the apex of the historical rationale hierarchy, in that it embraces but extends all the previous approaches. It is not sufficient to know the facts of our past or to understand or even to appraise our present; historical study needs to equip us to direct our future efficiently and ethically. This is where both knowledge and character merge, and so this is my overarching goal in teaching church history.

While this philosophical consideration has addressed the teaching of history, I am confident that every one of these rationale statements could be equally applied with minimal variation to virtually every other content area in the theological curriculum.

Following the establishment of our rationale, the next step is the strategic structural incorporation of graduate attributes into the curriculum, with the desired graduate attributes to the fore, as outlined in the recommended curriculum structure above.

At the first level of teaching, the emphasis is on the development of GA 1 (critically review and analyse complex knowledge), with the development of a workable historical hermeneutic. Students are led in how to work within a simple analytical grid of historical cause, course, and consequence, with a focused treatment of primary historical documents. They read the documents, find out the details of the historical context that led to the issue of the document, analyse the development of that issue by reference to the document and associated secondary literature, and identify the short- and long-term outcomes of the issue and/or the document itself. Guidelines for writing a formal analysis are given; sample analyses are provided for class analysis (that is, the sample analysis is itself analysed); practice in writing historical analyses is undertaken. The need to focus on the centrality of primary material informed by a wide range of reliable secondary commentary becomes an established modus operandi, which students may take with them into all sorts of disciplines and dialogues.

At the second level of teaching, the emphasis is on the development of GA 2 (exercise critical thinking and judgement), with the extended application of the first-level analytical tools to an expanded critical arena. There is now a movement from documentary analysis to engagement with historiography, which engages the students in the critical interpretation of course data through different eyes. In a recent exercise, students were provided with and led through guidelines on how to write an evidence-based historical essay. They were then given a two-page note on conflicting perspectives of Anabaptist history in the Sixteenth Century, a topic which has engendered heated debate and widely variant evaluation both in the Sixteenth Century and in the pages of history books ever since. They were then set the task of constructing a three-part essay or oral presentation, presenting a statement of advocacy for Anabaptism, followed by a denunciation of the movement, and a final statement on 'the proper place' of Anabaptists in history. There was no right or wrong answer in this; the students were required to arrive at a judgement based on evidence and critical interpretation of variant views to discern a way forward for balanced and credible dialogue. The resultant clarity of vision, respect for variant views, and ability to reach fair judgements spoke highly of ethical and well-informed character.

At the third level of teaching, the emphasis is on the development of GA 3 (take responsibility for their own learning and autonomy in decision-making). This involved a process of informed and autonomous decision-making, which went beyond the set texts. Students were required to deal empathetically with disparate perspectives on a topic close to the daily reality of their own experience, where voluminous references to scholarship may not always be available. The extension of the previous stage of learning was the need for students to identify such a topic (within guiding parameters), to locate and evaluate appropriate source material, and stand at a critical arm's length from a topic in which they may well be personally involved, either actually or potentially. The field of study was an issue in denominational history at the state level, a field which directly involved all the ministry candidates in that class. Examples of debates on issues were provided as a starting point, and some general direction was provided, but the rest of the task was based on self-directed research and judgement, a developmental exercise in autonomous learning and taking responsibility for that learning.

This scaffolded approach to developing the listed graduate attributes saw encouraging progress in students' learnt ability to act in critically informed ways, make ethical and balanced contributions to dialogue, and combine responsibility for their own firm conclusions with an authentic respect for the equally firmly held conclusions of others. This last point is worth emphasising, as it went beyond mere toleration of different views (which tends to imply, 'You're wrong but I won't argue'); rather, it attained genuine respect (which implies, 'Your view is different from mine but is nonetheless equally valid'). This is a mark of intellectual rigour merged with ethical character—and that is a graduate attribute worth developing.

5. Application to Character-Oriented Graduate Attributes

This paper has sought to show how the development of ethical character can comfortably sit beside the attainment of those traditional academic attributes that typify our qualifications frameworks. While such congruence may happen incidentally, it can be facilitated intentionally by means of curriculum that is strategically shaped towards such an end. Such realignment of curriculum philosophy and consequent structure requires a re-orientation away from mass content delivery and analysis as the core of curriculum to a focus on developing those disciplines within a person with reference to the content under study. It does not abandon content; rather, it sees content not as an end in itself but as a means of developing the desired character in graduates. The paper has taken three general academic attributes as an illustration of the sort of marriage of attributes that can be pursued in any course, regardless of its length or content.

There is, of course, a set of underlying assumptions in such a notion. It is assumed that developing the art and skills of independent judgement leading to evidence-based conclusions is likely to produce critically thinking people who are not merely whimsical crowd-followers. It is assumed that a well-developed ability to achieve respectful, informed, and balanced perspectives on difficult issues is a good defence against bigotry and ignorance-based polemic—the bane of much of our contemporary destructive dialogue. The establishment of such a constructively critical habitus in graduates is proposed as one means of producing decent human beings who act ethically and with integrity, in all areas of personal, professional, and societal life. From the perspective of history, analysing and interpreting all texts, all narratives, in terms of historical causation and outcomes assist in the development of fair-minded, ethically consistent, and autonomous problem-solving and social engagement at all levels. While the illustration has been taken from church history, the suggested curriculum principles are equally applicable to all other content disciplines.

From a reading of many recent reports and reviews, it appears that curriculum is the conservative sacred ground of theological education, which makes it easy to retain as is and plough it as deeply as we can. It takes courage to grow a curriculum, which makes it hard to cultivate and produce freshness. Student welfare and support sources have received much recent attention from official circles. They are indisputably important in theological education; however, they are not what defines that education. Curriculum is at the heart of any educational institution, the sine qua non of its existence: Everything else supports the curriculum. To focus all our energies on the peripheral elements of resources and support, important as they are, but to ignore curriculum, is tantamount to tinkering around the edges. If that is the limit of our reforms, then we run the real risk of remaining as tinkers rather than teachers. If we are to be serious about developing character as an integral part of our mission, then we need to address such an aspiration at the very heart of our educational delivery: the formal curriculum.

Bibliography

Australian Government, Tertiary Education Quality and Standards Agency. *Characteristics of Australian Higher Education Providers and Their Relation to First Year Student Attrition* (June 2017).

Australian Qualifications Framework Council. *Australian Qualifications Framework* (2nd edn; 2013).

Ball, L., *Transforming Theology. Student Experience and Transformative Learning in Undergraduate Theological Education* (Preston, VIC: Mosaic, 2012).

Brookfield, S. D. *The Skillful Teacher: On Technique, Trust, and Responsiveness in the Classroom* (3rd edn; San Francisco: Jossey-Bass, 2015).

Chenoweth, B. 'The Pedagogy of Biblical Fiction: Where Research and Creativity Collide', in Ball, L. & Bolt, P.G (eds.). *Wondering about God Together. Research-Led Learning and Teaching in Theological Education* (Macquarie Park, NSW: SCD Press, 2018): 284-302.

Cooper, T. 'Transformative Learning in Church History', in Ball, L. & Harrison, J. R. (eds). *Learning and Teaching Theology. Some ways Ahead* (Northcote, VIC: Morning Star, 2014): 201-210.

Council of Private Higher Education. *Benchmarking First Year Institutional Student Engagement, Pathways and Retention Across HE Institutions* (January 2017).

Dalziel, J. 'Developing Scenario Learning', in Debergue, Y. & Harrison J. R. (eds.). *Teaching Theology in a Technological Age* (Newcastle upon Tyne, UK: Cambridge Scholars, 2015): 17-25.

Hockridge, D. 'Rethinking our Approach to Student Formation in Australian Theological Education', in Bain, A. & Hussey, I. (eds.). *Theological Education. Foundations, Practices, and Future Directions* (Australian College of Theology Monograph Series, Eugene, OR: Wipf & Stock, 2018): 200-214.

Kreminski, K. & Frost, M. 'Theological Education for Missional Leadership', in Bain, A & Hussey, I. (eds.). *Theological Education. Foundations, Practices, and Future Directions* (Australian College of Theology Monograph Series, Eugene, OR: Wipf & Stock, 2018): 175-186.

Martin, K, 'Theology for the iGeneration', in Ball, L. & Harrison, J. R. (eds.). *Learning and Teaching Theology. Some Ways Ahead* (Northcote, VIC: Morning Star, 2014): 147-158.

Mudge, P. & Fleming, D. '"To Take You Where You Do Not Wish To Go": Extending the Telos of Online Theological Education – The "What" of the Institution That Teaches', in Ball, L. & Bolt, P. G (eds.). *Wondering about God Together. Research-Led Learning and Teaching in Theological Education* (Macquarie Park, NSW: SCD Press, 2018): 123-139.

Sherlock, C., *Uncovering Theology: The Depth, Reach and Utility of Australian Theological Education* (Adelaide, SA: ATF Press, 2009).

Smith, S. & O'Flynn, L. 'Responding to Complexity', in Ball, L. & Harrison, J. R. (eds.) *Learning and Teaching Theology. Some Ways Ahead* (Northcote, VIC: Morning Star, 2014): 119-128.

Taylor, S. & Dewerse, R. 'Curiosity and Doubt in Researching the Future: The Contribution of Flipped Learning to Sociality in Theological Innovation', in Ball, L. & Bolt, P. G. (eds.) *Wondering about God Together. Research-Led Learning and Teaching in Theological Education* (Macquarie Park, NSW: SCD Press, 2018), 426-452.

Les Ball
Australian College of Ministries, Sydney
les.j.ball@gmail.com

17 | THE VIRTUES OF RELIGIOUS HISTORY

MAKING A NECESSITY OF VIRTUE

Abstract

It is well known that the study of history can help students to acquire critical habits of mind, research skills, interdisciplinary acuity, and knowledge about the forces that shape their lives, individually and collectively. My own leadership and teaching of church history at St Mark's National Theological Centre (School of Theology, Charles Sturt University) since 2009 has focused on imparting these skills and understandings through study of the history of Christianity and its interactions with the great historical movements and worldviews in human history. In a pluralistic, globalised world where the vast majority espouse some kind of religious belief, graduates need more than ever an understanding of the historical trajectories of religious impulses and institutions that have profoundly shaped their own—and others'—histories. This in turn enhances graduates' capacity for citizenship and informed contributions to the public good, not least in regional communities. Charles Sturt University's recent adoption of new GLOs (Graduate Learning Outcomes) has directly affected the way I structure, teach, and plan the church history curriculum at St Mark's. The GLOs have also prompted some productive thinking about the place of history both in the academy generally, and in theological education specifically.

1. Introduction

A few years ago, my university, Charles Sturt University (CSU), informed our faculty of a revision of university graduate attributes and what are now called Graduate Learning Outcomes (or GLOs). Subsequent discussion of the University's graduate attributes and GLOs prompted me to think more intentionally about the knowledge and skills I wanted graduates of my religious history subjects to come out with. I realised, for example, that I wanted them to come out of their education with a sense of the broad sweep and movement of the history of Christianity (i.e. 'from Plato to NATO') rather than a traditionally narrow focus on the early church (typically up to the Council of Chalcedon in AD 451) and the European Reformations (typically up to 1700). Accordingly, as head of the religious history subdiscipline in our School of Theology, I reconfigured several of my subjects to ensure they offered students this more comprehensive scope and breadth. Around the same time, various Australian theological colleges were thinking hard about the transformational dimensions of theological education, one outcome of which was the publication of the important monograph *Transforming Theology*, followed by a companion volume, *Learning and Teaching Theology*.[1] The contemporary Australian discussion of the transformative task of theological education likewise prompted me to think intentionally about what kinds of graduates I wanted to come out of my courses—that is, the kinds of character attributes and dispositions (in other words, virtues) the discipline of religious history might help to form—an 'inner GLO', if you will. This chapter is the fruit of some of that thinking and practice over more than a decade of teaching religious history courses at bachelor, graduate diploma, masters and PhD levels. This teaching and thesis supervision has been done in a context that is relatively unusual for theological education in the Australian setting, namely a confessional Anglican theological college within the arts faculty of a mainstream Australian university: St Mark's National Theological Centre, Canberra, in the School of Theology, Charles Sturt University.

My argument, in short, is for the importance of religious history as a nursery for cultivating character-oriented attributes that, for reasons which will become clear, I am labelling 'historical', 'epistemic', and 'theological' virtues. These historical virtues include: a commitment to *truth-telling*, *honesty*, and *balance*; *humility*, *empathy*, *charity*, and *justice*; a deep commitment to engaging with

---

[1] Ball, Transforming Theology: Student Experience and Transformative Learning in Undergraduate Theological Education; Ball & Harrison, Learning and Teaching Theology: Some Ways Ahead.

tradition—which I call being 'tradition-al', which aids in further instilling the aforementioned virtues alongside theological virtues of *faith* and *hope*; *aesthetic virtues*, such as being able to write in lucid, compelling, and evocative ways; and virtues of *carefulness*, *patience*, *perseverance*, *diligence*, and *attentiveness*.[2] These are virtues that, I argue, can and should be embodied in academics and graduates as they serve churches, academic and scholarly communities, and civil society.

In framing and defining these virtues, I draw from recent work on the philosophy of history, epistemology, and the philosophical tradition of virtue ethics. I understand the latter, following Paul Martens' helpful definition, as 'a normative ethic that employs a Greek (usually Aristotelian or neo-Aristotelian) concept of virtue (*arete*, excellence of moral character) cultivated through *phronesis* (practical wisdom) oriented to *eudaimonia* (flourishing or happiness)'.[3]

I also employ the term 'religious history' to describe the sub-discipline in theology that deals with the history of Christianity within its larger social, intellectual, cultural, political, and economic settings. This nomenclature reflects a shift in recent decades away from the more narrowly conceived 'ecclesiastical history' and 'church history' approaches that predominated before the 1960s and tended to focus primarily on institutions and elites (usually the 'great men' of Christian history). Since then, historians of Christianity have expanded their methodology and scope to draw fruitfully from other disciplines (such as sociology and anthropology) and on broader trends within academic history, including the post-war rise of social history, focusing on questions of class location and formation, and getting beyond elites to the lived experience of common, working, and lower-middle-class people; women's, feminist, and gender history; cultural history, where questions of culture and identity predominate; postcolonial, colonial, imperial, and global histories; and post-structuralist, postmodern, and critical theoretical approaches to history. Many Christian (or 'confessional') historians have also brought robust theological thinking to bear on their history writing, especially since the crisis in world history during the 1930s (and a previous preoccupation with positivistic or 'scientific' views of

---

2   For the sake of clarity, I have rendered various virtues throughout in italics.
3   Martens, 'Virtue and Character', 214. Froeyman, 'Virtues of Historiography', 416, offers a similar definition: 'Virtue' may be described as 'an ethically preferable and stable disposition to act in a certain way, and/or as a certain trait of character which distinguishes good people from bad people'.

history).⁴ In the following, it can be taken as read that where I refer to the religious historian, I am also referring to the student of religious history.

I begin by considering what might be called a 'virtuous turn' in the modern university more broadly, and in the humanities more particularly (especially in the disciplines of the philosophy of history, epistemology, and ethics). I will then discuss some of the key virtues in religious history before offering some conclusions about the study of religious history in both theological education and the modern Australian university.

2. A 'Virtuous Turn' in History and the Humanities?

In terms of the larger setting of theological education, historical study represents the contribution of the humanities. The definition and role of the humanities have changed over time in the Western university. In the late medieval period, the 'humanities' referred to secular learning as opposed to theology—namely, the study of ancient Latin and Greek language, literature, and intellectual culture (as grammar, rhetoric, history, and philosophy), as well as classical scholarship. In the modern period, the humanities have encompassed that branch of learning that is concerned with human culture: Traditionally, its subjects have comprised history, literature, ancient and modern languages, law, philosophy, art, and music. Today, the humanities are distinguished from the *social sciences* in several ways: in having a significant historical element; in the use of interpretation of texts and artefacts, rather than experimental and quantitative methods; and in having an idiographic character (that is, concerned with the individual, or relating to single and unique facts and processes) rather than a *nomothetic* character (that is, concerning underlying laws).⁵ The beauty of history lies in the way it can wed the humanities to theological study: It incorporates the history of literature, art, philosophy, language, law, and music. But it can also draw fruitfully from the social sciences like sociology, anthropology, economics, and political science, which means that new insights

---

4   For Australian, British, and American accounts of a shift from 'church history' to 'religious history' since the 1960s, see Bradley and Muller, *Church History: An Introduction to Research Methods and Resources*, ch. 1; Webster, 'Religious History'; Outler, 'Theodosius' Horse: Reflections on the Predicament of the Church Historian'; Clark, 'The Lady Vanishes: Dilemmas of a feminist historian after the "Linguistic Turn"' Brooke, 'What is Religious History?'.
5   'Humanities', *Oxford English Dictionary*.

and developments in the humanities can be reflected in the study of theology via the historical discipline.

In a perceptive article on the role of the virtues in the humanities and in history, Anton Froeyman observes that philosophers of history after the Second World War focused largely on problems raised by the relationship between the past itself and the historical text. Prominent questions included how texts explained certain phenomena (in Carl Hempel's influential work, for example), or *if* and *how* a text could represent the past (in the work of Hayden White and Frank Ankersmit, for example). Most philosophers of history focused on finished historical texts, rather than on the historian's practices or the question of what a good historian was like. Likewise, in the wake of the Enlightenment, dominant Anglo-Saxon ethical theories—namely, deontological ethics and utilitarianism—tended to focus on what kind of actions were good or bad rather than on what kind of person acted in a good or bad way.[6]

Traditionally, this shift this was understood as part of a process by which longstanding traditions of virtue ethics in moral reflection came to a shuddering halt in the Eighteenth Century with Immanuel Kant's *Metaphysics of Morals*. On Kant's account, virtue was redefined as 'the moral strength of a human being's will in fulfilling his duty', which subordinated virtue ethics to deontology and oriented them to 'the autonomous will of the individual apart from social, physical, or emotional determinants of human behaviour'.[7] Virtue and character were subsequently replaced by 'utilitarianism, deontology, existentialism, emotivism, or some other mode of moral reasoning'.[8] Such 'declension narratives' of the post-Reformation period have, however, tended to understate the extent to which virtue continued to be present in the Christian moral imagination in Europe during the Nineteenth Century.[9] Nevertheless, it is clear that from around the 1960s, virtue ethics emerged with new force and clarity as a reaction against the influential deontological or utilitarian focus on moral action. The aim of virtue ethicists in this context—some of the most notable of whom were Elizabeth Anscombe, Philippa Foot, and Alasdair MacIntyre—was to move the focus back

---

6   Froeyman, 'Virtues of Historiography', 415-16.
7   Martens, 'Virtue and Character', 214, 216.
8   Martens, 'Virtue and Character', 214.
9   So Martens, 'Virtue and Character', 214-16. As Martens points out, virtue remains important in the moral imagination of influential post-Kantians in Europe: among both Protestants (Schleiermacher, G. W. F. Hegel, and Søren Kierkegaard) and Catholics (John Henry Newman). In the American context Marten notes Walter Rauschenbush, who had in turn been influenced by Albrecht Ritschl, among others.

to the moral agent. Their key concept was 'virtue'. From the 1990s onward, a similar shift in focus—from output to actor—emerged in the analytic tradition of philosophy in the English-speaking world via the discipline of epistemology, in turn giving birth to the subdiscipline of virtue epistemology. Virtue epistemologists, therefore, focused on 'which capacities a person should possess in order to generate true justified beliefs. These capacities were generally called intellectual or epistemic virtues, in contrast to the moral virtues of virtue ethics'.[10]

Philosophers of history have in recent years brought the insights of virtue ethics and virtue epistemology to bear on thinking about historians and their work. Working within the tradition of virtue epistemology, Herman Paul has advocated a shift in focus from historians' *output* to their *practices*—of reading, thinking, selecting, associating, defining, formulating, synthesising, associating, discussing, and writing, *inter alia*—and the ways in which the successful performance of historical scholarship demands the cultivation of certain skills, attitudes, and virtues. Paul has focused on these 'doings' of historians—the 'virtuous performances historians recognize as professional conduct'—in terms of 'epistemic virtues', a term Paul adapts from its longstanding use among philosophers of science. That is, historical scholarship is 'embedded in "practices" or "epistemic cultures," in which knowledge is created and warranted by means of such virtues as *honesty, carefulness, accuracy*, and *balance*'. Such epistemic virtues are not, however, 'etched in stone' because historians may highlight some, exchange one for another, or reinterpret their meaning'.[11] Elsewhere, Paul adds that historians' performances are 'ideally regulated by virtues such as *diligence, accuracy*, and *truthfulness*', which are exhibited in their day-to-day work. Likewise, 'professional' behaviour is thought of in terms of virtues (and unprofessional conduct in terms of vices).[12]

Such thinking has a long pedigree among historians, even in the nineteenth and twentieth centuries, the periods in which many traditional accounts have posited a declension or near absence of virtue thinking. David Hume, for example, wrote in 1777 that 'the historians have been the true friends of virtue', largely on account of their interest in characters and events that promoted 'a lively sentiment of blame and praise' (in contrast with the bloodless abstractions

---

10 Froeyman, 'Virtues of Historiography', 415-17.
11 Paul, 'Performing History: How Historical Scholarship is Shaped by Epistemic Virtues', 1. I am grateful to Professor Geoff Treloar for alerting me to both this article and Paul's broader scholarship on these issues
12 Paul, 'Performing History: How Historical Scholarship is Shaped by Epistemic Virtues', 4.

of philosophers), and a degree of disinterestedness that aided in rightly judging people's characters.[13] In their 1898 *L'Introduction aux études historiques* (*Introduction to the Study of History*), French historians Charles Langlois and Charles Seignobos declared that historical research required a 'scientific spirit' (or *wissenschaftliche Persönlichkeit*', as their German contemporaries put it). Ideally, such a scientific spirit excelled in *'minute accuracy'*, *'prudence'*, and *'complete disinterestedness'*, as well as in qualities of *'order, industry*, and *perseverance'*. Virtue language was employed directly to describe *'patience'* as 'the cardinal virtue of the scholar'. This was contrasted with vices of laziness, outspoken prejudice, blind devotion, carelessness, exaggeration, and hurriedness. Historical scholarship depended on virtuous behaviour and character formation, along with the avoidance of vicious behaviour and character traits. Similarly, in the mid-Twentieth Century, March Bloch wrote of an ideal 'intellectual ethic' consisting of virtues such as *'diligence, perseverance*, and *dedication'*.[14]

As noted above, in recent decades, philosophers have shown interest in virtues of this sort, increasingly classifying such things as *'carefulness, honesty, accuracy*, and *balance'* as 'epistemic virtues'. Epistemic virtues are further divided into cognitive abilities (such as a properly functioning memory) and personality traits (such as *intellectual courage* and *open-mindedness*, which are character traits that can be considered 'epistemic virtues' because they increase a person's chance of arriving at true beliefs).[15] Paul contends further that without the exercise of certain character virtues, there can be no acquisition of scholarly knowledge; Additionally, without '"scholarly selves," socialized into knowledge-seeking communities and disciplined to perform according to the standards set by those communities, scholarship is impossible'. This naturally draws us into the realm of sociology of knowledge and socialisation into epistemic virtues. Students develop research skills, working habits, and personal qualities under the influence of their teachers and peers' expectations and examples. In 'highly institutionalized contexts, where the pursuit of advanced degrees and future employment depends on a successful appropriation of collectively approved standards, students are likely to do their best to excel in those epistemic virtues that are considered markers of professional performance'.[16] It is in this sense that we might

---

13 Hume, 'Of the Study of History', 567-68.
14 Paul, 'Performing History: How Historical Scholarship is Shaped by Epistemic Virtues', 5–6 (emphasis mine).
15 Paul, 'Performing History: How Historical Scholarship is Shaped by Epistemic Virtues', 7–8.
16 Paul, 'Performing History: How Historical Scholarship is Shaped by Epistemic Virtues', 9.

understand the induction process of theology students over the course of their degrees, not least at the level of higher degrees at masters and doctoral levels.

Paul adds that the virtues prized by historians are shaped by historical contexts, with greater weight or emphasis placed on certain virtues at different times. By way of example, he points to the fetish for 'objectivity' that marked positivist traditions of nineteenth- and early-twentieth-century Anglo-Saxon history-writing; in turn, these approaches were challenged during the Twentieth Century by historians working in idealist traditions (and, later, it might be added, in post-structuralist traditions). Here, Paul also shows how an ideal like objectivity can, nevertheless, be conceived in terms of epistemic virtue:

> Just like the moral virtues of righteousness, fairness, and justice, objectivity is a regulative ideal. Even though this ideal may be unachievable—who can ever claim to be fully righteous or entirely objective?—it serves as a point of orientation. It focuses the historians' research and provides a standard by which to measure their achievements. Consequently, in order to be considered 'objective', historians need not reach the unreachable, but only have to practice the virtue of objectivity (or intellectual honesty, as Bevir suggests) to an extent considered sufficient by their peers.[17]

As Paul concedes, however, the historically and culturally conditioned nature of epistemic virtues raises the question of whether there are any rational criteria for judging epistemic virtues. On what grounds might one virtue or set of virtues be preferred over another? Are certain virtues—such as objectivity, for example—'more fundamental to the historian's work, and therefore less subject to change, than others?'[18] These are questions to which I shall return below.

In contrast, Anton Froeyman argues with some force that Paul's application of the concept of 'epistemic virtue' to historiography as too limited and straightforward, in the sense that truth is not the sole criterion for judging historical accounts. 'For every complex historical event', argues Froeyman in an invocation of the insights of Hayden White and Frank Ankersmit, 'there are many true stories to be told and many emplotments or narrative substances to be employed. There is no sure path that leads from the historical world to a historical representation. It depends for a large part on personal and often

---

17 Paul, 'Performing History: How Historical Scholarship is Shaped by Epistemic Virtues', 17.
18 Paul, 'Performing History: How Historical Scholarship is Shaped by Epistemic Virtues', 18.

unconscious decisions on behalf of the historian'.[19] Truth is still enacted through the criteria of source-critical enquiry and remains a precondition of historical writing (and a means of differentiating serious historiography from pseudohistory), but surely, argues Froeyman, there are many other matters in the mix, such as originality, scope, literary style, and ideology. The focus on epistemic virtues, Froeyman adds, risks suggesting that 'there is only one possible true representation given a certain arrangement of the world', a view that risks veering towards a kind of truth-obsessed neo-positivism.[20]

Froeyman proposes instead to steer away from the concept of 'epistemic virtue' toward the concept of 'virtue' as it is employed in the field of virtue ethics. Drawing on Alasdair MacIntyre's influential account of virtue ethics, he argues for the importance of the general ideal of being a good historian rather than merely the obsession to discover 'the historical truth'.[21] Another important concept for Froeyman, and one that has been associated with virtue ethics, is the 'uncodifiability thesis', which, like virtue ethics, finds its clearest early expression in Aristotle. More recently, it has been prominent in the work of John McDowell. The thesis states that it is *a priori* impossible to formulate a rule or general rules to guarantee a morally right choice in every situation. Hence, the emphasis in virtue ethics on character and the exercise of practical wisdom (*phronesis*) in any given situation. This, of course, flies in the face of rival accounts of ethics, namely the deontological and utilitarian. Likewise, argues Froeyman, there can be 'no general rule of algorithm on how to write history' given that a subjective factor is needed to link the world, historical facts, and historical representation. It is '*a priori* impossible to put all the do's and don'ts of historiography into a single manual that could allow a layman to make the right choice in every possible situation. It entails that there are some decisions in historiography which can only be made on personal grounds'.[22]

With MacIntyre and McDowell as his key interlocutors, Froeyman goes on to explain how, within the discipline of virtue ethics, virtues are dependent on an ideal notion of 'the good' and 'the good life', which translates to the ideal of a certain social role, such as being a good friend or a good mother.[23] This he expands to the ideal of being a 'good historian':

---

19   Froeyman, 'Virtues of Historiography', 418.
20   Froeyman, 'Virtues of Historiography', 419.
21   Froeyman, 'Virtues of Historiography', 431.
22   Froeyman, 'Virtues of Historiography', 421-22.
23   Froeyman, 'Virtues of Historiography', 427-28.

Becoming a historian consists of taking up certain habits and certain practices within a society. In seems quite natural that, in their practice, historians are then guided by the ideal to be a 'good historian'. As with other ideals, this ideal is in its turn dependent on historical context and personal background. Furthermore, as is the case with the ideal of a good friend, it is not possible to analyze the good historian as if she is an assembly of discrete properties which can be expressed in clear propositions. Rather, 'the good historian' is a certain vague overall idea, more constructed through family resemblance between concrete examples than by clear definition. Nevertheless, there are a number of virtues which historians quite generally agree to be more or less necessary to be a good historian.

As Froeyman points out, his list is not exhaustive, but it does provide an overall impression of what a view of a historian in terms of moral virtues (not merely epistemic virtues) might amount to:

A good historian should always be objective and fair, she should have *a strong empathy with her research subject* and *a keen eye for detail*, she should be *sensitive [to] the relevance of history for current-day society, conscious of her own point of view, open-minded, original* and she should be *able to write a clear but nevertheless compelling and evocative way*. In a traditional (non-virtue based) view on historiographic methodology, combining these traits would be a problem. How can a historian be objective and empathic at the same time? Or open-minded whilst at the same time having a political agenda? In a virtue approach, however, this is not the case, since what it means to be objective, open-minded or politically relevant in a concrete situation, or at which point it is better to be open-minded than engaged, is not determined in advance. It is left to the practical wisdom of the historian, and there is no general rule or calculus by means of which it is possible to articulate this. Therefore, the fact that different virtues seem to contradict each other is not really a problem. Rather, it is the possibility of practical judgment on behalf of the historian, and therefore a precondition of historical representation itself. As we have seen, this results in a view of the historian constantly balancing out different factors rather than steadily working her way up from a firm foundation.[24]

Just as in virtue ethics there is no guarantee of one solution to a moral problem, there is no guarantee that one historical account is the final word on that subject. There is always a degree of provisionality in historical judgments (new sources may emerge, for example, new perspectives be opened up). Accordingly, historical methodology is best transferred and taught as moral virtues are, as general dispositions of character that are shaped and moulded. The understanding of individual virtues and the development of practical wisdom 'implement and compare them' can be acquired by studying the classics of historiography and 'by seeing and understanding the qualities that made them classics in the first place'. In this sense, historians look to 'historical saints' for their practice as well as their products. Study of how virtues are embodied in exemplary historians' work also ensures that historical virtues do not remain too abstract and theoretical.[25]

What is clear in these discussions is the extent to which 'historical virtues' (or 'historiographical virtues', as Froeyman has it)—emerging from discussions in the fields of both virtue epistemology and virtue ethics—have become a focus of increasing attention for philosophers of history. The insights of Paul and Froeyman reflect the extent to which a renaissance in virtue ethics since the 1960s, and in epistemology and philosophy of history since the 1990s, has offered new insights in relation to agent-centred ethical theories in contrast to a prior focus on act-centred ethical theories. In turn, this thinking about virtues in historiography has opened up conceptual space and a vocabulary for historians generally—and religious historians more specifically—to think about and articulate within their own subdisciplines and practices as historians, and ways in which that can foster character-oriented attributes in the students they mentor and teach.

It is also worth noting a similar 'virtuous turn' in thinking about the broader humanities disciplines and the modern university over the last two decades. Jon Nixon, for example, is one among many recent thinkers who has drawn from virtue ethics to push for the reform of the academic profession and the modern Western university so that they articulate and inculcate virtues and 'virtuous dispositions' (For Nixon, these virtues comprise truthfulness, respect, authenticity, and magnanimity in the place of current emphases on managerial effectiveness

---

24 Froeyman, 'Virtues of Historiography', 428-29 (emphasis mine). Froeyman adds that 'only three of these (eye for detail, open-mindedness and consciousness of one's point of view) are truth-conducive and, on Paul's account, would qualify as virtues'.

25 Froeyman, 'Virtues of Historiography', 429-30.

in terms of economic efficiency, entrepreneurialism, self-promotion, and competitive innovation,). Such virtues are, in turn, a means of enriching civil society and the common good.[26] Other important initiatives, arising mainly in the British context, have included funded research centres, such as the Templeton-funded Jubilee Centre for Character and Virtues based at the University of Birmingham and the Oxford Character Project, a project on moral character and virtue in postgraduate education based at the University of Oxford.[27]

Paul and Froeyman differ in their emphasis; taken together, however, both of their schemes provide a useful (although not exhaustive) context for considering 'historical virtues' and their relevance for teaching religious history in the context of theological education.[28] This encompasses Paul's truth-enabling epistemic virtues (truthfulness, honesty, carefulness, aspirations to objectivity, accuracy, diligence, balance, open-mindedness, and intellectual courage) and Froeyman's 'moral virtues', several of which overlap with Paul's epistemic virtues (namely aspirations to objectivity, open-mindedness, an eye for detail, and fairness), and several of which move beyond truth-enabling virtues to other kinds of dispositions (empathy with research subjects, sensitivity to the relevance of history for contemporary society; and more aesthetic considerations such as originality and the ability to write in clear, compelling, and evocative ways). Both Paul and Froeyman stress the importance of induction and socialisation into 'knowledge-seeking communities' whose professional standards, expectations, and discipline aid in transmitting and forming historical and scholarly virtues.

There are further benefits in this regard for those within theological education, whether the committed ('confessional') Christian historian or the student of religious history. Not only are they able to draw from the insights and judgements of professional historians and philosophers of history about what constitutes moral and epistemic virtues (and vices), but they are able to draw from the rich

---

26 Nixon, Towards the Virtuous University: The Moral Bases of Academic Practice. I am grateful to Professor Ross Chambers for alerting me to the work of Nixon, among others. See also Higton, A Theology of Higher Education; Hauerwas, The State of the University: Academic Knowledges and the Knowledge of God.

27 See Arthur et al., Graduates of character—values and character: higher education and graduate employment; Brant and Lamb, 'Cultivating virtues in postgraduates: a case study from the Oxford Character Project'; Oxford Character Project, www.oxfordcharacter.org. For a helpful overview of these trends (and a more cautious approach to the teaching of virtues in higher education), see Carr, 'Virtue and Character in Higher Education'.

28 Here is not scope in this paper to pursue the conversation between Froeyman and Paul further, but those interested in their continuing conversation are advised to read Paul's rejoinder to Froeyman: Paul, 'Virtue Ethics and/or Virtue Epistemology: A Response to Anton Froeyman'.

and deep wells of Christian thought and practice, whether from philosophers (including philosophers of history and ethical thinkers reaching back to Jesus and the early church), theologians, or historians themselves. The Christian student of history is thus located within a distinct moral community that possesses a long and rigorous tradition of ethical thinking, practice, and a narrative with a defined *telos* and guiding set of virtues. Those virtues are, in turn, drawn from a deeper classical and Christian heritage, in which medieval Christian thinkers added the Pauline 'theological' virtues of faith, hope, and love (or charity) to the classical 'cardinal' or 'human' virtues of wisdom, temperance, courage, and justice.[29] Taken together, these moral, epistemic, and theological virtues provide valuable resources with which to articulate and explore the virtues of religious history.

3. Virtues of Religious History
3.1 Truth-Telling and Honesty

The first historical virtues I want to consider are *truthfulness* and *honesty*. These are historical virtues to which both Paul and Froeyman subscribe (for Paul they are, naturally, epistemic in nature). Both thinkers also discuss them in terms of an ideal of 'objectivity', 'truthfulness', and 'accuracy'. One might add Froeyman's 'keen eye for detail' and Paul's injunction to 'intellectual courage'. In a basic sense, the need for truth-telling and honesty is essential because although historians use the techniques of literature and fiction (narrative structure, emplotment, characterisation, and description) and rhetoric (appeals to *logos*, *pathos*, and *ethos*), they are always constrained by the extant evidence and traces of the past, whether textual or material.[30] Many years ago, when I was a PhD student, during one meeting with my supervisor (historian Brian

---

29 The student of history still, of course, faces the challenge, noted by Paul and Froeyman (and indeed by MacIntyre), that is posed by the culturally conditioned nature of historical virtues (as decided and debated by historians) and the consequent question of whether there are any rational criteria or grounds for judging virtues and preferring one virtue or set of virtues over another. But for the Christian historian, certain virtues are indeed 'more fundamental to the historian's work, and therefore less subject to change, than others'. See Paul, 'Performing History: How Historical Scholarship is Shaped by Epistemic Virtues', 18. This reality also picks up MacIntyre's emphasis in After Virtue on the importance of tradition in creating a coherent moral community and framework.

30 In classical rhetoric, *logos* denotes the appeal to reason, *pathos* the appeal to emotion and feeling, and *ethos* the appeal to authority.

Stanley), I asked him how he would characterise his philosophy of history. I settled back in my chair, waiting for the inevitably long and complex answer you would expect from a front-rank religious historian and Cambridge don with nearly forty years' experience of writing academic history. To my astonishment, however, the answer was a single, crisp phrase: 'Truth-telling. As far as that is humanly possible!'.

On reflection, it is a cogent (and admirably succinct) approach to history generally, and religious history specifically. The concept of truth-telling also encompasses virtues of *even-handedness* and *balance* (to cite two other virtues noted by Paul and Froeyman) that, on the one hand, help us to avoid propagandist, hagiographical, or whitewashed views of the past, while on the other help us to reject an overly suspicious hermeneutic or a 'black armband' focus on the evil that Christians do, which, alas, often leaves the good interred with Christian bones (and everyone *expecting* the Spanish Inquisition).

There is an important epistemological dimension to truth-telling that consists in instilling confidence in students about the possibility of apprehending and representing historical truth. Philosopher Dallas Willard has pointed out that although approaches to truth in the centuries during and after Socrates were profound and impressive, the most impressive view and experience of the moral life and devotion to truth in history has been the Christian tradition, which gave rise to the universities in the Western world and sustained them up until the end of the Nineteenth Century or so.[31] Willard adds that '[i]t is not an exaggeration to point out that no alternative to the Christian tradition has yet been discovered as a satisfactory basis for life', despite the best efforts of the best human minds since Descartes.[32] A virtue of historical study is that it presses students (not least those in theology courses) to think critically about epistemology and notions of truth, which naturally include theories of historical knowledge and historical truth. This is one of the benefits of incorporating intellectual history into religious history courses, at both masters and undergraduate levels, where this is scope to consider various 'meta' theories of truth that have emerged since ancient times: for example, a classical correspondence theory of truth since

---

31 Willard, 'How Reason Can Survive the Modern University'. Willard notes elsewhere Gertrude Himmelfarb's The De-Moralization of Society: From Victorian Virtues to Modern Values. New York. Vintage Books. 1996; MacIntyre, After Virtue, Notre Dame, IN. University of Notre Dame Press. 1984; Julie A. Reuben in her book, The Making of the Modern University: Intellectual Transformation and the Marginalization of Morality. Chicago. University of Chicago Press. 1996

32 Willard, 'How Reason Can Survive the Modern University'.

Aristotle, a naïve empiricism, or more recent 'coherence' and 'pragmatic' theories of truth (such as those of Richard Rorty).

There used to be a time when many historians were shy about such theorising, preferring to rely on correspondence, common sense, or naïve empiricist theories of truth. By the 1960s, however, as E. H. Carr memorably put it, many historians found themselves naked in the garden without a scrap of philosophical clothing to cover them. Since then, in the wake of the failure of neo-Marxist and other approaches to history, a renewal in continental philosophy of renewed post-Nietzschean scepticism (epistemic, ontological, and semantic) has fed some post-structuralist, postmodern, and 'new historicist' suspicions that 'historical descriptions, interpretations and explanations are [merely] expressions of historians' cultural milieu and social or political interests rather than accurate accounts of the past.'[33] We might add to this a pervasive cultural mood of relativism, an 'incredulity towards metanarratives' (which is also, of course, a metanarrative of sorts) and a resulting post-truth 'fake news' culture.[34] Most historians have rejected the wilder claims of the radical fringe of postmodern and critical theory while welcoming insights that have challenged the older and rather naïve positivistic claims to objectivity. Yet, any historians and history students worth their salt will still engage critically with the insights of philosophers and postmodern critics, and in so doing, forge intentionally reflective and sophisticated theories of truth.[35] In my masters-level philosophy of history subject, we compare conceptions of history ranging from cyclical ancient Greek and Eastern schemes to those of historicism, idealism, positivism, Marxism, and post-structuralism/postmodernism, as well as a wide range of Christian philosophies of history, from some of the earliest (namely, Augustine's *City of God*) to those of George Florovsky, Christopher Dawson, Herbert Butterfield, David Bebbington, and Paul Ricoeur (among others).

It is in this light, in the context of my teaching of masters-level method courses, that I introduce students to competing theories of truth, outlined above, as well as some of the fallibilistic theories that I have found most compelling and

---

33 McCullagh, *Logic of History*, p. 2.
34 'Iincredulity towards metanarratives' is, of course, Jean Lyotard's famous neologism from *The Postmodern Condition*.
35 For some important ways in to a vast literature, see Thompson, Postmodernism and History; Lundin, The Culture of Interpretation; Curthoys and Docker, Is History Fiction?; Clark, *History, Theory, Text: Historians and the Linguistic Turn*; Evans, Lying About Hitler: History, Holocaust, and the David Irving Trial; Jenkins, The Postmodern History Reader.

helpful. One such approach is that of philosopher of history Behan McCullagh, who has offered what he calls a 'correlation' or 'critical' theory of truth, building on the work of philosophers such as the nineteenth-century pragmatist Charles Sanders Peirce and, somewhat surprisingly, the twentieth-century anti-realist Michael Dummett. In brief, McCullagh recognises the post-Kantian worry that 'there are several reasons for denying the common-sense assumption that things in the world are as we perceive them'.[36] For example, we have no uninterpreted access to the world. 'Our perceptions might be mistaken: for instance, it is easy to perceive artificial flowers as real', while scientists 'tell us that the colours and sounds we perceive are really in our minds, the product of light and sound waves stimulating our eyes and ears and brains'.[37] In light of these valid concerns, argues McCullagh, we can adopt a theory like Peirce's where we say a historical description 'of the world is true if it is part of an ideal theory which explains all possible observations of the world; and, for 'an ideal theory of the world to be true there must exist in reality something which could cause all those perceptions, were people in a position to make them'.[38] On this view:

> [w]hen we call an historical description of the world true, we mean that there were things in the world that could have produced the possible perceptions which the description implies, had there been someone present to perceive them. In this way, it makes sense to say that true descriptions correlate with things in the world, but do not correspond to them. On this theory, the particular truth conditions of a true description of the world are those states of the world that would cause an observer to have the perceptions that the description, if true, is conventionally taken to imply. In this way, it makes sense to say that true descriptions correlate with things in the world, but do not correspond to them. On this theory, the particular truth conditions of a true description of the world are those states of the world that would cause an observer to have the perceptions that the description, if true, is conventionally taken to imply. Strictly speaking, this account of the truth of descriptions refers to a necessary but not sufficient condition for a description being true. After all, if I tell the children that Santa Claus came last night and

---

36 McCullagh, 'The Truth of Basic Historical Description', 115.
37 McCullagh, 'The Truth of Basic Historical Description', 115.
38 McCullagh, *Logic of History*, 5, 9-10.

put presents for them around the tree, the truth of this statement would seem to be confirmed when they see presents around the tree. But it is not the best explanation of the presence of those presents. True descriptions of the world are not only confirmed by observing their implications, but are also part of the best, indeed the ideal, explanation of the cause of those observations.[39]

McCullagh's account is, of course, only one among an efflorescence of specifically Christian contributions to epistemology and the philosophy of history, particularly in the wake of Alvin Plantinga's seminal work in the 1960s (In this area, I find it helpful to point students to the subsequent work of William Alston, Nicolas Wolterstorff, and Paul K. Moser.).[40] Approaches like McCullagh's offer cogent reasons to hold, in the face of the more radical claims of postmodern scepticism and the fact that we have no uninterpreted access to the world, that 'the best explanation of our experiences is that they are caused by things outside us, things in the world which we say we perceive'.[41] With such theories of truth, historians and students alike can be confident that although 'no knowledge of the world is infallible, it is often reasonable to believe many descriptions of the past are true'.[42]

Historians John D. Woodbridge and Frank A. James remind us that *honest* religious history is an 'academically responsible engagement with the facts of history as best as we can determine them, whether or not these facts comport with personal convictions ... such *honesty*, although at times painful, will ultimately serve the best interests of all, Christian or not'. This should not surprise us, given the biblical record of the flawed people of God and any robust anthropology that acknowledges human sinfulness and the flawed grandeur of humanity. Persecuted Christians 'can at another time be the persecutors. The history of the church reminds us that Christians can be culprits of foolishness, as well as bold titans for truth. They can be egoistic and self-serving; they can be humble and generous. A single individual can embody conflicting traits'.[43]

---

39 McCullagh, 'The Truth of Basic Historical Description', 115–16.
40 Key works in Plantinga's development of what he calls 'Reformed Epistemology' include *Warrant: The Current Debate* (1993), *Warrant and Proper Function* (1993), and *Warranted Christian Belief* (2000).
41 McCullagh, *Logic of History*, 5, 9–10.
42 McCullagh, *Logic of History*. I also remind students of the myth of neutrality, the implications of a Christian metanarrative in a contemporary intellectual climate that often displays 'incredulity' towards metanarratives, the limitations of our own finitude and fallenness, and the limits of unaided reason and the need for revelation, which means we will always need to take further steps towards the truth.
43 Woodbridge and James, *Church History*, 29.

But this should also cause us to think and write about people with *charity* and *empathy*, recognizing that, by virtue of us all being fallible and flawed human beings, we are not much different from them.

In terms of the complex issue of making moral judgements on the past, it is worth noting that—like all history—religious history and religious historians are culturally conditioned. 'The social norms that governed an earlier era may not be the social norms today. For example, today, we do not execute heretics (at least, not physically). However, 'even as we evaluate actions according to the cultural standards of the time', the Christian affirms 'doctrinal beliefs and ethical standards that are culturally transcendent'.[44] *Honesty* compels plain speaking when previous generations of Christians have failed to embody Christian virtues and ideals or have devalued the authority of Scripture and tradition. In terms of teaching, historical case studies can be useful in this light. In my undergraduate modern religious history course, for example, we consider in some depth the failure of German Christians and their associated forms of liberal Protestantism to oppose the Nazi state and its genocidal atheism, anti-semitism, prejudice, and racism after 1933. This is juxtaposed, however, against the uncompromising stand and theological reflection of the Confessing Church and leaders such as Bonhoeffer, Barth, and Niemoller.

In an oft-quoted passage, C. S. Lewis famously compared the reader of history to the person who has lived in many places and times.

> Most of all, perhaps, we need intimate knowledge of the past. Not that the past has any magic about it, but because we cannot study the future, and yet need something to set against the present, to remind us that the basic assumptions have been quite different in different periods and that much which seems certain to the uneducated is merely temporary fashion. A man who has lived in many places is not likely to be deceived by the local errors of his native village; the scholar has lived in many times and is therefore in some degree immune from the great cataract of nonsense that pours from the press and the microphone of his own age.[45]

A 'cataract of nonsense' is, of course, flowing in our own online age, such as the historically illiterate rants of some 'new atheists' with their facile claims that

---

44 Woodbridge and James, *Church History*, 30.
45 Lewis, Weight of Glory.

Christianity is opposed to science, or that it has been primarily a force for evil, violence, and war throughout its history. This is a reminder that there is also an apologetic dimension to history: It is useful for dismantling straw men and inaccurate caricatures of Christians in history. Surely, this is also a gift to any genuine seeker of truth.

3.2 Humility, Empathy, Charity, and Justice

Before we too easily judge motives, prejudices, or intentions, we must also ask how we would fare in others' sandals. We must make due allowance for context and the often-limited range of choices people in the past have may have had. We do well to say continually, 'There but for the grace of God go I'.[46] So, a related historical virtue is *humility*. It relates to the previous virtue of truth-telling, where we saw that although historians are well-qualified and -equipped to 'come up with the very best explanations of the evidence which relates to that field', and that it is reasonable to believe descriptions of the past to be true, this does not mean that their conclusions are always correct. A historian's knowledge is limited and fallible, and she is dealing with probabilities rather than certainty. New evidence may turn up, or a more comprehensive account may be offered. There is always, then, a certain degree of provisionality in historical judgements. This, in turn, fosters humility in judgements about the past—and regarding knowledge generally. Indeed, one of the benefits of the more moderate traditions of postmodern scholarship has been a greater awareness of what historian Shirley Mullen has described as any historian's 'locatedness' and perspective, regardless of whether that historian happens to be a Christian, a neo-Marxist, an apatheist, or an atheistic secularist (here, one could of course fold in locations of class, gender, race, and geography). But for the Christian student of history, as Mullen reminds us, recognising locatedness only increases the historian's burden 'to be fair and even-handed in treating any topic'. This is in part because Christian historians and students of history are 'boundary dwellers' who operate in various communities, both professional and non-professional (for instance, church, academy, public intellectual life, and civil society). As such, the Christian historian has

> a special responsibility for modeling and invoking *fair-mindedness* toward all subjects of history, and for cultivating the particular

---

46 Ferguson, *Church History*, 25.

balance of appreciation and criticism that is appropriate to any topic or person in this glorious but fallen world.[47]

In turn, this recognition of our own locatedness and context fosters a better understanding of the locatedness of both the historians we read and the historical actors we study. Here, I constantly remind students of the old maxim that they should study the historian as well as the history they write. But it is also just at this point, adds Mullen, that virtues of *charity* and *hospitableness* should be the stamp of the Christian historian:

> we as Christians ought to have something going for us that make us not one more identity group among others in the profession. For, integral to our very identity as Christians is the call to care about people besides other Christians. We are called to love the world as God loves the world, and to love our neighbors as we love ourselves. That is, Christian historians ought to be models of those who are seeking to portray the stories and concerns of others with the same love and appreciation, the same care and attention, and the same critical reflection with which we tell our own stories. Our work as Christian historians ought to be an extension of Christian hospitality. Christian historians ought to be, of all historians, the most gracious and fair-minded and evenhanded. That, at least, is the goal.[48]

Such an approach of *even-handedness*, *charity*, and *hospitality* towards one's neighbour resonates strongly with the moral virtue of *justice*, one of the four cardinal virtues the Catholic Church defines as the 'constant and firm will to give their due to God and neighbor [...] Justice toward men disposes one to respect the rights of each and to establish in human relationships the harmony that promotes equity with regard to persons and to the common good'.[49]

A posture characterised by virtues of *humility*, *empathy*, and *charity* further helps to forge what I call 'informed ecumenism', as opposed to ignorant sectarianism. I am occasionally surprised by just how ill-informed some of my Protestant students are about basic Roman Catholic or Orthodox doctrines and practices, let alone the rich 2000-year histories of these traditions from which

---

47 Mullen, 'History and Virtue', 8.
48 Mullen, 'History and Virtue', 8.
49 Catechism of the Catholic Church, Part 3, Section 1, Article 7, The Virtues, 1807, https://www.vatican.va/archive/ccc_css/archive/catechism/p3s1c1a7.htm.

Protestantism emerged. Gaining a deeper understanding of these traditions—of how and why they believe and do what they do—does not have to lead to agreement, but at least it promotes informed and more charitable engagement and possibly even the chance to learn from the insights of other traditions and denominations. This also gestures towards the value of providing students with a long vie —chronologically, thematically and geographically—of the history of Christianity. This provision of courses relating to all periods of Christian history has been a particular commitment of our history department at St Mark's National Theological Centre (This includes a course devoted to the medieval period—that Cinderella of history offerings in theological colleges, and, incidentally, a subject that I am not aware is being offered by any other Australian theological colleges).

3.3 Tradition and Virtue

Being 'tradition-al' is a commitment to helping students (and others) to engage critically and deeply with the rich and deep traditions of Christian experience and writing. In turn, this becomes a means of cultivating several of the virtues we have already considered, particularly those of *faith* and *hope*. Historian Everett Ferguson has suggested that church history 'is the study of the history of God's people in Christ, a theological claim, or, speaking more neutrally, of those who have *wanted to be* God's people in Christ'. It deals with the most influential religious community and movement in history. 'It is a human story of a divinely called people who wanted to live by a divine revelation. These are people who have struggled [just as we do] with the meaning of the greatest event in history, the coming of the Son of God'.[50] For the Christian lecturer and student, the church's history is our own corporate history and tradition—our family history, if you like. 'If we're in Christ', as one religious historian puts it:

> church history is the story of our own true community and family. My brothers and sisters from the fourth century, for example, compose my spiritual family. Though separated by time, we share one Lord, one faith, one baptism. The bond we share in Christ is as real and enduring as the connection we have with our families in the flesh.[51]

If we have a quarrel with the church in the past (and in the present), then, as

---

50 Ferguson, *Church History*, 25.
51 Hall, '13 Reasons We Need Church History'.

one of my theologian colleagues at St Mark's puts it, it is a lover's quarrel. G. K. Chesterton memorably described serious engagement with tradition as a means of 'giving a vote to most obscure of all classes, our ancestors. It is the democracy of the dead … Democracy tells us not to neglect a good man's opinion, even if he is our groom; tradition asks us not to neglect a good man's opinion, even if he is our father'. That engagement with tradition needs, of course, to be critical. Rowan Williams provides one of the more penetrating theological visions of such engagement, conceiving of it as a 'spiritual discipline'. He adds, however, that it will not be a spiritual discipline

> if it is not also critical; the development of some techniques of scientific history has been a good and welcome dissolving agent for self-serving, propagandist versions of the past. But to stop with this is to isolate ourselves from the unceasing conversation of the Body of Christ in time. Whether we use the past as an inflexible standard of correctness, or neglect it as a record of premodern error, we isolate ourselves from the real life of the past. And when the past in question is that of the Church, that real life in its ultimate depth is the life of Christ.

Williams adds that in the study of Christian history, we are also 'reminded that we are not our own authors, that we have not *just* discovered what it is to be human, let alone what it is to be Christian. And all this has the important consequence that, if we are free to listen to the strange and recognisable 'otherness' of the past, this may help us in dealing with what is strange to us now'.

> If we begin from our axiom of common membership in the Body, there will always be gifts to be received from the past; we can expect that we shall find something there that we had not grasped until a contemporary crisis had brought it into focus. Hence the extraordinary regularity with which radical renewal in the Church has come from a new appropriation of tradition in one sort of another. The Reformation is an obvious case, but the twentieth century offers some dramatic instances as well […] the movements of greatest theological vitality are all movements of 'recovery', *ressourcement*, rather than simple innovation or simple repetition.[52]

---

52 Williams, *Why Study the Past?*, 98.

Williams adds, by way of example, that:

> [t]he foremost Protestant theologian of the age, Karl Barth, abandoned the most fashionable and accessible intellectual models of theological modernity to think through afresh the themes of Paul, Anselm, Calvin and Kierkegaard as the most relevant and critical contribution possible to the unprecedented disasters of twentieth-century Germany.[53]

This steeping in tradition is also a rehearsing and passing on of, in the words of the psalmist, those 'things that we have heard and known, / that our ancestors have told us. / We will not hide them from their children; / we will tell to the coming generation /the glorious deeds of the Lord, and his might, / and the wonders that he has done'.[54] Such a disposition may teach us to rejoice in expressions of faithfulness and authentic witness and respond with gratitude and the desire to imitate.[55]

Finally, Mullen stresses the concreteness of historical writing, in terms of narrative and the canons of rhetorical and literary craft, and its power for what she describes as 'truth-showing' and 'enlargement':

> Historical narrative gets under the skin in a way that neither philosophical nor theological argument or imaginative literature has the power to do. Historical narrative, by its disarming power of telling a story, invites people to see things that might change their thinking in ways that abstract arguments will never do. And the fact that it purports to tell a true story (though I do not want to reject ultimately the sense in which good fiction also speaks truth, but that is another discussion) means that the historical narrative is harder to ignore than imaginative literature and poetry [...] [B]y what we choose to focus on in our illumination of the 'isness' of the world, we can invite concern beyond that 'isness' to moral and spiritual reflection about what might have been, and therefore what ought to be and what can be. When historical study shines light clearly on injustice or human stupidity or inadequacy of any sort, we invite people into the realm of questioning. Historians have a power to

---

53 Williams, *Why Study the Past?*, 98.
54 Psalm 78:3-4 (NRSV).
55 Ferguson, *Church History*, 25.

show, through the stories they choose to tell, to enlarge the worlds of both the historical communities they address and the Christian communities they address.[56]

Identifying Christian vitality and weakness in every age promotes sober reflection on our own contemporary expressions of Christianity.[57] We may find it disconcerting that our heroes are [...] flawed', notes another historian. 'To alleviate in part this dissonance', he offers the following aphorism: 'God works through sinners to accomplish his good purposes. Such words remind us all that despite our frailties, we are yet serviceable to God'.[58] In a real sense, being 'tradition-al' can nurture the great Christian virtues of *faith* and *hope*.

3.4 Other Virtues

The religious virtues considered above are far from exhaustive. Mullen's comments in the previous paragraph gesture towards literary and aesthetic virtues, echoing Froeyman's virtue of being 'able to write a clear but nevertheless compelling and evocative way'. Many more virtues might be noted: for example, the abovementioned virtues of *carefulness*, *patience*, and *diligence* (to which could be added *perseverance*) that are cultivated in the hard graft of historical reading, research, and writing. All require practice and a significant degree of attention to detail. Simone Weil reminds us that the cultivation of *attentiveness* to these relatively mundane aspects of scholarly endeavour can yield further unexpected benefits in helping us cultivate attentiveness in other areas of our lives: to others in our personal relationships; and to God in prayer.[59]

Conclusions

It is striking that CSU, like many modern Western universities, offers vague nods in its discussion of graduate attributes and graduate learning outcomes to ethics and being ethical (generally in a coherentist vein) and to the appropriation of wisdom ('to live well in a world worth living in') drawn from indigenous

---

56 Mullen, 'History and Virtue', 7-8.
57 On this point, I sometimes ask students to ponder what future historians might say 100 years from now (or 500 years from now) about our contemporary expressions of Christianity.
58 Woodbridge and James, *Church History*, 29.
59 On the link between study, attentiveness and spirituality, see Simone Weil's *Waiting on God*, 53-54.

Australian traditions, although nowhere does it make any mention of the word 'truth'.[60] That is not surprising given the post-nineteenth-century retreat and pluralistic confusion in universities with regard to questions of truth and moral knowledge. In contrast, our School of Theology's handbook entry stresses theology and religious history's 'emphasis on intellectual honesty and academic rigour', adding that '[i]t doesn't shy away from difficult questions or awful histories. It pursues facts *and truths*, even unsettling ones'. In this context, the practice and teaching of religious history, as we have seen, is an important nursery for cultivating what I have called historical, epistemic, and theological virtues: a commitment to *truth-seeking*, *truth-telling*, *honesty*, *balance*, and *even-handedness*; *humility*, *empathy*, *charity*, and *justice*; a commitment to deep engagement with tradition as a further means of cultivating Christian virtues of *faith*, *hope*, and *love*; *aesthetic virtues*, such as being able to write in lucid, compelling, and evocative ways; and virtues of *carefulness*, *patience*, *perseverance*, *diligence*, and *attentiveness*. The focus here on how the practitioner–teacher and student of religious history contributes to broader discussions of virtue, if not a 'virtuous turn', among philosophers of history, commentators on the role and character of the modern Western university, and a significant scholarship on the requisite virtues and intellectual posture of the Christian scholar and academic.[61] A common theme in the literature is the importance of virtue ethics and the humanities in the moral formation of students for the public good, over against what David Carr describes as:

> the instrumental and utilitarian drift of much modern (perhaps especially post-WW2) formal primary, secondary and higher education, under political pressures on schools to equip young people with the academic knowledge and vocational skills needed for the job market and national economic growth. But it has also been a common theme that such educational instrumentalism has been much reinforced by widespread loss of nerve on the part of

---

60 Although ethics is mentioned here, the references are somewhat vague: for example, 'applying ethical decision making' or understanding 'ethical approaches such as rights, utilitarianism and virtue ethics, and the need for moral awareness and reflection on moral values'. See <https://www.csu.edu.au/division/learning-and-teaching/home/csu-curriculum/graduate-learning-outcomes>.

61 For recent discussions of the vocation and posture of the Christian academic and intellectual, see Plantinga, 'Augustinian Christian Philosophy'; Noll, Jesus Christ and the Life of the Mind; Moser, 'Jesus And Philosophy: On The Questions We Ask'; Moser, Moreland and Gould, *Loving God with Your Mind: Essays in Honor of J. P. Moreland*; Crisp, *Christian Scholarship in the Twenty-First Century: Prospects and Perils*.

educationalists concerning the prospects and legitimacy of any wider formation of young people in common moral, communal and spiritual values in increasingly secular and/or culturally plural liberal democracies.[62]

This highlights the value of being a school of theology within a mainstream university, where such virtues can be promoted from within the academy—bringing a kind of leavening influence there, as well as in churches and civil society more broadly. This, in turn, enhances graduates' capacity for citizenship and informed contributions to the public good, especially in regional communities (given St Mark's and CSU's expertise in online and distance education), where many of our graduates exercise leadership as leaders (and thought leaders) within local churches and church agencies, and through service in social welfare, education, and the caring professions.

The importance of theological education to our wider academic and public culture is one that prominent theologians such as David Ford and Rowan Williams have recognised as crucial.[63] I conclude with Williams' related observation that education in religious history contributes more broadly to our share in the history of 'the West'. Western modernity, he contends, has been both deeply confused about its history and alarmed at challenges to its self-evident superiority in recent decades, whether from the teleological, secular vision of Marxism, or from Islam, which 'denies the possibility of rational social organisation independent of revelation'. Western modernity too easily resorts to a narrative of globalised communication and economic control that is evidence of its rational and universal triumph:

> Yet Christian history is part of modernity's buried and frequently denied biography. To disinter some of this biography is not only something that makes for the health of the Church; it is a seriously needed contribution to the intellectual and emotional well-being of the culture. A Church that shares the widespread and fashionable illiteracy of this culture about how religious faith worked in other ages is grossly weakened in its witness. That witness has to do with a promise of universal community that is grounded not in assumptions about universal right and reason but in a narrative

---

62   Carr, 'Virtue and Character in Higher Education', 111.
63   See, for example, Ford, 'The future of theology at a public university'.

displaying how communication is made possible between strangers by a common relatedness to God's presence and act in history—in an historical person. Trying to understand—and to celebrate—the full diversity of Christian history as the record of one community is also to offer to the world we are in a model of life together that does not depend on cultural homogeneity. Christian history shows how believers have constantly, if not reinvented the Church, then at least rediscovered and redefined its essence.[64]

The virtues of religious history clearly have an important role in shaping our common life. In terms of character-oriented attributes, then, the study of Christianity's past in the present has a future.

Bibliography

Arthur, J., Wilson, K., Godfrey, R., Gray, B. & Newton, N. (eds.) *Graduates of Character—Values and Character: Higher Education And Graduate Employment.* Project Report (Birmingham, UK: University of Birmingham, 2009).

Ball, L. J. *Transforming Theology, Student Experience and Transformative Learning in Undergraduate Theological Education* (Melbourne, Vic: Mosaic Press, 2012).

Ball, L. J., & Harrison, J. R. *Learning and Teaching Theology: Some Ways Ahead* (Eugene, Oregon: Wipf & Stock, 2015).

Bradley, J. E. & Muller, R. A. *Church History: An Introduction to Research Methods and Resources* (2nd edn; Michigan: Eerdmans, 2016).

Brant, J. & Lamb, M. 'Cultivating virtues in postgraduates: a case study from the Oxford character project. Paper presentation at the 'Cultivating Virtues' conference of the University of Birmingham's Jubilee Centre for Virtues and Character, Oriel College, Oxford, 8 January 2016. Oxford Character Project website at: www.oxfordcharacter.org.

Brooke, C. et al. 'What is Religious History?', History Today 35 (1985), 43-53.

Carr, D. 'Virtue and Character in Higher Education', *British Journal of Educational Studies* 65.1 (2017), 109-124.

Catechism of the Catholic Church, Part 3, Section 1, Article 7, The Virtues, 1807, https://www.vatican.va/archive/ccc_css/archive/catechism/p3s1c1a7.htm.

Clark, E. 'The Lady Vanishes: Dilemmas of a feminist historian after the 'Linguistic Turn', *Church History* 67.1 (1998), 1-31.

Crisp, T. M. *Christian Scholarship in the Twenty-First Century: Prospects and Perils* (Grand Rapids, Michigan: William B. Eerdmans, 2014).

---

64 Williams, *Why Study the Past?*, 112-13.

Ferguson, E. *Church History: the Rise and Growth of the Church in Its Cultural, Intellectual, and Political Context. Vol. 1: From Christ to the Pre-Reformation* (Grand Rapids: Zondervan, 2013).

Ford, D. 'The future of theology at a public university', *Verbum et Ecclesia* 38.1 (2017), 1-6.

Froeyman, A. 'Virtues of Historiography', *Journal of the Philosophy of History* 6 (2012), 415-431.

Himmelfarb, G. *The De-Moralization of Society: From Victorian Virtues to Modern Values* (New York: Vintage Books. 1996).

Hume, D. 'Of the Study of History', in Shirley A. Mullen (ed.), 'History, Virtue and the Conference of Faith and History', *Fides et Historia* 37/38.2/1 (2005/2006), 1-9.

Hauerwas, S. *The State of the University Academic Knowledges and the Knowledge of God* (Malden, MA: Blackwell Publishing, 2008).

Higton, M. *A Theology of Higher Education* (Oxford: Oxford University Press, 2012).

Lewis, C. S. 'Learning in War-Time', in *The Weight of Glory and Other Addresses* (Grand Rapids, Michigan: Eeerdmans, 1965): 50-51.

MacIntyre, A. *After Virtue* (Notre Dame, Indiana: University of Notre Dame Press, 1984).

Martens, P. 'Virtue and Character', in Rasmussen, J. D. S Rasmussen et al. (eds.), *The Oxford Handbook of Nineteenth-Century Christian Thought* (Oxford: Oxford University Press, 2019): 12-22.

Matthew, J. H. '13 Reasons We Need Church History' (3 June 2016) <https://www.thegospelcoalition.org/article/13-reasons-we-need-church-history/>.

Moreland, J. P. & Gould, P. M. *Loving God with Your Mind: Essays in Honor of J. P. Moreland* (Chicago, Il: Moody, 2014).

Moser, P. 'Jesus And Philosophy: On The Questions We Ask', *Faith and Philosophy: Journal of the Society of Christian Philosophers* 22.3 (2005), 261-83.

Mullen, S. A. 'History, Virtue and the Conference of Faith and History', *Fides et Historia* 37/38.2/1 (2005/2006), 1-9.

Nixon, J. *Towards the Virtuous University: The Moral Bases of Academic Practice* (New York: Routledge, 2008).

Outler, A. 'Theodosius' Horse: Reflections on the Predicament of the Church Historian', *Church History: Studies in Christianity and Culture* 57 (1988), 9-19.

Paul, H. 'Performing History: How Historical Scholarship is Shaped by Epistemic Virtues', *History and Theory* 50 (February 2011), 1-19.

Paul, H. 'Virtue Ethics and/or Virtue Epistemology: A Response to Anton Froeyman', *Journal of the Philosophy of History* 6.3 (2012), 432-446.

Reuben J. A. *The Making of the Modern University: Intellectual Transformation and the Marginalization of Morality* (Chicago, Il; University of Chicago Press. 1996).

Webster, P. 'Religious History' (London: Institute of Historical Research) <http://www.history.ac.uk/makinghistory/resources/articles/history_of_religion.html>.

Weil, S. *Waiting on God* (New York: Perennial Classics, 1950).

Willard, D. 'How Reason Can Survive The Modern University: The Moral Foundations Of Rationality', in Ramos A. & George, M. I. (eds), Faith, Scholarship, and Culture in the 21st Century (Washington DC: The Catholic University of America Press, 2002): 181–191 <http://www.dwillard.org/articles/individual/how-reason-can-survive-the-modern-university-the-moral-foundations-of-ratio>.

Williams, R. *Why Study the Past?* (London, UK: Darton, Longman and Todd, 2005).

Woodbridge, J. D., & James, F. A. *Church History: the Rise and Growth of the Church in Its Cultural, Intellectual, and Political Context. Vol. 2* (Grand Rapids, Michigan: Zondervan, 2013).

Michael Gladwin
Senior Lecturer in History | Editor, *St Mark's Review* St Mark's National Theological Centre, School of Theology Research Fellow,
Public and Contextual Theology Strategic Research Centre (PaCT)
Charles Sturt University
mgladwin@csu.edu.au

18 | 'BUT ONLY ONE THING IS NECESSARY'

CULTIVATING KEY VIRTUES IN TEACHERS WITH A PARTICULAR FOCUS ON 'COURAGE'

Abstract

To foster the emergence of exemplary graduates and teachers, theological institutions typically encourage the cultivation of certain virtues in their staff and students. The primary focus of this paper is classroom teachers and parishioners, with its insights equally applicable to tertiary graduates and online lecturers (hereafter all referred to as 'teachers'). Commencing with a brief reflection on Jesus' response to Martha, 'But only one thing is necessary' (Lk. 10:42; Virtue One), this paper then considers a range of more prominent 'necessary' virtues as a way of interrogating why certain virtues are more visible while others remain 'quieter'. It also urges a closer consideration of less obvious virtues, such as courage (Virtue Two). Finally, the paper makes a distinct contribution to this field by briefly referring to two innovative meta approaches—Quadrivial or 'four rivers' spirituality and a fourfold approach for the practical teaching of such virtues based on: (1) a theology of epektasis, (2) insights from the Divine Pedagogy, (3) from the theology of 'accompaniment', and (4) from the Socratic concept of aporia.

1. Introduction

To foster the emergence of exemplary students, those who will develop into ethical and humane leaders and act with integrity, theological institutions typically encourage the cultivation of certain virtues. This paper emerged from a reflection on Jesus' statement in Luke 10:42 – 'But only one thing is necessary'. I will reflect later on some of the deeper meanings behind this phrase and address it as Virtue One. However, suffice to say that this expression led to the question: 'What is the one virtue or cluster of virtues that is truly necessary or foundational'? In what follows, I will attempt to address this question by exploring what traditionally are numbered among the foundational or 'essential' virtues.

This paper asks: Are there some virtues that are silent, excised, or simply ignored?; And why is it that certain virtues are visible and popular, while others such as courage (treated as Virtue Two) rarely raise a virtuous eyebrow? This paper calls for a practical consideration of a fourfold meta approach (a framework or way of operating) that could assist cultivation of such virtues. Similar to the 'Quadrivial model ('four rivers') of spirituality' mentioned below (refer to Figure 2), the fourfold movements of *epektasis*, Divine Pedagogy, accompaniment, and *aporia* (refer to Figure 1) are described here as a 'meta approach'.

In his writings on 'shared Christian praxis', Thomas Groome describes a meta approach as 'neither a theory alone nor a method alone but a reflective mode of going about the historical tasks of [religious education, spirituality, virtue, and so on]'. He also characterises it as 'an overarching perspective and mode for proceeding that can be readily adapted to a great variety of teaching/learning occasions…'.

Elsewhere he considers the associated term of 'movement'. Each of the four rivers (Figure 2) can be visualised as a movement: 'I use the term *movement* intentionally. It implies that shared praxis is a free-flowing process to be orchestrated, much like the movements of a symphony or a dance. The movements have a logical sequence […] but in an actual event [or application] they overlap, recur, and recombine in other sequences'. Movements are 'dynamic activities and intentions to be consistently honoured over time rather than "steps" in a lockstep procedure'. They should not be programmed or translated into a 'pedagogical cycle' but instead be 'cultivated' among students or adults as a series of 'markers', 'intentions', or 'touchstones'. They can only be rendered intelligible within a concrete and intentional learning event—such as a class, seminar, sermon, retreat, lecture, or in a discussion about a particular virtue such as courage.

At this juncture, the paper will focus on the movements of the second 'virtue meta approach' (Figure 1) and provide a brief example of each in relation to courage—at a future stage, they will be developed into a paper in their own right: (1) *epektasis* as stretching towards one's full potential of Christ in God — for example, the teacher stretches the student from rudimentary notions of courage to a consideration of the role of prudence and the existence of formative and deformative approaches to courage; (2) an affinity with the *Divine Pedagogy*—the way in which God leads and 'teaches'. The teacher asks the student to reflect upon God's presence and absence during their journey towards authentic courage; (3) the theology of *accompaniment*—the teacher reflects with the student on how God accompanies them on their journey towards courage in light of various scripture texts (for example, what courage is required towards strangers when reflecting on this passage?: 'Do not neglect to show hospitality to strangers, for by doing that some have entertained angels without knowing it' (Heb. 13:2); and (4) the inclusion of *aporia* or the situation of being in doubt, perplexed, or confused about how best to proceed. For example, the student might experience *aporia* upon considering the nature of courage, when distinguishing between true and false courage, and reflecting upon the praxis of courage—how do they think they have or would respond during an event that involved violence and trauma?

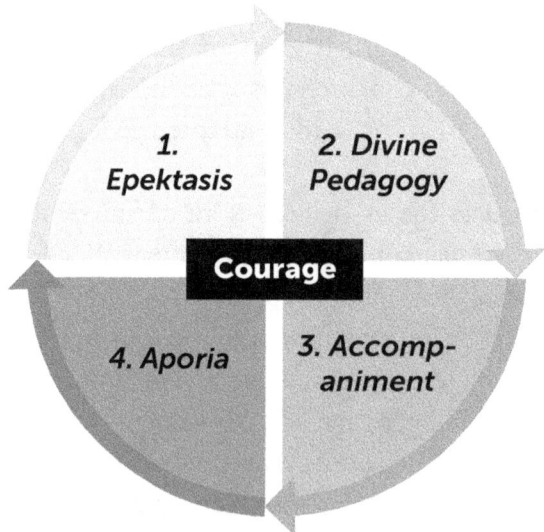

Figure 1 – *The meta approach that includes the movements of Epektasis, Divine Pedagogy, Accompaniment, and Aporia, applied to discussion of the virtue of courage.*

2. Some Prefacing Comments and 'Working Definitions'

Spirituality

This paper makes the following working assumptions about the nature of 'spirituality' and then of 'virtue'. With regard to *spirituality*, it proposes that the student could employ the following approach, both to cultivate spiritual wisdom and to provide a reliable calculus for teaching spirituality in a meaningful and practical way in the classroom. I refer to a model based on the research of Nancy Ammerman, who argues that spirituality is not simply a topic or discourse. It is a living, interwoven reality comprising traditions, narratives, practices, and values. My preference in the remainder of this paper is for the articulation of 'disciplines' rather than 'practices', and 'virtues' rather than 'values'. For example, a topic such as 'courage' needs to be understood and taught both as an interfaith reality connected to the Abrahamic religions and as a virtue symbiotically related to narratives and disciplines. In addition, in applying the Quadrivial or 'four rivers' meta approach to the virtue of courage, as the name suggests, one would need to consider the interwoven relationship between spiritual *traditions*, *narratives*, *disciplines*, and *virtues* (ST, SN, SD, and SV – refer to Figure 2).

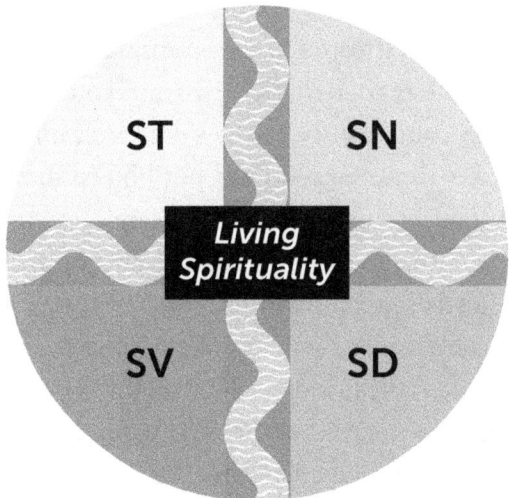

Figure 2 – *The Quadrivial or 'four rivers' meta approach to spiritual formation, leading to an integrated 'living spirituality'. It embraces spiritual traditions (Abrahamic), narratives, disciplines, and virtues: ST, SN, SD and SV. It is designed to be a series of free-flowing and interactive spiritual process, similar to the movements of a dance, artwork, or symphony.*

In this focus on 'courage', students can be challenged to discern links between courage in Christianity (for example, *tradition* and *narrative* are combined in the episode where Jesus defends the woman accused of adultery, John 7:53–8:11), *ometz* (אֹמֶץ, Hebrew for 'the willingness to take action')[1] in Judaism, and *shajaea* (شجاعة, Arabic for 'bravery, valour, guts, spunk')[2] in Islam. Students could then link these insights to the *discipline* of *lectio divina* (focusing on the same passage from John's Gospel) and then back in a circular trajectory to the *virtue* of 'courage'. If these four aspects are not intertwined during the teaching process, then focusing on one in isolation, such as the practice of *lectio divina*, risks spirituality being received by students as a dry and vacuous technique. Without its traditions and narratives (the upper half of the cycle), spirituality lacks its theoretical foundations. Without its disciplines and virtues (the lower half of the cycle), spirituality is deprived of its praxis and potential for transformation. Ammerman's integrated approach and my own Quadrivial model are also supported by the research of Puchalski and co-authors,[3] Bregman,[4] and Loue.[5]

3. Virtue and Virtues

The concept of *virtue* is well attested in the scriptures. Wisdom 1:1-2 lists several virtues and encourages the reader to 'Love virtue, you who are judges on earth, let honesty prompt your thinking about the Lord, seek him in simplicity of heart; since he is to be found by those who do not put him to the test, he shows himself to those who *do not distrust him*' (NRSV, my emphases). The Scriptures imply that those who live the Gospel and practise the virtues are like those who build their house on rock: 'Jesus said to his disciples: "Everyone then who hears these words of mine and acts on them will be like a wise [person] who built [their] house on rock. The rain fell, the floods came, and the winds blew and beat on that house, but it did not fall, because it had been founded on rock"' (Matt. 7:24–25). The reward of virtue is not in practising it, nor is it being praised for it. As St. Augustine says: 'The reward of virtue will be God..., who gave the virtue'.[6]

---

1   Ulpan La-Inyan, "How to say 'courage' in Hebrew."
2   Word Hippo, "How to say 'courage' in Arabic."
3   Puchalski et al., 'Improving the spiritual dimension of whole person care', 642-56.
4   Bregman, *The ecology of spirituality*.
5   Loue, *Handbook of Religion and Spirituality*.
6   Augustine, *Concerning the City of God Against the Pagans*, 22.30.

The author's home tradition of Catholic Christianity defines 'virtue' in the *Catechism of the Catholic Church* as 'an habitual and firm disposition to do the good. It allows the person not only to perform good acts, but to give the best of [themselves]. The virtuous person tends toward the good with all [their] sensory and spiritual powers; [he/she] pursues the good and chooses it in concrete actions' (The Holy See, n.1803). This definition is underscored by a quotation from Gregory of Nyssa: 'The goal of a virtuous life is to become like God' (citing *De beatitudinibus*, 1:PG 44, 1200D). This saying of the Nyssan parallels other theological categories within Christianity, such as the cultivation of the *imago dei* (that humans are made in the image and likeness of God) and the parallel Eastern Christian teachings of *theosis* and *deification*.[7]

As Trillo notes, the virtues do not stand alone. They are viewed by scholars in perpetual tension with the vices, such as an achievement of a healthy balance between attachment to comfort (sensual response) and austerity (temperate response). Any one virtue normally represents the mean between two extremes: for example, honour is 'the virtue intermediate between ambition and unambitiousness'.[8] Hence, the purpose of an authentic and struggling existence is to live a temperate or intermediate life governed by the virtues, in order to cultivate confidence, flourishing, and peace of mind.[9] Its further purpose is to cultivate a life of *eudaimonia*, meaning more than simple 'happiness', but a state where one strives towards one's full potential with head, heart, and hands, governed at the same time by a style of 'conative' or 'wisdom' knowing.[10]

3.1 Virtue One – Returning to 'the One Thing Necessary'

What exactly was Jesus referring to in Luke 10:38-42 (NRSV) when he spoke of 'the one thing necessary'? During this episode, when Jesus visits the home of Martha, Mary, and Lazarus, Martha complains that she is overwhelmed with domestic duties and that her sister Mary, sitting at the feet of the Teacher, ought to help her—a request that was potentially insulting to the visiting Jewish rabbi. Jesus replies: 'Martha, Martha, you are anxious and troubled by many things.

---

7 According to Dominican Vincent of Beauvais (c.1190–1264) the opposite of the *imago dei* is 'ignorance', since it is capable of destroying the divine image in us; in Evans, *Fifty Key Medieval Thinkers*, 124.
8 Aristotle, *The Nicomachean Ethics*, Book IV, Part 3.
9 Trillo, *Vices & Virtues*, 12. Refer to his chart in Trillo, *Vices*, 108, based on Aristotle and others, showing selected virtues and vices in tension.
10 Groome, *Sharing Faith*, 26-32.

But there is need for only one. Mary chose the good part. It won't be taken away from her' (Luke 10:41-42).

What then is this 'one thing necessary' that here the paper recontextualises as the 'one virtue necessary'? As Johnson points out, Mary is portrayed as 'listening to [Jesus] speak', meaning that she literally 'listened to his word (*logos*)'. She was attentive to what he was saying and therefore received him as he was, a prophet who spoke 'the word of God'.[11] Martha, on the other hand, is 'overwhelmed' or is 'being distracted' by so much serving since there was so much to be done (understandably) with the presence of so many guests.[12] In verse 41, Martha is described as 'anxious' and as one who is 'putting herself in an uproar'.[13] Jesus' expression 'there is need for only one' refers to 'the essential note of *hospitality* which is to pay attention to the guest; only that is necessary; the rest is optional'. By contrast, 'Mary chose the good part' (v. 42), meaning that she has acted ethically and with courage in listening to and receiving the person of the Prophet present in Jesus.[14] As we shall see, 'the one thing necessary' thus proliferates many equally important companion virtues—among them hospitality, compassion, attentiveness, receptiveness, listening, and the prioritisation of 'being'.

Jesus challenges the reader/listener in every age to go beyond the customary threshold of virtue—to cultivate compassion that is not simply a feeling but translates itself into the self-giving that takes risks, that disposes of the self and one's possessions, and then allows the other to leave without clinging; and to promote the hospitality that receives the other as the other wishes to be received, that listens.[15] Pope Francis cites Pope John Paul II about 'the one thing necessary' when he refers to the latter's seminal document *Novo millennio ineunte* ('At the beginning of the new millennium'): 'Our is a time of continual movement which often leads to restlessness, with the risk of "doing for the sake of doing". We must resist this temptation by trying "to be" before trying 'to do'.[16] Francis frames 'the one thing necessary' in this manner: 'In the being and vocation of every Christian is the personal encounter with the Lord. To seek God is to seek

---

11   Johnson, *The Gospel of Luke*, 173, n.39.
12   Johnson, *Luke*, 173, n. 40.
13   Johnson, *Luke*, 173, n. 41.
14   Johnson, *Luke*, 174, n. 42.
15   Johnson, *Luke*, 176.
16   *Novoe millennio ineunte*, 15, cited in Pope Francis. *The people wish to See Jesus*, 9.

his face, to enter into his intimacy'.[17] To summarise, Jesus' rabbinic conversation with Martha and Mary implies a suite of virtues under the banner of 'the one thing necessary'—among these one could list: listening or paying attention, hospitality, resting in the presence of Jesus, and compassion. These characteristics are also shared by the virtue of 'courage' to be examined below.

3.2 What is 'the One Virtue Necessary'?

What, then, do other saints and scholars identify as 'the one virtue necessary', whether singly or in a family cluster of virtues? Perhaps, Karen Armstrong would answer 'compassion'.[18] St Benedict might proffer 'charity' or 'humility'[19] or the associated qualities of 'dispossession' or 'poverty of spirit'.[20] Gregory of Sinai and Gregory Palamas from within the Eastern Christian 'hesychastic' tradition might submit the virtue of 'stillness'.[21] Others more attuned to the philosophy of language might say silence.[22] Henry David Thoreau preferred a minimalist virtue: 'Our life is frittered away by detail [therefore engage in] Simplicity! Simplicity! Simplicity!'[23] Pope Francis offers the tripartite echo of 'Dialogue, Dialogue, Dialogue!'—'When leaders in various fields ask me for advice, my response is always the same: dialogue, dialogue, dialogue. The only way for individuals, families, and societies to grow, the only way for the life of peoples to progress, is via the culture of encounter, a culture in which all have something good to give and all can receive something good in return'.[24] Martin Luther states: 'One thing, and only one thing, is necessary for Christian life, righteousness, and freedom. That one thing is the most holy Word of God, the gospel of Christ'.[25] Søren Kierkegaard instead avers that everyone who lives according to the truth 'is to will one thing [and] must be led to will the good'. It would be a 'drastic error of presumptuous, ungodly enthusiasm: to will the

---

17 Pope Francis, *The people wish to See Jesus*, 9.
18 Armstrong, *Twelve steps to a compassionate life*.
19 Chittister, *The Monastery of the Heart*, 169-186.
20 Casey, *Strangers to the City*, 76-90.
21 Zecher, *The Role of Death*, 6-7.
22 Sestigiani, 'Silence, the "Virtue of Speaking"', 481–496. For additional moral and theological perspectives, refer to: Pinckaers et al., 'The Virtue of Silence', 64-73. Refer also to: Brueggemann. *Interrupting Silence*. Brueggemann countenances the need to break the silence of oppression, poverty, racism, ecological devastation, and many other injustices; see also Rahner. *Encounters with Silence*.
23 Thoreau, *Walden or Life in the Woods*, 74.
24 Pope Francis, 'Meeting with Brazil's Leaders of Society'.
25 Luther & Grimm, *On Christian Liberty*.

great, no matter whether it is good or evil'. Human existence thus presents a stark choice—either choose the great and double-minded persona, accompanied by its visibility of triumph and superiority, or become that 'person who wills only one thing when he[she] wills the good *can will only the good in truth*'.[26]

Soon after my initial foray into this topic in 2016, I asked this same question about 'the one virtue necessary' of Dom David Barry, a priest, academic, and member of the Benedictine community of New Norcia, Western Australia—the only monastic town in Australia.[27] Dom Barry's answer was 'reverence'[28]:

> Reverence for God in the Divine Self (in older biblical and catechetical terminology, 'fear of God'). This reverence (the basis of humility) arises from an awareness based on reason and on faith [...]This is where detachment and compassion naturally emerge, and Christian believers engage in appropriate forms of service – appropriate to the perceived need and to the individual person's particular gifts and limitations.[29]

3.3 The 'Quieter' or Ignored Virtues?

As MacIntyre has shown, understandings of 'virtue' and what is considered the most important virtues have changed throughout history.[30] However, from a contemporary perspective, it is important to interrogate why certain virtues are more visible while others remain what Spencer terms more hidden and 'quiet'.[31] Spencer lists seven 'quieter virtues'—discernment, innocence, authenticity, modesty, reverence, contentment, and generosity.[32] Another commentator, Rolheiser, notes the routine obfuscation of 'gratitude' as a central virtue.[33] Chittister refers to humility as 'the lost virtue'.[34] For Thomas Aquinas, the most

---

26   Kierkegaard, 'Purity of heart is to will one thing', citations in order from 276, 272 & 271, italics occur in the original for the last quote.
27   The New Norcia Benedictine Community home page is at: https://www.newnorcia.wa.edu.au/
28   Barry is well-supported by other commentators on the topic. For example, Peter Fink SJ applauds reverence as a quality oriented towards both awe and fear of God and 'indicating a relational stance of deep respect before a person, or...any reality that is held to be sacred'. It is linked to prayer, symbolism, holy objects, and sacramentality. Refer to: Peter E. Fink, 'Reverence', 1098-1101.
29   Barry, Personal email correspondence, 7 May 2017.
30   MacIntyre, *After Virtue*, 211-237.
31   Spencer, *Awakening the quieter virtues*.
32   Spence, *Awakening*, 21-180 and passim.
33   Rolheiser, 'Gratitude: The basic virtue'.
34   Chittister, *Wisdom distilled from the Daily*, 51-66.

ignored and least understood virtue is 'prudence'.[35] Another largely overlooked virtue is that of 'courage'.

3.4 Virtue Two – Courage

On 15 March 2019, three weeks in the past when this paper was delivered, a gunman carried out terrorist attacks during Friday prayer at two mosques in Christchurch, New Zealand. The attacks targeted the Al Noor Mosque and the Linwood Islamic Centre, killing 50 people and injuring 50 others. Prime Minister Jacinda Ardern described the attacks as 'one of New Zealand's darkest days'. It was also the deadliest mass shooting in modern New Zealand history. Such a catastrophic and traumatic event demands a response in relation to our conference themes of 'virtue' and 'character' and especially in light of contemporary leanings toward a more 'practical theology'.[36] In this paper, I have sought to make a small contribution by focusing on one virtue required in such situations: 'courage'. One of Australia's most prominent Muslim leaders, Professor Mohamad Abdalla,[37] visited the injured, their families and friends following the attack and reflected on the calibre of their bravery: 'But the common thread in their response to the horrific events of 15 March is profound bravery, deep consideration and thoughtfulness, and a complete lack of desire for vengeance'.[38] In what follows, I would like to create a dialectic between the Christchurch event and a 'theology of the virtue of courage'.

Theologian and ethicist Stanley Hauerwas contemplates 'courage' in terms that we shall return to a number of times during the remainder of this paper. I

---

35 Holy See, *Catechism,* 1806. '[Prudence] is not to be confused with timidity or fear, nor with duplicity or dissimulation. It is called *auriga virtutum* (the charioteer of the virtues); it guides the other virtues by setting rule and measure...[and] guides the judgment of conscience', citing St. Thomas Aquinas, *STh* II-II, 47, 2.
36 Disappointingly, my consulted volume entitled Miller-McLemore (ed.), *The Wiley Blackwell Companion to Practical Theology* has no significant entries related to violence, terrorism, brutality, and its cognates (which it needs to address in terms of 9/11 and subsequent events), but it does contain significant treatments of 'Suffering' and 'Healing'.
37 Professor Mohamad Abdalla is one of Australia's most prominent and respected Muslim leaders, combining the roles of an academic scholar, public intellectual, community leader, and commentator. He is the founding Director of the Centre for Islamic Thought and Education, University of South Australia. Over the last 15 years, he has played a leading role in establishing Islamic Studies (Research and Teaching) as an academic area of study in Australia, including securing $8m to found the National Centre of Excellence for Islamic Studies (NCEIS), a collaboration between the University of Melbourne, Griffith University, and the University of Western Sydney. Summarised on 30 March 2019 from: http://people.unisa.edu.au/mohamad.abdalla
38 Abdalla, 'Finding dignity and grace...'.

quote from his advice on various virtues to his godson, comprising a series of letters on fifteen virtues.[39] He advises his godson that courage can be manifested in his willingness to transform and remain constant in a world of change and violence; to understand that courage is an everyday virtue; and realise that courage is not something you have or 'manufacture on demand' but is something that you discover you have *after the fact or event*.[40] Hauerwas counsels his godson that courage requires vulnerability, and comes into play when one confronts every unknown as a 'little death': 'In your lifetime you'll face many unknowns, and you'll have to be courageous'.[41] Courage, he proposes, names the determination to see one's beliefs and commitments through and the willingness to live them out and thus be open to transformation.[42] Perhaps, the most visceral advice on courage provided by Hauerwas is his conviction 'that the Crucifixion reveals a God who redeems nonviolently' and who thus displays and models courage. Courage is required 'to be committed to living nonviolently [...] [as did] Martin of Tours, Dorothy Day, and Martin Luther King'.[43] Finally, the author links the Crucifixion and non-violence to that larger story that impregnates his life with meaning—the Gospel as a proclamation of the kingdom—which then enables him to live dangerously and to take the risk of nonviolence and trust.[44] He concludes: 'Courage so understood is embodied in skills of speech and behaviour that make imaginative alternatives possible... [this is supported by] courageous friends [...] [who will assist his godson] to live courageously, that is, truthfully'.[45]

The word 'courage' (from the Latin *cor* meaning heart) typically connotes 'the power or quality of dealing with or facing danger, fear, [and] pain' along with 'the confidence to act in accordance with one's beliefs'.[46] Both aspects were exemplified during the Christchurch shootings. One instance among many (including police and people who confronted the gunman and were shot or killed) was the case of Abdul Aziz, praying with his four sons at the Linwood mosque who, instead of running from the gunshots, picked up the first object he could find, a credit card machine, and flung it at the attacker. He later chased him

---

39   Hauerwas, *The Character of Virtue: Letters to a Godson*.
40   Hauerwas, *Character of Virtue*, 109-111.
41   Hauerwas, *Character of Virtue*, 112-113; quote from 113.
42   Hauerwas, *Character of Virtue*, 113.
43   Hauerwas, *Character of Virtue*, 114.
44   Hauerwas, *Character of Virtue*, 116.
45   Hauerwas, *Character of Virtue*, 116-117.
46   McKeown (Sen. Ed.), *Collins Concise Australian Dictionary*, 381.

into the carpark and then smashed the gunman's car window with a discarded rifle. It is highly likely that Mr Aziz prevented the gunman from returning with another rifle to continue his attack and hence prevented further casualties.[47] However, as we shall see below, there is a distinction to be made between this act of genuine courage and others of false, deformative, or 'bad' courage.

For C. S. Lewis, courage is ranked as one of the most important virtues. In *The Screwtape Letters*, he pictures a senior devil advising a younger devil: '[God, 'The Enemy'] sees as well as you do that courage is not simply *one* of the virtues, but *the form of every virtue at the testing point*, which means at the point of highest reality'.[48] Hepburn also comments on the indispensability of courage: 'Given the nature of the human lifeworld, few worthwhile enterprises are possible for those who will take no avoidable risks: such a policy would entail (at the everyday level) no parenthood, little travel, few ventures in work or play; and (in extreme situations) no standing up to tyranny, no speaking out against injustice'.[49] One of Walter Brueggemann's latest books, *Interrupting Silence*, on the surface, is a treatment of ordinary 'silence'. However, it could be argued that its deeper concern is prophetic courage. Its subtitle is 'God's Command to Speak Out'. For Brueggemann, a referential icon of courage is the story of the widow's prayer, where Jesus exhorts his listeners 'to pray always and not to lose heart' (Luke 18:1). He observes that intercession and other forms of prayer represent an 'intrusion into the courts of power on behalf of another [and is] central to the church's action in prayer'.[50] Throughout the eight textual studies in his book, Brueggemann is struck by 'how silence breaking is evoked by attention to the body in pain'.[51] Such was also the case with the shooting incidents at the two mosques.

Particularly after the Christchurch event, the virtue of 'courage' has been epitomised in a range of statements from the survivors. The following views were expressed during that period to Mohamad Abdallah, who visited Christchurch at that time. Each was expressed without a hint of vengeance or resentment, with many respondees discerning the footholds of their courage in future hope and in Islamic tradition: 'terrorism must not scare us. Racism must not divide us' (Ahmad); 'We trust in God. Don't be scared to go to Mosques and

---

47 Cave, 'Quick Action, Near Miss and Courage in New Zealand Attacks'.
48 Lewis, *The Screwtape Letters*, 148–149; my emphases.
49 Hepburn, 'Courage', 169.
50 Brueggemann, *Interrupting Silence*, 4.
51 Brueggemann, *Interrupting Silence*, 7.

schools' (Mustafa); 'the Prophets of God were tested more severely' (young man in his 20s). Adnan Ibrahim lost his three-year-old son, the youngest victim of the twin shootings. 'In deep pain and sorrow, he showed grace and dignity. Verily we belong to God and to Him we shall return'. Equally courageous was Ambreen Nadeem, who lost both her husband and her 21-year-old son, Talha: 'I pity the killer because his heart was filled with hate, not love'.[52] Mohamad Abdallah concludes: 'anger, vengeance and resentment could take hold in a community so demolished by violence, I found the exact opposite. They were compassionate. They were forgiving. They were humane'.[53] These could be held up as some of the defining markers of true courage.

Yet, one could also diagnose forms of 'courage' that are negative or deformative, with both forms equally relevant to the Christchurch shootings and to any similar event characterised by suffering, brutality, or trauma. Pury and her co-authors ask: 'Is courage always a virtue?'[54] They conclude that 'the subjective nature of judging the worth of a goal may on occasion lead to "bad courage"'[55] and argue 'that some actions may involve the mechanism of courage when seen from the viewpoint of the actor but lead to non-virtuous and even bad outcomes from a different viewpoint'.[56] After examining the three common features of courageous action (Volition, Risk, and Value of Goal), they conclude: 'this study provides evidence for the existence of bad courage – instances where the individual voluntarily assumes a known personal risk to work toward a goal…that is both valuable to the actor but abhorrent to wider society'.[57] Petersen and Seligman draw a similar conclusion: 'Bravery raises the moral and social conscience of a society…Because bravery entails judgment, the ends that a person's action serves are part of the consideration about whether an act reflects bravery…Hence, we are reluctant to designate a murderer as courageous, even when he takes great risks to accomplish his crime'.[58]

From a biblical perspective, some echoes of courage at Christchurch can be found in texts that associate courage with situations in which 'one's heart goes out' to others in distress (Gen. 42:28), or where one's heart 'faints' (Job. 23:16)

---

52 Abdallah, 'Finding dignity and grace'.
53 Abdallah, 'Finding dignity and grace'.
54 Pury et al., 'Is courage always a virtue? Suicide, killing, and bad courage'.
55 Pury et al., 'Is courage…', 383.
56 Pury et al., 'Is courage…', 383.
57 Pury et al., 'Is courage…', 386.
58 Peterson & Seligman, *Character Strengths and Virtues*, 214.

or 'melts' (Ezek. 21:7).[59] Jesus is viewed as a model who displayed courage in the face of weakness, vulnerability, and brokenness. He moved 'beyond the outer limits of human courage by daring to die, not for good people but for sinners (Rom. 5:6-8)'.[60] Jesus 'endurance of the cross [and his ultimate martyrdom] (Heb. 12:2-3) is the model to which those who are "losing heart" should look…[the same author] closes with an exhortation to strengthen feeble arms and weak knees…to regain courage'.[61] Ultimately, the Jewish and Christian religions, in particular, are traditions of hope, resilience, and resurrection. Students at all levels can be encouraged to reflect on such passages in the twin context of practical theology and praxis. They should be invited where possible to consider concrete examples involving suffering, trauma, trial, persecution, and even death,[62] especially within the local Australian context.[63]

Conclusions and Future Directions

This paper has examined the areas of spirituality, virtue, and the quieter virtues. It has argued the importance of addressing the question raised by Virtue One: 'what is the one virtue necessary', whether as a sole virtue or a cluster of foundational virtues. It has explored 'courage' as Virtue Two in the context of the Christchurch shootings and proposes the usefulness of a dialectic between the virtue and the event—both framed within the ambit of practical theology. The entire paper has stressed the importance of establishing links between

---

[59] Passages and examples from: Ryken et al, *Dictionary of Biblical Image*, 176.

[60] Ryken et al., *Dictionary*, 176.

[61] Riken et al., *Dictionary*, 176. A claim supported by Qiaoying, 'Aquinas' Transformation of the Virtue of Courage', 482-484. The author argues that Aquinas has defined the principal act of perfect courage as martyrdom, thereby pointing to Christ as the perfect martyr and the paradigm of a courageous person. As in the case of the Christchurch gunman, one could of course consider oneself a martyr and courageous without this actually being the case in relation to authentic Christian courage.

[62] Refer, for example, to these themes in the scriptures and the lives of the saints but also modern catalogues such as '2019 Watch List', which states that one in nine Christians are persecuted for their faith, 50,000–70,000 Christians are believed to be in labour camps in Korea and, of the 4,136 recorded deaths of Christians directly resulting from persecution reported in the 2019 World Watch List, Nigeria alone accounts for about 90% (3,731). Retrieved on 2 April 2019 from: https://www.opendoors.org.au/persecuted-christians/blog/2019-world-watch-list-1-in-9-christians-persecuted-for-their-faith/ What type of courage would be required of students in such circumstances? Case studies of these and other contexts are recommended.

[63] See, for example, a discussion of 'Islam In Our Backyard' in Iner, *Islamaphobia in Australia*, 11; and the same author's contention that 'The antidote to Islamaphobia is for the Christian faith to play its part in nurturing the capacity for all "to live faithfully" in the midst of diversity', in Iner, *Islamaphobia*, 14.

theory and practice, between real-life events and the cultivation of practical virtues within students and graduates. It has also proposed two meta approaches—Quadrivial Spirituality and the four movements for cultivating virtue. In the second meta approach, it has argued that a pedagogy designed to cultivate virtuous character could profit by embracing the four movements of *epektasis*, the Divine Pedagogy, a theology of accompaniment, and the Socratic concept of *aporia*. Examples were provided to align each of these elements with the virtue of courage and to call forth a response from students.

Vulnerability is not always associated with a virtue such as courage. Yet, to be vulnerable is central to human experience,[64] and certainly to this event. Healing transpires through the wound, whether through physical, emotional, symbolic, or other manifestations and not by avoiding this difficult passage. Perhaps, potentially, the most courageous act to emerge from the Christchurch tragedy is an acceptance by each traumatised person that a transformation needs to occur within each of their individual selves—replacing shame, self-loathing, and any assumptions of guilt with compassionate acceptance.[65]

The 'Focus' for this conference called for the shaping of graduates as societal leaders who are also decent human beings and who act ethically and with humanity and integrity—with a view to building a better society and being capable of transforming others. Such aspirations are echoed in the words of one of the survivors of the Christchurch shootings. Professor Mohamad Abdallah's conversation with this survivor illuminates the need to pursue at greater length those more profound connections between the virtues (especially courage) but equally between woundedness (internal and external), vulnerability, healing, and embodiment of full humanity:

> I then visited Fuad, another middle-aged man originally from Afghanistan who also escaped death. He had been struck by a bullet in the back and another just missing the back of his head. His wounds were visible. He told me, with four children, he was just grateful to be alive. Not resentful or vengeful, he was full of praise for Prime Minister Jacinda Ardern and her deep expression of humanity.[66]

---

64 Refer to McCoy, *Wounded Heroes*.
65 Fisher, *Healing the Fragmented Selves of Trauma Survivors*.
66 Abdulla, 'Finding dignity and grace'.

Bibliography

Abdalla, M. 'Finding dignity and grace in the aftermath of the Christchurch attack', *The Conversation* (22 March 2019) <https://theconversation.com/finding-dignity-and-grace-in-the-aftermath-of-the-christchurch-attack-114072> [accessed 30 March 2019].

Ammerman, N. T. *Sacred Stories, Spiritual Tribes: Finding Religion in Everyday Life* (Oxford: OUP, 2013).

Aristotle, *The Nicomachean Ethics* (transl. David Ross, rev. & intro. Lesley Brown; Oxford, UK: OUP, 2009).

Armstrong, K. *Twelve Steps to a Compassionate Life* (London, UK: The Bodley Head, 2011).

Augustine. *Concerning the City of God Against the Pagans* (transl. H. Bettenson; New York: Penguin, 1984).

Barry, D., Fr. *Personal email correspondence on the central virtues*. Reply sent from Holy Trinity Abbey, New Norcia, WA on 7 May 2017. Refer also to: https://www.newnorcia.wa.edu.au/

Bregman, L. *The Ecology of Spirituality: Meanings, Virtues, and Practices in a Post-Religious Age* (New York, NY: Springer, 2014).

Brueggemann, W. *Interrupting Silence: God's Command to Speak Out* (Louisville, KY: Westminster John Knox, 2018).

Brueggemann, W. *The Prophetic Imagination* (Philadelphia, PA: Fortress, 1983).

Casey, M. *Strangers to the City: Reflections on the Beliefs and Values of the Rule of Saint Benedict* (Brewster, MA: Paraclete, 2005).

Cave, D. 'Quick Action, Near Miss and Courage in New Zealand Attacks', *The New York Times* (17 March 2019), 1-2. <https://www.nytimes.com/2019/03/17/world/asia/new-zealand-shootings-police-response.html> [accessed 29 March 2019].

Chittister, J. *The Monastery of the Heart: An Invitation to a Meaningful Life* (Katonah, NY: BlueBridge, 2011).

Chittister, J. D. *Wisdom distilled from the Daily: Living the Rule of St. Benedict Today* (New York, NY: HarperOne, 1990).

Division of Christian Education of the NCCC in the USA. *The Holy Bible: New Revised Standard Version* (London, UK: HarperCollinsPublishers, 1998).

Evans, G. P. 'Cardinal Virtues', in Michael Downey (ed.), *The New Dictionary of Catholic Spirituality* (Collegeville, MN: Liturgical Press, 1993): 114-117.

Evans, G. R. *Fifty Key Medieval Thinkers* (London & New York: Routledge, 2002).

Fink, P. E. 'Reverence', in Peter E. Fink (ed.), *The New Dictionary of Sacramental Worship* (Collegeville, MN: Liturgical Press, 1990): 1098-1101.

Fisher, J. *Healing the Fragmented Selves of Trauma Survivors: Overcoming Internal Self-Alienation* (London, UK: Taylor & Francis, 2017).

Groome, T. H. *Sharing Faith: The Way of Shared Praxis* (Eugene, OR: Wipf & Stock, 1998).

Hauerwas, S. *The Character of Virtue: Letters to a Godson* (intro. Samuel Wells; Grand Rapids, MI: William B. Eerdmans, 2018).

Hepburn, R. H. 'Courage', in Ted Honderich (ed.), *The Oxford Companion to Philosophy* (Oxford, UK: Oxford University Press, 1995): 169.

Iner, D. (ed.) with L. Briskman et al. (contribs). *Islamophobia in Australia 2014–2016* (Sydney, NSW: Centre for Islamic Studies and Civilisation, Charles Sturt University, 2017).

Johnson, L. T. (ed. D.J. Harrington). *The Gospel of Luke* (Collegeville, MN: Liturgical Press, 1991).

Kierkegaard, S. 'Purity of heart is to will one thing', in Howard V. Hong & Edna H. Hong (eds.), *The Essential Kierkegaard* (Princeton, NJ: Princeton University, 1997/1847): 271-276.

Lewis, C. S. *The Screwtape Letters* (London, UK: Fontana, 1955).

Loue, S. *Handbook of Religion and Spirituality in Social Work Practice and Research* (New York: Springer, 2017).

Luther, M. (author) and Grimm, H. J. (ed.). *On Christian Liberty* (Minneapolis, MN: Fortress, 2003/1520).

MacIntyre, A. *After Virtue: A Study in Moral Theory* (London & New York: Bloomsbury, 2007).

McCoy, M. B. *Wounded Heroes: Vulnerability as a Virtue in Ancient Greek Literature and Philosophy* (Oxford, UK: OUP, 2013).

McKeown, C. (Sen. Ed.), *Collins Concise Australian Dictionary* (Glasgow, UK: Collins, 2008).

Miller-McLemore, B. J. (ed.). *The Wiley Blackwell Companion to Practical Theology* (Oxford, UK: Wiley Blackwell, 2014).

Ospino, H. 'Theological horizons for a pedagogy of accompaniment,' *Religious Education* 105.4 (2010), 413-429.

Petcu, L. 'The doctrine of Epektasis. One of the major contributions of Saint Gregory of Nyssa to the history of thinking,' *Revista Portuguesa de Filosofia* 73.2 (2017), 771-782.

Peterson, C. & Seligman, M. E. P. *Character Strengths and Virtues: A Handbook and Classification* (Oxford & New York: Oxford University Press, 2004).

Pinckaers, S., Guevin, B. M., and Sherwin, M. 'The Virtue of Silence', in *Passions and Virtue* (Washington, D.C.: Catholic University of America, 2015): 64-73.

Pope Francis (Jorge Mario Bergoglio). *The People Wish to See Jesus: Reflections for those who Teach* (transl. Michael O'Hearn; New York: Claretian/Herder & Herder, 2014)

Pope Francis, 'Meeting with Brazil's Leaders of Society' (27 July 2013), para. 3 <http://w2.vatican.va/content/francesco/en/speeches/2013/july/documents/papa-francesco_20130727_gmg-classe-dirigente-rio.html> [accessed 25 March 2019].

Puchalski, C. M., Vitillo, R., Hull, S. K. & Reller, N. 'Improving the spiritual dimension of whole person care: Reaching national and international consensus', *Journal of Palliative Medicine* 17 (2014), 642-56.

Pury, C. L. S., Starkey, C. B., Kulik, R. E., Skjerning, K. L. & Sullivan, E. A. 'Is courage always a virtue? Suicide, killing, and bad courage', *The Journal of Positive Psychology* 10.5 (2015), 383-388.

Qiaoying, L. U. 'Aquinas' Transformation of the Virtue of Courage', *Frontiers of Philosophy in China* 8.3 (2013), 471-484.

Rahner, K. *Encounters with Silence* (transl. James M. Demske; South Bend, IN: St. Augustine's Press, 1960/1938).

Rolheiser, R. 'Gratitude: The basic virtue (1992)' <http://ronrolheiser.com/gratitude-the-basic-virtue/#.Wopz46huY2w> [accessed 19 February 2018].

Russi, J. 'A way through the moral maze', *The Tablet* (23 April 2016), 14.

Ryken, L., Wilhoit, J. C. & Longman III, T. (gen.eds.). *Dictionary of Biblical Imagery* (Downers Grove, IL: IVP Academic, 1998).

Sestigiani, S. 'Silence, the "Virtue of Speaking". David Malouf's An Imaginary Life and Walter Benjamin's Philosophy of Language', *Orbis Litterarum* 65.6 (2010), 481-496.

Spencer, G. *Awakening the Quieter Virtues* (Downers Grove, IL: IVP Books, 2010).

The Holy See. *Catechism of the Catholic Church*, Second Edition. Part Three, Life in Christ; Section One, Man's Vocation Life in the Spirit; Chapter One, The Dignity of the Human Person; Article 7, The Virtues (nn.1803-1845). (Strathfield, NSW: St Pauls, 2000).

Thoreau, H.D. (intro. W.S. Merwin, & afterword W. Howarth). *Walden or Life in the Woods and 'Civil Disobedience'* (London, UK: Signet Classics, 2012/1854).

Trillo, A.O. *Vices & Virtues: Knowing, Accepting and Improving Yourself* (transl. Carolina Gambini; Ligouri, MI: Ligouri Publications, 2015).

Ulpan La-Inyan, 'How to say "courage" in Hebrew' <https://ulpan.com/how-to-say-courage-in-hebrew/> [accessed 25 March 2019].

White, J. D. *The Way God Teaches: Catechesis and the Divine Pedagogy* (Huntington, IN: Our Sunday Visitor, 2014).

Word Hippo. 'How to say "courage" in Arabic' <https://www.wordhippo.com/what-is/the/arabic-word-for-a2d90f4e973af241b3b81461af2cfbe66acb0429.html> [accessed 25 March 2019].

Zecher, J. L. *The Role of Death in the Ladder of Divine Ascent and the Greek Ascetic Tradition* (Oxford, UK: OUP, 2015): 1-45.

Peter Mudge
Sydney College of Divinity
pjpmudge@gmail.com

PART 4

TEACHING FOR GRADUATE DEVELOPMENT: PRACTICAL CONSIDERATIONS

19 | FACILITATING STUDENT FORMATION IN TERTIARY EDUCATION

Abstract
This paper will build upon the foundations established in 'Student Formation' to suggest ways in which character formation might be better facilitated in the Christian tertiary context. This will include the contribution of Graduate Attributes, formal and informal elements of the College curriculum, assessment of efforts to encourage character growth, and the appropriate boundaries and expectations of what can be reasonably achieved.

1. The Company We Keep
This paper will build upon the foundations established in the paper 'God's Exemplary Graduates: Student Formation in Theological Education'. That paper suggested that Christian tertiary institutions have at their disposal considerable resources with which to think through how to better facilitate spiritual formation. The Scriptures suggest in broad terms the overarching shape of spiritual formation as movement towards Christlikeness. There are also hints of a process through the New Testament writers with an emphasis on the renewal of the mind and imitation of Christ facilitated by teaching and modelling the Christian faith. Behind this 'effort' lies an understanding that ultimately the work of formation is a spiritual one, worked within the believer by God's Spirit and is, in a very real sense, an already finished work because of what was achieved on the cross by the Lord Jesus Christ.

This paper will suggest ways in which character formation might be better facilitated in the Christian tertiary context. As such, it is looking very much on the human side. This is not at the expense of an acknowledgement of absolute dependence upon God, working by his Spirit (Jn. 15:5; 1 Cor. 3:6). For this reason, humble and dependent prayer will be an integral part of the Christian institution's spiritual development strategy, and this understanding, therefore, prefaces all that follows.

As ways to facilitate character formation are suggested, the contribution of graduate attributes and formal and informal elements of the college curriculum will be surveyed. The over-riding point is that a commitment to character formation in theological education requires a 'whole of institution' approach that encompasses both curriculum and culture. The question of how to assess efforts in this area and the appropriate expectations of what can be reasonably achieved given the constraints under which the enterprise takes place will also be discussed.

What follows will, at times, have an anecdotal feel as the author draws on his own experiences, either of teaching personally or practices observed in other places and the literature. This simply acknowledges the fine work that has been done and continues to be done in this area. It also acknowledges the power of collaboration and is an attempt to reproduce, in some sense one, of the main benefits of a conference: the sharing of ideas and practices amongst attendees.

The overall metaphor that guides the ensuing reflections is the idea of keeping company with Christ. This is intended to reflect the modelling/imitation strand of New Testament teaching that acknowledges the powerful shaping effect of relationships generally and the relationship with Christ, particularly (cf 1 Cor. 4:16; 11:1;15:33; Phil. 3:17; Heb. 6:12). While the student's relationship with Christ is mediated through Scripture, it is a real relationship nonetheless, and it is suggested that facilitating the student's engagement with Jesus Christ to enable that transforming relationship, in the power of the Holy Spirit, to develop is a key strategy of the Christian tertiary institution as it thinks about personal and spiritual formation.

2. Begin with the End in Mind

It is a truism to say that we cannot hit what we are not aiming at and that the establishment of clear goals is an important part of any planning process. This is no less true in spiritual formation. The question of the shape of our graduates, what they will 'look like' once finished their course of study is an important one to ask. One useful formal mechanism to facilitate clarity in this area is a list of graduate attributes or the formation of a graduate profile.[1]

Graduate attributes help the college to plan with the end in mind and provide a starting point (paradoxically) to work backwards from using the process of constructive alignment.[2] Clearly articulated goals at an institutional level help set direction and establish priorities, which enable a consistent approach and commitment to student learning, and for our interests, formation across all levels of the college's life and teaching.[3]

A statement of graduate attributes provides an opportunity to do much more than simply describe the 'product' at which the college is aiming. They provide a stimulus to important conversations about every aspect of the college's life and processes. In the case of formation, to articulate formational goals, colleges need to be clear about what they understand formation to mean, the goal of formation in their students, and the shape of formational processes. All of this might be related to personal, spiritual, ministry, pastoral, or leadership formation. The attempt to formulate a graduate profile facilitates this conversation.

It is a big picture exercise that involves a variety of stakeholders. The process of formulation should be widely consultative, and this, in turn, promotes ownership of the final product.

This is not a straightforward process. In the past, I have been on committees that have generated 'super-student 'profiles that are long and difficult to remember, and so the usefulness of the exercise is diminished by a lack of clarity and confusion. Attributes need to be a mix of achievable and slightly aspirational but not so aspirational as to be out of reach and, therefore, easily ignored or, worse, dispiriting.[4]

Once formulated, the statement of graduate attributes needs to be put to work. In their extensive survey, Oliver and de St Jorre (2018) suggest seven key actions so that institutions can work to ensure the effective use of graduate attributes:

---

1. Biggs & Tang, *Quality Learning* (2011) is a foundational discussion. See also Barrie 'Research-based' (2004), 'Understanding' (2006), Oliver & de St Jorre, 'Graduate Attributes' (2018), and Treloar, 'Graduate Attributes' (2019).
2. Biggs & Tang, *Quality Learning* (2011), 95-109.
3. D. Hockridge, 'Rethinking' (2018).
4. The SMART acronym applies: Specific, Measurable, Attainable, Relevant, Timely; My own variation: Scriptural, Memorable, Assessable, Relevant, and Trajectoried to reflect a slightly more contextual, aspirational emphasis in my own thinking.

1. Publish the attributes they focus on, aligning the emphasis with the needs of their students and the aims of their institution
2. Ensure the attributes are contextualised and communicated at a course level, including in the curriculum, course handbooks, and marketing materials
3. Be more explicit with students: Those who teach students and support their learning should communicate intended outcomes and explain their importance repeatedly throughout the course
4. Continue to emphasise attributes associated with global citizenship, teamwork, and communication; give more emphasis to independence, critical thinking and problem-solving, and the fundamental foundational skills of written and spoken communication
5. Draw on more objective measures to test achievement of the attributes by students, inculcating them more explicitly into assessments in the curriculum
6. Continue to use perception measures with stakeholder groups and wherever possible align skills in a similar fashion so that we can see where we are making headway, and where we still need to improve
7. Most importantly, continue to review and refresh the attributes regularly to ensure fitness for purpose in the rapidly changing environment within which we operate and within which our graduates will increasingly create or find work.

While their primary audience is universities, Oliver and de St Jorre suggest that these recommendations also apply to non-university providers.[5] Colleges in the theological sector may want to add or substitute more specifically scripturally informed formational goals at point 5, but there is good guidance in this list of recommendations.

The general point is that graduate attributes or the graduate profile must be a living document to be effective. Too often, it seems, these lists can be simply an exercise written, ticked off, and then shelved.[6]

Point 3 concerning student engagement is worth underlining. Bowden et al. (2000) and Oliver (2013) point to the integral part played in inculcating attributes by ensuring graduates know the attributes and can be challenged to

---

5   Oliver & de St Jorre 'Graduate Attributes', (2018), 833.
6   For example, Treloar, 'Graduate Attributes', (2019) observes the wide gap between the rhetoric and reality of graduate attributes amongst the colleges of the Australian College of Theology consortium. Oliver & de St Jorre 'Graduate Attributes' (2018), 824, observed that they were only able to find published attributes on 32 out of 82 non-university higher education provider websites, compared with 41 out of 42 university provider sites.

'buy-in' to what is intended for their learning and take some responsibility for their own achievement (Oliver and de St Jorre, 827). If formational goals are written into the graduate attributes, then the dissemination and repetition of these attributes immediately reinforce the importance of formational goals amongst all concerned in the learning process. In this sense, graduate attributes not only guide but publicise intentions amongst all interested parties.

As a penultimate comment on this matter of graduate attributes, the comments by Sherlock (2009, 105-8) and Ball (2012, 2) are noted where they observe that claims to formation lie more in the realm of aspiration and affirmation than deliberately planned and structured. If these observations are true, then concerted discussion and the formulation of graduate attributes would be a good place to start.

While it can be an arduous process, the formulation of GAs is the relatively easy first step in the long and difficult process of implementation.[7]

> **Some Thoughts on Practice**
>
> Meet annually at the beginning of the year to review and refresh, if necessary, the statement of graduate attributes.
>
> Turn the list of attributes into a prose description that may make it more memorable for students and/or choose the significant words in each attribute to emphasise.
>
> Use the graduate attributes as the basis of small group experience for students at the beginning of the year for the students to discuss, critique, affirm.
>
> Display the attributes physically in the college environment.
>
> Refer to the attributes in any formational assessment of the students offered towards the end of the year.

3. Everything is Important

Hockridge (2018, 203-4) points to the external requirements (TEQSA accreditation requirements, the AQF, and the possible tension operating in the higher

---

[7] Some suggestions for practice with respect to graduate attributes: Consider turning the list of attributes into a prose description that may make it more memorable for students; use the graduate attributes as the basis of small group experience for students at the beginning of the year for the students to discuss, critique, affirm; refer to the attributes in any formational assessment of the students offered towards the end of the year.

education environment brings when thinking about formational goals. Questions are raised concerning the possibility of teaching 'formation', should spiritual formation be included in College goals, and how can it be assessed with integrity.

It is often noted that, historically, Australian religious institutions have tended to rely on more informal elements of their programmes when it comes to spiritual formation.[8] These elements include chapels, discipleship groups, mission experiences, spiritual retreats and exercises, meals together, gathered and even residential communities.[9] Certainly, in the institutions I have taught at, much was made of the importance of the overall community context, and it was sobering to read Ball's research on this that suggested that faculty valued the overall community context much more highly than their students.[10] That said, my own 'anecdata' at this point suggests that many students do value the attempts a college makes at forming a community of learning.

One of the problems with informal structures is that it is often difficult to assess their effectiveness and impact. Another is that a reliance on these factors blinds us to the potential significance of other aspects of the college's life for formation, especially the more formal elements such as curriculum and classes, and may even preclude the formational significance of thought. Further, a reliance on these factors means that for an increasing number of students, they do not 'work' as numbers of both part-time and online students rise in the Australian theological tertiary context.

In the light of these preliminary comments, the point to be asserted here is that formation is not a function of the informal elements alone but is rather a holistic pursuit, encompassing formal and informal elements, inviting us to consider the entire culture of the organisation.

4. The Importance of Culture

It is increasingly commonplace to hear management experts point out the importance of attending to the culture of an organisation.[11] In educational

---

8   Ball, *Transforming* (2012), 5, 109.
9   Ball, *Transforming* (2012), 2.
10 Hockridge 'Rethinking' (2018), 204; Ball *Transforming* (2012), 5, 109. Adam, 'Education and Formation' (2009) while stressing the need for integration of various elements highlights these more informal elements as being integral to student formation.
11 According to Torben Rick 'Maintaining' (2020), the quote 'culture eats strategy for breakfast' was coined by management guru Peter Drucker and popularised by the President of Ford, US.

terms, we are used to considering the concept of the hidden curriculum: what our structures and ways of doing things inadvertently communicate about what is valued by the institution.[12]

Paying attention to the culture and ethos of our teaching colleges is important. While speaking from a business context, Rick's suggestion that culture is 'the lingering effect of every interaction' is worth contemplating regarding formational goals. In the whole context of the theological college, every interaction can have a formative effect. The whole formational effect will be made up of the sum of any number of interactions the student has with the college. In order to progress this line of thinking, we may benefit by thinking in almost sociological categories and attending to matters such as the myths, legends, heroes, icons, lore, festivals, rituals, and ceremonies of the institutions we are involved in.[13] These elements will all contribute to the culture that is forming our students from the moment they walk in the door.

I recall the helpful advice of educationalist Perry Shaw in a seminar I attended who urged us to pay attention to the language we used and encouraged us to think of pithy 'catch phrases' that embodied the values and concepts we wanted the students to imbibe. Focused attention in the formulation and regular repetition of these phrases continually reinforce the key concepts and values that are desirous of being inculcated.[14]

As students come and go, the burden of this culture shaping and maintenance is carried by the faculty and staff. This suggests that a united faculty on the cultural ethos is essential, as is some consistency of presence over time. Recruitment of future faculty from the existing pool of college graduates would seem to be an advisable way of continuing cultural continuity, but this must also be balanced against the need for new ideas and refreshment that occurs so that the culture is not becoming stagnant.

---

12 I recall a conversation once with a friend who advises corporations on cultural change. He was asking me about the values of the college I was teaching at, and I mentioned team ministry. He then asked about the organisational structures in our college and whether students would see the leadership structure of the college as embodying a sense of team. Shaw *Transforming* (2014), 82-90, suggests some common hidden messages in the way that theological institutions teach include: 'schooling' = 'education'; an academic approach to ministry; leader control; ministry is about competition and not co-operation.
13 These categories are drawn from the discussion by Weems' *Leadership* (2010) concerning the importance of thinking about culture for church leadership.
14 As an example, one phrase I use regularly with students is 'There is a God and it's not you'. Graduates of another college I am familiar with tend to answer questions 'it depends', indicating (in my view) time being taken to examine the context and theological possibilities of the question posed. This was very much a part of the culture of the college.

5. Community

This subset of culture is worth thinking about independently. Most of our institutions will speak a lot about the importance of the community as the context for the learning, with good cause. There is an impulse to community that derives from Scripture. The benefits that accrue from the unity amidst diversity model outlined in Paul's metaphor of the body (1 Cor. 12-14) are well known, as well as their tensions.

There are several dimensions to be considered when thinking about the role of community in spiritual formation.

5.1 The Benefit of Community

The drive to community in whatever shape that occurs points to an acknowledgement of the importance of time spent in the company of others, not only for instruction but also for the many intangible benefits that come from observing the behavior and lifestyle of others, and the opportunity to engage with the ideas and character of others. This includes both faculty and fellow learners. In the midst of the community, we can keep company with Christ in an attenuated sense as we keep company with his people. This provides the opportunity for formation (at least) in terms of modelling and learning to bear with one another.

One of the key benefits of a community context is the opportunity for modelling the Christian faith that can take place, as a function of the important strand in Scripture that commends modelling of the faith more generally.[15] Modelling is a function of the relationships in the learning community and can occur amongst all members of the community. It is not necessarily a one-way movement from teacher to student, although this will be a significant aspect to be considered. The importance of modelling has implications for faculty selection so that the college's criteria will not solely be academic. The important question will be asked as to the extent that the candidate for the faculty position embodies the values, ethos, and culture of the institution. In this context, we can point again to the value of recruiting graduates who have been shaped by

---

15 See, for example, Paul's letter to the Philippians where Paul commends Epaphroditus and Timothy to the Philippians as models in whom can be seen a glimpse of the mind and character of Christ in action (Phil. 2). Paul also regularly point to his own example as one to follow (1 Cor. 4:16; 11:1; 1 Thess. 1:6). Doubtless readers can recall significant models of aspects of the Christian faith in their own growth and development.

the institution and are also known quantities, having been observed through the course of their study.

It needs to be remembered that modelling is also taking place in lectures, tutorials, and other small group contexts that may be teacher-led. Subtle things like one's approach to the material being taught, the way that questions and responses during the class are dealt with, and illustrations of points made that are used that are personal examples can all have a shaping effect. Some of us may recall those magical moments in the lecture room or classroom where the mode of discourse suddenly shifted from telling to sharing, and a transformative thought or personal anecdote made a deep impression. Teachers need to be alert to the serendipitous teachable moments that move beyond the curriculum to these other areas.

As a final thought with respect to the role of faculty, perhaps more acknowledgement needs to be given of the different skill levels of individual faculty when it comes to the discipleship of students in a formational sense. Part of the role of modelling and encouraging spiritual growth will be engagement in the art of 'formational conversations' with students. These may be arranged or serendipitous and provide significant opportunities for making an impact in a student's life. But not everyone is adept at these. Perhaps, colleges need to consider putting resources into training their faculty to initiate and respond appropriately to the opportunities that emerge for spiritually formative conversations; to develop their emotional intelligence.

The focus to this point has been on teachers modelling before their students, but students are also clearly modelling to one another. This ranges from the positive learning and modelling that can take place as students share lives with one another formally in the classroom and informally outside. The use of group discussions and assignments can help students engage with one another at a formal level. Colleges will often try to keep a cohort together over the period of theological study to maximise the opportunity for long-term friendships to form in the context of ministry training and theological study.

Modelling requires visibility, time, and space. The question is posed to the college as to how things can be arranged to provide good time and space for relational development amongst teachers and students. This will include decisions regarding timetable, giving some open space to relate, the conduct of meals (will there be common eating times and spaces), and the geography of the campus (providing comfortable spaces to meet). Expectations of faculty interaction with students will also be a consideration, and colleges have discussions and differing policies concerning the availability of faculty to students at eating times and the general accessibility of students to faculty. Colleges may provide small group discussion experiences, prayer groups, sporting activities, and other structures to foster intermittent community interaction. Other ideas observed include the organisation of intensive residential units and cohort retreats or camps. The possible gold standard is full time and residential study. At the very least, the constant verbal encouragement to students to maximise the benefits of the (quasi) community situation in which they find themselves is an important part of the mix, including regular explicit discussion of the behaviours and covenant commitments that facilitate shaping communities.

Many of these measures are increasingly difficult to sustain due to their cost; rates of part-time students increasing, and a slow drift to online participation, or at least blended programmes as part of the drift to part-time.

5.2 Suffering and Community

One of the intriguing observations that emerges from the New Testament teaching is the place of suffering in character formation. This is explicit in Romans 5 and implicit at other points in the New Testament (1 Pet. 3-4: Heb. 12-13). Can this insight be leveraged in the college context?

From one perspective, it might be argued that any form of study brings with it its own measure of suffering, and we can compound this by placing people consistently in the company of others on the basis of Sartre's observation that 'hell is other people'. No doubt there is a truth to this, and there are many benefits from having to bear with one another as well as be shaped by all the good they bring to bear.

That said, there may be more to be said in analogous relation to the observation that much suffering spoken about in the New Testament with respect to the Christian faith comes in the context of testimony for Christ. In an extension of this observation, it is suggested that an analogy would be creating opportunities for students to be subjected to more scrutiny for their testimony and ideas through their course. Historically, written communication, evaluated by a single marker, has been the norm for testing ideas. Perhaps, greater consideration could be given to the creation of oral assessments where students are forced to articulate their ideas and have them subjected to the public scrutiny of the classroom at least. While not strictly speaking suffering (though students may have a different view on this), there are many benefits, not the least, further preparation for what are going to be, in the main, oral ministries. Both questioning and being questioned can lead to advances in empathy, listening, and responding graciously: formative experiences and possibly close to some of the formational attributes the college will have framed for its students.

Some colleges provide a mission experience annually or biannually for their students where the possibility of public testimony for the Christian faith is very much a live one. One of the legendary stories from my own undergraduate college experiences is of generations of past students participating in open-air preaching at a local railway station weekly.

6. Worship

Many, if not all, theological colleges will provide an opportunity for gathering to worship as part of the college experience, and this is a seminal shaping experience, not only formally in the preached word but also the experience of sitting under a liturgy in the company of God's people. For some students, depending on their liturgical background, this can be a confronting experience initially as well as an encouraging one.

7. Some Final Questions

Given the power of community to shape is there an optimal size for a college beyond which it gets increasingly difficult to gain the benefit of the community experience. Now, most private theological institutions are not in the position, enrolment-wise, to consider this question, but for some colleges, it may be a growing reality.

Second, the move to distance learning by a considerable number of students raises the question of effective spiritual formation in the online context.

8. Curriculum

Having addressed the broader, less formal culture and context, we turn to briefly consider the place of the curriculum in formation. We have noted the trend to rely on the less formal elements of the college context, but the fact is that most of the students' time during a theological course of study is oriented to the classroom and formal curriculum. Failure to consider the formational possibilities when considering curriculum structures and content, pedagogies, and teaching practices would appear to be, at least, an opportunity missed and, at worst, dereliction of duty.

In the first place, we ought not to underestimate the power of the Scriptures as the primary text for theological study and, therefore, its potential effects through the curriculum that is based upon their study. If we want to keep company with Christ, an evangelical understanding of the primary means of that occurring is in the company of his word. In the midst of his exposition of all that Christ has achieved and the desired transformation of lives, as a result, Paul urges the Colossians to let the word of Christ dwell amongst them richly (Col. 3:16).

Paul declares that transformation of the mind is one of the keys to the profound spiritual transformation (Rom. 12:1-2). One of the temptations of discussions on formation is to pit intellectual formation against personal and spiritual formation instead of seeing them, integrally connected. This is not to defend or excuse arid intellectualism, which those reading may have all suffered or even inflicted at some point, but to point to the reality that God works through his word to convey knowledge of himself, and the sum of beliefs that have the power to transform the mind and worldview of a person. They tell the Christian story that we inhabit, that inhabits us and slowly reshapes our identity as we see that we are loved and known by God and enabled in his grace to be his children.[16]

That is to say ,the study of the Scriptures in part and whole at the core of the classical theological studies curriculum is capable, in the power of the Spirit, of working to transform, even if it is being presented in an academic and even critical context.

That said, there are opportunities formally for formation-oriented units to be included in the formal curriculum and a series of initiatives that can be pursued to foster formation in the formal curriculum processes, including:

- Help students to develop frameworks to assist them in reflecting on and in practice and include opportunities for supervised practice (e.g. through fieldwork and internships).
- Expose students to, and ask them to engage with, different perspectives.
- Include learning activities and assessments that require students to apply their understanding to real contexts.

---

16 Wright, *Virtue* (2010), 221-233; Rosner, *Known* (2017), 249-51.

- Include intentionally formative outcomes and content (in all subjects).[17]

9. How Do We Know it is Working?

As Hockridge (2018, 209) notes, the evaluation of spiritual formation 'presents a significant challenge to theological educators'. The questions and concerns crowd in. How do we accurately assess spiritual formation? Is this too subjective to assess? Who is worthy of assessing the spiritual and personal growth of another, especially in a context where there are apparently explicit sanctions against judging another? What exactly are we evaluating and what criteria would we use to make such evaluations? The temptation will be simply to set up structures and practices that align with our theological understanding of formation and how it is facilitated and then simply trust the process.

However, effort must be made and, of course, is being made. The integrity of an educational process is very much tied up with the question of assessment. If the concept of spiritual formation is as significant a part of the process as has been implied, then we are obliged to assess our effectiveness in facilitating it; our students will expect some feedback, and there are parties interested in the graduates of our courses who are also interested and will be making their own assessment of the effectiveness or otherwise of the college's efforts regardless.

The question is not whether we assess spiritual formation but rather how can we do it effectively. To cycle back to the beginning of this paper, the discussion over graduate attributes is important and will contain within it a discussion of evaluation and how we know progress is being made in what is aspired to with respect to students. There are no easy answers here, but the discussion can be had (repeatedly). Elements such as the capacity for reflection, the sophistication of reflection, and the maturity of reflective frameworks can be assessed. The construction of assessments with elements of personal reflection, process diaries, pastoral application, interaction with alternate views, oral

---

17 The list is culled from Hockridge 'Rethinking' (2018), 208. In a case study based on a survey and focus group discussion with students on what contributes to spiritual formation, Hussey 'Contributors' (2018) found that elements such as faculty input, chapel, and reflection groups were affirmed. The surprising contributions in the study were the place of researching and writing essays, learning notes, and particular units of study. He concedes the study is small and contextually based, but the results are interesting, nonetheless, for the specific question asked and the Australian context in which the study was conducted. Cooper 'Church History' (2015) also reports, with examples, on the possibilities of transformative learning in Church history.

presentations with the fielding of questions, and other more overtly formative assessment instruments can be gainfully employed.

It also needs to be acknowledged that the assessment of formational goals inevitably veers to the qualitative and more subjective end of the assessment spectrum, and there is nothing wrong with that. Most people are used to making qualitative judgements concerning the character of others regularly. There may be a natural reticence or humility in this area, but this does not mean nothing can be said. It is suggested that one of the keys in the light of these considerations is to facilitate processes of shared qualitative judgement and multiply sources of perspective on students with respect to formational goals. This is a shared and not an individual responsibility.

This may mean several teachers meeting and swapping perspectives on students from the point of view of personal formation. This is dependent on some of the factors mentioned above…not the least a community context that reasonably allows the time and space for some of these judgements to form. The tentative nature of these judgements needs to be conceded, especially early in the student's engagement with the college; there may be more information available over the years a student is with the institution. Opinions formed ought to be as evidence/incident-based as possible. This is a process that will take time and may at times be fraught. The size of the student body will determine how and who is evaluated. Some larger colleges will restrict these kinds of assessments to vocational ministry candidates; smaller colleges may be able to deal with their entire student body. A decision will need to be made as to whether the form of reporting to the student will be formal or informal.[18]

Alongside this more formal process, should the college pursue this, is a more informal serendipitous approach of incidental conversations, encouragements, and evaluations between teachers and students and eventually into the whole culture of the institution. Such moments may, in fact, be more powerful sources of feedback as well as encouragement to grow as reflective and teachable moments occur. These will rarely form part of any formal assessment process but may well end up being a significant part of the overall goal of spiritual formation. Such moments are dependent on creating time and space where these interactions may occur.

---

18   One college's practice is to meet together as a group and draft a letter to each of their students from the faculty group as a whole. This letter notes both encouragements and observed growing edges for the student. The letter is then distributed, and time is given for personal reflection before a group reflection experience is undertaken reviewing the year.

There are other avenues to multiplying perspectives in assessment. Peers can be invited to assess one another; the individual student can be invited to make a self-assessment. In some cases, stakeholders/employers can be invited to assess students, though this level of feedback is more likely to be to the college on its performance than to the students directly.[19]

10. Knowing the Limits

It is an understandable temptation for the theological college to think it can do everything. But, as Shaw points out, the time the college has with students is extremely limited.[20] The theological study experience is one amongst many experiences that contribute to the ongoing maturity of its students. It does, of course, have significant advantages and input into students' lives in terms of concentrated time and resources, but there are limitations. The college has the student for one, three, four, or possibly eight to 10 years, in varying degrees of relational proximity and intensity. Much of that time is formally structured in classes and semesters. The college cannot do it all.[21]

What are the proper limits/expectations of what can be realistically achieved? There are no easy answers here, but it is important that the college reign in its expectations and aspirations, for its own sake and the sake of its students. Over-estimating the college's ability to deliver in this space can lead to over-bearing expectations on staff and students and the almost certain disappointment that comes from over-promising and under-delivering. It is best to think more about trajectories, nudges, processes, and contributions rather than products when it comes to student outcomes with respect to formation. In this respect, our graduate attributes may be veering towards the aspirational, but even here, a measure of balance and humility is advisable.

At the very least, the student can leave the college with a more integrated understanding of the Scriptures and Christian faith, a more theologically formed worldview. They can be established or grown in the prior trajectory of knowledge and service. The aim will be to develop a student in head, heart, and hand: knowledge, affections, and skills within a coherent framework that is cognisant

---

19   At least one college I know of has experimented with the creation of an employer survey based on their graduate attribute statement to try and garner more detailed and focused employer feedback.
20   Shaw, *Transforming* (2014), 20.
21   Hussey, 'Spiritual Formation' (2015), 149.

of God's grace and love and his intentions for his creation. This will be Christologically focused and oriented to the action of obedience to God and his will in the world. This will be commensurate with their length of time and depth of engagement with the college and its programmes. But perhaps this is to veer too far into the area of graduate attributes?

It is important also for the theological college to realise that it does not labour alone in forming students. The students who attend are part of other faith communities, which are also shaping and forming, and it would seem important to acknowledge and leverage those links where possible in the sense of partnership and shared interest in the formation of the students involved. There may also be partnerships with broader bodies, such as mission agencies and denominational authorities. One of the important questions here will be where the initiative lies with creating and maintaining these partnerships, and this may boil down to resources, especially time. Even if there is no partnership or contact, it remains important for the college to realise that it does not labour alone.

That said, there is a place for further thinking about contact and ongoing relationship with alumni and having further input at later stages of a graduate's formation.

There have been occasional nods to the fact that many students now choose to complete their study in distance mode, and it needs to be acknowledged that there is an entire other discussion to be had concerning the possibility and efficacy of formation in online study.[22]

Conclusion

The focus of this paper has been on the practice of spiritual formation in theological education. It has been a survey of thought and practices with many questions raised along the way. This is clearly an ongoing conversation. It is hoped that the combined burden of both papers in this volume is to show that there are tremendous resources in the Christian faith for both the theory and practice of spiritual formation. There will always remain the challenge that there is room to do better to what is being claimed to be done. To do this better, the college needs to consider all that it is doing and see that spiritual formation is a function of every activity that takes place within the college's sphere of influence.

---

22 See Lowe & Lowe, 'ecosystems' (2010), Taylor, 'Embodiment', (2015).

Bibliography

Adam, P. *Education and Formation for Ministry in Theological Education Today* (2009) <https://stjudes.org.au/wp-content/uploads/2017/07/Education-and-formation-for-ministry-in-Theological-and-Bible-Colleges-today-Peter-Adam.pdf>

Ball. L. *Transforming Theology. Student Experience and Transformative Learning in Undergraduate Theological Education* (Preston, VIC: Mosaic Press, 2012).

Ball. L & Harrison, J. (eds). *Learning and Teaching Theology: Some Ways Ahead* (Eugene, OR: Wipf & Stock, 2015)

Barrie, S. A research-based approach to generic attributes policy, *Higher Education Research and Development* 23 (2004), 26-76.

Barrie, S. Understanding what we mean by the generic attributes, *Higher Education* 51.2 (2006), 215-41.

Biggs, J & C. Tang. *Teaching for Quality Learning at University* (4th ed; Maidenhead, McGraw Hill, 2011).

Bowden, J., Hart, G., King, B. Trigwell, K, & Watts, O. *Generic Capabilities of ATN University Graduates*. Canberra: Australian Government Department of Education, Training and Youth Affairs (2000).

Cooper, T. 'Transformative Learning in Church History', in L. Ball & J. Harrison (eds.), *Learning and Teaching Theology: Some Ways Ahead*. (Eugene, OR: Wipf & Stock, 2015): 201-210

Dow, P. Virtuous Minds: Intellectual Character Development. (Downers Grove, ILL: IVP 2013).

Hockridge, D. 'Making the implicit explicit: exploring the role of learning design in improving formational learning outcomes', in L. Ball & J. Harrison (eds.), *Learning and Teaching Theology: Some Ways Ahead*. (Eugene, OR: Wipf & Stock, 2015): 131-145.

Hockridge, D. Rethinking our Approach to Student Formation in Theological Education, in A. Bain & I Hussey (eds.), *Theological Education: Foundations, Practices, and Future Directions* (ACT Monograph Series; Eugene, OR: Wipf & Stock, 2018): 200-213

Hussey, I. 'Spiritual formation in an Australian Baptist theological college: A survey-based case study', *Journal of Adult Theological Education* 12.2 (2015), 137-152.

Hussey, I. 'The contributors to spiritual formation in theological education: What the students say', in A. Bain & I Hussey (eds.), *Theological Education: Foundations, Practices, and Future Directions* (ACT Monograph Series; Eugene, Oregon: Wipf & Stock, 2018): 241-256.

Oliver, B. 'Graduate attributes as a focus for institution-wide curriculum renewal: Innovations and challenges', *Higher Education Research & Development* 32.3 (2013), 450-463.

Lowe, S.D & Lowe, M.E. 'Spiritual formation in theological distance education: an ecosystems model', *Christian Educators Journal* 3.7.1 (2010), 85-102.

Oliver, B. & se St Jorre, T.J. 'Graduate Attributes for 2020 and beyond: Recommendations for Australian higher education providers', *Higher Education Research & Development* 37.4 (2018), 821-836.

Rick, T. 'Maintaining cultural coherence across a company's portfolio should be an essential factor when determining a corporate strategy' (2020). <https://www.supplychain247.com/article/organizational_culture_eats_strategy_for_breakfast_lunch_and_dinner>.

Rosner, B.R. *Known by God. A Biblical Theology of Identity*. (Grand Rapids, MI: Zondervan, 2017).

Taylor, S. 'Embodiment and transformation in the context of e-learning', in L. Ball & J. Harrison (eds.), *Learning and Teaching Theology: Some Ways Ahead* (Eugene, OR: Wipf & Stock, 2015): 171-184.

Treloar G. 'Graduate attributes in the Australian College of Theology: Rhetoric or reality' (Unpublished paper based on a paper delivered at the SCD Teaching and Learning Conference, 2019).

Weems. L.J. Jnr. *Church Leadership: Vision, Team, Culture, Integrity* (Rev Ed; Nashville: Abingdon Press 2010).

Wright, N.T. *Virtue Reborn*. (London, UK: SPCK, 2010).

Bill Salier
Youthworks College, Sydney
bill.salier@youthworks.net

20 | EDUCATING FOR THE KINGDOM

THE DEVELOPMENT OF CHARACTER THROUGH PARTICIPATION IN PREPARATORY LEARNING ACTIVITIES

Abstract

Expansive learning activities are designed to prepare participants for engagement in other activities related to, but separate from, these learning activities. As students develop specific capacities associated with a particular cultural practice, they also developing their capacity to learn, building a range of dispositions that prepare them for engagement in a wide range of cultural activities.

In a similar manner, the writers of the New Testament describe the development of Christian character as something that occurs within this current age, in preparation for the age to come. According to Wright, the process of character development begins with habit formation. Such habits become dispositions to act in a certain way which, when clustered together, are described as virtues associated with a person's character. Educating for the kingdom, therefore, includes a focus on developing learning character through students' engagement in preparatory learning activities designed to promote the virtues of the new creation such as grace, humility, compassion, and kindness.

1. Introduction

Education has often been understood as a knowledge-sharing process. The teacher who possesses the knowledge shares this knowledge with students so that they, too, might possess this knowledge. Whether it is learning about mathematics, geography, or theology, this approach to education, which is sometimes called the transmission approach, has provided the mechanism by which cultures have passed their collective wisdom and worldview from one generation to the next. Such an approach focuses on propositions that are taught and assessed through examinations that typically require students to recall propositions covered in class.

Unsurprisingly, this approach to education has not gone unchallenged, and for much of the past 100 years, there have been voices of reform, arguing that such a model of education is grossly inadequate in our time, reflecting the values and beliefs of the Nineteenth Century rather than the twentieth (or the twenty-first). The voices of reform are not necessarily univocal, but there are common themes that have emerged. These voices argue for student-centred education rather than teacher-centred, focused on skills such as thinking and reasoning rather than knowledge, directed by student interests rather than set curriculum documents, and designed to subvert dominant paradigms rather than maintain them.

Yet despite these calls for reform, the revolution has not yet taken place. True, there exists greater diversity in educational practice today, yet knowledge continues to sit at the centre of current educational practice; curriculum documents still provide outcomes that students will 'learn about', identifying the big ideas that are regarded as important at this point in social-cultural-historical time. Teachers still teach much of the time, while students listen. There are pockets of change, however, evident in many schools. Sometimes, students collaborate, though typically under the guidance of a teacher. Sometimes, they lead lessons, pose questions, and seek to challenge existing ways of knowing and doing. Replacing knowledge transmission with knowledge co-construction, however, has proved more difficult than it might have first appeared.

2. Epistomology and Education

This debate between knowledge acquisition and knowledge construction is fundamentally an epistemological debate, which still, in the end, suggests that education is all about the accumulation of knowledge. Epistemology seems, at first, to provide an obvious foundation for the practice of education. If education is about the acquisition of knowledge, then the obvious place to start is with the questions 'what is knowledge?' and 'how do we know what we know?'. Is it possible, however, that this focus on knowledge and how we acquire it may need to be replaced by an alternate way of understanding education? Perhaps, we have been asking the wrong questions? Perhaps, instead of being focused on epistemology, we should begin by developing a clear picture of our anthropology that informs different approaches to education? What is our understanding of what it means to be human and how might this impact our approach to teaching and learning? And how do we understand the concept of becoming human?

In the Western tradition, many of the topics considered by philosophers were set out by Plato in his dialogues, which focus on arguments between Socrates and early Greek thinkers such as Protagoras, Parmenides, and Heraclitus. The nature of knowledge and how we know what we know are fundamental to Plato's arguments about learning, virtue, and the soul. Yet Plato's understanding of knowledge, with his emphasis on the eternal forms and the immutability of truth handed down by the gods, tended to be static rather than dynamic. This presented Plato with a major problem when it came to understanding the process of learning. In the *Meno*, Plato, through the character of Socrates, argues that the process of learning is simply the process of remembering what is already known. The student (in this case, Meno the uneducated slave) merely needs assistance to remember knowledge that he has had eternally as an immortal soul that has simply moved from one body to another. The question of how someone can learn something that they did not already know is avoided by assuming that through the process of transmigration of the soul from one generation to the next, knowledge, like the Forms and Ideas, is eternal and unchanging.

In the *Timaeus*, in which Plato sets out an explanation of the cosmos, he begins by distinguishing between two categories of existence—that which is, and is not becoming, and that which is becoming but never is. For Plato, his concern is with those unchanging aspects of the cosmos—mathematical truths and the Forms that sit behind the ever-changing material world that is most immediate to the senses.

In contrast to Plato, both Heidegger and Kierkegaard consider as their primary data the reality of human experience and consciousness, which they understood to be in a constant state of becoming, shaped by experience. At the most fundamental level, knowing who we are becomes an elusive goal without any anchor in an objective truth or reality. Our humanness is always in a state of becoming. So, too, is our understanding of the material and immaterial, since the way in which we know (epistemology) is fundamentally linked to who we are (anthropology). In the *Theaetetus*, Socrates quotes Protagoras as making the claim that 'Humanity is the measure of all things'. Knowledge is not fixed for all time but is constantly changing; it is in a constant state of Heraclitean flux (after Heraclitus who adopted the metaphor of fire to describe the fundamental essence of all things), being mediated by our senses and our own individual experience.

The epistemological quest of Plato to understand how we can know something with confidence becomes a futile exercise for philosophers such as Heidegger and Kierkegaard. While we may be aware of our existence, we have no knowledge of what this existence means, or will be. Heidegger identifies different aspects of the human experience of existence—one of which is that we are never complete in our being. Humanity is always 'becoming'. While there is the suggestion that other beings may have essences that are fixed and given, humanity cannot identify its essence, since it is constantly in the process of becoming its existence. Earlier, Kierkegaard had suggested, along a similar line, that the ego has no essence, but is in a state of becoming, directed by choice on the part of the individual. Part of being human from an existentialist perspective, therefore, is becoming; but for Kierkegaard (and Heidegger), who we are becoming can never be fully known, and so our choices that impact this process of becoming are a cause of anxiety and dread.

While Heidegger begins his analysis with an investigation of Being in *Being and Time* (*Sein und Zeit*), his focus shifts very quickly to understanding Dasein– that is, humanity who are aware of being and seek to understand it. In doing so, his analysis of Being is inexorably intertwined with the notion of Becoming (as is evident in the title that sees Being and Time being closely linked). Being and becoming, therefore, represent two fundamental tenets of existential thinking concerning the essence of human experience. Similarly, in Jesus' teaching, there is also a recognition of the importance of both being and becoming. The moral imperative of participating in the kingdom of God is immediate, even though the bringing together of heaven and earth into one reality is yet to come. In the current age, God's rule is disputed and hidden to some degree. In the age to come, God's rule is undisputed and universal. But both realities—the current reign of God and the final reign of God—are not independent of one another but are intimately connected in a unified whole.

> The liberating rule of God (in history) can...be understood as the immanence of the eschatological kingdom, and the coming kingdom can be interpreted as the transcendence of the believed and experienced rule of God in the present. This understanding forbids us to banish the lordship of God to a future world totally unrelated to our earthly, historical life. But it also forbids us to identify the kingdom of God with conditions in history, whether they be already existing or desired.[1]

Being who we are becoming represents a significant key for unlocking major themes within theology and philosophy. What, then, can we say about the process of learning and the activity of education more generally?

3. Learning and Education

Many different educational theories, such as sociocultural theory and cultural-historical activity theory, suggest that activities in the classroom should be related to cultural practices outside the school—that the becoming' should inform the 'being' in the classroom. However, not all schooling activities provide students opportunities to be who they are becoming. Engeström draws a distinction between two different types of activity evident in schools—'school-going' activity and 'expansive learning activity'[2]. According to Engeström, school-going activity is focused on achieving success, typically in the form of results. Within this activity, students are participants focused on grades, making use of different instruments for the purpose of recalling results, working independently and in competition with other students. In contrast, expansive learning activities are focused on mastery, particularly mastery that enables students to participate in other cultural activities.

Expansive learning activities are a distinct sub-category of cultural activities ontologically distinct from work activities. Work activities and other cultural activities are focused on transforming objects separate to the people engaged in the activity—perhaps, it is producing cars or providing a particular service. By way of contrast, the object of expansive learning activity is, in fact, the transforming of the participants engaged in this activity such that they can

---

1   Moltmann, *The Church in the Power of the Holy Spirit*, 190.
2   Engeström, *Learning by expanding*.

become better equipped to engage in other activities. Expansive learning activities, therefore, are not activities intended to be self-sustaining but other-activity sustaining. This fundamental distinction between school activity and work activity suggests that attempts to align school activities to reflect more accurately workplace activities may prove less than optimal for supporting the learning of students within the classroom.

Attempts to align school activity with work activities are often motivated by a desire to make learning in the classroom more authentic. John Dewey, for example, supported the establishment of rich, authentic learning environments[3]. Other theorists, however, have suggested that school activities are preparatory activities rather than participatory activities when it comes to the workplace. Beach describes classroom learning activities as *mediational* activities designed to simulate activities yet to be experienced[4]. While they might vary in their alignment with work activities, they maintain a mediational status as a 'third object' between where the participants are and where they are going developmentally. What teachers aim to do in the classroom is determine how best to support students' movement from their current participation in various learning activities to their future participation in other forms of activity.

As educators who locate themselves within the biblical narrative, there will be a commitment to preparing students for participation in cultural practices. Students need opportunities to be the people they are becoming—people who are lifelong learners, ready to participate in a wide range of cultural activities. Yet more than this, as God's people who look forward to the restoration of all things, there is a much larger picture of the types of human activities that students can be engaged in, associated with their participation in the new heavens and the new earth. With this understanding of the future, we seek to develop students' *learning character*, teaching them the 'language of heaven'[5] in anticipation of the coming together of heaven and earth in one reality. While not all students will choose to be a part of the new creation, the speaking of this language by teachers, other students, and staff creates an opportunity within our schools for students who live according to different metanarratives to gain an insight into God's plans and purposes for creation. The speaking of this language also challenges the dominant voices of our age that speak of

---

3   Wilson, Teslow, & Taylor, 'Instructional design perspectives on mathematics education with reference to Vygotsky's theory of social cognition'.
4   Beach, 'Consequential transitions'.
5   Wright, N. T., *Virtue Reborn*.

individuality, self-fulfilment, and greed. It has the potential to generate ways of thinking, acting, and doing that communicate something of God's character and the virtues that will characterise the coming kingdom of God.

The development of a kingdom-centred learning community, therefore, enables students (and teachers) to experience something of the kingdom of God. Although imperfect, being comprised of flawed human beings, such learning communities are characterised by the fruits of the Spirit. The way these communities approach learning, therefore, should be radically different to learning communities created without an appreciation of how the death and resurrection of Jesus provide hope of mercy, forgiveness, justice, and restoration.

As outlined earlier, rather than beginning with a particular epistemology, perhaps educational theory should begin with anthropology. Perhaps, we begin by asking the question 'What is our vision of human flourishing?'. This question will provide, in broad terms, a picture of the 'becoming' that will impact the 'being' in the classroom. In response to this question, the Christian might reply that humanity flourishes under the lordship of Jesus, restored to be in a relationship with God through the death and resurrection of Jesus, and renewed through the Spirit to be people of grace, compassion, kindness, humility, and justice. Kingdom-of-God-shaped learning activities that begin with this understanding of human flourishing are designed to give students an understanding and experience of what it looks like to be a person of the kingdom. Such learning activities encourage students to be gracious, compassionate, kind, humble, and ready to oppose injustice in the world.

Almost all vision statements developed by schools include the identification of desirable character traits (or virtues) that the school hopes its students will have at the conclusion of their formal schooling. The concept of virtue is not a foreign one in education. But the process by which virtues are formed through engaging in educational activity has received little attention in educational research.

According to Wright, virtues grow out of the habits that we form over a long period of time. Habits are appropriated through ongoing participation in different contexts or situations. They refer to those everyday actions which seem, on their own, innocuous enough, but, in fact, instantiate ways of knowing and doing. By developing culturally specific habits, we learn how to orient ourselves in our cultural context (which could be the way we do mathematics, for example, or the way we enter a science classroom), which Smith refers to as comporting oneself in the world and learning how to construct one's world[6]. They become part of our character, imprinted within and evident in our spontaneous action. They are the *second* nature that we take on rather than the nature into which we are born. Character formation begins with establishing these habits of action, habits of mind and, in the context of this discussion, learning dispositions.

But prior to developing habits and dispositions, we engage in certain routines of action that become habitual over time. For example, many of the thinking routines developed by the Visible Thinking team at Harvard are designed to be used repeatedly over time so that these routines become habitual. Habits refer to those actions or ways of thinking that are no longer the result of conscious reflection, but happen automatically. They are ways of thinking and acting that become grounded in our brains and bodies so that we can perform certain tasks 'intuitively'. Choosing the order in which you brush your teeth, for example, can become a deeply ingrained habit—so much so that you probably know exactly what path to follow without thinking about it.

Certain categories of habits, however, become indicative of different character traits. People who have developed a collection of associated habits may be described as having a certain disposition. For example, a fastidious person regarding their appearance (a disposition) may be known by a range of habits that identify them as such—routinely brushing their hair, checking the length of their nails each week, flossing every couple of days, etc. The disposition of being fastidious about one's appearance describes a person who displays this collection of associated habits.

Within the New Testament, we find an extended discussion concerning the development of character. Within Paul's letters to different churches, we find various lists of behaviours that Paul encourages his readers to 'put on' while also 'putting off the activities of the sinful nature (replacing our *first* nature with a *second* nature). It is in this way of setting before his readers guidelines for living that Paul identifies habits and ways of acting that lead to the development of virtues. In the letter to the Galatians, he uses the language of 'flesh' and 'spirit' to distinguish between the nature we are born with and the second nature we are called to put on. The works of the flesh include immorality, impurity, sensuality, idolatry, and much more. The fruit of the spirit, however, is 'love, joy, peace, patience, kindness, goodness, faithfulness, gentleness, self-control; against such

---

6   Smith, J. K. A. *Imagining the kingdom.*

things, there is no law'. (5:22). In his letter to the Colossians, Paul encourages his readers to put away anger, wrath, malice, slander, and obscene talk (3:8) and to put on compassionate hearts, kindness, humility, meekness, and patience (3:12), amongst many other virtues. And what binds all these virtues together is the ultimate virtue of love (3:14). In Ephesians, Paul describes how we should walk in the light submitting to one another out of reverence for Christ, encouraging one another with song, and singing praises to God, turning our backs on the activities of the darkness. In this way, we provide the ground for the seeds of virtue to grow. Rather than being drunk with wine, which leads to self-centred sensuality, we are encouraged to be filled with the Spirit, which enables us to become people who take on the outward-looking virtues of faith, hope, and love.

To strive for completeness requires the establishment of habits that will support the development of character. As well as encouraging each other in song and singing praises to God, Paul also includes a range of guidelines for living that promote habits that inform the development of virtues. Sometimes, these guidelines are expressed in general terms. In his letter to the Philippians, Paul exhorts his readers to think about things that are just, pure, true, honourable, excellent, or worthy of praise (4:8). At other times, Paul is more direct, providing guidance and practical advice. In his first letter to the Thessalonians, Paul hopes that the believers in Thessalonica might 'admonish the idle, encourage the fainthearted, help the weak, be patient with them all. See that no one repays evil with evil, but always seek to do good to one another and to everyone' (1 Thess, 5:14-15). Finally, Paul also identifies patterns of behaviour that are unhelpful for promoting the virtues of the complete humanity that he associates with the new creation. These include drunkenness, sexual immorality, greed, grumbling, obscene talk, stealing, lying, or letting our anger take control of us. In each case, there is a contrast between behaviours that are focused on being truly human in our treatment of other people, which Paul encourages his readers to put on and those behaviours that are focused on self-indulgence and being less than human in our treatment of others. Such behaviours, according to Paul, do not (in some cases he says 'cannot') result in the development of the character that we will one day have as part of the new heavens and the new earth.

Our task as Christian educators, therefore, is to identify the habits associated with each learning disposition which, through being strengthened over time, can result in the formation of specific character traits associated with the restored creation.

As part of his more general discussion about the development of virtue in

Virtue Reborn, Wright identifies five related elements associated with virtue formation that form a 'circle of virtue'. Each element informs the next element around the circle such that it does not matter where someone starts in this circle of virtue—eventually, all five elements will come into play to provide a context within which the people of God are challenged and encouraged to become people of Christian virtue. These five elements are the reading of scripture, sharing stories, following examples, being part of a faith community, and engaging in certain practices that form the habits of heart associated with virtue.

Wright outlines how these five elements operate and interact with each other in healthy Christian communities—typically in the form of church communities. However, these five elements are also evident in educational institutions that see their role as sharing the vision of the 'complete' humanity outlined in the New Testament. Schools and colleges whose purpose, character, and practices are shaped by the teachings of Jesus provide a context within which habit formation and subsequent character development are possible, incorporating the same five elements identified by Wright.

In the same way that churches come together around the reading of Scripture, educational institutions have their own 'texts' or 'voices' (using the notion of voices from Bakhtin's theory of dialogical spaces) that promote habits of mind (in particular) and ways of doing that are foundational for the development of character. Many of these voices are heard through Scripture, through the teaching of the Bible and conversations about the Christian worldview that emerges from the biblical story. Unlike most churches, however, schools are communities in which multiple voices contribute to the learning conversation. This conversation always includes the voice of Scripture, alongside other voices drawn from educational research, theories of education, and the experiences of teachers and students. This conversation can be shaped, prompted, and directed towards the development of learning character.

The second element identified by Wright is the sharing of stories. Claxton describes the activity of teaching as an 'epistemic apprenticeship'.[7] Whether intentionally or unintentionally, teachers communicate certain beliefs about learning character. Teachers regularly tell stories that communicate beliefs about students' capacity to improve their understanding—whether our learning capacities are relatively fixed, or whether it is always possible for us to develop as learners, for example. Teachers also tell students stories about how learning

---

7   Claxton, *School as an Epistemic Apprenticeship*.

occurs, whether this is primarily through drill and practice, through the communication of ideas with others, or by asking the teacher what the correct answer is. Teachers decide what the outcomes of learning are (particularly through what is measured in schools) and what types of learning are valuable.

Each of these stories also communicates something about the learning character that we seek to promote amongst our students. Our stories about learning are also stories about the type of people we hope our students will become. Will they be driven by their own learning goals, or by the collective learning of their school community? Is ability the metric by which we judge others? Do we encourage students to celebrate difference as they learn from each other or are our lessons designed to present a cultural hegemony that encourages our students to identify with a cultural elite?

Third, students follow examples, most notably their teachers. We model how to interact with different conceptual ideas each lesson, but more importantly, we model what learning looks like in our various disciplines. Our learning practice informs our students' practice. What do we do when we get stuck? How do we deal with the fact that our understanding of English/mathematics/science/history is also incomplete? How do we respond to questions that we cannot immediately answer? We need to model the same learning character that we hope our students will one day exhibit, being intellectually humble, people who ask questions that extend our thinking, who collaborate with others, displaying grace and compassion rather than arrogance and ego. We need to be people who listen to our students to hear their perspectives and value these perspectives as sources of new ways of understanding our subject area.

The fourth element in Wright's circle of virtue development is the engagement in a community. Kingdom-of-God-shaped learning activities take place within specific learning communities where the fruits of the spirit are found in abundance, where it is more than just a group of individuals seeking independently to be people of the kingdom. Learning communities that seek to be impacted by the present and future kingdom of God grow as groups of people whose communal character reflects, perhaps, only in some small part, the faith, hope, and love associated with the kingdom of God. It is within such learning communities that learning character of the kind described earlier has the greatest opportunities to grow and become deeply rooted in the lives of both students and teachers engaged in this community.

Finally, Wright identifies the fifth aspect of his virtuous circle as specific practices (sometimes rituals) within such communities that support the development of virtue. We have many opportunities to establish practices that become habit-forming in schools—students' engagement with meaningful rituals can be a powerful way of promoting habits of thinking and behaviour. School songs, prayers, and patterns of behaviour that reinforce the idea of respecting others, being grateful for the foundations provided by our predecessors on which we have been able to build, manners, ways of speaking, relating, acknowledging our debt to the indigenous people of the land—all of these in and of themselves may seem insignificant, but they can support the development of habits that can develop character and virtues.

In summary, learning character is promoted in classrooms in many different ways. Teachers model learning character, encourage students to adopt different aspects of learning character, tell stories about what 'good' learning involves and promote the development of learning communities that are genuinely expansive, preparing students to engage with others and flourish in a wide range of activities. Schools support the development of such communities of practice through the way they structure learning activities, the rituals that schools encourage amongst students, the language that is used to describe learning, and the way that all members of this community show an eagerness to learn and grow in maturity and understanding.

Bibliography

Beach, K. 'Consequential transitions: A sociocultural expedition beyond transfer in education', in Iran-Nejad, A. & Pearson, P. D. (eds.), *Review of Research in Education* (vol. 24; American Educational Research Association, Washington, DC, 1999): 101-39.

Claxton, G. *School as an Epistemic Apprenticeship: The Case of Building Learning Power* (32nd Vernon-Wall Lecture, Education Section of the British Psychological Society, 2013).

Engeström, Y. *Learning by Expanding: An Activity-Theoretical Approach to Developmental Research* (Helsinki: Orienta-Konsultit, 1987).

Heidegger, M., Macquarrie, J. & Robinson, E. S. *Being and Time.* (New York, NY: Harper, 1962. tr. from German, 1929).

Kierkegaard, S. & Lowrie, W. *The Concept of Dread.* (Princeton: Princeton University Press, 1967, tr. from Danish, 1844).

Moltmann, J. & Kohl, M. *The Church in the Power of the Holy Spirit: A Contribution to Messianic Ecclesiology,* (Fortress Press, Minneapolis, 1993, tr. from German, 1993).

Plato, Lee, H. D. P., & Johansen, T. K. *Timaeus and Critias* (London, New York: Penguin, 2008).

Plato & Waterfield, R. *Theaetetus.* (Harmondsworth, Middlesex, New York: Penguin Books, 1987).

Plato & Guthrie, W. K. C.. *Protagoras and Meno* (Harmondsworth, Middlesex New York: Penguin Books, 1956).

Smith, J. K. A. *Imagining the Kingdom: How Worship Works* (Grand Rapids, MI: Baker Academic, 2013).

Wilson, B. G., Teslow, J. L. & Taylor, L. 'Instructional design perspectives on mathematics education with reference to Vygotsky's theory of social cognition', *Focus on Learning Problems in Mathematics* 15 (1993), 65-86.

James Pietsch
Principal, Inaburra School
pietschj@inaburra.nsw.edu.au

21 | GOD'S EXEMPLARY GRADUATES IN TIMES OF ECOLOGICAL CRISIS

ENABLING FUTURE LEADERS TO BECOME AUTHENTIC PROMOTORS OF AN ECOLOGICAL CONVERSION

Abstract

Church leaders and theologians challenge individuals as well as society to undergo a spiritual ecological conversion and turn to more sustainable ways of living. This challenge calls theological higher education to include sustainability formation at the core of its curriculum for students to theoretically learn and practically experience ways of living as stewards of God's creation. Through action-oriented teaching and learning methods with a corresponding learning environment, prospective graduates of theological higher education should be enabled to undergo a spiritual ecological conversion and become role models and promotors of the same for others.

1. Introduction

The growth-based economic system and consumerism prevalent in most industrialised and emerging societies are instigating a major ecological crisis. Official church statements as well as theological and ethical publications from various denominational backgrounds have responded to this threat.[1] They widely argue that anthropogenic climate change, species extinction, littering, and destruction of the natural environment, with their harmful implications for present and future human generations, constitute both a violation of the biblical principle of human stewardship of creation and the Gospel at large. Taking action against the crisis can thus be understood as being an essential part of every Christian's mission in today's world. On a more fundamental level, there is a need for a spiritual ecological conversion of the individual and society within which a response to the crisis can be rooted and embedded.

The fourth Sydney College of Divinity Learning and Teaching Theology Conference explored the theme of character-oriented graduate attributes in theological higher education. This endeavour was motivated by the understanding that theological higher education is meant to not only provide students with professional knowledge and skills but also stimulate a transformation of character: It seeks to graduate future leaders 'who act ethically and with integrity' and are 'prepared to build a better society'.[2] In the light of the need for a spiritual ecological conversion and corresponding action against the ecological crisis, any leadership in church and society that arises out of the Christian ethos should promote such conversion and action. However, there is an increasing notion in the interdisciplinary discourse that only people who themselves try to pursue an ecologically sustainable lifestyle can be authentic and successful advocates for ecological change. Theological higher education should thus help their students to grow towards living more sustainably. This certainly includes theoretical learning as part of curricula. Experts in sustainability research agree, however, that the more pressing challenge is to help people make the leap from knowledge to action. Therefore, it is important to use action-oriented teaching and learning methods as well as create a corresponding learning environment, which together enables students to practically experience means and ways of living as good stewards of God's creation.

To elaborate this line of reasoning, I will firstly explore the idea of a spiritual ecological conversion. As a second step, I will briefly outline the need for authentic advocacy for ecological change. Thirdly, I will establish that and in what way sustainability formation is a core responsibility of (theological) higher

---

1   Cf. e.g. GreenFaith, *Christian Teachings*; WCC, *Climate Change*; Pope Francis, *Laudato Si'*; Chryssavgis, 'Ecumenical Patriarch'.
2   SCD, *God's Exemplary Graduates*.

education. In step four, I will explain why it is important to help students make the leap from knowledge to action, and what role action-oriented teaching and learning methods, an appropriate learning environment, and academic teachers play in this regard. Last, some examples will be given to illustrate how such teaching and learning methods as well as learning environments could be designed.

2. The Idea of a Spiritual Ecological Conversion

In 2001, Pope John Paul II coined the term 'ecological conversion' in an address given at one of his general audiences:

> We must therefore encourage and support the "ecological conversion" which in recent decades has made humanity more sensitive to the catastrophe to which it has been heading. Man is no longer the Creator's "steward", but an autonomous despot, who is finally beginning to understand that he must stop at the edge of the abyss.[3]

A year prior, the Catholic Bishops of the Boston Province (US) had already explained in a pastoral letter that an 'environmental examination of conscience' must lead to a conversion that 'will reclaim the common vocation we all have as stewards of all God's creation'.[4] In 2002, the Pope elaborated the notion further in a joint declaration with the Orthodox Ecumenical Patriarch Bartholomew. The two church leaders clearly identified a spiritual dimension within the current ecological crisis. Hence, they concluded that an ecological conversion first and foremost needs to happen on a spiritual, faith-related level—which for Christians, has a distinct Christological implication—while practical action is a consequence of this spiritual conversion.[5]

In subsequent years, the concept of an ecological conversion was adopted and further developed in various Catholic documents and publications.[6] The Australian Catholic Bishops employed it in their annual Social Justice Statement of 2002. According to their interpretation, Genesis 1 makes it clear that 'human beings are connected with all creatures, the natural world, indeed the whole

---

3   Pope John Paul II, *General Audience*, nos. 2–4.
4   Catholic Bishops of the Boston Province, *And God*.
5   Cf. Pope John Paul II, Ecumenical Patriarch Bartholomew, *Common Declaration*.
6   Cf. e.g. CCCB, *Our Relationship*; ICBC, *The Cry*.

universe'. This connectedness must be rediscovered as part of an ecological conversion so that humans can 'be reconciled with all creation'. The connectedness is not only rooted in the common creation of all things but also in their joint salvation through Jesus Christ. The Australian Bishops point this out by referring to Col. 1:15-20: It is in Jesus Christ that 'all things in heaven and on earth were created' and 'through him God was pleased to reconcile to himself all things'.[7]

Pope Francis incorporated the idea of an ecological conversion in his encyclical *Laudato Si'*, explicitly drawing on both John Paul II and the Australian Catholic Bishops.[8] He, too, makes it clear that an ecological conversion is a deeply spiritual matter and that 'a more passionate concern for the protection of our world' needs to be motivated and inspired by 'an ecological spirituality grounded in the convictions of our faith'.[9] He names several such convictions, including 'the security that Christ has taken unto himself this material world and now, risen, is intimately present to each being, surrounding it with his affection and penetrating it with his light'.[10] The Catholic theologian Denis Edwards highlights this nexus as a very important aspect of a specifically Christian approach to ecological conversion:

> For Christians, of course, the deepest reason for this conversion is that we see the Earth and all its creatures as God's good creation, the creation that God radically embraces in the incarnation of the Word made flesh. [...] God's creation of all things is deeply interconnected with God's presence with us in Christ.[11]

The Pope explains 'that a healthy relationship with creation is one dimension of overall personal conversion'.[12] While being a spiritual matter, an ecological conversion has to bear fruit in a change of behaviour and in corresponding actions so that the effects of people's 'encounter with Jesus Christ become evident

---

7   ACBC, *A New Earth*. Bible version cited in this paper: NRSV.
8   Cf. Pope Francis, *Laudato Si'*, nos. 5 + 218.
9   Pope Francis, *Laudato Si'*, no. 216.
10 Pope Francis, *Laudato Si'*, nos. 220-221.
11 Edwards, *Jesus*, 4-5. – In fact, Edwards considers the nexus between creation, incarnation and salvation in Jesus Christ to be 'not well represented in the encyclical'. He assumes that 'because of its attempt to speak to those who are not Christian, Laudato Si [...] is focused mainly on creation theology, and does not explore in any detail the interconnection between creation and incarnation' (Edwards, 'Sublime Communion', 378-379).
12 Pope Francis, *Laudato Si'*, no. 218.

in their relationship with the world around them. Living our vocation to be protectors of God's handiwork is essential to a life of virtue; it is not an optional or a secondary aspect of our Christian experience'.[13] Pope Francis also points out that 'self-improvement on the part of individuals will not by itself remedy the extremely complex situation facing our world today. [...] The ecological conversion needed to bring about lasting change is also a community conversion'.[14]

Although two popes have employed it most prominently, the idea of a spiritual ecological conversion is not an exclusively Catholic concept. Even though they do not use the exact same term, similar themes can be found in documents from various denominational backgrounds. Patriarch Bartholomew, for example, speaks of a necessary repentance and of manÐs reconciliation with God that results in man's reconciliation with nature.[15] In *The World is Our Host*, a delegation of Anglican bishops states that the ecological problem is 'spiritual as well as economic, scientific and political' and that 'climate justice for us as Christians demands a faith response'.[16] To give one more example, the Evangelical Environmental Network's *Evangelical Declaration on the Care of Creation* pronounces that 'God calls us to confess and repent of attitudes which devalue creation', that 'our actions and attitudes toward the earth need to proceed from the center of our faith', and that the 'presence of the kingdom of God is marked not only by renewed fellowship with God, but also by renewed harmony and justice between people, and by renewed harmony and justice between people and the rest of the created world'.[17]

Summing up the various statements, a spiritual ecological conversion and its counterpart, an ecological spirituality, comprise:

- an awareness that all things created reflect something of God;
- a recollection of humans' common vocation as stewards and protectors of God's creation;
- a recognition that through creation and—from a Christian point of view—also through incarnation and salvation, we are connected and in communion with all creatures, the natural world, and the whole universe;

---

13 Pope Francis, *Laudato Si'*, no. 217.
14 Pope Francis, *Laudato Si'*, no. 219. – For further interpretation of the concept of an ecological conversion in Laudato Si' see e.g. Edwards, 'Sublime Communion', 387-388; Edwards, 'Ecological Theology', 27-28; Ormerod, Vanin, 'Ecological Conversion'.
15 Cf. Ecumenical Patriarch Bartholomew, *Message* (2003) + *Message* (2011).
16 Anglican Bishops, *The World*, 2-3.
17 EEN, *Evangelical Declaration*.

- changes in behaviour, actions, and lifestyle towards greater care for creation and sustainability, which flow from a true conversion that is part of the transformative encounter with Jesus Christ;
- both individual and communal/societal conversion and change.

Denis Edwards adds that an ecological conversion 'involves not only a radical transformation in the way we see the wider natural world, but also in the way we feel for it and with it'.[18] He also explains that 'Christians are called to humbly stand with others who may have been involved with care for Earth long before' them, and that, in fact, a global 'movement of ecological conversion involves people from all kinds of religious backgrounds': Regardless of whether or not the ecological spirituality that drives the individual participant is Christian, 'this movement can be understood as a new form of global spirituality, and in Christian terms as a work of the Holy Spirit'.[19]

3. The Need for Authentic Advocacy for Ecological Conversion and Change

If 'living our vocation to be protectors of God's handiwork' is–as Pope Francis has clarified–not optional, but essential to leading a Christian life, so must be the spiritual ecological conversion that lets us (re)discover this vocation. Any leadership in church and society that arises out of the Christian ethos should, therefore, promote such a conversion as well as the changes in behaviour, actions, and lifestyle that can grow from it. Leaders can play an important role in the diffusion of more ecologically sustainable patterns of thinking and living.[20] However, can they successfully encourage others to change if they have not undergone or are not undergoing an ecological conversion themselves? The German economist Niko Paech not only doubts this, he even considers sustainability experts dangerous who do not embody what they try to convey. He criticises the large number of such experts that 'jet from continent to continent, non-stop, yet also non-effectively,' to communicate values of sustainability, try to convince people of the urgent need for change, present the latest research findings, give advice, etc. Paech's criticism points to the fact that

---

18   Edwards, 'Ecological Theology', 27-28.
19   Edwards, *Jesus*, 4.
20   Cf. Paech, 'Adiós', 290; Baden, Prasad, 'Applying Behavioural Theory', 338; Burns et al., 'Leadership'.

their restless, emissions-intensive lifestyle is a 'perfect antithesis' to what a sustainable lifestyle would look like. In his opinion, the only meaningful way to communicate and promote the latter is by setting examples: Smart presentations and lectures or consultation services cannot be a substitute for an expert or leader living out sustainability in an exemplary and imitable way.[21]

Obviously, examples can also be set by individuals or groups that are not in a formal leadership role: Anyone who has changed their behaviour and lifestyle towards greater care for the earth, and shows the results publicly enough, can potentially trigger change in others. What they do can serve as an experiment and model for the wider public to observe and learn that living more sustainably is possible and feasible.[22] Even though these individuals and groups often 'do not think of themselves as facilitators of a learning process' for their fellow citizens, they actually are.[23]

4. Sustainability Formation as a Core Responsibility of (Theological) Higher Education

There is a high chance for higher education graduates to take up positions in society in which they are bound to become leaders and/or role models for others. This could be in a formal leadership role, but also as teachers, managers, counsellors, staff in NGOs, or religious organisations, etc. Tertiary education institutions thus have an opportunity as well as a responsibility to equip their students with everything they need in order to become leaders and role models in living sustainably. This particularly applies to institutions that seek to educate and form their prospective graduates out of a Christian ethos—including those providing theological higher education. If their students are meant to undergo a transformation of character and be 'prepared to build a better society', in the current time of climate crisis, this should involve undergoing a spiritual ecological conversion, learning to lead a sustainable lifestyle, and becoming authentic promotors of that same conversion for others.

Naturally, this is not a call for higher education institutions to exclusively bear this responsibility, but they should have a share in it. At the international level, it has been proposed again and again that environmental and sustainability

---

21 Paech, 'Adiós', 290–293; tr. from German by S. Salaske-Lentern.
22 Cf. WBGU, *Welt*, 256–257 + 262; Rückert-John et al., 'Neue Formen', 78.
23 Van Poeck et al., 'An Exploration'.

matters should become an integral part of education at all levels and in all disciplines. Respective recommendations can be found, for example, in the 1992 Rio de Janeiro Earth Summit's *Agenda 21*, the 1997 UNESCO *Declaration of Thessaloniki*, or the 2002 Johannesburg Earth Summit's *Plan of Implementation*.[24] Agenda 21 also calls these matters 'a crosscutting issue', while the Declaration of Thessaloniki suggests a 'reorientation of education as a whole towards sustainability'.[25] The Australian Government named precisely such a reorientation in 'all sectors of Australia's formal education system' as one of the strategies outlined in its 2009 *National Action Plan for Education for Sustainability*.[26] One of the objectives listed as part of this strategy reads: 'Education for sustainability is integrated into all university courses/subject areas and campuses are managed in a sustainable way'.[27]

According to Prof. Kerry Shephard of the Higher Education Development Centre at the University of Otago, New Zealand, '[m]any Australian higher education institutions have inspirational initiatives that pilot and promote education for sustainability'.[28] Others, however, seem to 'have not yet committed themselves to the concept'.[29] The Australian Government admits in its National Action Plan that '[e]ducation for sustainability still has a long way to go before it could be said to be integral to shaping Australia's environmental, social and economic future'.[30] To further advance in this regard, it may be imperative to systematically 'develop the capability of [...] faculty to teach environmental literacy' to students.[31] Australian research indicates 'that while many teachers are aware that sustainability has some role to play in their teaching, some of them view that role in quite limiting ways' and assume that it mostly belongs in the domain of life sciences.[32]

---

24 Cf. UNCED, *Agenda 21*, nos. 36.3–36.5; UNESCO, *Declaration of Thessaloniki*, nos. 10 + 12; WSSD, *Plan*, no. 121.
25 UNCED, *Agenda 21*, no. 36.5.b + UNESCO, *Declaration of Thessaloniki*, no. 10.
26 DEWHA, *Living Sustainably*, 21.
27 DEWHA, *Living Sustainably*, 21.
28 Shephard, 'Higher Education's Role', 17. – Just as one example cf. Macquarie University, *Sustainability*, 12–13.
29 Shephard, 'Higher Education's Role', 16.
30 DEWHA, *Living Sustainably*, 10. – To be fair to tertiary education institutions: Whether they have the capacity to commit themselves to sustainability education is, of course, also a matter of funding. Shephard explains that '[w]ithout explicit funding, higher education has limited opportunities to have an impact and institutions that attempt to do so are doing it by redirecting funding allocated for other purposes and jeopardising their financial security' (Shephard, 'Higher Education's Role', 17).
31 ULSF, *The Talloires Declaration*, action no. 4. Cf. also Reid, Petocz, 'University', 121.
32 Reid, Petocz, 'University', 106 + 108.

Such a perception clearly contradicts sustainability's character as a crosscutting issue. By the same token, it falls short of realising that each academic discipline might have something to contribute to teaching sustainability matters more comprehensively and effectively so that 'the strengths of each traditional discipline can be used and leveraged with the strengths of other disciplines'.[33] According to Reid and Petocz, '[p]ractitioners in each discipline will need to explore the ways in which sustainability can be positioned as core business for the particular discipline rather than peripheral to it'.[34] For theological higher education, both contributing its own disciplinary expertise to a more 'holistic Education for Sustainable Development'[35] and embedding sustainability at the centre of its syllabi should somehow be related to ecological conversion and ecological spirituality. In this field, theological higher education really has something to offer, as the following statement by Italian-American professor of biology Bruno Borsari suggests. In his opinion, students need to be led to 'ponder that we humans are part of nature and that the sustenance of the whole system depends on our ability and wisdom in cooperating with it, rather than against it. Such cooperative attitude derives from values like stewardship, conservation, social justice'.[36] In the aforementioned statement *The World is Our Host*, the signatory bishops equally

> call for programmes of theological formation [...] to include in-depth components of eco-justice and ecotheology. We call for Anglican educational institutions to integrate issues of environmental sustainability and ethics into their curricula and community life and by teaching a theological approach to climate justice.[37]

5. Making the Leap from Knowledge to Action

The responsibility of higher education institutions is not limited to imparting environmental and sustainability-related knowledge. It also encompasses helping students to make the leap from knowledge to action and a change of behaviour. Many experts in sustainability research agree that one of the most

---

33 McKeown, Hopkins, 'EE≠ESD', 124.
34 Reid, Petocz, 'University', 121.
35 Cf. McKeown, Hopkins, 'EE≠ESD', 124.
36 Borsari, 'Curriculum', 75-76.
37 Anglican Bishops, *The World*, 6.

pressing challenges we currently face is not people's lack of knowledge about the ecological crisis and about means to deal with it, but the so-called mind-behaviour gap (also known as intention-behaviour gap, value-action gap, and by some other names). This term refers to the phenomenon that in most industrialised societies, it is commonly known how dangerous the situation has become and what could be done collectively and individually to live more sustainably. Several surveys have shown that a majority of citizens also endorses or even pledges themselves to the idea of respective change. Nevertheless, most people do not act or change their lifestyle accordingly.[38] Some scholars explain what seems like a conundrum by pointing to various factors that can possibly inhibit the step from knowledge to action, especially psychological factors (such as cognitive, attentional and perceptual weaknesses, behavioural tendencies, emotions, habits, and routines) and sociocultural factors (including influences from family, friends, schoolmates, work colleagues, etc. as well as cultural background, religion, subculture, peer group, mass media, opinion leaders, etc.).[39] Obviously, structural barriers also play an important role, such as limited availability and accessibility of sustainably sourced yet affordable consumer goods, or a lack of fast and affordable local and long-distance public transport.[40] A lot could be done by political and economic actors to reduce structural barriers and address some of the psychological and sociocultural inhibitors, but that is not the concern of this discussion.

Educational actors on their part can and should help bridge the gap by offering learning experiences that allow students to not just theorise but to practically try out and accustom themselves to means and ways of living more sustainably, thereby gaining what Jensen and Schnack call 'action competence'.[41] However, such learning experiences should not be attempts of behavioural modification; that is trying to change students' behaviour in a previously determined direction.[42] These views are widely shared by supporters of so-called

---

38 Cf. Kollmuss, Agyeman, 'Mind the Gap'; Barr, 'Environmental Action'; Huddart Kennedy et al., 'Why We Don't'; Heidbrink et al., 'Einleitung', 9–10. – Specifically within the context of higher education cf. Shephard, 'Higher Education's Role', 14: '[G]raduates may know much about sustainability and possess many of the skills needed to function sustainably, but unless they choose to put this knowledge and these skills to sustainable ends, their education (for sustainability) will have in some senses failed'.
39 Cf. Hofmann, Brand, 'Information', 98-100; Kleinhückelkotten, 'Konsumverhalten', 138-141 + 153; Reisch, Hagen, 'Kann der Konsumwandel', 221-233.
40 Cf. WBVE, *Verbraucherpolitik*, 8–9; Heidbrink, Schmidt, 'Die neue Verantwortung', 30.
41 Jensen, Schnack, 'The Action', especially 163 + 174; Michelsen, Fischer, *Nachhaltig konsumieren*.
42 Cf. Jensen, Schnack, 'The Action', 167–168, 176.

'Education for Sustainability' (EfS) approaches.[43] The latter explicitly go beyond 'education *about* sustainability (developing understanding and awareness)' and aim at building up students' motivation and capacity by engaging them in actions towards sustainability. To prevent behavioural modification, they seek to 'be a learner-centred approach, create situations for participants to become involved in decision-making, be collaborative and participatory throughout'. Furthermore, EfS is meant to also go beyond mere individual behaviour changes. It seeks to enable students to envision alternative ways of development, encourage them to partake in collective actions, and empower them to contribute to structural and systemic change. It advocates trying to put '[l]ess emphasis on seeing people as the problem and more on seeing people as agents of change'.[44]

How can tertiary institutions provide learning opportunities that meet these criteria? One key element is introducing action-oriented teaching and learning methods into classes, lectures, tutorials, etc. In this case, authenticity plays an important part: Some supposedly more action-oriented methods like simulations or roleplays have been criticised for merely creating 'as if'-situations instead of real action.[45] Such a need for authenticity will frequently result in the action having to be taken outside of the classroom as well as beyond class time, for example in the form of student projects, field trips, or service-learning.[46]

This last aspect leads to a second element: creating a learning environment that allows students to experience means and ways of living more sustainably. Two features of such an approach are campus management and campus design. By managing the campus sustainably, the institution can become a role model for its students.[47] It is pointed out in the Australian National Action Plan that managing the campus 'in line with what is learnt in the classroom reinforces formal learning and demonstrates the importance of the issues'.[48] Beyond this passive reinforcement, sustainable campus management and campus design ideally create spaces and opportunities for students to be challenged to make sustainable choices and to engage in sustainability-related action.[49] Apart from

---

43 Alternative names are 'Learning for Sustainability' (LfS) or 'Education for Sustainable Development' (ESD) (cf. Delgado, *Education*, 40-41).
44 Entire passage about EfS: Delgado, *Education*, 38-39 + 41 (direct quotes from this source) + Jensen, Schnack, 'The Action', 164 + 168 + 172-173.
45 Cf. Jensen, Schnack, 'The Action', 167, 175.
46 Cf. Borsari, 'Curriculum', 77; Radinger-Peer, Pflitsch, 'The Role', 165.
47 Cf. Shephard, 'Higher Education's Role', 14.
48 DEWHA, *Living Sustainably*, 21.
49 Cf. Borsari, 'Curriculum', 77; Barth, 'Nachhaltigkeit', 115-118.

that, active aspects can also be incorporated into sustainable campus management and design by inviting students to participate in shaping the respective policies and projects.[50] Another important part of creating a supportive learning environment is the establishment of a network of regional partners: NGOs, businesses, governmental organisation, etc. that have a focus on the environment and sustainability can facilitate students' practical experiences and action outside of the classroom and class time; for example, participating in an environmental campaign or co-developing a more sustainable product.[51]

A third element, besides action-oriented teaching and learning methods and a corresponding learning environment, relates to the role of lecturers, tutors, or supervisors: As has been pointed out, university teachers themselves need to undergo a formation that enables them to include environmental and sustainability matters in the teaching of their respective subjects.[52] Furthermore, they may struggle to convincingly accompany students through a learning and transformation process towards more sustainable living if they 'have not themselves embraced sustainable lifestyles'.[53] As much as prospective higher education graduates are needed to become leaders or role models for others, as much do they need their teachers to be leaders and role models for them.[54] This does not have to contradict the EfS' preference for 'student-centred rather than teacher-centred teaching'.[55] In fact, Borsari describes a good teacher-student relationship in the context of sustainability as a mutual 'circle of learning' from which 'true education emerges successfully' for both sides.[56] If the three elements are pursued with equal commitment, 'whole-of-institution change for sustainability' is underway.[57] Again, for theological higher education, all the above implicates the dimensions of an ecological conversion and an ecological

---

50 Cf. Barth, 'Nachhaltigkeit', 115–118; UNCSD, *The Future*, no. 234.
51 Cf. Radinger-Peer, Pflitsch, 'The Role', 165; Barth, 'Nachhaltigkeit', 120.
52 The Declaration of Thessaloniki suggests 'the strengthening and eventual reorientation of teacher training programmes' (UNESCO, *Declaration of Thessaloniki*, no. 24). In the Agenda 21, '[e]ducational authorities, with the appropriate assistance from community groups or non-governmental organizations, are recommended to assist or set up pre-service and in-service training programmes for all teachers, administrators, and educational planners, as well as non-formal educators in all sectors, addressing the nature and methods of environmental and development education' (UNCED, *Agenda 21*, no. 36.5.b).
53 Shephard, 'Higher Education's Role', 20.
54 Cf. Shephard, 'Higher Education's Role', 14; Aldrin, *University*.
55 Shephard, 'Higher Education's Role', 20–21. Cf. also Delgado, *Education*, 39.
56 Borsari, 'Curriculum', 76.
57 DEWHA, *Living Sustainably*, 23. Likewise, cf. Barth, 'Nachhaltigkeit', 107.

spirituality: Alongside action competence, students should be able to acquire an eco-spiritual competence that deepens their understanding and experience of living more sustainably, and links both to their religious identity.

6. Practical Examples

At the end of this paper, some examples shall illustrate how learning opportunities and learning environments in theological higher education can enable students to practically experience how to lead a life of sustainability and stewardship:

The Catholic University of Eichstätt-Ingolstadt in Southern Germany enjoys a reputation for being committed to sustainable development and has invested in building a respective learning environment. One part of it is a garden and model farm on campus; another one is partnering up with the local forest administration. The university offers several units in various subject areas—including theology—that combine theoretical learning about ecology matters with making use of the learning environment for practical experiences. One is titled 'Experiencing the forest: Outdoor education approaches to creation theology and their practical implementation'. Another one, 'Foundations and practical implementation of sustainable development', includes practical sessions in the garden, where students can get their hands into the earth and learn to live in a, at least partly, self-sustaining way, not having to buy all produce from a supermarket.[58]

Another example is tertiary institutions that, as part of their campus management, create incentives for students and staff to reduce the use of petrol-fuelled vehicles for getting to and around campus. Australian Monash University and La Trobe University offer free Bikeshare-systems on some of their campuses. La Trobe additionally has their own carpooling programme.[59] These are obviously big universities, but even small vocational colleges could introduce something alike on a smaller scale. Students may not make an immediate connection between work on ecological responsibility and spirituality in (theology) units and using the campuses' bike-sharing or carpooling facilities. However, if, for example, the units entailed some form of fieldwork, students

---

58 Cf. Katholische Universität Eichstätt-Ingolstadt, *Sechster Nachhaltigkeitsbericht*, 35–38 + 48; tr. from German by S. Salaske-Lentern.
59 Cf. Monash University, *Monash Bikeshare* + La Trobe University, *Carpooling* + La Trobe University, *Cycling*.

could be encouraged to make use of the facilities in that very context.

A final example is trying to work together with a local Christian NGO or parish that is particularly committed to environmental action out of a Christian spirit. Students could take part in some of their activities or campaigns to get some first-hand experience of how the themes discussed in class might translate into real life. A good opportunity could be local parishes' and churches' activities for the *World Day of Prayer for the Care of Creation* (1 September each year) or the *Season of Creation* (annually from 1 September to 4 October, the feast day of St Francis of Assisi). These activities are often aimed at combining prayer and practical action, which again is an important link for ecological spirituality and conversion.[60]

Conclusion

Challenged by the Christian idea of a spiritual ecological conversion, this paper has made a case for providers of theological higher education to pursue a path of 'whole-of-institution change' and include sustainability formation at the core of their curricula. This demand is backed by a wide range of political and educational declarations on an international as well as an Australian national level. Students should theoretically learn and practically experience what it means to live as stewards of God's creation. As such, they can become role models for others. This can be achieved particularly through action-oriented teaching and learning methods, a corresponding learning environment, and teachers who have been able to acquire the necessary teaching capabilities and ideally undergone a spiritual ecological conversion themselves. Some examples have indicated how these ambitious goals could be put into practice.

---

60 Cf. Global Catholic Climate Movement, *About the Season*.

Bibliography

ACBC (Australian Catholic Bishops Conference). *A New Earth: The Environmental Challenge* (2002) <https://www.socialjustice.catholic.org.au/files/SJSandresources/2002_SJSS_statement.pdf> [accessed 26 March 2019].

Aldrin, V. *University Teachers as Role Models for Being Sustainable – Doing Sustainability Together with Students through the Use of Professional Ethics* <https://www.diva-portal.org/smash/get/diva2:1051438/FULLTEXT01.pdf> [accessed 26 March 2019].

Anglican Bishops Gathered At Volmoed Conference and Retreat Centre, South Africa, 23 to 27 February 2015. *The World is Our Host: A Call to Urgent Action for Climate Justice* (2015) <https://acen.anglicancommunion.org/media/148818/The-World-is-our-Host-FINAL-TEXT.pdf> [accessed 26 March 2019].

Baden, D., Prasad, S. 'Applying Behavioural Theory to the Challenge of Sustainable Development: Using Hairdressers as Diffusers of More Sustainable Hair-Care Practices', *Journal of Business Ethics* 133.2 (2016), 335-349.

Barr, S. 'Environmental Action in the Home: Investigating the "Value-Action" Gap', *Geography* 91.1 (2006), 43-54.

Barth, M. 'Nachhaltigkeit in die Schule gebracht: Befunde aus einer empirischen Studie', in G. Michelsen, D. Fischer (eds.), *Nachhaltig konsumieren lernen: Ergebnisse aus dem Projekt BINK* ('Bildungsinstitutionen und nachhaltiger Konsum') (Bad Homburg, DE: Verlag für Akademische Schriften, 2013): 105-129.

Borsari, B. 'Curriculum Frameworks for Sustainability Education', *Academic Exchange Quartely* 16.1 (2012), 74-78.

Burns, H., Vaught, H. D., Bauman, C. 'Leadership for Sustainability: Theoretical Foundations and Pedagogical Practises That Foster Change', *International Journal of Leadership Studies* 9.1 (2015), 131-143.

Catholic Bishops of the Boston Province *And God Saw That It Was Good: A Pastoral Letter of the Bishops of the Boston Province* (4 October 2000) <http://fore.yale.edu/publications/statements/and-god-saw-that-it-was-good-> [accessed 26 March 2019].

CCCB (Canadian Conference of Catholic Bishops, Commission for Social Affairs). *Our Relationship with the Environment: The Need for Conversion* (Ottawa, ON: CCCB, 2008) <http://www.cccb.ca/site/images/stories/pdf/enviro_eng.pdf> [accessed 26 March 2019].

Chryssavgis, J. 'Ecumenical Patriarch Bartholomew: Insights into an Orthodox Christian Worldview', *International Journal of Environmental Studies* 64.1 (2007), 9-18.

Delgado, L. *Education for Sustainability in Local Government: Handbook* (Canberra, ACT: DEWHA, Australian Research Institute in Education for Sustainability (ARIES), 2007) <http://aries.mq.edu.au/handbook> [accessed 26 March 2019].

DEWHA (Australian Government Department of the Environment, Water, Heritage and the Arts). *Living Sustainably: The Australian Government's National Action Plan for Education for Sustainability* (Canberra, ACT: Commonwealth of Australia, 2009).

Ecumenical Patriarch Bartholomew. *Message by H.A.H. Ecumenical Patriarch Bartholomew upon the Day of Prayer for the Protection of Creation* (1 September 2003) <https://www.patriarchate.org/-/message-by-h-a-h-ecumenical-patriarch-bartholomew-upon-the-day-of-prayer-for-the-protection-of-creation-01-09-2003-> [accessed 26 March 2019].

Ecumenical Patriarch Bartholomew. *Message by H.A.H. Ecumenical Patriarch Bartholomew upon the Day of Prayer for the Protection of Creation* (1 September 2011) <https://www.patriarchate.org/-/menyma-tes-a-th-panagiotetos-tou-oikoumenikou-patriarchou-k-k-bartholomaiou-epi-tei-1ei-septembriou-hemerai-proseuches-dia-to-physikon-periballon-01-0?_101_INSTANCE_QnqPBbQ42NED_languageId=en_US> [accessed 26 March 2019].

Edwards, D. '"Sublime Communion": The Theology of the Natural World in Laudato Si", *Theological Studies* 77.2 (2016), 377-391.

Edwards, D. 'Ecological Theology: Trinitarian Perspectives', *Proceedings of the Catholic Theological Society of America* 72 (2017), 14-28.

Edwards, D. *Jesus and the Natural World: Exploring a Christian Approach to Ecology* (Mulgrave, VIC: Garratt, 2012).

EEN (Evangelical Environmental Network). *Evangelical Declaration on the Care of Creation*, <https://www.creationcare.org/evangelical_declaration_on_the_care_of_creation> [accessed 26 March 2019].

Global Catholic Climate Movement. *About the Season of Creation + History of the Season*, <https://seasonofcreation.org/about> [accessed 26 March 2019].

GreenFaith *Christian Teachings*, <https://greenfaith.org/christian_teachings> [accessed 26 March 2019].

Heidbrink, L., Schmidt, I. 'Die neue Verantwortung der Konsumenten', *Aus Politik und Zeitgeschichte* 32-33 (2009), 27-32.

Heidbrink, L., Schmidt, I., Ahaus, B. 'Einleitung: Der Konsument zwischen Markt und Moral', in L. Heidbrink, I. Schmidt, B. Ahaus (eds.), *Die Verantwortung des Konsumenten. Über das Verhältnis von Markt, Moral und Konsum* (Frankfurt a.M., DE et al.: Campus, 2011): 9-22.

Hofmann, J., Brand, M. 'Information gegen Irrationalität – Welche Faktoren beeinflussen Kaufentscheidungen?', in C. Bala, K. Müller (eds.), *Abschied vom Otto Normalverbraucher: Moderne Verbraucherforschung. Leitbilder, Information, Demokratie* (Essen, DE: Klartext, 2015): 95-109.

Huddart Kennedy, E., Beckley, T. M., McFarlane, B. L., Nadeau, S. 'Why We Don't "Walk the Talk": Understanding the Environmental Values/Behaviour Gap in Canada', *Human Ecology Review* 16.2 (2009), 151-160.

ICBC (Irish Catholic Bishops' Conference) *The Cry of the Earth: A Call to Action for Climate Justice: A Pastoral Reflection on Climate Change from the Irish Catholic Bishops' Conference* (2014) <https://www.catholicbishops.ie/wp-content/uploads/2014/09/The-Cry-of-the-Earth-A-Call-to-Action-for-Climate-Justice-2014.pdf> [accessed 26 March 2019].

Jensen, B. B., Schnack, K. 'The Action Competence Approach in Environmental Education', *Environmental Education Research* 3-2 (1997), 163-178.

Katholische Universität Eichstätt-Ingolstadt. *Sechster Nachhaltigkeitsbericht 2017/18 mit integrierter Umwelterklärung nach EMAS/EMASplus* (November 2018) <https://www.ku.de/fileadmin/190811/Downloads/NHB_1718_miUmwelterkl_kleiner_v3.pdf> [accessed 26 March 2019].

Kleinhückelkotten, S. 'Konsumverhalten im Spannungsfeld konkurrierender Interessen und Ansprüche: Lebensstile als Moderatoren des Konsums', in L. Heidbrink, I. Schmidt, B. Ahaus (eds.), *Die Verantwortung des Konsumenten. Über das Verhältnis von Markt, Moral und Konsum* (Frankfurt a.M., DE et al.: Campus, 2011): 133-156.

Kollmuss, A., Agyeman, J. 'Mind the Gap: Why Do People Act Environmentally and What Are the Barriers to Pro-Environmental Behavior?', *Environmental Education Research* 8.3 (2002), 239-260.

La Trobe University. *Carpooling and car share schemes*, <https://www.latrobe.edu.au/transport-central/carpool-and-car-share> [accessed 26 March 2019].

La Trobe University. *Cycling*, <https://www.latrobe.edu.au/transport-central/cycling> [accessed 26 March 2019].

Macquarie University. *Sustainability in the Curriculum Project* (2009) <https://www.mq.edu.au/lih/pdfs/039_sust_in_curric.pdf> [accessed 26 March 2019].

McKeown, R., Hopkins, C. 'EE≠ESD: Defusing the Worry', *Environmental Education Research* 9.1 (2003), 117-128.

Michelsen, G., Fischer, D. (eds.) *Nachhaltig konsumieren lernen: Ergebnisse aus dem Projekt BINK* ('Bildungsinstitutionen und nachhaltiger Konsum') (Bad Homburg, DE: Verlag für Akademische Schriften, 2013).

Monash University. *Monash Bikeshare*, <https://monashbikeshare.com> [accessed 26 March 2019].

Ormerod, N., Vanin, C. 'Ecological Conversion: What Does it Mean?', *Theological Studies* 77.2 (2016), 328-352.

Paech, N. 'Adiós Konsumwohlstand: Vom Desaster der Nachhaltigkeitskommunikation und den Möglichkeiten der Suffizienz', in L. Heidbrink, I. Schmidt, B. Ahaus (eds.), *Die Verantwortung des Konsumenten: Über das Verhältnis von Markt, Moral und Konsum* (Frankfurt a.M., DE et al.: Campus, 2011): 285-304.

Pope Francis. *Encyclical letter Laudato Si': On Care for our Common Home* (24 May 2015) <http://w2.vatican.va/content/francesco/en/encyclicals/documents/papa-francesco_20150524_enciclica-laudato-si.html> [accessed 26 March 2019].

Pope John Paul II. General Audience (17 January 2001) <http://w2.vatican.va/content/john-paul-ii/en/audiences/2001/documents/hf_jp-ii_aud_20010117.html> [accessed 26 March 2019].

Pope John Paul II, Ecumenical Patriarch Bartholomew. *Common Declaration by Pope John Paul II and Ecumenical Patriarch Bartholomew I* (10 June 2002) <https://www.patriarchate.org/common-declarations-between-popes-and-ecumenical-patriarchs/-/asset_publisher/mQachZJu0upV/content/common-declaration-by-pope-john-paul-ii-and-ecumenical-patriarch-bartholomew-i-10-june-2002-> [accessed 26 March 2019].

Radinger-Peer, V., Pflitsch, G. 'The Role of Higher Education Institutions in Regional Transition Paths towards Sustainability: The Case of Linz (Austria)', *Review of Regional Research* 37.2 (2017), 161-187.

Reid, A., Petocz, P. 'University Lecturers' Understanding of Sustainability', *Higher Education* 51.1 (2006), 105-123.

Reisch, L. A., Hagen, K. 'Kann der Konsumwandel gelingen? Chancen und Grenzen einer verhaltensökonomisch basierten sozialen Regulierung', in L. Heidbrink, I. Schmidt, B. Ahaus (eds.), *Die Verantwortung des Konsumenten. Über das Verhältnis von Markt, Moral und Konsum* (Frankfurt a.M., DE et al.: Campus, 2011): 221-233.

Rückert-John, J., John, R., Jaeger-Erben, M. 'Neue Formen des Konsums aus Sicht der Politik', *Forschungsjournal Soziale Bewegungen* 28.2 (2015), 77-89.

SCD (Sydney College of Divinity). *The fourth Sydney College of Divinity Learning and Teaching Theology Conference: 5–6 April 2019: God's Exemplary Graduates: Character-Oriented Graduate Attributes in Theological Education* (conference poster) <https://scd.edu.au/wp-content/uploads/2018/11/SCD_A4_Gods_Exemplary_Grad_CONF_Web-1.pdf> [accessed 26 March 2019].

Shephard, K. 'Higher Education's Role in 'Education for Sustainability", *Australian Universities Review* 52.1 (2010), 13-22.

ULSF (Association of University Leaders for a Sustainable Future). *The Talloires Declaration: 10 Point Action Plan* (1990) <http://ulsf.org/wp-content/uploads/2015/06/TD.pdf> [accessed 26 March 2019].

UNCED (United Nations Conference on Environment and Development). *Agenda 21* (Rio de Janeiro, BR, 1992) <https://sustainabledevelopment.un.org/content/documents/Agenda21.pdf> [accessed 26 March 2019].

UNCSD (United Nations Conference on Sustainable Development). *The Future We Want* (Rio de Janeiro, BR, 2012) <https://sustainabledevelopment.un.org/futurewewant.html> [accessed 26 March 2019].

UNESCO International Conference on Environment and Society: Education and Public Awareness for Sustainability. *Declaration of Thessaloniki* (1997) <https://unesdoc.unesco.org/ark:/48223/pf0000117772> [accessed 26 March 2019].

Van Poeck, K., Læssøe, J., Block, T. 'An Exploration of Sustainability Change Agents As Facilitators of Nonformal Learning: Mapping a Moving and Intertwined Landscape', *Ecology and Society* 22.2 (2017), article 33. <https://www.ecologyandsociety.org/vol22/iss2/art33> [accessed 26 March 2019].

WBGU (Wissenschaftlicher Beirat der Bundesregierung Globale Umweltveränderungen). *Welt im Wandel: Gesellschaftsvertrag für eine Große Transformation* (2nd edn; Berlin, DE: WBGU, 2011).

WBVE (Wissenschaftlicher Beirat Verbraucher- und Ernährungspolitik beim BMELV). *Verbraucherpolitik für nachhaltigen Konsum – Verbraucherpolitische Perspektiven für eine nachhaltige Transformation von Wirtschaft und Gesellschaft: Stellungnahme des Wissenschaftlichen Beirats Verbraucher- und Ernährungspolitik beim BMELV* (2013) <www.aloenk.tu-berlin.de/fileadmin/fg165/Aktuelles/Stellungnahme_Nachhaltiger_Konsum_-_final.pdf> [accessed 26 March 2019].

WCC (World Council of Churches). *Climate Change: WCC Documents Related to Climate Change*, <https://www.oikoumene.org/en/resources/documents/wcc-programmes/diakonia/climate-change/climate-change> [accessed 26 March 2019].

WSSD (United Nations World Summit on Sustainable Development). *Plan of Implementation of the World Summit on Sustainable Development* (Johannesburg, RSA, 2002) <http://www.un-documents.net/jburgpln.htm> [accessed 26 March 2019].

Sebastian Salaske-Lentern
University of Muenster (Germany), Faculty of Catholic Theology
sebastian.salaske@uni-muenster.de

22 | LANGUAGE LEARNING IN THEOLOGICAL EDUCATION

Abstract

In what ways can the study of Greek and other biblical languages shape Christian character? This paper explores this question through the misquoting of the Apostle Paul: 'We rejoice in our language studies, because we know that language study produces endurance, endurance produces proven character, and proven character produces hope. This hope will not disappoint us'. The essay will argue that the study of Greek, Hebrew, and Aramaic can indeed bring spiritual benefit—not just because these languages allow access to the text of Scripture as originally written but because the discipline, motivation, and purpose of language learning can be harnessed in the formation of Christian character.

1. Introduction

This essay addresses the meta-question about the place of Greek language teaching within theological education, and, more importantly, its role in developing Christian character. It seems the first part of that task is more straightforward than the second. It is quite a bit easier to discuss the merits of teaching and learning Greek for the study of theology than it is to articulate how such study might shape Christian character. That is especially the case since I have already written on the first topic. But the second element connects to the theme of this volume of essays and, to my knowledge, no one has written about language acquisition and Christian character before.

At first blush, it may take some imagination to claim that the study of biblical languages has any relationship to Christian formation at all. After all, the languages themselves do not have any direct connection to God, Jesus, or the Christian life. Anyone can study Ancient Greek, and one would not suppose that the experience would cause them to become conformed to Christ somehow. On the other hand, studying doctrine teaches us about God and his ways, and so may directly inform Christian formation. Learning about the themes and shape of the Old and New Testaments has likewise a direct bearing on the Christian life. The study of ethics, pastoral ministry, mission and—well, let's face it—just about any topic in theological study will help to shape the believer in positive ways. But surely something as dry, technical, and 'secular' as Ancient Greek could not possibly have a role to play.

In this paper, I will argue against that 'first blush' position and suggest that learning Ancient Greek and the other biblical languages does not only aid theological study but the formation of Christian character as well. To paraphrase a well-known statement of the Apostle Paul, we rejoice in our language studies because we know that language study produces endurance, endurance produces proven character, and proven character produces hope. This hope will not disappoint us.

2. Academic Reasons for Learning Greek

I have written previously about the academic reasons to learn Greek for the study of theology.[1] In this opening section on that same subject, I will shamelessly plagiarise myself before developing some new thoughts regarding how Greek can shape Christian character.

First, consider any university that is serious about the study of classical history. In any undergraduate classical history course, it is standard for students to learn both Greek and Latin. It is standard to assume that undergraduate students will read several of the primary texts in their original languages. The study of Aristotle, Plato, Thucydides, Herodotus, Lysias, and so on is conducted in Ancient Greek. This is because history takes the primary sources seriously. And taking the primary sources seriously means reading them in their original languages. And just to reiterate: This is the expectation of undergraduate students. These are not experts in the field. These are not renowned scholars and researchers. No, these are students just beginning their tertiary education.

---

1   Campbell, 'The Study of the Language of the New Testament'.

If the discipline of history holds such expectations for their undergraduate students, why is it unrealistic to expect that postgraduate students of theology will study Greek and Hebrew?

Second, we must resist the consistent dumbing down of expectations for preachers and pastors. The seriousness of training ministers in times past led to the foundation of the oldest universities in the Western world. Oxford, Cambridge, Harvard, Yale—alongside several others—all began as institutions devoted to theological training. The impetus that began Oxford has now dwindled to the attitude that a pastor does not even need to learn Greek. What a sorry state of affairs.

Third, if we believe that the preaching pastor is a doctor of souls, why would we tolerate sloppy and incomplete training? We would not tolerate incomplete training of a medical doctor or surgeon. After all, we put our lives in the hands of such people—they need to know what they are doing. How much more a doctor of souls? We put our eternal lives in the care of pastors and preachers, and yet we value their training less than that of the surgeon. Something is wrong with our perception of reality if we are willing to make such a concession. Either we do not believe in the seriousness of what's at stake, or we do not believe that training really makes much difference. Both are significant errors.

3. Endurance

We turn now to consider issues beyond the academic use of Greek for the study of theology. First, as our Pauline paraphrase indicates, we rejoice in our language studies because we know that language study produces endurance.

Endurance is a bit of an old school word. Our world is one of immediacy and convenience, with Wikipedia, Uber Eats, and Netflix. It was not that long ago that we used to wait for our TV show to air at the same time each week and then patiently endure advertisements as they interrupted our program. Now, we decide what to watch and when. And there are no ads. After five minutes of watching 'old school' TV, I find that I have run out of patience for it. The convenience of Netflix has dramatically undermined my endurance of advertisements and the patience required to wait for the next instalment of Homeland. Now, I can binge-watch Homeland without interruption.

Notwithstanding such developments, there are still some endeavours that require endurance. Learning a musical instrument, running a marathon, and raising children all require daily commitment that can be painful, unrewarding in the short-term, and frequently frustrating. None of these endeavours can go anywhere at all without endurance, or, as educationalists now prefer to call it—grit.

Grit has been shown to be the number one factor in success and achievement. It outweighs natural talent, economic advantage, and relational and familial support. Grit can literally project an uneducated woodcutter to the White House. Of course, natural talent helps. But grit helps more.

Now, if some endeavours have become automated, immediate, or can be performed through an app, there are other endeavours that simply cannot be done without grit. The key, then, is to figure out which tasks are which. Is learning Greek something that can be replaced by an app? Or is it a task that requires grit?

I'm sure you know where I'm going with this. Learning Greek cannot be replaced by an app, whether it be Accordance or Logos. Study of the Greek New Testament will always require knowledge of Greek. The apps simply cannot replicate first-hand knowledge because language knowledge is far more complex than vocabulary and parsing. It is like trying to have a conversation by using Google translate. That program is useful for looking up phrases and even whole paragraphs, but for a conversation, it is absolutely useless.

Like few other disciplines in theological study, language learning requires grit. Sure, it takes grit to read Karl Barth. It takes grit to master church history. And it takes grit to write an essay on the perichoretic unity and diversity within the Godhead according to the Fourth Gospel. But language-learning takes a different kind of grit. It's a grittier kind of grit. An essay might occupy you for a few weeks. Barth might take a lot longer, but there is no rush. Language study takes careful diligence, day in day out, for two years or more. And in order to keep the knowledge and skill you've acquired, it takes long-term maintenance grit.

For some, language-study grit is a fun exercise in personal discipline. Such people enjoy the long-term challenge of mastering something through a slow and steady bit-by-bit commitment. Other people hate it. For both types, but especially the second, learning Greek will achieve more than knowledge of a wonderful ancient tongue. It will develop grit. Or, to put it more biblically, it will develop endurance.

Endurance for its own sake is not especially noble. But endurance for a great cause is praiseworthy. We set our minds to accomplish something useful and necessary, and we push forward with it through thick and thin. There are times when you may want to quit. There are times you will feel defeated. There are times when you will be convinced that you are just wasting your time. But that is why it is called endurance. You must endure. And these are just the hardships through which we must endure.

The thing that is useful and necessary, in this case, is the right handling of the scriptures. Knowing the biblical languages informs good exegesis and proper interpretation. It is simply not possible to handle the text well as a teacher without access to the original languages in which these ancient texts are written.

4. Proven Character

Endurance produces proven character. This is because of what endurance is. By its nature, endurance is character-building. To overcome set-backs and discouragement, to honour a daily commitment, and to choose long-term gain over short-term pain strengthens character and enhances resolve. Such things help to make a person reliable and trustworthy.

4.1 Humility

Language learning also enhances other aspects of character development, such as humility. Irrespective of natural gifts or inclination, language learning is a humbling experience. Like learning a musical instrument, language acquisition cannot be faked and regularly reminds us of our weaknesses. Even the most gifted students are forced to admit what they don't know. And conversely, one can only improve by humbly acknowledging where the weaknesses are. That's righty—like many endeavours that require endurance, learning Greek and Hebrew can only be done well with a posture of humility.

Humility is also cultivated through the use of biblical languages. One of the trappings of pride is to think that we know what a text says before we even examine it carefully. But reading a text slowly, as originally written in Ancient Hebrew, Aramaic, or Greek—and reading it with careful attention to the nuances of language—requires humility. One must adopt a position of humble acknowledgement that perhaps there is more to know about a certain text. Or, even, one's pre-existing understanding of a text may require adjustment. In other words, you might be wrong.

Often the most illuminating exegesis occurs not with unknown texts, but with known texts. It occurs when a text you thought you knew well—one that is perhaps widely known and loved—is freshly expounded in a way you had not previously considered. Some nugget of new insight hits you between the eyes and you are once again reminded that there is yet more to learn, more to see, more to behold. Language-based exegesis arguably yields more such humbling insights than any other element of biblical interpretation.

4.2 Dependency

Closely linked to humility is dependency. This is likely the characteristic that Jesus endorses when he says that anyone who would enter the kingdom of Heaven must do so as a little child. It's not that little children are necessarily humble—sometimes quite the opposite—but that they are dependent.

If any endeavour will cultivate dependency, it is the learning of an ancient language. Again, like learning a musical instrument, someone may figure it out on their own, but it's highly unlikely. At very least, the student needs grammar to study. While it is possible to think through theological truths without an instructor, or interpret parts of the Bible without help, no one is going to learn Ancient Greek without some sort of guide—whether grammar, instructor, or usually both.

Of course, other areas of theological study may cultivate dependency too. Church history, for example, cannot be studied without either instructor or textbook. But it is possible to read a textbook on one's own. One may study primary historical sources without help. It's much more difficult to do the same with a language and with primary sources written in Greek or Hebrew. This is because language acquisition and language usage are actually skills, not simply knowledge. One must develop ability, not just understanding.

Dependency through language learning does not stop after the initial acquisition of Greek and Hebrew. Indeed, the further the student goes into these languages, the more dependent they become. Intermediate and advanced knowledge and skills are only developed in consultation with more rigorous and technical tools. And such tools will often require some level of instruction in order to navigate and use them well.

4.3 Love

Like all theological study, the learning of biblical languages is ultimately done out of love for God and neighbour. It is done out of respect for God's word and out of a desire to remain faithful to the text of Scripture. It is also done so that others may benefit more richly in their encounter with the Bible. Indeed, language acquisition is a major tool for preaching and teaching the Bible and has some fairly dramatic consequences for doing that faithfully and insightfully.

Thus, whether or not students develop a love for the biblical languages themselves, their study, nevertheless, ought to be motivated by love. As they endure the difficulties, allow themselves to be humbled, and increase in their dependency, language learning is ultimately an expression of the love of God and neighbour.

4.4 Hope

Language study produces endurance, endurance produces proven character, and proven character produces hope. But how does language-produced proven character result in hope?

First, humility induces hope. Humility involves the lowering of oneself for the sake of something greater. And the belief in something greater is an expression of hope. There is something greater than ourselves, with a greater purpose, and with greater resources that are already in play. All the answers do not rest with us. We are part of something bigger and beyond ourselves, and this grander reality constitutes our hope.

Second, the same can be said about dependency. Dependence on another acknowledges our belief that we rely on something or someone beyond ourselves. It acknowledges that someone is good. It acknowledges that our needs will be met by him. On whom are we ultimately dependent? The answer to that question is our hope.

Third, any activity conducted for the love of God and neighbour is necessarily hope-filled. It is performed in the hope that such efforts will be of service. Such efforts will bring honour to God and help to neighbour. Without such hope, love becomes somewhat empty because good intention alone is not effective. Loving acts move beyond intention to implementation.

In these ways and more, language-produced proven character produces hope. Learning the biblical languages is conducted in humility, with dependency and for love. And each of these characteristics require and foster hope.

4.5 Hope Will Not Disappoint

And this hope will not disappoint. Even if one day all your hard work in acquiring Greek and Hebrew disappears through the midst of time, neglect, and forgetfulness, the character-building aspects of the study will remain. It will have been an exercise in endurance that produced humility, dependency, and hope. It will have been an expression of hope.

And what if time, neglect, and forgetfulness do not have their way with you? What if that patient endurance leads to a permanent knowledge and skill set that will enrich your study and teaching of the Bible for the rest of your life? Well, then, you will be glad for that temporary pain for long-term gain.

Conclusion

The study of Greek, Hebrew, and Aramaic can indeed bring spiritual benefit; not just because these languages allow access to the text of Scripture as originally written. Though they certainly do that, language acquisition offers more direct benefit for the formation of Christian character—even apart from the fresh reading of text that it facilitates. The discipline, motivation, and purpose of language learning can all be harnessed for the formation of Christian character. Of course, it will be character-forming even apart from Christian commitment. But the point is that such character-formation can be directed toward Christian formation in positive and powerful ways.

In conclusion, we rejoice in our language studies because we know that language study produces endurance, endurance produces proven character, and proven character produces hope. This hope will not disappoint us.

Bibliography

Campbell, C. R. 'The Study of the Language of the New Testament', in Dockery, D. S. (ed.), *Theology, Church, and Ministry: A Handbook for Theological Education* (Nashville: B&H, 2017): chapter 8.

Constantine R. Campbell
Trinity Evangelical Divinity School
crcampbell@tiu.edu

23 | DESIGNING EFFECTIVE FIELDWORK EXPERIENCES

Abstract

International fieldwork experiences are prized by students as a great opportunity to see the world and explore other cultures and contexts. Whilst international travel is generally formational to some degree, many overseas trips are barely more than a guided tour with little attempt to address unit learning outcomes or to make assessments align with the experience. At ACOM and the Alliance Institute for Mission, we have attempted to overcome this disparity with a clear strategy to connect field experiences with learning content and unit outcomes. Pre- and post-assessments also help to frame the fieldwork experience within the course unit. In this paper, the design strategy for these fieldwork units will be discussed with two specific examples from recent fieldwork experiences. These fieldwork units involved both short (two weeks) and longer-term (two months) durations. Whilst still a work in progress, initial outcomes have proved positive with students applying the knowledge and skills gained through the fieldwork to course unit requirements.

1. Introduction

The use of local and international fieldwork programs is well-attested in scientific awards in which study of the content requires travel to where the content is physically located. Geology, geoscience, and archaeological awards are obvious examples. But many practical degrees, such as medicine, nursing, and related health care awards, also utilise fieldwork components as it is necessary to provide a context for students to apply their theoretical knowledge to real-world situations. In many cases, these fieldwork experiences are mandated as significant graduate outcomes are achieved through their implementation.

However, the case for fieldwork programs in humanity awards, such as we find in theological institutions, is not as clear cut. Universities, seminaries, and confessional bible colleges can, and do, produce theology and ministry graduates who have never had to stray from the safe confines of the classroom. Therefore, those of us who operate an international fieldwork program are open to the accusation that, at best, such programs are merely tangential to graduate outcomes and, at worst, are a barely concealed reach for market share. There remains, then, a valid question as to the value and place of these experiences within theological education.

From the outset, as the theme of this volume might suggest, any answer to this question must be connected to graduate outcomes. What particular outcomes are fieldwork experiences designed to achieve in the student? How can such outcomes be assessed? And perhaps most importantly, what structures and systems should be implemented in order to guarantee these outcomes? In what follows, I'd like to explore these questions and examine what we are doing at ACOM and the Alliance Institute for Mission in an endeavour to answer them.

2. Character Formation as Integral to Required Graduate Outcomes

The first point to stress is that fieldwork experiences are intentionally designed to be formational first, and knowledge or skills-based second. That is, fieldwork experiences should have a holistic impact even as they go some way to address key ministry skills. While learning outcomes rightly address both knowledge and skills, the goal of student formation is just as important, if not more so. The challenge, of course, is that student formation outcomes are far more difficult to quantify, and understandably, very few units are designed with formation in mind. However, formational experiences are a fundamental and integral component of theological education, and we need not apologise for intentionally finding space for it within our curriculum. It is not difficult to demonstrate that from the very beginning, Christian ministry training has had formation as a central and even essential focus. Bain notes in his discussion on *Theological*

Education in Early Christianity that a striking feature of the educational literature on the pastorate in late antiquity is its 'near total concern with matters of personal character and godliness'.[1] He goes on to say,

> Whether they are discussing questions of suitability, preparation, or the practice of formally-recognised ministry, matters of character are critical and receive almost all of the attention given ... these authors believed that the most critical factors relating to 'success' in ministry, and those most clearly providing reasons for failure, were questions of character rather than deficiencies in biblical or practical training.[2]

The importance of developing character in ministry and pastoral candidates has not diminished in the subsequent centuries, and so one of our main responsibilities as theological educators is to provide a context in which personal formation can take place. Of course, it is well-known that formation does not just happen but must be intentionally facilitated. Not that we can form the students ourselves —that remains the task of the Spirit of God. But we can create contexts in which formation can occur. In a 2018 publication, Ian Hussey reminded us that 'Students are formed by God in every context of their lives, not just when they are in lectures. The role of the college is then to be the *facilitator* of spiritual formation throughout the student's life (rather than the *provider*), whether that be in class, on a short-term mission trip, or anywhere in between'.[3] The goal of offering fieldwork experiences is the expectation that such experiences will facilitate this development.

Another aspect is the value of making these experiences cross-cultural in nature, for exposure to diversity as a means of fostering personal formation is well-known and attested.[4] Dana Harris suggests that the Scriptural example of the great multitude from every nation, tribe, people, and language in the throne room vision of Revelation 7 strongly points to the value of intercultural development. The point here is that there is formational value in encountering diversity because a healthy understanding of oneself will also include an awareness of others and, thus, the limitations of one's own context. Therefore, graduates who are self-aware are more open to engaging with the contexts of

---

1   Bain, 'Theological Education in Early Christianity', 50.
2   Ibid.
3   Hussey, 'The Contributors to Spiritual Formation in Theological Education', 244.
4   See the discussion in Harris, 'Theological Education and Spiritual Formation', 74-89.

others. Harris writes,

> The changing demographics and realities associated with globalization require increasing awareness of one's own context and appreciation of how it fits into the larger setting of God's global mission. Lack of such understanding may cause one to assume that one's own experience is universal and normative. Thus exposure to others reveals the vastness of God's world and fosters greater self-awareness.[5]

This focus on self-awareness is actually a fundamental element of effective adult learning. Smith and Healey have noted that effective learning takes place when students are able to make better sense of their world. This sense-making requires the student to be able to ground their learning in who they are and in how they see the world; thus, the relative importance of self-awareness.[6] It also has a cognitive impact for the student learns through noting and extracting cues from the environment and then interpreting those cues in the light of their developing values, beliefs, and experiences. Therefore, international fieldwork which places the student in a context that promotes the discovery of self-awareness through 'disorienting dilemmas' (to use another term from Smith and Healey) enables the student to face the discomfort of the unknown and apply it to their own self-journey of discovery. Such encounters are fundamentally formational and result in better sense-making and, thus, better learning for the student. The question is, how can all this best be accomplished in order to prevent fieldwork from merely reducing to 'feel good' experiences?

2. Fieldwork Integrated Learning - Intentional Planning

Simply sending students overseas and assuming that suitable formation will somehow take place in an ad hoc way is neither theologically appropriate, pedagogically sound, nor a good use of student time and resources. If fieldwork units are to be effective, then they must be rigorously planned from the beginning. By this, I don't mean that the institution must plan in detail the student's formation but rather plan in detail the context for formation. As

---

5 Ibid., 82.
6 Smith & Healey, 'On the Frontiers of Change', 154-55.

already noted, the role of the college is 'to be the *facilitator* of spiritual formation […] rather than the *provider*'.

The place to start is with the development of suitable units with carefully constructed learning outcomes and assessment strategies. An example of one of the units we have developed is the AQF7 unit, *Engaging in Intercultural Ministry (SCD: Cross Cultural Ministry Experience)*. The learning outcomes of this unit are given as follows:

1) Identify key issues involved in a specific cross-cultural ministry;
2) Articulate coherently the implications for ministry of the interrelationships of culture and gospel within that culture;
3) Analyse cultural elements in their own formation and propose adjustments needed for effectual cross-cultural ministry;
4) Engage effectively in a range of supervised cross-cultural ministry experiences;
5) Apply insights gained from the field experience to an actual or projected personal program in cross-cultural ministry.

There are a few points to note with these learning outcomes. The first is that they follow the standard SCD requirement of two knowledge, two skills, and one application-based outcome. But even within this normalised constraint, there is much flexibility and room for intentional formation and ministry skills to develop. Note particularly Learning Outcome 3. Here, the student is required to address the cultural elements of their own formation and reflect upon what may need to be adjusted in their own lives in order to engage effectively. This is a formation task even as it builds cross-cultural competence and prepares the student for Learning Outcome 4 and their actual fieldwork. Crucially, alongside these key learning outcomes is the unit threshold concept.

3. Threshold Concept

> Ministering cross-culturally demands clear discernment of what is core to the gospel and what is culturally shaped expression of the gospel, in order to avoid the potential errors of (a) identifying Christianity with a set cultural expression or (b) adopting cultural forms which are irreconcilable with the gospel.

It is clear that this threshold is irreducibly formational. The student is forced to wrestle with who they are as a Christian and what it requires to cross-cultural boundaries with the gospel message. This cannot be done lightly and requires significant engagement with themselves prior to any engagement with others. This leads then to an indication of the necessary assessment strategy. Of course, the holistic nature of spiritual formation raises concerns about how one can assess what a spiritually formed person looks like. Harris reminds us that 'factors such as maturity in Christlikeness, integration of oneself within a community, and yieldedness to the Spirit are nearly impossible to quantify'.[7] Whilst this is true, there are effective forms of assessment involving intentional reflection.

One possibility is the set of standard questions proposed by Smith in his doctoral work that enables the student to process not just what happened but how to respond to what happened. He suggests the following array[8]:

- What do I observe happening? (a focus on data)
- What do I feel about it? (a focus on emotional response)
- What do I think is going on? (a focus on cognitive analysis)
- What do I want to be different? (a focus on action for improved practice)

While it would not be realistic to assume that all students will grasp the nuances of these questions, they do, nonetheless, give the student a place to commence their personal reflection and, in particular, to address learning outcome 5 of the fieldwork unit. Helping the student to focus on these kinds of questions through the assessment strategy will guide them towards effective reflection. Once again, everything the student is asked to do should build in some way to meeting the unit learning outcomes. This is the major way in which to avoid a fieldwork trip from becoming a sight-seeing holiday.

How is this done within a fieldwork context? What we have implemented is a three-tier assessment strategy. It is essential that the first assessment demonstrates that the student has grasped the necessary knowledge to be able to engage in the fieldwork and learn successfully. This needs to be done prior to departure through an appropriate means. For us, this is interaction and analysis of such intercultural foundations as cultural intelligence and the realities of short-term mission. The second assessment must be an engagement with the

---

7   Harris, 'Theological Education and Spiritual Formation', 87.
8   Smith, 'Savouring Life', 38.

culture itself and a report on the fieldwork experience. That is, the student must reflect on the fieldwork integrated learning—this is, after all, the reason why the student is on the placement in the first place. If the fieldwork does not result in learning that is connected with the learning outcomes, then the placement itself is at fault, and not the student. A crucial component of this assessment is the fieldwork supervisor's report. This report provides third-party feedback to the student and the institution on the student's performance with the fieldwork tasks. Finally, the student must reflect on how their fieldwork-integrated learning can be applied to their own ministry context and future expectations. This is a formational task and helps to ground the entire experience in the student's overall learning journey.

4. How to Prevent Fieldwork Experiences from defaulting to 'Feel-Good' Experiences

An important element of managing the fieldwork experience is designing it in such a way that the student can achieve all the stated outcomes reliably and comprehensively. What needs to be avoided is the fieldwork defaulting to a field-good sightseeing experience. The latter is often the temptation because organising valuable and productive fieldwork for students who don't speak the language, are not used to the culture, and who are only on the ground for a relatively short period of time is incredibly difficult.

What we have done at ACOM is develop a fieldwork integrated learning guide that covers the details of any proposed fieldwork experience. Some key elements of that guide are:

1) Duration of fieldwork must be of a significant length to enable the student to engage satisfactorily in the task. We set a minimum of fourteen days but have had students embedded for up to two months.
2) There must be established, on-the-ground organisers who manage the fieldwork placement. This cannot be done remotely and cannot be effectively done by the institution itself—unless, of course, the institution has a permanent presence on the ground.
3) Fieldwork must involve direct engagement with the culture and community—this does not comprise church building, well drilling, or room painting activities but cross-cultural interaction. If the threshold

concept is to be grasped, then gospel discussions in the context of another culture must be experienced.

4) The fieldwork must be programmed before departure and cannot be decided 'on the day'. It is crucial that the program be developed well before the student arrives on the field. The student's fieldwork must be connected to the learning outcomes. This will not happen, unless the work itself is planned in advance.

Student support is also critical. The following table summarises the support required throughout the fieldwork program.

Prior to WIL Experience	During WIL Experience	After WIL Experience
Explain expectations, establish learning goals and assessments, and familiarise with fieldwork protocols	Assist students to make sense of the experience	Debrief with students and help reflect critically on learning
Prepare students for placement through orientation and pre-briefings	Assist students to deal with tensions, difficulties, cultural and health issues, including any placement-related conflict	Assist the student with final assessment tasks and integrating the field component of WIL with unit outcomes
Ensure student's travel, insurance, and medical requirements are up-to-date prior to departure	Assist students to connect their learning objectives with field practices	Evaluate the learning experience for future students
Assist students to complete any specific fieldwork partner requirements	Guide and support students in ethical behaviour	

Two of the support elements should be highlighted. The first is to assist the student in connecting their work with the learning outcomes of the unit whilst they are in the field. This helps the student understand why they are doing what they are doing and, in particular, focus their attention on the ultimate learning outcomes for the experience. The second task is post-return, guiding the student to reflect upon their experience as part of their overall formation. In the eighteen months we have been running these fieldwork units, we have found that students find them very intensive, both in relation to the academic outcomes and in their emotional experiences. There is a significant need for the processing of all elements of the fieldwork placement upon their return.

5. Real-World Examples

To help demonstrate how this can work, I'd like to give two examples: one for a short-term (three weeks) duration and the other of a long-term (two months) duration. Due to the limitations of the present context, we can only focus on specific aspects of each placement.

5.1 Example 1: Jordan

In this placement, the student was embedded with [name withheld] in Jordan for a three-week period. The principal task of the fieldwork was to engage in teaching English to the children of Syrian refugees who had fled the civil war. Additional time was also spent conversing with locals with whom the local ministry already had contact and with whom they were developing relationships. It is important to recognise that the prime purpose of these placements is not missionary activity but to provide contexts in which formation can occur. The practical ministry skills, while important, are secondary in nature.

So what were the results? One student's report noted some points of interest. In particular, the student demonstrated a level of self-awareness by identifying their cultural defaults and how they needed to be adjusted in order to engage with the local community. They commented that:

> In going from Australia, a developed western nation, with Christian foundations to Jordan, an Arabic, majority Muslim nation, there are adjustments to my perspective of normality that needed to be made in order to communicate, and relate in an honourable way. If I was to approach sharing the gospel in Jordan similarly to my approaches in Australia, this would be ineffective because of cultural differences.

This shows a forming awareness of the threshold concept. It was the third-party report, however, that demonstrated that the student had made significant steps in this direction whilst in the field. Here, the field supervisor wrote:

> Due to [the students} knowledge of the Qur'an and Mohammed, [the student] was able to enter into lengthy conversations with local people to understand more about what they believe, but also offer counter arguments. These conversations provided valuable insight into the people and how they think which [the student] used in future conversations to build more on [their] understanding. [The

student] made the gospel relevant to the people that [were] talked to, especially in referring to Jesus as a prophet in the Qur'an.

This is quite a positive report on the student's ability to address and respond to the cultural challenges in communicating the gospel. As far as formation goes, the student concluded their reflection piece with these words:

> It is only with practical experience that we can begin to realise and challenge our theoretical understandings. For this reason, I can confidently say that practical fieldwork in Jordan was highly valuable to me.

While this is just one example, it does demonstrate that fieldwork experiences can help in the obtainment of desired graduate outcomes.

5.2 Example 2: Indonesia

In this placement, the student was embedded with [name withheld] in Indonesia, for two months. Being a much longer duration afforded us the opportunity to develop and plan for a more in-depth fieldwork experience with the result that the student experienced deeper learning and a greater self-awareness.

An important component of facilitating this development was the student support prior to departure. Interviews with the field placement supervisor took place over Skype in order to ensure that expectations were well-established on both sides. An additional on-the-ground mentor who would meet with the student on a weekly basis was put in place. The student also prepared a version of her testimony and researched how to communicate appropriately within the Indonesian culture.

Once in the field, the placement was divided into four distinct experiences: language study, a homestay in a local Muslim home, English teaching for students aged sixteen to twenty-five, and because the student was female, a stint in a birthing home for unwed mothers. The student reported that the greatest formational impact took place during the homestay, primarily because of the untimely death of one of the family members during her time there. This was most definitely a 'disorientating dilemma', but the student faced that discomfort and, in the midst of the family's grief, was able to share her own testimony and hope in God. She comments:

> The welcoming and social nature of the Indonesian family helped me to feel welcomed wherever I went and taught me the humility to

> accept strangers as family [...] the death of one of the host family members [was hard] but [it] taught me how to comfort and support the family, which taught me to always pursue joy and understand empathy through love. [It also gave] me a chance to talk of my testimony and share of who God was to me.

The fact that a family member would die was, of course, not planned or desired, but it does demonstrate the opportunity that fieldwork experiences present to form students. Here, the student evidences the fourth of Smith's reflection questions in that she demonstrates what it is that she wanted to change or action on the basis of the experience.

Once again, the fieldwork supervisor's report showed evidence of grasping the threshold concept. The report states:

> [The student] proved to be quite observant in noticing subtleties in cultural norms. [She] was often evaluating how cultural practices lined up with Biblical truth.

This shows evidence of growth in how to apply biblical truth within the context of a culture and helps to demonstrate both learning outcomes 1 and 2 of the fieldwork unit.

Conclusion

These two examples have helped to demonstrate that when theological institutions work to facilitate contexts in which formation can take place, it becomes an expected and, indeed, anticipated outcome. In both cases, the student grew in character and self-awareness and was able to embed their learning in deep reflection. While it is clear that individual students will learn and reflect at different levels, the work done to establish and implement these fieldwork placements is proving to be worthwhile in the overall task of developing requisite graduate outcomes.

Bibliography

Bain, A. M. 'Theological Education in Early Christianity: The Contribution of Late Antiquity', in Bain, A. & Hussey, I. (eds.), *Theological Education: Foundations, Practices, and Future Directions* (Eugene, OR: Wipf and Stock, 2018): 47-59.

Harris, D. M. Theological Education and Spiritual Formation', in Dockery, D. S. (ed.), *Theology, Church, and Ministry: A Handbook for Theological Education* (Nashville: B&H Academic, 2017): 74-89.

Hussey, I. 'The Contributors to Spiritual Formation in Theological Education: What the Students Say', in Bain, A. & Hussey, I. (eds.), *Theological Education: Foundations, Practices, and Future Directions* (Eugene, OR: Wipf and Stock, 2018): 241-256.

Smith, S. & Healey, S. 'On the Frontiers of Change: Designing Bespoke Learning Architecture', in Debergue, Y. & Harrison, J. R. (eds.), *Teaching Theology in a Technological Age* (Cambridge, UK: Cambridge Scholars Press, 2015): 147-165).

Smith, S. 'Savouring Life: The Leader's Journey to Health and Effectiveness' (Unpublished Dissertation; Faculty of Health Sciences, University of Sydney, 2012).

Peter Laughlin
Australian College of Ministries
plaughlin@acom.edu.au

24 | CULTS IN THE CLASSROOM

THE CHALLENGE OF RELIGIOUS PLURALISM TO PEDAGOGY AND CURRICULUM IN AUSTRALIAN THEOLOGICAL EDUCATION

Abstract

The changing demographic nature of religion in Australian society has important repercussions for theological education. One area here is the approach to teaching theology graduates about non-traditional, alternative, and novel religious developments. This chapter looks at the history of theological education in this area, surveys some common challenges to student learning, and offers some suggestions for how theological educators might better integrate teaching about New Religions into the wider theological curriculum.

With the growth of religious pluralism and multiculturalism across the Australian religious landscape, theological education has increasingly turned its attention to how best to equip graduates to engage with those of other faiths and cultures. With these wider demographic changes, some combination of inter-faith or interreligious dialogue, the theology of religions, world religions, cross-cultural ministry, and missiology have now become mainstays within most theological curricula. Alongside subject offerings that inculcate a greater awareness and, in *some* instances, a greater respect for the so-called 'Great Traditions' of Islam, Judaism, Hinduism, and Buddhism, subjects have also appeared that tackle the broad phenomenon encompassed under the umbrella of New Religious Movements (NRMs)—sometimes less politely styled as 'cults' and 'sects'. While considerable theological reflection and resources have been brought to bear on how Christians might engage with mainstream world religions, and educate students about them, these smaller alternative religions have been the subject of surprisingly little serious theological reflection, and the approach to teaching that I call the 'cults subject' in theological curricula has often been surprisingly ill-informed and counterproductive.[1]

This chapter has three aims. First, I discuss the pedagogical and social background of the 'New Religions survey class' and its problematic integration into the increasingly over-crowded theological curriculum in the form of what I call the traditional 'counter-cult' apologetics class. Second, I look briefly at five points of student resistance and barriers to learning that I've encountered and how the traditional counter-cult approach exacerbates rather than resolves these difficulties. In conclusion, I make some observations about why maintaining such subjects is important for theology graduates and offer some preliminary suggestions for how we might better integrate such a subject into the wider theological curriculum and benefit from pedagogical approaches from the related fields of the sociology of religion and religious studies.

One note before going further. Throughout this chapter, I will use the terms New Religions and 'cults' interchangeably. The term 'cult' has now been more-or-less completely abandoned by serious researchers in this area outside of Christian counter-cult discourse and is an undesirable and unhelpful label for the analysis of groups that—whatever we might otherwise think of them—would be classified as religions by any reasonable criteria.[2] I recognise, regrettably however, that the term "cult," is unavoidable given its continued use by the media and in popular culture and as such I begrudgingly use it here.

1. The 'Cults Class'

The idea of a cult survey class in theological curricula has its roots in the 1970s and 1980s as the topic of 'cults' came to be seen as increasingly relevant to the

---

[1] For some of the few informed discussions, see the early collection Brockway & Rajashekar (ed.), *New Religious Movements and the Churches*. On evangelical responses, see Johnson, 'Apologetics, Mission and New Religious Movements', 99-100; Lausanne Movement, 'Christian Witness to New Religious Movements' and 'Religious and Non-Religious Spirituality in the Western World'. For other theological responses, see Saliba, 'The Christian Church and the New Religious Movements' and *Understanding New Religious Movements*, 167-197. On the challenges of dialogue approaches to NRMs, see Melton, 'New Religious Movements' and Saliba, 'Dialogue with the New Religious Movements'.

[2] See e.g. Richardson, 'Definitions of Cult'.

wider public—largely through its ubiquity in the media and popular culture and through dramatic events like the murders and mass suicides of members of the People's Temple in Jonestown in late 1978.[3] The apparent upsurge of young people joining what were in a Western context non-mainstream religious groups, such as the International Society of Krishna Consciousness (the Hare Krishnas), the Unification Church (the Moonies), the Children of God, and various other lesser-known groups on the fringes of mainstream religions, caused alarm in various sectors of society as these groups were seen as a threat to the family and to the churches.[4] In Australia, the groups viewed with the most concern were the Hare Krishnas, the Children of God, the Unification Church, Ananda Marga, the now-defunct Universal Brotherhood commune, and later and to a lesser degree, the Church of Scientology.

Different sectors of society responded to the so-called 'cult problem' in different ways, and space does not permit me to look in depth at each of these in great detail. What is important here is that many in the churches viewed these groups as both a threat to members of their flocks, but also as competitors in the religious marketplace. In response to this, a number of churches drew on a pre-existing tradition of anti-heretical apologetics—a veritable modern heresiology—which had been directed against groups on the fringes of Christianity since at least the early Nineteenth Century.[5]

The strategies of Biblical proof-texting and what has been called 'negative apologetics'[6] used in earlier anti-heretical pamphlet literature sought, in short, to examine the writings of various newer and seemingly heterodox Christian groups—for example, the Plymouth Brethren, Jehovah's Witnesses, British Israelites, Christadelphians, Christian Scientists, and the Church of Jesus Christ of Latter-day Saints—and to contrast these with mainstream Christian doctrine (as understood from the confessional position of the author[7]). By the 1970s, Christians—predominantly evangelical Protestants[8]—began to draw on this

---

[3] See e.g. Willis, 'The Urgent Need for Education About Cults'.
[4] The literature on this period is immense but for a good overview see Jenkins, *Mystics and Messiahs*, 166-226. See also Sharpe, 'New Religious Movements in Retrospect'.
[5] On the history of the counter-cult movement see Melton, 'Critiquing Cults' and Chryssides, 'From Deviance to Devotion'.
[6] See Cowan, 'Exits and Migrations', 348.
[7] Some representative examples of this approach which went into multiple printings are Davies, *Christian Deviations*; Sanders, *Heresies Ancient and Modern*; and van Baalen, *Chaos of the Cults*.
[8] Though Roman Catholic examples exist, see e.g. LeBar, *Cults, Sects, and the New Age*.

earlier tradition and to expand its remit to newer groups.[9] This body of literature and various para-church ministries that emerged to promote its ideas soon became known in sociology as counter-cult ministry or the 'counter-cult movement'.[10] In Australia, the first groups of this kind appeared in the late 1970s—though countercult style literature had been circulating since at least the 1850s. While some in the churches, particularly more liberal mainline denominations, gave limited attention to the topic, these counter-cult ministries became a continuing presence on the fringes of more conservative evangelical denominations and, as the only Christians paying sufficient attention to the 'cult problem'[11], their approach often proved influential when the cults class first began to enter theological curricula in the 1980s and early 1990s.

The logic and purpose of these initial 'cult classes' in theological curricula was well put by an article in *Christianity Today* about counter-cult ministries in 1991 in which the author argued that seminaries needed to do more 'to educate church leaders in contemporary doctrinal aberrations'.[12] For these early subjects, the logic was largely apologetic and, like much apologetic writing, functioned predominantly as a form of sociological 'boundary maintenance'—comparing and contrasting the teachings of these groups with a yardstick of normative Christian truth, such as Scripture or the Apostles Creed.[13] Unsurprisingly, the material used to construct syllabi was predominantly drawn from the plethora of counter-cult pamphlet literature and evangelical encyclopaedias that has been mass-produced and promoted by Christian bookstores and publishers, and the areas of focus continued to be, as it had in the Nineteenth Century, on groups on the Christian fringes, including the Jehovah's Witnesses and the Church of Jesus Christ of Latter-day Saints, later augmented by various New Age practices and attention to the popular New Religions of the 1970s, like the Children of God and the Unification Church.

The approach taken in these classes often encouraged an outdated form of aggressive and combative proselytism and gross mischaracterisation of target groups' beliefs, which almost completely failed to take seriously the sophisticated

---

9   For some notable examples of this perspective, see Larson, *Larson's Book of Cults*; Martin, *The Kingdom of the Cults*; Martin, Rische, and Van Gorden, *The Kingdom of the Occult*; Mather and Nichols, *Dictionary of Cults, Sects, Religions, and the Occult*.
10 See Cowan, *Bearing False Witness*.
11 Here, I use this in a social constructionist sense, see Barker, 'The Cult as a Social Problem'.
12 Jones, 'New Courses for a New Age'.
13 For this critique, see Melton, 'Emerging Religious Movements in North America'.

body of literature on the topic emerging from other disciplines. Indeed, it is indicative that the most complete sociological study of counter-cult ministry is poignantly entitled *Bearing False Witness?*[14] Sadly, in many quarters, including in Australia, this approach continues to be the default position in theological colleges, even while a quiet revolution has taken place in counter-cult circles calling for a more respectful and sophisticated missiological approach—spearheaded in some instances by Australian missiologists.[15]

Contemporaneously with the emergence of the traditional 'cult' as a subtopic within apologetics, however, the topic was receiving increased attention in sociology of religion and also in the field of religious studies, where multi-disciplinary perspectives were being applied to the study of New Religions.[16] This scholarship and the approaches being taken in related curricula, while not without its own challenges, problematised the simple view of 'cults' as theological aberrations and availed itself of more empathetic approaches drawn from the social sciences and the phenomenology of religion by exploring these New Religions as genuine—if perhaps misguided—attempts by sincere individuals in their search spiritual meaning that deserved to be treated alongside the 'Great Traditions' as part of the wider religious landscape.[17] While many of the pioneers in these other disciplines were in fact confessing Christians whose training was initially theological, their methodological orientation, and refusal to make sweeping judgements about the 'cults' as theological aberrations tended to contrast with those teaching similar classes in the theological education sphere and cross-fertilisation was often slow, problematic, and piecemeal.

Slowly, however, insights from religious studies and the social sciences have filtered across into theological classes, but this has been stalled by a suspicion held more widely amongst some theologians about the social sciences and about the alleged sympathies and activist approach of some religious studies scholars who were often labelled 'cult apologists' by those who disagreed with them. This is usually because of their strong adherence to a broader conception of religious tolerance and liberty and the refusal to uncritically accept 'atrocity

---

14 Cowan, *Bearing False Witness?*
15 On this 'quiet revolution' see e.g. the edited volume Hexham, Rost and Morehead (eds.), *Encountering New Religious Movements* and Johnson, 'Apologetics, Mission and New Religious Movements'. For perhaps the most strongly stated version of this shift, see Morehead, 'Walter Martin Was Wrong?'
16 See Ashcraft, *A Historical Introduction*.
17 See e.g. Bednarowski, *New Religions*.

stories' about these groups circulated by former members and in the media.[18]

Much of this resistance amongst theological educators, it must be said, came down to intransigence in recognising the weaknesses of the traditional counter-cult approach amongst Christian apologists and evangelists who had invested considerable time and resources in promoting this approach—and at times established lucrative ministries based on dubious claims, particularly regarding Satanism[19]—and over personal disputes between competing paradigms of interpretation.[20] Also apparent were the divergent positions held within the wider counter-cult community, which ranged from hard-nosed reformed apologists, through conspiracy-driven Pentecostals obsessed with spiritual warfare, to premillennialists who saw in the cults a sign of the end times.[21] The trends from the American Christian publishing industry, moreover, filtered into Australian theological libraries—most notably in the widespread American myths regarding the non-existent phenomenon of so-called Satanic Ritual Abuse (SRA) that found fertile ground in the imagination of some Australian Christians leading to the 'Satanic Panic' of the late 1980s and early 1990s.[22] What has resulted is that the 'cults' class has taken on a very different complexion between theological education providers often tied up with wider theological divergences in the theology of religions along the spectrum from exclusivists through inclusivists to pluralists.[23]

The key point here is that students studying cults in a theological context have often been, in a very real sense, deprived of an accurate analysis of the phenomenon they are purporting to study and have had their information literacy stifled by an approach to New Religions, which straight-jackets these groups into a one-size-fits-all apologetic model. What this does, I suggest, is have a negative effect on graduates by ill-equipping them both as ministers and witnesses to the Gospel and as global citizens.

---

18 On the contested nature of the field, see Robbins and Zablocki, *Misunderstanding Cults*.
19 The most famous of these are tele-exorcist Bob Larson and Mike Warnke. For this aspect, see the well-researched exposé by Hertenstein and Trott, *Selling Satan*.
20 See e.g. the published dialogue Enroth and Melton, *Why Cults Succeed Where the Church Fails*.
21 On these different strands, see Cowan, *Bearing False Witness?* and Johnson, 'Apologetics, Mission and New Religious Movements'.
22 On the SRA controversy in Australia, see e.g. Guilliatt, *Talk of the Devil* and Lynch, *Satan's Empire*. For a sensible Christian response see Smulo, 'Spiritual Warfare Profiles of Satanism'.
23 For these different positions, see e.g. Dupuis, *Christianity and the Religions*; Hick and Hebblethwaite, *Christianity and the Other Religions*; Kärkkäinen, *An Introduction to the Theology of Religions*; Knitter, *No Other Name?* and *Introducing Theologies of Religions*; Netland, *Encountering Religious Pluralism*.

2. Barriers to Learning

Bearing in mind this problematic integration of the cults class into various theological curricula and the mixed nature of the wider Christian response to the 'cult problem', it is unsurprising that many students electing to take a subject on this topic arrive with many preconceived ideas about what they will be studying and that these can present additional barriers to learning. Furthermore, the traditional counter-cult pedagogical approach I've outlined actually works to reinforce and exacerbate these barriers rather than challenge them. In my experience, there are six common points of student resistance what I've called experiential negativity; epistemological presupposition; methodological myopia; theological/confessional rigidity; normative/moral superiority; and ideological/political intransigence.

By experiential negativity, I mean largely that most students have had limited or no exposure to members of these groups, but what they have experienced they have tended to interpret through a negative lens. While I have taught a number of students over the years who are former members of groups that have been labelled 'cults'—a pedagogical situation worthy of a chapter in itself—in general, students have had little or no social intercourse with members of New Religions other than encountering Latter-day Saint and Jehovah's Witness door-knockers, Hare Krishnas panhandling at shopping centres, or having innocently taken the Oxford Capacity Test offered by the Church of Scientology only to discover that they have (according to this Scientology metric) a defective personality but that Scientology can help them with this for a nominal fee. These kinds of encounters are almost always episodic and often vicarious or anecdotal, however, they work to reinforce wider societal prejudices directed against these groups by generalising isolated incidents across a wider class of people. However, the reverse is also sometimes true, with students engaging in the 'good person' fallacy, whereby a similar episodic or positive encounter with members of New Religions is taken as a warrant to justify a carte blanche idea about groups—even those groups whose activities have been deeply problematic. This type of student resistance is unsurprising and, in general, supported by social psychology literature that measures levels of religious prejudice and has consistently found that encounters with groups labelled as 'cults' are subject to the same kinds of cognitive bias when it comes to prejudice against racial minorities and other stigmatised groups.[24]

For educational purposes of the theological curriculum, however, the traditional counter-cult pedagogy in this area discourages interaction with such groups outside of aggressive witnessing and scripted theological debate and creates a kind of theological *cordon sanitaire*. This is most unfortunate, as it has been shown in social psychology research that greater familiarity and exposure to stigmatised religious groups beliefs can work to reduce prejudice.[25] In sociological terms, the type of limited exposure and social distancing encouraged by the traditional counter-cult approach helps to reinforce negative stereotypes as the experience of students is mediated through other sources like the media and counter-cult literature.

This brings me to what I've called here epistemological presupposition. As is often the case with other topics discussed in the social sciences, in particular, academic discourse surrounding 'cults' differs considerably from popular discourse. This is the question of how do we know what we know about cults? Without labouring the point, most people continue to rely on the mainstream media and popular books for their information about 'cults'—I'm confident some readers have viewed harrowing docudrama series like *The Cult of the Family* (2018) or *Wild Wild Country* (2017), or seen the documentary *Going Clear* (2013). What this has meant is that, in general, mainstream society has privileged what media theorist Graham Murdock has called 'discourses of experience' over 'discourses of expertise'.[26] This sees the emphasis in popular analysis of 'cults' being almost invariably placed on the predominantly (though not entirely) negative accounts of former members depicted using docudrama media conventions and not the result of careful long-term empirical studies conducted by various social scientists or testimonies from current members.[27] What this inevitably does is reinforce the 'cult stereotype' rather than challenge preconceived ideas and permits the perpetuation of ideas, which, to serious researchers, are, at best, partial and selective and, at worst, complete nonsense.

Once again the counter-cult pedagogical approach—which discourages engagement with the groups themselves outside of a textual analysis framework—I suggest strengthens this point of resistance by adding a theological

---

24 See e.g. Olson, 'The Public Perception of "Cults" and "New Religious Movements" ' and Pfeifer, 'The Psychological Framing of Cults'.
25 See e.g. Hood, Williams and Morris, 'Changing Views'.
26 Murdock, 'Tales of Expertise and Experience'.
27 See e.g. Barbour, *Versions of Deconversion*.

veneer and justification to what often amounts to little more than popular prejudice and misinformation. This brings me to the third point of resistance: normative/moral superiority.

It is a long-truism in social psychology that, in general, when faced with negative behaviour by an out-group, we are more likely to generalise that behaviour across a class of people than if the same behaviour occurred by a member of our in-group.[28] By being different to mainstream society, isolated incidents of negative behaviour by 'cult' members are generalised to all members of that group. If you have any doubts about this, ask yourself how often an alleged or convicted criminal's religion is mentioned in news reports when they are a Baptist or Greek Orthodox Christian compared to if they were a Scientologist or member of the Plymouth Brethren Christian Church (the so-called 'Exclusive Brethren').

Similarly, more routine actions by members of cults are often viewed through a sinister lens that would not be applied if the same actions were being engaged in by a more mainstream religious group. In an Australian context, a great example of this for those interested is to compare media coverage of public fund-raising and soup-kitchens operated Christian charities like St Vincent de Paul and the Salvation Army with identical operations undertaken by the Hare Krishnas. In the former case, the charities actions are clearly depicted as informed by Christian notions of charity, in the latter case, the Hare Krishnas—less so today than forty years ago—are often depicted as dubious fund-raising to support the allegedly lavish lifestyle of leaders or philanthropy directed purely at attracting converts. We might call this a monopoly of moral concern, whereby only socially mainstream religious groups are attributed *bona fides* as genuine charities—whereas any prosocial activities by 'cults' are attributed to ulterior motives.[29]

This kind of double standard is again reinforced by the counter-cult pedagogical approach that reinforces the old heresiological trope that doctrinal error is almost always accompanied by a moral defect and that the latter often flows logically from the former. If a group's beliefs diverge from what is considered acceptable, then its actions must do likewise. Again, providing theological cover, the counter-cult approach fails to draw careful distinctions

---

28 See e.g. the classic study of Allport, *The Nature of Prejudice*.
29 The laudable involvement of Scientologists in exposing psychiatric abuses at the Chelmsford Private Hospital is a case in point. See Bromberger and Fife-Yeomans, *Deep Sleep*.

and instead reinforces a behavioural double standard.

What I call methodological myopia is quite simply a resistance to applying social science methodologies that might help in reality testing student ideas about groups or phenomenological approaches that encourage what Denise Cush has called 'epistemic humility'.[30] That there is validity to some theological critique of the social sciences or the phenomenological approach to religion is indisputable, but their use in various other areas of the theological curriculum—notably in practical theology and missiology—is rarely contested. This, however, is often not the case with the counter-cult pedagogical approach. Indeed, many counter-cult writers have accused those using social scientific and religious studies approaches with confusing an empathetic approach to cults with sympathy and labelling such scholars—not without a degree of irony I might add—'cult apologists'.[31]

Finally, I will treat ideological/political intransigence and theological/confessional rigidity together. In general, the students who struggle most with coming to terms with the study of 'cults' are those who hold strong ideological or theological commitments, who are unwilling or unable to entertain, even on a purely theoretical and heuristic level, alternative viewpoints.[32] As any educator knows, many students, in what has been called 'epistemic closure', are nowadays so ideologically entrenched in a particular worldview that they are unable or unwilling to entertain approaches or information that challenges this position.[33] This, I would note, is a wider educational problem and hardly requires further discussion. In terms of theological education, however, this most often manifests amongst students who hold an exclusivist or particularist approach to the theology of religions, whereby a defence of confessional truth at all costs is primary and diligent empirical inquiry and intellectual rigour are at best secondary. The counter-cult pedagogical approach is predominantly an exercise in boundary maintenance—like much apologetics—and actually works to reinforce epistemic closure and discourage further inquiry by rigidly policing the boundaries of acceptable belief and discouraging critical reflection.

It will be clear from what I have said that the counter-cult approach still

---

30 Cush, 'Engaged Religious Studies'.
31 On the debate over so-called 'cult apologists', see the collection Robbins and Zablocki, *Misunderstanding Cults*.
32 For instance, by applying the phenomenological method of 'bracketing', see Cox, *Introduction to the Phenomenology of Religion*.
33 On 'epistemic closure', see Nichols, *The Death of Expertise*.

enshrined in many theological institutions is unsatisfactory on any number of grounds. However, it is not the only approach nor indeed is it the approach taken more widely in academia outside of confessional theological colleges.

Conclusion and Future Directions

Rather than argue that other theological institutions should simply follow the multi-disciplinary approach that I have taken the cults subject at Charles Sturt University, which is heavily weighted to a social science and religious studies approach, I instead want to conclude with what might come as a surprising proposal. Initially in thinking through this chapter, I had intended to argue for greater emphasis being placed on social science and religious studies approaches to counter-balance what I see as the theologically unsophisticated and socially divisive nature of the traditional counter-cult approach. Clearly, these disciplines have taken the issue of teaching New Religions far more seriously.[34] However, the conclusion I have come to is that within the context of theological education—as distinct from religious studies and the sociology of religion—with our focus on forming the character of theological graduates, a much more satisfactory approach actually entails not a less theological approach, but, perhaps paradoxically, a more theological approach.

What I suggest is that theological education institutions who chose to retain a 'cults' subject on their curriculum—and in an increasingly multi-faith society I believe this is both warranted and necessary—need to actually avail themselves of a more integrated theological approach that borrows not only from the pedagogical work being done in the sociology of religions and religious studies but also from other theological sub-disciplines.

The chief pedagogical problem with the counter-cult approach I've discussed is not that an apologetic approach has no place at all in how we prepare theological graduates to engage with members of New Religions—being conversant in where we diverge from other religions plays an important function, and robust but respectful dialogue and debate here should not be discouraged—though certainly not in its current form. Rather, I believe that apologetics should

---

34 See e.g. Bromley (ed.), *Teaching New Religious Movements*; Neal, 'From Classroom to Controversy'; Perrin, 'When Religion Becomes Deviance'; Schmalz, 'Scientology and Catholicism Do Mix'; Smith, 'Teaching a Course on Deviant Groups'; Zeller, ' "But Aren't Cults Bad?"'.

not be the sole lens through which we approach this topic and that when apologetics is used, it needs to be undertaken in a more irenic manner that respects the adherents of New Religions as our neighbours and fellow citizens.

As an increasing number of evangelical missiologists have begun to realise; for example, the 'ministry toolbox' required for cross-cultural ministry not only provides more satisfactory methods for learning about cults but also allows for more effective evangelism directed to members of such groups—rather than the traditional counter-cult approach that has largely abandoned witnessing to these groups and, as such, has failed in the primary Christian call to live the Great Commission. Such missiologists, moreover, have seen engaging with social science and religious studies approaches as a benefit rather than a threat. This is, perhaps, counterintuitively for those involved in counter-cult ministry, hardly surprising—it is worth remembering that many of the founding figures of contemporary religious studies were actually missionaries who honed their methods of analysis in the field living and engaging with those of other faiths, and while many Christians today are uncomfortable with the postcolonial baggage of missionary encounters, there is still much we can learn from these experiences—not least about mutual respect and coexistence.[35]

However, areas of practical theology like missiology, evangelism, and cross-cultural ministry are only a few areas where the 'cults' subject could be better integrated with the wider theological curriculum—though they are those that are proving most fruitful amongst evangelicals who had previously championed the counter-cult approach. I would suggest, for example, that, in future, New Religions subjects could, for example, avail themselves of the tools of Biblical translation, exegesis, and hermeneutics to better understand; for example, how groups with a strong link to historical Christianity like the Jehovah's Witnesses and the Church of Jesus Christ of Latter-day Saints approach the Bible and how this relates to their other sacred texts.[36] Church history, with its study of the development of doctrine and tradition, could help students better appreciate the internal diversity within the Christian faith to better understand the origins and

---

35   See e.g. Cox, *A Guide to the Phenomenology of Religion*, and Sharpe, *Comparative Religion*.
36   See e.g. Barlow, *Mormons and the Bible* and Chryssides, *Jehovah's Witnesses*. See also the welcome anthology Maffly-Kipp, *American Scriptures*.

ideas of many New Religions and their appeals to various historical forebears.[37] Systematic theology, moreover, could help students to better map the ways in which New Religions have developed their teachings and the internal logic that drives their understandings of truth.[38] Perhaps, however, the most urgent area where a more integrated approach could be beneficial is in the area of interfaith dialogue and the theology of religions. While most churches have slowly developed a more sophisticated approach to major world faiths, their engagement with New Religions—for various understandable reasons—has been piecemeal and staggered in approach.

A more integrated approach in theological education will remind Christians that New Religions are a phenomenon that has always been with us and is one that will continue into the future. How we, as theological educators tasked with forming graduates, chose to engage with this phenomena is up to us. For my part, as I've suggested above, I believe that the traditional counter-cult apologetics course, as it is still being taught in some theological institutions, has had its day and is actually a barrier to creating more culturally aware and culturally competent Christian witnesses to the Gospel in increasingly multi-cultural and multi-faith societies. It will only be by better integrating the study of New Religions into our curricula that we will achieve any lasting good from teaching subjects in this area—if we choose instead to ignore what we can bring as theological educators to this question, we have failed, not only as educators but also as Christians.

Bibliography

Ahlstrom, S.E. *A Religious History of the American People* (Second ed.; New Haven: Yale University Press, 1972).

Allport, G. *The Nature of Prejudice* (Addison-Wesley: Reading, 1954).

Ashcraft, W.M. *A Historical Introduction to the Study of New Religious Movements* (London: Routledge, 2018).

Barbour, J.D. *Versions of Deconversion: Autobiography and the Loss of Faith* (Charlottesville: University of Virginia Press, 1994).

---

37 A good example here is the extensive diachronic anthology Trompf, Johnson and Mikkelson, *The Gnostic World,* which surveys various ideas surrounding "Gnosticism" from antiquity into the present. Other works of use might be Ahlstrom, *A Religious History of the American People*; Conkin, *American Originals* and Stein, *Communities of Dissent.*
38 See e.g. Bednarowski, *New Religions.*

Barker, E. 'The Cult as a Social Problem', in Titus Hjelm (ed.), *Religion and Social Problems* (London: Routledge, 2011): 198-212.

Barlow, P.L. *Mormons and the Bible: The Place of the Latter-day Saints in American Religion* (Oxford: Oxford University Press, 1991).

Bednarowski, M. *New Religions and the Theological Imagination in America* (Bloomington: Indiana University Press, 1989).

Bromberger, B. & Fife-Yeomans, J. *Deep Sleep: Harry Bailey and the Scandal of Chelsmford* (Roseville: Simon and Schuster, 1991).

Bromley, D.G. (ed.) *Teaching New Religious Movements* (AAR Teaching Religious Studies, Oxford: OUP, 2007).

Chryssides, G.D. 'From Deviance to Devotion: The Evolution of NRM Studies', in Eugene V. Gallagher (ed.), *'Cult Wars' in Historical Perspective* (London: Taylor and Francis, 2016): 43-54.

Chryssides, G.D. *Jehovah's Witnesses: Continuity and Change* (London: Routledge, 2016).

Conkin, P.K. *American Originals: Homemade Varieties of Christianity* (Chapel Hill: University of North Carolina Press, 1997).

Cowan, D.E. 'Exits and Migrations: Foregrounding the Christian Counter-Cult', *Journal of Contemporary Religion* 17.3 (2002), 339-354.

Cowan, D.E. *Bearing False Witness? An Introduction to the Christian Countercult* (Westport: Praeger, 2003).

Cowan, D.E. 'The Christian Countercult Movement', in Lewis, J. R. & Tøllefsen, I. (eds.), *The Oxford Handbook of New Religious Movements* (Vol. 2; Oxford: OUP, 2016): 143-151.

Cox, J.L. *A Guide to the Phenomenology of Religion: Key Figures, Formative Influences and Subsequent Debates* (London: Bloomsbury, 2006).

Cox, J. L. *An Introduction to the Phenomenology of Religion* (London: Bloomsbury, 2009).

Cush, D. 'Engaged Religious Studies', *Discourse* 4.2 (2005): 84-104.

Davies, H. *Christian Deviations: The Challenge of the Sects* (2nd edn; London: SCM, 1961).

Dupuis, J. *Christianity and the Religions: From Confrontation to Dialogue* (Maryknoll: Orbis, 2001).

Enroth, R. & Melton, J.G. *Why Cults Succeed Where the Church Fails* (Elgin: Brethren Press, 1985).

Gallagher, E.V. 'Responding to Resistance in Teaching about New Religious Movements', in Bromley, D. G. (ed.), *Teaching New Religious Movements* (Oxford: OUP, 2007): 273-290.

Guilliatt, R. *Talk of the Devil: Repressed Memory and the Ritual Abuse Witch-Hunt* (Melbourne: Text Publishing, 1996).

Hexham, I., Roost, S. & Morehead, J. *Encountering New Religious Movements: A Holistic Evangelical Approach* (Grand Rapids: Kregel Academic, 2004).

Hick, J. & Hebblethwaite, P. *Christianity and Other Religions: Selected Readings* (Oxford: One World, 2001).

Hood, R. W., Williamson, W.P., Morris, R.J. 'Changing Views of Serpent Handling: A Quasi-Experimental Study', *Journal for the Scientific Study of Religion* 39.3 (2000): 287-296.

Jenkins, P. *Mystics and Messiahs: Cults and New Religions in American History* (Oxford: OUP, 2000).

Jones, T. 'New Courses for a New Age', *Christianity Today* (October 7, 1991), 17.

Johnson, P. 'Apologetics, Mission and New Religious Movements: A Holistic Approach', *Lutheran Theological Journal* 36.3 (2002), 99-111.

Kärkkäinen, V-M. *An Introduction to the Theology of Religions: Biblical, Historical and Contemporary Perspectives* (Downers Grove: IVP Academic, 2003).

Knitter, P.F. *No Other Name? A Critical Survey of Christian Attitudes Toward the World Religions* (Maryknoll: Orbis Books, 1996).

Knitter, P.F. *Introducing Theologies of Religions* (Maryknoll: Orbis, 2002).

Larson, B. *Larson's Book of Cults (*Wheaton: Tyndale Publishing House, 1986).

Lausanne Movement. Christian Witness to New Religious Movements, *Lausanne Occasional Paper* 11 (1980). < https://www.lausanne.org/content/lop/lop-11> [accessed 22/11/19]

Lausanne Movement. Religious and Non-Religious Spirituality in the Western World, *Lausanne Occasional Paper* 45 (2004). < https://www.lausanne.org/content/lop/religious-non-religious-spirituality-western-world-lop-45> [accessed 22/11/19]

LeBar, J.J. *Cults, Sects, and the New Age* (Huntington: Our Sunday Visitor, 1989).

Lynch, T. *Satan's Empire: The Panic over Ritual Abuse in Australia* (Saarbrücken, VDM Verlag Dr. Müller, 2011).

Martin, W. *The Kingdom of the Cults* (Revised edn; Minneapolis: Bethany House, 2003).

Martin, W., Rische J.M., & Van Gorden, K. *The Kingdom of the Occult* (Dallas: Thomas Nelson, 2008)

Mather, G.A. & Nichols, L.A. *Dictionary of Cults, Sects, Religions and the Occult* (Grand Rapids: Zondervan, 1993).

Melton, J.G. 'Emerging Religious Movements in North America: Some Missiological Reflections', *Missiology* 28.1 (2000), 85-98.

Melton, J.G. 'The Modern Anti-Cult Movement in Historical Perspective', in Kaplan, J. & Lööw, H. (eds.), *The Cultic Milieu: Oppositional Subcultures in an Age of Globalization* (Walnut Creek: Altamira Press,2002): 265-289.

Melton, J.G. 'Critiquing Cults: An Historical Perspective', in Gallagher, E. V. & Ashcraft, M. W. (eds.), *Introduction to New and Alternative Religions in America: History and Controversies* (Westport: Greenwood Press, 2006): 126-142.

Melton, J.G. 'New Religious Movements: Dialgoues Beyond Stereotypes and Labels', in Hedges, P. & Race, A. (eds.), *Christian Approaches to Other Faiths* (London: SCM Press, 2008): 308-323.

Melton, J.G. *Encyclopedic Handbook of Cults in America* (New York: Garland Publishing, 1986).

Maffly-Kipp, L.F. (ed.) *American Scriptures: An Anthology of Sacred Writings* (New York: Penguin Books, 2010).

Morehead, J.W. 'From "Cults" to Cultures: Bridges as a Case Study in a New Evangelical Paradigm on New Religions', *The Asbury Journal* 65.2 (2010), 26-35.

Morehead, J.W. 'Walter Martin Was Wrong: A Critique and Alternative to the Counter-Cult Approach to Cults', *Journal of Asian Missions* 14.1 (2013), 3-28.

Murdock, G. 'Tales of Expertise and Experience: Sociological Reasoning and Popular Presentation', in Haslam, C. & Bryman, A. (eds.), *Social Scientists Meet the Media* (London: Routledge, 1994): 108-122.

Neal, L.S. 'From Classroom to Controversy: Conflict in the Teaching of Religion', *Teaching Theology and Religion* 16.1 (2009), 66-75.

Netland, H. *Encountering Religious Pluralism: The Challenge to Christian Faith and Mission* (Downers Grove: IVP Academic, 2001).

Nichols, T.M. *The Death of Expertise: The Campaign against Established Knowledge and Why it Matters* (Oxford: OUP, 2017).

Olson, P.J. 'The Public Perception of "Cults" and "New Religious Movements"', *Journal for the Scientific Study of Religion* 45.1 (2006): 97-106.

Perrin, R.D. 'When Religion Becomes Deviance: Introducing Religion in Deviance and Social Problems Courses', *Teaching Sociology* 29 (2001), 134-152.

Pfeifer, J.E. 'The Psychological Framing of Cults: Schematic Representations and Cult Evaluations', *Journal of Applied Social Psychology* 22.7 (1992), 531-544.

Richardson, J.T. 'Definitions of Cult: From Sociological-Technical to Popular-Negative', *Review of Religious Research* 34.4 (1993), 348-356.

Robbins, T. & Zablocki, B. (eds.). *Misunderstanding Cults: Searching for Objectivity in a Controversial Field* (Toronto: University of Toronto Press, 2001).

Saliba, J.A. 'The Christian Church and the New Religious Movements: Toward Theological Understanding', *Theological Studies* 43.3 (1982), 468-485.

Saliba, J.A. 'Dialogue with the New Religious Movements: Issues and Prospects', *Journal of Ecumenical Studies* 30.1 (1993), 51-80.

Saliba, J.A. *Christian responses to the New Age Movement: A Critical Assessment* (New York: Geoffrey Chapman, 1999).

Saliba, J.A. *Understanding New Religious Movements* (Grand Rapids: Eerdmans, 1995). (ESP pp. 167-197).

Sanders, J.O. *Heresies Ancient and Modern* (London: Marshall, Morgan and Scott, 1957 [1948]).

Schmalz, M.N. 'Scientology and Catholicism Do Mix: A Note on Teaching New Religions in a Catholic Classroom', *Teaching Theology and Religion* 9.1 (2006), 29-36.

Sharpe, E.J. *Comparative Religion: A History* (2nd edn; London: Duckworth, 1986).

Sharpe, E.J. 'New Religious Movements in Retrospect', *South Pacific Journal of Mission Studies* 1.4 (1991), 11-14.

Smith, D.H. 'Teaching a Course on Deviant Groups: A Neglected Aspect of Deviance', *Teaching Sociology* 24 (1996), 177-188

Smulo, J. 'Spiritual Warfare Profiles of Satanism: Are they Misleading?' *Lutheran Theological Journal* 36.2 (2002), 126-137.

Stafford, T. 'The Kingdom of the Cult Watchers', *Christianity Today* (October 7, 1991), 18-22.

Stein, S.J. Communities of Dissent: A History of Alternative Religions in America (Oxford: OUP, 2003).

Hertenstein, M. & Trott, J. *Selling Satan: The Evangelical Media and the Mike Warnke Scandal* (Chicago: Cornerstone Press, 1993).

Trompf, G.W., Mikkelsen, G.B. & Johnston, J. (eds.). *The Gnostic World* (London: Routledge, 2019).

Van Baalen, J.K. *The Chaos of Cults: A Study in Present-Day Isms* (4th edn; Grand Rapids: Eerdmans, 1962).

Willis, S.H. 'The Urgent Need for Education About Cults', *Phi Delta Kappan* 64.7 (1983), 500-502.

Zeller, B.E. '"But Aren't Cults Bad?": Active Learning, Productive Chaos, and Teaching New Religious Movements', *Teaching Theology and Religion* 18.2 (2015), 121-132.

Bernard Doherty
Course Director in School of Theology and Research Fellow Centre for Public and Contextual Theology, Charles Sturt University;
Adjunct Lecturer in School of Law, University of Notre Dame (Sydney).
bdoherty@csu.edu.au

PART 5
IMPLICATIONS FOR THE PASTORAL GRADUATE

25 | PRIVATE STUDY, SOCIAL LEARNING, AND EMBODIED PRACTICE

INSIGHTS FROM JOHN WESLEY'S FRAMEWORK FOR PREPARING EFFECTIVE MINISTERS IN EARLY METHODISM

Abstract

Facilitating new social behaviours involves cognitive inputs, engagement in life experiences, and the intentional formation of new habitual practices through the imitation of a practitioner. After a brief examination of some of the latest findings in neuroscience, social psychology, and higher education to frame the discussion, the focus of the chapter is on how John Wesley's model for ministry training anticipates many of these findings. He understood the potential for education to function as an instrument of personal and social reform, making the character of his preachers and leaders of vital importance, not just their intellectual preparation. This paper is an examination and discussion of John Wesley's approach to training people for ministry, paying attention to Wesley's focus on the importance of private reading, community conference, and personal involvement in the work. He clearly integrates the educational practices of personal study, group learning, and embodied practice.

1. Introduction

In some recent studies, it has been argued that facilitating new social behaviours involves cognitive inputs, engagement in life-experiences, and the intentional formation of new habitual practices through the imitation of an exemplar. This brings together the role of the teacher, the community, and an effective practitioner to help the student learn effectively. This chapter begins with a brief examination of the common Western education model and its limitations regarding character formation. It then examines some of the latest findings in neuroscience, social psychology, and higher education to frame an account of John Wesley's model for ministry training that anticipates many of these findings. He understood that the character of his preachers and leaders was of vital importance, and not just their intellectual abilities. By making use of 'The "Large" Minutes' of his Methodist Conferences and his 'Address to the Clergy', the elements that Wesley thought were critical for both personal and community transformation can be identified. This shows that he undoubtedly integrates the educational practices of personal study, group learning, and embodied practice in ministry preparation. The final section briefly reflects on the importance of incorporating all three elements of personal, social, and embodied learning for effective transformative learning to shape both character and practice when preparing people for effective ministry in an Australian context.

2. Western Theological Education Today

The major theologians in the early centuries of the church were usually pastors, bishops, abbots, or spiritual directors. These are roles devoted to the practical instruction and guiding of Christian communities in their engagement with daily life. In each case, the life of the practitioner could be closely observed by those who were being instructed. It was with the emergence of the university in the medieval period that we begin to see the theological task undertaken by a specialist whose primary vocation was academic instruction in theology by following a set curriculum.[1] As Methodist theologian Randy Maddox points out, it was not the move to the university as such that is the problem, but the specific model of education adopted—as a theoretical discipline focused primarily on knowledge and divorced from practice or regular community

---

1   Maddox, 'The Dynamics of Theology', 21.

involvement. This resulted in elevating the role of the university academic who researched and taught a purely theoretical subject (theology), while downplaying the role of the practitioner in a local church or community setting.[2] Given the increased emphasis on specialised knowledge that is evident in higher education today, there is much evidence of the stress on knowledge acquisition while ignoring, or only giving brief attention to, character formation that will shape responsible personal and community action. The general Enlightenment optimism about humanity that lies behind much of modern education practice assumed that moral goodness is inherent, 'so there is little emphasis on cultivating dispositions toward desirable actions'.[3] The failure to appreciate 'the malleable nature of character has left us susceptible to cultural captivity. If we want our members to have greater clarity about and greater consistency in embodying truly Christ-like life in our culture, we must own the need to cultivate competent Christ-like dispositions'.[4]

Our problems are compounded by the fact that much of modern Western education tends 'to separate knowledge into different silos—biology, economics, history, physics, and philosophy. In the real world, information is rarely divided into neatly defined categories'.[5] This increasing specialisation frequently limits access to alternative ways of looking at the world and our human relationships; this, in turn, closes down the range of possible solutions to many of complex issues facing our churches and the wider society. One of the things that is becoming more significant in the education process is an awareness of the mental models we use to think.

> A mental model is an explanation of how something works. It is a concept, framework, or worldview that you carry around in your mind [...]. Mental models guide your perception and behavior. They are the thinking tools that you use to understand life, make decisions, and solve problems. Learning a new mental model gives you a new way to see the world [...].[6]

Expanding our set of mental models is necessary if we are to solve the new questions that arise or visualise new ways of doing things. It has been well said

---

2   Maddox, 'The Dynamics of Theology', 23–25.
3   Maddox, 'The Dynamics of Theology', 27-28.
4   Maddox, 'The Dynamics of Theology', 28.
5   Clear, 'How to Train Your Brain to Think in New Ways'.
6   Clear, 'How to Train Your Brain to Think in New Ways'.

that 'Relying on a narrow set of thinking tools is like wearing a mental straight jacket'.[7] If the cognitive range of possibilities is limited, our ability to find new solutions is equally limited. 'This is why it is critical to not only learn new mental models, but to consider how they connect with one another. Creativity and innovation often arise at the intersection of ideas'.[8] Education is critical in this process, and that means we need to engage with a range of information and practice that is broader than our own narrow specialisation and experience.

David Setran notes how Christian college students in Western contexts undergo an education experience that develops dispositions focusing more on personal advancement, material security, and devotion to a narrow sphere of family and friends rather than being other-focused. There is a gap between their world-views and concrete 'ways of life'.[9] The 'new evangelicalism' often seems to have a focus on issues such as the environment, racial injustice, immigration, economic development, and human trafficking, but the rhetoric of social engagement is rarely matched by the student's lifestyle.[10] If this is to change, intentional formation is essential and will require a variety of 'activities aimed at invoking and shaping beliefs, affections, and character dispositions'.[11] Theological reflection is vital in this, both in fostering change but also in dealing with alternative perspectives. One of the elements that would seem to shape this lack of engagement is the student's worldview:

> [This] is not simply one set of beliefs/dispositions alongside others which he or she embraces; these specific beliefs/dispositions frame the perspective within which the person makes sense of, evaluates, and incorporates all other beliefs and dispositions. That is why the term theology should not be restricted to designating only knowledge of God (as the Greek roots of the word might imply). It is inadequate even to confine it to knowledge of general religious truths. It names instead the Christian practice of approaching all of life from, and placing all knowledge within, the perspective of God's revelation in Christ Jesus.[12]

---

7   Clear, 'How to Train Your Brain to Think in New Ways'.
8   Clear, 'How to Train Your Brain to Think in New Ways'.
9   Setran, 'From Worldview to Way of Life', 53.
10 Setran, 'From Worldview to Way of Life', 54-55.
11 Maddox, 'The Dynamics of Theology', 22.
12 Maddox, 'The Dynamics of Theology', 22.

Maddox believes that the critical pastoral (and educational) task is to form such a holistic worldview that will then profoundly shape the person's beliefs, affections, actions, and character.[13] He points out that at the heart of our character is the 'life narrative' that forms our unique sense of self over against other people. It is this 'story' that gives coherence to our inclinations, motives, and actions. 'While this narrative has unique elements, its plot self-consciously emulates a prototype—imbibed from those who surround us and/or chosen out of adoration. For Christians, this prototype is the "Christ story"'.[14] To be formed by this story requires much more than personal Bible study, reading Christian devotional literature or a range of theological works. Such formation can only occur through regular participation in a Christian community where we relate to and work alongside exemplars. This model is well-supported by recent developments in neuroscience.

3. The Neuroscience Background

We need to recognise that our current understanding of neuroplasticity challenges earlier beliefs that cognitive abilities are fixed and non-modifiable. The brain changes as it responds to its external environment, lived experiences, and training by means of a complex interaction of internal processes.[15] Since the rise of the Enlightenment, Western thought has long assumed that the mind, not the body, is the site of thinking and learning.[16] The brain has almost been regarded as a detached organ, rather like a computer, that simply makes use of a passive body. While we must acknowledge that the brain is essential for almost everything we do, it is critical to recognise that it is inextricably linked both to the body and to its environment. It is not an autonomous organ but is shaped by sensory input from within the body as well as the external environment.[17] 'Our practices and experiences have the power to reshape and rewire our brains, and our identities. […] brain function and behavior mutually inform one another in a two-way process'.[18] Recent studies in social neuroscience are

---

13 Maddox, 'The Dynamics of Theology', 22.
14 Maddox, 'The Dynamics of Theology', 29.
15 Brown, 'Equipping minds for Christian education', 150-51.
16 Tampio, 'Look up from your screen'.
17 Jasanoff, 'The Cerebral Mystique'.
18 Roozeboom, 'Rethinking Theological Anthropology', 79.

contributing to a renewed sense of the importance of social learning and the impact that relationships have on shaping our brains—learning cannot be focused on individual brains encased in an individual skull.[19] Human learning emerges out of our lived experience, not merely data acquisition. Failure to recognise this leads to an overemphasis on the role of the individual in learning and formation while discounting the role of relationships in their environmental and cultural contexts. The Western notion that we are primarily 'thinking beings' is so limiting; learning is more than a cognitive process. Current studies have shown that biology and physicality also shape human knowing, while our desires drive human behaviour more than mere rationalistic conceptions allow. If we are to 'form' students as a people who will live for others, we need to transform the body and not just the mind; words by themselves are insufficient to do that. For example, reflect on the difference it makes to studies on obstetrics if the student has borne and nursed a child compared to one who had not.[20] In learning to dance from a Cartesian perspective, the mind moves the body like a puppeteer pulls strings to move a puppet. You simply need to memorise a sequence of steps. Alternatively, the way to learn to dance is to move one's physical body in space until it becomes a deeply imprinted practice.[21] Both examples remind us of the power of habituated action in the process of learning and transformation. For truly effective learning, we a need to embrace physical, personal, and corporate practices, not just the mental acquisition of data.[22] An authentic and long-lasting transformation of our dispositions and inclinations requires that we continually participate in the routines and rituals of a tradition, as well as intentionally imitating the models upheld as exemplars by the tradition. Lasting character transformation is not primarily a matter of getting information, but of building good habits that construct character—moral formation happens by means of habituated practice.[23]

In his recent book, Marcus Holmes draws upon research on philosophy of mind, cognitive science and social neuroscience, to argue that physical copresence is essential to generate trust and empathy among human beings.[24] Folk psychology holds that when we see another person, we think for a moment

---

19 See Hogue, 'Brain Matters', 44.
20 Miller-McLemore, 'Embodied knowing, embodied theology', 746.
21 Tampio, 'Look up from your screen'.
22 Setran, 'From Worldview to Way of Life', 58–63.
23 Setran, 'From Worldview to Way of Life', 54.
24 Holmes, *Face-to-Face Diplomacy*, 5–8.

before deciding how to react. This is now an abundance of research to support this viewpoint as neuroscientists have diagrammed the 'mirroring system' that enables human beings to understand each other's intentions.[25] Mirror neurons are a class of visual/motor neurons that are discharged when a person watches another person performing an activity. This neural activity occurs in the same neural areas that would be activated if the individual were themselves performing the activity. 'Mirror neurons perform two essential functions: first, they allow humans to "personally" understand observed actions; second, they are the basis for human learning by imitation. We need to personally "experience" another person's emotions in order to understand or relate to the person; experience precedes empathy'.[26] While 'writing, calling or video-chatting often works fine for many forms of communication [...] people must meet in the flesh to achieve a high degree of trust or social bonding'.[27]

According to the new 'simulation theory', we actually feel what the other person feels as mirror neurons fire in just the same manner as if the experience was happening to us. The mirroring system enables advanced neural synchronisation between individuals, and they have a primary role in generating empathy.

> If this is true, then when someone is visiting a sick person and physically mirroring their facial and other movements, the mirrored expressions and movements will recreate the emotions of the person who is suffering. This is how mirror neurons "work": they create understanding by mirroring physical actions that recreate another person's emotions. As understanding of a person's suffering grows, love and compassion may grow as well as gratitude. The understanding created by the mirror neuron system permits a person's compassion for another to increase, allowing the visitor to grow in grace.[28]

This is not an automatic response on the part of the person visiting: 'Empathetic response requires initial mirroring, the acceptance or rejection of conditioned responses, and a conscious effort to recruit the feelings being experienced in order to empathize with the sufferer. While the first stage is involuntary, the next two require a motivated desire to empathize'.[29] Furthermore, the visitor

---

25 Iacoboni, 'Imitation, Empathy, and Mirror Neurons'.
26 Shrier and Shrier, 'Wesley's Sanctification Narrative', 234.
27 Tampio, 'Look up from your screen'.
28 Shrier and Shrier, 'Wesley's Sanctification Narrative', 235.
29 Shrier and Shrier, 'Wesley's Sanctification Narrative', 237.

must be physically present with the sick person for this to occur.[30] We are seeing an increasing convergence 'between cognitive models of imitation, constructs derived from social psychology studies on mimicry and empathy, and recent empirical findings from the neurosciences'.[31] There is little doubt that it requires a corporeal pattern of giving and receiving for us to be freed from the illusion of the autonomous self.[32]

4. Preparing for Ministry in Early Methodism

According to John Wesley, the whole purpose of the church is to help people, communities, and nations reach their full, holistic potential and to mature in Christlikeness. To do this effectively, 'Wesley…was deeply concerned to educate and direct pastors and preachers, society and band leaders in the spiritual care of people'.[33] The early Methodist movement was largely lay-led by Assistants, but it did have some ordained clergy who were university-trained. Because there were so few clergy, it was the role of the assistant that was critical to the ministry structure of Methodism. The Conference of 1744 gave guidance for the one who, in the absence of the ordained minister, was to 'feed and guide, to teach and govern the flock'. He (and it was a male, though women were prominent in many others way, which are beyond the scope of this paper to explore) was to do this by preaching, meeting the United Societies, the Bands, Select Societies, and Penitents every week; visiting the classes monthly; supervising the other leaders and meeting them weekly.[34] In terms of preparation for ministry, Wesley expected no less of the assistants than he did of the ordained clergy, even though they were rarely university trained. They were to view themselves 'As learners rather than teachers; as young students at the university, for whom therefore a method of study is expedient in the highest degree'.[35] They were to have minds always open to any further light God may give.[36] This is in harmony with our current understanding that a person's thoughts, beliefs, and motivations are

---

30 Iacoboni, 'Imitation, Empathy, and Mirror Neurons', 657.
31 Iacoboni, 'Imitation, Empathy, and Mirror Neurons', 653. See also p. 667.
32 Kim, 'The wounded grace', 374.
33 Maddix and Leclerc, *Pastoral Practices*, 15-16.
34 Wesley, *Works 10*, 139.
35 Wesley, *Works 10*, 179. See also p. 820.
36 Wesley, *Works 10*, 811.

usually transformed over time.[37] Wesley gave specific guidance on the use of time, managing relationships (especially with women), social actions, management of finances, and pastoral work. He expected them to model what they preached, and they were to be a servant of all by fetching wood, drawing water, and cleaning their own or the neighbour's shoes.[38] It was a program that combined both academic study and practical action and, as such, speaks to many of the current concerns about the limitations of current higher education.

4.1 Personal Study

To be an effective minister of the gospel required a firm commitment to being prepared for the task. This involved a mix of both intentional learning and practical application and was very demanding of both time and energy.[39] In his 'Address to the Clergy', Wesley wrote:

> Ought not a Minister to have, *First, a good understanding, a clear apprehension, a sound judgment, and a capacity of reasoning with some closeness?* [emphasis his] Is not this necessary in an high degree for the work of the ministry? Otherwise, how will he be able to understand the various states of those under his care; or to steer them through a thousand difficulties and dangers, to the haven where they would be?[40]

He wanted no less for his assistants and urged them to acquire both a broad and a deep knowledge in the areas of pastoral theology and practice, the Scriptures and their original languages, world history, church history, the sciences, medicine, logic, philosophy, the early church writers, the social sciences, poetry, and general wisdom.[41] He recommended a diverse range of readings, often accompanied by specific titles or authors to engage (many were classical authors from the first centuries of the church), including his own sermons, tracts, treatises, and abridgements. In order to do this well, they were to commit each morning (at least five hours) to the task. Such a broad curriculum would

---

37 Shrier and Shrier, 'Wesley's Sanctification Narrative', 229.
38 Wesley, *Works 10*, 140–42.
39 Wesley *Works 10*, 339.
40 Wesley, *Works* (Jackson) 10, 482. The rest of the document unpacks what he means here in some detail; see particularly 483-94.
41 See his reading lists in Wesley, *Works 10*, 144, 162-68, 179-80, 816-17, 820. Over 50 titles were kept at London, Bristol and Newcastle—see 162-68.

certainly help them to see new ways of looking at life and provide them with plenty of material for personal reflection and application. This reading was not simply to increase their store of information; it was to be a means of grace that God used for transforming their character and improving the quality of their ministry to others (both within the church and the wider community) by gaining an ever-deeper knowledge of, and ability to apply, the Scriptures:

> Do I meditate therein day and night? Do I think (and consequently speak) thereof, "when I sit in the house, and when I walk by the way; when I lie down, and when I rise up?" By this means have I at length attained a thorough knowledge, as of the sacred text, so of its literal and spiritual meaning? Otherwise, how can I attempt to instruct others therein? Without this, I am a blind guide indeed! I am absolutely incapable of teaching my flock what I have never learned myself; no more fit to lead souls to God, than I am to govern the world.[42]

Wesley left no one in any doubt that this program of study was essential for character formation: 'It cannot be that the people should grow in grace unless they give themselves to reading. A reading people will always be a knowing people […] we shall soon find why *the people* are not better, viz., because *we* are not more knowing and more holy'.[43] He was adamant that without constant reading of the kinds of material he had listed, the power and impact of preaching would diminish. He told one of his assistants who struggled to maintain his reading:

> What has exceedingly hurt you in time past, nay, and I fear to this day, is want of reading. I scarce ever knew a preacher read so little. And perhaps by neglecting it you have lost the taste for it. Hence your talent in preaching does not increase. It is just the same as it was seven years ago. It is lively, but not deep; there is little variety; there is no compass of thought. Reading only can supply this, with meditation and daily prayer. You wrong yourself greatly by omitting this. You can never be a deep preacher without it any more than a thorough Christian. O begin! Fix some part of every day for private exercises. You may acquire the taste for it which you have not; what

---

42 Wesley, *Works* (Jackson) 10, 494.
43 Wesley, *Letters* (Telford) 8, 247.

is tedious at first will afterwards be pleasant. Whether you like it or not, read and pray daily! It is for your life; there is no other way; else you will be a trifler all your days, and a pretty, superficial preacher.[44]

Wesley could not be plainer in stating that the quality of a person's ministry was tied to both the depth of their reading (education) and its personal and community application, addressing issues in both the church and the wider community.

4.2 Group Learning

Apart from regular attendance at church, he expected his ministers to be involved in the weekly class and other local society meetings. This gave an opportunity for social learning through Bible studies, group conversations, and sharing personal testimonies. There was a clear requirement to attend the annual conference and quarterly meetings, as well as other gatherings of the clergy and assistants with Wesley or other leaders. Conferences, in particular, were occasions to read and consider every point of the preceding conference. They were invited to speak freely and calmly about each decision, before deciding to retract, amend, or enlarge the statements.[45] The conferences were instrumental in helping to inform and then to guard Methodist values and practices in the face of relentless pressure from the surrounding culture.[46]

4.3 Embodied Practice

While the cognitive and personal character aspects of pastoral ministry were vital to Wesley, they were not seen as sufficient for faithful practice; book learning had to be put into practice by visiting the families in their care.[47] This expectation of active involvement in practical ministry was central to his deep conviction that Christians are formed in the likeness of Christ by practising ongoing acts of piety (the elements of personal and corporate worship) and acts of mercy (visiting and offering practical help to others).[48] In order to truly grow

---

44 Wesley, *Letters* (Telford) 4, 102.
45 Wesley *Works 10*, 811.
46 For example, see Maddox, 'The Dynamics of Theology', 25 regarding the impact of American Methodism on the slavery issue.
47 Wesley *Works 10*, 856.
48 McEwan, *Life of God in the Soul*, 102–04.

in love for God, Christians had to be deeply engaged with the people of their community, no matter who they were nor how pleasant this practice was personally. While he did not use the term empathy, he certainly understood its reality and how vital it was for growing in love to God and neighbour.

> Empathy is central for Wesley's belief that *acts of mercy* sanctify. He explained how to perform acts of mercy in his sermon "On Visiting the Sick." He wrote that visiting the sick is every Christian's obligation. Christians ought also to give money and other assistance, but not in place of personal visits. He explained that personal contact with the sick encouraged their souls. It also encouraged the visitor, who received grace through increased thankfulness to God for their health, increased sympathy and 'tenderness of spirit' for the afflicted person, and increased interest and activity in matters of social action.[49]

5. Some Implications for Higher Education Today

Perhaps, one of the greatest deficits arising from the loss of so many residential programs for ministry education is the loss of community that results. With the current demand for flexible learning, online classes, and video-streaming, it is much harder to maintain a cohort of learners who actually live together as a learning community. As we saw above, 'Social media highlights the importance of relationships, collaboration, and group life, but the personal, private, and distant nature of the online environment is counterproductive to the goal. Authentic community demands face-to-face interaction'.[50] If transformative education is merely the acquisition of intellectual data, this would be less of an issue. The widespread analogy of the brain to a computer simply reinforces the distancing of the brain from the rest of the body, and it 'fosters a misleading sense that the brain is the prime mover of our thoughts and actions', which causes us to pay less attention to factors outside the head and overemphasise the role of individuals and underemphasise the role of contexts.[51] While it may

---

49 Shrier and Shrier, 'Wesley's Sanctification Narrative'. 232.
50 Shirley, 'Overcoming Digital Distance', 398.
51 Jasanoff, 'The Cerebral Mystique'.

not always be possible to show how personal experience and knowledge are inter-related, there is no way to learn without bodily involvement.[52] That is why we need to encourage the engagement of students in a range of practices in a range of settings, and not simply intellectual exercises in a classroom space. For example, it is not enough to simply teach about mercy, but we need to find a way for the student to be mentored in performing acts of mercy in their local community.[53] Central to this is the 'interaction in which a mediator who possesses knowledge conveys a particular meaning or skill to a [person] and encourages him or her to transcend, that is, to relate meaning to some other thought or experience'.[54] Such a relationship helps the student to help expand cognitive capacity, especially in the face of new or challenging ideas. Without a mediator, we tend to reach a natural limitation.[55]

A regular connection with, and input from, practitioners who can model what we are seeking to teach is essential. This connection must not be restricted to isolated tutorial sessions or a limited field practice setting. The danger here is that the student does enough to meet the requirements of the class, but the practices never become habituated. This raises a real challenge in the face of the increasing demand to reduce the hours required for instruction and any required practical work. The use of supervised ministry placements following graduation certainly has its place, but it does tend to divorce the academic program from the life setting, creating an artificial barrier between the two. Students and lecturers both need to be actively involved in regular community practice in a local setting alongside exemplars who model the integration of knowledge and practice as well as Christian character. This provides the best opportunity to cultivate the range of habituated practices essential for spiritual and moral transformation, both personally and corporately. In our current adult education environment, this will be a real challenge.

Conclusion

While John Wesley was a man of the Eighteenth Century, there are still many things was can learn from his educational practice. His own life and the ministry

---

52 Tampio, 'Look up from your screen'.
53 Shrier and Shrier, 'Wesley's Sanctification Narrative', 240.
54 Brown, 'Equipping minds for Christian education', 154.
55 Brown, 'Equipping minds for Christian education', 154.

framework he established for Methodism in his lifetime all promoted a holistic approach to the formation of effective practitioners. In Wesley's understanding, both book learning and practical engagement with other people were equally essential for personal and community transformation. While it was rarely formal education for most of the lay assistants and other helpers, there are still elements that we can apply in the more formal higher education setting today. He emphasised the importance of academic study that was directed towards personal and community transformation. He expected it to occupy a significant number of hours per day, and it was to be life-long learning. However, the time given to formal learning was not to be at the expense of pastoral practice. The combination of personal study, social learning, and embodied practice through involvement with their local church and the guidance of mentors fostered the transformation of the whole person, and this, in turn, impacted their community setting. These elements—a sound and broad academic program, the role of a mentor, and regular involvement in a local community as part of the academic process—are no less important today. Our challenge is to find practical ways to establish a similarly comprehensive education program that will be equally effective in fostering personal and community transformation in our current setting.

Bibliography

Brown, C. T. 'Equipping minds for Christian education: Learning from neuroscience for Christian educators', *Christian Education Journal* 13.1 (2016), 147-68.

Clear, J. 'How to Train Your Brain to Think in New Ways' <https://jamesclear.com/feynman-mental-models> [accessed 18 March 2019].

Hogue, D. 'Brain Matters: Neuroscience, Empathy, and Pastoral Theology', *Journal of Pastoral Theology* 20.2 (2010), 25-55.

Holmes, M. *Face-to-Face Diplomacy: Social Neuroscience and International Relations* (Cambridge, UK: Cambridge University Press, 2018).

Iacoboni, M. 'Imitation, Empathy, and Mirror Neurons' *Annual Review of Psychology*, 60 (October 2008), 653-70.

Jasanoff, A. 'The Cerebral Mystique', *Aeon Newsletter* (8 May 2018) <https://aeon.co/essays/we-are-more-than-our-brains-on-neuroscience-and-being-human> [accessed 26 September 2018].

Judge, S. J. 'Nothing but a pack of neurons?' *Faraday Paper* 16 (The Faraday Institute for Science and Religion, March 2010), 1-4.

Kim, J. 'The wounded grace: memory, body and Salvation in EndÐ ShÐsaku and Rowan Williams', *The Expository Times* 124.8 (2013), 374-83.

McEwan, D. B. *The Life of God in the Soul: The Integration of Love, Holiness and Happiness in the Thought of John Wesley* (Milton Keynes, UK: Paternoster, 2015).

Maddix, M. & Leclerc, D. *Pastoral Practices: A Wesleyan Paradigm* (Kansas City, Kansas: Beacon Hill Press of Kansas City, 2014).

Maddox, R. L. 'The Dynamics of Theology in Christian Life', *Quarterly Review* 21.1 (Spring 2001), 20-32.

Miller-McLemore, B. J. 'Embodied knowing, embodied theology: what happened to the body?' *Pastoral Psychology* 62 (2013), 743-58.

Phillips, A. 'Being Human', *Theology* 118.4 (2015), 243-49.

Roozeboom, W. D. 'Rethinking Theological Anthropology: Constructing a Pastoral Theology of Wellness in Light of the Paradigm of Plasticity in Neuroscience' (PhD dissertation, Brite Divinity School, 2013).

Setran, D. 'From Worldview to Way of Life: Forming Student Dispositions toward Human Flourishing in Christian Higher Education', *Journal of Spiritual Formation & Soul Care* 11.1 (2018), 53-73.

Shirley, C. 'Overcoming Digital Distance: The challenge of developing relational disciples in the internet age', *Christian Education Journal* 14.2 (2017), 376-90.

Shrier, P. and C. Shrier, 'Wesley's Sanctification Narrative: A Tool for Understanding the Holy Spirit's Work in a More Physical Soul', *Pneuma* 31 (2009), 225-41.

Tampio, N. 'Look up from your screen'. *Aeon Newsletter* (5 June 2018) <https://aeon.co/essays/children-learn-best-when-engaged-in-the-living-world-not-on-screens> [accessed 26 September 2018].

Wesley, J. *The Bicentennial Edition of the Works of John Wesley*. (35 vols. projected, ed.-in-Chief, Frank Baker. Nashville: Abingdon Press, 1984-. vols. 7, 11, 25, and 26 of this edition originally appeared as the Oxford Edition of the Works of John Wesley. Oxford: Clarendon, 1975-1983).

Wesley, J. *The Letters of the Rev. John Wesley* (8 vols., ed. John Telford; London: Epworth Press, 1931).

Wesley, J. *The Works of John Wesley* (14 vols., 3rd ed., ed. Thomas Jackson; London: Wesleyan Methodist Book Room, 1872; Reprint, Kansas City: Beacon Hill Press of Kansas City, 1979).

David B. McEwan
Associate Professor of Theology and Pastoral Theology
Nazarene Theological College-Brisbane
Email: dmcewan@ntc.edu.au

26 | UNBOUNDING LEARNING COMMUNITIES

AN EDUCATIONAL STRATEGY FOR THE FUTURE OF LIFE-LONG LEARNING

Abstract

This chapter employs Richard Osmer's four core tasks for developing an educational strategy for leadership formation. The descriptive-empirical task involved action-research conducted by the Knox Centre for Ministry and Leadership across 2017-2018 into the life-long learning needs of leaders across the Presbyterian Church of Aotearoa New Zealand, beginning with interviews with fifty-five ordained ministers. The interpretive task employed the notion of habitus to locate inherited assumptions about theological education in relation to existing Reformed assumptions about ministerial identity and formation. The normative task invited reflection on how Jesus experienced and enacted the unbounding of learning. The research then required a pragmatic task of developing an educational strategy. The results challenge traditional assumptions lying within theological education and call for the unbounding of learning communities.

1. Introduction

In 2017, Knox Centre for Ministry and Leadership commissioned research, supported by the Thornton Blair Trust, to investigate and instigate life-long learning for ordained leaders in the Presbyterian Church of Aotearoa New Zealand (PCANZ). We could have assumed that we knew what was needed. As educators and theologians, we are experienced in delivering leadership formation informed by traditions in theology and in adult education, as well as notions of best practice in scholarship and academy. Paying attention to the voices of prospective students and their communities located in our changing contexts is crucial, however, if any educational endeavour is to be effective, relevant, and prophetic. In our case, what we heard was not what we had expected. From there, as a work of practical theology, the concrete words and actions of the church were critically evaluated in light of the gospel and of scholarly tradition in order to inform how we, seeking to serve the church, might, therefore, purpose and enact our educating.[1]

This chapter details the strategy that emerged from our research, taking as its frame Richard Osmer's four core tasks in a spiral of action-reflection,[2] as outlined in his book *Practical Theology*.[3] Drawing from qualitative data gathered and analysed, engaging inherited assumptions about theological education in critical dialogue with scholars, and reflecting upon Jesus in the gospels, we build the case for a strategy for the future of life-long learning that invites us to step beyond our suppositions and to unbound learning communities.

2. Methodology and Method: Educational Strategy as Practical Theology

In order to develop an educational strategy for leadership formation, Osmer argues for the outworking of four core tasks in both the academy and ministry, noting their resonance with the disciplines of practical theology, including preaching, spirituality, and Christian education.[4]

The descriptive-empirical task involves a priestly listening seeking to discern 'What is going on?' In our research, this involved gathering information about

---

[1] 'Practical theology is a dynamic process of reflective, critical inquiry into the praxis of the church in the world and God's purpose for humanity, carried out in the light of Christian Scripture and tradition, and in critical dialogue with other sources of knowledge'. Swinton, *From Bedlam to Shalom*, 12.
[2] For Swinton and Mowatt, practical theology is action-research as it generates solutions that articulate wider theological understandings that challenge current practices in seeking Gospel faithfulness. Swinton and Mowat, *Practical Theology*, 170.
[3] Osmer, *Practical Theology*, 1-29.
[4] Osmer, *Practical Theology*, 12-13.

the learning needs of leaders across the Presbyterian Church of Aotearoa New Zealand, given that for many, Presbyterian identity has become uncertain.[5] Initially, fifty-five ministers were chosen by random selection, aiming for a 30% representation of every Synod and Presbytery[6] Respondents were interviewed—most of them by phone or Skype. Their interviews were anonymised, transcribed, and coded with faculty of the Knox Centre for Ministry and Leadership (KCML), the ministerial provider of the PCANZ. Five themes emerged in areas of faith, community life, witness, leadership, and church form. A report gathered and wove interview material relevant to each theme and was sent to participants for their feedback. We (Taylor and Dewerse) have argued for the value of action-research in theological education, in which participatory research methods locate research within the organisation that cares deeply about resolving contextual concerns.[7] Hence, the data from ministers was workshopped with a further 230 lay and ordained participants in Presbyteries and key church committees, who provided feedback on the results and engaged around emerging ideas regarding future educational responses.

The interpretive task applies wisdom in seeking to understand 'Why is this going on?' The patterns in the data are considered in relation to general insights, with God as the author of the created world. Wider research is thus analysed, in this case, in relation to the social construction of theological learning communities.

The normative task offers prophetic discernment in seeking to articulate 'What ought to be going on?' This involved using theological concepts, in this case Jesus' experiences of learning, to interpret the shape of good practice in leadership formation.

The pragmatic task requires a servant leadership to articulate 'How might we respond?', understanding that action research invites the reforming of existing actions. What emerged from our data was a plea for formational education of ministry leaders to be located in and with the realities of their people—the local body of Christ. Because practical theology includes leading change, we, therefore, turned our attention to determining strategies of action

---

5   Johnston, 'New Zealand Presbyterian Predicaments', 13-16.
6   'Participants [in the interviews] included 37 men and 18 women and ranged from new graduates to long-experienced ministers close to retirement. They are located in rural, town, and urban contexts, serve in small churches, uniting churches/contexts, medium churches, large/hub churches, education centres and a hospital, and come from across the theological spectrum. Ethnic diversity and ethnically diverse congregations are represented'. Dewerse, 'A Report', 3.
7   Taylor & Dewerse, 'Researching the Future', 87-104.

for life-long learning, including graduate outcomes, a new host and means, and new communities of engagement.

Our educational strategy (pragmatic) of 'unbounding learning communities' is practical theology as informed listening (descriptive-empirical), considered in the light of critical theory (interpretive) and biblical reflection (normative).[8]

3. The Descriptive-Empirical Task: Listening Leadership[9]

In seeking to offer education for life-long leadership formation beyond the two or so years a person may spend in ministry training with us, we applied particular assumptions to our research.[10] We were keen to be offering postgraduate study options, linked to an accredited framework, that would offer a professionalised and, we hoped, innovative approach. But we were committed to grounding this in thorough-going research. We thus set in motion an action-research project to ensure any design would be shaped by the wisdom of leaders in context. Through interviews with ordained leaders, reflective analysis, and workshops across the PCANZ to test emerging themes and educational prompts, a particular picture began to emerge.

In asking 'What is going on?', we were told that there is a crisis of faith across the church. Biblical literacy is low, and theological understanding limited, too often creating less than Christ-like behaviour within our communities and neighbourly engagement without referencing Christ. Participants expressed a perceived danger in institutional postgraduate study: It could grow leaders in concepts and language too divorced from the realities and understanding of their people to empower effective ministry. We were asked not to focus future theological education initiatives on a few, removing them for long periods of time at an expense to instil knowledge in them out of an embodied context. We sought instead to create means for **teaching leaders with their people in the community** so that growth in Christ could occur together. With that plea established, three requests were made of us.

Firstly, for decades, the main teaching occurring in many church communities

---

8 Branson, 'The Practical Theology Cycle'.
9 Much of this section draws from the conference paper by Taylor & Dewerse, 'Unbounding Learning Communities'.
10 The model for training leaders for ordination combines internship with theological block courses. This model, established in 2007, began under the leadership of then principal, Rev. Dr. Graham Redding.

has been the sermon—a twenty-minute content download—doing, as one colleague observed, much of the 'heavy lifting' in terms of Christian education. According to one minister, 'We've bought into the whole Western Enlightenment idea that...the sermon will do the trick. But accountability, vulnerability, and trust [qualities integral to the journey of a disciple] don't happen well in a public space, in a sermon'.[11] If success in disciple-making was measured on the basis of numbers, the PCANZ would be failing: Membership has decreased by 25% in the last thirteen years, from 42,180 in 2005 to 31,491 in 2018.[12] Those who participated in our research asked that theological education as learning in a community be grounded in teaching **practices for living differently**.

Secondly, the urgency of the contextual situation makes it clear that a theological college on its own is unlikely to provide enough leaders to arrest declining membership and address the crisis of faith. The focus of theological education as learning in community, grounded in teaching practices for living differently, must thus be on **educating educators** so integrated knowledge can be quickly shared, modelled, embedded, and replicated. 'Who those educators are can [then] expand… and the education of the whole people of God is in view'.[13] Such an investment holds promise of ending the isolation that many we spoke with are feeling.[14]

Thirdly, in a context becoming pastorally complex, in which, as a number of our participants noted, 'respectful communication and deep listening' seem to be increasingly rare skills, there is a need in theological education for learning in community, and grounded in teaching practices for living differently, to be educating the educators **in relationally embodied ways.**[15] Particular critique was levelled at committees and the General Assembly: 'We don't really listen with the heart. We listen with half an ear and half a mind, but the other half of the mind is around the questions, "How is what this person is saying threatening what I believe and how can I bolster up what I believe and how can I respond to that?"'[16] Cultural and emotional intelligence—vital in an increasingly diverse and fractured world—require integrated human beings sure of their identity and grounded in God's love who are able to be fully present to others.

---

11   Dewerse, 'A Report', 13.
12   Soberly, in 2010 the PCANZ was a quarter of the size it had been in 1970. Johnston, 'Minister's Missional Capacities, 13.
13   Dewerse, 'Enlarging the Frame', 8.
14   Dewerse, 'Enlarging the Frame', 49.
15   Dewerse, 'Enlarging the Frame', 22.
16   Dewerse, 'Enlarging the Frame', 22.

4. The Interpretive Task: Data as Foil for Assumptions

The interpretive task invites us to analyse the empirical data in relation to inherited assumptions about theological education. Three themes—learning community, workplace learning, and habitus—help us do that.

College-based theological education claims to be formational. However, when these claims were tested in Australia, Les Ball found that talk of transformation far exceeded reality.[17] One of the impediments he noted was the perception among students 'of a sometimes contrived college community, which can be remote from other significant elements of life'.[18] One response is to try to make college more like real life, using case studies in class, utilising visiting lecturers from the so-called 'real world', and creating assignments that seek to mirror elements of ministry life. What is not addressed is a bigger question: Why is theological education detached from prior communities of learning in the first place?

The role of community in formation is helpfully parsed by Ascough.[19] He distinguishes between 'communities of practice', defined by Wenger et al. as a group of people 'who share a concern, a set of problems, or a passion about a topic, and who deepen their knowledge and expertise in this area by interacting on an ongoing basis'[20] and 'bounded learning communities' defined by Wilson et al. as 'groups that form within a structured teaching or training setting, typically a course', developing 'in direct response to guidance provided by an instructor, supported by a cumulative resource base'.[21] Using this frame, inherited theological education is a bounded learning community. Our participants were asking for communities of practice located in relation to local church communities.

The bounded learning community can be further interpreted by Bourdieu's notion of *habitus*. Bourdieu defined *habitus* as the 'systems of durable, transposable dispositions [...] which generate and organize practices and representations that can be objectively adapted'.[22] Applied to education, learning is 'a process that is situated within a particular social setting, and any knowledge derived is contingent upon that social setting'.[23] This invites us to interpret the social setting that is a theological college as occurring with a set of

---

17 Ball, *Transforming Theology*, 100.
18 Ball, *Transforming Theology*, 100.
19 Ascough, 'Welcoming', 132.
20 Wenger et al., *Cultivating Communities of Practice*, 4.
21 Wilson et al., 'Bounded Community'.
22 Bourdieu, *Logic of Practice*, 53.
23 Avis et al., 'Theorizing the Work-Based Learning of Teachers', 49.

rules, values and language; lectures, footnotes, and essays as assignments: 'the social game embodied and turned into a second nature'.[24]

In utilising *habitus*, Bourdieu sought to not only uncover the reproduction of bounded structures but simultaneously to recognise the fragility of those structures and hold out for the possibility of change.[25] For Bourdieu, while *habitus* was second nature, the social setting was always malleable. We can thus interpret our data as an invitation to re-imagine. How might life-long learning interface with the places where formation for ordination occurs? How might the *habitus* of a local church ministry context interplay with the *habitus* of higher theological education?

Existing theological education does involve elements of local church engagement, resonating with an interpretation through the lens of workplace learning. Avis et al. argue that workplace learning occurs in three modes: learning how the real world works, rehearsing workplace skills, and seeing the workplace as the context for learning.[26] What our data was suggesting was that the *habitus* of learning (the local church) be the workplace, facilitating in real time the other two modes.

Our participants were deeply aware of 'dispositions *acquired through experience*' in local settings by members.[27] The request for life-long learning in local contexts was not in order to 'dumb' down education or escape from rigorous thinking. Rather, it was in response to a more rigorous challenge: a diagnosis of the *habitus* of the local church and a vision of the formation and re-formation not of individuals in a classroom but of an entire church system. A trickle-down approach to formation, in which selected individuals are taken aside for formation and returned re-formed, was not seen as sufficient to meet the learning and formational challenges of the local context.

Our empirical data, interpreted, generated a pragmatic proposal: What might a theological college seeking to partner with local church communities, and unbounding learning in 'communities of formational practice', look like?

Before we addressed this question, we needed to undertake the re-normative task, that of reflecting on the ways that Jesus experienced and enacted the unbounding of learning.

---

24 Avis et al., 'Theorizing the Work-Based Learning of Teachers', 63.
25 Wiedner, 'Reflecting on the Use of Bourdieu's Tools', 223-230.
26 Avis et al., 'Theorizing the Work-Based Learning of Teachers', 48-57.
27 Bourdieu, *In Other Words*, 9.

5. The Normative Task: Jesus as Teacher and Learner

A Resourcing Ministers Day in 2018 prior to a PCANZ General Assembly provided an opportunity to present our empirical data to ministers. Aware that ministerial identity is framed in relation to the embodied Christ,[28] we undertook the normative task by dwelling in three Scriptures that located our interpreted empirical data in relation to the life of Christ. This involved lectio divina in order to 'seek truth with others', engaging the Bible as beggars, with the risk of disagreement, in the context of congregational practice of ministry—a posture Kiefert describes as 'the cutting edge of contemporary theological education'.[29] Each Scripture offered surprising insights when it came to themes of learning in community, practices for living differently, and educating the educators.

Jesus in the temple in Luke 2:41-52 locates Jesus as a learner in community—with his parents (41), as a participant with a 'group of travellers' (44), and as a listener in the temple (46). Learning in community is intergenerational; children have a voice and experience inquiry-based learning (46). Learning is holistic, an integration of wisdom, years, divine, and human favour (52). Practices for living differently involve pilgrimage and the movement between villages and capital centres in the context of extended family structures. Educating the educators involves a disturbance of normative expectations. Jesus' insights and answers cause amazement (47), yet Jesus listens to established teachers (46) and is obedient to his parents (51). This text encourages a community in which questions are welcomed and all are learning.

Jesus' encounter across cultures in Matthew 15:21-28 portrays a learning community that is at first disturbed by the cries of the Canaanite woman (22) and then enlarged, as Jesus affirms her great faith (28). Again, we see learning across the generations, with the needs of a child made central to the learning encounter. The woman and her child are the educators, challenging change; Jesus' practice of living differently includes a willingness to enlarge his understanding.

Jesus' response to the conflict in Matthew 5:43-46, juxtaposing 'love' and 'enemies', offers a particular relational challenge for living differently (Matt. 5:44; Lk. 6:27). Ministry includes conflict, yet in Jesus' teaching and example, it can become generative for learning, stimulating empathy and creativity. While conflict is challenging, the suggestion is that less than Christ-like behaviour within a local community can be a source of formation.

---

28 'The role of the ministry in the Church is to serve Christ alone'. APPENDIX D-4: ORDINATION AND THE MINISTRY OF WORD AND SACRAMENTS (Adopted by the General Assembly, 1966).
29 Kiefert, 'The Bible', 178.

These three Gospel narratives suggest that congregational settings are, in fact, learning communities. The questions of children, the cries of the perceived outsider, and the complexities of conflict are invitations to learning.

6. The Pragmatic Task: Unbounding Educational Design

In asking 'How might we respond?' strategically to the results of an investigation into what is going on and why that is so, informed by reflection on what ought to be, a key starting point is the naming of the outcomes one intends for one's graduates. Life-long learning could be, and often is, seen as an informal cousin to formal academic programmes. Such assumptions risk being untrue to biblical and formational tradition. We offer outcomes—though technically one never graduates from life-long learning—as markers for review and to benchmark expectations, as well as guide educational content and delivery.[30] These outcomes reflect the plea our participants made of us and their three requests, discussed in the light of scholarship and the life and teaching of Jesus.

> Our graduates will be leaders who are:
> 1. creatively and critically reflecting on praxis in real-time with and within the local community
> 2. modelling and enabling Christ-like practices for living differently
> 3. agile educators empowering the people of God
> 4. integrating the whole self in relationally embodied ministry and mission

The first outcome suggests an institutionalised model is too physically and socially bounded. What is required is flexibility of access—geographically, temporally, pedagogically, and in terms of academic level and commitment. The second suggests theological education must be approached through action-learning inquiry, informed application, and critical reflection grounded in Christ. The third outcome removes any elitism, addresses issues of resourcing, and mentors the replication of scholar-practitioners. The fourth demands that not just the head, but the heart and the hara—a Maori word for the whole self—being caught up in learning, grounded in meaningful and accountable relationships for the good of all.

---

30 We could name them 'learning outcomes', yet 'learning outcomes' typically lie at a course level, and what we are offering is an overall educational frame. Hence, we call them graduate outcomes.

6.1 A New Host for Life-Long Learning: The Living Library

The first challenge is how to host such an endeavour. Spiralling action-reflection alerted us to the need for a new way to bring the academy and local contexts together in order to disseminate quality resources 24/7 across the country, in ways that would enable connection and accountability on an as-needs basis, communicate a variety of structured learning opportunities, and empower those beyond a theological educator-core to efficiently and effectively harness means for empowering others.

We proposed and began to build a Living Library.[31]

This concept took as inspiration the great Christian tradition of libraries as a key resource at the heart of our theological institutions, the Danish innovation of the Human Library where one takes out a human for a story-encounter,[32] and the connective power of the internet.

The idea was that we would create a digital home in which knowledge was located in praxis and relationally embodied in practices. The challenge was to bring alive recommended and topical archival and printed resources, alongside articles, videos, art, music, opinion/blogs, study leave reports, websites, and podcasts via pithy monitored reviews offered by colleagues, as well as the opportunity to borrow a human for a conversation identified via an initial blurb published online, with contact mediated by permission. Also available would be opportunities to participate in one-off or regular 'book' clubs and webinars, lecture series, and interactive short courses. Mentoring would also be available, along with the ability to book a 'live expert' to visit a local community to lead workshops and retreats. (The digital platform would not preclude proactive offers made to communities not able to access it.) A blog could add a regular personal touch; community news could profile local church doings and link to SPANZ—the magazine of the PCANZ. The themes arising from our research—faith, community, witness, leadership, innovation—would inform the shape of our Living Library.

6.2 A New Means for Life-Long Learning: Click. Engage. Accredit

The second challenge is how to cater for a range of learning demands. We were hearing that while some wanted educational opportunities face-to-face, others

---

31 https://livinglibrary.org.nz/
32 https://humanlibrary.org

needed ultimate accessibility and flexibility. While some wanted to learn through informal means, others wanted options for (marked) feedback and the opportunity to gain formal recognition.

> We proposed and began to scaffold a frame expressed as 'Click. Engage. Accredit'.

The most accessible point of entry was that many recommended resources in the Living Library would be, literally, freely available to anyone at any time—at the click of a computer mouse. In terms of the human part of the library, access would also be freely available—or available for the price of a coffee—at a time mutually suitable to both parties. These investments would be a gift to individuals and communities across the church. For those keen to engage—to join with others or to build in accountability—a small fee or subscription would give them access to synchronous activities, such as online or local face-to-face book clubs, webinars, and even short courses. A fee per hour would provide supervision, mentoring, and/or marking of an agreed assessment. Meanwhile, the advent in educational circles internationally of nanodegrees, or micro-credentials in the New Zealand context, offers an opportunity to accredit—to synchronise the engage offerings with (optional) fee-charged, fully-assessed learning opportunities in small pieces that, educationally framed and stacked, could provide internal recognition or, potentially, external recognition of a theological qualification.[33] Within the PCANZ, the former offers an opportunity to provide fully flexible yet rigorous life-long learning. In addition, it might open pathways for locally ordained ministers (those ordained in situ to serve a particular context). It might also whet the appetite of lay as well as ordained leaders interested in theological or further theological study but not, at least initially, in a position to step into full-time, semesterised fee-paying study. Micro-credentials could enable staircasing to build modules toward the equivalent of a semesterised course, agreed via an MOU with a seminary or university.

---

33 Nanodegrees were pioneered by Udacity, an organisation offering massive open online courses (MOOCs): www.udacity.com. EdX, meanwhile, is a platform offering nanodegrees from top universities, for which you pay a flat fee: www.edx.org/. The New Zealand Qualifications Authority launched micro-credentials in August 2018. 'Micro-credentials system launched' (1 August 2018), www.nzqa.govt.nz/about-us/news/micro-credentials-system-launched/ [accessed 20 August 2019].

a. New Communities Engaging in Life-Long Learning: The Example of Listening in Mission

The third challenge is how to invite and enable new communities to engage in life-long learning, especially when human resources at the hub to invest in their development are limited, if we are to realise the leaders' request to educate them with their communities.

> We drew on a model already initiated, offering it to the wider church.

Steve and his colleague Mark Johnston, both lecturers at Knox Centre for Ministry and Leadership, created in 2017 a short course called 'Listening in Mission'. This involved an unbounding, in which part of an existing course taught to ordinands was made available to the wider church as a stand-alone offering through videoconferencing.

Delivered in five sessions, there is time in between for action. Leaders are given tools and equipped with readings and invited to invite others in their local church community to go on a journey with them of listening for the spirit of God in their neighbourhoods, ultimately discerning where they might join in (Graduate Outcomes 1 and 2). While Steve and Mark train the leaders (online), the leaders immediately train their group (face-to-face) in what they are learning (Outcome 3). Sessions using Zoom give the leaders the opportunity to return, share stories, reflect, and discuss missiologically with peers, participate in Lectio Divina on Luke 10:1-11, and pray (Outcome 4).[34]

The course—and a second entitled 'Experimenting in Mission'—further enable relational embodiment (exercises require the use of the senses and prioritise connection with land and with people).[35] Feedback from participants noted the decrease in isolation and the accountability around practices for living differently.

Conclusion

We have discovered that if we are to be effective, relevant, and prophetic as theological educators, we need to listen. What we have heard offers a strategy for life-long learning that, by unbounding learning communities, in fact, offers

---

[34] Paragraph taken directly from Taylor and Dewerse, 'Unbounding Learning Communities'.
[35] To date, students have come from Aotearoa, Australia and Scotland.

an opportunity for the Presbyterian Church of Aotearoa New Zealand to re-form the best of its tradition toward renewal.

Key to Presbyterian identity is that it is 'a genuinely educated church'.[36] Yet the low levels of biblical and theological literacy revealed in our research put the lie to this. The strategy they have inspired offers a redefinition to combat the shrinking reach of decades of specialised, bounded theological education. It breaks open embedded isolationism by harnessing possibilities for developing flexible and diverse networks with in-built accountability loops, ensuring theological education becomes an activity available to all and able to empower all. The strategy also challenges contemporary distortions of the ordained as professional generalists carrying the faith of the people. The strategy provides ways to empower a return to being 'ministers of word and sacrament', 'teaching elders' and 'guardian[s] of the Gospel' working alongside members, and enabling each one's 'study of the scriptures'.[37]

Such are the consequences and the potential of our asking 'What is going on?', 'Why is this going on?' 'What ought to be going on?', and 'How might we respond?' Through spiralling action-reflection investigating life-long learning, we have been challenged to critically review assumptions about the enterprise of theological education and unbound learning communities so that we, and those whom we seek to serve, might have a future.

Bibliography

Ascough, R. S. 'Welcoming Design – Hosting a Hospitable Online Course', *Teaching Theology and Religion* 10.3 (2007), 131-136.

Avis, J., K. Orr & Tummons, J. 'Theorizing the Work-Based Learning of Teachers', in Avis, J. et al. (eds.), *Teaching in Lifelong learning: A Guide to Theory and Practice* (Open University Press; Mc-Graw Hill: Maidenhead, UK): 48-57.

Ball, L. *Transforming Theology: Student Experience and Transformative Learning in Undergraduate Theological Education* (Melbourne: Mosaic Press, 2012).

Bourdieu, P. *Logic of practice* (Cambridge, UK: Polity Press; tr. Richard Nie, 1990).

Bourdieu, P. *In Other Words. Essays Towards a Reflexive Sociology* (Stanford, California: Stanford University Press; tr. Matthew Adamson 1990).

---

36 Expertly outlined in Dutney, *A Genuinely Educated Ministry*, 35-41.
37 PCANZ, 'The Book of Order', 6.1.2, 6.1.3; 1.4.2 b).

Branson, M.L. 'The Practical Theology Cycle', <https://vimeo.com/13948078> [accessed 20 March 2019].

Dewerse, R. 'A Report on the First Round of a Research Project Investigating Life-long Learning Needs of Ministry Leaders in the Presbyterian Church of Aotearoa New Zealand' (Knox Centre for Ministry and Leadership, 2017).

Dutney, A. *"A Genuinely Educated Ministry." Three Studies on Theological Education in the Uniting Church in Australia* (Sydney, NSW: Assembly of the Uniting Church, 2007).

Johnston, M. 'Minister's Missional Capacities: Cultivating Discernment in a Presbyterian Training System' (D. Min. thesis, Fuller Seminary, 2015).

Johnston, M. 'New Zealand Presbyterian Predicaments in Missional Leadership Education', *Australian Journal of Mission Studies* 12.1 XX (2018), 11-21.

Kiefert, P. 'The Bible and Theological Education', in Beverley Gaventa and Patrick Miller (eds.), *The Ending of Mark and the Ends of God: Essays in Memory of Donald Harrisville Juel* (Louisville: Westminster John Knox Press, 2005): 165-182.

Osmer, R. R. *Practical Theology: An Introduction* (Grand Rapids: Eerdmans, 2008).

Swinton, J. & Mowat, H. *Practical Theology* and Qualitative Research (London, UK: SCM, 2006).

Swinton, J. *From Bedlam to Shalom: Towards a Practical Theology of Human Nature, Interpersonal Relationships, and Mental Health Care* (New York, NY: Peter Lang, 2000).

Taylor S. & Dewerse, R. 'Unbounding Learning Communities: Action Research in Lifelong Ministerial Formation' (Learning and Teaching Theology conference paper, Sydney College of Divinity, 2019).

Taylor S. & Dewerse, R. 'Researching the Future: The Implications of Activist Research for Theological Scholarship in Teaching and Learning', in Ball, L. & Bolt, P. (eds.), *Wondering about God Together: Research-Led Learning and Teaching in Theological Education* (Sydney, NSW: SCD Press, 2018): 87-104.

'The Book of Order of the Presbyterian Church of New Zealand' (amended October 2018).

Wiedner, R. 'Reflecting on the Use of Bourdieu's Tools from Outside the Fields of Music and Music Education', in Burnard, P. et al. (eds.), *Bourdieu and the Sociology of Music Education* (Farnham: Surrey and Burlington: Ashgate, 2015): 223-230.

Wenger, E., McDermott, R. A. & Snyder. W. *Cultivating Communities of Practice: A Guide to Managing Knowledge* (Cambridge, MA: Harvard Business Review Press, 2002).

Wilson, B.G., Ludwig-Hardman, S., Thornam, C. L. & Dunlap, J. C. 'Bounded Community: Designing and Facilitating Learning Communities in Formal Courses', *International Review of Research in Open and Distance Learning* 5.3 (2004) <http://www.irrodl.org/index.php/irrodl/article/view/204/286> [accessed 9 February 2007].

Websites

'Micro-credentials system launched' (1 August 2018), https://www.nzqa.govt.nz/about-us/news/micro-credentials-system-launched/ [accessed 20 August 2019].

EdX: https://www.edx.org/

The Human Library: https://humanlibrary.org

The Living Library: https://livinglibrary.org.nz/

Udacity: https://www.udacity.com

Steve Taylor
Knox Centre for Ministry and Leadership, and Flinders University,
principal@knoxcentre.ac.nz

Rosemary Dewerse,
Unitec,
rosemarydewerse@gmail.com

27 | CURIOSITY-BASED LEARNING

STRETCHING FEARLESSLY INTO THE UNKNOWN

Abstract

The authors assert effective learning begins with curiosity. Curiosity is central to early childhood development and is maintained throughout life as a foundational dimension of our ability to learn, adapt, and change. This chapter explores curiosity as a motivator in the pursuit of learning. Information gap theory, the importance of safety and trust, and workplace stretch learning are also discussed. Two heuristic models are introduced to demonstrate the practical application of curiosity-based learning in action: The *Stretch Learning Matrix* and the *Action Coaching Approach*.

1. Introduction

Cats are notoriously inquisitive.

The old expression 'curiosity killed the cat' has a core meaning: *don't ask too many questions*. This is not a new idea, and rather comically, Augustine[1] suggests that, before creating heaven and earth, God 'fashioned hell for the inquisitive'. Later, in Don Juan,[2] Byron exclaimed, 'I loathe that low vice—curiosity'.

This expression about cats and curiosity has remained, perhaps, because in

---

1   Augustine, *Confessions* (Middlesex: Penguin Books, 1961).
2   Lord Byron, *Don Juan: In Sixteen Cantos* (Halifax: Milner and Sowerby, 1837).

many organisations, *questioning* can be perceived as *attacking the status quo* or challenging authority. History has revealed orthodoxy can be unkind to those who oppose it. This is reflected in old fables such as *The Emperor's New Clothes*,[3] where everyone shares a common lie for fear of consequence. In this fable, it is finally the most *curious*, a child, who exclaims, 'The Emperor is naked, he has no clothes!' And, suddenly, everyone feels free to admit their shared view of the world is flawed.

In ancient times, curiosity was the poor cousin of wonder. Wonder brought humility; whereas, curiosity was mischievous. Aristotle wrote *curiosity* is mostly a witless and aimless prying into things of no concern to us. In contrast, *wonder* is the root of true inquiry and the beginning of the love of wisdom (philosophy).[4] There appears to be one significant difference between the two concepts: *awe*. Wonder sees the unknown and is amazed; curiosity takes that wonder and asks, 'How does it work' and 'How can we do it better?'

We are all born with an insatiable curiosity. An essential aspect of learning is asking *why*. As we age, this curiosity may become more focused, with questions such as 'How can we improve?', 'What is a different perspective?' or 'Where can we get more information?' These questions fuel a lifelong journey of learning and discovery.

Curiosity has been defined as a need, thirst, or desire for knowledge. It is central to personal motivation[5], which is defined as the arousal, direction, and persistence of behaviour.[6] Curiosity is a motivational prerequisite for exploratory behaviour.[7] At the core of curiosity are three components: learning, exploration, and immersion.[8] Guo, Zhang, and Zhai describe this as *a sensory curiosity* (a focus on emotional experience), *epistemic curiosity* (a focus on the desire to gain new knowledge), and *perceptual curiosity* (a focus on what data is seen and heard).[9]

---

3   *The Emperor's New Clothes* was written by Hans Christian Anderson in 1837 and is based on a 1335 story from a medieval Spanish collection of short fables. In the story, two tailors make a new set of clothes for an emperor, saying their garment is so special that it is invisible to anyone who is stupid or unfit for their position. In reality, they make nothing, pretending they have made the most beautiful piece of clothing in the world. No one is willing to admit they cannot see it for fear of being seen as stupid and for challenging the shared lie. Finally, it is a child who yells from the crowd, 'He isn't wearing anything at all!' Everyone then laughs, and the fear is gone.
4   Ball, *Curiosity: How Science Became Interested in Everything*.
5   Fowler, *Curiosity and Exploratory Behaviour*.
6   Franken, *Human Motivation*.
7   Berlyne, *Conflict, Arousal, and Curiosity*.
8   Kashdan & Silvia, 'Curiosity and Interest: The Benefits of Thriving on Novelty and Challenge', 367-374.
9   Guo, Zhang, & Zhai, 'A Potential Way of Enquiry into Human Curios', E48–E52.

2. The Tantalising Information Gap

Curiosity tantalises us. It gives us the energy to pursue knowledge we do not have. In Greek mythology,[10] this is perhaps best illustrated by the story of Tantalus who, for his crimes, faced the punishment in Hades of having food and drink always in front of him, but every time he reached out for sustenance, the items moved slightly out of his grasp. Thus, the word 'tantalise' conveys a sense of being teased by the unobtainable.

There is an unsettling cognitive dissonance that exists in being tantalised by the hope of something just out of one's reach. This curiosity is an opportunity to test taken-for-granted assumptions and, therefore, to become aware of a gap in personal knowledge or skills. Lowenstein's information gap theory asserts that 'curiosity happens when we feel a gap in our knowledge'. To alleviate feelings of deprivation (i.e. missing out), Lowenstein[11] found the intensity of curiosity is linked to the likelihood of being able to fill this information gap. We work hard attempting to solve a puzzle until we can see what the image may be. Lowenstein also discovered we are more curious about knowledge gaps in areas we already know about. In other words, if we have a 7/10 knowledge of cats, we are more likely to want to fill in the gap than if we only had 1/10 knowledge of cats. In this way, curiosity is seen to enhance learning when knowledge gaps are posed as questions, puzzles, dilemmas, and cases.[12]

Given this, curiosity may increase the learner's motivation to think more often and more intently about the subject under consideration, resulting in 'deeper' learning rather than merely skimming and doing the bare minimum to get by.[13] This enhanced learning is brought about by a desire to resolve the dissonance often induced by curiosity.[14]

These information gaps need to be manageable for students, and educators, therefore, should be acutely aware of what those gaps are for their students. Lowenstein's[15] research suggests that, when the information gap is small, curiosity is heightened. This is consistent with the view presented by Litman et al.: 'When we know nothing, we aren't curious at all. We have nowhere to

---

10 Homer's *Odyssey*, Book XI.
11 Lowenstein, 'The Psychology of Curiosity: A Review and Reinterpretation', 75-98.
12 von Renesse & Ecke, 'Teaching Inquiry with a Lens Toward Curiosity', 148-164.
13 Marton & Saljo, 'On Qualitative Differences in Learning: Outcome and Process', 4-11.
14 Craik & Lockhart, 'Levels of Processing: A Framework for Memory Research', 671-84.
15 Craik & Lockhart, 'Levels of Processing', 75-98.

begin, and therefore no curiosity to drive us to acquire the knowledge'.[16] Litman et al. identified a 'tip of the tongue' phenomenon, explaining we are 'most curious when we feel the need to recall something that we are close to remembering'.[17] On the other hand, when we already know something, our curiosity has been satiated, and our desire for learning diminishes. In this way, curiosity is so personally motivating because it has very little to do with what we feel we 'have to do', and a lot to do with what 'we want to do'. This reinforces the idea that regular 'check-ins' with students to assess their current knowledge is essential in keeping curiosity alive.[18] Otherwise, it may slip into one of two extremes: *not enough information gap* equals boredom, and *too much information gap* equals a sense of being overwhelmed.

These information gaps can include a range of knowledge and skills,[19] particularly the following: (a) *Experiential knowing*, which comprises personal perceptions, observations, feelings, and intuitions that may be tacit and pre-verbal and embedded in the relationships within the situation; (b) *presentational knowing*, which is the experiences (tacit) participants share with others for mutual learning through exhibits in the form of words, images, or multimedia to generate sharing and mutual discovery; and (c) *propositional knowing*, which is sensemaking and is developed into statements, theories, and concepts. Challenging these models through a rigorous review is vital in adding depth to learning. The propositions are carried by exhibits (handouts, guides, reflections, and articles) to articulate the learning propositions. And, finally, there is (d) *practical knowing*, which refers to being aware of ways to improve what is being done. This is about competency and skill, which is grounded in know-how, and therefore, there is an opportunity for the integration of new knowledge (cognitive, behavioural, and affective) into a whole-of-life approach.

Building on the work of Knowles in their review of effective corporate learning and development practices,[20] Bingham et al.[21] asked, 'When do I learn deeply and effectively?' In response, they found the following:

---

16 Litman, Hutchins, & Russon, 'Epistemic Curiosity, Feeling-of-Knowing, and Exploratory Behaviour', 559–582.
17 Litman, Hutchins & Russon, 'Epistemic Curiosity', 566.
18 Ginsberg, '"Mind the Gap" in the Classroom', 74-80.
19 Heron, *Co-operative Inquiry,* 238-239; Heron & Reason, 'Extending Epistemology within a Co-operative Inquiry', 367.
20 Knowles, *The Adult Learner: A Neglected Species*.
21 Bingham, Healey, & Smith, *Global Best Practice in People Development*.

- I learn when I am involved in planning my own development,
- I learn through taking action and reflecting on ways to improve my practice,
- I learn when challenged by problems rather than merely hearing about solutions, and
- I learn when the subject is relevant and is something I care about.

As such, the starting point for learning is the curious interest of the learner. When referring to the gamification of learning, Greenlees[22] explained that 'the key learner question is: *What's in it for me?* This is the starting point for fun, engaging and effective online learning'. This leads to learners realising there is a gap in their knowledge and, thus, causes sufficient curiosity and motivation to fill that gap—which is central to the learning experience. As Schmitt et al. pointed out, 'stimulating curiosity is central to education and learning'.[23]

3. Curiosity and Personalised Stretch Learning

As people tend to believe they know more about something than they actually do, they may need help identifying their information gaps. The nuance is perhaps to withhold simple answers so they can explore and discover for themselves, allowing them to find out what they do not know rather than simply instructing them. Asking learners to 'have a go' and try to figure it out themselves (and then receiving feedback from them) has been shown to significantly raise their level of curiosity in terms of discovering what is next in their learning journey.[24]

Growing research into how adults learn reveals how important 'having a go' is to effective learning:

> [Learning] generally begins with a realisation of current or future need and the motivation to do something about it. This might come from feedback, a mistake, watching other people's reactions, failing or not being up to a task—in other words, from experience.[25]

---

22 Greenlees, *Gamification at WorkStar*.
23 Schmitt & Lahroodi, 'The Epistemic Value of Curiosity', 125–48.
24 Lowenstein, 'The Psychology of Curiosity', 75–98.
25 Lombardo & Eichinger, *The Career Architect Development Planner*, iii.

Theoretically, this is not new or insightful. Thirty-five years ago, Edgar Schon[26] described what the experience of learning in the field should look like:

> The practitioner allows himself to experience surprise, puzzlement, or confusion in a situation which he finds uncertain or unique. He reflects on the phenomenon before him, and on the prior understandings which have been implicit in his behaviour. He carries out an experiment which serves to generate both a new understanding of the phenomenon and a change in the situation.

'Having a go' carries with it curiosity and adventure. With this in mind, Smith and Bingham[27] tested a proof of concept in a large government department to encourage better managerial performance. This involved setting up *stretch assignments* designed to advance employees beyond their existing competency to new levels of professional development. Curiosity and the adventure of discovering new knowledge and skills are strong motivational drivers in the success of stretch learning.

The researchers designed workplace learning experiences that involved being 'stretched' in two directions: depth and breadth (Figure 1). *Depth* refers to increasing the level of responsibility, knowledge, and intensity of work within an area of work already known, and *breadth* refers to broadening work outside of areas of usual work. Accordingly, *depth* increases intensity, and *breadth* broadens experience. While Smith and Bingham[28] found that not every on-the-job learning activity needs to stretch the learner in both these ways, the experiences with the highest impact most certainly involve both dimensions.

---

26 Schon, *The Reflective Practitioner*, 68.
27 Smith & Bingham, *Report on Talent Management for BaptistCare*.
28 Smith & Bingham, *Report on Talent Management for BaptistCare*.

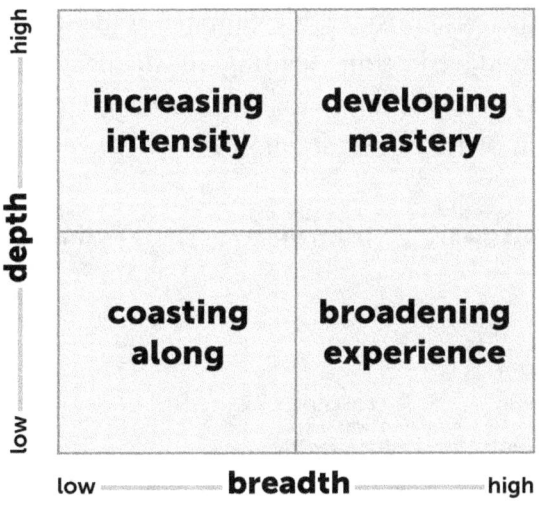

Figure 1. Stretch Learning Matrix.

In this way, the researchers sought to engage learner curiosity to motivate work-based development experiences, as follows:

- Adding different challenges to their current set of responsibilities,
- intentionally focusing on learning from one dimension of the work they are already doing, and/or
- taking on a new role with new responsibilities.

To supplement the application of this model, Smith and Bingham[29] developed and tested a second proof of concept: The *Action Coaching Approach* (Figure 2), where stretch goals are linked to the action learning cycle. Building on the work of Lewin,[30] Reg Revans[31] popularised action learning as an industry-focused system to improve professional practice, where 'the end of learning is action, not knowledge'.[32] Action learning is a form of peer learning and disciplined inquiry,[33] where a group of colleagues work on the real, live challenges they face.

The *Action Coaching* approach is built on iterative cycles of curious questions, usually in the form of the following: What did I *plan* to do? What *action* did I take? What did I observe? What are my *reflections*? Subsequently,

---

29 Smith & Bingham, *Report on Talent Management for BaptistCare*.
30 Lewin, 'Field Theory in Social Science'.
31 Revans, *Action Learning*.
32 Revans, *Action Learning*.
33 Goff, Gregg & May, 'Participatory Action Research'.

the cycle repeats. There is considerable support in the literature for this cyclical process of action and reflection, leading to further inquiry and action for change.[34] The approach investigates reality in order to transform it[35] and equally transforms reality in order to investigate it.[36]

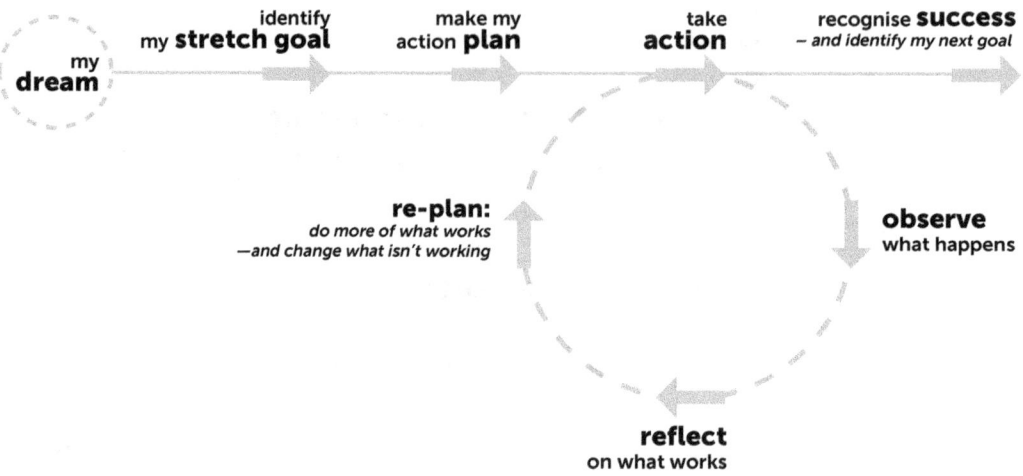

Figure 2. Action Coaching Approach.

Coaching is a very effective way to help people engage in curious learning, as '"learning must be equal to or greater than the rate of change'.[37] In this way, coaching helps the learner remain ahead of the information gap they have. This is described by Rapoport[38] as follows: 'Action research aims to contribute both to the practical concerns of people in an immediate problematic situation and to the goals of social science by joint collaboration within a mutually acceptable ethical framework'.

These two models are heuristic and have proven useful in a variety of settings. This Action Coaching approach, when used in conjunction with the Stretch Learning Matrix, employs the motivation underpinning curiosity and adventure by emphasising the following:

- Learning through action.

---

34 Burns, *Introduction to Research Methods*; Kolb, *Experiential Learning*; Parkin, *Managing Change in Healthcare Using Action Research*; Revans, *Action Learning*.
35 O Fals Borda, 'Investigating Reality in Order to Transform it', 33–55.
36 Kemmis, 'Critical Theory and Participatory Action Research'.
37 Revans, *Action Learning*.
38 Rapoport, 'Three Dilemmas in Action Research', 499.

- A clear alignment of curious learning to the professional skills required of potential employers.
- A focus on inquiry that is adaptive and useful.
- An iterative approach where observation and reflection ignite action and learning.
- It is immediately useful as a reward for curious exploration and discovery.

3. For Curiosity to Thrive, There Must be Safety and Trust

For curiosity to exist among members of a group, there must be trust. Heuristic models such as those espoused here do not function in a low-trust environment. People will not ask questions or imagine new ideas if there is a fear of being humiliated or put down. Teachers should create spaces built on psychological safety and trust, where people can take risks, and even share foolish or silly ideas while being supported, encouraged, and valued. For curiosity to thrive, it must be culturally okay to feel silly or incorrect.

Smith's research with global teams[39] found that, when people work in an environment that lacks trust, they *automatically* slip into a selfish, defensive position. With this negative mindset, many people hoard knowledge and experience, using them as weapons for personal gain rather than sharing knowledge cooperatively for the good of the organisation. Without a doubt, there is a direct positive correlation between the level of trust in a group and the effectiveness of their creativity and productivity.[40] Knowledge truly is power, and any organisation that is hindered by low trust and poor collaboration will be marked by a significant competitive disadvantage.

Fear of retribution kills trust. Without emotional and physical safety, people feel under threat of punitive responses. When leaders are overbearing, bullying, belligerent, or petty, a workplace becomes scary. Where there is the risk of embarrassment, ridicule, or insult, there is no opportunity for trust to flourish. Our brains trigger fear any time we are defensive, cautious, or uncertain. Specifically, when our amygdala is activated, it interferes with the functioning

---

39 Rapoport, 'Three Dilemmas in Action Research', 499
40 Smith, 'Connecting People: Improving Knowledge Sharing and Collaboration'.

of our prefrontal cortex.[41] In other words, we are dumber when we are stressed or afraid. Fear kills curiosity, as does the thought of doing anything that is a step into the unknown.

One way a teacher can help build a culture of trust is by modelling personal vulnerability. This may feel dangerous, but it demonstrates to learners that it is okay to take risks, have some fun, and explore together. Curiosity helps shift the mental frame of learners from 'work', where failure is punished, to 'play', where curiosity and imagination lead to the possibility of new adventures in learning. This sense of wonder at the unknown is crucial to learning, improvement, creativity, and innovation.

While trust is relational and grows slowly over time, it can also diminish quickly. This is why it is so important for those who are creating learning experiences to make it an absolute priority —whether online, in the classroom, or in the workplace. In this way, the most effective teachers work to ignite the curiosity of their learners to assist them on their journey of discovery.

4. Curiosity is Essential in Transformative Learning

Broadly speaking, there have been two dominant theories of learning. The *teacher-centred positivist* approach, which is grounded in the theory of behaviourism by Skinner, positions the learner as a passive empty vessel waiting to be filled by the expert with prescribed knowledge.[42] In contrast, the *learner-centred constructionist* approach, based on the theory of constructivism by Piaget,[43] positions learners as actively directing the development of their own knowledge creation through curious inquiry and drawing from personal experience with input from a broad range of sources. For Piaget, curiosity led to exploratory behaviour and was vital to childhood cognitive development.[44]

The behaviourist 'classroom-focused' approach has dominated education for centuries. In recent decades, however, constructivist approaches have gained popularity. This has been driven in part by the industry's growing need to solve

---

41 The prefrontal cortex controls our executive functioning. Among other things, this part of the brain helps us think clearly, explore possibilities, differentiate conflicting thoughts, predict outcomes, determine good and bad, and suppress unacceptable behaviours to avoid negative social outcomes.
42 Sagal, *Skinner's Philosophy*.
43 Piaget, *Studies in Reflecting Abstraction*.
44 Gorlitz, 'Exploration and Attribution'.

complex problems quickly and ensure learning can be applied to real-world business needs.[45] Constructivism is essentially 'a view of learning in which learners use their own experiences to construct understandings that make sense to them, rather than having understanding delivered to them in an already organised form'.[46]

Constructivist approaches usually begin with a problem to be solved or a current practice to be improved. All such approaches attempt to reverse traditional teaching methods, moving learners from a *passive* to an *active* position (i.e. constructivist) and emphasising self-directed and collaborative learning. This positions the role of the instructor as a facilitator of the learning process rather than being directly responsible for inputting information. Without curiosity, constructivist learning fails. There is wide support in the literature for the constructivist approach, where the deepest learning is achieved through (1) exposure to rich experiences, (2) opportunity to practice, (3) conversation and exchanges with others, and (4) reflection on action.

Curiosity is an essential dimension of this kind of active learning. Building on the foundational principles of learning theories such as experiential learning,[47] action learning,[48] reflective practice,[49] adult learning,[50] and transformational learning,[51] it is evident curiosity does not occur from the outside-in but, rather, from the inside-out. Accordingly, the role of a leader, manager, teacher, or coach is to create an environment conducive to curiosity.

5. The Advantages of Curious Learning

Constructivism is a child of curiosity. When we are curious, we are more resourceful. We ask more questions, such as what can I do to be better? Are there different ways I can solve this problem? Consequently, we naturally come up with interesting and innovative ideas. In this way, the following ensues:

- Curiosity quickly builds rapport, trust, and relationship quality.[52]

---

45 Revans, *Action Learning*.
46 Kauchak & Eggen, *Learning and Teaching*, 184.
47 Kolb, *Experiential Learning*.
48 Lewin, 'Field Theory in Social Science'.
49 Schon, *The Reflective Practitioner*.
50 Knowles, *The Adult Learner*.
51 Mezirow, *Transformative Dimensions of Adult Learning*.
52 Kashdan &. Roberts, 'Trait and State Curiosity in the Genesis of Intimacy', 792–816.

- Curiosity lures us out of our comfort zone. The unknown is not as scary when curiosity enables us to peek into the darkness, and while we know there will be surprises, our fear is overpowered by our curiosity as a result of our desire to discover something new.
- Curiosity helps us to frame difficult discussions in a friendly manner—for example, stating 'I'm curious about why you did it that way' is easier (and will likely be better received) than stating 'Why did you do it like that?'
- Curiosity advances empathy in professional carers (e.g. doctors, nurses, psychologists, and pastors),[53] as it helps us appreciate people's personal circumstances and perspectives.
- Curiosity improves workplace learning and increases job performance.[54]
- Curiosity allows us to be more solution-focused. It helps us explore possibilities and see things from different perspectives. For example, asking 'How can I improve that?' leads to innovation and new ways of facing the future.
- Curiosity helps improve our enjoyment of life and satisfaction with living.[55]
- Curiosity helps us find peace. When we are willing to stand in someone else's shoes, we can better understand the perspectives of others in a way that diminishes conflict and misunderstandings.
- Curiosity builds resilience and helps us manage change. Furthermore, it focuses us on the adventure of what might be ahead rather than on a fear of the unknown.
- Curiosity can enhance self-awareness—the key to personal learning. When we feel free to look within and be vulnerable, honest, and willing to question who we really are and what truly motivates us, we are then ready to learn and grow.

6. Moving from Curiosity to Learning to Action

Albert Einstein once said, 'I have no special talents. I am only passionately curious'.[56]

---

53 Halpern, *From Detached Concern to Empathy*.
54 Reio Jr. & Wiswell, 'Field Investigation of the Relationship among Adult Curiosity, Workplace Learning, and Job Performance', 5–30.
55 Kashdan, Rose & Fincham, 'Curiosity and Exploration', 291–305.
56 Albert Einstein, *Letter to Carl Seelig*, 39–013.

Curiosity is an important building block in engaging learners online, in the workplace, or in the classroom. Curiosity-based learning needs to be discussed further as a core component of modern andragogy. Curiosity is the vehicle by which the open-minded travel to undiscovered countries, explore different possibilities, and make world-changing discoveries. Curiosity fuels imagination and wonder as we are stretched fearlessly into the unknown.

This chapter explored curiosity as a motivator for lifelong learning, whether online, in the classroom, or in the workplace. It also explored information gap theory, the importance of safety and trust, and stretch learning in the workplace. Two heuristic models were introduced: The *Stretch Learning Matrix* and the *Action Coaching Approach*. Both approaches are powered by curiosity as a strong motivating force to be unleashed by those teachers and leaders who wish to lead individuals on an adventure of learning and discovery.

Bibliography

Augustine. *Confessions* (Middlesex: Penguin Books, 1961).

Ball, P. *Curiosity: How Science Became Interested in Everything* (Chicago, IL: University of Chicago Press, 2013).

Berlyne, D. E. *Conflict, Arousal, and Curiosity* (New York, NY: McGraw Hill, 1960).

Bingham, M., Healey, S. & Smith, S. *Global Best Practice in People Development* (Sydney, NSW: Robertson and Chang, 2014).

Burns, R. *Introduction to Research Methods* (Sydney, NSW: Addison Wesley Longman, 1996).

Byron, L. *Don Juan: In Sixteen Cantos* (Halifax: Milner and Sowerby, 1837).

Craik F. & Lockhart, R. 'Levels of Processing: A Framework for Memory Research', *Journal of Verbal Learning and Verbal Behavior* 11 (1972), 671-84.

Einstein, A. *Letter to Carl Seelig* (Letter, March 11, 1952) Einstein Archives 39-013.

Fals Borda, O. 'Investigating Reality in Order to Transform it: The Colombian Experience', *Dialectical Anthropology* 4 (1979), 33-55.

Fowler, H. *Curiosity and Exploratory Behaviour* (New York, NY: Macmillan, 1965).

Franken, R. E. *Human Motivation* (3rd ed; California, US: Brooks/Cole, 1994).

Ginsberg, S.M. '"Mind the Gap" in the Classroom', *Journal of Effective Teaching* 10 (2010), 74-80.

Goff, S., Gregg, J. & May, K. 'Participatory Action Research: Change Management in the "No Go" Zone', in Sankaran, S., Dick, B., Passfield, R. & Swepson, P. (eds.), *Effective Change Management using Action Learning and Action Research* (Lismore, NSW: Southern Cross University Press, 2001): 83-94.

Gorlitz, D. 'Exploration and attribution', in Gorlitz, D. & Wohlwill, J.F. (eds.), *Curiosity, Imagination, and Play: On the Development of Spontaneous Cognitive and Motivational Processes* (Mahwah, NJ: Lawrence Erlbaum Associates, 1987).

Greenlees, M. *Gamification at WorkStar* (Sydney, NSW: Catalyst6, 2015).

Guo, S., Zhang, G. & Zhai, R. 'A Potential Way of Enquiry into Human Curiosity', *British Journal of Educational Technology* 41.3 (2010), E48-E52.

Halpern, J. *From Detached Concern to Empathy: Humanizing Medical Practice* (London, UK: Oxford University Press, 2001).

Handy, C. 'Trust and the Virtual Organisation', *Harvard Business Review* 72.3.

Heron, J. *Co-operative Inquiry: Research into the Human Condition* (London, UK: Sage, 1996).

Heron, J & Reason, P. 'Extending Epistemology within a Co-operative Inquiry', in Reason, P. & Bradbury, H. (eds.), *The Sage Handbook of Action Research: Participative Inquiry and Practice* (London, UK: Sage, 2008): 199-210.

Homer. 'Odyssey', Book XI. 13, in Murray, A. (translator) *Odyssey Books 1–12* (Cambridge, UK: Harvard University Press, Loen Classical Library, 1995).

Kashdan, T. B & Silvia, P. J. 'Curiosity and Interest: The Benefits of Thriving on Novelty and Challenge', in *Oxford Handbook of Positive Psychology* (2nd ed; New York, NY: Oxford University Press, 2009): 367-374.

Kashdan, T. B. & Roberts, J. 'Trait and State Curiosity in the Genesis of Intimacy: Differentiation from Related Constructs', *Journal of Social and Clinical Psychology* 23.6 (2004): 792-816.

Kashdan, T. B., Rose, P. & Fincham, F. D. 'Curiosity and Exploration: Facilitating Positive Subjective Experiences and Personal Growth Opportunities', *Journal of Personality Assessment* 82.3 (2004), 291-305.

Kauchak, D & Eggen, P. *Learning and Teaching: Research-Based Methods* (Boston: Allyn & Bacon, 1998).

Kemmis, S. 'Critical Theory and Participatory Action Research', in Reason, P. & Brabury, H. (eds.) *The Sage Handbook of Action Research: Participative Inquiry and Practice* (London, UK: Sage, 2008): 199-210.

Knowles, M. *The Adult Learner: A Neglected Species* (3rd ed; Houston, US: Gulf Publishing, 1984).

Kolb, D. *Experiential Learning. Experience as the Source of Learning and Development* (Englewood Cliffs: Prentice-Hall, 1984).

Lewin, K. F. *Theory in Social Science: Selected Theoretical Papers* (New York, NY: Harper & Row, 1951).

Lombardo, M. & Eichinger, R. *The Career Architect Development Planner* (Boston, US: Center for Creative Leadership, 2010).

Lowenstein, G. 'The Psychology of Curiosity: A Review and Reinterpretation', *Psychology Bulletin* 116.1 (1994), 75-98.

Marton F. & Saljo, R. 'On Qualitative Differences in Learning: Outcome and Process', *British Journal of Educational Psychology* 46 (1976), 4–11.

Mezirow, J. *Transformative Dimensions of Adult Learning* (San Francisco, CA: Jossey Bass, 1991).

Parkin, P. *Managing Change in Healthcare Using Action Research* (London, UK: Sage, 2009).

Piaget, J. *Studies in Reflecting Abstraction* (Hove: Psychology Press, 2001).

Rapoport, R.N. Three Dilemmas in Action Research', *Human Relations* 23 (1970).

Reason, P. & Bradbury, H. *Handbook of Action Research* (London, UK: Sage, 2001).

Reio, T. G. Jr. & Wiswell, A. 'Field Investigation of the Relationship among Adult Curiosity, Workplace Learning, and Job Performance', *Human Resource Development Quarterly* 11.1 (2000), 5-30.

von Renesse, C. & Ecke, V. 'Teaching Inquiry with a Lens toward Curiosity', *Problems, Resources, and Issues in Mathematics Undergraduate Studies* 27.1 (2017), 148-164.

Revans, R. W. *Action Learning: New Techniques for Management* (London, UK: Blond & Briggs, 1980).

Revans, R. *Action Learning* (Bromley: Chartwell Bratt, 1982).

Sagal, P. *Skinner's Philosophy* (Washington, US: University Press of America, 1981).

Schmitt F. & Lahroodi, R. 'The Epistemic Value of Curiosity', *Educational Theory* 8 (2008), 125-48.

Schon, D. *The Reflective Practitioner* (New York, NY: Basic Books, 1983).

Smith, S. 'Connecting People: Improving Knowledge Sharing and Collaboration' (PhD thesis, Southern Cross University, 2003).

Smith, S. & Bingham, M. *Report on Talent Management for BaptistCare: 70:20:10 Initiatives for Continuous Learning* (Sydney, NSW: Robertson and Chang, 2016).

Stephen Smith
Australian College of Ministries
ssmith@acom.edu.au

Murray Bingham
The Colloquium Group
murray@colloquiumgroup.com

Catherine Kleemann
Australian College of Ministries
ckleemann@acom.edu.au

28 | SHOULD MINISTERS BE GRADUATES ANYWAY?

Abstract

The question this essay addresses has been one asked frequently within Churches of Christ from the arrival of that religious tradition in Australia to quite recent times. The subject is approached historically from the viewpoint of that tradition because Churches of Christ is in many ways quite different from what are usually termed the 'mainstream denominations'. Churches of Christ are the Australian embodiment of the Restoration Movement, which had its origins in both the United Kingdom and the United States in the closing decades of the eighteenth and the early decades of the nineteenth centuries. While the movement embraces elements of Evangelical Protestantism, it is first and foremost Restorationist. The essay does not address that differentiation, but suffice it to say the tradition has a different outlook.

1. Introduction

On my study wall, there hangs a college diploma. On it is the statement 'having completed a prescribed course of study in the Bible College and having maintained a good Christian character during his connection therewith'.[1] For Churches of Christ, Christian character is important for ministry. This essay

---

1   This statement is found on the unaccredited Diploma of Ministry issued to every graduate of the college, now known as the Australian College of Ministry, from 1942 until the formation of the Sydney College of Divinity. From then, the diploma was issued only to students without the necessary qualification to undertake a Bachelor of Theology degree.

provides an explanation for that statement.

An unashamed historical approach is taken to this study. The way in which one religious tradition has dealt with the question of theological education and training is traced from the various origins of the Restoration Movement to its present-day expression in Australia, and New South Wales in particular.

2. How It All Began

The Restoration Movement developed in parallel in the United States and in Great Britain.[2] Thomas Campbell, an Irish Presbyterian clergyman, who migrated to the United States in 1807, delivered the defining document of the Churches of Christ, *The Declaration and Address*, to the Christian Association of Washington on 17 August 1809.[3] In it, he presented thirteen propositions, the summation of which is a plea for Christian unity on the basis of restoring the New Testament church with the Scriptures as the sole authority for faith and practice. Two of the notions that emerged from the address are the importance of the priesthood of all believers (mutual ministry) and the autonomy of the local church. The latter has been a blessing and a curse, but has a place in this discussion. A third notion was the disavowal of what they termed a 'clergy class'.

Thomas Campbell's son and successor, Alexander, was loved and revered. His intellect, his years of labour and self-sacrifice, and his method of work all commended themselves. To promote the ideals of *The Declaration and Address*, he established an educational department in his great scheme. From his home in Bethany, Virginia, came many of the leading evangelists in the early days of the movement, among them those who became the teachers at the College of the Bible, Lexington, Kentucky; and 'though the great founder passed to his grave, his glorious work moved on with most triumphant march'.[4] Ministerial education in the community was from the outset part of the American scene. In Great Britain, it was quite different. The movement educated its ministers on an apprenticeship model.[5] These differences are noticeable in Australia.

---

2   For a brief account of the origins of Churches of Christ see Elliott, *Bridge Builders in Restoration*. The appendix is an abridged version of the thirteen propositions of the *Declaration and Address*.
3   Campbell, *Declaration and Address*, 15-17.
4   Kingsbury, 'What Steps Must We Take'.
5   Breward. "Historical Perspectives on Theological Education in Australia", 9. The British churches moved away from the apprenticeship model and started Overdale College (1920) of which the sometime principal was the astute theologian William Robinson.

3. Early Days in Australia

When Britain lost the American colonies, she turned her eyes to the recently 'discovered' Great South Land. After all, she had to find somewhere to house her unwanted convicts. The history of Churches of Christ in Australia may be summarised thus: 'the British churches planted, United States evangelists watered, God gave the increase'.[6]

By the time the Restoration Movement arrived in Australia in the 1850s, the denominations had already established patterns of ministerial education having 'a variety of models from which to choose'.[7] By the close of the Nineteenth Century, the Catholics (1838), Church of England (1856), Congregationalists (1864), Presbyterians (1873), and Baptists (1891) had all established colleges to train their ministers. However, the initial action was to import clergy from the 'old country'.[8]

The origin of the Churches of Christ in every Australian colony was British, and in its early days, Churches of Christ in Sydney was very British and essentially a lay movement; its preachers were not college graduates. The same held true throughout the Commonwealth. However, in the last third of the Nineteenth Century, Victoria and South Australian had the benefit of American graduate evangelists. One of them, Thomas Gore, trained George Moysey on the apprenticeship model in 1872 in Adelaide.[9]

Churches of Christ in Sydney had its birth in 1853 when Albert Griffin and Henry Mitchell set up the 'Lord's Table' in the former's grocery store on the corner of Goulburn and Pitt Streets, Sydney. Griffin was influenced by reading tracts from St. Pancras Church of Christ, London. Others joined the small group, and soon a church was established that met first in Newtown and then in Enmore.[10] From 1853 to December 1864, there was no evangelist, as they were later to call their ministers, until the church 'set aside one of their number, Edward Lewis, as evangelist'.[11] The movement in New South Wales did not

---

6   Stephenson, 'Where Two Streams Met', 6.
7   Breward, 'Historical Perspectives', 9.
8   For a fuller discussion on the development of theological education in Australia, see the articles by Ian Breward and Stuart Piggin in Treloar, *The Furtherance of Religious Beliefs,* and Banks 'Fifty Years of Theology in Australia'.
9   *Australian Christian Standard* 1 (1885): 62.
10   The early history of Churches of Christ in Australia is discussed in Picton, 'Primitive Christianity in New South Wales', 206; Davies, E. *The Story of an Earnest Life*, 348f.; Elliott, *Bridge Builders in Restoration*, 28-46; Stephenson, *Victories of a Century*, 11-17; Chapman, *No Other Foundation*, 2-160;
11   Hayward, and Nutt, *Enmore Incorporated*, 5.

receive its first graduate Australian evangelists until 1887 in the persons of Charles Forscutt and Peter Dickson, both of whom had studied at the College of the Bible, Lexington, Kentucky. George Walden and Thomas Bagley, also Lexington graduates, joined them in the 1890s. The movement relied very much on Mutual Improvement Societies and bible classes. Thomas Bagley and George Walden got their start in both places. The centrality in the worship of the Lord's Supper and lay presidency militated against the graduate ministry.

Churches continued to be planted in city and country with laymen as their evangelists, and by 1905, New South Wales had eighteen churches with ten full-time evangelists of whom three were graduates. The other eight churches were all led by 'preaching brethren'. Throughout the Australian colonies, there were 152 churches with eighty-eight evangelists, of whom fourteen were graduates, twelve American, and two British trained.[12]

Did even three graduates make a difference in New South Wales? The 1908 Annual Conference Report quoted some growth statistics. For the five years from 1898 to 1903, the membership in New South Wales increased by forty-nine per cent. This was due almost entirely to the growth of three churches: Enmore, City Temple, and Paddington, all with graduate evangelists. So, yes, it did make a difference. For the years 1903 to 1908, the increase was ninety-one per cent.[13] This upsurge corresponded with the arrival of five additional graduates of the College of the Bible, Lexington, Kentucky. These young Australians brought with them two things: the ability to organise and the capacity to communicate effectively. They also brought American methods such as the 'protracted meeting' and the tent mission.[14]

The churches were delighted to have them, but they did not displace the practice of appointing non-graduate evangelists. An illustration of this is that in 1905, the Lismore Church of Christ members decided on a forward movement into the surrounding district. They reported it thus:

> During the week we had our quarterly business meeting, and we decided on a forward movement by engaging one of our local men

---

12 The figures are extracted from the Annual Conference statistics published in the *Australian Christian* volumes 1-8.
13 *Australian Christian* 11.18 (30 April 1908), 232.
14 These were George Walden (1898), Thomas Bagley (1905), Horace Kingsbury (1905), Arthur Day (1905), and George Verco (1906). Walden remained at Enmore for sixteen years and, during that time, had over 1000 additions to the Church. Bagley planted two significant churches and had a term as State Evangelist.

to labour in word and doctrine for three days every week in the outlying districts of the Richmond and Brunswick Rivers. The one chosen [Ethelbert Davis] is a man of considerable ability, of good character and has the confidence of the whole church.[15]

This was local autonomy in action and was replicated in numerous churches across the Commonwealth. Character and proficiency were all that was needed. But the American 'bug' was catching. For the years 1902 to 1907, forty-eight young men, many of whom were already engaged in church ministry, travelled the path to the United States from all States of the Commonwealth: ten were from New South Wales.[16] In 1905, there were twelve Australian men at Lexington. But there were problems with this: six came home to minister, two of whom went back and forth to the United States. Six never returned, and the Australian churches could ill-afford the loss of such talent. Nevertheless, the teachers at Lexington, James McGarvey in particular, exercised an ongoing influence in Australia. McGarvey's *Commentary on Acts* was used at Glen Iris until the late 1930s. Gordon Stirling, a vice-principal of the College of the Bible at Glen Iris, remarked that the commentary was 'like using the Bible until something better turned up'.

There was a societal aspect to it as well. Higher education was not a concomitant part of the level of society that Churches of Christ reached. The members were mostly lower-middle-class, although there were wealthy upper-middle-class businessmen who focussed on things other than education. The Enmore Board of Officers had eight of Sydney's leading businessmen on it. They were not anti-intellectual, but they were not overly interested in higher education either. Still, there were highly educated men among them: veterinarians, doctors, lawyers, etc.[17] This group recognised the loss to New South Wales of the ten young men who had once been in local church ministry.

---

15 *Australian Christian* 8.45 (1905), 590.
16 *Australian Christian* 8.11 (1905), 133.
17 Hon. David Hall, for example, was a barrister who served two terms in the New South Wales Legislative Assembly, as Minister for Housing and then as Minister for Justice. He was also a New South Wales Senator in the Federal Parliament. John Hindle, owner of Samuel Taylor Pty Ltd, also served a term in the State Parliament.

4. Impetus to a Graduate Ministry

The need for a critical level of membership to support the capital costs of a training institution hindered progress. However, along with the growth of membership in Churches of Christ emerged an awareness of the need for better ministerial education. The practice of 'mutual edification' or the preaching of biblically literate but untrained elders was not adequate in a more sophisticated and better-educated society. It must be understood that Churches of Christ had, and still have, a high view of eldership. Leaders across the Commonwealth began to discuss what could be done to stem the losses and address societal expectations.

The outcome was a symposium held in March 1905 in Melbourne. The subject addressed was 'What Steps Must We Take to Prevent Our Young Men Going to America to Study?'[18] Ten evangelists, of whom two were graduates of American colleges, gave addresses. David Ewers expressed the underlying feeling thus:

> Let evangelists, church officers and others rouse the whole [movement] by voice and pen to a realisation of the serious loss sustained by the Australian Churches through the manufacture of the cream of their intellectual youth into butter *for American consumption.*[19]

All ten speakers supported the establishment of a College of the Bible in Australia. Character and biblical literacy were still important, but proficiency was to be enhanced by education. The solution? Apply a counter-irritant in the form of active work—give the young men, as much as possible, the same opportunities for preaching and studying as they would have had in America. The outcome? In 1907, the College of the Bible was established in Melbourne under the leadership of Henry Harward, a native of Bendigo, but a graduate of Eureka College in the United States. His assistant, James Johnston, MA, from South Australia, was a Lexington graduate. Harward's resignation in 1910 produced an interesting dichotomy. His replacement, Alexander Main, was a Masters graduate in Arts from the Melbourne University but had no formal theological education. His vice-principal, Thomas Scambler, was a graduate of

---

18 *Australian Christian* 8.14 (1905), 173-178. The issue contained short extracts from the speeches.
19 *Australian Christian* 8.14 (1905), 173. David Ewers was one of the early untrained evangelists. His son, William Ewers, was a graduate of the College of the Bible, Lexington, Kentucky. Hence, David Ewers's stated position.

one of the movement's American theological colleges. This was to cause some tension between them.

5. Progress to a Fully Graduate Ministry

With the establishment of the College, were people still asking 'Should ministers be graduates anyway?' For some, the answer was 'Well, yes'. For others, it was 'No'. To bolster the view that graduate ministers were 'a good thing', the college number of the *Australian Christian* in 1921 contained a double-page spread of photographs and names of college graduates who had gained university successes. There are seven with completed degrees and eleven in their final university year.[20] All had started on their university courses while in college. Ernest Hinrichsen, one of the Churches of Christ's leading tent evangelists, commented in September 1923:

> In these days one would think that such an institution as the College of the Bible too well understood and appreciated to be quibbled about in the question box. We have many 'speaking brethren', but too often the one least qualified is most anxious to exhort.[21]

Clearly, there was still some strength in the position that the minister did not need to be a graduate. In New South Wales, for example, in 1929, there were fifty-six churches. Of these, thirty-nine had ministers and, of that number, twenty-five were graduates and fourteen non-graduates. 'Preaching brethren' led the seventeen churches without paid ministers. In that year, the College of the Bible celebrated its twenty-first birthday, and Charles Vawter, from the United States, visited Sydney for a series of tent missions.

In an article entitled 'The Importance of College Training',[22] Vawter entered wholeheartedly into the debate. He countered the argument that three characteristics alone made for a good minister: spirituality, energy, and eloquence. While acknowledging their value, he concluded that to excel in them was not essential to success. He wrote:

---

20 Australian Christian 23.37 (1921), 594-595.
21 *Australian Christian* 26.38 (1923)m 602. Hinrichsen was a graduate of the College of the Bible, Glen Iris, Melbourne.
22 Vawter, 'The Importance of College Training', 615. The immediate following quotations, unless indicated otherwise, are from this article.

> I find that the man who leads is always one whose native ability has been given power by good training, and that this training is practically always that which is afforded by a good college or university. The uneducated preacher never reaches the top.

In essence, he argues that while the three characteristics are a great asset, education is necessary. He further observes that in the 'old times', when schools were rarer and fewer people were educated, it was different. But now that every child had to go to school for some time, and many went through to university, the religious leaders must be educated. He was realistic enough to note that 'some Bible colleges deepen faith and some shatter it. Some develop men spiritually as well as mentally, while others destroy spiritually'.

He refuted the argument that college graduates would look for soft jobs and avoid the hard fields by citing an example of the opposite. Vawter wrote:

> In New South Wales I know a young man who was trained in the College of the Bible at Glen Iris. He went to a little church with nine members. They had no building, and no block on which to build. They had twenty-five shillings in their treasury, and they had already been saving for some months to get that much ahead. They now have a good, strong, self-supporting church, and in the course of time will have their own building. That young man faced discouragement and accepted heartache, and he did it uncomplainingly. He was a hard student, a good speaker and had extraordinary musical ability. He is big enough for any pulpit anywhere. He could have made, as a musician, many times the salary he received as a preacher. But through college trained, he didn't dodge the hardest place. His name is Roy Greenhalgh.

Roy Greenhalgh went on to fulfil Vawter's assessment that 'he is big enough for any pulpit anywhere'. In his ministerial career, he filled two of the prime ministerial appointments in Australian Churches of Christ. Further, as Youth Director in New South Wales for twenty years, he influenced several generations of young graduates, this writer included. To character and eloquence, Vawter added commitment as essential. His was a useful contributor to the debate, but it did not settle the issue.

A misunderstanding of a more critical approach to Scripture was one of the drivers of the continuing opposition. To talk about the critical methods was considered to be 'modernism'. This view clung on tenaciously, and almost ten years later, a motion was put to a Federal Conference 'that all regular lecturers in Biblical and Doctrinal subjects at the College from 1938 onwards shall be fundamentalist rather than modernist in their view of Biblical interpretation'.[23] This attitude was much more prevalent in New South Wales and Queensland, states that did not have the benefit of the graduate American evangelists in their foundational days.[24] Some used the 'modernist' fear to argue that a graduate from such an institution might lead the flock astray.

The idea that the College of the Bible might be 'liberal' or 'modernist' in its teaching and practice took hold in New South Wales and Queensland. It was mere perception, but it led to distrust. Ultimately, the opinion-formers in New South Wales decided that the time had arrived for a college in their state that would have 'restoration' as its guiding principle. One of the instigators, a College of the Bible, Glen Iris, graduate remarked: 'An expanding communion needs a College loyal to the New Testament'.[25] In 1942, the Woolwich Bible College, now Australian College of Ministries, was established.

There were now two colleges preparing men and women for ministry, whether for home or overseas. And there were two faculties, each of which was an amalgam of graduate and non-graduate lecturers.

The first intake of the Bible College of New South Wales numbered nine. Eight of them were already 'preaching brethren' in smaller churches, and all in the city. At the time, there were thirteen non-graduate ministers in the state from a total of forty-two.[26] Fast-forward forty years to 1982 and the situation was only slightly different. There were still eight ministers without any formal theological education.[27] Local autonomy was still strong.

---

23 *Federal Conference Reports* 1938, 73. 'Fundamentalist' meant 'conservative'. Churches of Christ in Australia were not greatly affected by the Fundamentalist Movement *per se*, although it influenced a few individuals.
24 During the thirty years from 1868 to 1898, Victoria enjoyed the ministries of T.J. Gore, H.S. Earl, J.J. Halley, O.A. Carr, G.L. Surber, A.G. Bennett, and A.B. Maston after lengthy stays. All trained at the Lexington College of the Bible. Only Carr and Halley ministered briefly in New South Wales. None of them ministered in Queensland. With the exception of Gore and Maston, all returned to the United States.
25 Nutt, *A Crucible of Faith and Learning*, 23.
26 There were still six American-trained graduates ministering in New South Wales' churches. All bar one had studied before 1905.
27 This figure is drawn from the list of ministers in the *New South Wales Annual Conference Reports*, 1982, 58-65.

6. Acceptance of a Graduate Ministry

The next move towards a fully graduate ministry came in 1982 with the advent of the Sydney College of Divinity. It cost the board and faculty of the New South Wales College a considerable amount of time and effort to convince their constituency of the value of a theological college whose students could study for a degree.[28] Permission was given, nevertheless, certain constraints were laid upon the College: a course of study true to the principles of the Restoration Movement and the development of Christian character.[29] There was, however, a sociological aspect to the College's desire to join the Sydney College of Divinity. Education in broader society was changing. Australian society had become aspirational. A university degree was now a desired educational outcome. The educational level of congregations was rising, and it was considered that the minister needed to be as well-educated as the society at large and with most of his congregation. For too long, the movement had been swimming against the tide.

Do we need a college, and should ministers be graduates anyway? The question was asked in the 1980s because it was known that there were a few who would answer in the negative. There were still those who objected to a college-educated man or woman. They feared the creation of a 'clergy class' and had visions of the movement drifting. They were sincere, in many cases having a strong belief in the 'priesthood of all believers', and they could not be put on one side with a wave of the hand or pen.

That there were some grounds for the fears under certain circumstances was conceded. But that those circumstances existed was not admitted. What they feared was the creation of a class known as ministers, evangelists, pastors, preachers, or anything else who, because of intellectual standing, demanded a right to be heard above others.

A breadth of vision is one of the essentials of a successful minister, and this is not so readily developed in the isolation of the average local congregation. When those who are seeking the same goal get together in the environment of a college, their mutual cooperation, with the natural interchange of ideas, has one result only; that is, to broaden their vision. No minister has a right to be a sectarian in these days, and the college graduate is less likely to be such.

---

28 This battle had been fought and won in Victoria many years before when the College of the Bible at Glen Iris joined the Melbourne College of Divinity.
29 Initially, students had a choice between taking a degree or the unaccredited Diploma of Ministry. Degree students were required to take practical elements of the Diploma.

7. A Change in Emphasis

When a fully graduate ministry was accepted, further questions began to be heard: What type of graduate ministry do we need? What of the student who struggles to pass the varying subjects that must be taken to graduate, but who has a spiritual gift of evangelism? Does such a person need to be a graduate to be effective in ministry? The writer has known several who barely passed their college course at diploma level but still turned out to be very effective in ministry. To them, the major benefit of their college experience related to the practical side of ministry. Thus, there began agitation for different 'streams' within the college program: pastoral, youth, missionary, evangelistic, etc. And what of the character and spirituality aspects?

They are good questions, and the Churches of Christ colleges continue to grapple with them. Formation, once rejected by the constituency as being 'a catholic thing', has now found acceptance and become integral to all ministerial training. Units on spirituality are taught as core even in management degrees.

Should a minister be a graduate? While I value the worth of a theologically literate person without a theological education—I know a specialist medical doctor who is as theologically literate as I am—I believe that in this day and age, the minister of a congregation should be a graduate. The function of the college is to educate those who go there to the high calling of Word and Sacrament, and to that end, imparts to them the higher standard of education, both religious and technical, which is calculated to enable them to minister in a capable and effective manner.

However, their education must not cease with graduation. Life-long learning has to be an essential part of their ministerial experience. If this is the case, then they will always be on the path of deeper learning that goes beyond mere formal study.

Conclusion

Do we need colleges? If we need ministers, we certainly do. The days through which we are passing are days when ministers capable of commanding the respect of those to whom pronouncements are made must follow up any pronouncement on matters of faith. Ministers must be able to commend the Word they proclaim, first of all in their life and character, as well as in the way in which they present their message. Faith is not simply a matter of education, but it comes publicly with greater force from an educated person.

Preachers cannot advise young men or women to this service as they might advise concerning ordinary business or professional life. The work, the demands, the equipment, and the rewards are not the same. No mistake is quite so serious as the mistake made in connection with the ministry of the Word. To enter this work with a false estimate of oneself, or through the urgent persuasion of indiscreet friends, is bound to lead to disappointment and disaster.

But, if a young man or woman has a natural gift of speech, physical health to endure the strain, mental equipment for the task, a great love for Jesus Christ, a great passion for the souls of men, and a yearning, longing desire to preach the gospel, then I say, 'Yes', they should give themselves to the work of the ministry and undertake the education it requires.

We need ministers of the soul; ministers with a heart to their people's distress, and 'soul' and 'heart' should be fostered in the college. We need more and more ministers, who in an age of doubt proclaim both salvation and the force of the Word of God in the world, those who will command the respect and confidence of their people because of their zeal, loyalty, faith, and piety. Colleges should keep such an ideal before every student.

Bibliography

Banks, R., 'Fifty Years of Theology in Australia, 1915–1965', *Colloquium* 9.1 (1976), 36-42.

Breward, I. 'Historical Perspectives on Theological Education in Australia', in Treloar, G. (ed.), *The Furtherance of Religious Beliefs* (Sydney, NSW: EHAA, 1997): 8-23.

Campbell, T. *Declaration and Address* (Birmingham, UK: Berean Press, 1951): 15-17.

Chapman, G.E. *No Other Foundation—A Documentary History of Churches of Christ in Australia Vol. I 1846–1864*, 2-160

Davies, E. *The Story of an Earnest Life* (Cincinnati, US: Central Book Concern, 1881): 348f.

Elliott, A.G. *Bridge Builders in Restoration* (Sydney, NSW: Christian Unity Committee, 1970).

Federal Conference Reports. 1938, 73.

Hayward, H.E. & Nutt, D. *Enmore Incorporated* (Sydney, NSW: Freshhope, 2014): 5.

Kingsbury, H. 'What Steps Must We Take to Prevent Our Young Men Going to America to Study?' *Australian Christian* 8.14 (1905), 173.

New South Wales Annual Conference Reports. 1982, 58-65.

Nutt, D.C. *A Crucible of Faith and Learning* (Sydney, NSW: ACOM Press, 2017): 23.

Picton, H.G. 'Primitive Christianity in New South Wales', *Christian Pioneer* (1897), 206.

Piggin, S. 'A History of Theological Education in Australia', in Treloar, G. (ed.), *The Furtherance of Religious Beliefs* (Sydney, NSW: EHAA, 1997): 24-43.

Stephenson, A.W. *Victories of a Century* (Melbourne, VIC: Vital Publications, 1984): 11-17.

Stephenson, A.W. 'Where Two Streams Met', *Christian Messenger* 49.4 (1972), 6.

Vawter, C.R.L. 'The Importance of College Training', *Australian Christian* 32.39 (1929), 615.

Dennis Nutt
Australian College of Ministries
pdnutt@bigpond.com

29 | EPILOGUE: THEOLOGICALLY-SHAPED CHARACTER IN AN INCREASINGLY POLARIZED ENVIRONMENT

PETER G. BOLT

Upon request, the master teacher taught his closest learners to pray (Matt 6:9–13; Luke 11:1–4):

> Our Father in heaven,
> [...] Your kingdom come,
> Your will be done on earth as it is in heaven [...]
> And deliver us from the Evil One.

The benevolent Father in heaven, now known once and for all time by the appearing of his Son on earth, stands ready to receive our prayers — 'more ready to hear than we to pray, and to give more than we either desire or deserve'.[1] The benevolent character of our Father in heaven, now known once and for all time by the appearing of his Son on earth, then becomes the basis of our prayer that the character of life on earth might come to reflect (however imperfectly) his character as it is known (so perfectly) in heaven. For although the content

---

1   *Book of Common Prayer* (1662), Collect for 12th Sunday after Trinity: 'Almighty and everlasting God, who art always more ready to hear than we to pray, and art wont to give more than either we desire, or deserve; Pour down upon us the abundance of thy mercy; forgiving us those things whereof our conscience is afraid, and giving us those good things which we are not worthy to ask, but through the merits and mediation of Jesus Christ, thy Son, our Lord'.

of our prayer is shaped by the context of the life of heaven, the need for our prayer arises from the context of life on earth. This earthly context was what called for the coming of the Son into the world in the first place and it continues to require his grace.

Reflecting upon our broken and divided world and the unseen forces that lie behind it, with dramatic apocalyptic language and courageous apocalyptic expectations Jesus of Nazareth looked to the end:

> If a kingdom is divided against itself, that kingdom cannot stand. If a household is divided against itself, that household cannot stand. And if Satan opposes himself and is divided, he cannot stand; his end has come. (Mark 3:24–26).

In the meantime, those who know 'the God and Father of our Lord Jesus Christ' (Rom 15:6; 2 Cor 1:3; 11:31; Eph 1:3; 1 Peter 1:3; Rev 1:6), pray 'deliver us from the Evil One'. As we pray, we work in the hope that as the character of God in heaven is made known through the gospel of Christ, this will continue to shape the character of human life on earth.

This is the framework within which Theological Education operates. This perspective supplies the superordinate goal which stands ever over and beyond the goals of the theological curriculum. The more theological students think like God rather than like mere human beings (cf. Mark 8:33), the more they will develop a theologically-shaped character, renewed by the Spirit to conform to the image of the Son who is the image of the Father. Theological Education will produce God's exemplary graduates because of these same prayers directed towards the Father: Your kingdom come; Your will be done on earth as it is in heaven; Deliver us from the Evil One.

Although it was far too early in human history for Jesus to make any observations about universities and modern Western democracies (or their opponents), I suspect that his recommendations would have been along the same lines. The character and will of God have not changed. Neither has our world. In fact, even the lofty realms of Higher Education are simply part of 'our broken and divided world'—Adamic, fallen, suffering, needing redemption, and so much in need of God's mercy.[2]

---

2   *An Australian Prayer Book* (1978), 96: 'God of the nations, whose kingdom rules over all, have mercy on our broken and divided world. Shed abroad your peace in the hearts of all men and banish from them the spirit that makes for war; that all races and people may learn to live as members of one family and in obedience to your laws; through Jesus Christ our Lord'.

As this volume was waiting for this Epilogue before going to press, Professor Brian Schmidt, Vice Chancellor of the Australian National University delivered his 2021 'State of the University' address.[3] Warning that 'democracy and truth are under siege', being threatened by 'extreme forms of populism' (apparently, non-extreme populism would be okay?), the Nobel Laureate urged that 'because they exist to establish what is true, universities are needed like never before' and they have 'a special responsibility to show leadership'. Three years earlier, as an astrophysicist, Professor Schmidt entitled his Professor Walter Stibbs Lecture at the University of Sydney 'the State of the Universe'.[4] This year, as Vice Chancellor his 'State of the University' speech to his own university (with an eye on the crowd) identified science in particular as having a strong part to play in that leadership:

> In fighting the [COVID-19] pandemic, academics have not only enhanced the reputation of universities, they have enhanced the reputation of science—the crucial discipline that needs to retain, and in some places regain, the world's trust.[5]

So, universities are still needed 'to establish what is true', especially through the pursuit of science. Although once taken for granted almost universally, this is certainly an interesting perspective to propound in the contemporary Higher Educational climate.

The pre-advertising for Professor Schmidt's address particularly alluded to 'recent events in the United States [...] including the storming of the Capitol', and warned against 'extreme forms of populism', that are 'leading to violence and autocracy, besieged parliaments and mass arrests'. If he was speaking after 1789, he could have been referring to the French 'chaotic bloodbath', that 'played a critical role in shaping modern nations by showing the world the power inherent in the will of the people'.[6] As one of its lasting legacies, the French Revolution bequeathed the language of 'Left' and 'Right', which continues to befuddle political discourse, just as surely as it so deeply polarizes contemporary society, by the assumption that this dichotomy is the sole Dictator before whom all must bow. The polarity always looks strange to the Christian

---

3   My citations come from the preadvertising on the ANU website, 'Unis must continue to defend truth', as well as the *Campus Morning Mail* of the same day, 'Universities "the ramparts of democracy" says ANU VC'.
4   Usyd, 'The State of the Universe'.
5   Campus Morning Mail, 'Universities "the ramparts of democracy" says ANU VC'. Schmidt's particular concern is 'tackling climate change'.
6   Editors, 'The French Revolution'.

who is conscious of the early Apologist's description of our tribe situated alongside 'Jew' and 'Greek' as 'the Third Race' (Aelius Aristides, *Apol.* 2)—alongside, but nevertheless outside such humanly conceived cultural conceptions.

Speaking early in 2021, Schmidt was, of course, alluding to the troubles on American streets provoked by the democratic ousting of President Donald Trump, which were—after the French typology—'Right-wing', as so eagerly noted by members of the media, so frequently—after the same typology—leaning heavily Left. And, no matter how much the violence of the original Left might be justified (or conveniently forgotten), the contemporary violence of the Right must be exposed for the evil that it truly is. Confirming any initial guesses at the true nature of his concerns, Schmidt quickly added another usually Right-directed swearword. Apparently, the contemporary 'populism' (at least in its 'extreme' form) against which universities seeking to establish truth, and especially academics in the scientific fields, needed to do battle, was 'at times and in places approaching fascism'.[7]

In the same month that the Vice-Chancellor insisted that seeking truth especially through science ought to lead the way out of the present university malaise, his own university hit the headlines because of its *Gender-Inclusive Handbook* (published in 2019), aimed at 'any ANU student or staff member' involved in teaching.[8] With claims that 'heterosexual and woman-focused lactation language ... can misgender, isolate, and harm transmasculine parents and non-heteronormative families', the document recommended use of the terms '"breast/chest feeding" and "human/parent's milk", rather than "breast-feeding" and "mother's milk" to describe lactation' and '"gestational" or "birthing" parent rather than "mother", and the terms "nongestational" or "nonbirthing" parent rather than "father"'. Despite the rather quaint-sounding words about 'truth' and 'science' coming out of the Vice-Chancellor's office, clearly the segment of ANU still drunk on post-modern madness had long-since given up on truth in favour of ideology and dispensed with any last shreds of science in favour of radical gender reconstructions, in its attempt to enforce politically-correct speech upon both staff and students of what is purportedly 'the country's leading university'. It must have further damaged Schmidt's hope to redeem the public reputation of the role of universities in recovering a better future when, one month later, the Australian Senate responded by banning

---

7   See ANU website and *Campus Morning Mail*.
8   Chung, 'ANU urges staff'.

'distorted' gender-neutral language from official documents.⁹ The motion declared that 'broad scale genuine inclusion cannot be achieved through distortions of biological and relational descriptors' and that 'an individual's right to choose their descriptors and pronouns for personal use must not dehumanise the human race and undermine gender'. Although the motion passed only narrowly, it remains to be seen whether it marks a turning-point in the ground-swell of opinion that political-correctness has gone way too far—even amongst the very minorities supposedly being protected by its dogmas!¹⁰

But to return to Schmidt's fear of fascism. I consulted Robert Soucy's *Encyclopedia Britannica* article to refresh my memory about this usually-left-ill-defined term.¹¹ I was reminded that this political ideology (usually including an opposition to Marxism) took its name from Benito Mussolini's party and that between the years 1922 and 1945 it spawned a whole variety of mass movements in Europe, which then spilled over to elsewhere. Although Soucy therefore wrote of fascism in the past tense, he moved towards the present tense by acquainting his readers with the 'neofascism' of the post-WWII period before taking them on a global journey ending in 2016, with 'the unexpected electoral victory of Republican presidential candidate Donald J. Trump'. Without going into who it was who didn't expect this result, and passing over many upstanding American citizens without comment, he noted that Trump's supporters included 'white supremacists', 'white nationalists', and 'neo-Nazis', and that 'the immediate aftermath' of his election was an increase in 'hate crimes directed at minorities'. Referring to the revised labels introduced post-WWII by 'scholars of fascism', Soucy passed over 'quasi-fascist', 'proto-fascist', and 'semi-fascist', to quickly defend Trump against being a 'fascist or neofascist' by agreeing with the said scholars that he was 'arguably a borderline fascist', just like Vladimir Putin of Russia and Jair Bolsonaro of Brazil. Interesting friends.

It was apparently of no relevance to Soucy's exposition of the 'immediate aftermath' to Trump's election, that across 2017 American Universities experienced such civic disturbances and violence that some have compared it to

---

9   Chung, 'Senate votes'.
10 See, for example, Donnelly, *How Political Correctness is Destroying Australia; How Political Correctness is Destroying Education; How Political Correctness is Still Destroying Australia*; Pluckrose & Lindsay, ~~Critical~~ *Cynical Theories*. The November 2019 Australia Talks Survey found that 68% of Australians believe political correctness has gone too far; see R. Conaghan, 'Apparently Most Australians'. US polls have shown similar results; see, e.g., Mounk, 'Americans Strongly Dislike PC Culture'; Abrams, 'Student surveys'.
11 Soucy, 'Fascism'.

the student protests of 1968. One of the early outbreaks of violence was at the University of California's Berkeley campus, ten days after Trump's inauguration, when 'an estimated 1,500 protesters surrounded the building where Milo Yiannopoulos, a young, British, gay,[12] Trump supporter, was scheduled to speak'.[13] On the French typology, this was an initiative not of the Right, but of the Left. Calling themselves 'antifascists', the protestors' aim was 'to prevent the speech from happening', and a wave of vandalism, violence, and attacks on police ensued across the campus and throughout the town, with property damage exceeding $500,000. Coming after several years of escalating troubles over 'freedom of speech', in which students (not universities) were the ones initiating demands that certain ideas must not be spoken in classes or on campuses,[14] the 'Milo Riot'

> marked a turning point—an escalation of conflicts over campus speakers. [...] Since then, many students on the left have become increasingly receptive to the idea that violence is sometimes justified as a response to speech they believe is "hateful". At the same time, many students on the right have become increasingly eager to invite speakers that are likely to provoke a reaction from the left.[15]
>
> [It] marked a major shift in campus protests. Violence was used successfully to stop a speaker; people were injured, and there were (as far as we can tell) no costs to those who were violent. Some students later justified the violence as a legitimate form of "self-defense" to prevent speech that they said was violent.[16]

As First Amendment Lawyer Greg Lukianoff and psychologist Jonathan Haidt document the spread of these largely Left-led troubles across USA campuses, they lay the blame at the feet of 'Three Bad Ideas' that have become deeply rooted in Western society, which arrived on American campuses with the iGen in 2013. In exposing the untruths of fragility, that ideas actually harm people; of emotional reasoning, in which events are interpreted in the light of emotional

---

12 Recently Yiannopolous has become 'ex-gay' after a Christian conversion experience; McEachen, 'Milo Yiannopolous [sic]'.
13 Lukianoff & Haidt, *Coddling*, 82.
14 For a view of these pressures from the perspective of an Australian Professor of Poetry and Poetics (now retired), see Spurr, 'Academic Freedom'.
15 Lukianoff & Haidt, *Coddling*, 83. Although the final sentence becomes problematic if it attributes motives for these invitations, rather than being simply descriptive of outcomes.
16 Lukianoff & Haidt, *Coddling*, 97.

reactions not logical thought; and of 'us versus them', in which humanity is divided into tribe-like 'identities' over against other 'identities', their book, *The Coddling of the American Mind*, aims towards wiser kids, wiser universities, and wiser societies. Rather than the destructive cycle presently dividing and conquering the Western world and its Higher Education systems, they hope for better child-rearing, better students, better graduates, together producing a better society. It is a grand vision, with a top reaching for the heavens, but whether it is achievable depends on how much it resembles the statue with feet of clay (Gen 11:1-9; Daniel 2).

The 2017 troubles were not confined to American universities, but campuses in the United Kingdom, Canada, and Australia were similarly afflicted.[17] At the end of that year Australia endured a referendum as to whether marriage in the Commonwealth Marriage Act should no longer be defined as being between a man and a woman. When a handful of students at the University of Sydney made speeches holding banners 'it's ok to say no', they were quickly surrounded by a crowd of about 200 megaphone-assisted students seeking to drown out their voices and forcing police to intervene.[18] The year before, in the interests of 'accessibility and inclusion' the USyd student union decreed that the practice of associations requiring particular beliefs of their executive 'is no less exclusionary than requiring candidates to be of a particular sexuality or gender identity'. To put their money where their mouth was, the Sydney University Evangelical Union was threatened with expulsion, despite being one of the oldest student associations on campus. When the SUEU pointed out that even the United Nations recognises that protecting diversity requires the protection of the rights of diverse groups to associate freely (such as political parties), the student union's decision was defended by its vice-president pointing out that their board was not a signatory to the UN.[19] Obviously well-informed.

In August 2018, the University of Western Australia gave in to protests and, citing 'risk management', cancelled a talk by US academic Quentin Van Meter

---

17   Lukianoff & Haidt, *Coddling*, 11. For a further catalogue of such violent encounters in 2016–2017 on campuses in the USA, UK, and Canada, see Lesh, *Free Speech*, 4–5.
18   Singhal, 'Police called'.
19   Judd, 'University of Sydney's Evangelical Union'. The same philosophical position is reflected in the University of Chicago's suite of approaches to the freedom of expression. Diversity is not protected by a uniformity of ideology, but by protecting the freedom of every individual to express their point of view, no matter how unpopular it may be to others, but always within the confines of a respect for a common humanity.

who is known for questioning the science used to support transgenderism.[20] After facing a protest at La Trobe University in the same month, sex therapist Bettina Arndt faced another at the University of Sydney in September, causing riot police to enter the campus after some 40 students, led by the Wom*n's Collective, attempted to block access to her talk questioning whether there is a 'rape culture' on Australian campuses.[21] In 2019, after the provocateur at the centre of the Californian 'Milo Riot' found himself *persona non gratia* wherever his presence was expected, his mooted Australian tour was cancelled. Scott Morrison's freshly elected Liberal Government surprised other conservative voices by revoking his visa in response to inflammatory comments he had made about Islam after an attack on a mosque in Christchurch.[22]

But even if by 2017 a new wave of 'cancel-culture' was finding fertile ground,[23] censorship initiated by Left-led student groups had already been a growing feature of Australian campus life for at least two decades.

The student newspapers of the 60s and 70s often spearheaded the anti-censorship campaign, even if often only through the publication of outrageous sexual or blasphemous articles overtly designed to shock the sensibilities of wider society. Whenever this aim was achieved, they cried out against censorship and stood in solidarity with the censored. Student papers were 'a training ground for journalists, writers, artists and politicians' who later became household names in Australia (e.g. Cyril Pearl, Alan Moorehead, Donald Horne, Brian Fitzpatrick, Jack Lindsay, P.R. Stephensen, Max Harris; L.F. Crisp; Bob Ellis; Clive James; Richard Walsh; Laurie Oakes; Geoffrey Blainey; Lindsay Tanner; Christos Tsiolkas; Michael Leunig; Humphrey McQueen; Julianne Schultz; John Bannon; Julian Disney; David Penberthy; Nick Xenophon; Kate Ellis).[24]

As student activism centred on the Vietnam War, apartheid, women's liberation, gay rights, Aboriginal land rights, nuclear energy, the environment and Watergate, many student newspapers were radicalised.[25] The formation of the Australian Union of Students (AUS) in 1970 was part of an increased commitment to student representation and activism, and editors of student

---

20 Carmody, 'UWA cancels talk'.
21 Fernando, 'Riot Squad Called'.
22 Wahlquist, 'Australia Cancels Milo Yiannopoulos's visa'.
23 See Donnelly (ed.), *Cancel Culture*.
24 Griffin-Foley & Walker, 'Student Newspapers'.
25 Griffin-Foley & Walker, 'Student Newspapers'.

papers began to receive small honoraria, student newspapers and their print runs became larger, and changes in typesetting technology enabled last-minute publication to beat the censors.[26] Across the seventies student papers lost some of their activist energy, as the campuses generally became more settled and conservative, perhaps epitomised by the collapse of AUS in 1984 and its replacement with the National Union of Students.

But despite this changing mood, earlier anti-censorship commitments still surfaced occasionally. Perhaps the most celebrated example was the 1995 controversy arising after La Trobe University's student newspaper *Rabelais* published an article entitled 'The Art of Shoplifting'. Condemned by police and major retail chains, the editors defended the article as raising legitimate (albeit Marxist-oriented) issues of wealth distribution and private property in Australia, as well as crowd-pleasing concerns about financial support for students. After the public outcry, the editors were prosecuted for ignoring a ban issued by Victoria's Chief Censor. When seven other student papers linked arms by reprinting the article, their editors were not charged, and *Rabelais* also escaped unharmed.[27]

But examples of the shoe being found on the other foot along the French political scale were also beginning to appear. After previously writing a few articles and reviews for the University of New South Wale's student paper *Tharunka*, in the year 2000 Michael Shane joined the editorial team. As a twenty-year-old idealist who thought he could make a difference, he assumed that a university was the place for the free exchange of ideas in the quest of truth and the betterment of humanity. But he soon found out that the days when reality reflected that theory had apparently long gone.

In March the pseudonymist 'Kilroy Montgomery' presented data from a survey of issues in the newspaper from 1997 to 1999, reporting that 123 articles addressed women's issues but only 5 addressed male; 101 were pro-gay/lesbian but only 7 were concerned with heterosexual sex; 42 were sexually explicit; and 10 were explicitly anti-male, and another 11 were misogynistic or homophobic.[28] As a result, somewhere in the editorial corridors the idea was floated that *Tharunka* should redress the balance and publish an edition examining issues of particular relevance to men. Sight unseen this mooted edition was quickly

---

26 Griffin-Foley & Walker, 'Student Newspapers'.
27 Griffin-Foley & Walker, 'Student Newspapers'.
28 Montgomery, 'Tharunka: Ruled by Feminists?'.

'panned as the "white heterosexual male edition"'.[29] It never saw the light of day. It was aborted long before it could be strangled at birth.

Reflecting on these events four years later in a piece including similar censorship in student papers from Wollongong and Melbourne, Joe Stella explained that the Guild Council had forbidden the editors from publishing on men's issues, 'claiming that the move would "undermine" the women's, gay, lesbian, indigenous, and ethic [sic] affairs departments'.[30] He also noted that this same Guild Council was derided by the left's Nick Salzberg, who edited *Tharunka* in 2001, as 'right wing'. After Kilroy's article in March, the Guild also banned an issue criticizing the University Union as incompetent, before in August the Guild President—without constitutional warrant—demanded that all content had to be signed off by him and the Women's Department. Moving even further in the same oppressive direction, after a 'decidedly left-wing' Guild Council was elected in September, a committee of three students was appointed to oversee *Tharunka*'s production. They were also granted the right to withhold *Tharunka*'s budget to give some teeth to their censorship decisions.

In March, Kilroy's survey had noted 5 articles that 'called for a censorship of non PC debate' and 6 articles that 'called for free debate'. Having come to the paper keen to make some improvements, Michael Shane stood firm with the latter, but across his difficult year as editor he discovered that the real power rested upon those who marched with the former until the latter were trampled down. The only words printed on page 36 of the October *Tharunka*, the last for the year, read: 'This is an anti-censorship protest by the editors'. Page 37 offered the following explanation:

> The Executive Editors of *Tharunka* 2000 have been firmly committed to a "zero censorship, zero-bias" policy. The final edition of *Tharunka* conflicts with that policy following a motion passed at the last Student Guild Council:
>
> > That Guild Council approve $7,000 to *Tharunka* for use until 31/12/00. This money shall be conditional upon the approval of the Secretary / Treasurer Elect, Women's Representative, Queer Representative and Ethnic Affairs Representative and be granted in pieces as they see fit or not be granted as they see fit.

---

29 Stella, 'Censorship'.
30 Stella, 'Censorship'.

> The committee appointed by the Council effectively consisted of only two individual representatives both from the incoming elect-guild. The newly elected Secretary / Treasurer, the new Ethnic / Queer Representative (both positions have been jointed). The committee now has absolute censorial and directional power over *Tharunka*.
>
> In the final edition the "committee" insisted on the removal of three articles from this edition: two articles defending Campus Bible Studies [sic] (written in response to Sex, Lies and Campus Bible Study *Tharunka* #12) and one article concerning IVF. The articles were authored by Skye Macleod, Alan Ma and Kilroy Montgomery respectively. The committee also directed *Tharunka* not to print ANY information about the motion or their censorial actions. This page has been printed against their explicit instruction.
>
> The editors strongly oppose the decision to censor *Tharunka*, to dismiss the zero-censorship, zero-bias policy and the actions of this "committee".

As the year closed, another member of the editorial team that year fired some parting shots at Kilroy Montgomery, while also arguing that space should be given in the paper to indigenous, homosexual, and women's issues, but never to men's issues. Evidently a champion of the censorship that had occurred that year, she added a slogan which sniggered on the usual swearword: 'Let's put the Sshhhhh! back in Fascist, I say'.[31]

By 2017, according to the Fre*e Speech on Campus Audit* published by Melbourne's *Institute of Public Affairs*, 'Australia's universities are failing to protect free speech on campus'. The report systematically analysed 'over 165 policies and actions at Australia's 42 universities', rating their support of free speech, especially through noting those that 'limit the diversity of ideas on campus'.[32] To repeat the report's 'Executive Summary':

- The majority of Australia's universities limit the diversity of ideas on campus:
    - Thirty-four of Australia's 42 universities (81 per cent) received a Red rating for policies and actions that are hostile to free speech on campus, an increase from 33 in 2016.

---

31 Creighton, 'On Life and Leaving'.
32 Lesh, *Free Speech*, 'Executive Summary', 2.

- Seven of Australia's universities (17 per cent) received an Amber rating for policies and actions that threaten free speech on campus.
- One university, the University of New England, received a Green rating for supporting free speech on campus.

- Just eight of Australia's 42 universities (19 per cent) have an explicit policy that protects intellectual freedom, as mandated by the Higher Education Support Act 2003.
- There is evidence of increasing censorship at Australia's universities, as well as a growing number and scope of speech codes since the previous Audit in 2016:
  - The number of universities which have Red ranked policies has increased from 28 to 31 since the 2016 Audit.
  - The number of universities where there have been actions intended to limit the diversity of ideas has increased from 9 to 16 since the 2016 Audit.
- The institutions most hostile to intellectual freedom are the University of Sydney (36), Charles Sturt University (15), followed by James Cook University (14) and Monash University (14), according to the new Hostility Score which measures the aggregate number of problematic policies and actions.
- University policies prohibit a wide variety of speech, including 'insulting' and 'unwelcome' comments, 'offensive' language, and, in some cases, 'sarcasm' and hurt 'feelings'.
- There have been a growing number of censorious actions at Australian universities, including violent protests against the presence of speakers, venue cancellations for controversial speakers, students required to pay selective security fees, activist students demanding censorship of course content, universities censuring academics for their speech, students instructed to not express their viewpoint, and the growing use of trigger warnings.

Anticipating Lukianoff and Haidt's observations about 'safetyism' amongst current student bodies on American campuses and its impact upon university administrations (i.e. ideas will do you harm),[33] the IPA *Audit* noted amongst its '5 Worst Policies': a Bullying Prevention statement defining bullying to include

---

33 Lukianoff & Haidt, *Coddling*, chs. 1 and 10.

hurting another person's feelings; a Discrimination and Harassment policy, Bullying Prevention Guidelines, and an Anti-Racism Policy forbidding sarcasm; and another definition of bullying including 'unintentional offence' and forbidding language that causes 'emotional injury'; and several others banning behaviour that is 'unwelcome'; and a social media policy forbidding students, in activities both related to the university and personal usage, from making comments that 'might be construed' to be 'offensive'.

The 5 worst actions of 2017 were listed as: a student union attempting to block the screening of a film, claiming that the mere showing of a video could 'physically threaten women on campus' (Sydney); the first formal introduction of trigger warnings as part of course guides (Monash); misconduct action against an academic for claiming that the Great Barrier Reef was healthy (James Cook); withdrawal of a textbook and suspension of an academic, after a Quiz question offended international students from China (Monash); and the obligation for conservative students to pay hefty security fees not charged for activities of other student groups (Sydney).

As the IPA report sounded an alarm bell that 'freedom of speech on campus is in peril', it noted:

> Today, a censorious culture has developed at universities. Speakers are cancelled and violently protested because certain groups disagree with their ideas. Students are self-censoring for fear of social ostracism and academic repercussions. Trigger warnings, alerts before content that could cause emotional discomfort, and safe spaces are coddling students from intellectual challenge. Activists are demanding course censorship on the basis that they dislike the content. Meanwhile, speech codes have institutionalised restrictions on free speech. It is of serious concern that universities, the institutions designed to facilitate a flourishing debate, have instead become hotbeds of censorship and are lacking in viewpoint diversity.[34]
>
> The failure to protect freedom of expression is seriously imperilling the discovery of truth, the core purpose of Australia's universities; student development, which requires debate and challenge; and the future of Australian society, which depends on a tolerance and openness to debate. In order to protect free speech, it

---

34 Lesh, *Free Speech*, 4.

is recommended that Australia's universities: (1) abolish policies that limit free speech; 2) introduce a policy that protects intellectual freedom, as mandated by legislation; and (3) commit to the University of Chicago's sector-leading statement on free expression.[35]

In the United States, the University of Chicago has stood firm against the current campus cancel-culture, arguing that freedom of speech is the very basis of a true education.[36] Mid-way through the tumultuous 2017, President Zimmer declared that:

> universities that aspire to excellence must embrace and defend free expression as a value that is necessary to fulfilling their mission. Only in this way will they be fulfilling their obligations to all their students in preparing them well and empowering them for the challenges and opportunities of their future life.[37]

Meanwhile in Australia, when Janet Albrechtsen, a journalist with *The Australian*, asked the University of Sydney, the University of Melbourne, Monash University, the University of New South Wales, the University of Queensland, Queensland University of Technology and the Australian National University whether they supported a letter from the University of Chicago to new students which encouraged them 'to speak, write, listen, challenge and learn without fear of censorship', she found that no Australian university was willing to endorse the letter.[38] While many on the Left persisted with the spin that there is no problem about free speech on Australian campuses,[39] the March 2020 French Report considered that it did in fact need protection and the Minister for Education urged Australian Higher Education to adopt a form of French's recommended code. Given the disarray found by the 2017 *Institute of Public Affairs* report, it was surprising to learn from a November 2020 independent review, just how quickly the universities could report alignment to French's model code.[40]

---

35 Lesh, *Free Speech*, 2, Executive Summary conclusion.
36 See the various documents relating to University of Chicago and Free Expression Statement on the bibliography.
37 Zimmer, 'Chicago Humanities Festival Address'.
38 Lesh, *Free Speech*, 5.
39 As one example, see the comments from some panel members when Jordan B. Peterson made a guest appearance on the ABC's *Q & A*, 25/2/2019.
40 For access and discussion see Higher Education Reviews and Consultations.

As this book was going to press (just as soon as my Epilogue was completed), both houses of Parliament in the Australian State of Victoria passed the most draconian Bill ever to be presented in Australia. The 'Change or Suppression (Conversion) Practices Prohibition Bill 2020', 'casts a very wide net in seeking to outlaw any religious practice that might challenge question or denigrate a person's self-perceived sexual orientation or gender identity'.[41] Since no other community groups are mentioned in the bill, it seems to be specifically targeted at Christian churches, with the expectation that they will be monitored under powers given to the Human Rights Commission, who can receive a complaint from anyone. There is no acknowledgement of 'interfering with the religious freedoms of groups who want to teach the traditional religious views. It doesn't signal any interest in balancing the rights of people or consider the dangers of suppressing religious free speech'.[42] It is blatantly ideological, seeking to teach people what is normal, at pain of criminal prosecution: 'to affirm that a person's sexual orientation or gender identity is not broken and in need of fixing [and] affirm that no sexual orientation or gender identity constitutes a disorder, disease, illness, deficiency or shortcoming'. 'Change suppression measures' are not permitted even for people who decide they want them, making 'areas of sexual and gender identity the most important to a person's identity and authenticity'. Despite Australia's Federalism, it even seeks to control what happens outside the State of Victoria. This enshrining of a particular ideologically-driven agenda is not the result of any Right-wing Fascism. It is the result of the Left, having gained power, then suppressing dissent and punishing those who do not bow before their ideological tyranny—which is made even more horrendous by the fact that the supporters of the legislation seem to feel this is acceptable in a liberal democracy.

Surely the lessons of the 20th century should have taught us that, in the end, the problem is not Right versus Left, but those who think they only are right because they have worked so hard to ensure that they are the only ones left! There was little difference between the atrocities committed by the 'fascist' Nazis in Germany and those of the Leninist-Stalinist regime in Russia. Every one of the features of fascism listed by Soucy can be paralleled almost exactly by those of the Soviets. Soucy certainly agrees that there were similarities

---

41 Editor, 'Suppression or Oppression?'.
42 Neil Foster, Associate Professor in the Law School at the University of Newcastle (Australia), interviewed in Editor, 'Suppression or Oppression?'.

between fascism and Soviet communism but beginning the list with the rather lame observations that they were both mass movements, and that both emerged in the years following World War I in circumstances of political turmoil and economic collapse, almost domesticates the next item on the list: that they both employed terror and violence without scruple when it was expedient to do so. But in his favour, Soucy acknowledges that both sought to create totalitarian systems after they came to power, after concealing their totalitarian ambitions beforehand. This is undoubtedly the most significant thing they held in common.

Turning again to the *Encyclopedia Britannica*,[43] Duignan's article defines totalitarianism as 'a form of government that theoretically permits no individual freedom and that seeks to subordinate all aspects of individual life to the authority of the state'. Another term coined by Mussolini, the dictator described it as 'all within the state, none outside the state, none against the state'. It is 'characterized by strong central rule that attempts to control and direct all aspects of individual life through coercion and repression'.

> The totalitarian state pursues some special goal, such as industrialization or conquest, to the exclusion of all others. All resources are directed toward its attainment, regardless of the cost. Whatever might further the goal is supported; whatever might foil the goal is rejected. This obsession spawns an ideology that explains everything in terms of the goal, rationalizing all obstacles that may arise and all forces that may contend with the state. The resulting popular support permits the state the widest latitude of action of any form of government. Any dissent is branded evil, and internal political differences are not permitted. Because pursuit of the goal is the only ideological foundation for the totalitarian state, achievement of the goal can never be acknowledged.

On this definition, post-modernism and critical theory have become totalitarian, since, in the words of Pluckrose and Lindsay's subtitle, 'Activist Scholarship [has] Made Everything about Race, Gender, and Identity'.[44] Duignan notes that Nazism and Stalinism were both examples of 'popular totalitarianism', 'in which the state achieved overwhelming popular support for its leadership', assisted by modern developments in communication. But now that the Left has

---

43 Duignan, 'Totalitarianism'.
44 Pluckrose & Lindsay, ~~Critical~~ Cynical Theories.

such control of the Internet and its social media, what will this new totalitarianism manage to achieve as the echo-chambers continue to reverberate the anger and invective which is by now infamous in those versions of underworld?

> Under totalitarian rule, traditional social institutions and organizations are discouraged and suppressed. Thus, the social fabric is weakened and people become more amenable to absorption into a single, unified movement. Participation in approved public organizations is at first encouraged and then required. Old religious and social ties are supplanted by artificial ties to the state and its ideology. As pluralism and individualism diminish, most of the people embrace the totalitarian state's ideology. The infinite diversity among individuals blurs, replaced by a mass conformity (or at least acquiescence) to the beliefs and behaviour sanctioned by the state.

To return to the present-day polarizations on and off Western campuses, fuelled by a 'common-enemy identity politics' and with violence strangely justified in the name of anti-discrimination[45]—let alone Victoria's 'Conversion Suppression' Bill—Duignan's description of previous totalitarian regimes sounds nothing but chilling.

> Large-scale organized violence becomes permissible and sometimes necessary under totalitarian rule, justified by the overriding commitment to the state ideology and pursuit of the state's goal. In Nazi Germany and Stalin's Soviet Union, whole classes of people, such as the Jews and the kulaks (wealthy peasant farmers) respectively, were singled out for persecution and extinction. In each case the persecuted were linked with some external enemy and blamed for the state's troubles, and thereby public opinion was aroused against them and their fate at the hands of the military and police was condoned.

Totalitarianism stifles the expression of alternative viewpoints and demands acceptance of the viewpoints of those who assert themselves in power against the rest. A Totalitarianism of the Right is little different from a Totalitarianism of the Left. Here is the real evil that lies on both sides of the French Left/Right divide. The suppression of the freedom of the individual in service of the grand ideology.

---

45 Lukianoff & Haidt, *Coddling*, chs. 4 & 5.

As a member of 'the Third Race', Karl Barth named this 'political absolutism' as the first of the 'lordless powers' that hold humanity in slavery, as our alienation from God produces a consequent alienation from each other.[46]

> World history, being the history of man and humanity, of adamic humanity which has fallen from God, is also the history of innumerable absolutisms of different kinds, of forces that are truly and properly man's own but that have won a certain autonomy, independence, and even superiority in relation to him. There they are, powerful enough in and in spite of their impotence to be too much for the one who can and should be their lord and to take him to task, to master him who should master them, influencing, determining, and controlling his thought and speech and also his purposes and enterprises for himself and in his common life with others. If they are only pseudo-objective realities, strangely enough they are still powerful realities which make a fine display of their lying objectivity.[47]

Barth notes that such lordless powers—including ideologies with their slogans and propaganda—are

> the hidden wirepullers in man's great and small enterprises, movements, achievements, and revolutions. They are not just the potencies but the real factors and agents of human progress, regress, and stagnation in politics, economics, scholarship, technology, and art, and also of the evolutions and retardations in all the personal life of the individual. It is not really people who do things, whether leaders or the masses. Through mankind's fault, things are invisibly done without and above man, even above the human individual in all his uniqueness, by the host of absolutisms, of powers that seek to be lordless and that make an impressive enough attempt to exhibit and present themselves as such.[48]

The individual members of the 'Third Race' are not called to stand over against any human being, in the kind of 'common enemy identity politics' currently rife in the polarized West.[49] Instead, in the kind of 'common-humanity identity

---

46 Barth, *The Christian Life*, 213–222. Other 'lordless powers' are Mammon, and ideologies.
47 Barth, *The Christian Life*, 216.
48 Barth, *The Christian Life*, 216; for ideology and its slogans and propaganda, see 224–28.
49 Lukianoff & Haidt, *Coddling*, ch. 3.

politics' encouraged by Lukianoff and Haidt,[50] Barth notes that the New Testament sees human beings as 'pushed as well as pushing, moved as well as moving', 'self-alienated in their alienation from God' and therefore no match for the lordless powers,

> those impalpable but supremely efficacious potencies, factors, and agents, those imaginary gods and lords that are so active in their imaginary character. While asserting and not denying man's responsibility, [the New Testament] sees and understands the irrational and harmful nature of human attitudes and acts in terms of man's having fallen under the binding sway of these factors and agents. As the message of God's freeing of man from this bondage it constantly proclaims to all what God has done for them, and will do, in Jesus Christ. It thus proclaims to them faith in him, not (even incidentally) as faith in these forces, but as resolute unbelief in their reality and efficacy, even though these may not be denied but have to be taken soberly into account.[51]

This is still the earthly context in which Theological Education works towards 'God's exemplary graduates'. A broken and divided world already invaded by the Prince of Peace. Under the heading 'The Struggle for Human Righteousness', Barth noted that:

> Christians pray to God that he will cause his righteousness to appear and dwell on a new earth under a new heaven. Meanwhile they act in accordance with their prayer as people who are responsible for the rule of human righteousness, that is, for the preservation and renewal, the deepening and extending, of the divinely ordained human safeguards of human rights, human freedom, and human peace on earth.[52]

Theological Education serves the larger agenda of individuals and a society reflecting the values of heaven, with a view to the coming Kingdom of God. Your kingdom come. Your will be done. Deliver us from the Evil One, whose end—because of the death and resurrection of Christ—has most certainly come.

---

50   Lukianoff & Haidt, *Coddling*, 60–62, 74–76, 221, 244.
51   Barth, *The Christian Life*, 218.
52   Barth, *The Christian Life*, 205.

Bibliography

Abrams, S.J. 'Student surveys show that Trump is right about campus political correctness', *Washington Examiner* 20/10/2020, www.aei.org/op-eds/student-surveys-show-that-trump-is-right-about-campus-political-correctness.

ANU, 'Unis must continue to defend truth and democracy' (10/2/2021); www.anu.edu.au/news/all-news/unis-must-continue-to-defend-truth-and-democracy.

Barth, K. *The Christian Life. Church Dogmatics Volume IV, Part 4: Lecture Fragments* (G.W. Bromiley, transl.; London: T&T Clark, 2004 [1981]).

Campus Morning Mail 'Universities "The Ramparts of Democracy" says ANU VC', 10/2/2021. https://campusmorningmail.com.au/.

Carmody, J. 'UWA cancels talk by transgender sceptic Quentin Van Meter after protests', 17/8/2018. www.abc.net.au/news/2018-08-17/uwa-cancels-talk-by-controversial-academic-transgender-views/10132400.

Chung, F. 'ANU urges staff to say "chestfeeding" instead of "breastfeeding", "gestational parent" instead of mother', *News.com.au* 16/2/2021.

Chung, F. 'Senate votes to ban "distorted" gender-neutral language such as "chestfeeding" from official materials', *News.com.au* 18/3/2021

Conaghan, R. 'Apparently Most Australians Think Political Correctness Has Gone Too Far', https://junkee.com/australia-political-correctness-too-far/230659.

Creighton, L. 'On Life and Leaving', *Tharunka*, 3/10/2000.

Donnelly, K. (ed.) *Cancel Culture and the Left's Long March* (Melbourne: Wilkinson Publishing, 2021).

Donnelly, K. *How Political Correctness is Still Destroying Australia. The Latest Articles* (Melbourne: Wilkinson Publishing, 2020).

Donnelly, K. *How Political Correctness is Destroying Education and your Child's Future* (Melbourne: Wilkinson Publishing, 2018).

Donnelly, K. *How Political Correctness is Destroying Australia. Enemies Within and Without* (Melbourne: Wilkinson Publishing, 2018).

Duignan, B. 'Totalitarianism', https://www.britannica.com/topic/totalitarianism. Duignan, is the most recent reviser, Aug 07, 2019.

Editor 'Suppression or Oppression? Victoria's Anti-Conversion Bill', 10/12/2020, *The Gospel Coalition Australia*. https://au.thegospelcoalition.org/article/suppression-or-oppression.

Editors 'The French Revolution' (9/11/2009; updated 4/2/2021). www.history.com/topics/france/french-revolution.

Fernando, G. 'Riot Squad called to Sydney University over protests to sex therapist Bettina Arndt', *News.com.au* 12/9/2018. www.news.com.au/lifestyle/real-life/news-life/riot-squad-called-to-sydney-university-over-protests-to-sex-therapist-bettina-arndt/news-story/0698b147e38b44f2b13fc3766664385c .

Griffin-Foley, B., & S. Walker, 'Student Newspapers', B. Griffin-Foley (ed.), *A Companion to the Australian Media* (Kew: Australian Scholarly Publishing, 2014), 442–444. www.austlit.edu.au/austlit/page/9566701.

Higher Education Reviews and Consultations, www.dese.gov.au/higher-education-reviews-and-consultations/independent-review-adoption-model-code-freedom-speech-and-academic-freedom.

Judd, A. 'University of Sydney's Evangelical Union shouldn't have to give up its faith in fight against discrimination', *Sydney Morning Herald*, 23/3/2016.

Lesh, M. *Free Speech on Campus Audit 2017* (Melbourne: Institute of Public Affairs, Dec 2017).

Lukianoff, G., & J. Haidt *The Coddling of the American Mind. How Good Intentions and Bad Ideas are Setting up a Generation for Failure* (New York: Penguin, 2019).

McEachen, B. 'Milo Yiannopolous [sic] Gives Up Being Gay to Follow Jesus', Eternity 10/3/2021. https://www.eternitynews.com.au/world/milo-yiannopolous-gives-up-being-gay-to-follow-jesus/.

Montgomery, K. 'Tharunka: Ruled by Feminists?', *Tharunka* 21/3/2000, 10.

Mounk, Y. 'Americans Strongly Dislike PC Culture', *The Atlantic* 10/10/2018, https://www.theatlantic.com/ideas/archive/2018/10/large-majorities-dislike-political-correctness/572581/.

Pluckrose, H., & J. Lindsay, C̶r̶i̶t̶i̶c̶a̶l̶ *Cynical Theories. How Activist Scholarship Made Everything about Race, Gender, and Identity — and Why This Harms Everybody* (Durham, NC: Pitchstone, 2020).

Singhal, P. 'Police called as hundreds of protesters surround Sydney University's "vote no" rally', *Sydney Morning Herald*, 14/9/2017.

Soucy, R. 'Fascism', www.britannica.com/topic/fascism.

Spurr, B. 'Academic Freedom in the Thought-Policed University. Challenges for Christian Educators Today', in L. Ball & P.G. Bolt (eds.), *Wondering about God Together. Research-Led Learning & Teaching in Theology* (Macquarie Park, NSW: SCD Press, 2018), 189–202.

Stella, J. 'Censorship', *Tharunka*, 27/5/2004.

University of Chicago, University of Chicago and Free Expression Statement. See: https://freeexpression.uchicago.edu/history/ https://freeexpression.uchicago.edu/foundational-principles/ https://freeexpression.uchicago.edu/leadership-communications/ https://cpb-us-w2.wpmucdn.com/voices.uchicago.edu/dist/3/337/files/2019/01/Free-Speech-Is-the-Basis-of-a-True-Education-WSJ-1v5hqit.pdf https://provost.uchicago.edu/sites/default/files/documents/reports/FOECommittee Report.pdf

University of Sydney 'The State of the Universe'; www.sydney.edu.au/engage/events-sponsorships/sydney-ideas/2018/the-state-of-the-universe.html.

Wahlquist, C. 'Australia Cancels Milo Yiannopoulos's visa after Christchurch comments', *The Guardian*, 16/3/2019. www.theguardian.com/australia-news/2019/mar/16/australian-government-urged-to-ban-milo-yiannopoulos-after-christchurch-massacre.

Zimmer, R.J. 'Chicago Humanities Festival Address', 29/7/2017. https://president.uchicago.edu/page/chicago-humanities-festival-address.

www.ingramcontent.com/pod-product-compliance
Lightning Source LLC
Chambersburg PA
CBHW081331080526
44588CB00017B/2589